Economic development in the Third World

Economic development in the Third World

An introduction to problems and policies in a global perspective

Michael P. Todaro

Deputy Director
Center for Policy Studies
The Population Council
New York

Longman
London and New York

Longman Group Limited London

Associated companies, branches and representatives throughout the world

Published in the United States of America by Longman Inc., New York

© Michael P. Todaro 1977

First published 1977

Library of Congress Cataloging in Publication Data

Todaro, Michael P
    Economic development.

    Includes bibliographies.
    l. Economic development. 2. Underdeveloped areas.
I. Title.
HD82.T552   338 .09172 4   76-49626
ISBN 0-582-44628-7

Set in 9/10 VIP Times
and printed in United States of America

Contents

Part II   Problems and policies – domestic

A note to the student on the organizational structure and operating procedure for analyzing development problems in parts II and III

Part IV   Possibilities and prospects

Preface

The field of development economics has undergone profound changes during the 1970s. Old clichés and shibboleths about necessary conditions and historical determinants have been replaced by a healthy agnosticism and a refreshing willingness to focus on specific problems and real issues. The very meaning of the term 'development' has been altered from an almost exclusive preoccupation with aggregate economic growth to a much broader interpretation that encompasses questions of poverty, inequality and unemployment as well as aggregate growth. If nothing else, the 1970s will be remembered as a decade during which the problems of domestic and international poverty and income distribution rose to the top of the agenda of the development debate. Moreover, the 1970s ushered in a new era of international instability and global economic disorder which shattered the complacency and security of the developed world and forced it to take seriously its pious rhetoric about global interdependence. Whatever else happens, the system of economic relationships between the developed and the underdeveloped world will never be quite the same again; nor will the field of development economics.

In a constantly changing world, outmoded and outdated textbooks have a special proclivity for survival. Long after academic researchers have discarded irrelevant or incorrect theories and have thoroughly reoriented their discipline towards new issues and problems, many leading textbooks continue to focus on discarded concepts and inappropriate models. Nowhere is this more evident than in the rapidly changing field of development economics[1]. It is in the hope of rectifying this situation that this book is conceived and structured (see the Introduction for a detailed description of the organization and orientation of the text).

Note

1. In his major survey of the recent evolution of development theory and policy, for example, Derek Healey concluded that, 'there can be little doubt that a thorough survey of opinion on the problem of economic development would show that at the end of the 1960s and the beginning of the 1970s a new consensus began to emerge. Like all new attitudes, it arose not in a vacuum but in response to the demonstrable failure of past beliefs and practices. For it is difficult to alter accepted notions – we have invested too much intellectual capital in them. It is difficult to admit that what once appeared axiomatic is in fact subject to the limitations of time and space and must now be doubted.' Derek T. Healey, 'Development policy: new thinking about an interpretation', *Journal of Economic Literature*, September 1972, 792–4.

Acknowledgments

I am indebted to a great number of friends (far too many to mention individually) in both the developing and the developed world who have directly and indirectly helped to shape my ideas about development economics and on how an economic development text should be structured. To my former students in Africa and the United States and my colleagues in Latin America and Asia, I owe a particular debt of gratitude for their probing and challenging questions. Two good friends and colleagues, Edgar O. Edwards and Lloyd G. Reynolds, were particularly helpful at an earlier stage, and valuable comments and suggestions for improvement were received from Mathew Edel and three anonymous referees.

I wish also to mention my good friends and former colleagues at The Rockefeller Foundation, particularly John H. Knowles, M.D., Joseph E. Black and R. Kirby Davidson for their moral as well as financial support, without which this book would not have been possible.

Finally, to my lovely wife, Donna Renée, who typed the entire manuscript and provided the spiritual and intellectual inspiration to persevere under difficult circumstances, I can do no more than reaffirm my eternal devotion.

Michael P. Todaro
New York, January 1977

We are grateful to the following for permission to reproduce copyright material:

American Ecomomic Association and author Derek T. Healey for table from 'Development Policy: New Thinking About an Interpretation' *Journal of Economic Literature*, Vol. 10. No. 3, Sept. 1972; Cambridge University Press and author David Morawetz for table from 'Employment Implications of Industrialisation in Developing Countries' *Economic Journal* No. 84, Sept. 1974; Center for Migration Studies for diagram from 'Rural-Urban Migration in Africa: Theory, Policy and Research Implications' by D. Byerlee from *International Migration Review* Vol. 8 No. 4, Winter 1974; Columbia University Press for table from *Peasant to Farmer: A Revolutionary Strategy for Development* By R. Weitz (1971) and table by John G. Gurley 'Rural Development in China: 1949–1972 and the lessons to be learned from it' from *Employment in Developing Nations* Ed. K.O. Edwards (1974); The Economist for tables from Report by Chairman of Development Assistance Committee, Development Corporation Review, 1974, reprinted in *The Economist* Feb. 1975; Elsevier North-Holland Inc., for table 8.2 by G. G. Psacharopoulos from *The Returns to Education: An International Comparison*; The Ford Foundation for table by Edgar O. Edwards from *Employment in Developing Countries*; International Labour Office for tables 1, 2, 3A and 8 from *Bulletin of Labour Statistics*, Spec. Edn. 1974; Intergovermental Committee for European Migration for table from 'Italian Emigration: Some Aspects of Migration in 1964' *International Migration* Vol. IV.2 (1966); International Labour Office for table 3 and appendix 'Employment and Unemployment 1960–90' by Yves Sabalo © International Labour Organisation, Geneva, reprinted from *International Labour Review* Vol.112 No.6 Dec. 1975: The Johns Hopkins University Press for table 1 'Income Distribution Estimates' by Irma Adelman and Cynthia Taft Morris from *Society, Politics and Economic Development; A Quantative Approach*, Johns Hopkins U.P. © 1967 and table by P. A. Coombs and Munzoor Ahmed from *Attacking Rural Poverty: Noncomformal Education Can Help*, Johns Hopkins U.P. 1974; Organisation for Economic Co-operation and Development for table by David Turnham and Ian Jaeger from report *The Employment Problem in Less Developed Countries*, June 1970 and tables 2 and 4 from 'Flow of Resources from OPEC Members to Developing Countries 1974' *Document no.DD-103*, Dec. 1974, published by OECD, Paris; Oxford University Press for tables and figures from *Redistribution of Growth* by Hollis Chenery, Montek S. Ahluwalia, C. L. G. Bell, John H. Duloy and Richard Jolly publ for World Bank and the Inst. of Develpment Studies, Univ. of Sussex by Oxford U.P.; Penguin Books Ltd., for extracts from *International Trade and Economic Development* © G. K. Helleiner 1972 (penguin Educ. 1972); Pergamon Press Ltd. for extracts from articles by Sartaj Aziz Vol.2 No.2 Feb. 1974 and Paul Streeten Vol.1 No. 6, table by K. Griffen from 'Agrarian Policy: The Political and Economic Context' Vol.1 No.11. 1973 table 1 by Pazos 'Regional Integration of Trade among Less Developed Countries' Vol.1 No.7 1973 and text of 'Santiago Declaration of Third World' Vol.1 1973 all reprinted from *World Development*; Praeger Publishers Inc. and Permagon Press Ltd. for table from *By Bread Alone* by Lester R. Brown with Erik P. Eckholm © 1974 by Overseas Development Council, reprinted by permission of Praeger Publishers, Inc. and material from *The United States and the Developing World: Agenda for Action 1974* by James W. Howe and Staff of Overseas Development Council © 1974 ODC., by permission of Praeger Publishers, Inc; Prentice-Hall Inc. for table 13-D by T. E. Weisskopf from *The Capitalist System* by R. C. Edwards, M. Reich and T. E. Weisskopf due for publication 1977; The Population Council for tables by Thomas Frejka from *The Future of Population Growth* (1973) and tables by Bernard Berelson from 'World Population: Status Report 1974' *Reports on Population/Family Planning* No.15 (Jan. 1974); Random House Inc. for table from *World Without Borders* by Lester R. Brown; Department of State for table from *Communist States and Developing Countries: Aid and Trade in 1973*; United States Department of Agriculture for table From *World Agricultural Situation, June 1975*; The World Bank for Diagram by John Simmons from 'Investments in Education: National Strategy Options for Developing Countries' *Working Paper 196*, Feb. 1975, table by Rbt. S. McNamara 'Address to the Board of Governors of the World Bank Group' *World*

Bank 1974, data from *World Bank Atlas 1974* and chart 5-5 'Trends in Developing Countries' *World Bank Group 1973*. Whilst every effort has been made to trace the owners of copyright in a few cases this had proved impossible and we take this opportunity to offer our apologies to any authors/publishers whose rights may have been unwittingly infringed.

Introduction

The nature, scope and organization of the text

This book is designed for use in undergraduate university courses focusing on the economics of development in Africa, Asia, and Latin America – regions often collectively referred to as the 'Third World'[1]*. It is structured and written *both* for students who have had some basic training in economics *and* for those with little or no formal economics background. For the latter group, those essential principles and concepts of economics which appear to be of particular relevance for analyzing and reaching policy conclusions about specific development problems are explained at appropriate points throughout the text. Thus, the book should be of special value for those undergraduate development courses which presently attract or seek to attract students from a variety of disciplines. Yet the material is sufficiently broad in scope and rigorous in coverage to satisfy most undergraduate economics requirements in the field of development while still being intelligible and, hopefully, informative to the lay reader[2].

The book has a rather unique organization and orientation for development texts. Furthermore, it embodies a number of important pedagogic innovations which, in our opinion, represent significant improvements over existing books in the field. Among these innovations, the following are perhaps the most significant.

First, it is oriented exclusively towards the teaching of economic

*Numerals in square brackets refer to Notes at ends of the chapters.

development within the context of a major set of problems and issues faced by Third World nations – i.e., *the focus is on 'real world' development problems* like poverty, inequality, unemployment and rural stagnation rather than on abstract and often unrealistic models of how countries develop or sterile debates about comparative aggregate economic performances.

Second, it focuses on a wide range of developing countries not only in their capacity as independent nation states but also in relation to one another and in their interaction with rich nations, both capitalist and socialist.

Third, it recognizes the necessity of treating the problems of development and underdevelopment from an *institutional* and *structural* (i.e. a 'non-economic') as well as an economic perspective with appropriate modifications of the received 'general' economic principles, theories, and policies. We thus try to incorporate relevant theory with realistic institutional analyses.

Fourth, it views development and underdevelopment in both a domestic and a global context stressing the increasing *interdependence of the world economy* in areas such as food, energy, natural resources, technology and financial flows.

Fifth, it takes a *problem- and policy-oriented approach* to the teaching of development economics on the dual assumption that

(a) students can best grasp and eventually apply important economic concepts when these are explicated in the context of actual development problems, and

(b) a central objective of any development economics course should be the fostering of a student's ability to understand contemporary Third World economic issues and to reach independent judgements and policy conclusions about their possible resolution.

Sixth, it approaches development problems systematically by following a *standard procedure* with regard to the analysis and exposition of each problem. Each chapter begins by stating the general nature of the problem (e.g., population, poverty, rural development, education, income distribution, unemployment, etc.), its principal issues, and how it is manifested in the various developing countries. It goes on to discuss main goals and possible objectives, the role of economics in illuminating the problem, and some possible policy alternatives and their likely consequences. We believe that this approach will not only assist students to think systematically about major current development issues but, more importantly, will provide them with a methodology and operating procedure for analyzing and reaching policy conclusions about other contemporary and future development problems.

Seventh, it is based on the conviction that it is possible to design and structure a broadly based development economics textbook which simultaneously utilizes the best available cross-section data from Africa, Asia, and Latin America and appropriate theoretical tools to illuminate common Third World problems. While recognizing that these problems will differ in both scope and magnitude when dealing with such diverse countries as India, Indonesia, Kenya, Nigeria, Brazil, Mexico and Guatamala, the fact remains that they all *do* face very similar development problems. Widespread poverty and growing income and asset inequalities, rapid population growth, low levels of literacy and nutritional intake, rising levels of urban unemployment and underemployment, stagnating agriculture and relative rural neglect, inadequate and often inappropriate educational and health delivery systems, inflexible institutional and administrative structures, significant vulnerability to external economic, technological and cultural forces of dominance and dependence, and the difficult choices regarding trade-offs between 'modernization' and cultural preservation; these and other problems are a pervasive phenomenon and, in fact, often define the nature of underdevelopment in Third World nations.

Finally, it views the many economic, social and institutional problems of underdevelopment as *highly interrelated* and requiring *simultaneous and coordinated approaches to their solution at both the national and international levels*. It is based on the premise that economic development even when defined in terms of *both* the rapid growth and more equitable distribution of national incomes and opportunities is a *necessary* but not *sufficient* condition for 'development'. The problem is that one simply cannot talk about economics for development without placing economic variables squarely in the context of socio-political systems and institutional realities. To ignore 'non-economic' factors in an analysis of so-called 'economic' problems such as poverty, unemployment and inequality, both within and between nations, would do students a great disservice.

Organization and orientation

The book is organized into four parts. Part I focuses on the nature and meaning of underdevelopment and its various manifestations in Third World nations. It also examines the historical growth experience of the now developed countries and ascertains the degree to which this experience is relevant to contemporary developing nations.

Parts II and III form the core of the book. They focus on major development problems and policies, both domestic and international. Topics of analysis and review include economic growth, poverty and income distribution, population, unemployment, migration, technology, agricultural and rural development, education, international trade and finance, foreign aid and private foreign investment.

Finally, Part IV reviews the possibilities and prospects for Third World development. After discussing the theory and practice of development planning and the role and limitations of public policy in the development process, it analyzes the evolving world economy of the 1970s and the place of less developed nations in an increasingly interdependent, but highly unequal global system. The impact of the recent energy, food, and fertilizer crises on the economies of developing nations is closely examined and growing Third World demands for a 'new international economic order' in the context of greater collective 'self-reliance' are reviewed and analyzed.

In all four parts of the book we ask the fundamental questions: what kind of development is most desirable; and, how can Third World nations best achieve these economic and social objectives either individually or, better, in cooperation with one another and, it is to be hoped, with appropriate and meaningful assistance from the more developed countries of the world.

In our discussion and analysis of critical development problems we give the diverse and often conflicting viewpoints of development economists, other social scientists, planners and those actually on the 'firing line' in Third World government ministries and/or departments.

If we reveal a bias, it is probably in trying always to put forward the viewpoints of Third World social scientists and development practitioners who recently have begun to articulate their shared perceptions of the meaning of development as never before[3].

The locus of intellectual influence on development thinking is rapidly shifting from the First (Advanced Capitalist) and Second (Advanced Socialist) Worlds to the Third World. It is in these nations that the ultimate answers must be found and appropriate strategies formulated. And it will be the nationals of these countries who will increasingly exert the major influence on the form and content of these strategies. Yet, unless students from economically advanced nations possess a broad knowledge and understanding of the real 'meaning' of underdevelopment and its various manifestations in diverse Third World nations, the probability of enlightened developed country policies towards the plight of the world's poor, who comprise over two-thirds of our global population, will be even more remote than at present.

One further introductory comment seems in order. It is that in the final analysis we must realize that the development of *every* person depends directly or indirectly on the development of *all* persons. Third World nations are an integral part of the ever-shrinking global economic and political organism. Their economic role and influence are likely to increase over the coming decades. A thorough understanding, therefore, of the unique nature of their economic problems and aspirations, as well as the direct and indirect linkages between these problems and aspirations and the economic well-being of people in the developed nations should be an essential component in the education of all university economics students. It is our hope that the present book contributes in some small way to this broadening of student perspectives and that it will lead to a better understanding of the contemporary problems, possibilities, and prospects for economic and social development in the diverse nations of Africa, Asia and Latin America.

Notes

1. The ninety-seven African, Asian and Latin American member countries of the United Nations often collectively refer to themselves as the 'Third World'. They do this primarily to distinguish themselves from the economically advanced 'Capitalist' ('First World') and 'Socialist' ('Second World') countries. Although the origin of the term 'Third World' is obscure, it has become widely accepted and utilized by *economically poor nations themselves*, especially in their negotiations with economically rich nations on critical international controversies relating to trade, aid, energy, natural resource depletion, and dwindling world food supplies. While it is unfortunate that numbers such as 'First', 'Second' and 'Third' occasionally bear the regrettable connotation of superiority and inferiority when used in reference to different groups of nations, the fact remains that the term 'Third World' *is* widely used among developing nations primarily in an effort to generate and represent a new sense of common identity and a growing unity of purpose. Accordingly, we will often use the expression 'Third World' when referring to the developing countries as a whole with the clear understanding at the outset that it is always being used in its positive sense of a common identity and a growing unity of purpose.
2. A glossary at the end of the book provides a quick source of information on the meaning of various economic concepts and institutional acronyms (e.g. IBRD, ILO, etc) used in the text.
3. See, for example: Padma Desai, 'Third World social scientists in Santiago', *World Development*, **1** no. 9 (1973); 'Self-reliance and international reform', *Overseas*

Development Council Communiqué, no. 24 (1974); Mahbub ul Haq, 'Crisis in development strategies', *World Development*, no. 1 (1973); and finally, the first *Communiqué* of fifty leading economists from developing nations who met as members of the 'Third World Forum' in Karachi, Pakistan in January 1975. Both the Santiago Declaration and the Karachi Communiqué are reproduced as Appendices to Chapter 17.

For Donna Renée and Lenora Jean

Principles and concepts

Part I

| Chapter 1 | **Economics, institutions and development: A global perspective** |

The Third World, with 70 per cent of the world population, subsists on only 20 per cent of the world income – and even this meagre income is so maldistributed internally as to leave the bulk of its population in abject poverty.
Santiago Declaration of Third World Economists, 1973

Human needs have to be seen in a global framework.
Communiqué of Third World Social Scientists, 1974[1]

Introduction: How the other two-thirds live

Throughout the world people awake each morning to face a new day in very different circumstances. Some live in comfortable homes with many rooms. They have more than enough to eat, are well clothed, in good health and can look forward to a reasonable degree of financial security. Others – and these constitute more than two-thirds of the earth's four billion people – are much less fortunate. They may have little or no shelter and an inadequate food supply. Their health is poor, they cannot read or write, they are unemployed, and their prospects for a better life are bleak or uncertain at best. Let us, therefore, begin our study of economic development by briefly examining a sample of these living conditions in different parts of the globe.

If we looked first at an average family in North America, it would probably be a family of four with an annual income of approximately $8,000 to $10,000. They would live in a reasonably comfortable city apartment or a suburban house with a small garden. The dwelling would have many comfortable features including perhaps a separate bedroom for each of the two children. It would be filled with numerous consumer goods and electrical appliances, many of which were manufactured outside North America in countries as far away as South Korea, Argentina and Taiwan. There would always be three meals a day and many of the food products would be imported from overseas; for example, coffee from Brazil, Kenya or Colombia; tinned fish and fruit from Peru, Japan, and Australia; and bananas and other tropical fruits from Central America. Both children would be healthy and attending school. They could expect to complete their secondary education and probably go to a university, choose from a variety of careers to which they are attracted and live to an average age of 72 years.

On the surface, this family, which is typical of many rich nations, appears to have a reasonably good life. The parents have both the opportunity and the necessary education or training to secure regular employment, to shelter, clothe, feed and educate their children and to save some money each year for later life. But against these 'economic' benefits, there are always 'non-economic' costs. The competitive pressures to 'succeed' financially are very strong and the mental strain and physical pressure of trying to provide for a family at levels that the community regards as desirable can take its toll on the health of both parents. Their ability to relax, to enjoy the simple pleasures of a country stroll and to breathe clean air, drink pure water and see a crimson sunset are rapidly disappearing with the onslaught of economic progress and environmental decay. But, on the whole, theirs is an economic status and life style towards which many millions of other less fortunate people throughout the world seem to be aspiring.

Now let us examine a typical family in rural Asia. It is likely to be a family of 10 or more, including parents, 5 to 7 children, 2 grandparents and some aunts and uncles. They have a combined annual income, both in money and in 'kind' (i.e. they consume a share of the food they grow), of from $150 to $200. Together they live in a one-room poorly constructed house as tenant farmers on a large agricultural estate owned by an absentee landlord who lives in the nearby city. The father, mother and uncle as well as the older children must work all day on the land. None of the adults can read or write, and of the five school age children only one attends regularly and he cannot expect to proceed beyond 3 or 4 years of primary education. There is only one meal a day; it rarely changes nor is it usually sufficient to alleviate the constant hunger pains experienced by all the children. The house has no electricity, sanitation or fresh water supply. There is much sickness but qualified doctors and medical practitioners are far away in the cities attending to the needs of wealthier families. The work is hard, the sun is hot and aspirations for a better life are constantly being suffocated. The daily struggle for physical survival in this part of the world finds its only relief in the spiritual traditions of its people.

Shifting to another part of the world, suppose we now were to visit a large and beautiful city situated along the coast of South America. Immediately we would probably be struck by the sharp contrasts in living conditions from one section of this sprawling city to another. There is a modern stretch of tall buildings and wide, tree-lined boulevards along the edge of a gleaming white beach, while just a few hundred meters back and up the side of a steep hill, squalid shanty houses are pressed together in precarious balance.

If we were to examine two representative families – one a wealthy family from the local ruling class and the other of peasant background – we would no doubt also be struck by the wide disparities in their individual living conditions. The wealthy family lives in a multiroom complex on the top floor of a modern building overlooking the sea, while the peasant family is cramped tightly into a small makeshift shack in a 'favella' or squatter slum on the hill behind that sea-front building.

For illustrative purposes, let us assume that it is a typical Saturday evening and both families should be preparing for dinner. In the penthouse flat of the wealthy family a long table with expensive imported dishes, silverware and fine linen is being set by one of the domestic servants. Russian caviar and French champagne will constitute the first of several courses. The family's eldest son is home from his university in North America while the other two children are on vacation from their boarding schools in France and Switzerland. The father is a prominent surgeon trained in the United States with a clientele of wealthy local and foreign dignitaries and businessmen. In addition to his practice, he owns a considerable amount of land in the countryside. Annual vacations abroad, imported luxury automobiles and the finest food and clothing are commonplace amenities for this fortunate family in the penthouse flat.

And what about the poor family living in the shack on the hill? They too can view the sea but, somehow, it seems neither scenic nor relaxing. The stench of open sewers makes such enjoyment rather remote. There is no long dinner table to be set; in fact, there is no dinner. Most of the seven illiterate children are out on the streets begging for money, shining shoes or occasionally even trying to steal purses from unsuspecting persons as they stroll along the boulevard. The father migrated to the city from the rural hinterland a few years ago and the rest of the family recently followed. He has had part-time jobs over the years but nothing permanent. The family income is less than $120 per year. The children have been in and out of school many times, as most are forced to help out financially in any way they can. Occasionally the eldest teenage daughter who lives with 'friends' across town seems to have some extra money – but no one ever asks where it comes from or how it is obtained.

One could easily be disturbed by the sharp contrast between these two ways of life. However, had we looked at almost any other major city in Latin America, Asia and Africa, the contrasting scene would have been much the same (although the extent of inequality might not be so pronounced).

As a final aspect of this brief view of living conditions around the world, consider the eastern part of Africa where many small clusters of tiny huts dot a dry and barren land. Each cluster contains a group of 'extended' families, all participating in and sharing the work. There is no 'money' income here because all food, clothing, shelter and worldly goods are made and consumed by the people themselves – theirs is a 'subsistence' economy. There are no roads, schools, hospitals, electricity or water supplies and life here seems to have been unchanged for thousands of years. In many respects it is as stark and difficult an existence as that of the people in that Latin American favella across the ocean. Yet, perhaps it is not as psychologically troubling because there is no luxurious penthouse by the sea to emphasize the relative deprivation of the very poor. Life here seems to be eternal and unchanging – but not for much longer.

One hundred kilometres away a road is being built which will pass near this village. No doubt it will bring with it the means for prolonging life through improved medical care. But it will also inexorably bring information about the world outside along with the 'gadgets' of modern civilization. The possibilities of a 'better' life will be promoted and the opportunities for such a life will become feasible. Aspirations will be raised, but so will frustrations. In short, the 'development' process will have been set in motion.

Before long, exportable tropical fruits and vegetables will probably be grown in this now sparsely settled region. They may even end up on the dinner table of the rich South American family in the seaside penthouse. Meanwhile, transistor radios made at the other end of the earth in Southeast Asia and playing music recorded in northern Europe will become a prized possession in this African village. Throughout the world, remote subsistence villages such as this one are gradually but inexorably being linked up with modern civilization. The process is now well under way and will become even more intensified in the coming years.

Upon concluding this first fleeting glimpse of life in different parts of our planet, various questions might arise. Why does such obvious affluence coexist with such dire poverty not only across different continents but also within the same country or even the same city? How can traditional, low productivity, subsistence societies be transformed into modern, high productivity, high income nations? To what extent are the development aspirations of poor nations helped or hindered by the economic activities of rich nations? By what process and under what conditions do rural subsistence farmers in the remote regions of Nigeria, Brazil or the Philippines evolve into successful commercial farmers? These and many other questions concerning international as well as national differences in levels of living including health and nutrition, education, employment, population growth and life expectancies might be posed on the basis of even this very superficial look at life around the world.

It is hoped that this book will assist students to obtain a better understanding of the major problems and prospects for economic development by focusing specifically on the plight of the two-thirds of the world's population where poverty and low levels of living are an inexorable fact of life. However, as we shall soon discover, the development process in Third World nations cannot be analyzed realistically without also considering the role of economically developed nations in directly or indirectly promoting or retarding that development. Perhaps even more important to students in the developed nations is the need to recognize that as our earth shrinks with the spread of modern transport and communications, the futures of *all* peoples on this small planet are becoming increasingly 'interdependent'. What happens to the health and economic welfare of the poor rural family and many others in Southeast Asia, Africa or Latin America will in one way or another, directly or indirectly, affect the health and economic welfare of their counterparts in Europe and North America, and vice versa. The 'hows' and 'whys' of this growing economic interdependence will unfold in the remaining chapters. But it is within this context of a 'common future' for all mankind in a rapidly shrinking world that we now commence our study of Third World development.

1.1 Economics and development studies

The study of economic development is one of the newest, most exciting, and most challenging branches of the broader disciplines of economics and political economy. Although one might claim that Adam Smith was the first 'development economist' and that his *Wealth of Nations*, written in 1776, was the first treatise on economic development, the systematic study of the problems and processes of economic development in the Third World has emerged only over the past three decades. There are some who would nevertheless still claim that development economics is not really a distinct branch of economics in the same sense as is say macroeconomics and micro-economics or public finance and monetary economics. Rather they would assert that it is simply an amalgamation of all these traditional fields, but with a specific focus on the individual economies of Africa, Asia and Latin America.

We strongly disagree with this viewpoint. While development economics may draw upon certain principles and concepts from other branches of economics in either a traditional or modified form, for the most part it is a field of study which is rapidly evolving its own distinctive theoretical and methodological structure. We begin therefore by contrasting modern development economics with 'traditional' Western economics and then devote the bulk of this initial chapter to an analysis of those economic, institutional and structural factors, both domestic and international, which form an essential part of any analysis of development problems and prospects.

1. The nature of development economics 'Traditional' economics is concerned primarily with the efficient, least-cost allocation of scarce productive resources, and with the optimal growth of these resources over time so as to produce an ever expanding range of goods and services. (By 'traditional' economics we simply mean the classical and neoclassical economics that is taught in (mostly) American and British textbooks. See below for a further elaboration.) 'Political economy', on the other hand, goes beyond traditional economics to study among other things the social and institutional processes through which certain groups of economic and political elites influence the allocation of scarce productive resources now and in the future for their own benefit, or for that plus the wider benefit of the larger population. Political economy is therefore concerned with the relationship between politics and economics, with a special emphasis on the role of 'power' in economic decision making.

Development economics has an even greater scope. In addition to being concerned with the efficient allocation of existing scarce (or idle) productive resources and with their sustained growth over time, it must also deal with the *economic, social* and *institutional* mechanisms, both public and private, necesssary for bringing about *rapid (at least by historical standards) and large scale improvements in levels of living* for the masses of poverty-striken, malnourished and illiterate peoples of Africa, Asia and Latin America. Thus, development economics to a greater extent than 'traditional' economics or even political economy is concerned with the economic and political processes necessary for affecting *rapid structural and institutional transformations of entire societies in a manner that will most efficiently bring the fruits of economic progress to the broadest segments of their populations.* As such, the role of government and the need for some degree of coordinated economic planning and broad-based economic policies is usually viewed as an essential component of development economics.

2. Why study development economics?: some critical questions An introductory course in development economics should help students to gain a better understanding of a number of critical questions relating to the economies of the Third World. The following is a sample list of sixteen such questions which illustrate the kinds of issues faced by almost every developing nation and, indeed, every development economist.

1. What is the real meaning of 'development' and how can certain economic principles and theories contribute to a better understanding of the development process?
2. What are the sources of national and international economic growth? Who benefits most from such growth and why? Why do some countries and groups of people continue to get richer while others remain abjectly poor?
3. Why is there so much unemployment, especially in the cities of the Third World, and why do people continue to migrate to the cities from rural areas even though their chances of finding a job are very slim?
4. What is development planning all about? Why plan at all?
5. Should foreign private 'multinational' corporations be encouraged to invest in the economies of poor nations and, if so, under what conditions?
6. What about the impact of 'foreign aid' from rich countries? Should it continue to be sought after by developing countries, under what conditions, and for what purposes? On the other hand, should developed countries continue to offer aid, under what conditions and for what purposes?
7. Should exports of primary products such as agricultural commodities be promoted or should all less developed countries (LDCs) attempt to industrialize by developing their own heavy manufacturing industries as rapidly as possible?
8. When and under what conditions should Third World governments adopt a policy of exchange control, raise tariffs and/or set quotas on the importation of certain 'non-essential' goods in order to ameliorate chronic balance of payments problems?
9. Is international trade desirable from the point of view of the development of poor nations? Who really gains from trade and how are the advantages distributed among nations?
10. What has been the impact of the rapid rise in international oil prices on the economies of the non-oil exporting developing nations? What future role might the now wealthy OPEC oil countries play in furthering the development of other less fortunate Third World nations?
11. What is the best way to promote agricultural and rural development where 80 to 90 per cent of most LDC populations still reside?
12. How does the spread of inflation and unemployment among the economies of rich nations affect the levels of living of people in poor nations? Do poor nations have any recourse, or must they be passive but vulnerable spectators at an international economic power game?
13. Are there economic factors influencing levels of fertility in poor nations? What are the economic and social consequences of rapid population growth? Is the 'population problem' simply a question of numbers or is it also related to the impact of rising affluence in developed nations on resource depletion throughout the world?
14. Will there be chronic world food shortages? If so, which nations will be most adversely affected and how might such shortages best be avoided in the future?
15. Do contemporary Third World educational systems really promote economic development or do they simply act as a rationing or selection device by which certain select groups or classes of people

are perpetuated in positions of wealth, power and influence? And finally,

16. What is the origin and basis of growing Third World demands for a 'new international economic order'? Is such a new world economic order possible and, if so, what might be its main features and how might it affect the economies of developed nations?

These and many other similar questions will be analyzed and explored in the following chapters. The answers are often more complex than one might think. Remember that the overriding purpose of any course in economics, including development economics, should be to help students to *think systematically* about economic problems and issues and to formulate judgements and conclusions on the basis of the application of 'relevant' analytical principles and 'reliable' statistical information. Since the problems of Third World development are in many cases unique in the modern world and often not easily understood through the use of traditional 'Western' economic theories, we may often need unconventional approaches to what may appear to be conventional economic problems. Traditional Western economic principles can play a useful role in enabling us to improve our understanding of development problems; but they should not blind us to the realities of local conditions in these countries. Traditional theories of economic growth and development often require modification in both assumptions and procedures before they can shed light adequately on complicated and economically unprecedented development issues. We shall have more to say about the role and limitations of traditional economic theory later in the chapter.

3. The important role of 'values' in development economics

Economics is a 'social science'. It is concerned with man and the social systems by which he organizes his activities to satisfy basic material needs (food, shelter, clothing, etc.) and non-material wants (education, knowledge, beauty, spiritual fulfillment, etc.) Economists are 'social scientists' who are in the unusual position that the objects of their studies – i.e., human beings in the ordinary business of life – and their own activities are rooted in the same social context. Unlike the 'physical sciences', the 'social science' of economics can claim neither scientific 'laws' nor 'universal truths'. In economics there can only be 'tendencies'; and even these are subject to great variations in different countries and cultures and at different times. Many so-called 'general' economic models are often based on a set of implicit assumptions about human behavior and economic relationships which may have little or no connection with the realities of developing economies. To this extent, their 'objectivity' may be more assumed than real. Economic investigations and analyses, therefore, cannot simply be lifted out of their institutional, social and political context, especially when one must deal with the human dilemmas of hunger, poverty and ill-health which plague two-thirds of the world's population.

It is necessary, therefore, to recognize from the outset that ethical or normative 'value' premises about what is or is not desirable are central features of the economic discipline in general, and of development economics in particular. The very concepts of 'economic development' and 'modernization' which we shall be discussing in succeeding chapters represent implicit as well as explicit value premises about desirable goals for achieving what Gandhi once called the 'realization of the human potential'. Concepts or goals such as economic and social equality, the elimination of poverty, universal education, rising levels of living, national independence, modernization of institutions, political and economic participation, grass roots democracy, self-reliance and personal fulfilment all derive from subjective value judgements about what is good and desirable and what is not. So also for that matter are opposite values – for example, the sanctity of private property and the right of individuals to accumulate unlimited personal wealth, the preservation of traditional social institutions and rigid, inegalitarian class structures, and the supposed 'natural right' of some to lead while others follow.

When we deal in Parts II and III with such major issues of development as poverty, inequality, unemployment, population growth, rural stagnation and international 'dependence', the mere identification of these topics as 'problems' conveys the value judgement that their improvement or elimination is desirable and therefore good. The fact that there *is* widespread agreement among many diverse groups of people – politicians, academics and ordinary citizens – that these *are* desirable goals does not alter the fact that they arise not only out of a reaction to an objective empirical or 'positive' analysis of 'what is', but ultimately from a subjective or 'normative' value judgement with regard to 'what should be'.

It follows that value premises, however carefully disguised, *are* an integral component both of economic analysis and economic policy. Economics cannot be 'value free' in the same sense, as say, physics or chemistry. Thus, the validity of economic analysis and the correctness of economic prescriptions should always be evaluated in light of the nature of the underlying assumptions and/or value premises. Once these subjective values have been agreed upon by a nation or, more specifically, by those charged with the responsibility for national decision making, then specific development goals (e.g. greater income equality) and corresponding public policies (e.g. taxing higher incomes at higher rates) based on 'objective' theoretical and quantitative analyses can be pursued. However, where serious value conflicts and disagreements exist among decision makers, the possibility of a consensus either about desirable goals or appropriate policies will be considerably diminished. In either case, it is essential that one's value premises, especially in the field of development economics, always be made clear [2].

4. The nature of 'Western' economic theory

To analyze the diversity of critical development problems, some basic understanding of general economic concepts and principles is needed. Unfortunately, many of the fundamental economic concepts and principles of traditional economics, being derived from and relating to the special economic, institutional and structural characteristics of advanced industrial nations, are neither relevant nor appropriate to the understanding or solution of economic problems of developing countries.

Let us, therefore, quickly review economic theory and briefly sketch the reasons why many of the so-called 'Western' economic models and theories are thought to be inappropriate for the study of Third World development. Having done this, we will be in a better position to appreciate the distinctive nature of modern development economics.

Economic theory represents the way in which economists conceptually organize the interdependent facts of economic life including production, consumption, incomes, prices, employment, exports, imports, savings and investment. While 'economics' as a discipline is concerned with the way in which scarce human and material resources are most efficiently employed for the social good, 'economic theory' consists of a generally accepted body of concepts and principles about economic behavior which if properly formulated and correctly arranged, can help us to understand and explain better the workings of an economic system. The 'method' or 'thought process' of economic theory is largely 'deductive' in nature – that is, on the basis of a known or assumed set of facts about the essential characteristics of an economy an hypothesis is established and a 'model' is set up. The 'model' may be very simple, or quite complex, but the essence of all models are that they are simplifications of reality. Conclusions about the functioning of an economy or an economic system can then be logically 'deduced' either from the characteristics of the model or from experiments within the model. To be worthwhile, however, models need to be tested constantly against reality through the use of statistics and statistical methods.

The first essential of any economic theory or model is that it should be capable of explaining the economic realities of nations and regions. Any theory or set of principles must of necessity be based on simplifying *assumptions* and *abstractions*; but the type of assumptions or abstractions chosen cannot be decided in a vacuum. *They must fit the realities of nations and must be appropriate to the characteristic features of economic life as recorded by observation and experience.* Moreover, theories and principles which might be valid and appropriate for one type of economy in a given region or at a given moment may not be valid for other societies at the same or at different times. This brings us to an important point about 'economics' and 'development' – one which provides a principal rationale for the structure and design of this book.

1.2 The limited relevance of 'traditional' theory

Most 'development economists' and students of development today agree that what has come to be known as 'traditional' or 'Western' neo-classical and neo-Keynesian economic theory as such is of very limited relevance for understanding the characteristic features of both the economies and the economic processes of many Third World nations. Perhaps the eminent Nobel prize-winning Swedish economist, Gunnar Myrdal[3], best stated the case against the uncritical use of traditional economic concepts and theories in poor nations when he observed that:

Economic theorists, more than any other social scientists, have long been disposed to arrive at general propositions and then postulate them as valid for every time, place, and culture. There is a tendency in contemporary economic theory to follow this path to the extreme . . . when theories and concepts designed to fit the special conditions of the Western world – and thus containing the implicit assumptions about social reality by which this fitting was accomplished are used in the study of underdeveloped countries, where they do not *fit, the consequences are serious.*

Professor Paul Streeton of Oxford University was even more succinct when he noted that 'the whole paraphernalia of contemporary neo-classical economics seems to have become suddenly obsolete'[4].

Without going into the specific details at this stage of the extensive criticism of Western economic models as guides to understanding and/or ameliorating conditions of underdevelopment in poor nations, a few general comments are needed.

Neo-classical economics as taught in the developed nations and as generally transferred to and taught in developing nations through the importation of 'Western' textbooks has traditionally been divided into three broad catagories: micro-economics, macro-economics and international economics. Micro-economics focuses on the behavior and activities of individual economic units – primarily producers and consumers. Macro-economics looks at the economy as a whole in terms of 'aggregate' or 'macro' economic variables such as consumption, saving, investment, the money supply, gross domestic product, employment, and the overall price level. International economics examines the trading and monetary relationships between nation-states both as producers of exports and consumers of imports and thus represents a mixture of elements of both micro- and macro-economic theory.

The conceptual framework and behavioral assumptions which unite each of these broad areas of traditional neo-classical economic analysis are the threefold 'ideals' of consumer sovereignty, perfect competition, and profit maximization. *Neo-classical economics is the economics of 'equilibrium' and stability in a developing world of disequilibrium and instability.* It is the economics of 'marginal' choice, of 'a little more or a little less' in a developing world where major fundamental choices must be made to secure 'a lot more' in as short a time period as possible.

In micro-economic theory, the basic questions of what and how much to produce are assumed to be determined by the aggregate preferences of all consumers as revealed by their market demand curves for different goods and services. Producers are assumed simply to respond to these 'sovereign' consumer preferences and, motivated by the desire to maximize profits, they are assumed to compete with each other *on equal terms* in the purchase of resources and the sale of their products. The neo-classical economist's notion of 'perfect competition' is central to this whole process. It assumes that all prices, wages, interest rates, etc, are determined by the free play of the forces of supply and demand and that each of the millions of consumers and thousands of producers is so small in relation to total demand and supply that they cannot individually influence to any extent the market prices and quantities of goods, services and resources bought and sold. The ultimate rationale for the efficacy of this theory or model of economic activity is Adam Smith's famous notion of the 'invisible hand' of capitalism which postulates that if each individual consumer, producer, and supplier of resources pursues his or her own self interest, they will, 'as if by an invisible hand', be promoting the overall interests of society as a whole.

Unfortunately, the facts of economic life in *both* the developed and the less developed nations of the world are such as to render much of traditional micro-economic theory of negligible importance either for analysis or policy[5]. Consumers as a whole are rarely sovereign about anything, let alone with regard to questions of what goods and services are to be produced, in what quantities and for whom. Producers, whether private or public, have great power in determining market prices and quantities sold. The ideal of competition is typically just that – an 'ideal' with little relation to reality[6]. Finally, the so-called 'invisible hand' often acts not to promote the general welfare of all but, to lift up those who are already well-off while pushing down that vast majority of the population which is striving to free itself from poverty, malnutrition and illiteracy.

Briefly, macro-economic theory (whether in its 'Keynesian' or 'monitarist' form) also views the economy and its institutions through competitive equilibrium, supply and demand spectacles. Here, however, one is dealing with the determinents of 'aggregate' supply-and-demand for national output. The greater the level of aggregate demand, the higher the level of equilibrium employment and prices in the economy. Policy prescriptions for government intervention in the economy flow naturally from this theory. For example, in the Keynesian model unemployment is due to a deficiency of aggregate demand for the 'potential' output of a nation (i.e. the goods and services which the nation as a whole could produce at maximum capacity). By increasing aggregate demand, therefore (e.g. by expanding government expenditures and/or lowering taxes), governments can accelerate economic activity, and consequently induce higher levels of employment. Conversely, when aggregate demand exceeds the productive capacity (aggregate supply) of the economy so that inflation results, the role of government is to spend less and tax people more in order to reduce consumer demand and thus curtail general price increases.

Like micro-theory, traditional Keynesian macro-theory reveals many inadequacies when applied to the realities of economic life in the developing world[7]. This is particularly true in those economies with highly fragmented product, resource and financial markets. Such market fragmentation typically results from the coexistence of 'modern' and 'traditional' ways of doing things in both agriculture and industry. It is compounded by inadequate and malfunctioning credit systems and a general LDC vulnerability to powerful foreign economic influences.

This general irrelevance of traditional Keynesian macro-economics for Third World development should not be surprising. The 'general' theory was in fact formulated in response to the *special* Western economic and institutional circumstances of the Great Depression of the 1930s. Indeed, a good deal of Keynesian macro-theory is considered somewhat irrelevant today even in the developed nations where the major problems are no longer simply unemployment *or* inflation but 'stagflation' – i.e. unemployment accompanied by structural as well as demand inflation (see Ch. 8). Manipulating aggregate supply and demand curves by general government monetary and fiscal policies appears to have lost much of its effectiveness. As a result, Keynesian economics has come under increasing criticism even from many of its formerly most ardent proponents in the developed nations [8].

If such a gap between macro-theory and economic reality exists in the industrial nations, how much more irrelevant it must seem for the underdeveloped countries whose institutions and economic systems don't even approximate to those of the developed nations, now or in the past! In fact, as we shall see in Chapter 9 the traditional Keynesian policy for alleviating industrial unemployment, i.e. the creation of more urban jobs through expanded government-induced aggregate demand, may under certain real world conditions in poor countries actually *increase* the level of urban unemployment as a result of induced rural–urban migration. It may simultaneously also exacerbate domestic inflationary pressures. And, as we shall also see in Part II, this is not an isolated case of 'perverse' results which may occur when standard Western theory is applied uncritically to the problems of Third World development. Many other phenomena which might at first appear to be theoretical 'paradoxes' of development economics become less surprising when appropriate modifications of traditional theories are made in light of the unique characteristics of developing nations.

Finally, in Chapter 12, we discover that much of the traditional theory of international trade, based as it is on the same competitive assumptions of micro-economics, offers only limited guidance for an understanding of the actual mechanics of international economic relations between rich and poor nations in the 1970s. Who benefits most from trade, how the gains are distributed and how international commodity prices are determined often bear little resemblance to the dictates of traditional models of trade and growth.

1.3 Economies as 'social systems': the need to go beyond simple economics

Up to this point we have confined our introductory comments about traditional neo-classical economics largely to questions of its nature, scope and limitations for dealing with the complex and multi-dimensional problems of Third World development. But economics and 'economic' systems, especially in the Third World, need to be viewed in a much broader perspective – i.e. within the context of the overall 'social system' of a country. By a social system we mean the interdependent relationships between so-called economic and 'non-economic' factors. The latter include attitudes towards life, work and authority, public and private bureaucratic and administrative structures, patterns of kinship and religion, cultural traditions, systems of land tenure, the authority and integrity of government agencies, the degree of popular participation in development decisions and activities, and the flexibility or rigidity of economic and social classes.

Throughout this book we shall discover that the achievement of development and the solution to development problems is a much more complicated task than some people would lead us to believe. Increasing national production, raising levels of living, and promoting widespread employment opportunities are as much a function of the values, incentives, attitudes and beliefs, and the institutional and power arrangements of a society as they are the direct outcomes of the manipulation of strategic economic variables such as savings, investment and foreign exchange rates. Just as some economists occasionally make the mistake of confusing their 'science' with universal truth, so they also sometimes mistakenly dismiss these 'non-economic' variables as 'non-quantifiable' and *therefore* of dubious importance.

But, as we shall see in Parts II, III and IV, many of the failures of development policies in Third World nations have arisen precisely because these 'non-economic' factors, for example the importance of land reform for rural development or the role of foreign corporations in influencing urban wages and thus indirectly levels of urban unemployment, were intentionally or unintentionally excluded from the analysis. While the main focus of this book is on the nature of development economics and its usefulness in understanding problems of economic and social progress in poor nations, we shall continually be reminding students of the manner in which values, attitudes and institutions do play a crucial role in the overall development process.

1.4 Third World social systems as part of an interdependent international social system

We can extend the above analysis even further. Just as the economic life of developing nations is inevitably linked with its social, political and cultural life, so these domestic social systems are interconnected with the international social system: the organization and rules of conduct of the global economy. An important aspect of this linkage is the phenomenon of the *dominance* and *dependence* that exists between many developed and less developed nations (see Ch. 3). Dominance and dependence relationships can indeed be pervasive. They are found in a wide range of international economic affairs including foreign aid, private foreign investment and the transfer of technology where the LDCs as a group often appear to be at the mercy of the global power of rich nations and their multinational corporations. But dominance and dependence relationships may also exist in the political, intellectual and cultural sphere. Here many of the values, ideas, symbols, laws, attitudes and institutions of rich nations permeate, influence and shape the social systems of diverse Third World countries.

Conversely, there are many areas where the developed nations are beginning to recognize their own ultimate economic dependence on the developing countries. This applies increasingly with respect to the access to natural resources and raw materials, especially when dominant LDC suppliers are able to coordinate their activities. The prime example is the enormous destablizing impact which the quadrupling of international oil prices had in 1974 on the economies of all oil-importing nations (see Ch. 17).

But oil is not the only resource where formerly dependent economies can begin to exert influence on the rich industrial nations. A substantial amount of the world's raw material resources are located in Third World countries. In many cases, however, their control and management may still reside primarily with powerful multinational corporations from developed countries. For example, Zambia, Chile, Peru and a few other Third World countries supply almost 80 per cent of the world's copper. Malaysia and Sri Lanka supply over 50 per cent of the world's natural rubber. Bolivia, Malaysia and Thailand account for 85 per cent of world trade in tin. Third World countries including Jamaica, Surinam and Guyana supply almost 90 per cent of developed nation imports of bauxite. Other critical minerals where Third World nations are major suppliers include manganese (Gabon, Brazil and Zaire), iron ore (Venezuela and India) and lead (Peru, Mexico and others).

In the area of commodity exports Brazil, Colombia, Kenya, the Ivory Coast, Uganda and El Salvador produce almost the entire world supply of coffee, while Brazil and Ghana produce most of the world's cocoa. India, Sri Lanka, East Africa and China produce most of the world's tea while India, Pakistan, Bangladesh, Thailand and Nepal produce over two-thirds of the world's jute. As mentioned earlier, the Persian Gulf Arab states alone control almost 60 per cent of the world's known oil reserves although they constitute less than 1 per cent of the world's population.

These statistics stress the now widely recognized fact that the economies of the world today are becoming more and more economically interdependent. Such interdependence is likely to become even more significant in the future. Nevertheless, Third World nations as a whole have always been and still on balance remain much more dependent on the economic and political policies of the dominant rich countries. It is impossible to talk about their development without dealing with this dependence phenomenon even though, in recognition of this fact, many developing countries are attempting either singularly or collectively to pursue more 'self-reliant' development strategies while pressing their demands for a 'new international economic order' (see Ch. 17). As international political disputes move away from the cold war politics of the 1950s and 1960s and begin to focus more on the growing competition for increasingly scarce natural resources, many of which are located in Third World nations, the possibility of North–South (i.e. rich country–poor country) economic confrontation will take on added importance. This is a crucial emerging issue of global importance and one which we shall discuss further in Part IV.

Any study of development economics, therefore, which does not recognize and deal with the dual phenomena of persistent LDC economic, technological and institutional dependence on rich nations and the growing rich country dependence on Third World resource policies would be overlooking one of the most important elements in the long-run success or failure of diverse development efforts. Consequently, in the chapters that follow, and especially in Parts II and III we shall constantly try to frame our discussions of critical development problems such as poverty, inequality and unemployment not only within the broad context of the social systems of individual developing countries, but also within an international framework that views developing nations as part of an increasingly interdependent but still highly unequal global economic system. We shall discover that many common forces are at work in this system and many curious economic paradoxes become clarified when problems of underdevelopment are viewed, as they should be, in both a domestic *and* a global context.

Summary and conclusions

Development economics is a distinct yet very important extension of both traditional economics and political economy. While necessarily also being concerned with efficient resource allocation and the steady growth of aggregate output over time, development economics focuses primarily on those economic, social and institutional mechanisms necessary to bring about *rapid and large-scale* improvements in levels of living for the masses of poor people in Third World nations. As such, *development economics must be concerned with the formulation of appropriate public policies designed to affect major economic, institutional and social transformations of entire societies in the shortest possible time.* Otherwise the gap between aspiration and reality will continue to widen with each passing year. It is for this reason that the public sector assumes a much broader and more determining role in development economics than it does in traditional (Western) economic analysis.

As a 'social science', economics is concerned with people and how best to provide them with the material means to help them realize their full human potentials. But the question 'what constitutes the good life' is perennial and, as such, economics must of necessity be concerned with 'values' and value-choices. Our very concern with promoting development represents an implicit value-choice about good (development) and evil (underdevelopment). But 'development' may mean a lot of different things to a lot of different people. Therefore, the nature and character of that development and the meaning which we attach to it needs to be carefully spelled out. This will be our task in Chapter 3 and elsewhere throughout the book.

The central economic problems of all societies include traditional questions such as what, where, how, how much and for whom goods and services should be produced. But they should also include the fundamental question at the national level about who or which groups actually make or influence economic decisions and for whose principal benefit are these decisions made. Finally, at the international level, the question of which nations and which powerful groups within particular nations exert the most influence with regard to the use and deployment of scarce global food and mineral resource supplies must also be considered. Moreover, for whom do they exercise this power?

Any realistic analysis of development problems necessitates the supplementation of strictly economic variables such as income, investment and saving with equally relevant 'non-economic' factors including the nature of land tenure arrangements, the influence of social and class stratifications, the structure of credit, education and health systems, the organization and motivation of government bureaucracies, the machinery of public administration, the nature of popular attitudes towards work, leisure and self-improvement, and the values, roles and attitudes of political and economic elites. Economic development strategies which seek to raise agricultural output, create employment and eradicate poverty have often failed in the past because economists and other policy advisers neglected to view the economy as an interdependent 'social system' where economic and non-economic variables are continually interacting, sometimes in self-reinforcing ways and other times in contradictory manners.

We conclude this introductory chapter by stressing the importance of viewing these internal 'social systems' of developing nations within the broader context of the 'international social system' of all nations, rich and poor. Here, the phenomena of small but different power groups, mostly from rich nations, influencing global strategies and the corresponding 'vulnerability' of Third World nations caught in a dominance and dependence situation vis-à-vis the industrial nations of both East and West is often emphasized. An analogous vulnerability and dominance/dependence relationship often also exists between the great masses of people and the relatively small but powerful elites in the developing nations themselves.

Nevertheless, the evolution of the world economy in the mid-1970s and the emergence of global raw material and natural resource scarcities has underlined, as no other event had previously, the increasing dependence of rich nations on poor ones and thus the growing 'interdependence' of all nations and peoples within the international social system. What happens to life in Caracas, Cairo and Calcutta will in one way or another have important implications for life in New York, London and Moscow. It was once said that 'when the United States sneezes, the world catches pneumonia'. A more fitting expression for the 1970s and 1980s would perhaps be that 'the world is like the human body, if one part aches, the rest will feel it; if many parts hurt, the whole will suffer'.

Third World nations constitute these 'many parts' of the global organism. The nature and character of their future development, therefore, should be a major concern of *all* nations irrespective of their political, ideological or economic orientations. In the latter part of the twentieth century and in the twenty-first, there can no longer be 'two futures' – one for the few rich and the other for the very many poor. In the words of a poet, 'there will be only one future, or none at all'.

Notes

1. *World Development,* **2,** no. 6 (1974), 54.
2. For an excellent dissection of the role of values in development economics, see Gunnar Myrdal, *The Challenge of World Poverty,* Pantheon, New York (1970), Ch. 1. A more general critique of the idea that economics can be 'value free' is to be found in Robert Heilbroner's, 'Economics as a "value free" science', *Social Research,* **40,** (Spring 1973) 129–43.
3. Gunnar Myrdal, *Asian Drama: An Inquiry into the Poverty of Nations,* Pantheon, New York (1968), 16–17.
4. *World Development,* **2,** nos 4 and 5 (1974), 83.
5. For a critique of the relevance of neo-classical economics, even for Western developed economies, by three well-known economists, see: E. Phelps-Brown, 'The underdevelopment of economics'; G. D. N. Worswick, 'Is progress in economic science possible?'; and N. Kaldor, 'The irrelevance of equilibrium economics'; all in the *Economic Journal,* 1972.
6. Although monopolies of resource purchase and product sale are a pervasive phenomenon in most developing nations, the traditional theory of monopoly offers little insight into the day-to-day activities of these public, parastatal and private corporations. Decision rules can vary widely with the social setting so that profit maximization may be a low priority objective in comparison with, say, employment creation or the replacement of expatriate managers with local personnel.
7. One of the earliest and most powerful critiques of the relevance of Keynesian economics for developing nations can be found in Dudley Seers' seminal paper, 'The limitations of the special case', *Bulletin of the Oxford Institute of Economics and Statistics,* May 1965.
8. See, for example, J. K. Galbraith, 'Power and the useful economist' *American Economic Review,* March 1973 and W. Leontief, 'Theoretical assumptions and non-observed facts', *American Economic Review,* March 1971, 1–7. However, for a staunch defence of Keynesian economics and Keynesian policies for developed countries, see W. Heller, 'What's right with economics', *American Economic Review,* March 1975, 1–26.

Concepts for review

traditional (Western) economics	'laws' versus 'tendencies'
political economy	values and value premises
development economics	social system
economic theory	non-economic variables
economic model	interdependence
consumer sovereignty	economic and social 'institutions'
'Western' economic theory	economic system – domestic and
First World	international
Second World	subsistence economy
Third World	dominance/dependence relationships
social science	

Questions for discussion

1. Why do you think economics is so central to an understanding of the problems of Third World development?
2. Do you think that the concept of the 'Third World' is a useful one? Why or why not?
3. Why should one be skeptical about any claims of universal applicability of traditional 'Western' economic theories? Explain.
4. What is the meaning of our assertion that although assumptions and propositions of

economic theories may differ from one society to the next, the 'thought processes' of economics should be similar? Can you give some examples of common thought processes?

5. Do you think that the wide diversity of living conditions found by our brief trip around the world can also be found within most Third World countries? What do we mean by the notion of different 'levels of living'?

6. What do you hope to gain from this course in Development Economics (that is, besides a passing grade!)?

7. Why are values and value premises so important in economics? Can economics ever be truly 'value free'? Why or why not?

8. Why is it important to view economies as 'social systems' and to go beyond simple economic factors in analyzing development problems?

9. What do you think is meant by the expression 'interdependent international social system'? In what ways are national economies becoming more interdependent as we approach the end of the twentieth century?

Further readings For an enjoyable and lively layman's exposition of the nature of neo-classical economics see Robert A. Mundell, *Man and Economics*, McGraw-Hill, New York (1968), Ch. 1–3. In addition to Note 5 and the Seer's article referred to in Note 7 an extensive critique of assumptions, methodology and relevance of contemporary neo-classical economics can be found in J. Kornai, *Anti-Equilibrium: On Economic Systems, Theory and the Tasks of Research*, North-Holland (1971); and especially, in M. Hollis and E. J. Neil, *Rational Economic Man: A Philosophical Critique of Neo-Classical Economics*, Cambridge U.P., New York (1975). On the role of values, institutions and theories in traditional economics and their limited relevance for Third World countries, see Gunnar Myrdal, *The Challenge of World Poverty*, Pantheon, New York (1970), Pt One.

Diverse structures and common characteristics of developing nations	Chapter 2

Of course there must be differences between developing countries . . . [but] to maintain that no common ground exists is to make any discussion outside or across the frontiers of a single country meaningless.
  Julian West, Oxford University

The Third World is important because of the massiveness of its poverty.
  Padma Desai, Delhi School of Economics and Harvard University

Introduction: similarity within diversity

It is hazardous to try to generalize too much about the 118 nations that constitute the 'less developed countries' of the Third World. While almost all are poor in money terms, they are diverse in culture, economic conditions and social and political structures. Thus, for example, low income countries include India with over 600 million people and seventeen states as well as Gambia with less than 500,000 people, fewer than a single borough of New York City. Large size entails complex problems of national cohesion and administration while offering the benefits of relatively large markets, a wide range of resources and the potential for self-sufficiency and economic diversity. On the other hand, many small countries present quite different problems including limited markets, shortages of skills, scarce physical resources, weak bargaining power and little prospect of significant economic self-reliance.

Analysts, therefore, sometimes prefer to distinguish among *three* major groups of countries within the Third World; the forty-two poorest countries designated by the United Nations as 'least developed'[1], the sixty-three non-oil exporting 'developing' nations[2], and the thirteen petroleum-rich OPEC countries whose national incomes have jumped dramatically during the 1970s. Appendix 2.2 provides a complete listing of all 118 Third World countries classified according to the above three groupings, as well as the thirty-five developed nations with important economic and social data for each.

Despite the obvious diversity, however, most Third World nations do share a set of common and well-defined goals. These include among others the reduction of poverty, inequality and unemployment, the provision of minimum levels of education, health, housing and food to every citizen, the broadening of economic and social opportunities and the forging of a cohesive nation-state. Related to these economic, social and political goals are the common problems shared in varying degrees by most developing countries – e.g. widespread and chronic absolute poverty, high and rising levels of unemployment and under-employment, wide and growing disparities in the distribution of income, low and stagnating levels of agricultural productivity, sizable and growing imbalances between urban and rural levels of living and economic opportunities, antiquated and inappropriate educational and health systems, and substantial and increasing dependence on foreign and often inappropriate technologies, institutions and value systems. It, therefore, *is* possible and useful to talk about the similarities of critical development problems and to analyze these problems in a broad Third World perspective. This will be our task in Parts II and III.

For the present, however, we attempt to identify some of the most important structural *differences* among developing countries and then provide relevant data to delineate some of their most *common* characteristic features. In spite of obvious physical, demographic, historical, cultural and structural differences, most Third World nations do share a common set of economic and social dilemmas that define their state of underdevelopment.

2.1 An overview of the diverse structure of Third World economies

With regard to the structural diversity of developing nations, we can list seven major components. These include:
1. the size of the country (geographic, population and income);
2. its historical evolution;
3. its physical and human resource endowments;
4. the relative importance of its public and private sectors;
5. the nature of its industrial structure;
6. its degree of dependence on external economic and political forces; and
7. the distribution of power and the institutional and political structure within the nation.

Let us briefly consider each with specific reference to similarities and differences in Africa, Asia and Latin America.

1. Size and income level Obviously, the sheer physical size of a country, its population and its level of national income per capita are important determinants of its economic potential and a major factor differentiating one Third World nation from another. Of the 97 developing countries which are full members of the United Nations, 72 have less than 15 million people and 51 less than 5 million. There are large and populated nations like Brazil, India, Egypt and Nigeria existing side by side with small countries like Paraguay, Nepal, Jordan and Chad. Large size usually presents advantages of diverse resource endowment, large potential markets and a lesser dependence on foreign sources of materials and products. But it also creates problems of administrative control, national cohesion and regional imbalances. As we shall see in Chapter 5, there is no necessary relationship between a country's size, its level of per capita national income and the degree of equality or inequality in its distribution of that income. Even excluding the wealthy OPEC oil states, India with a population of over 600 million has an annual per capita income level of less than $125 while nearby Singapore with less than 2·5 million people has an annual GNP per capita of over $1,300.

Most African and Asian nations were at one time or another colonies of Western European countries – primarily Britain and France but also Belgium, the Netherlands, Germany, Portugal and Spain. Their economic structures as well as their educational and social institutions, therefore, have typically been modelled upon those of their former colonial rulers. Countries like those in Africa which only recently gained their independence are, therefore, likely to be more concerned with consolidating and evolving their own national economic and political structures than simply with promoting rapid economic development. Their policies (for example, the rapid Africanization of former colonial held civil service jobs) may therefore reflect a greater interest with these political issues.

2. Historical background

In Latin America, a longer history of political independence plus a more common colonial heritage (i.e. Spanish and Portuguese) has meant that in spite of geographical and demographic diversity, the countries possess relatively similar economic, social and cultural institutions and face similar problems. In Asia, different colonial heritages and the diverse cultural traditions of the indigenous peoples have combined to create quite different institutional and social patterns in countries such as India (British), the Philippines (Spanish and American), Laos (French) and Indonesia (Dutch).

A country's potential for economic growth is greatly influenced by its *physical* resource endowment (its land, minerals and other raw materials) and by its endowment of human resources (i.e. both numbers of people and their level of skills). The extreme case of the blessings of favourable physical resource endowments is, of course, the Persian Gulf oil states. At the other extreme are countries like Togo, Laos, Haiti and Bangladesh where endowments of raw materials and minerals as well as fertile land are relatively minimal.

3. Physical and human resource endowments

In the realm of *human* resource endowments, not only are sheer numbers of people and their skill levels important but so also are their cultural outlooks, attitudes towards work and desire for self-improvement. Moreover, the level of administrative skills will often determine the ability of the public sector to alter the structure of production and the time in which such structural alteration can occur. Here one gets involved with the whole complex of interrelationships between culture, tradition, religion, ethnic and tribal fragmentation or cohesion. Thus, the nature and character of a country's human resources are important determinants of its economic structure (see Chapter 11) and these clearly differ from one region to the next.

Most Third World countries have 'mixed' economic systems; there is both public and private ownership and use of resources. The division between the two and their relative importance is mostly a function of historical and political circumstances. Thus, in general, Latin American nations have larger private sectors than do Asia and especially

4. Relative importance of public and private sectors

African nations. The degree of foreign ownership in the private sector is another important variable to consider when differentiating among LDCs. A large foreign-owned private sector usually creates economic and political opportunities as well as problems not found in countries where foreign investors are less prevalent. Often countries like those in Africa with severe shortages of skilled human resources tend to put greater emphasis on public sector activities on the assumption that their limited skilled manpower can be best used by coordinating rather than fragmenting administrative and entrepreneurial activities.

Economic policies, for example those designed to promote more employment, will naturally be different for countries with large public sectors in comparison with those with sizable private sectors. In economies dominated by the public sector, direct government invest-ment projects and large rural works programmes will take precedence while in private oriented economies governmental policies designed to induce private businessmen to employ more workers through special tax allowances might be more likely than direct public employment creation. Thus, although the problem (widespread unemployment) may be similar the solution can differ in countries with significant differences in the relative importance of their public and private sec-tors.

5. Industrial structure The vast majority of developing countries are agrarian in economic, social and cultural outlook. Agriculture, both subsistence and com-mercial, forms the principal economic activity in terms of the occupa-tional distribution of the labour force, if not in terms of proportionate contributions to the gross national product. As we shall see in Chapter 10, farming is not only an occupation, it is a way of life for most people in Asia, Africa and Latin America. Nevertheless, the structure of agrarian systems and patterns of land ownership show great differ-ences between, say, Latin America and Africa, with Asian agrarian systems somewhat closer to those of Latin America in terms of pat-terns of land ownership. Nevertheless, there are substantial cultural differences, which even modify these similarities between Latin America and Asia.

It is in the relative importance of the manufacturing and service sectors that we find the widest variation among developing nations. Most Latin American countries, having a longer history of indepen-dence and, in general, higher levels of national income than African or Asian nations, possess more advanced industrial sectors. But in the 1960s countries like Taiwan, South Korea and Singapore greatly accelerated the growth of their manufacturing outputs and, in the case of the first two countries, are rapidly becoming industrialized states. In terms of sheer size, India has one of the largest manufacturing sectors in the Third World but this sector is nevertheless small in relation to its enormous rural population. Table 2.1 provides information on the percentage distribution of labor force and GDP between agriculture and manufacturing in seventeen developing countries as well as in the US and UK. The contrast between the industrial structures of these countries is striking, especially in terms of the relative importance of agriculture.

In spite of common problems, therefore, Third World development strategies may vary from one country to the next depending on the nature, structure and degree of interdependence among its primary (agriculture, forestry and fishing), secondary (mostly manufacturing) and tertiary (commerce, finance, transport and services) industrial sectors.

	Per cent of labor force in		Per cent of GDP in	
	Agriculture	Manufacturing	Agriculture	Manufacturing
Africa				
Tanzania	86	6	37	9
Kenya	80	8	31	11
Nigeria	67	9	49	7
Uganda	86	8	55	8
Zaire	78	3	8	19
Asia				
Pakistan*	70	11	45	15
India	68	10	45	13
Indonesia	70	3	48	9
Philippines	70	11	30	16
Sri Lanka	52	9	33	9
South Korea	58	13	28	22
Latin America				
Mexico	47	17	11	23
Guatamala	63	11	27	16
Colombia	45	13	27	19
Brazil	44	18	13	20
Peru	46	13	19	21
Venezuela	26	19	8	17
USA	4	24	3	26
UK	3	35	3	28

Table 2.1
Industrial structure in seventeen developing countries in comparison to USA and UK: 1970

Sources: (a) Labor force and GDP data for Agriculture, ILO 1974 World Population Year, *Labour Force and World Population Growth,* Geneva (1974), Table A.
(b) GDP data for Manufacturing, United Nations, *Statistical Year Book 1973,* New York (1974), Table 178.
(c) Labor force data for Manufacturing, D. Morawitz, *Employment Implications of Industrialization in Developing Countries: A Survey,* Economics Department, Hebrew University (October 1973), Table 1.
*Including present Bangladesh.

Related mostly to a country's size, resource endowment and political history will be its degree of dependence on foreign economic, social and political forces. For most Third World countries this dependence is substantial. In some cases, it touches almost every facet of life. Most small nations are very dependent on their foreign trade with the developed world (see Ch. 12). Almost all are dependent on the importation of foreign and often 'inappropriate' technologies of production (Ch. 8). This fact alone exerts an extraordinary influence on the 'character' of the growth process in these dependent nations.

6. External dependence: economic, political and cultural

But even beyond the strictly economic manifestations of dependence in the form of the international transfer of goods and technologies, is the international transmission of institutions (most notably, systems of education and health), values, patterns of consumption and attitudes towards life, work and self. Later chapters show that this transmission phenomenon brings very mixed blessings to most LDCs and especially to those with the greatest potential for more self-reliance. A country's ability to chart its own economic and social destiny will depend to a great extent on its degree of dependence on these and other external forces.

7. Political structure, power and interest groups In the final analysis, it is often not the correctness of economic policies alone that determine the outcome of national approaches to critical development problems. The political structure and the vested interests and allegiances of ruling elites (large landowners, urban industrialists, bankers, foreign manufacturers, trade unionists, etc.) will typically determine what strategies are possible and where the main roadblocks to effective economic and social change may lie.

The constellation of interests and power among different segments of the populations of most developing countries will itself be the result of their economic, social and political histories, and is likely to differ from one country to the next. Nevertheless, whatever the specific distribution of power among the large landowners of Latin America, the politicians and high level civil servants in Africa, the oil sheiks and financial monguls of the Middle East, or the landlords, moneylenders and wealthy industrialists of Asia, most developing countries are ruled directly or indirectly by small and powerful elites to a greater extent than are the developed nations.

Effective social and economic change requires, therefore, either that the support of elite groups be enlisted through persuasion or coercion or that they be pushed aside by more powerful forces. Either way, and this point will be repeated often throughout this book, *economic and social development will often be impossible without corresponding changes in the social, political and economic 'institutions' of a nation* (e.g. land tenure systems, educational structures, labor market relationships, the distribution and control of physical and financial assets, laws of taxation and inheritance, provision of credit, etc.).

2.2. Common characteristics of developing nations

The preceding section should have demonstrated why it is sometimes risky to generalize too much about such a diverse set of nations as those in Africa, Asia and Latin America. Nevertheless, there are common characteristic economic features of developing countries which permit us to view them in a broadly similar framework. In this section we attempt to identify these similarities and provide illustrative data to demonstrate their existence. For convenience, we can classify these common characteristics into six broad catagories:

1. Low levels of living.
2. Low levels of productivity.
3. High rates of population growth and dependency burdens.
4. High and rising levels of unemployment and underemployment.
5. Significant dependence on agricultural production and primary product exports.
6. Dominance, dependence and vulnerability in international relations.

1. Low levels of living In developing nations, general levels of living tend to be very low for the vast majority of people. This is true not only in relation to their counterparts in rich nations but often also in relation to small elite groups within their own societies. These low levels of living are manifested quantitatively and qualitatively in the form of low incomes (poverty), inadequate housing, poor health, limited or no education, high infant mortality, low life and work expectancy and, in many cases, a general sense of malaise and hopelessness. Let us look at some recent statistics comparing certain aspects of life in the underdeveloped countries with that of the more economically advanced nations. Although these statistics are national aggregates, often have substantial errors of measurement and in some cases are not strictly comparable due to exchange rate variations, they do provide at least a summary indication of relative levels of living in different nations.

The Gross National Product (GNP) per capita is often used as a summary index of the relative economic well-being of people in different nations. GNP itself is the most commonly used measure of the overall level of economic activity. For example, in the early 1970s the total production of all the nations of the world was valued at more than 3,200,000 million US dollars, of which more than 2,700,000 million originated in the economically developed regions while less than 500,000 million were generated in the less developed nations. When one takes account of the distribution of world population, this means that approximately 85 per cent of the world's total income is produced in the economically developed regions by less than one third of the world's people. More than two-thirds of the world's population, therefore, is producing only 15 per cent of total world output. More importantly, on the income side, the Third World, with almost 70 per cent of the world's population, subsists on less than 20 per cent of the world's income. The collective *per capita* incomes of the under-developed countries average less than one-fourteenth of the per capita incomes of rich nations.

A. Per capita national incomes

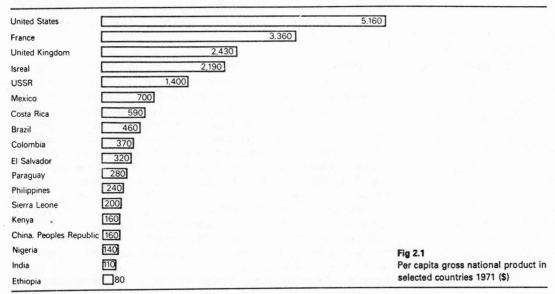

Fig 2.1
Per capita gross national product in selected countries 1971 ($)

Source: World Bank Atlas 1974, Washington DC. World Bank Group, 1974.

As an illustration of the per capita income 'gap' between rich and poor nations, look at Fig. 2.1. Notice that in 1971 the world's richest nation, the United States, had almost sixty-five times the per capita income of one of the world's poorest countries, Ethiopia, and almost fifty times that of one of the world's largest nations, India. Appendix 2.1 gives per capita income figures as well as other pertinent social and economic indicators of development for all nations of the world in 1972[3].

B. Relative growth rates of national (and per capita) incomes

In addition to having very much lower levels of per capita income, Third World countries as a whole have experienced slower GNP growth rates during the last decade than most of the developed nations. For example, the forty-two poorest countries designated by the United Nations classification system as 'least developed' showed an average annual GNP growth amounted to only $1 \cdot 1$ per cent between 1965 and 1974. The remaining fifty-five member nations classified by the UN as 'developing' showed an average growth rate of approximately $3 \cdot 3$ per cent during this same period. Taken all together, non-oil producing Third World nations showed an average GNP growth rate of approximately $2 \cdot 5$ per cent per annum.

In contrast, the average annual growth rate among all developed countries during this period was approximately $4 \cdot 6$ per cent. This means that the 'income gap' between rich and poor nations *widened* at a rate of more than 2 per cent per year. Moreover, when one takes account of the fact that the overall average annual rate of population growth in the developing countries is approximately $2 \cdot 5$ per cent while that of the developed world is only $0 \cdot 8$ per cent (see below), then the actual 'gap' between *per capita* incomes in all developed and less developed countries widened at an annual rate of $3 \cdot 8$ per cent, the rate at which per capita incomes grew in the more developed nations[4]. What is even more striking is the fact that there was *no improvement* in per capita income levels for all Third World countries taken as a group (i.e. their populations grew at the same rate as GNP) during the late 1960s – the so-called United Nations 'Development Decade'![5] No wonder one often hears the expression 'the rich get richer, while the poor get children!'

C. The distribution of national income

The growing gap between per capita incomes in rich and poor nations is not the only manifestation of the widening economic disparities between the world's rich and poor. It is also necessary to look at the growing gap between rich and poor *within* individual less developed countries to appreciate the breadth and depth of Third World poverty. We discuss the question of income distribution and equity more fully in Chapter 5 but a few remarks at this point seem appropriate.

First, all nations of the world show some degree of inequality. One finds large disparities between incomes of the rich and poor in *both* developed and underdeveloped countries. However, the gap between rich and poor is generally greater in the less developed nations than in the developed nations. For example, if we compare the share of national income which accrues to the poorest 40 per cent of a country's population with that of the richest 20 per cent as an arbitrary measure of the degree of inequality, we discover that countries like Brazil, Ecuador, Colombia, Peru, Mexico, Venezuela, Kenya, Sierra Leone, Philippines and Malaysia have substantial income inequality; others like India, Tanzania, Chile, France, Denmark and West Germany have moderate inequality, while Taiwan, Libya, Israel, Yugoslavia, Canada, Japan, the United States and Czechoslovakia have relatively lesser inequalities in their overall income distribution. Moreover, there is no obvious relationship or correlation between levels of per capita income and the degree of income inequality. The Philippines, with the same *low* per capita income as Taiwan, has a much wider income disparity between the top 20 per cent and bottom 40 per cent of the population. Similarly, Venezuela, with almost the same *high* per capita income as Japan, had a much lower percentage of its income distributed to the

	Per Capita GNP 1969	Population, 1969	Population below $50 Per Capita		Population below $75 Per Capita	
				(percentage of		(percentage of
	($)	(millions)	(millions)	population)	(millions)	population)
Latin America*	545	244·5	26·6	10·8	42·5	17·4
Ecuador	264	5·9	2·2	37·0	3·5	58·5
Honduras	265	2·5	0·7	28·0	1·0	38·0
El Salvador	295	3·4	0·5	13·5	0·6	18·4
Dominican Republic	323	4·2	0·5	11·0	0·7	15·9
Colombia	347	20·6	3·2	15·4	5·6	27·0
Brazil	347	90·8	12·7	14·0	18·2	20·0
Guyana	390	0·7	0·1	9·0	0·1	15·1
Peru	480	13·1	2·5	18·9	3·3	25·5
Costa Rica	512	1·7	†	2·3	0·1	8·5
Jamaica	640	2·0	0·2	10·0	0·3	15·4
Mexico	645	48·9	3·8	7·8	8·7	17·8
Uruguay	649	2·9	0·1	2·5	0·2	5·5
Panama	692	1·4	0·1	3·5	0·2	11·0
Chile	751	9·6	†	†	†	†
Venezuela	974	10·0	†	†	†	†
Argentina	1,054	24·0	†	†	†	†
Puerto Rico	1,600	2·8	†	†	†	†
Asia*	132	872·0	320·0	36·7	499·1	57·2
Burma	72	27·0	14·5	53·6	19·2	71·0
Sri Lanka	95	12·2	4·0	33·0	7·8	63·5
India	100	537·0	239·0	44·5	359·3	66·9
Pakistan	100	111·8	36·3	32·5	64·7	57·9
Thailand	173	34·7	9·3	26·8	15·4	44·3
Korea, Republic of	224	13·3	0·7	5·5	2·3	17·0
Philippines	233	37·2	4·8	13·0	11·2	30·0
Turkey	290	34·5	4·1	12·0	8·2	23·7
Iraq	316	9·4	2·3	24·0	3·1	33·3
Taiwan	317	13·8	1·5	10·7	2·0	14·3
Malaysia	323	10·6	1·2	11·0	1·6	15·5
Iran	350	27·9	2·3	8·5	4·2	15·0
Lebanon	570	2·6	†	1·0	0·1	5·0
Africa*	303	83·8	23·8	28·4	36·6	43·6
Chad	75	3·5	1·5	43·1	2·7	77·5
Dahomey	90	2·6	1·1	41·6	2·3	90·1
Tanzania	92	12·8	7·4	57·9	9·3	72·9
Niger	94	3·9	1·3	33·0	2·3	59·9
Malagasy Republic	119	6·7	3·6	53·8	4·7	69·0
Uganda	128	8·3	1·8	21·3	4·1	49·8
Sierra Leone	165	2·5	1·1	43·5	1·5	61·5
Senegal	229	3·8	0·9	22·3	1·3	35·3
Ivory Coast	237	4·8	0·3	7·0	1·4	28·5
Tunisia	241	4·9	1·1	22·5	1·6	32·1
Rhodesia	274	5·1	0·9	17·4	1·9	37·4
Zambia	340	4·2	0·3	6·3	0·3	7·5
Gabon	547	0·5	0·1	15·7	0·1	23·0
South Africa	729	20·2	2·4	12·0	3·1	15·5
Total*	228	1,200·3	370·4	30·9	578·2	48·2

Table 2.2
Population below the poverty line, forty-four developing countries, 1969

Source: Hollis Chenery *et al.*, *Redistribution with Growth*, Oxford U.P., London, for World Bank and Institute of Development Studies, University of Sussex (1974), 12.
*Covers only listed countries.
†Negligible.
‡Includes Bangladesh.

bottom 40 per cent of its population[6]. This phenomenon underlines the important point that *economic development cannot be measured solely in terms of the level and growth of overall income or income per capita; one must also look at how that income is distributed among the population* – i.e. who benefits from development.

D. Extent of poverty   The concept of 'absolute poverty', that is, the number of people below a specified minimum level of subsistence income necessary to secure the bare essentials of food, clothing and shelter (e.g. 50 US dollars annually) – a kind of 'international poverty line' – has recently been used to estimate magnitude of world poverty. Consider, for example, Table 2.2, which shows the proportion of the populations of forty-four selected less developed nations whose income in 1969 was below $50 and $75 per year – two rough measures of the income necessary to sustain an absolute minimum standard of living at 1969 prices.

The countries listed in Table 2.2 account for almost half of the total population of all Third World nations and more than one-third of the world population. We see from the bottom figure of column 3 that a staggering 370 million people are subject to the crushing burden of absolute poverty. If we extend these figures to the rest of the Third World which had a total population of approximately 2·5 billion in 1969, we arrive at an absolute poverty estimate of almost 750 million or three out of every ten people in the less developed countries. This works out to over 20 per cent of the *total* world population. Moreover, if instead of using a 50-dollar international poverty line we use the 75-dollar minimum, the total numbers for the countries listed in Table 2.2 increases to 570 million people or almost 50 per cent of the total population of these countries. Again extending these figures to all other Third World countries, we conclude that in 1969 *almost 35 per cent of the world's population – 1·3 billion people – was attempting to subsist at bare minimum levels of living*! There is little reason to assume that there has been any improvement over the past decade. If anything, the situation is probably much worse today than it was in 1969.

Finally, we can again note from Table 2.2 that high per capita incomes do not necessarily guarantee that there is no 'absolute poverty' problem. Since the actual share of national income that accrues to different population groups varies between countries, the international poverty problem can be equally serious in countries with widely divergent per capita income levels. For example, if we compare Ecuador with Korea, we discover that even though Ecuador had a higher GNP per capita in 1969, it still had 37 per cent of its population below the $50 poverty line compared with Korea, which had less than 6 per cent. Even adjusting for errors in measurement, these results are quite striking.

E. Health   In addition to struggling on low income, many people in Third World nations fight a constant battle against malnutrition, disease and ill-health. Among the forty-two 'least developed' countries of the world, life expectancy averages approximately 43 years as compared with 54 years among other Third World countries and 71 years in developed nations. Infant mortality rates (that is, the number of children who die before their first birthday out of every 1,000 live births) average about 155 in the least developed countries compared with approximately 110 in other less developed countries and 27 in the developed countries. Some specific examples of countries are shown in Fig. 2.2.

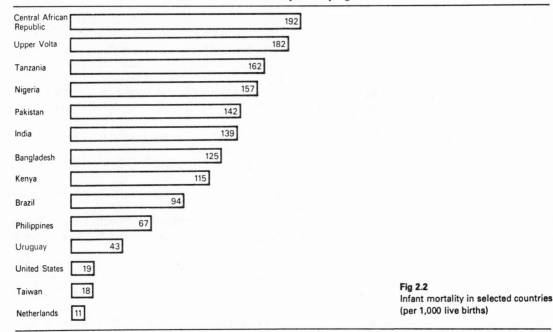

Fig 2.2
Infant mortality in selected countries
(per 1,000 live births)

Source: Overseas Development Council, *Agenda for Action: 1974*, Praeger, New York
(1974), 142 and 144–7.

Per capita daily protein consumption which is often used as a measure of malnutrition may vary from as much as 97 g in the United States
to 63, 48, and 43 g per day in Brazil, India and Ghana respectively.
Moreover, in terms of world grain consumption (i.e. wheat, rice and
corn), while the developed nations including the Soviet Union averaged approximately 650 kg per person in 1973, grain consumption in
Third World countries averaged only about 180 kg per person.

Finally, medical care is an extremely scarce social service in many
parts of the developing world. Recent data reveals that the number of
doctors per 100,000 people averages only 27 in the LDCs as compared
to 135 in the developed countries. The ratio of hospital beds to
population is similarly divergent between the two sets of nations.
Moreover, when one realizes that most of the medical facilities in
developing nations are concentrated in urban areas where only 25 per
cent of the populations reside, then the woefully inadequate provision
of health care to the masses of poor people becomes strikingly clear.
For example, in India 80 per cent of the doctors practice in urban areas
where only 20 per cent of the population resides. In Kenya, the
population to doctor ratio is 672 to 1 for the capital city of Nairobi and
20,000 to 1 in the rural countryside where 90 per cent of the Kenyan
population actually lives.

As a final illustration of the very low levels of living which permeate
Third World nations, consider the spread of educational opportunities.
The attempt to provide primary school educational opportunities has
probably been the most significant of all LDC development efforts. In
most countries, education takes the largest share of the government
budget. And, yet, in spite of some impressive quantitative advances in
school enrolments, literacy levels remain strikingly low compared with

F. Education

the developed nations. For example, among the forty-two least developed countries, literacy rates average only 10 to 15 per cent of the population (see Appendix 2.2). The corresponding rates for other Third World nations and the developed countries are approximately 50 and 97 per cent respectively. Moreover, as we point out in Chapter 11 much of the education provided for those children who are able to attend school is ill-suited and often irrelevant to the development needs of the nation.

Summarizing our discussion so far, we can list the following characteristics of developing countries:

1. Low relative levels, and in many countries, slow growth rates of national income.
2. Low levels and, in many countries, stagnating rates of income per capita growth.
3. Highly skewed patterns of income distribution with the top 20 per cent of the population often receiving five to ten times as much income as the bottom 40 per cent.
4. As a result of 1–3 above, great masses of Third World populations suffering from absolute poverty, with anywhere from 650 to 1,200 million people living on subsistence incomes of 50 to 75 US dollars or less per year.
5. Large segments of the populations suffering from ill health, malnutrition and debilitating diseases – with infant mortality rates running as high as ten times the rate in developed nations, and finally,
6. In education, low levels of literacy, significant school dropout rates, and inadequate and often irrelevant educational curricula and facilities.

Most important, is the interaction of *all* the characteristics which tends to reinforce and perpetuate the pervasive problems of 'poverty, ignorance and disease' that restrict the lives of so many people in the Third World.

2. Low levels of productivity In addition to low levels of living, countries are characterized by relatively low levels of labor productivity. The concept of a production function systematically relating outputs to different combinations of factor inputs for a given technology is often used to describe the way in which societies go about providing for their material needs. But, the technical, economic concept of a production function needs to be supplemented by a broader conceptualization which includes among its 'other' inputs managerial competence, worker motivations and institutional flexibilities. Throughout the developing world, levels of labor productivity (output per worker) are extremely low compared with those in developed countries. This can be explained by a number of basic economic concepts.

For example, the principle of diminishing marginal productivity states that if increasing amounts of a variable factor (labor) are applied to fixed amounts of other factors (capital, land, materials, etc.), then beyond a certain number the extra or marginal product of the variable factor declines. Low levels of labor productivity can, therefore, be explained by the absence or severe lack of 'complementary' factor inputs such as physical capital and/or experienced management.

⌐To raise productivity, according to this argument, domestic *savings* and foreign *finance* must be mobilized to generate new investment in physical capital goods and also to build up the stock of 'human capital' (e.g. managerial skills) through investment in education and training. Institutional changes are also necessary to maximize the potential of this new physical and human investment. These changes might include such diverse activities as the reform of land tenure, corporate, tax, credit and banking structures, the creation or strengthening of an independent, honest and efficient administrative service and the restructuring of educational and training programs to make them more appropriate to the needs of developing societies. These and other non-economic inputs into the 'social' production function must be taken into account if strategies to raise productivity are to succeed. An old proverb says that 'you can lead a horse to water, but you cannot make him drink'. In underdeveloped nations it is equally true that 'you can create the economic opportunities for self improvement, but without the proper institutional and structural arrangements you cannot succeed'.

One must also take into account the impact of worker and management *attitudes* towards self improvement, their degree of alertness, adaptability, ambition and general willingness to innovate and experiment, and their attitudes towards manual work, discipline, authority and possibly, also, exploitation. Added to all these must be the physical and mental capacity of the individual to do his or her own job satisfactorily.

It is with regard to the state of a person's physical health that the close *linkage* between low levels of income and low levels of productivity in developing nations is most clearly revealed. It is well known, for example, that poor nutrition in childhood can severely restrict the mental as well as the physical growth of individuals[7]. Poor dietary habits, inadequate foods and low standards of personal hygiene in later years can cause further deterioration in a worker's health and, therefore, can adversely influence his attitudes toward his job and the people around him. His low productivity may be due not so much to a lack of 'complementary' resources but to his physical lethargy and inability, both physical and emotional, to withstand the daily pressures of competitive work.

We may conclude, therefore, that *low levels of living and low productivity are self-reinforcing social and economic phenomena in Third World countries, and, as such, are the principal manifestations of and contributors to their underdevelopment*. Myrdal's well-known theory of 'circular and cumulative causation' in underdeveloped countries is based upon these interactions between low living levels and low productivity[8].

3. High rates of population growth and dependency burdens

Of the total population of approximately 4 billion people in the mid-1970s, more than two-thirds live in Third World countries and less than one-third in the more developed nations. Birth and death rates are strikingly different. Birth rates in less developed countries are generally at very high levels, on the order of 40 per 1,000 or more, while those in the developed countries are less than half that figure. Indeed, as shown in Table 2.3 the crude birth rate (the yearly number of live births per 1,000 population) is probably one of the most efficient ways of distinguishing the less developed from the more developed countries. There is hardly a less developed country with a birth rate below 30 per 1,000 or a developed nation with a birth rate above it.

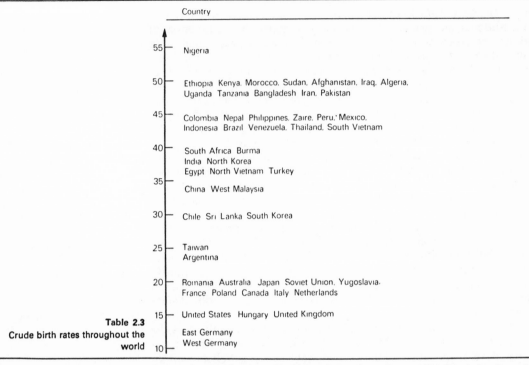

Source: Bernard Berelson, *World Population: Status Report 1974*, Population Council, New York, January 1974.

Even though death rates in Third World countries are also high relative to the more developed nations, because of improved health conditions and the control of major infectious diseases, the LDC–DC death rate differences are substantially smaller than the corresponding differences in birth rates. As a result, the average rate of population growth is now about 2·5 per cent per year in Third World countries compared with population growth rates of only about 1 per cent in the developed world.

A major implication of high LDC birth rates is that the proportion of children under the age of 15 is almost one-half of the total population in these countries, while in the developed countries the ratio is approximately a quarter of the total population. Thus the active labour force in most developing countries has to support proportionally almost twice as many children as it does in richer countries. On the other hand, the proportion of older people over the age of 65 is much greater in the developed nations. Older people as well as children are often referred to as an economic 'dependency burden' in the sense that they are non-productive members of society and therefore must be supported financially by a country's labor force (usually defined as those between the ages of 15 and 64). The overall dependency burden (i.e. both young and old) represents only about one-third of the populations of developed countries compared with half of the populations of the less developed nations. Moreover, in the latter countries, over 90 per cent of the dependents are children, whereas only 66 per cent are children in the richer nations.

We may conclude, therefore, that not only are Third World countries characterized by higher rates of population growth, they also must contend with greater dependency burdens than rich nations. The circumstances and conditions in which rapid population growth becomes a deterrent to economic development is, however, another question; one to be carefully examined in Chapter 7.

One of the principal manifestations of and factors contributing to the low levels of living in developing nations is their relatively inadequate or inefficient utilization of labor in comparison with the developed nations. Underutilization of labor is manifested in two forms. First, it occurs as 'underemployment' – those people, both rural and urban, who are working less than they could (daily, weekly or seasonally). Underemployment includes also those who are normally working full-time but whose productivity is so low that a reduction in hours would have a negligible impact on total output. The second form is open unemployment – those people who are able and often eager to work but for whom no suitable jobs are available.

4. High and rising levels of unemployment and underemployment

Current rates of open unemployment in Third World areas average from 10 to 15 per cent of the urban labor force. But this is only part of the story. Unemployment among young people aged 15 to 24, many of whom have a substantial education, is typically almost twice as high as the overall average. Table 2.4 provides some rough estimates of unemployment by age for eight selected Third World urban areas.

Urban Area	Ages 15–24	Ages 15 and over (Total)
Ghana, large towns	21·9	11·6
Bogota, Colombia	23·1	13·6
Buenos Aires, Argentina	6·3	4·2
Chile, urban areas	12	6
Caracas, Venezuela	37·7	18·8
Bangkok, Thailand	7·7	3·4
Philippines, urban areas	20·6	11·6
Singapore	15·7	9·2

Table 2.4
Rates of urban unemployment by age: Selected urban areas of LDCs

Source: Edgar O. Edwards, *Employment in Developing Countries*, Ford Foundation, New York (1973), Table 2.

The data shown in Table 2.4 represent, however, only the tip of the iceberg of LDC labor underutilization. When the *under*employed are added to the openly unemployed *almost 30 per cent of the combined urban and rural labor forces in Third World nations is unutilized* (see Ch. 8, Table 8.1).

With LDC populations growing rapidly, their labor forces will also be increasing fast for some time to come. This means that jobs will have to be created at equivalent rates simply to keep pace with the growth of labor supply. Moreover, in urban areas where rural–urban migration is causing the labor force to 'explode' at annual rates of 6 to 9 per cent in many countries (especially those in Africa), the prospects for coping effectively with rising levels of unemployment and underemployment and for dealing with the frustrations and anxieties of an increasingly vocal, educated, but unemployed youth are, to say the least, frightening. We will have more to say on the dimensions and implications of the unemployment and migration problem in Third World countries in Chapters 8 and 9.

The vast majority of people in Third World nations live and work in the rural areas. Almost 80 per cent are rurally based compared to less than

5. Substantial dependence on agricultural production

and primary product exports

A. Small-scale agriculture

35 per cent in the economically developed countries. In terms of the proportions of their labor forces engaged in agriculture, the figure for less developed regions is 66 per cent compared with 21 per cent for developed nations. Moreover, agriculture contributes about 32 per cent of the gross national product of the former while it amounts to only 8 per cent of the GNP of the latter.

Table 2.5 provides a breakdown of population, labor force and agricultural production by regions of the developed and the less developed world. Note in particular the striking difference between the proportionate size of the agricultural population in Africa and Asia (66 to 72 per cent) in comparison with North America (5 per cent). In terms of actual numbers, there are almost 635 million agricultural labor force members in Asia and Africa producing an annual volume of output valued at US $136 million in 1970[9]. On the other hand, in North America, less than 1 per cent of this total number of agricultural workers ($4 \cdot 5$ million) produced almost a quarter as much total output ($32 million). This means that the average productivity of agricultural labor expressed in US dollars is almost thirty-five times greater in North America than in Asia and Africa combined. While international comparative figures such as these are often of extremely dubious quality both with regard to their precision and methods of measurement, they do nevertheless give us rough orders of magnitude. Even adjusting them for, say, undervaluing Third World non-marketed agricultural output, the differences in agricultural labour productivity would still be very sizeable.

Region	Population (millions)	Urban (%)	Rural (%)	Labor Force in Agricultural (%)	Agricultural Share of GNP (%)
World	3,632	37	63	51	12
Less developed regions	2,542	25	75	66	31
More developed regions	1,090	66	34	21	8
Africa	344	22	78	72	25
South Asia	1,126	21	79	68	36
East Asia	826	23	77	66	43
Latin America	244	53	47	45	15
Europe	462	63	37	22	8
USSR	243	57	43	32	22
North America	228	74	26	5	3
Japan	103	72	28	21	7

Table 2.5
Population, labor force and production in 1970: Developed and less developed regions

Source: ILO, *1974 World Population Year: Bulletin of Labour Statistics*, Geneva (1974), Tables 1 and 2.

The basic reason for the concentration of people and production in agricultural and other primary production activities in developing countries is the simple fact that at low income levels the first priorities of any person are for food, clothing and shelter. Agricultural productivity is low not only because of the large numbers of people in relation to available land but also because LDC agriculture is often characterized by primitive technologies, poor organization and limited physical and human capital inputs. Thus, technological backwardness arises because Third World agriculture is predominantly non-commercial, peasant farming. In many parts of the world, especially in Asia and Latin America, it is characterized further by land tenure arrangements in which peasant proprietors usually rent rather than own their small plots of land. As we shall see in Chapter 10, such land tenure arrangements take away much of the economic incentive for output expansion and productivity improvement. Even where there is abundant land, primitive techniques and the use of hand ploughs, drag harrows and animal (oxen buffalo, donkeys, etc.) or raw human power necessitate that typical family holdings be not more than 5 to 8 hectares (12 to 20 acres). In fact, in many countries average holdings can be as low as 1 to 3 hectares. The number of people that this land must support both directly (through on the farm consumption) and indirectly (through production for urban and non-farm rural food consumption) often runs as high as 10 to 15 people per hectare. It is no wonder, therefore, that efforts to improve the efficiency of agricultural production and to increase the average per-hectare yields of rice, wheat, maize, soybeans and millet are now and will continue to be top priority development objectives.

B. Dependence on exports

Most economies of less developed countries are oriented towards the production of primary products as opposed to 'secondary' (manufacturing) and 'tertiary' (service) activities. These primary commodities form their main exports to other nations (both developed and less developed). For example, Table 2.6 shows that in 1971 for all Third World countries, these primary products (food, raw materials, fuels and base metals) accounted for almost 80 per cent of all exports. But except for those few countries blessed with abundant supplies of petroleum and other valuable mineral resources, basic foodstuffs and raw materials alone account for most LDC exports.

As we shall see in Chapter 14, most poor countries need to obtain foreign exchange in addition to domestic savings in order to finance priority development projects. While private foreign investment flows, plus foreign aid, are a significant source of such foreign exchange, exports of primary products typically account for 60 to 75 per cent of the annual flow of total foreign currency earnings into the developing world.

Category	Developed countries	Less developed countries	
Primary commodities			
Food. Food products and raw materials	18 4	39 39	
Fuels			
Manufactures			
Chemicals	9	2	
Engineering products	36	2	
Manufactures (non-metallic mineral and other)	31	17	Table 2.6
Unspecified	2	1	Composition of world exports 1971 (percentages of manufactured
Total	100	100	and primary products)

(Developed countries: 24% Primary, 76% MFGS; Less developed countries: 79% Primary, 21% MFGS)

Source: Overseas Development Council, *Agenda for Action 1974*, Washington (1974), p. 164.

Even though exports loom so important in many developing nations, over the past 20 years export growth (excluding oil exports) has not kept pace with that of developed countries. Consequently, even in their best years, the developing nations have been losing ground in terms of their share of total world trade to the more developed countries. In 1950, for example, their share was nearly 33 per cent. It has fallen in almost every year since, and by 1973 had fallen to nearly 16 per cent. At the same time, the developed countries have increased their share of world trade (mostly by trading with each other) from 60 to 74 per cent. Moreover, the percentage of total Third World exports going to each other dropped from 23 per cent in 1960 to 19 per cent by 1973. Thus, the less developed countries have become even more dependent upon the rich countries for outlets for their products while their overall share of world trade has been declining[10].

This growing LDC dependence on rich country economies for flows of foreign exchange brings us to one last major common characteristic of Third World nations – their dependence upon and occasional dominance by rich nations in the world economy.

6. Dominance, dependence and vulnerability in international relations For many less developed countries, a significant factor contributing to the persistence of low levels of living, rising unemployment and growing income inequality is the highly unequal distribution of economic and political power between rich and poor nations. As we shall see later, these unequal strengths are manifested not only in the dominant power of rich nations to control the pattern of international trade, but also in their ability often to dictate the terms in which technology, foreign aid and private capital are transferred to developing countries.

But there are other equally important aspects of the international transfer process which serve to inhibit the development of poor nations. One subtle but nonetheless very significant factor contributing to the persistence of underdevelopment has been the transfer of First and Second World values, attitudes, institutions and standards of behaviour to Third World nations. Examples include the transfer of often inappropriate educational structures, curricular and school systems, the formation of Western-style trade unions and the organization and orientation of health services also following the Western model, and, finally, the structure and operation of public bureaucratic and administrative systems which also may be out of tune with both the priority needs and the available manpower supplies in developing nations. Of even greater potential significance, however, may be the influence of rich country social and economic standards on developing country salary scales, elite life styles and general attitudes towards the private accumulation of wealth. Such attitudes can often breed corruption and economic plunder by a privileged minority. Finally, the penetration of rich country attitudes, values and standards also contributes to a problem widely recognized and referred to as the 'international brain drain' – i.e. the loss through emigration of highly educated and skilled personnel who may or may not have been trained in the local country.

The net effect of all these factors is to create a situation of 'vulnerability' among Third World nations in which forces largely outside their control can have decisive and dominating influences on their overall economic and social well-being. Many countries – most of the forty-two 'least developed' certainly – are 'small' and their economies 'dependent' with very little prospect for self-reliance. Their withdrawal from the world economy is virtually impossible. But, as we shall see in Chapter 13, hope can be found in their joining forces economically to promote 'collective' self-reliance. Such cooperation can also strengthen the joint bargaining power of small nations and enable them to scrutinize more carefully and be more selective about foreign investment and technical assistance.

For that larger number of Third World nations who possess greater assets and relatively more bargaining power, the phenomenon of dominance becomes manifested more in the general tendency of the rich to get richer, often at the expense of the poor. But this is not simply a matter of rich *nations* growing at a faster pace than poor nations. It is also a matter of the rich and dominating sectors or groups *within* the LDC economy (e.g. the 'modern' industrial or agricultural sector; landlords, trade union leaders, industrialists, politicians, bureaucrats and civil servants in positions of power) growing richer often at the expense of the much larger but politically and economically less powerful masses of poor people. This dual process of rich nations and powerful groups within poor nations simultaneously prospering while others stagnate is by no means an isolated phenomenon. We shall see that it is a rather common characteristic of international economic relations when we discuss the concept of 'dualism' and 'dual societies' in the next chapter.

Conclusion

The phenomenon of underdevelopment needs to be viewed both in a national and an international context. Economic and social forces, both internal and external, are responsible for the poverty, inequality and low productivity that commonly characterize most Third World nations. The successful pursuit of economic and social development will require not only the formulation of appropriate strategies within the Third World, but also a modification of the present international economic order to make it more responsive to the development needs of poor nations. But in order to formulate such domestic strategies and to suggest such international modifications, it is essential that we start with a fairly clear idea about what we mean when we use the words 'development' and 'underdevelopment'. This will be our objective in Chapter 3.

Notes

1. These countries are sometimes even referred to as the 'Fourth World' to underline their situation as the 'poorest of the poor' Third World countries and their special need for international assistance. For a description and analysis, see H. C. Low and J. W Howe, 'Focus on the Fourth World' in *The US and World Development: Agenda for Action 1975*, published for the Overseas Development Council by Praeger, New York (1975), 35–54.
2. Whether or not most of these countries are actually 'developing' is a moot point. It all depends on one's definition of development (see Ch. 3). However, for expository convenience and in order to avoid semantic confusion we will use the adjectives 'developing', 'less developed' and 'underdeveloped' interchangably throughout the text when referring to Third World countries as a whole. To do otherwise would unnecessarily complicate the discussion.
3. By the end of the 1974–5 oil price boom, countries like Kuwait, Qatar and the United Arab Emirates all had per capita incomes greatly in excess of that of the United States. Yet in terms of total 'wealth' (i.e. accumulated physical and financial assets) the United States is still far ahead of the rest of the world even though, according to the 1976 edition of the *World Bank Atlas* in per capita terms, both Sweden ($6,720) and Switzerland ($6,650) had surpassed the United States ($6,640).
4. Recall that the rate of growth of per capita income is simply measured as the difference between GNP growth (4·6 per cent) and population growth (0·8 per cent).

5. Naturally, within the group of Third World nations there are instances of much better and much worse economic performances than the overall average (see Appendix 2.1).
6. For specific country-by-country data, see Hollis Chenery *et al.*, *Redistribution With Growth*, Oxford U.P., London (1974), 8–9.
7. See, for example, Alan Berg *et al.* (eds), *Nutrition, National Development and Planning*, MIT Press, Cambridge and London (1973), Parts One and Two.
8. See, for example, Gunnar Myrdal, *Asian Drama*, Pantheon, New York (1968), Appendix 2.
9. The total value of actual agricultural output was probably somewhat higher than this figure since much of the food output in LDCs is consumed directly by farm families and, therefore, not always estimated in aggregate production figures.
10. The share has risen slightly since 1973 but this has been due solely to the spectacular increase in export earnings of OPEC nations. For the rest of the Third World, there has been a continuing decline in their share of world trade (see Ch. 12).

Concepts for review

dependency burden	literacy
per capita income	labor productivity
income 'gap'	crude birth rate
income inequality	death rate
'absolute' poverty	open unemployment
levels of living	underemployment
infant mortality	exports
malnutrition	foreign exchange

Questions for discussion

1. Explain the many ways in which Third World countries may differ in their economic, social and political structures. They are linked together by a range of common problems. What are these common problems? Which do you think are the most important? Why?
2. Explain the distinction between low levels of living and low per capita incomes. Can there exist low levels of living simultaneous with high levels of per capita income? Explain and give some examples.
3. What are some common characteristics of less developed countries? Can you think of others not mentioned in the text?
4. What are the advantages and disadvantages of using a concept such as an 'international poverty line'. Do you think that a real annual income of $50 in, say, Mexico has the same meaning as in, say, Nigeria or Thailand? Explain your answer.
5. Do you think that there is a strong relationship between health, labor productivity and income levels? Explain.
6. What is meant by the statement that many Third World nations are subject to 'dominance, dependence and vulnerability' in their relations with rich nations? Can you give some examples?

Further readings

1. For a concise but very informative summary of the diverse structures and the major economic characteristics of Third World Nations, see Lester Pearson *et al.*, *Partners in Development: Report of the Commission on International Development*, Praeger, New York (1969), Annex I, pp. 231–353. See also J. A. Raffaele, *The Economic Development of Nations*, Random House, New York (1971). For regional surveys, see Gunnar Myrdal, *Asian Drama*, Pantheon, New York (1968); P. Robson and D. Lury (eds), *The Economies of Africa*, George Allen and Unwin Ltd., London (1969); and Celso Furtado, *Economic Development in Latin America*, Cambridge U.P., London (1970).
2. Information on current economic trends within individual Third World countries and regions can best be obtained from various United Nations publications including the annual *Statistical Yearbook* and the regular publications of the UN Economic Commission for Latin America (ECLA), for Africa (ECA) and for Asia and the Far East (ECAFE). Concise statistical summaries can also be obtained from the annual *World Bank Atlas*. The World Bank (IBRD) and International Monetary Fund (IMF) also carry out studies of individual countries – see their current publications list for the most recent titles.

Appendix 2.1

Relative ranking of fifteen selected Third World countries by various indices of development

I. Per capita income levels (highest to lowest)	II. Per capita growth rates (highest to lowest)	III. Income distribution: ratio bottom 40% to top 20% of population (lowest to highest)
1. Mexico	1. South Korea	1. Taiwan
2. Brazil	2. Taiwan	2 South Korea
3. Peru	3. Brazil	3. Pakistan
4 Taiwan	4. Thailand	4. India
5. Zambia	5. Kenya	5. Zambia
6. Colombia	6. Nigeria	6. Thailand
7. South Korea	7. Pakistan	7. Philippines
8. Ghana	8. Mexico	8. Colombia
9. Philippines	9. Philippines	9. Mexico
10. Thailand	10. India	10. Peru
11. Kenya	11. Colombia	11. Brazil
12. Nigeria	12. Zambia	12. N.A. – Kenya
		Nigeria
		Ghana
		Bangladesh
13. Pakistan	13. Peru	
14. India	14. Bangladesh	
15. Bangladesh	15. Ghana	

IV. Literacy (per cent of population) (highest to lowest)	V. Population growth rates (lowest to highest)	VI. Infant mortality rates (lowest to highest)
1. Taiwan	1. South Korea	1. Taiwan
2. Mexico	2. Taiwan	2. South Korea
3. Colombia	3. Nigeria	3. Philippines
4. Philippines	4. India	4. Thailand
5. South Korea	5. Bangladesh	5. Mexico
6. Thailand	6. Brazil	6. Colombia
7. Brazil	7. Ghana	7. Brazil
8. Peru	8. Zambia	8. Peru
9. India	9. Peru	9. Kenya
10. Nigeria	10. Kenya	10. Bangladesh
11. Ghana	11. Pakistan	11. India
12. Kenya	12. Philippines	12. Pakistan
13. Bangladesh	13. Mexico	13. Ghana
14. Zambia	14. Thailand	14. Nigeria
15. Pakistan	15. Colombia	15. Zambia

Appendix 2.2

Selected social and economic indicators of development: by groups of countries	Population, mid-1975 (mil.)	Per capita GNP, 1972 ($)	Per capita GNP growth rate, 1965–72 (%)	Life expectancy at birth, 1970–5 Average (yrs.)	Birth rate per 1,000, 1970–5 Average	Death rate per 1,000, 1970–5 Average
Poorest Third World countries						
Afghanistan	19·3	80[a]	0·8[a]	40	49·2	23·8
Bangladesh	73·7	70[a]	−1·6[a]	36	49·5	28·1
Bhutan	1·2	80[a]	0·4[a]	44	43·6	20·5
Botswana	0·7	240[a]	10·0[a]	44	45·6	23·0
Burundi	3·8	70[a]	1·1[a]	39	48·0	24·7
Cameroon	6·4	200	3·8	41	40·4	22·0
Central African Rep.	1·8	160	2·3	41	43·4	22·5
Chad	4·0	80	1·6	38	44·0	24·0
Dahomey	3·1	110	1·7	41	49·9	23·0
El Salvador	4·1	340	1·2	58	42·2	11·1
Ethiopia	28·0	80	1·2	38	49·4	25·8
Ghana	9·9	300	1·0	44	48·8	21·9
Guinea	4·4	90	−0·3	41	46·6	22·9
Guyana	0·8	400	1·3	68	32·4	5·9
Haiti	4·6	130	1·3	50	35·8	16·5
Honduras	3·0	320	1·7	54	49·3	14·6
India	613·2	110	1·4	50	39·9	15·7
Ivory Coast	4·9	340	4·1	44	45·6	20·6
Kenya	13·3	170	4·1	50	48·7	16·0
Khmer Rep. (Cambodia)	8·1	120[a]	−3·8	45	46·7	19·0
Laos	3·3	130[a]	3·1[a]	40	44·6	22·8
Lesotho	1·1	90[a]	1·1[a]	46	39·0	19·7
Malagasy Republic	8·0	140	1·4	44	50·2	21·1
Malawi	4·9	100	2·9	41	47·7	23·7
Maldives	0·1	100[a]	0·6[a]	n.a.	46·0	23·0
Mali	5·7	80	1·3	38	50·1	25·9
Mauritania	1·3	180	2·0	38	44·8	24·9
Nepal	12·6	80	0·1	44	42·9	20·3
Niger	4·6	90	−5·1	38	52·2	25·5
Pakistan	70·6	130	1·7	50	47·4	16·5
Rwanda	4·2	60[a]	2·1[a]	41	50·0	23·6
Senegal	4·4	260	−0·7	40	47·6	23·9
Sierra Leone	3·0	190	1·8	44	44·7	20·7

Key: [a] Tentative estimate.
[b] 1972 figure.
[c] United Nations, *Monthly Bulletin of Statistics*, Vol. 29, No. 1, January 1975.
[d] US Agency for International Development, Bureau for Population and Humanitarian Assistance, *Population Program Assistance: Annual Report, FY 1973* (Washington, DC: US Government Printing Office, 1973).
[e] August 1974 figure.
[f] October 1974 figure.
[g] March 1974 figure.
[h] November 1974 figure.
[i] December 1974 figure.
[j] September 1974 figure.
[k] June 1971 figure.
[l] Mid-1973 figure.
[m] 1966 figure.
[n] 1971 figure.
[o] December 1973 figure.
[p] f.o.b.
[q] June 1974 figure.
[r] Associate Member of OPEC.
[s] Belgium-Luxembourg.
[t] See Belgium.
[u] Includes Botswana, Lesotho, Namibia, and Swaziland.

Infant mortality per 1,000 live births	Liter- acy	Per capita energy consump- tion, 1971	Total exports, f.o.b., 1973	Total imports, c.i.f., 1973	Net bilat. ODA from DAC countries and multilat. conces- sional flows, 1973	Inter- national reserves, January 1975
	(%)	(kg coal equiv.)	($ mil.)	($ mil.)	($ mil.)	($ mil.)
182	8	27	90[bc]	181[bc]	57·4	74
132	22[d]	n.a.	357	874	425·4	n.a.
n.a.	n.a.	n.a.	n.a.	n.a.	0·5	n.a.
97	20	n.a.	n.a.	n.a.	35·0	n.a.
150	10	11	30[c]	31[c]	26·1	162
137	10-15	97	353	334	61·5	98[e]
190	5-10	60	39[bc]	34[bc]	25·6	2[e]
160	5-10	27	38[c]	82[c]	40·9	8[e]
185	20	38	47[bc]	94[bc]	26·2	32[f]
58	49	223	352	373	12·8	92[f]
181	5	32	240	215	64·3	278
156	25	192	619	450	40·7	104
216	5-10	108	n.a.	n.a.	20·5	n.a.
40	76	996	135	164	7·6	24[g]
150	10	29	52	74	7·2	15[h]
115	45	234	237	262	13·9	44[i]
139	28	186	2,958	3,236	771·4	1,508[h]
164	20	265	·858	710	62·1	77[f]
135	20-25	171	461	615	95·9	205
127	41	24	7[b]	80[b]	144·8	n.a.
123	15	91	3[b]	44[b]	73·5	n.a.
181	59	n.a.	n.a.	n.a.	11·7	n.a.
170	39	71	203	203	52·4	48
148	15·	49	99	142	28·6	79
n.a.	n.a.	n.a.	n.a.	n.a.	0·5	n.a.
188	5	25	54[c]	115[c]	67·9	5[e]
187	1-5	133	100[b]	69[b]	22·5	96[h]
169	9	9	n.a.	n.a.	31·2	138[f]
200	5	22	56[c]	68[c]	69·6	47[f]
132	16[d]	n.a.	961	981	270·9	380
133	10	10	31[c]	28[c]	37·8	13[i]
159	5-10	129	195	361	76·8	12[j]
136	10	109	132	158	14·1	48

Sources: Unless otherwise indicated, figures for population, life expectancy, birth rate, death rate, and infant mortality are from Population Reference Bureau, '1975 World Population Data Sheet;' per capita GNP and per capita GNP growth rates are from *World Bank Atlas, 1974: Population, Per Capita Product, and Growth Rates* (Washington, DC: World Bank Group, 1974); figures for literacy and per capita energy consumption are from United Nations, *Handbook of International Trade and Development Statistics: Supplement 1973*, Publication Sales No. E/F.74.11.D.7, pp. 102–15; exports, imports, and international reserves are from International Monetary Fund, *International Financial Statistics,* Vol. 28, No. 3, March 1975; and figures for net flow of bilateral ODA and multilateral concessional flows are from Report by the Chairman of the Development Assistance Committee, *Development Cooperation, 1974 Review* (Paris: OECD, 1974), pp. 266–7. All data compiled by the Overseas Development Council, Washington, DC.

Appendix 2.2 contd.

Selected social and economic indicators of development: by groups of countries	Population, mid-1975 (mil.)	Per capita GNP, 1972 ($)	Per capita GNP growth rate, 1965–72 (%)	Life expectancy at birth, 1970–5 Average (yrs.)	Birth rate per 1,000, 1970–5 Average	Death rate per 1,000, 1970–5 Average
Poorest Third World countries contd.						
Somalia	3·2	80[a]	1·1[a]	41	47·2	21·7
Sri Lanka	14·0	110	2·0	68	28·6	6·4
Sudan	18·3	120[a]	−1·1[a]	49	47·8	17·5
Tanzania	15·4	120	2·9	44	50·2	20·1
Uganda	11·4	150	2·0	50	45·2	15·9
Upper Volta	6·0	70	0·6	38	48·5	25·8
Western Samoa	0·2[acl]	150[a]	0·4[a]	63[bd]	42·0[bd]	8·0[bd]
Yemen, Arab Rep.	6·7	90[a]	2·4[a]	45	49·6	20·6
Yemen, People's Rep.	1·7	100[a]	−7·2[a]	45	49·6	20·6
Other Third World countries						
Angola	6·4	390	5·5	38	47·3	24·5
Argentina	25·4	1,290	2·9	68	21·8	8·8
Bahamas	0·2	2,240[a]	0·6[a]	n.a.	23·8	5·7
Bahrain	0·3	670	6·0	47	49·6	18·7
Barbados	0·2	800	6·2	69	21·6	8·9
Bolivia	5·4	200	1·4	47	43·7	18·0
Brazil	109·7	530	5·6	61	37·1	8·8
Burma	31·2	90	1·0	50	39·5	15·8
Chile	10·3	800	2·2	63	27·9	9·2
China, People's Rep.	822·8	170[a]	2·6[a]	62	26·9	10·3
Colombia	25·9	400	2·4	61	40·6	8·8
Congo, People's Rep.	1·3	300	1·4	44	45·1	20·8
Costa Rica	2·0	630	4·1	68	33·4	5·9
Cuba	9·5	450[a]	−1·0[a]	70	29·1	6·6
Cyprus	0·7	1,180	6·4	71	22·2	6·8
Dominican Rep.	5·1	480	5·0	58	45·8	11·0
Egypt	37·5	240	0·6	52	37·8	14·0
Equatorial Guinea	0·3	240	−1·5	44	36·8	19·7
Gambia, The	0·5	140	1·4	40	43·3	24·1
Grenada	0·1	420[a]	5·0[a]	69	27·9	7·8
Guadeloupe	0·4	910[a]	5·0[a]	69	29·3	6·4

Key: [a]Tentative estimate.
[b]1972 figure.
[c]United Nations, *Monthly Bulletin of Statistics*, Vol. 29, No. 1, January 1975.
[d]US Agency for International Development, Bureau for Population and Humanitarian Assistance, *Population Program Assistance: Annual Report, FY 1973* (Washington, DC: US Government Printing Office, 1973).
[e]August 1974 figure.
[f]October 1974 figure.
[g]March 1974 figure.
[h]November 1974 figure.
[i]December 1974 figure.

[j]September 1974 figure.
[k]June 1971 figure.
[l]Mid-1973 figure.
[m]1966 figure.
[n]1971 figure.
[o]December 1973 figure.
[p]f.o.b.
[q]June 1974 figure.
[r]Associate Member of OPEC.
[s]Belgium-Luxembourg.
[t]See Belgium.
[u]Includes Botswana, Lesotho, Namibia, and Swaziland.

Infant mortality per 1,000 live births	Literacy	Per capita energy consumption, 1971	Total exports, f.o.b., 1973	Total imports, c.i.f., 1973	Net bilat. ODA from DAC countries and multilat. concessional flows, 1973	International reserves, January 1975
	(%)	(kg coal equiv.)	($ mil.)	($ mil.)	($ mil.)	($ mil.)
177	5	31	57	112	35·1	51
45	70-80	163	388	421	52·9	74
141	10-15	119	434	436	46·3	67
162	15-20	70	368	488	94·8	50
160	20	72	326	163	13·4	44[k]
182	5-10	13	24[c]	63[c]	57·3	74[j]
57[dm]	97	112	6	19	1·8	n.a.
152	10	14	8[c]	125[c]	20·9	n.a.
152	10	639	121	170	6·9	68[e]
203	10-15	157	728	529	8·9	n.a.
60	91	1,773	3,269	2,241	13·4	1,323[h]
33	85	5,600	531	757	0·4	n.a.
138	29	7,186	246[n]	280[b]	0·7	n.a.
31	91	1,238	54	170	4·8	n.a.
108	32	224	280	256	22·5	191
94	61	500	6,199	6,999	63·3	5,531[f]
126	60	68	128	102	70·9	162
71	84	1,516	1,231	941[b]	39·7	221[n]
55	25[d]	561	n.a.	n.a.	–	n.a.
76	73	638	1,084	876	133·3	412
180	20	250	125[c]	134[c]	27·2	22[e]
54	84	446	339	451	15·7	14[n]
25	78	1,152	803[bc]	1,292[bc]	4·9	n.a.
33	76	1,451	179	447	6·0	273
98	65	264	442	486	19·5	100
103	30	282	1,119	905	73·0	603[j]
165	20[d]	183	n.a.	n.a.	–	n.a.
165	10	68	25[c]	31[c]	6·2	35[f]
34	76[d]	n.a.	n.a.	n.a.	–	n.a.
46	83	452	64	201	83·5	n.a.

Sources: Unless otherwise indicated, figures for population, life expectancy, birth rate, death rate, and infant mortality are from Population Reference Bureau, '1975 World Population Data Sheet;' per capita GNP and per capita GNP growth rates are from *World Bank Atlas, 1974: Population, Per Capita Product, and Growth Rates* (Washington, DC: World Bank Group, 1974); figures for literacy and per capita energy consumption are from United Nations, *Handbook of International Trade and Development Statistics: Supplement 1973*, Publication Sales No. E/F.74.11.D.7, pp. 102–15; exports, imports, and international reserves are from International Monetary Fund, *International Financial Statistics,* Vol. 28, No. 3, March 1975; and figures for net flow of bilateral ODA and multilateral concessional flows are from Report by the Chairman of the Development Assistance Committee, *Development Cooperation, 1974 Review* (Paris: OECD, 1974), pp. 266–7. All data compiled by the Overseas Development Council, Washington, DC.

Appendix 2.2 contd.

Selected social and economic indicators of development: by groups of countries	Population, mid-1975 (mil.)	Per capita GNP, 1972 ($)	Per capita GNP growth rate, 1965–72 (%)	Life expectancy at birth, 1970–5 Average (yrs.)	Birth rate per 1,000, 1970–5 Average	Death rate per 1,000, 1970–5 Average
Guatemala	6·1	420	2·2	53	42·8	13·7
Guinea-Bissau	0·5	230	3·4	38	40·1	25·1
Hong Kong	4·2	980	5·7	70	19·4	5·5
Jamaica	2·0	810	3·9	70	33·2	7·1
Jordan	2·7	270	−2·8	53	47·6	14·7
Korea, Dem. Rep.	15·9	320[a]	4·0[a]	61	35·7	9·4
Korea, Republic of	33·9	310	8·5	61	28·7	8·8
Lebanon	2·9	700	1·4	63	39·8	9·9
Liberia	1·7	250	4·0	44	43·6	20·7
Malaysia	12·1	430	2·9	59	38·7	9·9
Martinique	0·4	1,050[a]	4·6[a]	69	29·7	6·7
Mauritius	0·9	300	0·6	66	24·4	6·8
Mexico	59·2	750	2·8	63	42·0	8·6
Mongolia	1·4	380[a]	0·6[a]	61	38·8	9·4
Morocco	17·5	270	3·0	53	46·2	15·7
Mozambique	9·2	300	5·6	44	43·1	20·1
Netherlands Antilles	0·2	1,500[a]	0·6[a]	74	19·7	4·7
Nicaragua	2·3	470	1·5	53	48·3	13·9
Oman	0·8	530	22·5	47	49·6	18·7
Panama	1·7	880	4·5	66	36·2	7·2
Papua-New Guinea	2·7	290	7·5	48	40·6	17·1
Paraguay	2·6	320	2·1	62	39·8	8·9
Peru	15·3	520	1·1	56	41·0	11·9
Philippines	44·4	220	2·4	58	43·8	10·5
Réunion	0·5	1,010[a]	4·6[a]	63	31·2	8·5
Rhodesia	6·3	340	2·9	52	47·9	14·4
Singapore	2·2	1,300	10·3	70	21·2	5·2
Surinam	0·4	810	4·7	66	41·6	7·5
Swaziland	0·5	260[a]	5·3[a]	44	49·0	21·8
Syrian Arab Rep.	7·3	320	3·8	54	45·4	15·4
Taiwan	16·0	490	6·9	69	24·0	5·0
Thailand	42·1	220	4·2	58	43·4	10·8
Togo	2·2	160	3·3	41	50·6	23·5
Tonga	0·1[acl]	320[a]	2·0[a]	56[bd]	39·0[bd]	10·0[bd]

Key: [a] Tentative estimate.
[b] 1972 figure.
[c] United Nations, *Monthly Bulletin of Statistics*, Vol. 29, No. 1, January 1975.
[d] US Agency for International Development, Bureau for Population and Humanitarian Assistance, *Population Program Assistance: Annual Report, FY 1973* (Washington, DC: US Government Printing Office, 1973).
[e] August 1974 figure.
[f] October 1974 figure.
[g] March 1974 figure.
[h] November 1974 figure.
[i] December 1974 figure.

[j] September 1974 figure.
[k] June 1971 figure.
[l] Mid-1973 figure.
[m] 1966 figure.
[n] 1971 figure.
[o] December 1973 figure.
[p] f.o.b.
[q] June 1974 figure.
[r] Associate Member of OPEC.
[s] Belgium-Luxembourg.
[t] See Belgium.
[u] Includes Botswana, Lesotho, Namibia, and Swaziland.

Infant mortality per 1,000 live births	Literacy (%)	Per capita energy consumption, 1971 (kg coal equiv.)	Total exports, f.o.b., 1973 ($ mil.)	Total imports, c.i.f., 1973 ($ mil.)	Net bilat. ODA from DAC countries and multilat. concessional flows, 1973 ($ mil.)	International reserves, January 1975 ($ mil.)
79	38	250	442	431	18·3	218
208	n.a.	103	n.a.	n.a.	8·6	n.a.
17	71	1,040	5,051	5,637	0·9	n.a.
26	82	1,338	392	668	15·6	174
99	35-40	318	58	335	88·8	472
n.a.	n.a.	2,294	n.a.	n.a.	–	n.a.
60	71	860	3,220	4,219	279·0	1,056[l]
54	86	841	573	1,184	11·7	1,672
159	9	368	324	193	10·0	n.a.
75	43[d]	n.a.	2,950	2,402	42·7	1,618[l]
32	85	660	55[c]	244[c]	101·8	n.a.
65	61	183	132	171	11·9	139
61	78	1,270	2,631	4,146	12·6	1,280[f]
n.a.	95[d]	945	n.a.	n.a.	–	n.a.
149	14	205	872	1,099	91·2	417[l]
165	7	178	304[c]	478[c]	3·9	n.a.
25	n.a.	n.a.	950	1,250	22·0	n.a.
123	50	389	277	327	26·2	166[l]
138	n.a.	62	260[b]	134[b]	0·1	n.a.
47	78	2,121	133	489	22·2	2,303[o]
159	29	133	511[c]	316[cp]	195·0	n.a.
84	74	142	127	122	14·7	89
110	61	621	1,047	863	73·8	551[o]
78	72	298	1,788	1,773	220·4	1,607
43[adn]	52	334	50[b]	196[b]	176·3	n.a.
122	25-30	618	499[bc]	417[bcp]	0·9	n.a.
20	75	851	3,605	5,063	25·7	1,392[q]
30	84	2,229	172[b]	144[b]	29·4	n.a.
149	36	n.a.	n.a.	n.a.	10·3	n.a.
93	35	485	339	595	10·4	773[f]
28	85	n.a.	4,378	3,797	-20·5	1,191[l]
65	68	296	1,584	2,057	60·5	1,905
179	5-10	73	61[c]	101[c]	25·8	47[j]
107[dm]	90-95[d]	n.a.	n.a.	n.a.	0·9	n.a.

Sources: Unless otherwise indicated, figures for population, life expectancy, birth rate, death rate, and infant mortality are from Population Reference Bureau, '1975 World Population Data Sheet;' per capita GNP and per capita GNP growth rates are from *World Bank Atlas, 1974: Population, Per Capita Product, and Growth Rates* (Washington, DC: World Bank Group, 1974); figures for literacy and per capita energy consumption are from United Nations, *Handbook of International Trade and Development Statistics: Supplement 1973*, Publication Sales No. E/F.74.11.D.7, pp. 102–15; exports, imports, and international reserves are from International Monetary Fund, *International Financial Statistics*, Vol. 28, No. 3, March 1975; and figures for net flow of bilateral ODA and multilateral concessional flows are from Report by the Chairman of the Development Assistance Committee, *Development Cooperation, 1974 Review* (Paris: OECD, 1974), pp. 266–7. All data compiled by the Overseas Development Council, Washington, DC.

Appendix 2.2 contd.

Selected social and economic indicators of development: by groups of countries	Population, mid-1975 (mil.)	Per capita GNP, 1972 ($)	Per capita GNP growth rate, 1965–72 (%)	Life expectancy at birth, 1970–5 Average (yrs.)	Birth rate per 1,000, 1970–5 Average	Death rate per 1,000, 1970–5 Average
Trinidad and Tobago	1·0	970	3·6	70	25·3	5·9
Tunisia	5·7	380	3·7	54	40·0	13·8
Turkey	39·9	370	4·3	57	39·4	12·5
Uruguay	3·1	760	0·4	70	20·4	9·3
Vietnam, Dem. Rep.	23·8	110[a]	−0·1[a]	48	41·4	17·9
Vietnam, Republic of	19·7	170	−0·7	40	41·7	23·6
Zaire	24·5	100[a]	3·9[a]	44	45·2	20·5
Zambia	5·0	380	−0·1	44	51·5	20·5
OPEC countries						
Algeria	16·8	430	3·5	53	48·7	15·4
Ecuador	7·1	360	3·8	60	41·8	9·5
Gabon[r]	0·5	880	10·0	41	32·2	22·2
Indonesia	136·0	90	4·3	48	42·9	16·9
Iran	32·9	490	7·2	51	45·3	15·6
Iraq	11·1	370	1·8	53	48·1	14·6
Kuwait	1·1	4,090	−1·3	67	47·1	5·3
Libyan Arab Rep.	2·3	1,830	8·1	53	45·0	14·8
Nigeria	62·9	130	5·4	41	49·3	22·7
Qatar	0·1	2,530	6·1	47	49·6	18·7
Saudi Arabia	9·0	550[a]	6·8[a]	45	49·5	20·2
United Arab Emirates	0·2	3,220	16·2	47	49·6	18·7
Venezuela	12·2	1,240	1·1	65	36·1	7·1
Developed countries						
Albania	2·5	530	5·7	69	33·4	6·5
Australia	13·8	2,980	3·1	72	21·0	8·1
Austria	7·5	2,410	5·0	71	14·7	12·2
Belgium	9·8	3,210	4·6	73	14·8	11·2
Bulgaria	8·8	1,420	5·9	72	16·2	9·2
Canada	22·8	4,440	3·2	72	18·6	7·7

Key: [a]Tentative estimate.
[b]1972 figure.
[c]United Nations, *Monthly Bulletin of Statistics*, Vol. 29, No. 1, January 1975.
[d]US Agency for International Development, Bureau for Population and Humanitarian Assistance, *Population Program Assistance: Annual Report, FY 1973* (Washington, DC: US Government Printing Office, 1973).
[e]August 1974 figure.
[f]October 1974 figure.
[g]March 1974 figure.
[h]November 1974 figure.
[i]December 1974 figure.

[j]September 1974 figure.
[k]June 1971 figure.
[l]Mid-1973 figure.
[m]1966 figure.
[n]1971 figure.
[o]December 1973 figure.
[p]f.o.b.
[q]June 1974 figure.
[r]Associate Member of OPEC.
[s]Belgium-Luxembourg.
[t]See Belgium.
[u]Includes Botswana, Lesotho, Namibia, and Swaziland.

Infant mortality per 1,000 live births	Literacy	Per capita energy consumption, 1971	Total exports, f.o.b., 1973	Total imports, c.i.f., 1973	Net bilat. ODA from DAC countries and multilat. concessional flows, 1973	International reserves, January 1975
	(%)	(kg coal equiv.)	($ mil.)	($ mil.)	($ mil.)	($ mil.)
35	89	3,962	658	776	1·3	394
128	30	255	386	608	129·7	418[l]
119	46	516	1,318	2,091	82·4	1,861[i]
40	91	958	322	285	15·8	216[h]
n.a.	65	165	n.a.	n.a.	–	n.a.
n.a.	60	290	59	620	447·2	240[l]
160	35-40	77	691[b]	787[b]	139·2	140[l]
157	15-20	458	1,142	604	45·2	221[h]
128	25-30	492	1,802	2,338	108·3	1,497
78	68	315	561	532	29·1	336
229	12	1,028	287	160	34·1	47[e]
125	43	123	3,211	2,347	589·2	1,624
139	23	895	6,914	3,370	–3·3	8,513
99	20	650	2,292	899	12·4	3,273[i]
44	47	7,888	3,789	1,042	–3·2	1,654
130	27	571	4,085	1,723	12·9	3,523
180	25	59	3,358	1,874	72·8	5,981
138	10-15[d]	2,025	332[b]	128[b]	0·4	n.a.
152	5-15	988	8,638	1,993	3·3	14,285[l]
138	20[d]	802	1,510	800	0·1	n.a.
50	76	2,518	4,727	2,813	8·3	6,191
87	70[d]	631	n.a.	n.a.	–	n.a.
17	98[d]	5,359	9,517	7,658	–	4,194
24	98[d]	3,231	5,287	7,119	–	3,608
17	97[d]	6,116[s]	22,488[s]	21,988[s]	–	5,529
26	95[d]	4,029	3,301[c]	3,266[cp]	–	n.a.
17	98	9,326	26,309	24,918	–	5,802

Sources: Unless otherwise indicated, figures for population, life expectancy, birth rate, death rate, and infant mortality are from Population Reference Bureau, '1975 World Population Data Sheet;' per capita GNP and per capita GNP growth rates are from *World Bank Atlas, 1974: Population, Per Capita Product, and Growth Rates* (Washington, DC: World Bank Group, 1974); figures for literacy and per capita energy consumption are from United Nations, *Handbook of International Trade and Development Statistics: Supplement 1973*, Publication Sales No. E/F.74.11.D.7, pp. 102–15; exports, imports, and international reserves are from International Monetary Fund, *International Financial Statistics*, Vol. 28, No. 3, March 1975; and figures for net flow of bilateral ODA and multilateral concessional flows are from Report by the Chairman of the Development Assistance Committee, *Development Cooperation, 1974 Review* (Paris: OECD, 1974), pp. 266–7. All data compiled by the Overseas Development Council, Washington, DC.

Appendix 2.2 contd.

Selected social and economic indicators of development: by groups of countries	Population, mid-1975 (mil.)	Per capita GNP, 1972 ($)	Per capita GNP growth rate, 1965–72 (%)	Life expectancy at birth, 1970–5 Average (yrs.)	Birth rate per 1,000, 1970–5 Average	Death rate per 1,000, 1970–5 Average
Czechoslovakia	14·8	2,180	4·5	69	17·0	11·2
Denmark	5·0	3,670	3·7	74	14·0	10·1
Finland	4·7	2,810	4·9	70	13·2	9·3
France	52·9	3,620	4·8	73	17·0	10·6
Germany, Dem. Rep.	17·2	2,100	3·5	73	13·9	12·4
Germany, Fed. Rep.	61·9	3,390	4·1	71	12·0	12·1
Greece	8·9	1,460	7·3	72	15·4	9·4
Hungary	10·5	1,520	4·2	70	15·3	11·5
Iceland	0·2	2,800	1·8	74	19·3	7·7
Ireland	3·1	1,580	3·7	72	22·1	10·4
Israel	3·4	2,610	7·1	71	26·5	6·7
Italy	55·0	1,960	4·3	72	16·0	9·8
Japan	111·1	2,320	9·7	73	19·2	6·6
Luxembourg	0·3	3,190	3·0	71	13·5	11·7
Malta	0·3	950	7·4	71	17·5	9·0
Netherlands	13·6	2,840	4·3	74	16·8	8·7
New Zealand	3·0	2,560	1·8	72	22·3	8·3
Norway	4·0	3,340	3·8	74	16·7	10·1
Poland	33·8	1,500	4·0	70	16·8	8·6
Portugal	8·8	780	5·3	68	18·4	10·1
Romania	21·2	810	6·7	67	19·3	10·3
South Africa	24·7	850	2·1	52	42·9	15·5
Spain	35·4	1,210	5·0	72	19·5	8·3
Sweden	8·3	4,480	2·5	73	14·2	10·5
Switzerland	6·5	3,940	2·9	72	14·7	10·0
USSR	255·0	1,530	5·9	70	17·8	7·9
United Kingdom	56·4	2,600	2·0	72	16·1	11·7
United States	213·9	5,590	2·0	71	16·2	9·4
Yugoslavia	21·3	810	5·5	68	18·2	9·2

Key: [a] Tentative estimate.
[b] 1972 figure.
[c] United Nations, *Monthly Bulletin of Statistics*, Vol. 29, No. 1, January 1975.
[d] US Agency for International Development, Bureau for Population and Humanitarian Assistance, *Population Program Assistance: Annual Report, FY 1973* (Washington, DC: US Government Printing Office, 1973).
[e] August 1974 figure.
[f] October 1974 figure.
[g] March 1974 figure.
[h] November 1974 figure.
[i] December 1974 figure.

[j] September 1974 figure.
[k] June 1971 figure.
[l] Mid-1973 figure.
[m] 1966 figure.
[n] 1971 figure.
[o] December 1973 figure.
[p] f.o.b.
[q] June 1974 figure.
[r] Associate Member of OPEC.
[s] Belgium-Luxembourg.
[t] See Belgium.
[u] Includes Botswana, Lesotho, Namibia, and Swaziland.

Infant mortality per 1,000 live births	Literacy (%)	Per capita energy consumption, 1971 (kg coal equiv.)	Total exports, f.o.b., 1973 ($ mil.)	Total imports, c.i.f., 1973 ($ mil.)	Net bilat. ODA from DAC countries and multilat. concessional flows, 1973 ($ mil.)	International reserves, January 1975 ($ mil.)
21	100[d]	6,615	6,288[c]	6,137[cp]	–	n.a.
14	99[d]	5,327	6,248	7,802	–	918
10	99[d]	4,334	3,828	4,333	–	594
16	97[d]	3,928	36,659	37,727	–	9,007
18	99[d]	6,308	7,521[c]	7,854[cp]	–	n.a.
20	99[d]	5,223	67,502	54,552	–	33,075
27	80[d]	1,470	1,440	3,456	−12·3	936
34	97[d]	3,291	4,433[c]	3,919[c]	–	n.a.
12	99[d]	4,311	291	359	–	39
18	98[d]	3,285	2,135	2,794	–	1,242
21	84[d]	2,710	1,449	4,240	186·1	1,202
26	93-95[d]	2,682	22,224	27,796	–	6,630
12	98[d]	3,267	36,982	38,347	–	13,509
16	98[d]	t	t	t	–	n.a.
24	83	981	98	240	26·9	407
12	98[d]	5,069	24,071	24,735	–	7,284
16	98[d]	2,934	2,599	2,179	–	658
13	99[d]	5,189	4,692	6,245	–	1,827
28	98[d]	4,374	6,374[c]	7,814[cp]	–	n.a.
44	65[d]	805	1,836	3,007	–	2,352
40	98-99[d]	2,975	3,698[c]	3,468[cp]	–	n.a.
117	35[d]	2,895[u]	3,435[c]	5,020[c]	–	1,188
15	86[d]	1,614	5,164	9,522	−8·8	6,277[h]
10	99[d]	6,089	12,201	10,628	–	1,786
13	98[d]	3,575	9,477	11,613	–	8,200
26	99[d]	4,535	21,463[c]	21,108[cp]	–	n.a.
18	98-99[d]	5,507	30,535	38,847	–	7,021
18	98[d]	11,244	71,339	73,575	–	16,262
43	80[d]	1,608	3,024	4,776	120·4	1,201

Sources: Unless otherwise indicated, figures for population, life expectancy, birth rate, death rate, and infant mortality are from Population Reference Bureau, '1975 World Population Data Sheet;' per capita GNP and per capita GNP growth rates are from *World Bank Atlas, 1974: Population, Per Capita Product, and Growth Rates* (Washington, DC: World Bank Group, 1974); figures for literacy and per capita energy consumption are from United Nations, *Handbook of International Trade and Development Statistics: Supplement 1973*, Publication Sales No. E/F.74.11.D.7, pp. 102–15; exports, imports, and international reserves are from International Monetary Fund, *International Financial Statistics*, Vol. 28, No. 3, March 1975; and figures for net flow of bilateral ODA and multilateral concessional flows are from Report by the Chairman of the Development Assistance Committee, *Development Cooperation, 1974 Review* (Paris: OECD, 1974), pp. 266–7. All data compiled by the Overseas Development Council, Washington, DC.

Chapter 3	# The meaning of development

It matters little how much information we possess about development if we have not grasped its inner meaning.
Denis Goulet, The Cruel Choice

Development must be redefined as an attack on the chief evils of the world today; malnutrition, disease, illiteracy, slums, unemployment and inequality. Measured in terms of aggregate growth rates, development has been a great success. But measured in terms of jobs, justice and the elimination of poverty, it has been a failure or only a partial success.
Paul P. Streeten, Chairman of Editorial Advisory Board, World Development

Introduction: everyone wants development – but what does it mean?

Every nation strives after development; it is an objective that most people take for granted. While economic progress is an essential component of development, it is not the only one. This is because development is not purely an economic phenomenon. In an ultimate sense, it must encompass more than the material and financial side of people's lives. Development should, therefore, be perceived as a *multidimensional* process involving the reorganization and reorientation of entire economic and social systems. In addition to improvements in incomes and output, it typically involves radical changes in institutional, social and administrative structures as well as in popular attitudes and, in many cases, even customs and beliefs. Finally, although development is usually defined in a *national* context, its widespread realization may necessitate fundamental modifications of the *international* economic and social system as well. However, before analyzing the complexities of development, we start by discussing two major conceptual approaches to the study of 'economic' development. We will then review the important notion of 'dualism' and dual societies.

3.1 Two major approaches to the study of economic development

The literature on economic development over the past 25 years has been dominated by two major strands of thought:

1. the 'stages of economic growth' theories of the 1950s and early 1960s;
2. the 'structural–internationalist' models of the late 1960s and early 1970s.

The thinking of the 1950s and early 1960s was focused mainly on the concept of 'stages of economic growth' in which the process of development was viewed as a series of successive stages through which all countries must pass. It was primarily an 'economic' theory of development in which the right quantity and mixture of saving, investment and foreign aid were all that was necessary to enable Third World nations to proceed along an economic growth path which historically had been followed by the more developed countries. Development thus became synonymous with economic growth.

This stages approach has now been replaced to a great extent by what we might call the 'structural–internationalist' school of thought. This approach views underdevelopment in terms of international and domestic power relationships, institutional and structural economic rigidities, and the resulting proliferation of dual economies and dual societies both within and among the nations of the world. Structuralist theories tend to emphasize external and internal 'institutional' constraints on economic development. Emphasis is placed on policies needed to eradicate poverty, to provide more diversified employment opportunities and to reduce income inequalities. These and other egalitarian objectives are to be achieved within the context of a growing economy, but economic growth *per se* is not given the exalted status accorded to it by the linear stages model. We will now look at each of these alternate approaches in greater detail.

1. The linear 'stages' model

When the interest in the poor nations of the world really began to materialize following the Second World War, economists in the industrialized nations were caught off guard. They had no readily available conceptual apparatus with which to analyze the process of economic growth in largely peasant, agrarian societies characterized by the virtual absence of 'modern' economic structures. But they did have the recent experience of the 'Marshall Plan' in which massive amounts of US financial and technical assistance enabled the war-torn countries of Europe to rebuild and modernize their economies in a matter of a few years. Moreover, was it not true that all modern industrial nations were once undeveloped peasant agrarian societies too? Surely, their historical experience in transforming their economies from poor agricultural subsistence societies to 'modern' industrial giants had important lessons for the 'backward' countries of Asia, Africa and Latin America? The logic and simplicity of these two strands of thought – i.e., the need for massive injections of capital and the historical pattern of the now developed countries – was too irresistible to be refuted by scholars, politicians and administrators in rich countries to whom people and ways of life in the Third World were often no more real than UN statistics or scattered chapters in anthropology books.

A. Rostow's 'stages of growth'

Out of this somewhat sterile intellectual environment and fuelled by the 'Cold War' politics of the 1950s and early 1960s with the resulting competition for the allegiance of newly independent nations came the doctrine of the 'stages of economic growth'. Its most influential and outspoken advocate was the American economic historian, W. W. Rostow. According to the Rostow doctrine, the transition from under-development to development can be described in terms of a series of steps or stages through which *all* countries must proceed. As Professor Rostow wrote in the opening chapter of his book[1]:

This book presents an economic historian's way of generalizing the sweep of modern history. . . . It is possible to identify all *societies, in their economic dimensions, as lying within one of five categories: the traditional society, the pre-conditions for take-off into self-sustaining growth, the drive to maturity, and the age of high mass consumption . . . These stages are not merely descriptive. They are not merely a way of generalizing certain factual observations about the sequence of development of modern societies. They have an inner logic and contin-uity . . . they constitute, in the end, both a theory about economic growth and a more general, if still highly partial, theory about modern history as a whole.*

The advanced countries, it was argued, had at various times in history passed the stage of 'take-off into self-sustaining growth' and the underdeveloped countries which were either still in the 'traditional society' or the 'preconditions' stage had only to follow a certain set of rules or 'tricks' of development to 'take off' in their turn into self-sustaining economic growth.

One of the principal 'tricks' of development necessary for any take-off was the mobilization of domestic and foreign savings in order to generate sufficient 'investment' to accelerate economic growth. The economic mechanism by which more investment leads to more growth can be described in the following macro-economic terms.

B. The Harrod–Domar growth model Every economy must save a certain proportion of its national income if only to replace worn out or impaired capital goods (buildings, equip-ment, materials). However, in order to grow, new *investments* repre-senting net additions to the capital stock are necessary. If we assume that there is some direct economic relationship between the size of the total capital stock, K, and total GNP, Y – for example, if 3 dollars of capital are always necessary to produce a 1 dollar stream of GNP – then it follows that any net additions to the capital 'stock' in the form of new investment will bring about corresponding increases in the 'flow' of national output (GNP).

Suppose this relationship, known in economics as the capital/output ratio, is roughly 3 to 1. If we define the capital/output ratio as k and assume further that the national *savings ratio, s,* is a fixed proportion of national output (e.g. say 6 per cent) and that total new investment is determined by the level of total savings, we can construct the following simple 'model' of economic growth:

1. Saving (S) is some proportion, s, of national income (Y) such that we have the simple equation

$$S = s . Y \tag{1}$$

2. Investment (I) is defined as the change in the capital stock, K and can be represented by ΔK such that

$$I = \Delta K \tag{2}$$

But since the total capital stock, K, bears a direct relationship to total national income or output, Y, as expressed by the capital/output ratio, k, then it follows that

$$\frac{K}{Y} = k \quad \text{or,} \quad \frac{\Delta K}{\Delta Y} = k \text{ or, finally } \Delta K = k \, \Delta Y \tag{2a}$$

3. Finally, since total national savings S must equal total investment, I, we can write this equality as

$$S = I \tag{3}$$

But from equation (1) above we know that $S = s . Y$ and from equations (2) and (2a) we know that $I = \Delta K = k \Delta Y$.

It therefore follows that we can write the 'identity' of saving equalling investment shown by equation (3) as

$$S = s . Y = k \Delta Y = \Delta K = I \text{ or, simply as} \tag{3a}$$

$$s . Y = k \Delta Y \tag{3b}$$

Now by dividing both sides of equation (3b) first by Y and then by k we obtain the following expression

$$\frac{\Delta Y}{Y} = \frac{s}{k} \tag{4}$$

Note that the left-hand side of equation (4), $\Delta Y/Y$, represents the rate of change or rate of growth of GNP – i.e. it is the percentage change in GNP.

Equation (4), which is a simplified version of the famous Harrod–Domar equation in the theory of economic growth[2], states simply that the rate of growth of GNP ($\Delta Y/Y$) is determined *jointly* by the national saving ratio, s, and the national capital/output ratio, k. More specifically, it says that the growth rate of national income will be directly or 'positively' related to the savings ratio (i.e. the more an economy is able to save – and invest – out of a given GNP, the greater will be the growth of that GNP) and inversely or 'negatively' related to the economy's capital/output ratio (i.e. the higher is k, the lower will be the rate of GNP growth).

The economic logic of equation (4) is very simple. In order to grow, economies must save and invest a certain proportion of their GNP. The more they can save, and, therefore, invest the faster they can grow. But the actual rate at which they can grow for any level of saving and investment depends on how productive that investment is. The productivity of this investment – i.e. how much additional output can be had from an additional unit of investment – can be measured by the inverse of the capital/output ratio, k, since this inverse, $1/k$, is simply the output/capital or output/investment ratio. It follows that multiplying the *rate* of new investment, $s = I/Y$, by its productivity, $1/k$, will give us the rate by which national income or GNP will increase.

$$\left[\text{Since } s = \frac{S}{Y}, \text{ and } \frac{1}{k} \text{ can be written as } \frac{1}{I/\Delta Y}, \text{ it follows that} \right.$$

$$\left. s \cdot \frac{1}{k} = \frac{I}{Y} \cdot \frac{\Delta Y}{I} = \frac{\Delta Y}{Y} \right]$$

Now, returning to the stages of growth theories, and using equation (4) of our simple Harrod–Domar growth model, we learn that one of the most fundamental 'tricks' of economic growth is simply to increase the proportion of national income which is saved (i.e. not consumed). If we can raise s in equation (4), then we can increase $\Delta Y/Y$, the rate of GNP

C. Obstacles and constraints

growth. For example, if we assume that the national capital output ratio in some less developed country is, say $3 \cdot 0$ and the aggregate savings ratio is 6 per cent of GNP, it follows from equation (4) that this country can grow at a rate of 2 per cent per year since

$$\frac{\Delta Y}{Y} = \frac{s}{k} = \frac{6\%}{3} = 2 \text{ per cent}$$

Now if the national savings rate can somehow be increased from 6 to, say, 15 per cent – e.g. through increased taxes, foreign aid and/or general consumption sacrifices – then GNP growth can be increased from 2 to 5 per cent since now

$$\frac{\Delta Y}{Y} = \frac{s}{k} = \frac{15\%}{3} = 5 \text{ per cent}$$

In fact, Rostow and others defined the 'take-off' stage precisely in this way. Countries which were able to save 15 to 20 per cent of their GNPs could grow ('develop') at a much faster rate than those who saved less. Moreover, this growth would then be self-sustaining. The 'tricks' of economic growth and development, therefore, are simply a matter of increasing national savings and investment.

The main 'obstacle' to or 'constraint' on development according to this theory was the relatively low level of new capital formation in most poor countries. But if a country wanted to grow at, say, a rate of 7 per cent per year and if it could *not* generate savings and investment at a rate of 21 per cent of national income (assuming that k, the final aggregate capital output ratio, is 3) but could only manage to save 15 per cent, then it could seek to fill this 'savings gap' of 6 per cent either through foreign aid or private foreign investment.

Thus, the 'capital constraint' stages approach to growth and development became an intellectual and (in terms of cold-war politics) opportunistic tool to justify the massive transfers of capital and technical assistance from the developed to the less developed nations. It was to be the 'Marshall Plan' all over again, but this time for the 'under-developed' nations of the Third World!

D. Necessary versus sufficient conditions: some criticisms of the stages model

Unfortunately, the 'tricks' of development embodied in the theory of stages of growth did not always work. And the basic reason why they didn't work was not because more saving and investment isn't a *necessary* condition for accelerated rates of economic growth – which it is – but rather because it is not a *sufficient* condition. Once again we are faced with an example of what we discussed in Chapter 1: the inappropriateness and/or irrelevance of many of the *implicit* assumptions of 'Western' economic theory for the actual conditions in Third World nations. The Marshall Plan for Europe worked because the European countries receiving aid possessed the necessary structural, institutional and attitudinal conditions (e.g. well-integrated commodity and money markets, highly developed transport facilities, well-trained and educated manpower, the motivation to succeed, an efficient government bureaucracy, etc.) to convert new capital effectively into higher levels of output. The Rostow–Harrod–Domar models implicitly assume the existence of these same attitudes and arrangements in underdeveloped nations. But in many cases they are not present nor are the complementary factors such as managerial competence, skilled labor and the ability to plan and administer a wide assortment of development projects always present in sufficient quantities.

But even at a more fundamental level, the stages theory fails to take into account the crucial fact that contemporary Third World nations are part of a highly integrated and complex international system in which their best and most intelligent development strategies can sometimes be nullified by external forces beyond their control. (The case of Chile under the Allende regime in the early 1970s is a striking, if somewhat extreme, example of this point.) One simply cannot claim, as many economists did in the 1950s and 1960s, that development is simply a matter of 'removing obstacles' and supplying various 'missing components' like capital, foreign exchange, skills and management – a task in which the developed countries could theoretically play a major role. It was because of numerous failures and the growing disenchantment with this strictly 'economic' theory of development (especially among Third World intellectuals) that a more recent approach has emerged – one that attempts to combine economic and institutional factors into a 'social systems' model of international development and underdevelopment.

2. International–structuralist models

The second major approach to the study of underdevelopment has recently gained increasing support as a result of a growing disenchantment with the earlier 'stages' and economic 'constraints' approach. This approach, which we have called the 'international–structuralist' model, essentially views Third World countries as being beset by institutional and structural economic rigidities and caught up in a 'dependence' and 'dominance' relationship to rich countries. There are two major streams of thought in the international–structuralist model.

A. The 'neo-colonial' dependence model

The first, which might be called the 'neo-colonial dependence model, is an outgrowth of Marxist thinking. It attributes the existence and maintenance of Third World underdevelopment primarily to the historical evolution of a highly unequal international capitalist system of rich country–poor country relationships. Whether intentionally exploitive or unintentionally neglectful, the coexistence of rich and poor nations in an international system dominated by such unequal power relationships between the 'center' and the 'periphery' renders attempts by poor societies (the periphery) to be self-reliant and independent in their development efforts difficult, and sometimes, even impossible[3]. Certain groups in the developing countries (e.g., landlords, entrepreneurs, merchants, salaried public officials and trade union leaders) who enjoy high incomes, social status and political power constitute a small elite ruling class whose principal interest, whether knowingly or not, is in the perpetuation of the international capitalist system of inequality and conformity by which they are rewarded. Directly and indirectly, they serve (are dominated by) and are rewarded by (dependent upon) special interest power groups including multinational corporations, national bilateral aid agencies, and multilateral donor organizations such as those in the UN system whose main allegience and/or funding comes from wealthy capitalist countries. Their activities and viewpoints often serve to inhibit any genuine reform efforts which might benefit the wider population. In some cases these activities can actually lead to even lower levels of living, or, using Baran's well-known phrase, to the 'development of underdevelopment'. In short, the neo-Marxist, neo-colonial, structural view of underdevelopment attributes a large part of the Third

World's continuing and worsening poverty to the existence and policies of the industrial capitalist (and socialist) countries of the northern hemisphere and their extensions in the form of small but powerful elite or 'comprador' groups in the less developed countries[4].

One of the most forceful statements of the international dependence school of thought is that of Theotonio Dos Santos[5] of Latin America who argues that:

> *. . . underdevelopment, far from constituting a state of backwardness prior to capitalism, is rather a consequence and a particular form of capitalist development known as dependent capitalism . . . dependence is a* conditioning *situation in which the economies of one group of countries are conditioned by the development and expansion of others. A relationship of interdependence between two or more economies or between such economies and the world trading system becomes a dependent relationship when some countries can expand through self-impulsion while others, being in a dependent position, can only expand as a reflection of the expansion of the dominant countries, which may have positive or negative effects on their immediate development. In either case, the basic situation of dependence causes these countries to be both backward and exploited. Dominant countries are endowed with technological, commercial, capital and socio-political predominance over dependent countries – the form of this predominance varying according to the particular historical moment – and can therefore exploit them, and extract part of the locally produced surplus. Dependence, then, is based upon an international division of labour which allows industrial development to take place in some countries while restricting it in others, whose growth is conditioned by and subjected to the power centres of the world.*

B. The 'false paradigm' model The second approach to development, which we might call the 'false paradigm' model, attributes Third World underdevelopment to faulty and inappropriate advice provided by well-meaning but often uninformed international 'expert' advisers from both developed country assistance agencies and multinational donor organizations (like the World Bank, UNESCO, the ILO, UNDP and the International Monetary Fund). These 'experts' offer sophisticated concepts, elegant theoretical structures and complex econometric models of development which often lead to inappropriate or simply incorrect policies. Because of institutional and structural factors such as the highly unequal ownership of land, disproportionate control over domestic and international financial assets and very unequal access to credit, these policies often merely serve the vested interests of existing power structures, both domestic and international.

In addition, according to this argument, leading university intellectuals, trade unionists, future high-level government economists and other civil servants all get their training in developed country institutions where they are unwittingly served an unhealthy dose of alien concepts and models camouflaged behind a smokescreen of excessive sophistication and esoteric irrelevance. Having little or no really useful knowledge to enable them to come to grips in an effective way with real development problems, they often tend to become unknowing or reluctant 'apologists' for the existing system of elitist policies and institutional structures. In university economics courses, for example, this typically entails the perpetuation of the teaching of false, or at least irrelevant, 'Western' concepts and models, while in government policy discussions too much emphasis is placed on the notion of capital/output ratios, savings and investment ratios and growth rates of GNP. As a result, desirable institutional and structural reforms, many of which we have mentioned in previous sections, are neglected or are given only cursory attention.

Whatever their ideological and institutional differences of emphasis, both the 'neo-colonial, dependence' and the 'false paradigm' components of the international–structuralist model of underdevelopment reject the exclusive emphasis on accelerating the growth of GNP as an index of development. Instead, more emphasis is placed on needed structural and institutional reforms (both domestic and international) in order to eradicate absolute poverty, provide expanded employment opportunities, lessen income inequalities and raise the general levels of living (including health, education and cultural enrichment) of the masses of people. While some structuralists would go as far as to say 'growth doesn't matter', the majority of thoughtful observers recognize that the most effective way to deal with these diverse social problems is to alter the *character* of the growth process itself so that wider segments of Third World populations can participate in and benefit from its realization.

C. Conclusions

3.2 Dualism and the concept of dual societies

Implicit in the international–structuralist view of the world, in both its 'neo-colonial' and 'false paradigm' models, is the notion of a world of dual societies – rich nations and poor nations internationally and pockets of wealth within broad areas of poverty in developing countries. 'Dualism' is a concept widely discussed in development economics. It represents the existence and persistence of *increasing divergences* between rich and poor nations and peoples on various levels. Specifically, the concept of dualism embraces four key elements[6]:

1. *Different sets of conditions* of which some are 'superior' and others 'inferior' can *coexist* in a given space at the same time. For example, the coexistence of 'modern' and 'traditional' methods of production in urban and rural sectors, the coexistence of wealthy, highly educated elites with masses of illiterate poor people, and the coexistence of powerful and wealthy industrialized nations with weak, impoverished peasant societies in the international economy – these are all obvious manifestations of this first element of dualism.

2. *This coexistence is chronic* and not merely transitional. It is not due to a temporary phenomenon which with time will eliminate the discrepancy between superior and inferior elements. In other words, the international coexistence of wealth and poverty is *not* simply an historical phenomenon which will be rectified in time. This what the 'stages of growth' theory implicitly assumes but which the facts of growing international inequalities emphatically refute.

3. The degrees of superiority or inferiority not only fail to show any signs of rapidly diminishing, they even have an inherent *tendency to increase*. For example, the productivity gap between industries in developed countries and their counterparts in the LDCs seems to widen with each passing year.

4. The interrelations between the 'superior' and 'inferior' elements
are such that *the existence of the superior element does little or
nothing to pull up the inferior element*. In fact, it may actually serve
to push it down – to 'develop its underdevelopment'.

1. International dualism These four components of dualism provide a near perfect description
of the contemporary situation in the international economic system.
First, there are, as we have seen in Chapter 2, great differences in per
capita incomes and levels of living currently coexisting between different countries, races, continents and climatic zones of the world. Second, these differences are clearly not short-term but chronic. The
disparity between economic levels of living between, say, England and
France on the one hand and India and Sub-Saharan Africa on the other
have persisted not for decades but for centuries. Third, these differences show signs of increasing rather than decreasing. We saw in
Section 2.2 how growth rates of GNP and especially GNP per capita
had widened in favour of the developed countries during the past
decade. Fourth and finally, the interrelations between the rich and
poor countries in the international economy, at least in the judgement
of most members of the structural–dependence school of development
thought, contain many elements which make the rapid growth of the
former only marginally helpful and, in some cases, absolutely harmful
to the development of the latter. These so-called international 'backwash' effects inhibiting the sustained development of Third World
nations include, among others, the following forces of international
dominance and dependence:

1. The power of strong countries to control and manipulate world
   resource and commodity markets to their advantage.
2. The spread of international capitalist domination of domestic
   LDC economies through the foreign investment activities of private multinational corporations.
3. The privileged access of rich nations to scarce raw materials.
4. The export of unsuitable and inappropriate science and technology.
5. The freedom for industrialized countries to 'impose' their products on fragile Third World markets behind import-substituting
   tariff barriers for monopolistic multinational corporations.
6. The transfer of outmoded and irrelevant systems of education to
   societies where education is perceived as a key component in the
   development process.
7. The ability of rich countries to disrupt efforts at industrialization
   by poor countries by 'dumping' cheap products in these controlled
   markets.
8. Harmful international trade theories and policies which lock
   Third World countries into primary product exports with declining international revenues.
9. Harmful aid policies which often merely serve to perpetuate and
   exacerbate internal dualistic economic structures.
10. The creation of elites in poor countries whose economic and
    ideological allegiance is to the external world, both capitalist and
    socialist.
11. The transfer of unsuitable methods of university training for
    unrealistic and often irrelevant international professional stan-
    dards, as induced by the externally conceived degree require-
    ments for doctors, engineers, technicians and economists.

12. The corresponding capacity of rich countries to lure trained personnel away from LDCs with attractive financial rewards (the international 'brain drain'); and finally,
13. The demoralizing 'demonstration effect' of luxury consumption on the part of the wealthy both at home and abroad as propagated, for example, in imported foreign movies and magazine advertisements.

As we pointed out in the previous section, it is easy and rather reassuring, but often unrealistic, to attempt to lay the blame for all the evils of underdevelopment at the international doorstep of rich nations. However, on the other hand, it is equally naive to believe that many of the serious problems of underdevelopment do not originate abroad. Clearly, the continued economic growth of rich nations helps to make it possible for poor countries to maintain growth rates of output which are high by historical standards. At the same time, however, it is difficult to refute Professor Singer's observation that:

the very forces which are set in motion by the rapid growth of the richer countries – specifically the development of even more sophisticated, costly and capital-intensive technologies, and of mortality-reducing health improvements and disease controls – are such as to create forces within the poorer countries – specifically a population explosion, rising unemployment and inability to develop their own technological capacities, which may in fact assure that they will not *have the time needed for the continued maintenance of current growth rates, let alone their acceleration, so as to result in acceptable levels of development* [7].

2. Domestic dualism

Our fourfold definition of dualism is equally descriptive of the internal economic structures of many Third World countries. First, standards of living vary greatly between the top 20 per cent and bottom 40 per cent of the population with ratios as high as 6 and 12 to 1 being quite representative (see Ch. 5). The majority of those few with very high incomes live in urban areas while the great clusters of mass poverty are generally to be found in rural regions. However, even within most Third World urban areas one typically finds pockets of great wealth coexisting with spreading slums.

But this initial element of dualism – the coexistence of 'superior' with 'inferior' phenomena – is not limited to the distribution of wealth, income and power. It also exists in the technological nature of Third World industrial production. Small enclaves of 'modern' industries (mostly urban manufacturing) using modern imported capital-intensive production methods to produce sophisticated products in large quantities coexist with traditional labour-intensive, small-scale activities catering for limited local needs.

Second, the coexistence of small modern enclaves in the midst of traditional societies, and of a small group of 'progressive' wealthy elites amid masses of poor, shows no sign of disappearing. The vast majority of Third World peoples seem today as untouched by 'development' as they were, say, 10 to 15 years ago.

Third, the gap between the rich and poor and between modern and traditional methods of production shows signs of growing even wider not only within individual LDCs but also among the developing countries as a group. Countries such as Brazil, Panama, Costa Rica, Singapore, Taiwan, Thailand, Korea, Cyprus, Sierra Leone and Kenya have experienced relatively high rates of per capita income growth for a number of years now while Bangladesh, Haiti, Mali, the Sudan, Ghana, India and Peru and many others have shown little or no per capita growth at all over the past decade. Within many nations, however, the gap between rich and poor seems in many cases to be widening. This is especially true in those Third World countries with markedly dualistic industrial structures like Brazil, Mexico, the Philippines, Venezuela, Peru, Kenya, Zambia and India.

Finally, the 'spread effects' between the rising wealth of modern enclaves and the improvement in the levels of living of the traditional society are less than obvious in most LDCs. In fact, there seem to be little or no spread effects whatsoever. Many observers claim with some justification that it is the very growth of the stronger or 'superior' component of dualistic societies that pushes down or at least is achieved at the expense of the weaker or inferior element. We shall see precisely how this process has tended to be prolonged and intensified when we discuss the problems of poverty, income distribution, unemployment, rural development, education, trade, aid and technology transfer in Parts II and III.

3.3 What do we mean by 'development'?

Let us now try to pull together many of the threads of previous sections of this chapter and, indeed, of previous chapters in an attempt to define what we really mean by 'development'.

1. Traditional economic measures In strictly economic terms, 'development' for the past two decades has meant the capacity of a national economy, whose initial economic condition has been more or less static for a long time, to *generate* and *sustain* an annual increase in its gross national product at rates of perhaps 5 to 7 per cent or more. For example, the 1960s were dubbed the 'Development Decade' by a resolution of the United Nations and 'development' was conceived largely in terms of the attainment of a 6 per cent annual target growth rate of GNP. An alternative common economic index of development has been the use of rates of growth of *per capita* GNP to take into account the ability of a nation to expand its output at a rate faster than the growth rate of its population. Levels and rates of growth of 'real' *per capita* GNP (i.e. 'monetary' growth of GNP per capita *minus* the rate of inflation) are typically used to measure in a broad sense the overall 'economic' well-being of a population – that is, how much of real goods and services are available for consumption and investment for the average citizen.

Economic development has in the past also been typically seen in terms of the planned alteration of the structure of production and employment so that agriculture's share of both declines, whereas that of the manufacturing and service industries increases. Development strategies, therefore, have usually focused on rapid urban industrialization often at the expense of agriculture and rural development. Finally, these principal economic measures of development were often supplemented by casual reference to and general acceptance of 'non-economic' social indicators: gains in literacy, schooling, health conditions and services, provision of housing, for instance.

But on the whole development in the 1950s and 1960s was nearly always seen as an economic phenomenon in which rapid gains in overall and per capita GNP growth would either 'trickle down' to the masses in the form of jobs and other economic opportunities, or create the necessary conditions for the wider distribution of the economic and social benefits of growth. Problems of poverty, unemployment and income distribution were of secondary importance to 'getting the growth job done'.

Unfortunately the experience of the 1950s and 1960s, when a large number of Third World nations *did* achieve the overall UN growth targets but the levels of living of the masses of people remained for the most part unchanged, signalled that something was very wrong with this narrow definition of 'development'. A clamour was raised by an increasing number of economists and policy makers for the 'de-thronement of GNP' and the elevation of direct attacks on widespread absolute poverty, increasingly inequitable income distributions and the spectre of rising unemployment. In short, *economic development was redefined in terms of the reduction or elimination of poverty, inequality and unemployment within the context of a growing economy.* 'Redistribution from Growth' became a common slogan. Professor Dudley Seers [8] posed the basic question about the meaning of development succinctly when he asserted that:

2. The new economic view of development

The questions to ask about a country's development are therefore: What has been happening to poverty? What has been happening to unemployment? What has been happening to inequality? If all three of these have declined from high levels, then beyond doubt this has been a period of development for the country concerned. If one or two of these central problems have been growing worse, especially if all three have, it would be strange to call the result 'development' even if per capita income doubled.

The above assertion is not idle speculation or the description of an hypothetical situation. There were, for example, a number of developing countries which experienced relatively high rates of growth of per capita income during the 1960s but which simultaneously showed no improvement or witnessed an actual decline in employment, equality and the real incomes of the bottom 40 per cent of their populations. By the earlier 'growth' definition, these countries were 'developing' in the 1960s. By the more recent poverty, equality and employment criteria, however, they were not.

But the phenomenon of 'development' or the existence of a chronic state of 'underdevelopment' is not only a question of economics or the simple quantitative measurement of incomes, employment and inequality. Underdevelopment is a real fact of life for over 2 billion people of the world – a state of mind as much as a state of national poverty. As Denis Goulet[9] has so forcefully portrayed it:

3. Beyond narrow economic criteria

Underdevelopment is shocking: the squalor, disease, unnecessary deaths, and hopelessness of it all! No man understands if underdevelopment remains for him a mere statistic reflecting low income, poor housing, premature mortality or underemployment. The most empathetic observer can speak objectively about underdevelopment only after undergoing, personally or vicariously, the 'shock of underdevelopment'. This unique culture shock comes to one as he is initiated to the emotions which prevail in the 'culture of poverty'. The reverse shock is felt by those living in destitution when a new self-understanding reveals to them that their life is neither human nor inevitable . . . The prevalent emotion of underdevelopment is a sense of personal and societal impotence in the face of disease and death, of confusion and ignorance as one gropes to understand change, of servility toward men whose decisions govern the course of events, of hopelessness before hunger and natural catastrophe. Chronic poverty is a cruel kind of hell; and one cannot understand how cruel that hell is merely by gazing upon poverty as an object.

The condition of underdevelopment in its totality is thus a consciously experienced state of deprivation rendered especially intolerable as more and more people acquire information about the development of other societies and realize that technical and institutional means for abolishing poverty, misery and disease do indeed exist.

Development must, therefore, be conceived of as a multidimensional process involving major changes in social structures, popular attitudes and national institutions as well as the acceleration of economic growth, the reduction of inequality and the eradication of absolute poverty. Development, in its essence, must represent the entire gamut of change by which an entire *social system*, tuned to the diverse basic needs and desires of individuals and social groups within that system, moves away from a condition of life widely perceived as 'unsatisfactory' and towards a situation or condition of life regarded as materially and spiritually 'better'.

4. Three 'core' values of development

Is it possible to define or broadly conceptualize what we mean when we talk about development as the sustained elevation of an entire society and social system towards a 'better' or 'more humane' life? The question 'What constitutes the good life?' is as old as philosophy and man himself. It is a timeless and perennial question which needs to be re-evaluated and freshly answered with the changing environment of world society. The appropriate answer for Third World nations in the last quarter of the twentieth century is not necessarily the same as it would have been in the second or third quarters. But we believe with Professor Goulet and others that at least three basic components or core 'values' should serve as a conceptual basis and practical guideline for understanding the 'inner' meaning of development. These core values are *life-sustenance, self esteem* and *freedom*, representing common goals sought by all individuals and societies[10]. They relate to fundamental human needs which find their expression in almost all societies and cultures in all times. Let us, therefore, examine each in turn.

A. Life-sustenance: the ability to provide basic necessities

All people have certain basic needs without which life would be impossible. These 'life-sustaining' needs include indisputably, food, shelter, health and protection. When any of these is absent or in critically short supply we may state, without reservation, that a condition of 'absolute underdevelopment' exists. *A basic function of all economic activity, therefore, is to provide as many people as possible with the means of overcoming the helplessness and misery arising from a lack of food, shelter, health and protection.* To this extent, we may claim that economic development *is* a *necessary* condition for the improvement in the 'quality of life' which is 'development'. Without sustained and continuous economic progress at the individual as well as the societal level, the realization of the human potential would not be possible. One clearly has to 'have enough in order to be more'[11]. Rising per capita incomes, the elimination of absolute poverty, greater employment opportunities, and lessening income inequalities, therefore, constitute the *necessary* but not the *sufficient* conditions for 'development'[12].

A second universal component of the good life is self-esteem – a sense of worth and self-respect, of not being used as a tool by others for their own ends. All peoples and societies seek some basic form of self-esteem, although they may call it authenticity, identity, dignity, respect, honour or recognition. The nature and form of this self-esteem may vary from society to society and from one culture to another. However, with the proliferation of the 'modernizing values' of developed nations, many societies in the Third World countries which previously may have possessed a profound sense of their own worth suffer from serious cultural confusion when they come in contact with economically and technologically advanced societies. This is because national prosperity has become an almost universal measure of worth. Because of the significance attached to material values in 'developed' nations, worthiness and esteem are nowadays increasingly conferred only on those countries who possess economic wealth and technological power – i.e. those who have 'developed'. Again, we may quote Professor Goulet[13]:

B. Self-esteem: to be a person

The relevant point is that underdevelopment is the lot of the majority of the world's population. As long as esteem or respect was dispensed on grounds other than material achievement, it was possible to resign oneself to poverty without feeling disdained. Conversely, once the prevailing image of the better life includes material welfare as one of its essential ingredients it becomes difficult for the materially 'underdeveloped' to feel respected or esteemed . . . nowadays the Third World seeks development in order to gain the esteem which is denied to societies living in a state of disgraceful 'underdevelopment' . . . Development is legitimized as a goal because it is an important, perhaps even an indispensable, way of gaining esteem.

A third and final universal value which we suggest should constitute the meaning of development is the concept of 'freedom'. Freedom here is not to be understood in the political or ideological sense (e.g. the 'free world'), but in the more fundamental sense of freedom or emancipation from alienating material conditions of life; and, freedom from the social servitudes of men to nature, ignorance, other men, misery, institutions and dogmatic beliefs. Freedom involves the expanded range of choices for societies and their members together with the minimization of external constraint in the pursuit of some social goal which we call 'development'. W. Arthur Lewis stressed the relationship between economic growth and freedom from servitude when he concluded that 'the advantage of economic growth is not that wealth increases happiness, but that it increases the range of human choice[14]. Wealth can enable man to gain greater control over nature and his physical environment (e.g. through the production of food, clothing and shelter), than if he remained poor. It also gives him the freedom to choose greater leisure, to have more goods and services or to deny the importance of these material wants and live a life of spiritual contemplation.

C. Freedom from servitude: to be able to choose

We may conclude that *'development' is both a physical reality and a state of mind* in which society has, through some combination of social, economic and institutional processes, secured the means for obtaining

5. The three objectives of development

a better life. Whatever the specific components of this better life, development in all societies must have at least the following three objectives:

1. To increase the availability and widen the distribution of basic life-sustaining goods such as food, shelter, health and protection.
2. To raise levels of living including: in addition to higher incomes, the provision of more jobs, better education and greater attention to cultural and humanistic values, all of which will serve not only to enhance material well-being but also to generate greater individual and national self-esteem.
3. To expand the range of economic and social choice to individuals and nations by freeing them from servitude and dependence, not only in relation to other peoples and nation-states but also to the forces of ignorance and human misery.

We may, therefore, reformulate and broaden Professor Seers' questions about the meaning of development as follows:

1. Have general levels of living expanded within a nation to the extent that absolute poverty (i.e., deprivation of life-sustaining goods), the degree of inequality in income distribution, the level of employment and the nature and quality of educational, health, and other social and cultural services improved?
2. Has economic progress enhanced individual and group esteem both internally vis-à-vis one another and externally vis-à-vis other nations and regions?
3. Finally, has economic progress expanded the range of human choice and freed people from external dependence and internal servitude to other men and institutions, or has it merely substituted one form of dependence (e.g., economic) for another (e.g. cultural)?

If the answer to each of the above three questions is 'yes', then clearly these phenomena constitute real 'development' and a nation in which they are manifested can unquestionably be called 'developed'. If only the first question (which is equivalent to Seers' three questions) can be answered affirmatively while the other two remain negative, then such a country may properly be designated as 'economically more developed' even though it still remains 'underdeveloped' in a more fundamental sense. In this sense, it is more proper to refer to the rich nations of the world as 'economically developed' and reserve judgement as to whether or not they are actually 'developed' to a more throughgoing social, political and cultural analysis. To paraphrase Seers, if the second and third of these central questions for all societies evokes a negative response – i.e. if people feel less self-esteem, respect or dignity and if their freedom to choose has been constrained – then even if the provision of life-sustaining goods and improvements in levels of living are occurring, it would be misleading to call the result 'development'.

3.4 Underdevelopment and development: a multidimensional schematic summary

Figure 3.1 represents a schematic attempt to portray and summarize some of the main economic and non-economic aspects of what we mean by 'underdevelopment'. In it we have listed our three primary components of underdevelopment – low levels of income (life-sustenance), low self-esteem and limited freedom – as three rectangular boxes with arrows indicating general lines of causation. The upper half of the chart relating to the determinants of levels of living portrays the principal economic aspects of underdevelopment. The two boxes on the bottom of the chart – self-esteem and freedom to choose – are what are typically referred to as 'non-economic' aspects of development.

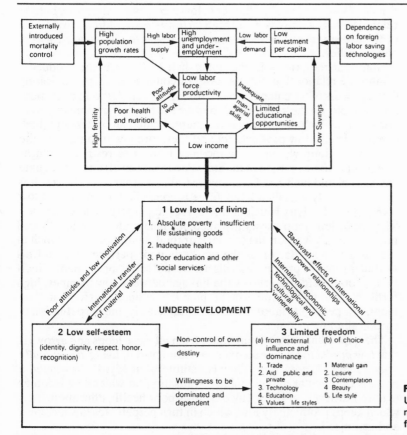

Fig 3.1
Underdevelopment: a multidimensional schematic framework

In fact, economic forces impinge on all three boxes while important non-economic factors like attitudes and institutions are also vital components of the determinants of levels of living. *It is simply not possible to separate economic from non-economic phenomena when dealing with real world development problems*. But, in order fully to understand the concepts and processes portrayed in our schematic framework of underdevelopment, let us look briefly at how the three components are interrelated.

First, we see that low levels of living (insufficient life-sustaining goods and inadequate or non-existent education, health and other social services) are all related in one form or another to low incomes. These low incomes result from the low average productivity of the *entire* labor force, not just those working. Low labor force productivity can result from a variety of factors, including on the supply side poor health, nutrition and work attitudes, high population growth and high unemployment and underemployment. On the demand side inadequate skills, poor managerial talents and overall low levels of worker education may, along with the importation of developed country, labor-saving techniques of production, result in the substitution of capital for labor in domestic production. The combination of low labor demand and large supplies results in the widespread underutilization of labor. Moreover, low incomes lead to low savings and investment which also restrict the total number of employment opportunities. Finally, as we shall see in Chapter 6, low incomes are also thought to be related to large family size and high fertility since children provide one of the few sources of economic and social security in old age for very poor families.

Note that the arrows in the upper half of Fig. 3.1, the productivity–income relationship, form a series of continuous 'loops', indicating that a process of 'circular causation' or 'vicious circles' is in operation. For example, on the 'outer right' loop we see that low incomes result in low savings which means low investment, limited labor demand, high unemployment, low productivity and therefore low incomes. On the 'inner right' loop we have low incomes leading to restricted educational opportunities (both at the state and family level) and inadequate managerial and high-level manpower training programs. The result is that a relatively unskilled labor force is compelled to produce at low levels of productivity which in turn serves to perpetuate low incomes. The 'inner left' loop shows low incomes leading to poor health and nutrition in the worker due to a lack of food, sanitation, etc., which in turn is a primary factor in the worker's poor performance and his attitudes towards promptness, discipline and self improvement. Finally, the 'outer left' loop shows the linkage between low incomes, high fertility, rapid population growth, high labor supply, high unemployment, low per capita labor productivity and, lastly, the perpetuation of chronically low incomes.

The important point to remember from all these loops and arrows is that *low productivity, low incomes and low levels of living are mutually re-enforcing phenomenon*. They constitute what Myrdal has called a process of 'circular and cumulative causation' in which low incomes lead to low levels of living (income plus poor health, education, etc.) which keeps productivity low, which in turn perpetuates low incomes, and so on[15].

But low levels of living, broadly defined, do not by themselves define underdevelopment. They only reflect one, although we would argue the most crucial, component of the inner meaning of development and underdevelopment. Boxes (2) and (3) in Fig. 3.1 – low self-esteem and limited freedom of choice – comprise the two other poles of the tripod of underdevelopment. Both are strongly influenced by low levels of living; both in turn contribute to these low levels. For example, there is nothing inherent in low levels of living to cause low esteem or dignity among the very poor *except* when their identity and worth in other peoples' eyes are largely determined by their material well-being. Thus the international transfer of material-oriented values from rich nations (through the cinema, television, newspaper, magazines, educational systems, foreign 'experts', and community 'developers', etc.) can and usually does alter the determinants of self-esteem so that low living levels cause individuals to feel a low sense of their real worthiness. Conversely, low self respect can contribute to low levels of living as a result of poor attitudes towards life, work, cleanliness, punctuality and self-improvement. These phenomena are depicted by the arrows leading to and from boxes (1) and (2).

Low levels of living also influence and are influenced by limited freedom (box 3 and arrows between boxes 1 and 3). They make people and nations vulnerable to, dependent upon, and often dominated by those who are materially better off and greatly limit their range of choice regarding alternative national and personal life-styles. Conversely, limited freedom greatly weakens nations and people and forces them to accept an international economic order in which the progress of the rich may have a chronic 'backwash' effect perpetuating the low living levels of the poor.

Finally, note that boxes (2) and (3) are also connected by arrows showing cause and effect. Limited freedom means that nations and individuals have little or no control over their own destinies. They are, therefore, likely to have a lower opinion of themselves and to lose some respect in the eyes of others. Conversely, nations and people with low self-esteem often do not have the economic, psychological or physical strength to resist domination and a loss of their freedom to choose.

Taken together, the three boxes in Fig. 3.1 present a concise portrait of the nature and inner meaning of underdevelopment. While low levels of living, low self-esteem and limited freedom all work in a cumulative cause and effect process to perpetuate underdevelopment, it is clear that without improving the level of living of people within a nation, the prospects for 'development' should be non-existent. *It follows that the first priority of moving from a chronic state of underdevelopment to one of development must be the improvement of peoples' levels of living.* For this reason *economics must play a central role in the development process.* However, the impact of that role will be greatly diminished, even nullified, if at the same time the importance of attending to the determinants of national and personal esteem and of striving to broaden society's freedom to choose are not also afforded priority attention by Third World politicians and planners alike.

Notes

1. W. W. Rostow, *The States of Economic Growth, A Non-Communist Manifesto,* Cambridge U.P., London (1960), 1, 3, 4 and 12. For an extensive and critical review of the Rostow stages doctrine from a Marxist perspective see, P. Baran and E. Hobsbaum, 'The stages of economic growth', *Kyklos,* **14** (1961), 234–42.
2. Named after two famous economists, Sir Roy Harrod of England and Professor Evesey Domar of the United States, who separately but concurrently formulated a variant of the model in the early 1950s.
3. For one of the most comprehensive introductions to the neo-marxist view of international development and underdevelopment, see Paul Baran, *The Political Economy of Growth,* Monthly Review Press, New York and London (1962).
4. A provocative and well-documented application of this argument to the case of Kenya can be found in Colin Leys, *Underdevelopment in Kenya: The Political Economy of Neo-Colonialism,* Heinemann Educational Books, London (1975).
5. T. Dos Santos, 'The crisis of development theory and the problem of dependence in Latin America', *Siglo,* **21** (1969). See also Benjamin J. Cohen, *The Question of Imperialism: The Political Economy of Dominance and Dependence,* Basic Books, New York (1973).
6. Hans Singer, 'Dualism revisited: a new approach to the problems of dual society in developing countries', *Journal of Development Studies,* **7,** no. 1 (1970), 60–1.
7. Ibid. p. 62.
8. Dudley Seers, 'The meaning of development', *Eleventh World Conference of the Society for International Development,* New Delhi (1969), 3.

9. Denis Goulet, *The Cruel Choice: A New Concept in the Theory of Development,* Athenium, New York (1971), 23.
10. Ibid, pp. 87–94.
11. Ibid. p. 124.
12. For a recent attempt to specify and quantify the concept of basic needs, see ILO, *Employment, Growth and Basic Needs,* Geneva (1976).
13. D. Goulet, op. cit., pp 89, 90. For an even more provocative discussion of the meaning of individual self-esteem and respect in the context of Latin American development, see Paulo Freise, *Pedagogy of the Oppressed,* Penguin Books (Education Series), London (1972).
14. W. Arthur Lewis, 'Is economic growth desirable', in *The Theory of Economic Growth,* Allen and Unwin, London (1963), 420.
15. See G. Myrdal, *Asian Drama,* Pantheon, New York (1968), Appendix 4.

Concepts for review

development	capital stock
underdevelopment	savings ratio
self-esteem	Harrod–Domar equation
circular cumulative	necessary and sufficient
causation	conditions
spread effects	structural theory of
freedom to choose	underdevelopment
dominance	'neo-colonial' dependence model
dependence	dualism
vulnerability	'false-paradigm' model
'stages of growth'	life-sustenance
theory of development	vicious circle
capital-output ratio	

Questions for discussion

1. Explain the essential distinction between the 'stages of growth' theory of under-development and the 'international–structuralist' theories, both the 'neo-colonial' and 'false paradigm' models. Which do you think provides a better explanation of the situation in most Third World nations? Explain.
2. Explain the meaning of dualism and dual societies. Do you think that the concept of dualism adequately portrays the development picture in most Third World countries? Explain.
3. Some people claim that international dualism and domestic dualism are merely manifestations of the same phenomenon. What do you think they mean by this and is it a valid conceptualization? Explain.
4. Briefly describe the various definitions of the meaning of 'development' encountered in the text. What are the strengths and weaknesses of each approach? Do you think that there are other dimensions of development not mentioned in the text? If so, please describe them. If not, please explain why you believe that the textual description of the meaning of development is adequate.
5. Why is a strictly economic definition of development inadequate? What do you understand 'economic' development to mean? Can you give hypothetical or real examples of situations in which a country may be developing economically but still be 'underdeveloped'?
6. Why is an understanding of the meaning of development crucial to policy formulation in Third World nations? Do you think it is possible for a nation to agree on a rough definition of development and orient its strategies for achieving these objectives accordingly? What might be some of the roadblocks or constraints in realizing these development objectives – both economic and non-economic?

Further readings

1. On the complex question of what is the real meaning of 'development' and under-development', see: Dudley Seers, 'The meaning of development', in Nancy Bastor (ed.), *Measuring Development,* Frank Cass Publishers, London (1972); Gunnar Myrdal, *The Challenge of World Poverty,* Pantheon, New York (1970), Ch. 1–4; Celso Furtado, *Development and Underdevelopment,* University of California Press (1964), especially Ch. 4; Denis Goulet, *The Cruel Choice: A New Concept on the Theory of Development,* Antheum, New York (1971), Ch. 2; Mahbub ul Haq, 'Crisis in development strategies', *World Development,* **7,** No. 1 (1973); Irma Adelman, 'Development economics: a reassessment of goals', *American Economic Review,* **65,** No. 2 (1975); and the various readings in Henry Bernstein (ed.), *Underdevelopment and Development: The Third World Today,* Penguin Books, Middlesex, England (1973).

2. For a survey of various theories of development, see: Everett Hagen, *The Economics of Development,* Irwin (1968), Chs. 6 and 7;   C. P. Kindleburger, *Economic Development,* McGraw-Hill (1965), Part One;   Hollis Chenery, 'The structuralist approach to development policy', *American Economic Review,* **65**, No. 2 (1975).

3. For an excellent summary statement of the concept of dualism and dual societies, see: Hans Singer, 'Dualism revisited: a new approach to the problems of dual society in developing countries', *Journal of Development Studies,* **7,** No. 1 (1970).

4. Among a number of recent surveys of the 'dependence' literature as applied to problems of underdevelopment the following are perhaps the best: (*a*) F. H. Cardoso, 'Dependence and development in Latin America', *New Left Review,* July–August 1972, 83–95;   (*b*) P. O'Brien, 'A critique of Latin American theories of dependency', in I. Oxaal *et al.* (eds), *Beyond the Sociology of Development,* Routledge and Kegan Paul, London (1975);   (*c*) Sanjaya Lall, 'Is 'dependence' a useful concept in analysing underdevelopment?', *World Development,* **3,** Nos. 11 and 12 (1975), 799–810;   (*d*) G. Kay, *Development and Underdevelopment: A Marxist Analysis,* Macmillan, London (1975).

Chapter 4	# Historic growth and contemporary development: Lessons and controversies

The growth position of the less developed countries today is significantly different in many respects, from that of the presently developed countries on the eve of
their entry into modern economic growth.
Simon Kuznets

Introduction: the growth game

For the past two decades the primary focus of world economic attention has been on measures to accelerate the real growth rates of
national incomes. Economists and politicians alike from all nations,
rich and poor, capitalist, socialist and mixed, have worshipped at the
shrine of economic growth. At the end of every year, statistics are
compiled for all countries of the world showing their relative rates of
GNP growth. 'Growthmanship' has become a way of life. Governments can rise or fall if their economic growth performance ranks high
or low on this global score card. As we have seen, Third World
development programs are often assessed by the degree to which their
national outputs and incomes are growing. In fact, for many years the
'conventional wisdom' equated 'development' with the rapidity of
national output growth.

In view of the central role that this concept has assumed in
worldwide assessment of relative national economic performance, it is
important to understand the nature and causes of economic growth. In
this chapter, therefore, we start by examining some of the basic concepts of the theory of economic growth, using the simple production
possibility framework to portray the level, composition and growth of
national output. After looking briefly at the historical record of
economic growth in contemporary rich nations, we then isolate six
principal economic, structural and institutional components which
appear to have characterized all growing economies. We then con-

clude by asking the question: of what relevance is the historical growth experience of contemporary developed countries to the plans and strategies of present-day Third World nations?

4.1 The economics of growth: some basic concepts and illustrations

The major factors in or components of economic growth in any society are:

1. *Capital accumulation,* including all new investments in land, physical equipment and human resources.
2. *Growth in population* and thus, although delayed, growth in the labor force.
3. *Technological progress*[1]. Let us look briefly at each.

Capital accumulation results when some proportion of present incomes are saved and invested in order to augment future outputs and incomes. New factories, machinery, equipment and materials increase the physical 'capital stock' of a nation (i.e. the total 'net' real value of all physically productive capital goods) and make it possible for expanded output levels to be achieved. These 'directly productive' investments are supplemented by investments in what is often known as social and economic 'infrastructure' – i.e., roads, electricity, water and sanitation, communications, etc. – which facilitate and integrate economic activities. For example, investment by a farmer in a new tractor may increase the total output of the vegetables which he can produce. But without adequate transport facilities to get this extra product to local commercial markets his investment may not add anything to national food production.

1. Capital accumulation

There are other less direct ways to invest in a nation's resources. The installation of irrigation facilities may improve the 'quality' of a nation's agricultural land by raising productivity per hectare. If 100 hectares of irrigated land can produce the same output as 200 hectares of non-irrigated land using the same other inputs, then the installation of such irrigation is the equivalent of doubling the quantity of unirrigated land. Use of chemical fertilizers and the control of insects with pesticides may have equally beneficial effects in raising the productivity of existing farmland. All these forms of investment are ways of improving the quality of existing land resources. Their effect in raising the total 'stock' of productive land is, for all practical purposes, indistinguishable from the simple clearing of hitherto unused but usable land.

Similarly, investment in 'human resources' can improve its quality and thereby have the same or even a more powerful effect on production as an increase in human numbers. Formal schools, vocational and on-the-job training programs and adult and other types of 'informal' education may all be made more effective in augmenting human skills and resources as a result of direct investments in buildings, equipment and materials (books, projectors, science equipment, vocational tools and machinery like lathes and grinders, etc.). The advanced and relevant training of teachers as well as good textbooks in economics may make an enormous difference in the quality, leadership and productivity of a given labor force. The concept of investment in human resources is therefore analogous to that of improving the quality and thus the productivity of existing land resources through strategic investments.

All of the above phenomena and many others are forms of investment which lead to 'capital accumulation'. Capital accumulation may add new resources (e.g. the clearing of unused land) or upgrade the quality of existing resources (e.g. irrigation, fertilizer, pesticides, etc.) but its essential feature is that it involves a 'trade-off' between present and future consumption – giving up a little now so that more can be had later.

2. Population (and labor force) growth Population growth and the associated, although delayed, increase in the labor force has traditionally been considered a positive factor in stimulating economic growth. A larger labor force means more productive manpower while a larger overall population increases the potential size of domestic markets. However, it is questionable whether rapidly growing manpower supplies in 'labor surplus' developing countries exert a positive or negative influence on economic progress (see Chapter 6 for a lengthy discussion of both the pros and cons of population growth for economic development). Obviously, it will depend on the ability of the economic system to absorb and productively employ these added workers – an ability largely associated with the rate and type of capital accumulation and the availability of other related factors, such as managerial and administrative skills.

Given an initial understanding of these first two fundamental components of economic growth and disregarding for a moment the third (technology), let us see how they interact via the production–possibility curve to expand society's potential total output of *all* goods. Recall that for a given technology and a given amount of physical and human resources, the production–possibility curve portrays the *maximum* attainable output combinations of any two commodities, say rice and radios, when all resources are fully and efficiently employed.

Suppose now that with unchanged technology the quantity of physical and human resources were to double, either as a result of investments that improved the quality of the existing resources or investment in new resources – land, capital and, in the case of larger families, labor. Figure 4.1 shows that this doubling of total resources will cause the entire production possibility curve to shift uniformly outward from $P—P$ to $P'—P'$. More radios and more rice can now be produced.

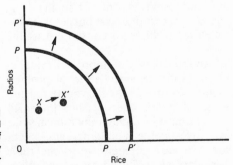

Fig 4.1
The effect of expanded physical and human resources on the position of society's production–possibility frontier

Since these are assumed to be the only two goods produced by this economy, it follows that the gross national product (i.e. the total value of all goods and services produced) will be higher than before. In other words, the process of economic growth is underway.

Note that even if the country in question is operating with under-utilized physical and human resources as at point X in Fig. 4.1, a growth of productive resources can result in a higher total output combination as at point X', even though there may still be widespread unemployment and underutilized or idle capital and land. But note also that there is nothing deterministic about the necessity of resource growth leading to higher output growth. This is not an economic law and there are many contemporary developing countries whose poor growth record bears witness to this phenomenon. Nor is resource growth even a necessary condition for *short-run* economic growth since the better utilization of idle existing resources can raise output levels substantially, as portrayed in the movement from point X to X' in Fig. 4.1. Nevertheless, in the *long run,* the improvement and upgrading of the quality of existing resources as well as new investments designed to expand the quantity of these resources are a principal means of accelerating the growth of national output.

Now instead of assuming the proportionate growth of *all* factors of production, let us assume that say, only capital, or only land is increased in quality and quantity. Diagrams (*a*) and (*b*) of Fig. 4.2 show that if radio manufacturing is a *relatively* large user of capital equipment while rice production is a *relatively* land-intensive process, then the shifts in society's production possibility curve will be more pronounced for radios (Fig. 4.2a) when capital grows rapidly and rice (Fig. 4.2b) when land quantity or quality grow relatively faster. However, since under normal conditions both products will require the use of both factors as productive inputs, albeit in very different combinations, the production–possibility curve still shifts slightly outward along the rice axis in (*a*), when capital is increased, and along the radio axis in (*b*), when only the quantity and/or quality of land resources are expanded.

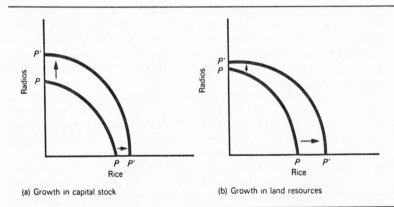

(a) Growth in capital stock   (b) Growth in land resources

Fig 4.2
Non-symmetrical shifts in production–possibility curves when (*a*) only the capital stock expands and (*b*) only land increases in quantity and/or quality

It is now time to consider the third, and to many economists the most important, source of economic growth – technological progress. In its simplest form, *technological progress results from new and improved ways of accomplishing traditional tasks* such as growing maize, making clothing or building a house. There are three basic classifications of technological progress: 'neutral', labor-saving and capital-saving.

'Neutral' technological progress occurs when higher output levels are achieved with the same quantity and combinations of factor inputs. Simple innovations like those that arise from the 'division of labor' can

3. Technological progress

result in higher total output levels and greater consumption for all individuals. In terms of production possibility analysis, a 'neutral' technological change which, say, doubles total output is conceptually equivalent to a doubling of all productive inputs. The outward shifting production possibility curve of Fig. 4.1, therefore, could also be a diagrammatic representation of 'neutral' technological progress.

On the other hand, technological progress may either be 'labor-saving' or 'capital-saving' – i.e. higher levels of output can be achieved with the same quantity of labor or capital inputs. The use of electronic computers, automated textile looms, high-speed electric drills, tractors and mechanical ploughs – these and many other types of 'modern' machinery and equipment can be classified as 'labor-saving'. As we shall discover in Chapter 8, the history of technological progress in the twentieth century has been largely one of rapid advances in labor-saving technologies of producing anything from beans to bicycles to bridges.

'Capital-saving' technological progress is a much rarer phenomenon, only because almost all of the world's scientific and technological research is conducted in the developed countries where the mandate is to 'save labor', not capital. But in the labor-abundant (capital-scarce) countries of the Third World, capital-saving technological progress is what is most needed. Such progress results in 'more efficient' (i.e. lower cost) labor-intensive methods of production – for example, hand- or rotary-powered weeders and threshers, foot-operated bellows pumps, back-mounted mechanical sprayers, etc., for small scale agriculture[2]. As we show in Chapter 8, the indigenous LDC development of low-cost, efficient, labor-intensive (capital-saving) techniques of production is one of the most essential ingredients in any long-run employment-oriented development strategy.

Technological progress may also be labor- or capital-'augmenting'. *Labor-augmenting technological progress* occurs when the quality or skills of the labor force are upgraded – for example, by the use of videotapes, televisions and other electronic communications media for classroom instruction. Similarly, capital-augmenting technological progress results in the more productive use of existing types of capital goods as, for example, the substitution of steel for wooden ploughs in agricultural production.

We can use our production–possibility curve for rice and radios to examine two very specific examples of recent technological progress as it relates to output growth in developing countries. In the 1960s, agricultural scientists at the International Rice Research Institute in the Philippines developed a new and highly productive hybrid rice seed, known as 1R-8 or 'miracle rice'. These new seeds, along with later further scientific improvements, enabled some rice farmers in parts of Southeast Asia to double and triple their per hectare yields in a matter of a few years. In effect, this technological progress was 'embodied' in the new rice seeds (one could also say it was 'land augmenting') which permitted higher output levels to be achieved with essentially the same complementary inputs (although more fertilizer and pesticides were recommended). In terms of our production possibility analysis, the higher yielding varieties of hybrid rice could be depicted as in Fig. 4.3 by an outward shift of the curve along the rice axis with the intercept on the radio axis remaining essentially unchanged (i.e., – the new rice seeds could not be directly used to increase radio production).

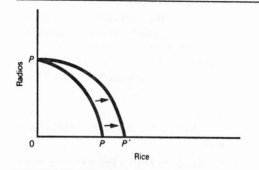

Fig 4.3
The new high-yielding rice varieties
cause the P–P curve to shift outward
along the 'rice' axis

In terms of the technology of radio production, the invention of transistors probably has had as significant an impact on communications as did the discovery of the steam engine in transportation. Even in the remotest parts of Africa, Asia and Latin America, the transistor radio has become a prized possession. Without the need for complicated, unwieldy and fragile tubes, radio production grew enormously with the introduction of the transistor. The production process became less complicated and workers were able to increase significantly their total productivity. Figure 4.4 shows that, as in the case of higher yielding rice seeds, the technology of the transistor can be said to have caused the production–possibility curve to rotate outward along the vertical axis. For the most part, the rice axis intercept remains unchanged (although perhaps the ability of rice paddy workers to listen to music on their transistor radio while working may have made them more productive!).

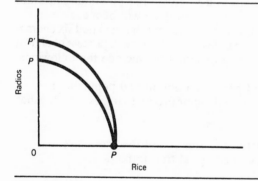

Fig 4.4
The invention of the transistor
causes the P–P curve to shift outward
along the 'radio' axis

Conclusion

We may summarize the discussion so far by saying that the sources of economic progress can be traced to a variety of factors, but by and large, *investments which improve the quality of existing physical and human resources increase the quantity of these same productive resources and raise the productivity of all, or specific resources through invention, innovation, and technological progress have been and will continue to be primary factors in stimulating economic growth in any society.* The production possibility framework conveniently allows us to analyze the production choices open to an economy, to understand the output and 'opportunity cost' implications of idle or underutilized resources, and to portray the effects on economic growth of increased resource supplies and improved technologies of production.

Having provided this introduction to the simple economics of growth, we can now look more carefully at the historical experience of economic growth in contemporary 'developed' nations in order to analyze in detail the nature of both these economic and 'non-economic' factors that are basic to long-term growth. We shall then see what relevance all this has for the growth prospects of developing countries.

4.2 The historical record: Kuznets' six characteristics of modern economic growth

Professor Simon Kuznets, who received the Nobel Prize in economics in 1971 for his pioneering work in the measurement and analysis of the historical growth of national incomes in developed nations, has defined a country's economic growth as 'a long-term rise in capacity to supply increasingly diverse economic goods to its population, this growing capacity based on advancing technology and the institutional and ideological adjustments that it demands'[3]. All three principal components of this definition are of great importance.

1. The *sustained rise in national output* is a manifestation of economic growth and the ability to provide a wide range of goods is a sign of economic maturity.
2. *Advancing technology* provides the basis or preconditions for continuous economic growth – a necessary but not sufficient condition. In order to realize the potential for growth inherent in new technology, however,
3. *Institutional, attitudinal and ideological adjustments* must be made. Technological innovation without concomitant 'social' innovation is like a light bulb without electricity – the potential exists but without the complementary input nothing will happen.

In his exhaustive analysis Professor Kuznets has isolated six characteristic features which were manifested in the growth process of almost every contemporary developed nation. They include the following:

Two aggregate economic variables:	1. High rates of growth of per capita output and population; 2. High rates of increase in total factor productivity, especially labor productivity;
Two structural transformation variables:	3. High rates of structural transformation of the economy; 4. High rates of social and ideological transformation;
Two factors affecting the international spread of growth:	5. The propensity of economically developed countries to reach out to the rest of the world for markets and raw materials; 6. The limited spread of this economic growth to only a third of the world's population.

Let us briefly examine each of these six characteristics.

1. High rates of per capita output and population growth In the case of both per capita output and population growth, all contemporary developed countries have experienced large multiples of their previous historical rates during the epoch of modern economic growth – roughly from around 1770 to the present. For the non-Communist developed countries, *annual* growth rates over the past 200 years averaged almost 2 per cent for per capita output, 1 per cent for population and therefore 3 per cent for total output (i.e. real GNP). These rates – which imply a doubling time of roughly 35 years for per capita output, 70 years for population and 24 years for real GNP – were far greater than those experienced during the entire era before the start of the industrial revolution in the late eighteenth century. For example, per capita output during the last two centuries has been estimated to be at almost ten times that of the pre-modern era; population has grown at a multiple of four or five times its level in the earlier period, and the acceleration in the growth rate of total output or GNP is therefore estimated to have been some forty or fifty times as large as that experienced before the nineteenth century!

The second aggregate economic characteristic of modern growth is the relatively high rate of rise in total factor productivity (i.e., output per unit of all inputs). In the case of the major productive factor (labor), rates of productivity increase have also been large multiples of the rates in the pre-modern era. For example, it has been estimated that rates of productivity increase account for anywhere from 50 to 75 per cent of the historical growth of per capita output in developed countries. In other words, *technological progress including the upgrading of existing physical and human resources accounts for most of the measured historical increases in per capita GNP.* We shall discuss the crucial role which technological advance played in generating and sustaining economic growth shortly.

2. High rates of productivity increase

The historical growth record of contemporary developed nations reveals a third important characteristic; the high rate of structural and sectoral change inherent in the growth process. Some of the major components of this structural change include the gradual shift away from agricultural to non-agricultural activities and, more recently, away from industry to services; a significant change in the scale or average size of productive units – i.e. away from small family and personal enterprises to the impersonal organization of huge national and multinational corporations, and finally, a corresponding shift in the spatial location and occupational status of the labor force away from rural, agricultural and related non-agricultural activities towards urban-oriented manufacturing and service pursuits. For example, in the United States the proportion of the total labor force engaged in agricultural activities was 53·5 per cent in 1870. By 1960 this figure had declined to less than 7 per cent. Similarly, in an old European country like Belgium, the agricultural labor force dropped from 51 per cent of the total in 1846 to 12·5 per cent in 1947 and less than 7 per cent in 1970. In view of the fact that it took many centuries for agricultural labor forces to drop to even 50 per cent of the total labor supply prior to the nineteenth century, a drop of 40 to 50 points in the last 100 years in countries such as the United States, Japan, Germany, Belgium and Great Britain underlines the rapidity of this structural change.

3. High rates of economic structural transformation

For a significant economic structural change to take place in any society, concomitant transformations in *attitudes, institutions* and *ideologies* are often necessary. Obvious examples of these social transformations include the general urbanization process and the adoption of the ideals, attitudes and institutions of what has come to be known as 'modernization'. Gunnar Myrdal has provided a lengthy list of these modernization ideals in his seminal treatise on underdevelopment in Asia[4]. They include the following characteristics:

4. High rates of social, political and ideological transformation

(a) *Rationality* – i.e. the substitution of 'modern' methods of thinking, acting, producing, distributing, and consuming for age-old and traditional practices. According to the first Indian Prime Minister, Jawaharlal Nehru, what underdeveloped nations need is 'a scientific and technological society. It employs new techniques whether it is in the farm, in the factory or in transport. Modern technique is not a matter of just getting a tool and using it. Modern technique follows modern thinking. You can't get hold of a modern tool and have an ancient mind. It won't work'[5]. The quest for rationality implies that opinions about economic strategies and policies should be logically valid inferences rooted as deeply as possible in knowledge of relevant facts.

(b) *Planning* – i.e. the search for a rationally coordinated system of policy measures that can bring about and accelerate economic growth and development (see Ch. 15).

(c) *Social and economic equalization* – i.e the promotion of more equality in status, opportunities, wealth, incomes and levels of living, and finally,

(d) *Improved institutions and attitudes* – Such changes are envisaged as necessary to increase labor efficiency and diligence; promote effective competition, social and economic mobility and individual enterprise; permit greater equality of opportunities, make possible higher productivity, raise levels of living and promote 'development'. Included among social institutions needing change are outmoded land tenure systems, social and economic monopolies, educational and religious structures, systems of administration and planning, etc. In the area of attitudes, the concept of 'modern man' embodies such ideals as efficiency, diligence, orderliness, punctuality, frugality, honesty, rationality, change-orientation, integrity and self-reliance, cooperation and willingness to take the long view.

In Part Two we will look more carefully at some of these characteristics of modernization as they relate to contemporary Third World countries to see how and in what manner they fit into a 'development'-oriented economic strategy.

5. International economic outreach The last two characteristics of modern economic growth deal with the role of developed countries in the international arena. The first of these relates to the propensity of rich countries to 'reach out' to the rest of the world for primary products and raw materials, cheap labor and lucrative markets for their manufactured products. Such outreach activities are made possible economically by means of the increased power of modern technology, particularly in transport and communication. These had the effect of unifying the globe in ways that were not possible before the nineteenth century. They also opened the possibilities for political and economic dominance of poor nations by their more powerful neighbours to the north. In the nineteenth and early twentieth century, the establishment of colonies and the 'opening up' or 'partitioning' of previously inaccessible areas such as sub-Saharan Africa and parts of Asia and Latin America provided the expanding economies of the northern hemisphere with cheap raw materials and with export markets for their growing manufacturing industries.

6. Limited international spread of economic growth In spite of the enormous increases in world output over the past two centuries, the spread of modern economic growth is largely still limited to less than one-third of the world's population. As we discovered in Chapter 2, this minority of the world's population enjoys almost 85 per cent of the world's income. Moreover, as we also saw later in that chapter, unequal international power relationships between developed and underdeveloped countries have a tendency to exacerbate the 'gap' between the rich and poor. The further economic growth of the former is often achieved at the expense of the latter.

4.3 Conclusions: the interdependence of growth characteristics

The six characteristics of modern growth reviewed here are highly interrelated and mutually reinforcing. High rates of per capita output result from rapidly rising levels of labor productivity. High per capita incomes in turn generate high levels of per capita consumption, thus providing the incentives for changes in the structure of production (since as incomes rise the demand for manufactured goods and services rises at a much faster rate than the demand for agricultural products). Advanced technology needed to achieve these output and structural changes causes the scale of production and the characteristics of economic enterprise units to change in both organization and location. This in turn necessitates rapid changes in the location and structure of the labor force and in status relations among occupational groups (e.g. the income shares of landlords and farmers decline while those of manufacturers and industrialists tend to rise). It also means changes in other aspects of society including family size, urbanization and the material determinants of self-esteem and dignity. Finally, the inherent dynamism of modern economic growth coupled with the revolution in the technology of transportation and communication necessitates an international outreach on the part of those countries which developed first. But the poor countries affected by this international outreach may either, for institutional, ideological or political reasons, not be in a position to benefit from the process or may simply be weak victims of the policies of rich countries designed to exploit them economically.

If the common ingredient and linkage in all of these interrelated growth characteristics is, as Professor Kuznets suggests the 'mass application of technological innovations', then the rapid growth which makes possible the economic surplus to finance further programs in scientific research has a built-in tendency to be self-generating. In other words, *rapid economic growth makes possible basic scientific research which in turn leads to technological inventions and innovations which propel economic growth even further.*

We have an important hint here why the growth process seems to benefit the already rich nations disproportionately in relation to the poor ones: almost 98 per cent of all scientific research is undertaken in rich countries and on their problems. This research and the resulting technological progress which it engenders are of little direct benefit to poor nations whose resource and institutional conditions differ greatly from those of the developed nations. Wealthy nations can afford basic scientific research; poor ones cannot. Developed countries can therefore provide a continuous mechanism for self-sustaining technological and economic advance that is beyond the financial and technical capabilities of most developing countries. This is one of the real underlying economic reasons why the gap between rich and poor nations seems to widen every year.

4.4 Some lessons and implications

A basic question emerging from our discussion of the six characteristics of modern economic growth is, 'Why did the growth experience of the more developed nations not spread more rapidly to the less developed nations?' Two broad explanations come immediately to mind. The first relates to the internal initial conditions of most Third World countries and the other to the contemporary nature of international economic and political relationships between rich and poor nations.

Economic growth, as we have seen, results not only from the growth in quantity and quality of resources and improved technology but also from a social and political structure that is conducive to such change. Growth demands a stable but flexible social and political framework which is capable of accommodating and even encouraging rapid structural change. It also requires a social environment capable of resolving the inevitable interest group and sectoral conflicts that accompany such structural change, for example, the transition from a land-based, rural agrarian society to a highly skilled, urban oriented industrial and service economy. Shifts in relative power and influence from, say, the rural aristocracy to the new urban industrialists or from a few large landlords to many smaller commercial farmers who own rather than lease their land are examples of structural transitions involving potential conflicts of interest.

In short, unless local attitudes and institutional conditions exist which are amenable to structural change and, without holding back the growth-promoting groups in society, still provide opportunities for wider segments of the population to participate in the fruits of economic progress, efforts to stimulate growth through narrowly conceived economic policies are likely to fail. As we shall discover in many of the chapters in Part II, the apparent failure of some developing countries to generate more rapid rates of economic growth in spite of heavy investments in human and physical resources and the importation of sophisticated technological practices can be traced largely to the inflexibility of their social and political institutions and the reactionary power of certain vested interest groups.

The second, and not unrelated, explanation for the limited spread effects of modern economic growth derives from the economic and political policies of the developed countries themselves vis-à-vis the developing nations. As we discovered in Chapter 2, the dominant power of rich nations collectively to influence and control the conditions of their international trading relationships with poor countries and to transfer their economic, social, political and cultural values and institutions as well as their technology to these societies in opportunist ways may have greatly inhibited the latter's economic progress. There are three reasons to explain this phenomenon. First, such wholesale transfers tend to create and perpetuate dominance/dependence relationships between rich and poor in which the latter remain largely incapable of controlling their own economic destiny or evolving an indigenous ethos of self-reliance. Second, the transfers themselves may be largely inappropriate and counterproductive to the development aspirations of many Third World countries. Finally, it may simply not be in the private long-run economic and political interests for the one-third of the world's population who now control four-fifths of the world's production to share this abundance with the other two-thirds.

A world of increasingly scarce resources and commodities may not be compatible with truly global economic progress especially when the relative distribution of power is so unequal.

The analogy here between inflexible and reactionary domestic social structures and elite power groups inhibiting national economic growth and similar inflexibilities and reactionary policies among a small group of elite nations is obvious. Just as the economic growth of individual nations required flexible social and political institutions capable of resolving conflicts and promoting structural change, so too any realistic notion of 'world development' must accept that without an analogous flexibility at the international level (i.e. a genuine commitment on the part of developed nations to assist or, at least, not impede the economic progress of poor societies), 'global' economic progress will probably never occur. Without such flexible global institutions (e.g. world trade and aid relationships) and an international rather than provincial outlook on the part of world leaders, it is not unreasonable to anticipate the emergence of growing conflict and perhaps even worldwide violence between those few who prosper with the many who do not. In the face of inflexible social and political structures, domestic civil wars have often broken out to resolve economic conflicts in the developed nations; the American Civil War in the 1860s is an example. Recently, such violent conflicts related to struggles between small elites and the masses of poor, usually represented by other elites, have occurred with growing frequency in a number of developing countries (Sri Lanka, Pakistan, Algeria, Libya, Nigeria, Thailand, Chile, Haiti, Ethiopia, Vietnam, Cambodia, Laos, Sudan, Mozambique, etc.). In the absence of a more equitable distribution of the fruits of world economic growth and more flexible international institutions, Third World nations may well grow impatient with the present international system and begin as a group to exercise their own potential power. The outcome may or may not be violent. But the underlying conditions for such potential violence seem to grow with each passing year. (In Chapter 17 we will examine the question of prospects for international cooperation or conflict in the context of the Third World's growing demands for a 'new international economic order'.)

4.5 The limited value of the historical growth experience: differing initial conditions

One of the principal failures of development economics of the 1950s and early 1960s was its inability to recognize and take into account the limited value of the historical experience of economic growth in the West for charting the development path of contemporary Third World nations. Such theories as the 'stages of economic growth' and related models of rapid industrialization gave too little emphasis to the very different and less favorable initial economic, social and political conditions of today's developing countries. The fact is that the growth position of these countries today is in many important ways significantly different from that of the presently developed countries as they embarked on their era of modern economic growth. We can identify, for example, at least eight significant differences in initial conditions – differences that require a much amended analysis of the growth prospects and requirements of modern economic development:

1. resource endowments – physical and human,
2. per capita incomes and levels of GNP in relation to the rest of the world,
3. climate,
4. population size, distribution and growth,
5. historical role of international migration,
6. international trade benefits,
7. basic scientific and technological research and development capabilities,
8. stability and flexibility of political institutions.

Each of these conditions is discussed below with a view to formulating a more realistic set of requirements and priorities for generating and sustaining rapid economic growth in the last quarter of the twentieth century.

1. Resource endowment, physical and human

Contemporary Third World countries are on the whole often less well endowed with natural resources than were the presently developed nations when they began their modern growth. (*Note:* We are not here talking about the present very depleted natural resource situation of many rich countries, but what they possessed on the eve of their development.) With the exception of those few Third World nations blessed with abundant supplies of petroleum, other minerals and raw materials with growing world demands, most less developed countries, like those in Asia where almost one-third of the world's population resides, are poorly endowed with natural resources. Moreover, in parts of Latin America and especially in Africa where natural resources are more plentiful, heavy investments of capital are needed to exploit them. Such finance is not easy to come by without sacrificing substantial autonomy and control to the powerful developed country multinational corporations who alone are at present capable of large-scale, efficient resource exploitation.

The historical difference in skilled human resource endowments is even more pronounced. The ability of a country effectively to exploit natural resources is dependent on, among other things, the managerial and technical skills of its people. The populations of today's Third World nations are on the whole less educated, less experienced and less skilled than were their counterparts in the early periods of economic growth in the west (or, for that matter, the Soviet Union and Japan at the outset of their more recent growth processes).

2. Relative levels of per capita income and GNP

The two-thirds of the world's population presently living in developing countries have on the average a much lower level of real per capita income than their counterparts had in nineteenth-century England, North America or France or in early twentieth-century Russia and Japan. As we discovered in Chapter 2, well over three-quarters of the population of Third World countries is attempting to subsist at bare minimum levels. Obviously, the average standard of living in, say, early nineteenth-century England was nothing to envy or admire. But it was not as economically debilitating and precarious as it is today for most people in the Third World, especially those in the forty or so 'least developed' countries.

Secondly, at the beginning of their modern growth era, today's developed nations were economically in advance of the rest of the world. They could, therefore, take advantage of their relatively strong financial positions to widen the income gaps between themselves and other less fortunate countries. On the other hand, today's LDCs begin their growth process at the low end of the international per capita income scale. Their relatively weak position in the world economy is analogous to that of a 1,500 metre race between a young athlete and an old man where the former is given a 1,000 metre start. Such backwardness is not only economically difficult to overcome or even reduce but, psychologically, it creates a sense of frustration and a desire to 'grow' at any cost. This can in fact inhibit the long-run improvement in national levels of living.

Almost all Third World countries are situated in tropical or subtropical climatic zones. *It is an historical fact that all successful examples of modern economic growth have occurred in temperate zone countries.* Such a dichotomy cannot simply be attributed to coincidence: it must bear some relation to the special difficulties caused directly or indirectly by differing climatic conditions.

3. Climatic differences

One obvious climatic factor directly affecting conditions of production is that in general the extremes of heat and humidity in most poor countries contribute to deteriorating soil qualities and the rapid depreciation of many natural goods. It also contributes to the low productivity of certain crops, the weakened regenerative growth of forests and the poor health of animals. Finally, and perhaps most important, these extremes of heat and humidity not only cause discomfort to workers but also weaken their health, reduce their desire to engage in strenuous physical work and generally lower their levels of productivity and efficiency.

In Chapter 6 we will discuss in detail some of the development problems and issues associated with rapid population growth. At this point we merely note that Third World population size, density and growth constitute another important difference between less developed and developed countries. Before and during their early growth years, Western nations experienced a very slow secular trend in population growth. As industrialization proceeded, population growth rates increased primarily as a result of falling death rates but also because of slowly rising birth rates. However, *at no time during their modern growth epoch did European and North American countries have natural population growth rates in excess of 2 per cent per annum.*

4. Population size, distribution and growth

By contrast, the populations of most Third World countries have been increasing at annual rates in excess of 2·5 per cent over the past few decades and some are rising even faster today. Moreover, the concentration of these large and growing populations in a few areas means that most LDCs today start with considerably higher man/land ratios than did the European countries in their early growth years. Finally, in terms of comparative absolute size, it is a fact that, with the exception of the USSR, no country that embarked on a long-term period of economic growth approached the present-day population size of India, Egypt, Pakistan, Indonesia, Nigeria or Brazil. Nor, as we have just seen, were their rates of natural increase anything like that of present-day Mexico, Kenya, Philippines, Bangladesh, Zaire or Colombia. In fact, many observers even doubt whether the industrial revolution and the high long-term growth rates of contemporary developed countries could have been achieved or proceeded so fast and with such minimal setbacks and disturbances, especially for the very poor, had their populations been expanding so rapidly.

5. The historical roles of international migration

Of perhaps equal historical importance to the differing rates of natural population increase is the fact that in the nineteenth and early twentieth centuries there was a major outlet for excess rural populations in international migration.

As Table 4.1 reveals, international migration was both widespread and large in scale. In countries such as Italy, Germany and Ireland, periods of severe famine or pressure on the land often combined with limited economic opportunities in urban industry to 'push' unskilled rural workers towards the labor-scarce nations of North America and Australasia. Thus, as Brinley Thomas argues in his treatise on migration and economic growth in the nineteenth century, the 'three outstanding contributions of European labor to the American Economy – 1,187,000 Irish and 919,000 Germans between 1847 and 1855, 418,000 Scandinavians and 1,045,000 Germans between 1880 and 1885, and 1,754,000 Italians between 1898 and 1907 – had the character of evacuations.[6].

Table 4.1
Average annual overseas emigration from Europe 1846–1949 (in thousands)

	Total European overseas emigration	Total	British Isles	(Ireland)	Germany	Norway, Sweden, Denmark	Switzerland, France, Low Countries	Total	Italy	Austria, Hungary, Czechoslovakia	Russia, Poland, Lithuania, Finland	Spain, Portugal	Balkans
1846–50	256·6	254·3	199·1	(118·8)	35·5	4·3	14·4	2·3	0·2	1·6	0·1	0·4	
1851–55	342·3	331·3	231·7	(139·0)	74·9	6·9	17·8	11·0	0·7	4·0	0·2	6·1	
1856–60	197·1	184·7	123·5	(43·7)	49·4	4·5	7·3	12·5	4·2	2·2	0·2	5·9	
1861–65	219·3	202·9	143·6	(39·1)	43·5	9·7	6·1	16·4	8·2	2·2	0·3	5·9	
1866–70	354·9	308·4	170·8	(47·8)	83·4	39·3	14·9	37·4	18·7	5·7	0·6	12·4	
1871–75	370·7	310·1	193·9	(59·0)	79·0	22·1	15·1	60·6	23·3	10·5	5·0	21·8	
1876–80	258·0	192·8	114·9	(28·4)	46·2	23·2	8·5	65·2	28·9	11·8	7·2	17·3	
1881–85	661·3	480·7	228·0	(67·1)	171·5	58·4	22·8	180·6	64·0	34·6	17·1	64·5	0·4
1886–90	737·7	407·2	214·8	(62·0)	97·0	60·8	34·6	330·5	134·2	52·5	45·5	96·7	1·6
1891–95	674·8	273·9	128·4	(45·5)	80·5	48·1	16·9	400·9	150·2	67·6	72·2	108·9	2·0
1896–1900	543·3	137·5	81·0	(30·2)	24·9	22·1	9·5	405·7	165·7	77·2	55·8	102·4	4·6
1901–05	1.038·9	253·0	156·0	(36·8)	28·4	53·9	14·7	785·9	320·6	203·0	143·4	97·4	21·3
1906–10	1.436·7	322·2	234·6	(31·0)	26·4	43·7	17·6	1,114·3	402·4	265·4	211·6	185·4	49·5
1911–15	1.365·3	325·6	265·7	(38·4)	15·8	28·6	15·5	1,039·5	312·2	243·6	216·8	220·2	46·7
1916–20	405·5	123·9	101·1	—	2·4	11·2	9·2	281·8	126·6	11·5	7·8	121·3	14·6
1921–25	629·5	295·2	197·7	—	58·9	26·2	12·2	334·4	130·9	23·8	56·8	96·3	26·5
1926–30	555·6	253·5	163·3	—	54·0	23·9	13·3	302·2	89·4	23·0	75·5	74·7	39·6
1931–35	130·8	50·0	30·4	—	12·7	3·1	3·8	81·0	28·2	5·1	20·9	19·6	7·2
1936–39	147·4	60·4	30·3	—	17·3	4·2	5·6	87·2	23·6	6·3	20·8	27·4	9·1

Sources: Dudley Kirk, *Europe's Population in the Interwar Years* (Princeton: League of Nations, 1946), p. 279. For Ireland, Brinley Thomas, *Migration and Economic Growth*, Cambridge, U.P. (1954), 284.

Whereas the main thrust of international emigration up to the First World War was both long-distant and permanent in nature, the period since the Second World War has witnessed a resurgence of international migration within Europe itself which is essentially over short distances and to a large degree mostly temporary in nature. However the economic forces giving rise to this migration are basically the same, that is, during the 1950s and especially the 1960s surplus rural workers from Southern Italy, Greece, and Turkey flocked into areas of labor shortages, most notably West Germany and Switzerland. Table 4.2 gives an example of the magnitude and direction of Italian migration between 1960 and 1964.

The fact that this contemporary migration from regions of surplus labor in Southern and Southeastern Europe is of both a permanent and a non-permanent nature provides a valuable dual benefit to the relatively poor areas from which these unskilled workers migrate. In addition to relieving home governments of the costs of providing for people who in all probability would remain unemployed, the opportunity to earn money in nearby countries and to send a large percen-

Region	1960	1961	1962	1963	1964	
European Economic Community	170,580	175,266	158,900	107,578	113,200	
Total Europe	309,876	329,597	313,400	235,134	236,600	
North America	34,219	29,754	27,876	26,492	26,466	
Central/South America	18,823	10,252	6,568	3,837	3,322	
Australasia	19,629	16,379	14,411	11,539	10,890	
Africa	1,283	1,022	706	589	1,128	
Asia	78	119	255	20	178	**Table 4.2**
Grand Total	383,908	387,123	363,216	277,611	278,584	Italian emigration (1960–64)

Source: 'Italian emigration: some aspects of migration in 1964', *International Migration,* IV, 2 (1966), p. 122.

tage of these earnings home provides a valuable and not insignificant source of foreign exchange to the country in which the worker is permanently domiciled[7].

In view of the above discussion, one might reasonably ask why the large numbers of impoverished peoples in Africa, Asia and Latin America do not follow the example of workers from Southeastern Europe and seek temporary or permanent jobs in areas of labor shortage. Historically, at least in the case of Africa, migrant labor both within and between countries was rather common and did provide some relief for locally depressed areas. Even today, considerable benefits accrue and numerous potential problems are avoided by the fact that thousands of unskilled laborers in Upper Volta are able to find temporary work in neighboring Ivory Coast. The same is true for Malawians in South Africa, Tunisians, Morrocans and Algerians in Europe and Mexicans in the United States. With these possible exceptions, however, the fact remains that *there is very little scope for reducing the pressures of overpopulation in Third World countries today through massive international emigration.* The reasons for this relate not so much to a lack of local knowledge about opportunities in other countries but to the combined effects of geographical (and thus economic) distance and, more important, to the very restrictive nature of immigration laws in modern developed countries. Moreover, the irony of international migration today is not merely that this historical outlet for surplus people has effectively been closed, but that a large percentage of those people who do, in fact, migrate from poor to richer lands are the very ones whom the less developed countries cannot afford to lose: the highly educated and skilled. Since the great majority of these migrants move on a permanent basis, this perverse 'brain drain' not only represents a loss of valuable human resources but, more important, a loss of a productive factor which could prove to be a serious constraint on the future economic progress of Third World nations. For example, during the past 10 years the emigration of high-level professional and technical manpower from the developing to the developed countries of the United States, Canada and the United Kingdom alone amounted to over 400,000 skilled workers (see Table 11.4). The fundamental point remains, however, that the possibility of international migration of *unskilled* workers on a scale resembling that of the nineteenth and early twentieth centuries no longer exists to provide an effective 'safety valve' for the contemporary surplus populations of Africa, Asia and Latin America.

6. The growth stimulus of international trade

International trade has often been referred to as the 'engine of growth'

which propelled forward the development of the presently economically advanced nations during the nineteenth and early twentieth
centuries. Rapidly expanding export markets provided an additional
stimulus to growing local demands that led to the establishment of
large-scale manufacturing industries. Together with a relatively stable
political structure and flexible social institutions, these increased
export earnings enabled the newly developing country of the nineteenth century to borrow funds in the international capital market at
very low interest rates. This capital accumulation in turn stimulated
further production, made possible increased imports and led to a more
diversified industrial structure. All countries in the nineteenth century
were able to participate in this dynamic growth of international
exchange largely on the basis of relatively free trade, free capital
movements and the unfettered international migration of unskilled
surplus labor.

Today, the situation is very different. *Developing countries face
formidable difficulties in trying to generate rapid economic growth on
the basis of world trade.* While being a latecomer to the international
economic system in the nineteenth century was often a real advantage,
it has been a serious disadvantage in the twentieth century. Ever since
the First World War, most developing countries have experienced a
deteriorating trade position. Their exports have expanded but not as
fast as the exports of developed nations. Their terms of trade (i.e. the
price they receive for their exports relative to the price they have to pay
for imports) have declined steadily. Exports have had to grow faster
just to earn the same amount of foreign currencies as in previous years.
Moreover, the developed countries are so far out ahead of the LDCs
economically that they can afford through their advanced science and
technology to remain more competitive, develop more new products
(often synthetic substitutes for traditional LDC primary commodity
exports), and obtain international finance on much better terms.
Finally where developing countries are lower cost producers of competitive products with the developed countries (e.g. textiles, clothing,
shoes, some light manufactures, etc.) the latter have typically resorted
to various forms of tariff and non-tariff barriers to trade including
import quotas, sanitary requirements and special licensing arrangements.

We discuss the economics of international trade and finance in detail
in Chapters 12 to 14. For the present, it is sufficient to point out that
the so-called 'international engine of growth' that roared across the
northern hemisphere in the nineteenth century has for the most part
struggled and crawled for lack of sufficient fuel and need of repairs for
most newcomers to the growth game in the twentieth century.

7. Basic scientific and technological research and development capabilities

A recurrent theme throughout this chapter has been the crucial role
played by basic scientific research and technological development in
the modern economic growth experience of contemporary developed
countries. Their high rates of growth have been sustained by the
interplay between mass applications of many new technological innovations based on a rapid advancement in the stock of scientific knowledge and further additions to that stock of knowledge made possible
by growing surplus wealth. But even today the process of scientific and
technological advance in all its stages – from basic research to product
development – has been heavily concentrated in the rich nations. We
discovered earlier that almost 98 per cent of all world research and

development expenditures originate in these countries. Moreover, research funds are spent on solving the economic and technological problems of concern to rich countries in accordance with their own economic priorities and resource endowments. Rich countries are mainly interested in the development of sophisticated products, large markets and technologically advanced production methods using large inputs of capital and high levels of skills and management while economizing on their relatively scarce supplies of labor and raw materials. The poor countries by contrast are much more interested in simple products, simple designs, saving of capital, use of abundant labor and production for smaller markets. But they have neither the financial resources nor the scientific and the technological know-how at present to undertake the kind of research and development that would be in their best long-term economic interests. Their dependence on 'inappropriate' foreign technologies creates and perpetuates the internal economic dualism of which we spoke in Chapter 3.

We may conclude, therefore, that in the important area of scientific and technological research, contemporary Third World nations are in an extremely disadvantageous competitive position vis-à-vis the developed nations. In contrast, when the latter countries were embarking on their early growth process they were scientifically and technologically greatly in advance of the rest of the world. They could consequently focus their attention on staying ahead by designing and developing new technology at a pace dictated by their long-term economic growth requirements.

The final distinction between the historical experience of developed countries and the situation faced by contemporary Third World nations relates to the nature of social and political institutions. One very obvious difference between the now developed and the underdeveloped nations is that well before their industrial revolutions the former were independent consolidated nation-states able to pursue national policies on the basis of a general consensus of popular opinions and attitudes towards 'modernization'. As Professor Myrdal[8] has correctly pointed out:

8. Stability and flexibility of political and social institutions

... they [the now developed countries] formed a small world of broadly similar cultures, within which people and ideas circulated rather freely ... Modern scientific thought developed in these countries (long before their industrial revolutions) and a modernized technology began early to be introduced in their agricultural and their industries, which at that time were all small-scale.

In contrast to those pre-industrial culturally homogeneous, materially-oriented and politically unified societies with their emphasis on rationalism and modern scientific thought, many Third World countries of today have only recently gained their political independence and have yet to become consolidated nation-states with an effective ability to formulate and pursue national development strategies. Moreover, the modernization ideals embodied in the notions of rationalism, scientific thought, individualism, social and economic mobility, the work-ethic and dedication to national material and cultural values are concepts largely alien to many contemporary Third World societies, except perhaps for their educated ruling elites. Until stable and flexible political institutions can be consolidated with broad public support, the present social and cultural fragmentation of many developing countries is likely to inhibit their desires to accelerate national economic progress.

Conclusions

In view of the above discussion we may conclude that due to very different initial conditions the historical experience of Western economic growth is only of limited relevance for contemporary Third World nations. Nevertheless, one of the most significant and relevant lessons to be learned from this historical experience is the critical importance of concomitant and complementary technological, social and institutional changes that must take place if long-term economic growth is to be realized. Such necessary transformations apply not only within individual developing countries but perhaps more importantly within the international economy as well. In other words, unless there is some major structural, attitudinal and institutional reform in the world economy, one which accommodates the rising aspirations and rewards the outstanding performances of individual developing nations, internal economic and social transformation within the Third World may be insufficient. This realization provides one of the principal rationales for growing Third World demands for a 'new international economic order'. We take up this important issue once again in Part III and finally in Chapter 17.

Notes

1. Algebraically, these components can be written in the standard neo-classical 'production function' format as $Y = P(L,K,t)$ where Y is national output, L is labor, K is capital and t is technological progress.
2. For a more formal classification of neutral, labor- and capital-saving innovation in the context of neo-classical economics, see Appendix 4.1.
3. Simon Kuznets, 'Modern economic growth: findings and reflections', Nobel lecture delivered in Stockholm, Sweden, December 1971. Much of the information and analysis in this section is based on Kuznets' path-breaking work.
4. G. Myrdal, *Asian Drama,* Pantheon, New York (1971), 57–69.
5. Jawaharlal Nehru, 'Strategy of the Third Plan' in *Problems in the Third Plan: A Critical Miscellany,* Ministry of Information and Broadcasting, Government of India (1961), 46.
6. Brinley Thomas, *Migration and Economic Growth,* Cambridge U.P. (1954), p. viii.
7. For a description and analysis of the economic implications of international migration from the Mediterranean area to Western Europe, see W. R. Böhnung. 'Some thoughts on emigration from the Mediterranean area', *International Labour Review,* **14** (1975).
8. G. Myrdal, *The Challenge of World Poverty,* Pantheon, New York (1970), 30–1.

Concepts for review

capital accumulation
technological progress
labor and capital 'augmenting'
  technological progress
labor and capital 'saving'
  technological progress
inventions versus innovations
economic growth
social and institutional
  innovations
economic structural
  transformation

modernization ideals
rationality
resource endowment
economies of scale
trade as an 'engine of growth'
flexible versus rigid political
  and social institutions
relation between 'basic science'
  and technological innovation
research and development
  (R and D)

1. How would you describe the economic growth process in terms of the production–possibility analysis? What are the principal sources of economic growth and how can they be illustrated using *P–P* frontier diagrams?
2. What does the historical record reveal about the nature of the growth process in the now developed nations? What were its principal ingredients?
3. Of what relevance is the historical record of modern economic growth for contemporary Third World nations? How important are differences in 'initial conditions'? Give and describe some examples of the kinds of initial conditions in a Third World country with which you are familiar that make it different from most contemporary developed nations at the beginning of their modern growth experience.
4. What is meant by the statement 'social and institutional innovations are as important for economic growth as technological and scientific inventions and innovations'? Explain your answer.
5. What do you think were the principal reasons why economic growth spread rapidly amongst the now developed nations during the nineteenth and early twentieth century; but has failed to spread to an equal extent to contemporary less developed nations?

On the historical record of economic growth the classic study is that of the Nobel prize winning Harvard economist Simon Kuznets whose lifetime work is best revealed in two volumes: (1) *Modern Economic Growth: Rate, Structure and Spread,* New Haven, Yale U.P. (1966) and (2) *Economic Growth of Nations: Total Output and Production Structure,* Harvard U.P., Massachusetts (1971). But the best and most concise summary of Kuznets' findings can be found in Simon Kuznets, 'Modern economic growth: findings and reflections', *American Economic Review,* lxiii, No. 3 (1973), 247–58. See also Barry E. Supple (ed.), *The Experience of Economic Growth,* Random House, New York (1963), especially Part II for a comparison of the growth experience in a number of contemporary developed countries. For the most comprehensive general statement of the nature of economic growth as applied to less developed countries, see W. Arthur Lewis' classic work, *Theory of Economic Growth,* Unwin University Books, London (1955).

An extensive critique of the historical growth record of developed nations as applied to Third World countries can be found in Gunnar Myrdal, *The Challenge of World Poverty,* Pantheon, New York (1970), Ch. 2 and in his *Asian Drama,* Pantheon (1968), Ch. 14. See also Louis Lefeber, 'on the paradigm for economic development', *World Development,* **2,** No. 1 (1974). A somewhat different view stressing what can be learned from the historical growth experience and applied to contemporary developing nations can be found in A. J. Youngson (ed.), *Economic Development in the Long Run,* St. Martins Press, New York (1973).

Appendix 4.1 The classification of innovations

The classification of inventions and innovations as labor-saving, capital-saving or neutral can be demonstrated with the use of elementary 'isoquant' analysis. For those unfamiliar with this concept, an 'isoquant' or 'equal-product line' is a locus of all combinations of, say, capital (K) and labor (L) that, for a given technology, result in an *identical* level of physical output. Consider Fig. 4.5.

We start with a given isoquant, Y_0, representing an output level of say 60 units. Assume that the current factor price ratio is such that the minimum cost point is at P with K_0 capital and L_0 labor being used. Technological progress can then be represented by a new isoquant which passes through P, but now denoting an output level of say 100 units. In Fig. 4.5, three such new 100 unit isoquants are depicted; dotted lines Y_2 and Y_3 as well as solid line Y_1 which coincides with the original Y_0. Technological progress is classified according to whether the slope of the new isoquant at point P (i.e., the new ratio of marginal physical products) is

(1) *unchanged* $\dfrac{MP_L}{MP_K}(Y_1) = \dfrac{MP_L}{MP_K}(Y_0)$ denoting 'neutral' progress;

(2) *lower* $\dfrac{MP_L}{MP_K}(Y_2) < \dfrac{MP_L}{MP_K}(Y_0)$ denoting 'labor-saving' progress.

or

(3) *higher* $\dfrac{MP_L}{MP_K}(Y_3) > \dfrac{MP_L}{MP_K}(Y_0)$ denoting 'capital-saving' progress.

For purposes of illustration we have assumed the existence of conventional, continuous, convex neo-classical isoquants in Fig. 4.5. This implies an infinite choice of techniques, ranging from very labor-intensive (low K/L ratios) to very capital intensive (high K/L ratios). In actual practice, most developing countries face a very limited range of technical choice largely dictated by the availability of foreign technology and the influence of multinational corporations (see Ch. 8).

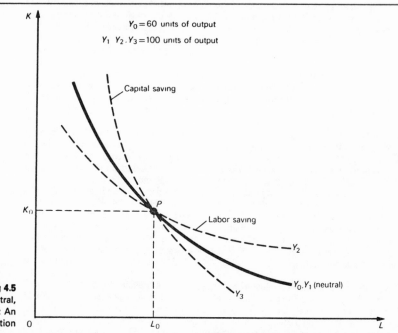

Fig 4.5
Technological progress: neutral, labor-saving and capital-saving: An illustration

Problems and policies
Domestic

Part II

Introduction to Parts II and III

A note to the student on the organizational structure and operating procedure for analyzing development problems in Parts II and III In Part I of this text, we examined the major characteristics of Third World nations, reviewed some basic concepts of development economics and explored the nature and meaning of 'economic growth' and 'development'. In Parts II and III we analyze a number of critical problems which are priority issues in almost all developing countries. Our task here is not only to describe the nature of these problems but also to demonstrate how economic analysis can contribute to their ultimate resolution. It is of little value to understand basic economic concepts and principles if one is not also able to apply them to real world development problems.

Accordingly, the problem-focused chapters in Parts II and III are, in general, organized around a common five-stage operating procedure. We believe that this procedure provides a convenient methodology for analyzing and solving any problem, whether in economics or any other field. The five stages – of problem analysis are:

1. problem statement and principal issues;
2. importance of the problem in developing countries;
3. possible goals and objectives;
4. role of economics;
5. policy alternatives and consequences.

Step No. 1: Statement of problem Each discussion begins with an analysis of what it is we are trying to understand (e.g. population growth, unemployment, poverty, etc.). Basically, four questions are asked:

1. What is the problem all about?
2. Why is it a problem?
3. How important is it?
4. What are the principal issues?

The purpose of this first step is to clarify the nature and importance of the problem so that the student can recognize why so much attention is given to the issue in newspapers, development plans, political speeches and international writings of scholars and journalists.

Step No. 2: Significance and variations of problems in developing countries Here we attempt to provide a capsule statistical summary of the relative importance of the particular problem under review in diverse developing nations. How does it vary from one country to the next and what, if any, are the qualitative as well as quantitative differences in Africa, Asia and Latin America? It is clear, for example, that while rising unemployment and underemployment is a common phenomenon in developing nations, the nature, extent and significance of the problem may be quite different in sub-Saharan Africa as compared with, say, Latin America or South Asia. Our purpose is not to overload the student with comparative Third World statistics. Rather, it is to give him a feel for the ubiquitous nature of certain development problems while advising him that the significance and principal manifestations of the problem may vary from country to country and region to region. As a result, policy approaches designed to cope with the problem can and often do differ in their scope and content.

Step No. 3: Possible goals and objectives Our next step is to set out the likely development goals and objectives as they relate to this particular issue. Here unavoidably we must deal with value judgements and priorities. For example, if greater equality is an overall objective of government policy, then factors such as the distribution of income, the spread of educational opportunities and the role of labor-intensive rural development projects take on a certain significance. However, if the objective is maximum growth of GNP irrespective of its distribution, then these same criteria may carry less weight. The point is that any attempt to deal with real world development problems must be based on explicit economic and social value premises about what is 'desirable' and what are the priorities among different desirable goals. In fact, the very selection of specific problems to be discussed and analyzed in Parts II and III (e.g. poverty, inequality, unemployment, population growth, education, rural development, trade, aid, technology, etc.) reflects a value judgement on the part of the author, albeit one which seems to be rooted in the consensus opinion of a great diversity of those who study and act on Third World development problems.

After setting forth a possible set of goals and objectives to a specific development problem, we ask the following pertinent questions for economists:

Step No. 4: The role of economics and economic principles

1. What are the economic components of the problem?
2. How can economic concepts and principles help us to understand better and possibly solve the problem?
3. Do the economic components dominate the problem and, if so or if not, how might they be related to the non-economic components?

The final step in our problem-solving procedure is to set forth alternative economic policy approaches and their possible consequences for the problem under review. Policy options expounded at the end of each chapter are intended primarily to stimulate group discussion and individual analysis. Students are encouraged therefore to formulate their own conclusions and to feel free to disagree with those put forward by the author. The nature of the policy options available to governments depends on the economic aspects of the overall problem. Each policy alternative needs to be evaluated in light of a variety of priority development goals. As a result, the possibility of 'trade-offs' between goals must always be considered. For example, the goal of rapid GNP growth may or may not be compatible with the elimination of unemployment or the eradication of rural poverty. Similarly, the encouragement of private foreign investment may not be compatible with the desire to be more self-reliant. In either case, when such a conflict of goals becomes apparent, choices have to be made on the basis of priorities and the socio-economic consequences of giving up or curtailing one objective in favor of another. It is at this final stage of evaluating the *indirect* consequences which a particular policy designed to eliminate one problem might have on the exacerbation of other problems that the wisdom of the broad-gauged development economist can be most important.

Step No. 5 Policy alternatives and consequences

By following the above five-step problem-solving procedure, students will not only secure a more comprehensive understanding of critical development issues, but more important, they will be better able to approach and reach independent judgements about other contemporary or future development problems. In the long run, we believe that the possible 'costs' of trying to cram all problems into a somewhat rigid five-step pattern rather than following a less tightly organized discussion will be greatly outweighed by the benefits.

Chapter 5	# Growth, poverty and income distribution

No society can surely be flourishing and happy, of which by far the greater part of the numbers are poor and miserable.
  Adam Smith, 1776

The fact of poverty is not new: what *is* new is the suspicion that economic growth by itself may not solve or even alleviate the problem.
  Montek S. Ahluwalia, 1974

Introduction: the growth controversy

The early 1970s witnessed a remarkable change in public and private perceptions about the ultimate nature of economic activity. In both rich and poor countries disillusionment grew about the relentless pursuit of growth as the principal economic objective of society. In the developed countries, the major emphasis seemed to shift away from growth towards more concern for the 'quality of life'. This concern was manifested principally in the environmental movement. There was an outcry against the onslaught of industrial growth and the consequent pollution of air and water, the depletion of natural resources and the destruction of many natural beauties. A major influential book, entitled *The Limits to Growth,* appeared in 1972 which purported to document the fact, first expounded in the early nineteenth century by Ricardo and especially by Malthus, that the earth's finite resources could not sustain a continuation of high growth rates without major economic and social catastrophes. It is a testimony to the mood of the period that in spite of obvious flaws in logic and many dubious assumptions, this book became widely publicized and acclaimed.

In the poor countries the main concern focused on the question of growth versus income distribution. Many Third World countries which had experienced relatively high rates of economic growth by historical standards in the 1960s began to realize that such growth had brought little in the way of significant benefits to their poor. For these hundreds of millions of people in Africa, Asia and Latin America, levels of living seemed to stagnate and, in some countries, even to decline in real terms. Rates of rural and urban unemployment and underemployment were on the rise. The distribution of incomes between rich and poor seemed to widen with each passing year. Many people felt that rapid economic growth had failed to eliminate or even reduce the wide-spread absolute poverty that remains a fact of economic life in all Third-World nations. In both the developing and developed worlds the call for the 'dethronement of GNP' as the major objective of economic activity was widely heard. In its place concern for the prob-lems of poverty and equality became the major theme of the second development decade. Mahbub ul Haq of Pakistan seemed to speak for a great number of observers when he succinctly asserted that 'we were taught to take care of our GNP as this will take care of poverty. Let us reverse this and take care of poverty as this will take care of the GNP'[1].

Since the elimination of widespread poverty and growing income inequalities is at the core of all development problems and, in fact, defines for many the principal objective of development policy, we begin Part II of this book by focusing on the nature of the poverty and inequality problem in Third World countries. Although our principal focus is on economic inequalities in the distribution of incomes and assets, the student should be aware that these are only a small part of the broader inequality problem in the developing world. Of parallel or even greater importance are inequalities of power, prestige, status, recognition, job satisfaction, conditions of work, degree of participa-tion, freedom of choice and many other dimensions of the problem that relate more to our second and third components of the meaning of development, self-esteem and freedom to choose. But as in most social relationships, one cannot really separate the economic from the non-economic manifestations of inequality. Each reinforces the other in a complex and often interrelated process of cause and effect.

Our basic problem-solving approach will be as outlined in the Intro-duction to Parts II and III. First, we define the nature of the poverty and income distribution problem and consider its quantitative sig-nificance in various Third World nations, then set forth possible goals and objectives, examine in what ways economic analyses can shed light on the problem and, finally, explore alternative possible policy approaches directed at the elimination of poverty and the reduction of excessively wide disparities in Third World distributions of income. A thorough understanding of these two fundamental economic manifes-tations of underdevelopment provides the basis for analysis of more specific development issues including population growth, unemploy-ment, rural development, education, international trade, and foreign assistance in succeeding chapters.

5.1 'Who' gets 'how much' of 'what'? a simple illustration

A simple and convenient way to approach the twin problems of pov-erty and income distribution is to utilize the production–possibility framework. To illustrate our point, however, let's divide production in our hypothetical developing economy into two classes of goods. First, there are *necessity* goods such as staple foods, simple clothing, minimum shelter, etc. – goods essential to basic subsistence. The second class of goods, luxuries, might include expensive cars and houses, sophisticated consumer goods, fashionable clothes, speciality foods, etc. Assuming for the present that production occurs on the possibility frontier (i.e. that all resources are fully and efficiently employed), the question arises as to what combination of economic necessities and luxuries will actually be chosen by the 'society' in question. Who will do the choosing and how?

Figure 5.1 illustrates the issue. On the vertical axis we have aggregated all luxury goods and on the horizontal axis are grouped all necessities. The production–possibility curve, therefore, portrays the maximum combinations of both types of goods which this economy could produce by making efficient use of all available resources with the prevailing technological know-how. But it does *not* tell us precisely *which* combination among the many possible ones will *actually* be chosen. For example, the same *real* GNP would be represented at

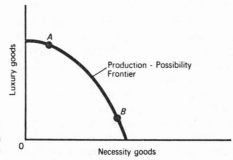

Fig 5.1
Choosing what to produce: Luxuries versus necessities

points A and B in Fig. 5.1. At point A many luxury goods and very few necessities are being produced, while at point B few luxuries and many necessities are being supplied to the population. One would normally expect the actual production combination in low-income countries to be somewhere in the vicinity of point B. But, with the exception of 'command' economies where production and distribution decisions are centrally planned, the basic determinant of output combinations in market and mixed economies is the level of effective aggregate demand exerted by all consumers. This is because the position and shape of society's aggregate demand curve for different products is determined primarily by the level and especially the distribution of national income.

Take, for example, the simple case of an economy consisting only of two consumers and two goods, luxuries and necessities. We know from both historical and cross-country expenditure studies that individuals or families with low incomes spend very high proportions of their incomes on basic necessities such as food, clothing and simple shelter. On the other hand, relatively rich people spend a low proportion of their income on these necessities and a relatively high proportion on what we have called luxury goods – luxurious at least in the context of what poor societies can afford. For our illustration, let us suppose that a person is poor if he has 5 units or less of income per year. Such a person might spend 90 per cent of his income on 'necessities', – that is his 'propensity to consume' necessities will be $0 \cdot 9$, which when multiplied by his income level will show his total consumption or expenditure on necessities. The remaining 10 per cent will be spent on 'luxuries', a propensity to consume $0 \cdot 10$. On the other hand, a rich person – i.e. one who was more than say 5 units per year – will spend on the average only 20 per cent of his income on necessities (a propensity to consume of $0\cdot2$) and 80 per cent (or a propensity of $0\cdot8$) on luxuries. We are assuming, therefore, for simplicity that all income is expended on these two goods.

Now suppose that the total GNP is 8 units and that this income is divided *equally* into 4 units of personal income for each individual, where Y stands for the level of personal income. Table 5.1 shows that in such a situation each individual with a propensity to spend 90 per cent of his 4 units of income on necessities will allocate $3\cdot6$ units of his income ($0\cdot9 \times 4 = 3\cdot6$) on these goods so that the total demand for necessity goods will be $7\cdot2$ units. On the other hand, each person will spend only $0\cdot4$ (i.e. $0\cdot1 \times 4$) on luxuries so that a total of only $0\cdot8$ units of income will be spent on luxury goods. If this demand is translated into production, the point on the production–possibility curve where this economy will be operating will be in the vicinity of B in Fig. 5.1.

Now, assume that this same national income of 8 units is distributed *very unequally*, with individual No. 1 getting 7 units and individual No. 2 only 1 unit. Table 5.2 shows that in the case of the coexistence of relative wealth and extreme poverty, total demand for necessity goods will amount only to $2\cdot3$ units (i.e. the rich person will spend $1\cdot4$ and the poor person $0\cdot9$ units respectively) while the total demand for luxury goods is $5\cdot7$ units ($5\cdot6$ for the rich individual and $0\cdot1$ for the poor one). Production will take place in the vicinity of Point A in Fig. 5.1.

	Individual No. 1	Individual No. 2
Personal Income (Y)	$Y = 4$	$Y = 4$
Propensity to consume and expenditures on:		
1. Necessities ($0\cdot9 \times Y$ if $Y \leqslant 5$)	$3\cdot6 (= 0\cdot9 \times 4)$	$3\cdot6$
or ($0\cdot2 \times Y$ if $Y > 5$)		
2. Luxuries ($0\cdot1 \times Y$ if $Y \leqslant 5$)	$0\cdot4 (= 0\cdot1 \times 4)$	$0\cdot4$
or ($0\cdot8 \times Y$ if $Y > 5$)		

Total demand for
1. Necessities $= 7\cdot2 (= 3\cdot6 + 3\cdot6)$
2. Luxuries $= 0\cdot8 (= 0\cdot4 + 0\cdot4)$
Total expenditure $= 8\cdot0$ (per capita
($=$ total GNP)   income $= 4\cdot0$)

Table 5.1
Expenditure and production patterns for an hypothetical two-person, two-good economy with equal incomes

We see, therefore, that in spite of the relative poverty of the country as a whole, the very unequal distribution of income means that the rich individual can dictate the overall pattern of production since his

	Individual No. 1	Individual No. 2
Personal Income (Y)	$Y = 7$	$Y = 1$
Propensity to consume and expenditures on:		
1. Necessities ($0\cdot9 \times Y$ if $Y \leqslant 5$)		$0\cdot9 (= 0\cdot9 \times 1)$
or ($0\cdot2 \times Y$ if $Y > 5$)	$1\cdot4 (= 0\cdot2 \times 7)$	
2. Luxuries ($0\cdot1 \times Y$ if $Y \leqslant 5$)		$0\cdot1 (= 0\cdot1 \times 1)$
or ($0\cdot8 \times Y$ if $Y > 5$)	$5\cdot6 (= 0\cdot8 \times 7)$	

Total demand for
1. Necessities $= 2\cdot3 (= 1\cdot4 + 0\cdot9)$
2. Luxuries $= 5\cdot7 (= 5\cdot6 + 0\cdot1)$
Total expenditure $= 8\cdot0$ (per capita
($=$ total GNP)   income $= 4\cdot0$)

Table 5.2
Expenditure and production patterns for an hypothetical two-person, two-good economy with highly unequal incomes

demand preferences carry more weight in the consumer goods market than those of the poor person. In both examples GNP (8) and per capita income (4) were exactly the same. But, given the very different distribution of this income, significant differences in production and consumption patterns ensued.

Tables 5.1 and 5.2 illustrate a basic point about the relationship between income distribution and the pattern of demand. Two countries with the same levels of GNP and income per capita may have entirely different production and consumption structures (i.e. they may be operating at different points on the same production–possibility curve) depending on whether or not personal incomes are distributed equitably. *For a given low level of GNP and per capita income, the more unequal the distribution of income, the more aggregate demand will be influenced by the consumption habits of the rich.* In spite of the fact that they may constitute only a small proportion of the population, the rich can control a very disproportionately large share of national resources. Their dominant purchasing power can bias production towards manufactured luxury goods even while the masses of people are barely subsisting. This provides a good example of a situation in which the traditional theory of consumer sovereignty, as manifested in market demand curves, represents in fact the sovereignty not of all consumers but of the very few rich ones who dominate the market and determine what goods should be produced.

As a result of highly unequal income distributions, we find a number of low-income Third World countries devoting a sizeable proportion of their financial, technical and administrative resources to the production of sophisticated consumption goods with large import contents (television sets, stereophonic equipment, electronic components, etc.) to cater for the demands of a very small but economically powerful minority located mostly in urban areas. If incomes were more equitably distributed, the pattern of demand would be geared more towards the production of basic foods and other necessities which would further help to eliminate rural poverty and raise levels of living for broader segments of the population. An additional implication (to be discussed in Chapter 8) of a demand pattern biased towards expensive consumption goods is that these products normally require relatively sophisticated capital-intensive production techniques compared with the relatively more labor-intensive technology of necessity good production. As a result, fewer jobs are available, profits (including those of resident foreign corporations) are higher and the distribution of income tends to widen even further.

For the remainder of this chapter we examine the following five critical questions about the relationship between economic growth, income distribution and poverty:

1. What is the extent of relative inequality in Third World countries and how is this related to the extent of absolute poverty?
2. Who are the poor and what are their economic characteristics?
3. What determines the 'character' of economic growth – i.e. who benefits?
4. Are rapid economic growth and more equitable distributions of income compatible or conflicting objectives for low-income countries? Alternatively, is rapid growth achievable only at the expense of greater inequalities in the distribution of income or can a lessening of income disparities contribute to higher growth rates?
5. What types of policies are required to reduce the magnitude and extent of absolute poverty?

5.2 Some basic concepts: size and functional distributions of income

We can get some idea of the answers to questions 1 and 2 relating to the extent and character of inequality and poverty in developing countries by pulling together some recent evidence from a variety of sources. In this section, we define the dimensions of the income distribution and poverty problems and identify some similar elements which characterize the problem in many Third World nations. But first we should be clear about what we are measuring when we speak about the distribution of income.

Economists usually like to distinguish between two principal measures of income distribution both for analytical and quantitative purposes: (1) the 'personal' or 'size' distribution of income and (2) the 'functional' or 'distributive factor share' distribution of income.

1. Size distributions

The *personal or size distribution of income* is the measure most commonly used by economists. It simply deals with individual persons and the total incomes they receive. The way in which that income was received is not considered. What matters is how much each earns irrespective of whether or not the income was derived solely from employment or from other sources such as interest, profits, rents, gifts, inheritance, etc. Moreover, the locational (urban or rural) and occupational sources of the income (e.g. agriculture, manufacturing, commerce, services, etc.) are neglected. If Mr X and Mr Y both receive the same annual personal income, they are classified together irrespective of the fact that Mr X may work 15 hours a day on his farm while Mr Y doesn't work at all but simply collects interest on his inheritance.

Economists and statisticians, therefore, like to arrange all individuals by ascending personal incomes and then divide the total population into distinct groups or 'sizes'. A common method is to divide the population into successive 'quintiles' (i.e. five groups) or 'deciles' (ten groups) according to ascending income levels and then determine what proportion of the total national income is received by each income group. For example, Table 5.3 shows an hypothetical but fairly typical distribution of income for a developing country. In this table twenty 'individuals', representing the entire population of the country are arranged in order of ascending annual personal incomes ranging from the individual with the lowest income ($0 \cdot 8$ units) to the one with the highest ($15 \cdot 0$ units). The total or national income of all individuals amounts to 100 units and is the sum of all entries in column 2. In column 3 the population is grouped into 'quintiles' or five groups of 4 individuals each. The first quintile represents the bottom 20 per cent of the population on the income scale. This group receives only 5 per cent (i.e. a total of 5 money units) of the total national income. The second quintile (individuals 5–8) receives 9 per cent of the total income. Alternatively, the bottom 40 per cent of the population (quintiles one plus two) is receiving only 14 per cent of the income while the top 20 per cent (the fifth quintile) of the population receives 51 per cent of the total income.

A common measure of income inequality which can be derived from column 3 is the ratio of the incomes received by the bottom 40 per cent compared to the top 20 per cent of the population. This ratio is often used as a measure of the degree of inequality between the two extremes of very poor and very rich in a country. In our example, this

Growth, poverty and income distribution

	Individuals	Personal income (money units)	Percentage share in total income	
			Quintiles	Deciles
	1	0·8		
	2	1·0		1·8%
	3	1·4		
	4	1·8	5%	3·2%
	5	1·9		
	6	2·0		3·9%
	7	2·4		
	8	2·7	9%	5·1%
	9	2·8		
	10	3·0		5·8%
	11	3·4		
	12	3·8	13%	7·2%
	13	4·2		
	14	4·8		9·0%
	15	5·9		
	16	7·1	22%	13·0%
	17	10·5		
	18	12·0		22·5%
	19	13·5		
	20	15·0	51%	28·5%
Totals	20	(National income) 100·0	100%	100%

Table 5.3
A hypothetical (but typical) size distribution of LDC personal income by income shares – quintiles and deciles

[Measure of inequality → Ratio of bottom 40% to top 20% = 14/51 = 0·28]

inequality ratio is equal to 14·0 divided by 51·0 or approximately 1 to 3·7, or 0·28.

To provide a more detailed breakdown of the size distribution of income, 'decile' or 10 per cent shares are listed in column 4. We see, for example, that the bottom 10 per cent of the population (the two poorest individuals) is receiving only 1·8 per cent of the total income while the top 10 per cent (the two richest individuals) receives 28·5 per cent. Finally, if we wanted to know what the top 5 per cent receives, we would divide the total population into 20 equal groups of individuals (in our example, this would simply be each of the 20 individuals) and calculate the percentage of total income received by the top group. In Table 5.3, we see that the top 5 per cent of the population (the 20th individual) receives 15 per cent of the income, a higher share than the combined shares of the lowest 40 per cent.

2. Lorenz curves Another common way to analyze personal income figures is to construct what is known as a Lorenz curve[2]. Figure 5.2 shows how it is done.The numbers of income recipients are plotted on the horizontal axis, not in absolute terms but in *cumulative percentages*. For example, at point 20 we have the lowest (poorest) 20 per cent of the population, at point 60, the bottom 60 per cent, and at the end of the axis all 100 per cent of the population has been accounted for. The vertical axis portrays the share in total income associated with or received by each percentage of population. It also is cumulative up to 100 per cent so that both axes are equally long and the entire figure is then enclosed in a square. A diagonal line is drawn from the lower left hand corner (the origin) of the square to the upper right hand corner. At every point on that diagonal, the percentage of income received is *exactly equal* to the percentage of income recipients – for example, the point half-way along the length of the diagonal represents 50 per cent of the income being distributed to exactly 50 per cent of the population. At the three-quarter point on the diagonal, 75 per cent of the income would be distributed to 75 per cent of the population. In other words, the diagonal line in Fig. 5.2 is representative of 'perfect equality' in the size distribution of income. Each percentage group of income recipients is receiving that same percentage of the total income; for example, the bottom 40 per cent receives 40 per cent of the income while the top 5 per cent receives only 5 per cent of the total income[3].

The Lorenz Curve shows the *actual* quantitative relationship between the percentage of income recipients and the percentage of the total income which they did in fact receive during, say, a given year. In Fig. 5.2 we have plotted this Lorenz curve using the 'decile' data contained in Table 5.3. In other words, we have divided both the horizontal and vertical axes into ten equal segments corresponding to each of the ten decile groups. Point A shows that the bottom 10 per cent of the population receives only 1·8 per cent of the total income. Point B shows that the bottom 20 per cent is receiving 5 per cent of the total income – and so on for each of the other eight cumulative decile groups. Note that at the halfway point, E, 50 per cent of the population is in fact receiving only 19·8 per cent of the total income.

The more the Lorenz line curves away from the diagonal (perfect equality), the greater the degree of inequality represented. The extreme case of perfect inequality, i.e. a situation in which one person receives *all* of the national income while everybody else receives nothing, would be represented by the coexistence of the Lorenz curve

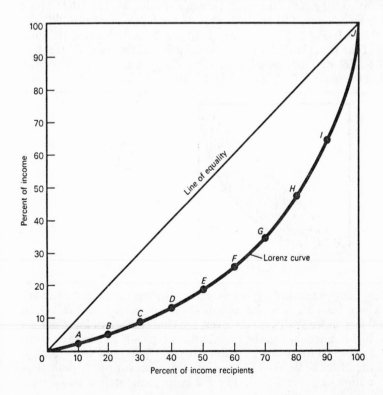

Fig 5.2
The Lorenz curve

with the bottom horizontal and the right-hand vertical axes. Since no country exhibits either perfect equality or perfect inequality in its distribution of income, the Lorenz curves for different countries will lie somewhere to the right of the diagonal in Fig. 5.2. The greater the degree of inequality, the more 'bend' and the closer to the bottom horizontal axis will be the Lorenz curve. Two such representative distributions are shown in Fig. 5.3.

(Can you explain why the Lorenz curve could not lie above or to the left of the diagonal at any point?)

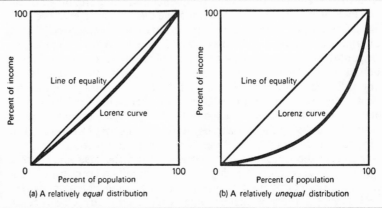

Fig 5.3
The greater the curvature of the Lorenz line, the greater the relative degree of inequality

(a) A relatively *equal* distribution

(b) A relatively *unequal* distribution

3. Gini coefficients and aggregate measures of inequality

A final and very convenient shorthand summary measure of the relative degree of income inequality in a country can be obtained by calculating the ratio of the 'area' between the diagonal and the Lorenz Curve as compared to the total area of the half-square in which the curve lies. In Fig. 5.4 this is the ratio of the shaded area A to the total area of the triangle BCD. This ratio is known as the 'Gini Concentration Ratio' or more simply, the *Gini Coefficient,* named after the Italian statistician C. Gini who first formulated it in 1912.

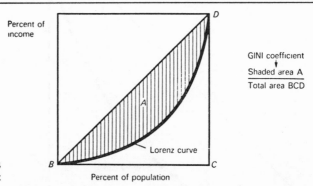

GINI coefficient

$$\frac{\text{Shaded area A}}{\text{Total area BCD}}$$

Fig 5.4
Estimating the GINI coefficient

Gini coefficients are aggregate inequality measures and can vary anywhere from zero (perfect equality) to one (perfect inequality). In actual fact, as we shall soon discover, the Gini coefficient for countries with highly unequal income distributions typically lies betwen 0·50 and 0·70 while for countries with relatively equitable distributions, it is of the order of 0·20 to 0·35. The coefficient for our hypothetical distribution of Table 5.3 and Fig. 5.2 is approximately 0·61 – a relatively unequal distribution.

The second common measure of income distribution used by economists, the *'functional' or 'factor share distribution'*, attempts to explain the share of total national income that each factor of production receives. Instead of looking at individuals as separate entities, the theory and measure of functional income distribution inquires into the percentage that 'labor' receives as a whole and compares this with the percentages of total income distributed in the form of rent, interest and profit (i.e. the returns to land and financial and physical capital). Although individuals may receive income from all these sources, it is not a matter of concern for the functional approach.

A sizable body of theoretical economic literature has been built up around the concept of functional income distribution. It attempts to explain the income of a factor of production by the contribution that this factor makes to production. Supply and demand curves are assumed to determine the unit prices of each productive factor. When these unit prices are multiplied by quantities employed on the assumption of efficient (i.e. minimum cost) factor utilization, one gets a measure of the total payment to each factor. For example, the supply of and demand for labor are assumed to determine its market wage. When this wage is then multiplied by the total level of employment, one gets a measure of total wage payments, also sometimes called the total wage bill.

4. Functional distributions

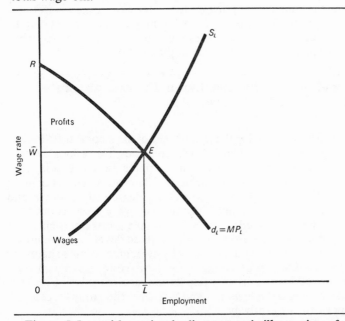

Fig 5.5
Functional income distribution in a market economy: An illustration

Figure 5.5 provides a simple diagrammatic illustration of the traditional theory of functional income distribution. We assume that there are only two factors of production: capital, which is a fixed (given) factor and labor, which is the only variable factor. Under competitive market assumptions, the demand for labor will be determined by labor's marginal product – i.e. additional workers will be hired up to the point where the value of their marginal product equals their real wage. But, in accordance with the principle of diminishing marginal products, this demand for labor will be a declining function of the numbers employed. Such a negatively sloped labor demand curve is shown by line d_L in Fig. 5.5. With a traditional neo-classical upward sloping labor supply curve S_L the 'equilibrium' wage will be equal to $0\overline{W}$ and the equilibrium level of employment will be $0\overline{L}$. Total national output (= total national income) will be represented by the area $OREL$[4]. This national income will be distributed in two shares – $OWEL$ going to workers in the form of wages and $\overline{W}RE$ remaining as capitalist profits (i.e. the return to owners of capital). In a competitive market economy with constant returns to scale production functions, therefore, factor prices are determined by factor supply and demand curves, while factor shares always combine to exhaust the total national product. Income is distributed by 'function' – laborers receive 'wages', owners of land receive 'rents' and capitalists obtain 'profits'. It is all a very neat and logical theory since each and every factor gets paid only in accordance with what it contributes to national output – no more, no less.

Unfortunately, the relevance of the functional theory is greatly vitiated by its failure to take into account the important role and influence of 'non-market' forces such as 'power' in determining these factor prices – e.g. the role of collective bargaining between employers and trade unions in the setting of 'modern sector' wage rates and the power of monopolists and wealthy landowners to manipulate prices on capital, land and output to their own personal advantages. We shall have more to say about the relative strengths and weaknesses of the size versus the functional approach to analyzing income distribution later in the chapter. But first let us use some recent empirical data to get a more precise idea of the magnitude of the problems of inequality and poverty in a wide range of developing nations.

5.3 A review of evidence: inequality and absolute poverty in Third World countries

1. Inequality: variations among countries As a first step in determining the significance of the income distribution and poverty problems in Third World countries, let us look at data collected from forty-two countries on the percentage shares in total national income going to different percentile groups. This is done in Table 5.4. Though methods of collection, degree of coverage and specific definitions of personal income may vary from country to country, the figures recorded in Table 5.4 give a first approximation of the magnitude of income inequalities in these developing countries. For example, we see from the last row by averaging income shares for different percentile groups among all forty-two countries that on average the *poorest* 20 per cent of the population receives only 5·6 per cent of the income while the *highest* 5 and 20 percentile groups receive 30 and 56 per cent respectively.

Now, consider the relationship, if any, between levels of per capita income and degrees of inequality for a large sample of both developed and less developed countries. Table 5.5 presents a cross-classification of these countries into three groups. The groupings correspond to high, moderate and low degrees of inequality as measured by specified ranges of the Gini coefficients and to high, middle and low income levels in accordance with specified ranges of real GNP per capita. As an alternative inequality measure to the Gini coefficient, Table 5.5 also provides a measure of the degree of concentration of incomes at the lowest and highest levels of the distribution scale by showing for each country the ration of the income share of the lowest 40 per cent to the highest 20 per cent of the respective populations.

	Poorest 20%	Poorest 60%	Middle 40–60%	Highest 5%	Highest 20%
Argentina	7·00	30·40	13·10	29·40	52·00
Bolivia	4·00	26·60	8·90	35·70	59·10
Brazil	3·50	22·70	10·20	38·40	61·50
Burma	10·00	36·00	13·00	28·21	48·50
Ceylon	4·45	27·47	13·81	18·38	52·31
Chad	12·00	35·00	12·00	23·00	43·00
Chile	5·40	27·00	12·00	22·60	52·30
Colombia	2·21	15·88	8·97	40·36	68·06
Costa Rica	6·00	25·40	12·10	35·00	60·00
Dahomey	8·00	30·00	12·00	32·00	50·00
Ecuador	6·30	35·70	13·40	21·50	41·80
El Salvador	5·50	23·60	11·30	33·00	61·40
Gabon	2·00	15·00	7·00	47·00	71·00
Greece	9·00	34·10	12·30	23·00	49·50
India	8·00	36·00	16·00	20·00	42·00
Iraq	2·00	16·00	8·00	34·00	68·00
Israel	6·80	38·80	18·60	11·20	39·40
Ivory Coast	8·00	30·00	12·00	29·00	55·00
Jamaica	2·20	19·00	10·80	31·20	61·50
Japan	4·70	31·10	15·80	14·80	46·00
Kenya	7·00	21·00	7·00	22·20	64·00
Lebanon	3·00	23·00	15·80	34·00	61·00
Malagasy	7·00	23·00	9·00	37·00	59·00
Mexico	3·66	21·75	11·25	28·52	58·04
Morocco	7·10	22·20	7·70	20·60	65·40
Niger	12·00	35·00	12·00	23·00	42·00
Nigeria	7·00	23·00	9·00	38·38	60·90
Pakistan	6·50	33·00	15·50	20·00	45·00
Panama	4·90	28·10	13·80	34·50	56·70
Peru	4·04	17·10	8·30	48·30	67·60
Philippines	4·30	24·70	12·00	27·50	55·80
Rhodesia	4·00	20·00	8·00	60·00	65·00
Senegal	3·00	20·00	10·00	36·00	64·00
Sierra Leone	3·80	19·20	9·10	33·80	64·10
South Africa	1·94	16·27	10·16	39·38	57·36
Sudan	5·60	29·30	14·30	17·10	48·10
Surinam	10·70	37·00	14·74	15·40	42·40
Tanzania	9·75	29·25	9·85	42·90	61·00
Trinidad and Tobago	3·60	18·52	9·16	26·60	57·00
Tunisia	4·97	20·57	9·95	22·44	65·00
Venezuela	4·40	30·00	16·60	23·20	47·40
Zambia	6·27	26·55	11·10	37·50	57·10
Averages	5·60	26·00	12·00	30·00	56·00

Table 5.4
Some income distribution estimates

Source: Table 1, Income Distribution Estimates from *Society, Politics and Economic Development: A Quantitative Approach* by Irma Adelman and Cynthia Taft Morris, Johns Hopkins.

A number of specific and interesting conclusions emerge from a careful examination of Table 5.5.

1. All countries, whether capitalist, socialist or 'mixed', show some degree of inequality. This is important because we need to have some idea of what kinds of distributions are practical and feasible, in other words, to establish some reasonable 'benchmarks' or 'targets' towards which a country might strive rather than to attempt to achieve the idealized but impractical goal of perfect equality.

2. Socialist countries such as Czechoslovakia, Hungary, Poland and Bulgaria have the highest degree of equality in their distributions of incomes (e.g. they have the lowest Gini coefficients).

Growth, poverty and income distribution

Table 5.5
Classification of countries by income
levels and inequality

	Country*	Year	Per capita income†	Ratio‡	Gini	Country*	Year	Per capita income†	Ratio‡	Gini	Country*	Year	Per capita income†	Ratio‡	Gini
	High inequality Gini > 0·50					**Moderate inequality** Gini — 0·40–0·50					**Low inequality** Gini < 0·40				
Low income <US $300	Brazil§	1970	231	6·5/66·7	0·61	Dahomey§	1959	65	15·5/50·0	0·44	Ceylon	1969–70	155	17·0/46·0	0·37
	Colombia§	1970	251	9·4/59·5	0·54	El Salvador§	1969	248	12·7/52·0	0·45	Taiwan	1964	201	20·4/40·1	0·32
	Ecuador§	1970	202	6·4/73·5	0·66	Guyana	1955–6	272	14·0/45·7	0·40	Chad	1958	63	18·0/43·0	0·35
	Gabon§	1960	261	6·0/71·0	0·65	India	1961–4	84	14·0/54·0	0·46	Ivory Coast	1959	139	17·5/55·0	0·43
	Honduras§	1967–8	224	7·3/67·5	0·61	Philippines	1965	150	11·6/55·4	0·50	Korea, South	1970	180	18·0/45·0	0·36
	Iraq§	1956	172	6·8/68·0	0·61	Sudan	1963	91	14·2/50·3	0·43	Libya	1962	220	23·5/37·0	0·26
	Madagascar§	1960	93	13·5/61·0	0·52	Tanzania	1967	70	14·0/57·0	0·48	Malaysia	1957–8	208	17·7/43·9	0·36
	Peru	1970–1	297	6·5/60·0	0·57	Thailand	1962	92	12·9/57·7	0·50	Niger§	1960	73	18·0/42·0	0·36
	Rhodesia§	1968	214	8·2/69·0	0·62	Tunisia§	1961	156	10·5/55·0	0·50	Pakistan (E/W)	1963–4	83	17·5/45·0	0·37
	Senegal§	1960	171	10·0/64·0	0·56	Zambia	1959	150	14·6/57·0	0·49	Uganda§	1969–70	110	17·1/47·1	0·38
Middle income US $300—750	Jamaica	1958	388	8·2/61·5	0·56	Argentina	1961	681	17·3/52·0	0·42	Bulgaria§	1962	407	26·8/33·2	0·21
	Lebanon	1955–60	454	13·0/61·0	0·52	Chile	1968	427	13·0/56·8	0·49	Greece§	1957	341	21·0/49·5	0·37
	Mexico	1968	464	10·2/65·8	0·58	Costa Rica	1971	423	14·7/50·6	0·43	Israel§	1957	686	20·2/39·4	0·30
	Panama§	1969	560	9·4/59·3	0·54	Uruguay	1967	460	14·3/47·4	0·42	Poland§	1964	649	23·4/36·0	0·25
	South Africa§	1965	530	6·2/58·0	0·56						Spain	1964–5	572	17·0/45·2	0·38
	Venezuela	1962	750	9·7/58·0	0·52						Surinam	1962	311	21·7/42·6	0·31
											Yugoslavia	1968	451	18·5/41·5	0·33
High income >US $750						Denmark	1968	1,838	13·6/47·6	0·42	Canada	1965	2,057	20·0/40·2	0·32
						Finland	1962	1,193	11·1/49·3	0·45	Czechoslovakia§	1964	880	27·6/31·0	0·18
						France	1962	1,373	9·5/53·7	0·50	Hungary§	1969	870	24·0/33·5	0·24
						Germany, W.§	1964	1,614	15·4/52·9	0·45	Japan	1963	780	20·7/40·0	0·31
						Netherlands§	1967	1,437	13·6/48·5	0·43	New Zealand§	1968–9	1,800	15·5/42·0	0·37
						Puerto Rico	1963	988	13·7/50·6	0·44	Norway§	1963	1,609	16·6/40·5	0·35
											Sweden§	1963	2,220	14·0/44·0	0·39
											United Kingdom	1968	1,599	18·8/39·0	0·32
											United Sates§	1970	3,603	19·7/38·8	0·31

* The data on countries without the section mark is based on house size distribution.
† Per capita income is in 1964 US $ to the closest 2 years.
‡ Ratios are ratio of bottom 40 per cent to top 20 per cent.
§ The data is based on active workers income distribution.

Source: Montek Ahluwalia, 'Dimensions of the problem', in Chenery, Duloy and Jolly (eds), *Redistribution With Growth: An Approach to Policy*, IBRD, Washington (1973), (2) 4 (mimeo.).

3. Developed countries on the whole exhibit a relatively more equal distribution than *most* Third World countries. This is primarily because most economically advanced countries have been able to develop effective mechanisms over the years to transfer some proportion of their incomes from rich to poor. For example, progressively higher income tax rates combined with public expenditures, social security payments, unemployment compensation, food stamps and other outright welfare payments to the very poor are methods used to temper the wide income disparities which might normally result in the course of private economic activity. Such income transfer mechanisms are still either largely non-existent or ineffectively administered in most developing countries.

4. Third World countries have a significant variation in their degree of inequality as shown by the wide range of their Gini coefficients.

5. Perhaps more important, there seems to be no apparent relationship between levels of per capita income and the degree of income concentration. Even within the group of very low income countries (i.e. those with per capita incomes of less than $300) we see from Table 5.5 that the share of income accruing to the bottom 40 per cent varies from 6·5 per cent (Brazil) to over 20 per cent (Taiwan).

2. 'Absolute' poverty: extent and magnitude

Now let's switch our attention from relative income shares of various percentile groups within a given population to the more significant question of the extent and magnitude of 'absolute poverty' in developing countries. In Chapter 2, remember, we saw that 'absolute poverty' can be defined by the number of people living below a specified minimum level of income – an imaginary 'international poverty line'. Such a line knows no national boundaries and is independent of the level of national per capita income. Absolute poverty can and does exist, therefore, just as readily in New York city as it does in Calcutta, Cairo, Lagos or Bogota – although its magnitude may be much less in terms of total numbers or percentages of the total population.

In Table 2.2 (page 27) we provided some rough estimates on the absolute numbers of people living below two arbitrary minimum levels of personal income in 1969 as expressed in constant (1964 based) US dollars. Obviously standards and costs of living will vary from country to country and comparative cross-country income estimates are subject to wide margins of error. Nevertheless, the figures in that table showed the enormous magnitude of the poverty problem in developing countries. The forty-four countries listed account for almost half of the total population of the Third World (excluding China). We found that over 370 million people or approximately 31 per cent of the populations of these forty-four countries had annual incomes that were less than US $50 per capita in 1969. When we defined the international poverty standard in 1969 as an annual income of less than US $75, we saw (columns 5 and 6) that almost 580 million people or 48·2 per cent of the total populations of these countries could be classified as absolutely poor. Even allowing for errors of measurement and the failure to estimate accurately subsistence incomes, the figures reported in Table 2.2 provide dramatic evidence of the enormous and crushing burden of poverty in the vast majority of Third World countries.

One final point, analogous to conclusion No. 5 above regarding the apparent absence of any necessary relationship between levels of per capita income and the distribution of that income, needs to be mentioned. It is that *high per capita incomes per se do not guarantee the absence of significant numbers of absolute poor*. Since the share of income accruing to the lowest percentile of a population can vary widely from one country to another, it is possible for a country with a high per capita income to have a larger percentage of its population below an international poverty line than a country with a lower per capita income. Thus, for example, if we look again at Table 2.2 we see that Taiwan and Iraq had approximately the same level of real per capita income in 1969 even though the proportion of Iraq's population below the $50 poverty line is almost 150 per cent greater than that of Taiwan. Similarly, Korea with half the per capita income level of Peru has less than one-third the proportion of its low income people below the $50 poverty line than Peru (5·5 compared with 18·9 per cent of their respective populations). This simply shows that problems of poverty and highly unequal distributions of income are not just the result of natural economic growth processes. Rather, they depend on the *character* of that economic growth and the political and institutional arrangements according to which rising national incomes are distributed among the broad segments of the population.

5.4 Economic characteristics of poverty groups

So far we have painted a broad picture of the income distribution and poverty problem in developing countries by showing how the magnitude of absolute poverty results from a combination of low per capita incomes and highly unequal distributions of that income. Clearly, for any given distribution of income, the higher the level of per capita income, the lower will be the numbers of the absolutely poor. But, as we have seen, higher levels of per capita income are no guarantee of lower levels of poverty. An understanding of the nature of the size distribution of income, therefore, is central to any analysis of the poverty problem in low income countries.

But painting a broad picture of Third World poverty is not enough. Before we can formulate effective policies and programs to attack poverty at its source, we need some specific knowledge of who these poverty groups are and what are their economic characteristics. As we show in a later section when we deal with alternative policies to combat poverty, it is *not* sufficient simply to focus on raising growth rates of GNP in the expectation or hope that this national income growth will 'trickle down' to improve levels of living for the very poor. On the contrary, direct attacks on poverty by means of poverty-focused policies and plans appear to be more effective both in the short and longer runs. But one cannot attack poverty directly without detailed knowledge of its location, extent and characteristics.

Perhaps *the most valid generalization about the poor is that they are disproportionately located in the rural areas* and that they are primarily engaged in agricultural and associated activities. Data from a broad cross-section of Third World nations supports this generalization. We find, for example, that about two-thirds of the very poor scratch out their livelihood from subsistence agriculture either as small farmers or low-paid farm workers. The remaining one-third are located partly in rural areas (engaged in petty services) and partly on the fringes and marginal areas of urban centers where they engage in various forms of self-employment such as street-hawking, trading, petty services and small-scale commerce. But, on the average, we may conclude that *about 75 to 80 per cent of all target poverty groups are located in the rural areas of Africa and Asia and about 70 per cent in Latin America.*

It is interesting to note in light of the rural concentration of absolute poverty that the largest share of most LDC government expenditures over the past two decades has been directed towards the urban area and, within that area, towards the relatively affluent modern manufacturing and commercial sectors. Whether in the realm of directly productive economic investments or in the fields of education, health, housing and other social services, this urban modern sector bias in government expenditures is at the core of many of the development problems which will be discussed in succeeding chapters. We need only point out here that, in view of the disproportionate numbers of the very poor who reside in rural areas, any policy designed to alleviate poverty must necessarily be directed to a large extent towards rural development in general and the agricultural sector in particular (see Ch. 9).

5.5 Economic growth and the extent of poverty

We mentioned in the previous section that exclusive reliance on the natural forces of economic growth to reduce significantly the extent of absolute poverty in most developing countries would probably be insufficient. This issue is so central to development theory and policy that it warrants further examination. The basic question is the following: 'Does the pursuit of economic growth along traditional GNP maximizing lines tend to improve, worsen or have no necessary effect on the distribution of income and the extent of poverty in developing countries?' Unfortunately, economists do not at present possess any definitive knowledge of the specific factors that affect changes in the distribution of income over time for individual countries. Professor Kuznets, to whom we owe so much for his pioneering analysis of the historical growth patterns of contemporary developed countries, has suggested that in the early stages of economic growth the distribution of income will tend to *worsen* while at later stages it will improve. Although long-run data for Western nations do seem to support this proposition, a look at recent data from developing nations is less convincing.

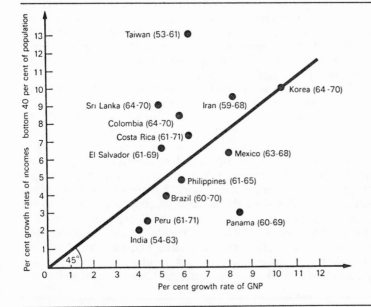

Fig 5.6
A comparison of rates of GNP growth
and income growth rates of the
bottom 40 per cent in selected LDCs

In Fig. 5.6 we have plotted rates of growth of GNP for some thirteen developing countries on the horizontal axis and the growth rate of income of the lowest 40 per cent of their population along the vertical axis. The data are for two points in time, shown in parentheses after each country, and the scatter is intended to reveal any obvious relationships between growth rates of GNP and improvements in income levels for the very poor. Each country's data, therefore, is plotted in the figure at a point reflecting its combination of GNP growth and the income growth of the lowest 40 per cent of its population. Countries above the 45° line are those countries where the distribution of income has improved – i.e. the incomes of the bottom 40 per cent grew faster than the overall GNP growth rate – while countries below the 45° line have experienced a worsening of their income distributions over the indicated period.

The scatter of points in Fig. 5.6 does *not* reveal any strong or obvious relationship between GNP growth and the distribution of income. High growth rates do not necessarily worsen the distribution of income as some have suggested. Indeed, countries like Taiwan, Iran, and Korea have experienced relatively high rates of GNP growth and had improved, or at least unchanged, distributions of income. Nevertheless, there are countries like Mexico and Panama which have grown just as fast but experienced a deterioration of their income distribution. On the other hand, there does not seem to be a necessary relationship between low GNP growth and improved income distribution. In several developing countries like India, Peru and the Philippines low rates of GNP growth appear to have been accompanied by a deterioration of the relative income shares of the bottom 40 per cent. And yet, Sri Lanka, Colombia, Costa Rica and El Salvador with similarly low GNP growth rates managed to improve the relative economic well-being of their low-income populations.

Although admittedly sketchy and limited to a short period of time, these data do suggest once again that it is the 'character' of economic growth (i.e. how it is achieved, who participates, which sectors are given priority, what institutional arrangements are designed and emphasized, etc.) that determines the degree to which that growth is or is not reflected in the improved living standards of the very poor. Clearly, it is not the mere fact of rapid growth *per se* that determines the nature of its distributional benefits.

This 'character of economic growth' argument is further reinforced by a recent extensive empirical study of forty-three developing nations in which the relationship between the shares of income accruing to the poorest 60 per cent of the population on one hand and a country's aggregate economic performance on the other were analyzed[5]. It was found that the principal impact of economic development on income distribution has been, on average, to *decrease* both the absolute and the relative incomes of the poor. There was no evidence of any automatic 'trickle-down' of the benefits of economic growth to the very poor. On the contrary, the growth process experienced by these forty-three LDCs has typically led to a 'trickle-up' in favor of the small middle class and especially the very rich. The authors, therefore, conclude that 'economic structure, not level or rate of economic growth, is the basic determinant of patterns of income distribution'[6].

5.6 Redefining development goals – growth with improved income distribution

The necessity of reorienting development priorities away from exclusive preoccupation with maximizing rates of GNP growth and towards broader social objectives such as the eradication of poverty and the reduction of excessive income disparities is now widely recognized throughout the Third World. The gap between problem redefinition and specific action, however, can be quite enormous. Abstracting from the serious political, institutional and power structure problems of a reorientation of development strategy towards greater concern for the very poor, economics itself has very little in the way of either a received theory of how economies grow and what types of investment strategies can maximize economic growth rates. Moreover, there is relatively little consensus among economists on what strategies should be followed and whether any strictly economic strategy can eliminate or greatly reduce the incidence of poverty. This is not only because the problems of poverty and income distribution are also political and institutional in origin, but because the theoretical determinants of income distribution are very poorly understood in the developed countries towards which the bulk of existing economic theory has been directed – let alone, the underdeveloped countries where much of this theory is irrelevant.

But the history of economics has been marked by the evolution of theories and concepts that have grown out of responses to specific real world economic problems and not merely as a natural organic process, unrelated to the world at large. The Malthusian theory of population, the Marxist theory of the increasing misery of the masses, the neo-classical theory of maximizing behavior and atomistic competition, the Keynesian theory of income and employment determination, and the Harrod–Domar theories of economic growth all represented direct responses to what were perceived to be the principal economic and social problems of the times. Given the current emphasis on problems of poverty and income distribution, therefore, it is not unreasonable to anticipate that as economists increasingly turn their attention away from exclusive concern with growth, new and better theories and policies will emerge to comprehend and cope with these very serious problems that are the daily scourge of hundreds of millions of people.

Although rapid economic growth does not automatically provide the answer, it nevertheless remains an essential ingredient in any realistic poverty-focused program of development. Moreover, rapid economic growth and more equitable distributions of income are not necessarily incompatible as development objectives. The choice is not between more growth and more equality but about the type of economic growth Third World countries wish to pursue – one that principally benefits the very rich or one in which the benefits are more widely distributed. In the next section we present some of the economic arguments why growth and equality are not in conflict. For present purposes, however, we may conclude that *development strategy requires not only a concern with accelerating economic growth but also a direct concern with improving the material standards of living for those very sizable segments of Third World populations who have been largely bypassed by the economic growth of the last two decades.*

A principal development objective, therefore, should be to generate a desired pattern of overall and broad-based income growth with special emphasis on accelerating the growth of incomes of 'target' poverty groups. Such an aim requires a very different strategy from one which is simply oriented towards maximizing the growth rate of GNP, irrespective of the distributional consequences.

5.7 The role of economic analysis: redistribution from growth

Although much of economic analysis has been strangely silent on the relationship between economic growth and the resulting distribution of income, there is a large body of theory which in essence asserts that highly *unequal* distributions are *necessary* conditions for generating rapid growth[7]. In fact, for the past two decades, the explicit and implicit acceptance of this proposition by economists from both developed and underdeveloped countries tended to turn their collective and individual attentions away from problems of poverty and income distribution. If wide inequalities are a necessary condition of maximum growth and if in the long run maximum growth is a necessary condition of rising standards of living for all through the natural 'trickle-down' processes of competitive and mixed economic systems, then it follows, according to this theory, that direct concern with the alleviation of poverty would be self-defeating. Needless to say, such a

1. Growth versus income distribution

A. The traditional argument: factor shares, savings and economic growth viewpoint, whether correct or not, provided a psychological, if not conscious, rationalization for the accumulation of wealth by powerful elite groups.

The basic economic argument to justify large income inequalities was that high personal and corporate incomes were necessary conditions of *saving* which made possible investment and economic growth through a mechanism such as the Harrod–Domar model described in Chapter 3. If the rich save and invest significant proportions of their incomes while the poor spend all their income on consumption goods, and if GNP growth rates are directly related to the proportion of national income which is saved, then apparently an economy characterized by highly unequal distributions of income would save more and grow faster than one with a more equitable distribution of income. Eventually, it was assumed that national and per capita incomes would be high enough to make possible sizable redistributions of income through tax and subsidy programs. But until such a time is reached, any attempt to redistribute incomes significantly would only serve to lower growth rates and delay the time when a larger income pie could be cut up into bigger slices for all population groups[8].

B. A counter-argument There are four general reasons why many development economists now believe the above argument to be *incorrect* and *why greater equality in developing countries may in fact be a condition for self-sustaining economic growth.*

First, common sense supported by a wealth of recent empirical data bear witness to the fact that, unlike the historical experience of the now developed countries, the rich in contemporary Third World countries are *not* noted for their frugality nor for their desire to save and invest substantial proportions of their incomes in the *local* economy[9]. Instead, landlords, businessmen, politicians and other rich elites are known to squander much of their incomes on imported luxury goods, expensive houses, foreign travel and investment in gold, jewellery and foreign banking accounts. Such 'savings' and 'investments' do not add to the nation's productive resources. In fact, they represent substantial drains on these resources in that the income so derived is extracted from the sweat and toil of common, uneducated and unskilled laborers. In short, the rich do not necessarily save and invest significantly larger proportions of their incomes (in the real economic sense of 'productive' domestic saving and investment) than the poor. Therefore, a growth strategy based on sizable and growing income inequalities may in reality be nothing more than an opportunistic myth designed to perpetuate the vested interests and maintain the *status quo* of the economic and political elites of Third World nations, often at the expense of the great majority of the general population. Such strategies might better be called 'anti-developmental'[10].

Second, the low incomes and low levels of living for the poor which are manifested in poor health, nutrition and education can lower their economic productivity and, thereby, lead directly and indirectly to a slower growing economy. Strategies to raise the incomes and levels of living of, say, the bottom 40 per cent would therefore contribute not only to their material well-being but also to the productivity and income of the economy as a whole.

Third, raising the income levels of the poor will stimulate an overall increase in the demand for locally produced necessity products like food and clothing. On the other hand, the rich tend to spend more of their additional incomes on imported luxury goods. Rising demands for local goods provide a greater stimulus to local production, local employment and local investment. It thus creates the conditions for rapid economic growth and a broader popular participation in that growth.

Fourth, and finally, a more equitable distribution of income achieved through the reduction of mass poverty can stimulate healthy economic expansion by acting as a powerful material and psychological *incentive* to widespread public participation in the development process. On the other hand, wide income disparities and substantial absolute poverty can act as a powerful material and psychological *disincentive* to economic progress. It may even create the conditions for its ultimate rejection by the masses of frustrated and politically explosive people, especially those with considerable education.

2. GNP as a 'biased' index of national development and welfare

We have already criticized reliance on GNP and its growth rate as the principal indicator of development and economic well-being. Figures for GNP per capita give no indication of how national income is actually distributed and who is benefiting most from the growth of production. We have seen, for example, that a rising level of absolute and per capita GNP camouflage the fact that the poor are no better off than before.

Many people (including some economists) are often unaware that the calculation of the rate of GNP growth is in reality largely a calculation of the rate of growth of the incomes of the upper 40 per cent of the population who receive a disproportionately large share of the national product. GNP growth rates, therefore, should *not* be used as an index of improved welfare. To give an extreme example, suppose an economy consisted of only ten people, nine of whom had no income at all and the tenth received 100 units of income. The GNP for this economy would therefore be 100 and per capita GNP would be 10. Now suppose that everyone's income increases by 20 per cent so that GNP rises to 120 while per capita income grows to 12. For the nine individuals with no income before and still no income now (i.e. $1 \cdot 20 \times 0 = 0$), such a rise in per capita income provides no cause for rejoicing. The one rich individual still has all the income. GNP, instead of being a welfare index of society as a whole, is merely measuring the welfare of a single individual!

The same thought processes apply to the more realistic situation where incomes are very unequally distributed, although not perfectly unequal as in the above example. Taking the figures from Table 5.3, where we divided the population into quintiles and showed that the bottom 20 per cent received only 5 per cent of the income while the remaining four quintile groups received 9, 13, 22, and 51 per cent income shares respectively, we found that together these income levels in each income class are a measure of their relative economic welfare and that the rate of income growth in each quintile is a measure of the economic welfare growth of that class, we can approximate the growth in total welfare of society as the simple weighted sum of the growth of income in each class. This in fact is what the rate of GNP growth measures – where the weights applied to each income class, however, are their respective shares of national income. To be specific, in the case of a population divided into quintiles according to rising income levels, we would have[11]:

$$G = w_1g_1 + w_2g_2 + w_3g_3 + w_4g_4 + w_5g_5 \qquad (1)$$

where G = a weighted index of growth of social welfare,

           g_i = the growth rate of income of the ith quintile (where the i quintiles are ordered 1, 2, 3, 4, and 5 in our example),

and w_i = the 'welfare weight' of the ith quintile (i.e. in our example $w_1 = 0·05$, $w_2 = 0·09$, $w_3 = 0·13$, $w_4 = 0·22$ and $w_5 = 0·51$).

As long as the weights add up to unity and are non-negative, our overall measure of the growth of social welfare, G, must fall somewhere between the maximum and minimum income growth rates in the various quintiles. In the extreme case of all income accruing to one individual or one group of individuals in the highest quintile and where the 'welfare weights' are the income shares (as they are with GNP growth calculations), equation (1) would be written as:

$$G = 0g_1 + 0g_2 + 0g_3 + 0g_4 + 1·0g_5 = 1·0g_5 \qquad (2)$$

The growth of 'social welfare' would, therefore, be associated exclusively with the growth of incomes of the top quintile of the population! In the example derived from Table 5.3, the GNP income share weighted index of social welfare would be written as:

$$G = 0·05g_1 + 0·09g_2 + 0·13g_3 + 0·22g_4 + 0·51g_5 \qquad (3)$$

Now suppose the income growth rate of the bottom 60 per cent of the population is zero (i.e. $g_1 = g_2 = g_3 = 0$) while that of the top 40 per cent is 10 per cent (i.e. $g_4 = g_5 = 0·10$). Equation (3) could therefore be written as:

$$G = 0·05(0) + 0·09(0) + 0·13(0) + 0·22(0·10) + 0·51(0·10) = 0·073$$

and the 'social' welfare index would rise by over 7 per cent, which is the rate of growth of GNP (i.e. GNP would rise from 100 in Table 5.3 to 107·3 if the incomes of the 4th and 5th quintiles grew by 10 per cent). Thus, we have an illustration of a case where GNP rises by 7·3 per cent, implying that social well-being has increased by this same proportionate amount even though 60 per cent of the population is no better off than before. These bottom 60 per cent still have only 5, 13 and 22 units of income respectively! Clearly, the distribution of income would be worsened (the relative shares of the bottom 60 per cent would fall) by such a respectable growth rate of GNP.

The numerical example given by equation (3) illustrates our basic point. The use of the growth rate of GNP as an index of social welfare and as a method of comparing the 'development' performance of different countries can be very misleading, especially where countries have markedly different distributions of income. The 'welfare weights' attached to the growth rates of different income groups are very unequal, with a heavy social 'premium' being placed on the income growth of the highest quintile groups. In the example of equation (3), a 1 per cent growth in the income of the top quintile carries over 10 times the weight of a 1 per cent growth in the lowest quintile (i.e. $0·51$ compared with $0·05$) because it implies an absolute increment which is ten times larger. In other words, *using the measure of GNP growth as an index of improvements in social welfare and development accords to each income group a 'welfare valuation' that corresponds to their respective income shares* – i.e. a 1 per cent increase in the income of the richest 20 per cent of the population is implicitly assumed to be over 10 times as important to society as a 1 per cent increase in the income of the bottom 20 per cent. It follows that the best way to maximize 'social welfare' is to maximize the rate of growth of the incomes of the rich while neglecting the poor! If ever there was a case for *not* equating GNP growth with 'development', the preceding example should provide a persuasive illustration.

An alternative to using the simple rate of GNP growth (the 'distributive share' index) of social welfare would be to construct an 'equal-weights' or even a 'poverty-weighted' index. The latter two indices might be especially relevant for those countries which are concerned with the elimination of poverty as a major development objective. As the name sounds, an 'equal-weights' index weighs the growth of income in each income class not by the proportion of total income in that class but by the proportion of the total population in each class – that is, all people are treated ('weighted') equally. In an economy which is divided into quintiles, such an index would give a weight of 0.2 to the growth of income in each quintile. Thus a 10 per cent increase in the income of the lowest 20 per cent of the population would have the same bearing on the overall measure of social welfare improvement as a 10 per cent increase in the top 20 per cent group or in any other quintile group, even though the absolute increase in income for the bottom group will be much smaller than for the upper groups.

3. Constructing a 'poverty-weighted' index of social welfare

Using an 'equal weights' index in our example of a 10 per cent income growth of the top two quintiles while the bottom three remain static, we would have

$$G = 0{\cdot}20g_1 + 0{\cdot}20g_2 + 0{\cdot}20g_3 + 0{\cdot}20g_4 + 0{\cdot}20g_5 \qquad (4)$$

or, inserting growth rates for g_1 through g_5,

$$G = 0{\cdot}20(0) + 0{\cdot}20(0) + 0{\cdot}20(0) + 0{\cdot}20(0{\cdot}10) + 0{\cdot}20(0{\cdot}1) = 0{\cdot}04$$

Social welfare will have increased by only 4 per cent, compared to the $7{\cdot}3$ per cent increase recorded by using the distributive shares or GNP growth rate index. Even though recorded GNP still grows by $7{\cdot}3$ per cent, this alternative welfare index of 'development' shows only a 4 per cent rise.

Finally, consider a developing country which is genuinely and solely concerned with improving the material well-being of, say, the poorest 40 per cent of its population. It might therefore wish to construct a 'poverty-weighted' index of development which places 'subjective' social values *only* on the income growth rates of the bottom 40 per cent. In other words, it might arbitrarily place a welfare weight on w_1 of say $0{\cdot}60$, and w_2 of say $0{\cdot}40$ while w_3, w_4 and w_5 are given zero weights. Using our same numerical example, the social welfare group index for this country would be given by the expression:

$$G = 0{\cdot}60g_1 + 0{\cdot}40g_2 + 0g_3 + 0g_4 + 0g_5 \qquad (5)$$

which, when substituting $g_1 = g_2 = g_3 = 0$ and $g_4 = g_5 = 0{\cdot}10$ becomes

$$G = 0{\cdot}60(0) + 0{\cdot}40(0) + 0(0) + 0(0{\cdot}10) + 0(0{\cdot}10) = 0$$

The poverty-weighted index therefore records *no* improvement in social welfare – i.e., no development – even though recorded GNP has grown by $7{\cdot}3$ per cent!

Although the choice of welfare weights in any index of development is purely arbitrary, it does represent and reflect important social 'value judgements' about goals and objectives for a given society. It would certainly be interesting to know, if this were possible, what are the *real* implicit welfare weights of the various development strategies of different Third World countries. Our main point, however, is that so long as the growth rate of GNP is explicitly or implicitly used to compare development performances, we know that a 'wealthy weights' index is actually being employed.

To put some real world flavor into the preceding discussion of alternative indices of improvements in economic welfare and to illustrate the usefulness of different weighted growth indices in evaluating the economic performance of various countries, consider the data in Table 5.6 presented in a paper by two World Bank economists, Chenery and Aluwahlia. The table shows the growth of income in fourteen countries as measured first by the rate of growth of GNP, second by an 'equal weights' index and third by a 'poverty weights' index where the actual weights assigned to income growth rates of the lowest 40 per cent, the middle 40 per cent and the top 20 per cent of the population are 0·6, 0·4 and 0·0 respectively. Some interesting conclusions emerge from a review of the last three columns of Table 5.6.

1. Economic performance as measured by 'equal' and 'poverty'-weighted indices is notably worse in some otherwise high GNP growth countries like Brazil, Mexico and Panama. Since these countries all experienced a deterioration in their income distribution and a growing concentration of income growth in the upper groups over this period, the equal and poverty weights indices naturally show a less impressive development performance than does the simple GNP measure.
2. In four countries (Colombia, El Salvador, Sri Lanka, and Taiwan) the weighted indices show a better performance than GNP growth. This is because the relative income growth of lower income groups proceeded more rapidly over the period in question in those four countries than that of the higher income groups.
3. In five countries (Costa Rica, Korea, Peru, Philippines and Yugoslavia) little change in income distribution during the period in question results in little variation between the GNP measure and the two alternative weighted indices of social welfare.

We may conclude, therefore, that *a useful summary measure of the degree to which economic growth is biased towards the relative improvement of high-income or low-income groups is the positive or negative 'divergence' between a weighted (equal or poverty) social welfare index and the actual growth rate of GNP.*

Finally, our analysis leads us to conclude that the presumed trade-off between rapid economic growth and a more equitable distribution of income is in reality better expressed as a trade-off between income growth rates among different income groups. If a weighted welfare index is used to measure economic development, then it is not only possible but may even be desirable for a lower growth rate of GNP to be associated with a higher rate of economic development, at least in terms of the specific value judgements of a particularly egalitarian society.

4. Combining the economics of growth and distribution

The reformulation of indices of development to take account of alternative social premiums for different income groups takes us a long way towards a better understanding of the relationship between economic growth and income distribution. For one thing, the use of such indices underlines the importance of focusing on the *direct* improvement in living standards for the lowest income groups rather than worrying

No.	Country	Period	I. Income growth			II. Annual increase in welfare		
			Upper 20%	Middle 40%	Lowest 40%	(A) GNP weights	(B) Equal weights	(C) Poverty weights
1	Korea	1964–70	12·4	9·5	11·0	11·0	10·7	10·5
2	Panama	1960–9	8·8	9·2	3·2	8·2	6·7	5·2
3	Mexico	1963–8	8·8	5·8	6·0	7·8	6·5	5·9
4	Taiwan	1953–61	4·5	9·1	12·1	6·8	9·4	11·1
5	Costa Rica	1961–71	4·5	9·3	7·0	6·3	7·4	7·8
6	Canada	1961–5	7·0	5·3	6·5	6·2	6·1	6·1
7	Colombia	1964–70	5·2	7·9	7·8	6·2	7·3	7·8
8	El Salvador	1961–9	3·5	9·5	6·4	5·7	7·1	7·4
9	Philippines	1961–5	5·0	6·7	4·4	5·5	5·4	5·2
10	Brazil	1960–70	6·7	3·1	3·7	5·2	4·1	3·5
11	United States	1960–6	5·6	5·2	4·1	5·2	4·8	4·5
12	Finland	1952–62	6·0	5·0	2·1	5·1	4·0	3·1
13	Sri Lanka	1963–70	3·1	6·3	8·3	5·0	6·5	7·6
14	Yugoslavia	1963–8	5·0	5·0	4·3	4·9	4·7	4·5
15	France	1956–62	5·6	4·5	1·4	4·8	3·5	2·4
16	Peru	1961–71	3·9	6·7	2·4	4·6	4·4	3·8
17	India	1954–63	5·3	3·5	2·0	4·2	3·3	2·5

Table 5.6
Income distribution and growth

Source: Ahluwalia and Chenery, op. cit. (3), 5.

about non-existent conflicts between growth and distribution or about the overall pattern of income distribution in Third World countries. On the other hand, the recognition that real development entails direct attacks on the sources of poverty within a country is useless without a better understanding of the factors that determine income shares and the relative rates of growth within different income groups. Unfortunately economic theory offers little guidance since it has always been concerned not with the size distribution of income (i.e., who gets what) but rather with the determinants of the functional distribution of income (i.e., how much of the total GNP is attributable to the total productivity of labor, capital, land, etc.). Even if the traditional theory of the determinants of functional income distribution had relevance for understanding the economic processes of contemporary developing nations (which, as we saw in a previous section, it does not, due to unreal assumptions about factor pricing, competitive markets and the influence of power), knowledge of how incomes are functionally distributed would not help us to understand how and why incomes tend to be concentrated in certain population groups. For this we need to know how income-earning factors of production are distributed among different groups of people. We know, for example, that personal income consists not only of income derived from the supply of an individual's labor but also, and primarily for upper income groups, from an individual's control over other income earning assets such as land and capital (both physical and financial).

When we analyze the real determinants of highly unequal distributions of income, *it is the very unequal distribution of the ownership of productive assets such as land and capital within different segments of Third World populations that largely accounts for the wide income divergence between rich and poor.* The concentration of physical and financial capital as well as land in the hands of small economic and political elites enables them to expand their stock of human capital through education and thereby to control even greater shares of the national product. As in the international sphere, it is another case of the rich getting richer while the poor stagnate. Any attempt to improve the living standards of the poor significantly must therefore focus not only on increasing the economic returns to the limited factors they possess (i.e. raising the returns to their labor through more employment) but also on progressively altering the existing pattern of concentration of both physical and human capital towards low income groups. Such redistribution can probably best be achieved in a growing economy. This leads us directly to our concluding sections on alternative policy approaches.

5.8 The range of policy options: some basic considerations

Those developing countries which aim to reduce poverty and excessive inequalities in their distribution of income need to know how best to achieve their aim. What kinds of economic and other policies might LDC governments adopt to reduce poverty and inequality while maintaining or even accelerating economic growth rates? Since we are concerned here with moderating the size distribution of incomes in general and raising the income levels of, say, the bottom 40 per cent of the population in particular, it is important to understand the various determinants of the distribution of income in an economy and see in what ways government intervention can alter or modify their effect.

1. Areas of intervention We can identify *four broad areas of possible government policy intervention* which correspond to the following four major elements in the determination of a developing economy's distribution of income:

1. Functional distribution – the returns to labor, land and capital as determined by factor prices, utilization levels and the consequent shares of national income that accrue to the owners of each factor.
2. Size distribution – the functional income distribution of an economy can be translated into the size distribution by knowledge of how ownership and control over productive assets and labor skills are concentrated and distributed throughout the population, and with the growth of these assets over time. It is the distribution of these asset holdings and skill endowments that ultimately determine the distribution of personal income.
3. Moderating (reducing) the size distribution at the upper levels through progressive taxation of personal income and wealth. Such taxation increases government revenues and converts a market-determined level of personal income into a fiscally corrected, 'disposable' personal income. It is an individual or family's disposable income which is the actual amount available for expenditure on goods and services and for saving.
4. Moderating (increasing) the size distribution at the lower levels through public expenditures of tax revenues to raise the incomes of the poor either directly (e.g., by outright money transfers) or indirectly (e.g. through public employment creation, the provision of free or subsidized primary education, etc.). Such public policies raise the real income levels of the poor *above* their market determined personal income levels.

2. Policy Options Third World governments have many options and alternative possible policies to operate in the four broad areas of intervention outlined above. Let us briefly identify the nature of some of them.

This is the traditional economic approach. It is argued that as a result of institutional constraints and faulty policies, the relative price of labor (basically, the wage rate) is higher than that which would be determined by the free interplay of the forces of supply and demand. For example, the power of trade unions to raise minimum wages to artificially high levels (i.e. higher than that which would result from supply and demand) even in the face of widespread unemployment is often cited as an example of the 'distorted' price of labor. From this it is argued that measures designed to reduce the price of labor relative to capital (e.g. through lower wages in the public sector, public wage subsidies to employers, etc.) will cause employers to substitute labor for capital in their production activities. Such factor substitution increases the overall level of employment and ultimately raises the incomes of the poor, who typically possess only their labor services.

A. Altering the functional distribution of income through policies designed to change relative factor prices

On the other hand, it is often also correctly pointed out that the price of capital equipment is 'institutionally' set at artificially low levels (i.e. below what supply and demand would dictate) through various public policies such as investment incentives, tax allowances, subsidized interest rates, overvalued exchange rates and low tariffs on capital good imports such as tractors, automated equipment, etc. If these special privileges and capital subsidies were removed so that the price of capital would *rise* to its true 'scarcity' level, producers would have a further incentive to increase their utilization of the abundant supply of labor and lower their uses of every scarce capital. Moreover, owners of capital (both physical and financial) would not receive the artificially high economic returns that they now enjoy. Their personal incomes would thereby be reduced.

Since factor prices are assumed to function as the ultimate signals and incentives in any economy, 'getting these prices right' (i.e. lowering the relative price of labor and raising the relative price of capital) would not only increase productivity and efficiency but would also reduce inequality by providing more wage paying jobs for currently unemployed or underemployed unskilled and semi-skilled workers. It would also lower the artificially high incomes of owners of capital. Removal of such factor-price distortions would, therefore, go a long way towards combining more growth efficiently generated, with higher employment, less poverty and greater equality.

We deal more extensively with the important question of factor-price distortions, employment generation and choice of 'appropriate' production techniques in Ch. 8. For the present we may conclude that there is much merit to the traditional factor-price distortion argument and that 'getting the prices right' should contribute to a reduction in poverty and an improved distribution of income. How much it actually contributes will depend on the degree to which firms and farms switch to more labor-intensive production methods as the relative price of labor falls and the relative price of capital rises – i.e. on the elasticity of factor substitution. This is an important empirical question, the answer to which will vary from country to country (see Ch. 8). But some improvement can be expected.

Given resource prices and utilization levels for each type of productive factor (labor, land and capital), we can arrive at estimates for the total earnings of each asset. But in order to translate this functional income into personal income, we need to know the *distribution* and *ownership concentration* of these assets among and within various segments of the

B. Modifying the size distributions through progressive redistribution of asset ownership

population. Here we come to what is probably the most important fact about the determination of income distribution within an economy. *The ultimate cause of the very unequal distribution of personal incomes in most Third World countries is the very unequal and highly concentrated patterns of asset ownership within these countries.* The principal reason why less than 20 per cent of their populations receive over 50 per cent of the national income is that this 20 per cent probably owns and controls well over 50 per cent of the productive resources, especially physical capital and land but also human capital in the form of better education. Correcting factor prices is certainly not sufficient to reduce income inequalities substantially nor to eliminate widespread poverty where the physical asset ownership and educated skills are highly concentrated.

It follows that *the second and, perhaps more important, line of policy to reduce poverty and unequality is to focus directly on reducing the concentrated control of assets, the unequal distribution of power and the unequal access to educational and income-earning opportunities which characterize many developing countries.* A classic case of such redistribution as it relates to the rural poor who comprise 70 to 80 per cent of the target poverty group, is *land reform.* The basic purpose of land reform is to transform tenant cultivators into smallholders who will then have an incentive to raise production and improve their incomes. But as we shall see in Chapter 10, land reform may be a weak instrument of income redistribution if other institutional and price distortions in the economic system prevent small farmholders from securing access to much needed critical inputs such as credit, fertilizers, seeds, marketing facilities and agricultural education.

In addition to the redistribution of existing productive assets, there are 'dynamic' redistribution policies which could be gradually pursued. For example, Third World governments could transfer a certain proportion of annual savings and investments to low-income groups so as to bring about a more gradual and perhaps politically more acceptable redistribution of *additional* assets as they accumulate over time. This is what is often meant by the expression 'redistribution from growth'. Whether such a gradual redistribution from growth is any more possible than a redistribution of existing assets is a moot point, especially in the context of very unequal power structures. But some form of asset redistribution, whether static or dynamic, appears to be a necessary condition for any significant reduction of poverty and inequality in most Third World countries.

Human capital in the form of education and skills is another example of the unequal distribution of productive asset ownership. Public policy, therefore, should promote a wider access to educational opportunities as a means of increasing income-earning potentials for more people. But, as in the case of land reform, the mere provision of greater access to education is no guarantee that the poor will be any better off, unless complementary policies – for example, the provision of more productive employment opportunities for the educated – to capitalize on this increased human capital are adopted. The relationship between education, employment and development is discussed further in Chapter 11.

C. Modifying (reducing) the size distribution at the upper levels through progressive income and wealth taxes

Any national policy attempting to improve the living standards of the bottom 40 per cent must secure sufficient financial resources to transform paper plans into program realities. The major source of such development finance is the direct and progressive taxation of both income and wealth. Direct progressive income taxation focuses on personal and corporate incomes with the rich required to pay a progressively larger percentage of their total income in taxes than the poor. Taxation on wealth (i.e. the stock of accumulated assets and income) typically focuses on personal and corporate property taxes but may also include progressive inheritance taxes. In either case, the burden of the tax is designed to fall most heavily on the upper income groups.

Unfortunately, in many developing countries (and developed countries as well) the gap between what is supposed to be a progressive tax structure and what different income groups actually pay can be substantial. Progressive tax structures on paper often turn out to be 'regressive' in practice, that is to say, the lower and middle income groups pay a proportionately larger share of their incomes in taxes than do the upper income groups. This is largely because the poor are often taxed at the source of their incomes or expenditures (by withholding taxes from wages, general poll taxes or 'indirect' taxes levied on the retail purchase of goods such as cigarettes and beer). On the other hand, the rich derive by far the largest part of their incomes from the return on physical and financial assets which often go unreported. They often also have the power and ability to avoid paying taxes without fear of government reprisal. Policies to enforce progressive rates of direct taxation on income and wealth, especially at the highest levels, are what is most needed in this area of redistribution activity (see Ch. 16 for a further discussion of taxation for development).

The direct provision of tax-financed public consumption goods and services to the very poor is another potentially very important instrument of a comprehensive policy designed to eradicate poverty. Examples include public health projects in rural villages and urban fringe areas, primary school lunch and pre-school nutritional supplementation programs and the provision of clean water and electrification to remote rural areas. Moreover, direct money transfers and subsidized food programs for the urban and rural poor as well as direct government policies to keep the price of essential foodstuffs low represent additional forms of public consumption subsidies. All of these policies have the effect of raising the real personal income levels of the very poor beyond their actual market derived monetary incomes.

D. Modifying (increasing) the size distribution at the lower levels through direct transfer payments and the public provision of goods and services

To summarize our discussion of alternative policy approaches to the problem of growth, poverty and inequality in Third World countries, the need is not for one or two isolated policies but for a 'package' of complementary and supportive policies, including the following three basic elements:

3. Summary and conclusions: the need for a 'package of policies'

1. A policy or set of policies designed to *correct factor price distortions* so as to insure that market or institutionally established prices provide accurate (i.e. socially correct) signals and incentives to both producers and resource suppliers. 'Getting the price right' should help to contribute to greater productive efficiency, more employment and less poverty. Equally important may be the promotion of indigenous technological research and development on efficient, labor-intensive methods of production (see Ch. 8).
2. A policy or set of policies designed to bring about far-reaching *structural changes in the distribution of assets, power and access to education and associated income-earning (employment) oppor-*

tunities. Such policies go beyond the narrow realm of economics and touch upon the whole social, institutional, cultural and political fabric of the developing world. But without such radical structural changes and asset redistributions, whether immediately achieved (e.g. through popular revolutions) or gradually introduced over time (through established political processes), the chances of improving significantly the living conditions of the masses of rural and urban poor will be highly improbable, perhaps even impossible.

3. A policy or set of policies designed to *modify the size distribution of income* at the upper levels through the enforcement of legislated progressive taxation on incomes and wealth and at the lower levels through direct transfer payments and the expanded provision of publically provided consumption goods and services.

4. A final question The above policy package would, we suggest, provide a comprehensive agenda for any national attack on the pervasive problems of mass poverty and income inequality. Within the context of such a comprehensive three-pronged national policy, however, one needs to ask a final but far from trivial question: 'Can Third World countries actively pursue policies to reduce poverty and promote equality while remaining open to and dependent upon the public financial resources, private investments, imported technology and products and, most importantly, the values, symbols, ideals, attitudes and institutions of advanced industrial countries?' In other words, 'can growth with equity be realistically pursued in isolation (as in the case of China) or, if not, can Third World countries collectively become more self-reliant masters of their own economic and social destinies while still actively participating in an increasingly interdependent yet highly unequal global system?' It is a difficult and perplexing question, but one which every developing nation and every thoughtful individual needs to ponder. We raise it again and attempt to provide some possible answers in the concluding chapter of the book.

Notes

1. Mahbub ul Haq, 'Employment and income distribution in the 1970s: a new perspective', *Development Digest,* October (1971), 7.
2. Named after Conrad Lorenz, an American statistician who in 1905 devised this convenient and widely-used diagram to show the relationship between population groups and their respective income shares.
3. A more precise definition of perfect equality would take into account the age structure of a population and expected income variations over the 'life cycle' of all households within that population. See M. Paglin, 'The measurement and trend of inequality: a basic revision', *American Economic Review,* Sept. 1975.
4. The summation of each worker's 'marginal' product must equal total national product (GNP), which will be distributed as the national income. For the mathematically inclined, total product is simply the integral of the marginal product curve between O and $\overline{L}$. This is because the marginal product function is the derivative of the total product curve – i.e. $TP = f(L, \overline{K})$; $MP_L = f'(L)$.
5. I. Adelman and C. T. Morris, *Economic Growth and Social Equity in Developing Countries,* Stanford U.P. (1973).
6. Ibid., p. 186.
7. One of the earliest and most well-known articles on the subject is that of Walter Galenson and Harvey Leibenstein, 'Investment criteria, productivity and economic development', *Quarterly Journal of Economics,* August 1955, 343–70.
8. The formal neo-classical growth model most often used to justify this argument is briefly described and illustrated in Appendix 5.1.

9. See, for example, various UN studies on sources of savings which show that small farmers and individuals seem to be among the highest savers. Also see Gustav Ranis, 'Investment criteria, productivity and economic development: an empirical comment', *Quarterly Journal of Economics,* May 1962 and K. L. Gupta, 'Personal saving in developing countries: further evidence', *Economic Record,* June 1970.

10. For empirical support of this argument with regard to rural saving and investment see Keith Griffin, 'Rural development: the policy options', in E. O. Edwards (ed.), *Employment in Developing Nations,* Columbia Press, New York (1974), 190–1.

11. This illustration is derived from Ahluwalia and Chenery, 'A conceptual framework for economic analysis' in Chenery, Duloy and Jolly, *Redistribution with Growth: an approach to policy,* IBRD, Washington (1973), (3), 2–4 (mimeo).

		Concepts for review
luxury versus necessity goods	'trickle down' theory of development	
consumer demand and income distribution	welfare index	
'size' distribution of income	GNP index	
'functional' distribution of income	equal weights index	
quintiles and deciles	poverty-weighted index	
highly 'skewed' distribution of income	asset ownership	
income inequality	factor-price distortions	
Lorenz curve	redistribution policies	
GINI coefficient	progressive income and wealth taxes	
absolute poverty	'regressive' tax	
'scatter' diagram	indirect tax	
'character' of economic growth	subsidy	
	'package' of policies	

1. Most development economists now seem to agree that the level and rate of growth **Questions for discussion** of GNP and per capita income do not provide sufficient or even accurate measures of a country's 'development'. What is the essence of their argument? Give some examples.

2. Distinguish between 'size' and 'functional' distributions of income distribution in a nation. Which do you feel is the more appropriate concept? Explain.

3. What is meant by 'absolute' poverty? Why should we be concerned with the measurement of absolute poverty in Third World nations?

4. What are the principal economic characteristics of poverty groups? What do these characteristics tell us about the possible nature of 'poverty-focused' development strategy?

5. In the text, when we examined statistics from a wide range of Third World countries, we found *no* direct relationship (positive or negative) between a country's level of GNP, GNP per capita, and rate of economic growth and its extent of absolute poverty or the degree of equality in its distribution of income. Assuming that these data are indeed correct, what do they tell us about the importance of the 'character' of a nation's growth process, and about its institutional structure?

6. What is the relationship between a Lorenz curve and a Gini coefficient? Give some examples of how Lorenz curves and Gini coefficients can be used as summary measures of equality and inequality in a nation's distribution of income.

7. In the text it is asserted that the major determinant of a country's income distribution was its distribution of productive and income-earning assets. Explain the meaning of this statement giving examples of different kinds of productive and income earning assets.

8. Are rapid economic growth (either GNP or per capita GNP) and a more equitable distribution of personal income necessarily conflicting objectives? Summarize the arguments both for and against the presumed conflict of objectives and state and explain your own view.

9. GNP is said to be a 'biased' index of national development and economic welfare. Explain the meaning of this statement, giving a specific hypothetical or real example of such a 'bias'.

10. What is the value of constructing an 'equal weights' or especially a 'poverty-weighted' index of social welfare? Under what conditions will these welfare indices differ from GNP? Explain your answer.

11. Economic growth is said to be a 'necessary but not sufficient condition' to eradicate absolute poverty and reduce inequality. What is the reasoning behind this argument?

12. Outline the range of major policy options available to LDC governments to alter and modify the size distribution of their national incomes. Which policy or policies do your believe are absolutely essential and which are important but not crucial? Explain your answer.

Further readings A comprehensive description of the various meanings and measures of income distribution can be found in Jan Pen, *Income Distribution,* Penguin, London (1971), Chs. 1–3. See also A. B. Atkinson, *The Economics of Inequality,* Oxford U.P., New York (1975).

For the most up-to-date summary of the poverty and income distribution problem in LDCs using recent cross-country data with appropriate analysis and alternative policy strategies, see Hollis Chenery *et al., Redistribution With Growth,* Oxford U.P., London and IBRD, Washington (1974) and *The Assault on World Poverty,* John Hopkins U.P., Baltimore, 1975.

Other useful readings include: (a) William R. Cline, *Income distribution and economic development: A survey, and tests for selected Latin American cities,* The Brookings Institution, Washington *DC (1973);* (b) G. Ranis, J. C. H. Fei and G. Fields, 'Growth, employment and the size distribution of income: a progress report', *Discussion Paper No. 208,* Yale Economic Growth Center, June 1974; (c) D. B. Keesing, 'Income distribution from outward-looking development policies', Research Memorandum No. 59, Williams College, Williamston, Massachusetts, April 1974; (d) Gunnar Myrdal, 'Equity and Growth', *World Development,* **1,** No. 11 (1973); (e) Felix Paukert, 'Income distribution at different levels of development: a survey of evidence', *International Labour Review,* August–September, 1973; (f) A. B. Atkinson, 'On the measurement of inequality', *Journal of Economic Theory,* September 1970; (g) I. Adleman and C. T. Morris, 'An anatomy of income distribution patterns in developing nations', *Development Digest,* October 1971; (h) Arun Shourie, 'Growth, poverty and inequalities', *Foreign Affairs,* **51,** No. 2 (1973); (i) Roger D. Hansen, 'The emerging challenge: global distribution of income and economic opportunity', in Overseas Development Council, *Agenda for Action 1975,* Praeger, New York (1975); (j) D. L. Meadows et al., *The Limits to Growth,* Universe Books, New York (1972).

Appendix 5.1

Factor shares, savings and growth: a diagrammatic illustration The traditional argument presented in the text that unequal incomes will best promote savings (and thus growth) is typically illustrated by using the standard neo-classical (i.e., variable factor proportions) growth model. Assume the existence of an aggregate production function in the form of

$$Y = f(K,L,t) \tag{A5.1}$$

where K is the capital stock, L the labor force, and t a trend variable denoting technological change. Assuming neutral technological progress, production function (A5.1) can be rewritten as:

$$Y = A(t)f[K,L], \tag{A5.2}$$

where $A(t)$ is some constant such as $1 \cdot 06$ per year. Finally, it is assumed that the production function is linear, homogeneous so that $\alpha Y = A(t)[\alpha K, \alpha L]$.
Setting $\alpha = 1/l$, then, we obtain:

$$\frac{Y}{L} = A(t)f\left[\frac{K}{L}, 1\right] = A(t)f\left[\frac{K}{L}\right] \cdot 1 \tag{A5.3}$$

Equation (A5.3) can be used to portray graphically the *theoretical* relationship between output per worker (Y/L), and thus by inference output per capita, and technological change and changes in the capital/labor ratio (K/L). It can also be used to depict the two-way relationship between functional income shares and economic growth under the assumed savings conditions. This is done in Fig. 5.7.

In the upper right-hand quadrant is the production function as given by expression (A5.3) for any given level of technology; changes in technology shift this function upwards. Since we have designated the y-axis below the origin as constituting the amount of labor input, the areas $OQRS$ is the amount of capital stock employed $(OQ.RS = K/L.L = K)$. Similarly, the x-axis to the left of zero measures labor input $(OST$ being an isosoles triangle) while the total area $OAZT$ in the upper left quadrant is the amount of real output produced $(OT.OA = L.Y/L = Y)$.

Now let us define P as 'profit', or the share of national output which is a return to capital, and W as labor's share of national output, so that

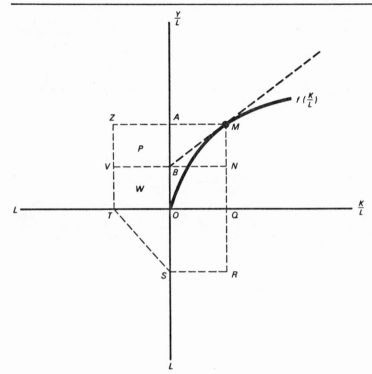

Fig 5.7
Economic growth and income distribution

$$\frac{P}{K} = \frac{Y - W}{K} = \frac{Y/L - W/L}{K/L} = \frac{f(K/L) - W/L}{K\ L} \qquad (A5.4)$$

According to some writers, producers may be expected to adopt a capitál–labor ratio (K/L) which maximizes the profit per unit of capital employed, (P/K). This presumably does, or could maximize 'business saving' and 'reinvestment' over some time period, increasing potential output over that period, with resources then at the end of this (indefinite) time period shifted to consumption and so maximizing consumption *at that point in time*. This is the essence of the argument underlying the 'big push' theory of economic development, as advanced, for example, by Galenson and Leibenstein[2]. Let us see what this implies.

If we differentiate expression (A5.4) for (P/K) with respect to (K/L) and set it equal to zero, we have:

$$\frac{d(P/K)}{d(K/L)} = \frac{(K/L).f'(K/L) - f(K,L)}{(K/L)^2} + \frac{W/L}{(K/L)^2} = 0, \qquad (A5.5)$$

or

$$f(K/L) = Y/L = (K/L).f'(K/L) + W/L, \qquad (A5.7)$$

where f' (K/L) is the derivative of the function f (K/L). But since (Y/L) — (W/L) = (P/L), which then from the above is equal to (K/L). f' (K/L), the distance AB = MN in Fig. 5.7 must equal (P/L); the tangent to the production function at M is f' (K/L) = (P/L) ÷ (K/L) = P/K for any point M along the production function. By definition, then, if distance AB is (P/L), distance OB must be (W/L). Thus, the point where the tangent to the production function intersects the y-axis can be used to show the relative income share going to wage earners, *OB/OA,* and that going to those who contribute capital to the productive process, *BA/OA*.

From all this it can be seen that rates of return plus relative and absolute shares of income going to labor and capital depend on the relative growth rates of labor and capital. If they grow evenly, the rates of return and relative income shares will be unchanged, while the absolute shares increase. If labor grows faster than the capital stock so that (K/L) falls, the rate of return to labor falls, but the rate of return to capital may rise or fall. Technological change which shifts the production function upward will be 'neutral' if the ratio $W/L / P/K$ is unchanged, i.e. if the distance OB relative to MN/BN is unchanged.

Growth, poverty and income distribution

To maximize $f'(K/L) = P/K$ at any point in time involves maximizing the slope of BM, which ostensibly will occur where point B is at point O in Fig. 5.7, i.e. where the absolute share of income going to labor ($OBVT$, or area W) is zero! Of course neo-classical growth economists recognize that this is absurd. Clearly workers must be paid at least a subsistence wage. But their point is that holding wages at this level, and so maximizing P/K with this constraint, will maximize saving over some time period and therefore consumption at some (unspecified) future point in time. But see pp.112–13 in the main text for a criticism of this model.

Notes

1. Taken from: Robert Solow, 'Technical progress and the aggregate production function', *Review of Economics and Statistics*, August 1957, 312–20.
2. Galenson and Leibenstein, op. cit. (note 7, Ch. notes, p. 122). The authors suggest, for example, that 'successful economic development under present conditions . . . hinges largely upon the introduction of modern technology on as large a scale as possible'. What is needed, therefore, is 'up-to-date equipment and relatively high initial capital/labor ratios'. (p. 370).

The central issue of our time may well turn out to be how the world addresses the problem of ever expanding human numbers.
  James Grant, President, Overseas Development Council

Consideration of population problems cannot be reduced to the analysis of population trends only.
  World Population Plan of Action, *Bucharest, August 1974*

Introduction: numbers and controversies

On 29 March 1976, the world's population was estimated to have passed the 4 billion mark. Optimistic projections by the United Nations placed the figure at over $6 \cdot 5$ billion people by the end of the twentieth century. Nearly two-thirds of that population will inhabit the developing world. What will be the economic and social implications for levels of living, national and personal esteem, and freedom of choice – that is, for 'development' – if such quantitative projections are realized? Are such projections inevitable, or will they depend on the success or failure of Third World development efforts? Finally, and more significantly, is rapid population growth *per se* as serious a problem as many in the developed world believe; or is it a manifestation of more fundamental problems of underdevelopment and the unequal utilization of global resources between rich and poor nations, as many others (mostly in the developing world) believe?

These and other questions lie at the core of the current worldwide interest in and debate about world population growth and human welfare. The main elements of this debate were clearly evident at the first World Population Conference held in Bucharest in August 1974. The first half of the present chapter, therefore, attempts to analyze the nature and context of the current population debate both as it relates to the domestic concerns of many developing countries and in its worldwide context. In Chapter 7 we look more closely at the economics of population and examine various policies that *both* the developing *and* the developed world might pursue in a joint effort to deal with the global population dilemma.

6.1 The basic issue: population growth and the quality of life

Every year between 75 and 80 million people are being added to a world population of just over 4 billion. About 65 million of these additional people will be born each year in Third World countries. These increases are unprecedented in the history of mankind. But the problem of population growth is not simply a problem of numbers. It is a problem of human welfare and of 'development' as defined in Chapter 3. Rapid population growth can have serious potential consequences for the well-being of mankind throughout the world. If 'development' entails the improvement in peoples' levels of living – their incomes, health, education and general well-being – and if it also encompasses their self-esteem, respect, dignity and freedom to choose, then the really important question about population growth is: *'How does the contemporary population situation in many Third World countries contribute to or detract from their chances of realizing the goals of development, not only for the current generation but also for future generations? Conversely, how does "development" affect population growth?'*

Among the major issues relating to this basic question are the following:
1. Will Third World countries be capable of improving the *levels of living* for their people with the current and anticipated levels of population growth? To what extent does rapid population increase make it more difficult to provide essential social services including housing, transport, sanitation and security?
2. How will the developing countries be able to cope with the vast increases in their labor forces over the coming decades? Will *employment opportunities* be plentiful or will it be a major achievement just to keep unemployment levels from rising?
3. What are the implications of higher population growth rates among the world's poor for their chances of overcoming the human misery of *absolute poverty*? Will *world food supply* and its distribution be sufficient not only to feed the anticipated population increase in the coming decades but also to improve nutritional levels to the point where all humans can have an adequate diet?
4. Will developing countries be able to extend the coverage and improve the quality of their *health and educational systems* so that everyone can at least have the chance to secure adequate health care and a basic education?
5. To what extent are low levels of living an important factor in limiting the *freedom of parents to choose* a desired family size? Is there a relationship between poverty and family size?
6. To what extent is the *growing affluence* and the desire to grow further among the economically more developed nations an important factor preventing poor nations from accommodating their growing populations? Is the inexorable pursuit of increasing affluence among the rich an even more detrimental force to rising living standards among the poor than the absolute increase in their numbers?

In view of the above questions, it becomes essential to frame the population issue not simply in terms of numbers, or densities, or rates, or movements but, as Bernard Berelson, former President of the Population Council, has said[1], with full consideration of

... the qualities of human life: prosperity in place of poverty, education in place of ignorance, health in place of ignorance and death, environmental beauty in place of deterioration, full opportunities for the next generations of children in place of current limitations. .... Population trends, if favorable, open man's options and enlarge his choices. Thus, population policy is not an end, but only a means – a means to the better life. That is what the concern about population is about, or ought to be.

6.2 A review of numbers: population growth – past, present and prospective[2]

Throughout most of the 2 million years of man's existence on earth, his numbers have been few. When he first started to cultivate food through agriculture some 12,000 years ago, the estimated world population was no more than 5 million, less than the number of people living today in Mexico City, Lagos, Buenos Aires or Bangkok (see Table 6.1). At the beginning of the Christian era nearly 2,000 years ago, world population had grown to nearly 250 million, less than half the population of India today. From the year AD 1 to the beginning of the industrial revolution around 1750 it increased twofold to 728 million people, approximately the same number as those living in China today. During the next 200 years (1750–1950), an additional 1·7 billion people were added to the earth's numbers. But in the last 25 years (1950–75) almost the same number of people (1·5 billion) have been added, bringing total world population at the end of 1975 to almost 4 billion people. If this trend continues to the year 2000, the world's population will then be almost 6·5 billion people.

1. World population growth through history

Year	Estimated population	Estimated annual increase in the intervening period
Circa 10000 BC	5,000,000	
AD 1	250,000,000	0·04
1650	545,000,000	0·04
1750	728,000,000	0·29
1800	906,000,000	0·45
1850	1,171,000,000	0·53
1900	1,608,000,000	0·65
1950	2,486,000,000	0·91
1970	3,632,000,000	2·09
1975	3,978,000,000	2·10

Table 6.1
Estimated world population growth through history

Source: Based on Carr-Saunders in W. S. Thompson and D. T. Lewis *Population Problems* (5th ed: New York: McGraw Hill, 1965) p. 384; United Nations, Demographic Yearbook for 1971. Raw data from UN sources are extrapolated throughout.

Turning from absolute numbers to percentage growth rates, we can see from Table 6.2 that for almost the whole of man's existence on earth until approximately 300 years ago the human population grew at an annual rate not much greater than zero – i.e., 0·002 per cent or 20 per million. Naturally, this overall rate has not been steady since there have been many ups and downs in the earth's numbers as a result of natural catastrophes and variations in growth rates among regions. By

1750, the population growth rate had accelerated by 150 times from 0·002 per cent to 0·3 per cent per year. By the 1950s, the rate had again accelerated, this time by threefold to about 1·0 per cent per year. Today, slightly more than 25 years later, the world's population growth rate has more than doubled to a remarkable 2·1 per cent per year.

Period	Approximate growth rate (per cent)	Doubling time (years)
Appearance of man to early historical times	0·002	35,000
1650–1750	0·3	240
1850–1900	0·6	115
1930–1940	1·0	70
Present	2·0	35

Table 6.2 World population growth rates and doubling times: An historical review

Source: Carr-Saunders, op. cit., p. 384.

The relationship between annual percentage increases and the time it takes for a population to double in size is shown in the last column of Table 6.2. We see that before 1650 it took nearly 35,000 years or about 1,400 generations for the world population to double. Today, in less than 35 years, little more than one generation, world population will double[3]. Moreover, whereas it took almost 1,750 years to add 480 million people to the world's population between AD 1 and the onset of the industrial revolution, at current growth rates this same 480 million people are being added to the earth's numbers every 6 years!

The reason for the sudden change in overall population trends is that for almost all man's recorded history the rate of population change, whether up or down, had been strongly influenced by the combined effects of famine, disease, malnutrition, plague and war – conditions that resulted in high and fluctuating death rates. Now, in the twentieth century, such conditions are coming increasingly under man's technological and economic control. As a result, human mortality (the death rate) is lower than at any other point in man's existence. It is this decline in mortality resulting from rapid technological advances in modern medicine and the spread of modern public measures throughout the world, particularly in the last 20 years, that has resulted in the unprecedented increases in world population growth – especially in Third World countries. For example, death rates in Africa, Asia and Latin America have fallen by as much as 50 per cent during the last 20 to 30 years while birth rates have remained relatively high.

In short, *population growth today is primarily the result of a rapid 'transition' from a long historical era characterized by high birth and death rates to one in which death rates have fallen sharply while birth rates, especially in developing countries, have not yet fallen much from their historic high levels.*

2. The structure of the world's population The world's population is very unevenly distributed by geographic region, by fertility and mortality levels, and by age structures.

A. Geographical region Of the world's total population in 1977, more than two-thirds live in developing countries and less than one-third in the economically developed nations. Figure 6.1 shows the regional distribution of the world's population as it existed in 1950 and as it is projected for the year 2000.

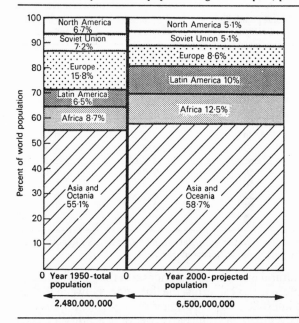

Fig 6.1
World population by region: 1950 and 2000 (projected)

Source: Based on United Nations Demographic Yearbook for 1971, and Population Division, Working Paper, no. 37 (17 December 1970) mimeo.

Given current population growth rates in different parts of the world (significantly higher in the LDCs), the regional distribution of the world's population will inevitably change by the year 2000. By that time it is likely there will be 4 billion *more* people on the earth than in 1950. However, over 60 per cent or almost 2·5 billion of the added people will be in Asia where overall population size should have increased by some 300 per cent during the 50-year period. The corresponding increases in Africa and Latin America are estimated at almost 400 per cent with an addition of almost 1 billion people. Together these three Third World continents will probably constitute over 80 per cent of the world's population by the year 2000 as contrasted with 70 per cent in 1950. Correspondingly, the proportion of the world's population living in Europe, the Soviet Union and North America will have fallen from 30 to less than 20 per cent of the total.

Consider finally the distribution of national populations. Table 6.3 lists the fifteen largest countries in the world in the mid-1970s. Together they account for about 70 per cent of the world's population. While these countries come from all the continents and from both developed and underdeveloped regions, it is instructive to note that in terms of annual increases in world population, countries such as India, Indonesia, Brazil, Bangladesh, Pakistan, Nigeria and Mexico all add more to the world's annual population increase than do most of the economically more developed countries. For example, Mexico, ranked fourteen in size, adds much more to the absolute growth of the world's population than does the United States, ranked as the fourth largest country. Similarly, Brazil, ranked seventh, adds more people annually than does the Soviet Union and so too Nigeria compared with Japan.

The *rate of population increase* is quantitatively measured as the percentage yearly net relative increase (or decrease, in which event it is negative) in population size due to *natural increase* and *net interna-*

B. Fertility and mortality trends

The population debate

Country	Total population (millions)	Rate of natural increase	Annual increase (millions)
China	800	2·0	16·0
India	580	2·2	12·8
Soviet Union	250	1·0	2·5
United States	210	0·6	1·2
Indonesia	130	2·3	3·4
Japan	105	1·3	1·3
Brazil	100	3·0	3·0
Bangladesh	80	2·8	2·4
Pakistan	65	2·8	1·8
Nigeria	60	2·5+	1·5
West Germany	60	−0·04	0·0
United Kingdom	56	0·3	0·2
Italy	55	0·7	0·4
Mexico	55	3·5	1·9
France	52	0·6	0·3

Table 6.3 The fifteen largest countries in the world and their annual population increases

Source: Calculated from United Nations Population and Vital Statistics Report 25, no. 2 (series A), 1973, and Demographic Yearbook for 1971.

tional migration. Natural increase simply measures the excess of births over deaths or, in more technical terms, the difference between *fertility* and *mortality.* Net international migration is of negligible importance today (although in the nineteenth and early twentieth century it was an extremely important source of population increase in North America, Australia and New Zealand and corresponding decrease in Western Europe). Population increase in Third World countries, therefore, depends almost exclusively on the difference between their birth and death rates.

The difference between developing and developed nations in terms of their rates of population growth can be explained simply by the fact that birth rates (fertility) in developing countries are generally much higher than in the rich nations. Third World death rates (mortality) are also higher. However, these death rate differences are substantially smaller than the differences in birth rates. As a result, the average rate of population growth in the developing countries is now about 2·5 per cent per year whereas most of the economically developed countries have annual growth rates of only about 1 per cent (see the second column of Table 6.3). Let us look briefly at contrasting fertility and mortality trends in these two sets of nations.

As just noted, the major source of difference in population growth rates between the less developed and the more developed countries is the sizable difference in birth or fertility rates between the former and the latter. Recall from Chapter 2 that almost all Third World nations have birth rates ranging from 30 to 55 per thousand. By contrast, in almost all developed countries the rate is less than 30 per thousand (see Table 2.3). Moreover, LDC birth rates today are substantially higher than they were in pre-industrial western Europe. This is largely because of early and almost universal marriage in contemporary Third World countries. But there are signs of the beginnings of a substantial decline in LDC fertility, especially in those countries like Taiwan, South Korea, Singapore and Hong Kong where rapid economic and social development have taken place.

On the other hand, there has been a narrowing of the gap in mortality rates between developed and less developed countries. The primary reason is undoubtedly the rapid improvement in health conditions throughout the Third World. Modern vaccination campaigns against malaria, smallpox, yellow fever and cholera as well as the proliferation of public health facilities, clean water supplies, improved nutrition and public education have all worked together over the past 25 years to lower death rates by as much as 50 per cent in parts of Asia and Latin America and by over 30 per cent in much of Africa and the Middle East. Nevertheless, the average duration of life remains almost 20 years greater in the developed countries. But even this gap has been sharply reduced in the last 25 years. For example, in 1950 life expectancy at birth for people in Third World countries averaged 35–40 years compared to 62–65 years in the developed world. By 1975 the difference had fallen to 19 years as life expectancy in the LDCs increased to 52 years (a gain of 40 per cent) while in the industrial nations it had risen to 71 years (an increase of 12 per cent). Today, because of still relatively high infant mortality rates Africa has the lowest life expectancy, 46 years, while the most favorable region is Europe where life expectancy at birth now averages about 72 years.

World population today is very youthful. Children under the age of 15 constitute almost half the total population of Third World countries while they make up only a quarter of the populations of developed nations. For example, 45 and 48 per cent of the population of Nigeria and Kenya respectively were below 15 years in 1972; for Brazil the comparable figure was 42 per cent and for Indonesia, India and the Philippines it was 45, 42 and 43 per cent respectively. In countries with such an age structure, the youth dependency ratio – that is, the proportion of youths (below 15 years) to economically active adults (ages 15–64) – is very high. Thus the working force in developing countries must support almost twice as many children as they do in the wealthier countries. For example, in Sweden and the Soviet Union the working force age group (15–64) amounts to almost 65 per cent of the total population. This work force has to support only 21 and 27 per cent respectively of the population who are its youthful dependants. By contrast, in countries like Egypt and Ghana the economically active work forces and the child dependants both approach 50 per cent of the total population. In general, the more rapid the population growth rate, the greater will be the proportion of dependent children in the total population and the more difficult it becomes for those who are working to support those who are not.

C. Age structure and dependency burdens

Whatever the line of causality, high birth rates are generally associated with national poverty. However, it would be a mistake simply to claim that since high birth rates are generally associated with countries having low per capita incomes (the less developed nations), while low birth rates generally are found in countries with high per capita incomes (the more developed nations), it follows that raising per capita levels of income will lead to lower birth rates.

3. Birth rates: their relationship to income levels, GNP growth rates and income distribution

Consider, for example, Table 6.4. Twelve Third World countries are listed according to their 1971 per capita income levels, their per capita GNP growth rates during the late 1960s, their income distribution ratios measuring the income multiple of the top 20 per cent to the bottom 40 per cent of the income scale, and the magnitude of their crude birth rates.

The three diagrams in Fig. 6.2 graphically portray the relationship, or 'non-relationship' as the case may be, between each of the three major income variables and the birth rate as shown in Table 6.4. For

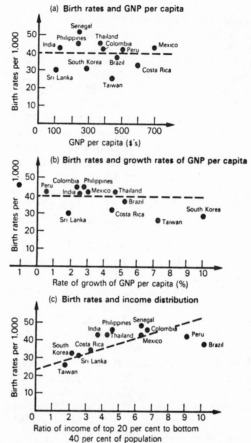

Fig 6.2
The relationship between incomes and birth rates in twelve Third World countries

example, in Fig. 6.2 (a) we have plotted the birth rate for each country against its *level* of per capita income to test the widely held hypothesis that there exists a close negative association between birth rates and per capita incomes. In Fig. 6.2 (b) these same country birth rates are plotted against *growth rates* in per capita incomes to see if more rapid rates of income growth are closely associated with lower fertility levels. Finally, in Fig. 6.2 (c) birth rates are plotted against *income distribution* ratios to see if lower ratios (i.e. more equal distributions of income) are associated with lower birth rates.

Taking Fig. 6.2 (a) first, it is immediately evident that there is no apparent direct or inverse relationship between levels of per capita income and birth rates, at least for the twelve countries under consideration. Countries with similar relatively high birth rates like Colombia, the Philippines, Peru and Thailand have widely varying levels of per capita income. Similarly, countries with close but relatively low birth rates like Sri Lanka, South Korea, Taiwan and Costa Rica have national incomes varying from 100 US dollars to 590 dollars per capita. So, we can reject the simple hypothesis that higher per capita incomes necessarily are associated with higher or lower birth rates, at least over the range of incomes represented by the twelve LDCs in our sample.

Looking now at Fig. 6.2 (b), we see that there also appears to be no clear relationship between growth rates of GNP per capita and birth levels. Again countries like Peru, India, Colombia, the Philippines, Mexico and Thailand, which have a variation of only three points in their birth rates (i.e. from 42 to 45 per thousand), have wide variations in their income growth performances (ranging from a rate of 0·5 per cent per annum in Peru to 4·7 per cent in Thailand). On the other hand, countries with the same relatively low birth rates like Sri Lanka and South Korea have variations of over 500 per cent in their respective GNP growth rates (1·8 per cent for Sri Lanka compared to 10 per cent for South Korea)[4].

Finally, if we compare relative country birth rates with their relative degrees of income inequality as in Fig. 6.2 (c), we discover that there *does* appear to be some relationship between lower (higher) birth rates and less (more) inequality in the distribution of income. Our twelve countries seem to fall roughly into two distinct groups – those with relatively low inequality ratios and relatively low birth rates (Taiwan, Sri Lanka, South Korea and Costa Rica) and the others with moderate to high inequality ratios and relatively higher birth rates (India, Thailand, Philippines, Senegal, Mexico, Colombia, Peru and Brazil).

We may tentatively conclude, therefore, that *countries which strive to lessen the inequality in their distribution of income or, alternatively, attempt to spread the benefits of their economic growth to a wider segment of the population may be better able to begin to lower their birth rates than countries where the benefits of growth are more unevenly shared,* even though these latter countries may have *both* higher levels and faster growth rates of per capita income[5]. However, given a development policy oriented towards a more equitable pattern of income distribution, higher rates of GNP growth are likely to result in even greater reductions in fertility – contrast, for example, South Korea and Taiwan with, say Brazil and Thailand.

The reason why direct attacks on poverty and low levels of living are probably more effective measures to lower birth rates than simple growth maximization is that higher levels of living provide the neces-

Country	Per capita GNP (1971), $'s	Per capita GNP growth rate (1965–71)	Income distribution (rates of top 20% to bottom 40%)	Birth (rate per 1,000)
Brazil	460	5·1	10·2	38
Colombia	370	2·3	6·8	45
Costa Rica	590	4·5	3·5	34
India	110	2·4	3·9	42
Mexico	700	2·9	6·5	43
Peru	480	0·5	9·3	42
Philippines	240	2·7	4·8	45
Senegal	250	−1·2	6·4	48
South Korea	290	10·0	2·5	31
Sri Lanka	100	1·8	2·7	30
Taiwan	430	7·3	2·0	27
Thailand	210	4·7	4·5	43

Table 6.4
The relationship between national per capita incomes, growth rates, income distribution and birth rates: Selected Third World countries

Sources: Cols. (1), (2), and (4): *Agenda for Action,* published for Overseas Development Council by Praeger Washington 1974, Table A–4. Co. (3) Calculated from IBRD, *Redistribution With Growth,* Washington 1973, p. (2) 4, Table 1.

sary *motivations* for families to *choose* to limit their size. Widespread poverty tends to sustain high birth rates for the obvious reason that families living without adequate incomes, employment, health, education and social services have little security for the future other than reliance on their children. They are caught in an 'underdevelopment trap' vis-à-vis their family size not only because their *levels of living* are low but also because their self-esteem and dignity may thereby be questioned and their *freedom to choose* a desired family size, however large, is constrained by their poverty and economic uncertainty.

Perhaps the least understood aspect of population growth is its tendency to continue even after birth rates may have declined substantially. Population growth has a built-in tendency to continue, a powerful *momentum* which like a speeding automobile when the brakes are applied tends to keep going for some time before coming to a stop. In the case of population growth this momentum can persist for decades after birth rates drop.

4. The 'hidden momentum' of population growth
There are two basic reasons for this hidden momentum. First, high birth rates cannot be altered substantially overnight. The social, economic and institutional forces which have influenced fertility rates over the course of centuries do not simply evaporate even at the urging of national leaders. We know from the experience of European nations that such reductions in birth rates can take many decades. Consequently, even if developing countries assign top priority to the limitation of population growth, it will still take many years to lower national fertility to desired levels.

The second and less obvious reason for the hidden momentum of population growth relates to the age structure of LDC populations. We saw in the previous section that nations with high birth rates have large proportions of children and adolescents in their population (sometimes as high as 50 per cent). In such a high fertility population, young people greatly outnumber their parents, and when their generation reaches adulthood the number of potential parents will inevitably be much larger than at present. It follows that even if these new parents have only enough children to replace themselves (say, two per couple as compared with their parents who may have had four children) the fact that the total number of couples having two children is much greater than the number of couples who previously had four children means that the total population will still increase substantially before levelling off.

To give an example, suppose for simplicity we assume that country X has a total population of 600, consisting only of 100 married couples, each of which has 4 children (2 girls and 2 boys). When these 400 children grow up, suppose they all marry, forming 200 new couples of childbearing age. Assume now that instead of 4 children per family, these new couples have only 2 children each (1 boy and 1 girl). Assuming the death of the first generation of parents, the total population of country X will have grown from 600 to 800 people (i.e. 200 families of 4 people in each family). Now when the children of these 2-child families grow up and get married, if they too have only 2 children per couple, then there will again be 200 families with 4 people in each for a total population of 800 people. Country X will, therefore, have been able to stabilize its population *only* after two generations or approximately 50 years! This is why it takes many years to curtail population growth in high fertility countries. Too often politicians, planners and even economists are unaware of the mathematics of population momentum. They assume incorrectly that population growth rates can be manipulated in the short-run with the same ease as the manipulation of, say, saving and investment rates or the levels and rates of taxation.

Suppose that we now make the extremely optimistic and unreal assumption that by the period 1980–5 fertility rates in all developing countries will have declined to the 'replacement' levels now characteristic of most developed countries (roughly two children per family). Even given such unrealistically optimistic assumptions, the population of the Third World would still continue to grow for many decades. In fact, it would not level off until it had reached a size fully 88 per cent greater than its 1970 level – i.e. an increase of more than 2·2 *billion* people! And those heavily populated countries like Mexico, India, Bangladesh, Indonesia, Nigeria and others would all also experience very substantial increases as a result of the momentum which is *already* built into the age structure of their current populations.

If we take a less optimistic but somewhat more realistic assumption that LDC fertility declines to 'replacement levels' not by 1980–5 but instead by the years 2000–2005, 20 years later, we obtain an entirely different set of figures. In this case the population of the Third World would not level off until its built-in momentum had resulted in an overall increase of 158 per cent and an additional 4 billion people had been born. This would be more than the total world population in 1975! These figures emphasize dramatically the importance to eventual population size of the date at which countries are able to lower their fertility levels. In the above example, a mere 20 years meant an additional 1·8 billion people, almost two-thirds of the present population of the entire Third World.

Table 6.5 strikingly illustrates the 'arithmetic' of population momentum using actual data and projections for a number of developing countries.

Country	Population circa 1970 (in millions)	Eventual population size in 2050 (in millions)		Per cent increase from 1970 level	
		Replacement by 1980–5	Replacement by 2000–5	Replacement by 1980–5	Replacement 2000–5
India	534	1,002	1,366	+ 88%	+156%
Brazil	94	192	266	+104	+183
Bangladesh	69	155	240	+125	+248
Nigeria	65	135	198	+108	+205
Pakistan	57	112	160	+ 96	+181
Mexico	51	111	168	+118	+229
Philippines	38	79	119	+108	+213
Egypt	34	64	92	+ 88	+171
All LDCs	2,530	4,763	6,525	+ 88	+158
All developed countries	1,122	1,482	1,610	+ 32	+ 44
World	3,652	6,245	8,135	+ 71	+123

Table 6.5
Population 'momentum' and projected population increases under two alternative (optimistic) fertility assumptions

Source: Tomas Frejka, reference tables to *The Future of Population Growth,* The Population Council, New York (1973).

We see that countries like Bangladesh, Mexico, the Philippines and Nigeria with high current birth rates have the highest built-in momentum of population growth. Note also that even though a country like India has approximately the same percentage growth momentum as

Egypt, its current size means that it stands to gain almost 750 million more people than Egypt even if both achieve replacement birth rates by the year 2000.

These illustrations vividly demonstrate the extent to which most Third World countries are *already* virtually assured of substantial population increases, whatever happens to fertility levels. As they set goals for desirable future population sizes, they may as well accept the fact that increases of the order of 80 to 125 per cent are coming *irrespective of any policy strategies*. But this should not be a cause for despair or a diminished commitment on the part of those countries which genuinely believe that slowing down population growth is in their best national interest. For, as we have seen from the above example, every year that passes without a reduction in fertility means a larger multiple of the present total population size before it can eventually level off.

6.3 The population debate: some conflicting opinions

Before discussing specific goals and objectives it must be recognized that there is substantial disagreement, particularly between the developed and the developing world, regarding whether or not rapid population growth is in fact as serious a problem as some make it out to be. Nowhere was this conflict more evident nor the debate more vocal than at the first World Population Conference held in Bucharest in 1974[6]. On the one hand, one must recognize that population growth is not the only, or even the primary, source of low levels of living, eroding self-esteem and limited freedom in Third World nations. On the other hand, it would be equally naïve to argue that rapid population growth in many countries and regions is *not* a serious *intensifier* and multiplier of our three integral components of underdevelopment, especially the first and third. The following summary of some of the main arguments for and against the idea that rapid population growth is a serious development problem forms the basis for discussion of whether some 'consensus' of opinion can be identified from which specific goals and objectives can be postulated[7].

1. Population growth is not a real problem We can identify three general lines of argument on the part of those individuals, primarily from Third World countries, who assert:

1. that the problem is not population growth but some other issue;
2. that population growth is a false issue deliberately created by dominant rich country agencies and institutions to keep LDCs in their underdeveloped 'dependent' conditions;
3. that for many developing countries and regions population growth is, in fact, desirable.

A. 'Some other issue' There are many knowledgeable people from both rich and poor nations who argue that the real problem is not population growth *per se* but:

1. Underdevelopment If correct strategies are pursued which lead to higher levels of living, greater esteem and expanded freedom, population will take care of itself. Eventually, it will disappear as a 'problem' as it has in all of the present economically advanced nations. According to this argument *underdevelopment is the real problem and 'development' should be the only goal*. With it will come economic progress and social mechanisms which will more or less automatically regulate population growth and distribution. As long as the vast majority of people in Third World countries remain impoverished, uneducated and physically and psychologically weak, the large family will constitute the only real source of 'social security' (i.e. parents will continue to be denied the 'freedom to choose' a small family, if they so desire). Proponents of the underdevelopment argument then conclude that birth control programs will surely fail, as they have in the past, where there is no *motivation* on the part of poor families to want to limit their size.

Population can only be an economic problem in relation to the availability and utilization of scarce natural and material resources. The fact is that the developed countries, with only one-third of the world's population, consume almost 80 per cent of the world's resources. For example, the average North American or European consumer uses up, directly and indirectly, almost sixteen times as much of the world's food, energy and material resources as his counterpart in Third World countries. In terms of the depletion of the world's limited resources, therefore, the addition of another child in the developed countries is as significant as the birth of sixteen additional children in the underdeveloped countries. According to this argument, the *developed* nations should curtail their excessively high consumption standards; rather than the less developed nations restrict their population growth. The latter's high fertility is really due to their low levels of living, which in turn are largely the result of the 'over-consumption' of the world's scarce resources by rich nations. It is this combination of rising affluence and extravagant, selfish consumption habits in rich countries and among rich people in poor countries which should be the major world concern, *not* population growth.

2. World resource depletion

According to this third argument, it is not numbers of people *per se* which are causing population problems but their *distribution* in space. Many regions of the world (e.g. sub-Saharan Africa) and many regions within countries (e.g. the northeast and Amazon regions of Brazil) are in fact *underpopulated* in terms of available or potential resources. Others simply have too many people concentrated in too small an area (e.g. central Java or most urban concentrations in LDCs). What is needed, therefore, instead of moderating the quantitative rate of population growth is governmental efforts to reduce rural–urban migration and to bring about a more natural spatial distribution of the population in terms of available land and other productive resources.

3. Population distribution

The second main line of argument denying the significance of population growth as a major development problem is closely allied to the neo-colonial dependence theory of underdevelopment discussed in Chapter 3. Basically, it is argued that the frenetic overconcern in the rich nations with the population growth of poor nations is really an attempt by the former to hold down the development of the latter in order to maintain the international status quo for their own special self interest. Rich countries are pressuring poor nations to adopt aggressive population control programs even though they themselves went through a period of sizeable population increase which accelerated their own development processes.

B. 'A deliberately contrived false issue'

An extreme version of this argument views population control efforts by rich countries and their allied international agencies as racist or genocidal attempts to reduce the relative or absolute size of those poor, largely non-white populations of the world who may someday pose a serious threat to the welfare of the rich, predominantly white, populations. World-wide birth control campaigns are seen, therefore, as manifestations of the fears of the developed world in the face of a possible radical challenge to the international order by the people who are its first victims.

C. 'Population growth is desirable'   A more conventional economic argument is that of population growth as an essential ingredient to stimulate economic development[8]. Larger populations provide the needed consumer demand to generate favorable economies of scale in production, to lower production costs and to provide a sufficient and low-cost labor supply to achieve higher output levels. Moreover, it is argued that many rural regions in the Third World are in reality *underpopulated* in the sense that there is much unused but arable land that could yield large increases in agricultural output if only more people were available to cultivate it. Many regions of tropical Africa and Latin America and even parts of Asia are said to be so situated.

In Africa, for example, it has even been argued that there are many regions which had *larger* populations in the remote past than exist today[9]. Their rural depopulation resulted not only from the slave trade, but also from compulsory military service, confinement to 'reservations' and the forced labor policies of former colonial governments. For example, the sixteenth century Congo Kingdom is said to have had a population of approximately 2 million. But by the time of the colonial conquest and after 300 years of slave trade, the population of the region had fallen to less than one-third of that figure. Today's Zaire has barely caught up to the sixteenth century numbers[10]. Other regions of west and eastern Africa provide similar examples – at least in the eyes of those who advocate rapid population growth in Africa.

In terms of ratios of population to arable land (i.e. land under cultivation, fallow land, pastures and forests), Africa south of the Sahara is said by these supporters of population expansion to have a total of 1,400 million arable hectares. Land actually being cultivated, however, amounts to only 170 million hectares or about 1 hectare per rural inhabitant. Thus, only 12 per cent of all potential arable lands is under cultivation and this very low rural population density is therefore viewed as a serious drawback to raising agricultural output[11]. Similar arguments have been expounded with regard to such Latin American countries as Brazil and Argentina.

Three other 'non-economic' arguments, each found to some degree in a wide range of developing countries, complete the 'population-growth-is-desirable' viewpoint. First, many countries claim a need for population growth to protect currently underpopulated border regions against any expansionist intentions of neighboring nations. Second, there are many ethnic, racial and religious groups within less developed countries whose differential attitudes towards family size have to be protected both for moral and political reasons. Finally, military and political power are often seen as dependent upon a large and youthful population.

Many of these arguments have a certain realism about them; if not in fact, then at least in the perceptions of vocal and influential individuals within the developing world. Clearly, some of the arguments have greater validity for some Third World countries than others. The important point is that they represent a considerable range of opinions and viewpoints within the Third World and therefore need to be seriously weighed against the counter arguments of those (mostly in the developed world) who believe that rapid population growth is indeed a real and important problem for underdeveloped countries. Let us now look at some of these counter arguments.

Positions supporting the need to curtail population growth through special programmes and policies are typically based on one or more of the following four arguments[12].

2. Population growth is a real problem

The extreme version of the population-as-a-serious-problem position attempts to attribute almost all of the world's economic and social evils to excessive population growth. Unrestrained population increase is seen as the major crisis facing mankind today. It is claimed to be the principal cause of poverty, low levels of living, malnutrition and ill-health, environmental degradation, and a wide array of other social problems. Value-laden and incendiary words such as the 'population bomb' or 'population explosion' are tossed around at will. Indeed, dire predictions of world food catastrophes and ecological disaster are attributed almost entirely to the growth in world numbers[13]. Such an extreme position, therefore, leads some of its advocates to assert that 'world' (i.e. LDC) population stabilization or even decline is the most urgent contemporary task even if it requires severe and coercive measures such as compulsory sterilization to 'control' family size in some of the most populated Third World countries like India and Bangladesh.

A. The population 'hawk' argument

A much less extreme and draconian anti-population growth argument asserts that there are many families in Third World countries who would *like* to limit their size, if only they had the *means* to do so. Hence, the main problem is to provide modern birth control devices such as the pill, the interuterine device (IUD), and increasingly 'voluntary' sterilization through male vasectomy. Family planning programs with clinics throughout the country, therefore, need to be established both to 'educate' people about modern methods of fertility control and to provide them with cheap and safe means to practise it.

B. The provision of family planning services

At a United Nations convention held in Teheran, Iran, in 1968 a resolution was adopted asserting that 'it is a fundamental human right for each person to be able to determine the size of his or her own family'. A more contemporary version of this position, at least in the more affluent societies, asserts that every woman has the fundamental right to the control of her own bodily reproductive processes – including the right to legal abortion as well as contraception. Since maternal and child health are also related to the ability of parents to space their children at greater intervals, the human rights position bases its 'freedom to choose' advocacy of family planning on grounds of health as well as family size.

C. Human rights

This is by far the principal argument advanced by a majority of those who hold that a too rapid population growth should be a real concern of Third World countries. Its basic proposition is that population growth intensifies and exacerbates the economic, social and psycholog-

D. 'Development' plus population programs

ical problems associated with the condition of 'underdevelopment', especially since it retards the prospects for a better life for those already born. It also severely draws down limited government revenues simply to provide the most rudimentary economic, health and social services to the additional people. This in turn prevents an improvement in the levels of living of the existing generation.

As we have seen, widespread absolute poverty and low levels of living are a major cause of large family size, due in part to parental desires for economic security when they grow old. It follows that economic and social 'development' are *necessary* conditions for bringing about an eventual slowing down or cessation of population growth at low levels of fertility and mortality. But, according to this argument, it is not a *sufficient* condition – that is, 'development' provides people with the *incentives* and *motivations* to limit their family size but family planning programs are needed to provide them with the technological *means* to avoid unwanted pregnancies. Even though countries like France, Japan, the United States, Great Britain and, more recently, Taiwan and South Korea, were able to reduce their population growth rates without widespread family planning clinics, it is argued by advocates of the development-plus-population-program position that the provision of these services will enable other countries desiring to control excessive population growth to do so more *rapidly* than if these family planning services were not available.

6.4 Goals and objectives: towards a 'consensus'

In spite of what at first sight may appear to be diametrically opposing arguments between those 'for' and 'against' population growth, there does appear to be a common ground, an intermediate position, which both sides can agree upon, that is with the possible exceptions of those who advance the extreme versions of either the population 'hawk' or the pro-natalist positions. The ethical 'values' which provide the basis for this consensus are rooted in what we have called in Chapter 3 the 'inner meaning' of 'development' in conjunction with the United Nations' 'human rights' declaration of 1968 referred to in the previous section. The following four propositions constitute the essential components of this intermediate or consensus opinion:

1. *Population growth is* not *the primary cause of low levels of living, gross inequalities or the limited freedom of choice which characterize much of the Third World.* The fundamental causes of these problems must be sought rather in the 'dualistic' nature of the domestic and international economic and social order.
2. *The 'problem' of population is not simply one of numbers but of the qualities of human life and its material well-being.* Thus, LDC population size must be viewed *in conjunction with developed country affluence* in relation to the quantity, distribution and utilization of world resources – not just in relation to 'indigenous' resources of the LDCs themselves.
3. *But, rapid population growth does serve to intensify problems of 'underdevelopment'* and make prospects for 'development' that much more remote. As we have seen, the momentum of growth means that, barring catastrophe, the population of developing countries will increase dramatically over the coming decades, no matter what fertility control measures are adopted now. It follows that high population growth rates, while not the principal cause of

underdevelopment, are nevertheless important contributing factors in specific countries and regions of the world.

4. *Many of the real problems of population arise not from its overall size but from its concentration,* especially in urban areas as a result of accelerated rural–urban migration (see Chapter 9). A more rational and efficient spatial *distribution* of national populations thus becomes a viable alternative, in some countries, to the mere slowdown of overall population growth.

In view of the above propositions and the explicit 'development' and 'human rights' value premises implicit in them, we may conclude that the following three *goals* and *objectives* might be included in any realistic approach to the issue of population growth in many developing countries.

1. In those countries or regions where the population size, distribution and growth is viewed as an existing and/or potential problem, the primary objective of any strategy to limit its further growth must deal *not only* with the population variable *per se* but also with the underlying social and economic conditions of *underdevelopment.* Goals such as the elimination of absolute poverty, gross inequality, widespread unemployment especially among females, limited female access to education, malnutrition, and poor health facilities need to be given high priority both as necessary concomitants of 'development' and as the fundamental motivational basis for the expanded *freedom* of the individual to choose an optimal and, in many cases, smaller than present family size.

2. In order to maximize the achievement of smaller families through 'development' induced motivations, family planning programs providing both the education and the technological means to regulate fertility *for those who wish to regulate it* need to be established.

3. Developed countries need to assist developing countries to achieve their lowered fertility and mortality objectives, not only by providing contraceptives and funding family planning clinics but, more importantly, (*a*) *by curtailing their own excessive depletion of non-renewable world resources* through programs designed to cut back on the unnecessary consumption of products that intensively utilize scarce raw materials and non-renewable resources; (*b*) *by making genuine commitments* to eradicating poverty, illiteracy, disease and malnutrition in Third World countries as well as their own; and (*c*) by recognizing in both their rhetoric and their international economic and social dealings that *'development' is the real issue, not simply population control.*

With these observations in mind, we can now turn to a more specific analysis of the 'economics' of population in Chapter 7. We would encourage readers, however, to reach their own independent judgement about the validity of the various arguments which have been presented in this chapter as part of the continuing worldwide debate on the 'pros' and 'cons' of population growth.

Notes

1. Bernard Berelson, *World Population: Status Report 1974,* Reports on Population Family Planning, no. 15 (January 1974), 47.
2. The information in this section is derived primarily from Berelson, op. cit., pp. 3–20.

3. For those interested, a convenient shorthand method of calculating 'doubling times' is simply to divide any growth rate into the number 72. For example, something (an asset, population, GNP, etc.) growing at 2 per cent per year will double its value in approximately 35 to 36 years.

4. For further statistical evidence of the lack of any clear relationship between rates of population growth and rates of GNP per capita growth for a sample of seventy-nine Third World nations, see: Derek T. Healey, *'Population Growth and Real Output Growth in Developing Countries: A Survey and Analysis'*, Dept. of Economics, University of Adelaide, South Australia (mimeo.), 1974.

5. For recent empirical support of the proposition that reducing income inequality will tend to lower fertility levels in developing nations, see A. K. Bhattacharyya, 'Income inequality and fertility: a comparative view', *Population Studies, 29,* no. 1 (1975), 5–19, Robert Repetto, 'The interaction of fertility and the size distribution of income', *Research Paper No. 8,* Center for Population Studies, Harvard University, October 1974 and Julian L. Simon, 'Income, wealth and their distribution as policy tools in fertility control,' in R. Ridker (ed.), *Population and Development: The Search for Selective Interventions,* John Hopkins U. P., 1976, Ch. 2.

6. For an analysis of this conflict, see J. Finkle and B. Crane, 'The politics of Bucharest: population, development and the new international economic order', *Population and Development,* **1,** no. 1 (1975), 87–114.

7. For a more detailed discussion of these divergent opinions, see Michael Teitelbaum, 'Population and development: is a consensus possible?', *Foreign Affairs,* July 1974, 749–57.

8. See, for example, Colin Clark, 'The "population explosion" myth', *Bulletin of the Institute of Development Studies,* Sussex, May 1969.

9. See Samir Amin, 'Underpopulated Africa', paper given at the African Population Conference, Accra, December 1971.

10. Ibid., fn. 2.

11. Ibid., p. 3.

12. Teitelbaum, op. cit., p. 752–3.

13. For example, see Paul R. and Anne H. Ehrlich, *Population, Resources and Environment: Issues in Human Ecology* (rev. edn.), W. H. Freeman, San Francisco (1972), and Lester R. Brown, *In the Human Interest: A Strategy to Stabilize World Population,* W. W. Norton, New York (1974).

Concepts for review		
general fertility rate	life expectancy at birth
doubling time	dependency ratio
infant mortality rate	age structure of population
rate of population increase	'hidden momentum' of
rate of natural increase	population growth
crude birth rate	'replacement' fertility
crude death rate	population distribution

Questions for discussion

1. Population growth in Third World nations has proceeded at unprecedented rates over the past few decades. Compare and contrast the present rate of population growth in less developed countries with that of the modern developed nations during their early growth years. What has been the major factor contributing to rapid Third World population growth since the Second World War? Explain.

2. What is the relationship between the age structure of a population and its dependency burden? Is the so-called dependency burden higher or lower in Third World countries? Why?

3. Does there appear to be any distinctive statistical relationship between Third World birth rates and (*a*) levels of per capita GNP; (*b*) rates of per capita GNP growth and/or (*c*) degree of equality or inequality in income distributions? If so, explain why you think such a relationship between birth rate and one or more of the above variables might exist.

4. Explain the meaning of the notion of the 'hidden momentum' of population growth. Why is this an important concept for projecting future population trends in different Third World nations?

5. Outline and comment briefly on some of the arguments *against* the idea that population growth is a serious problem in Third World nations.

6. Outline and comment briefly on some of the arguments *in favor* of the idea that population growth is a serious problem in Third World nations.

1. For an excellent summary of the world population picture in the mid-1970s see: **Further readings**
   Bernard Berelson, *World Population: Status Report 1974,* Population Council
   Report No. 15 (1974). Further detailed statistical information on specific countries
   can be obtained from the International Labour Organization's Bulletin of Labour
   Statistics 1974 Special Edition, *1974 World Population Year,* Geneva (1974).
2. For a concise and informative summary of the debate on population and development, both 'for' and 'against', see Michael S. Teitelbaum, 'Population and development: is a consensus possible?', *Foreign Affairs,* July 1974.
3. A good literature survey of the inter-relationship between population growth and
   economic development can be found in Michael E. Conroy and Nancy R. Folbie,
   *Population Growth as a Deterent to Economic Growth: A Reappraisal of the Evi-
   dence,* Institute of Society, Ethics and Life Sciences, February 1976 (mimeo.).

| Chapter 7 | **Economics of population and development** |

The basis for an effective solution of population problems is, above all, socio-economic transformation.
World Population Plan of Action, Bucharest, August 1974

Introduction

In recent years economists have begun to focus increasing attention on the relationship between economic development and population growth. The most difficult problem for such an analysis, however, is to be able somehow to separate cause from effect. Does economic development accelerate or retard population growth rates; or does rapid population growth contribute to or retard economic development? What are the linkages, how strong are they, and in what direction do they operate? In this chapter we shall examine three major approaches to the economics of population analysis: the theory of demographic transition, the Malthusian 'population trap' and the new 'micro-economics' of fertility. Our aim is to assess the degree to which these various approaches do or do not shed light on the main goals and objectives enumerated in the previous chapter. We conclude with an analysis of alternative policy approaches for dealing with the world population issue in both developing and developed countries.

7.1 The theory of demographic transition

The theory of 'demographic transition' attempts to explain why all contemporary developed nations have more or less passed through the same three 'Stages' of modern population history. Before their economic modernization, these countries for centuries had stable or very slow growing populations as a result of a combination of *high birth rates* and almost equally *high death rates*. This was *Stage I*. *Stage II* began to occur when modernization, associated with improved public health methods, better diets, higher incomes, etc., led to a marked reduction in mortality which gradually raised life expectancy from under 40 years to over 60 years. However, the decline in death rates was not immediately accompanied by a decline in fertility. As a result, the growing divergence between *high birth rates* and *falling death rates* led to sharp increases in population growth compared to past centuries. Stage II thus marks the beginning of the demographic transition, i.e. the transition from stable or slow growing populations to rapidly increasing numbers. Finally, *Stage III* occurs when the forces and influences of modernization and development cause fertility to begin to decline so that eventually *falling birth rates converge with lower death rates,* leaving little or no population growth.

Figure 7.1 roughly depicts the three historical stages of the demographic transition in Western Europe.

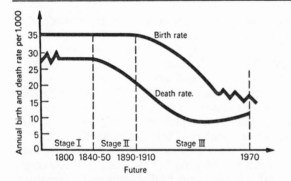

Fig 7.1
The demographic transition in western Europe

Before the early nineteenth century, birth rates hovered around thirty-five per thousand while death rates fluctuated around thirty per thousand. This resulted in population growth rates of around five per thousand, or less than one-half of 1 per cent per year. Stage II, the beginning of Western Europe's demographic transition, was initiated around the first quarter of the nineteenth century by slowly falling death rates as a result of improving economic conditions and the gradual development of disease and death control through modern medical and public health technologies. The decline in birth rates (Stage III) did not really begin until late in the nineteenth century with most of the reduction concentrated in the current century – many decades after modern economic growth had begun and long after death rates began their descent. But since the initial level of birth rates was generally low in Western Europe as a result of late marriage and celibacy, overall rates of population growth seldom exceeded the 1 per cent level, even at their peak. By the end of Western Europe's demographic transition in the second half of the twentieth century, the relationship between birth and death rates which marked the early 1800s had reversed with birth rates fluctuating and death rates remaining fairly stable or slightly rising. This latter phenomenon is simply due to the older age distributions of contemporary European populations.

Figure 7.2 shows the contrasting population histories of contemporary Third World countries.

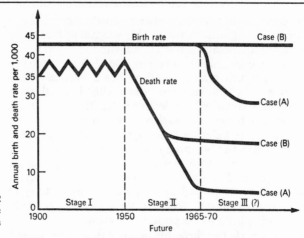

Fig 7.2
The beginning of a demographic
transition in Third World countries

Source: Based on *The Growth of World Population*, Publication 1091 (Washington, D.C.: National Academy of Sciences 1963) 15.

Birth rates in underdeveloped countries today are considerably higher than they were in pre-industrial Western Europe. This is because most people in LDCs marry at an earlier age than in pre-industrialized Europe. As a result there are both more heads of families for a given population size and more years in which to have children. Beginning in the 1940s and especially in the 1950s and 1960s Stage II of the demographic transition occurred throughout most of the Third World. The application of highly effective imported modern medical and public health technologies caused LDC death rates to fall much more rapidly than in nineteenth-century Europe. Given their historically high birth rates at over forty per thousand in many countries, this has meant that Stage II of the LDC demographic transition has been characterized by population growth rates well in excess of 2 to 2·5 per cent per annum.

With regard to Stage III, we can distinguish between two broad classes of developing countries. In case (A) in Fig. 7.2 modern methods of death control *combined with rapid and widely distributed rises in levels of living* have resulted in death rates falling as low as ten per thousand and birth rates alsò falling rapidly to levels between twenty-five and thirty per thousand. These countries, most notably Taiwan, South Korea, Chile and Sri Lanka, have thus entered Stage III of their demographic transition and have experienced rapidly falling rates of overall population growth.

On the other hand, most Third World countries fall into the category of Case (B) Fig. 7.2. After an initial period of rapid decline, the further decline of death rates has not occurred largely because of the persistence of widespread absolute poverty and low levels of living. Moreover, the persistence of high birth rates as a result of these low levels of living causes overall population growth rates to remain relatively high. These countries, consisting of most of Latin America, South and Southeast Asia, the Middle East and Africa, are still in Stage II of their demographic transition.

The important question, therefore, is when and under what conditions are Third World nations likely to experience falling birth rates and a slower expansion of population. On this issue many of both the traditional and modern economic theories of population and development have been constructed. Two of the best known are the traditional Malthusian 'population trap' model and the most recent 'micro-economic' theory of fertility.

7.2 The Malthusian 'population trap'

More than 175 years ago the Reverend Thomas Malthus put forward a theory of the relationship between population growth and economic development which still survives today. Writing in 1798 in his *Essay on the Principle of Population,* and drawing on the concept of diminishing returns, Malthus postulated a universal tendency for the population of a country, unless checked by dwindling food supplies, to grow at a 'geometric' rate, doubling every 30 to 40 years[1]. At the same time, because of diminishing returns to the fixed factor, land, food supplies could only expand roughly at an arithmetical rate. In fact, with each member of the population having less land to work with, his marginal contribution to food production would actually start to decline. Since the growth in food supplies could not keep pace with the burgeoning population, per capita incomes (defined in an agrarian society simply as per capita food production) would have a tendency to fall so low as to lead to a stable population barely existing at or slightly above the subsistence level. Malthus, therefore, contended that the only way to avoid this condition of chronic low levels of living or 'absolute poverty' was for people to engage in 'moral restraint' and limit the numbers of their progeny. Thus, one might regard Malthus as the 'father' of the modern birth control movement.

Modern economists have given a name to the Malthusian idea of a population being inexorably forced to live at subsistence levels of income. They have called it the 'low level-equilibrium population trap' or, more simply, the Malthusian 'population trap'. Diagrammatically, the basic Malthusian model can be illustrated by comparing the shape and position of curves representing population growth rates and aggregate income growth rates when these two curves are each plotted against levels of per capita income. This is done in Fig. 7.3.

On the vertical axis we plot numerical percentage changes, both positive and negative, in the two principal variables under consideration, i.e. total population and aggregate income. On the horizontal axis are levels of per capita income. Look first at the curve P portraying the assumed relationship between rates of population growth (measured vertically) and levels of per capita income, Y/P (measured horizontally). At a very low level of per capita income, y_0, the rate of population change will be nil so that there exists a stable population. y_0 might, therefore, represent our concept of 'absolute poverty'. Birth and death rates are equal and the population is barely holding its own absolute level. It is thus analagous to Stage I of the Demographic Transition Theory. At per capita income levels beyond (to the right of) y_0, it is assumed that population size will begin to increase under the pressure of falling death rates. Higher incomes mean less starvation and disease. And, with birth rates always assumed to be at the biological maximum, falling death rates provide the impetus for an expanding population (i.e. Stage II).

In Fig. 7.3, population growth achieves its maximum rate, roughly $3 \cdot 3$ per cent at a per capita income level of y_2. It is assumed to remain at that level until much higher per capita income levels are realized. Thereafter (i.e. beyond y_5), in accordance with Stage III of the Demog-

1. The basic model

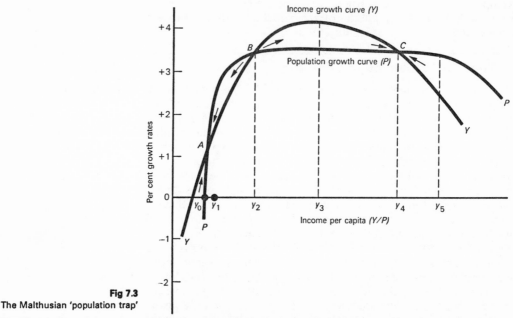

Fig 7.3
The Malthusian 'population trap'

raphic Transition, birth rates will begin to decline and the population growth rate curve becomes negatively sloped and once again approaches the horizontal axis.

The other part of the Malthusian theory requires us to plot a relationship between the growth rate of aggregate income (in the absence of population growth) and levels of per capita income. We can then compare the two rates, i.e. aggregate income and total population. If aggregate income (total product) is rising faster, per capita income by definition must be increasing; if total population is growing faster than total income, per capita income must be falling. In Fig. 7.3 the rate of aggregate income growth (also measured vertically) is assumed at first to be positively related to levels of per capita income; that is, the higher level of per capita income, the higher the rate of increase in aggregate income. The economic reason for .this positive relationship is the assumption that savings vary positively with income per capita. Countries with higher per capita incomes are assumed to be capable of generating higher savings rates and thus more investment. Given a Harrod–Domar type model of economic growth (see Ch. 3, pp. 52), higher savings rates means higher rates of aggregate income growth. Beyond a certain per capita income point (y_3), however, the income growth rate curve is assumed to level off and then begin to decline as new investments and more people are required to work with fixed quantities of land and natural resources. This is the point of diminishing returns in the Malthusian Model (note that the possibility of technological progress is not considered). The aggregate income growth curve therefore is conceptually analogous to the total product curve in the basic theory of production.

Observe that in Fig. 7.3 the curves are drawn so that they intersect at three points: A, B and C. Point A represents the point at which the Malthusian 'population trap' level of per capita income (y_1) is attained. It is a stable equilibrium point – any small movement to the left or right of point A will cause the per capita income equilibrium point to return to y_1. For example, as per capita income rises from y_1 towards y_2, the rate of population increase will exceed the rate of aggregate income growth, i.e. the P curve is vertically higher than the Y curve. We know that whenever population is growing faster than income, per capita income must fall. The arrow pointing in the direction of A from the right, therefore, shows that per capita income must fall back to its very low level at y_1 for all points between y_1 and y_2. Similarily, to the left of point A incomes grow faster than population, causing the equilibrium per capita income level to rise to y_1.

According to Malthus and the neo-Malthusians, poor nations will never be able to rise much above their subsistence levels of per capita income unless they initiate 'preventive' checks (i.e. birth control) on their population growth. In the absence of such preventive checks, 'positive' checks (starvation, disease, wars) on population growth will inevitably provide the restraining force.

Completing our description of the 'population trap' model portrayed in Fig. 7.3, we see that point B is an 'unstable' equilibrium point. If per capita income can somehow jump rapidly from y_1 to y_2 (e.g. as a result of 'big push' investment and industrialization program) before Malthusian positive checks take their toll, it will continue to grow until the other stable equilibrium point C at per capita income level y_4 is reached. Point B is an unstable equilibrium point in the sense that any movement to the left or right will continue until either A or C is reached.

The Malthusian 'population trap' model provides a simple and in many ways appealing theory of the relationship between population growth and economic development. Unfortunately it is based on a number of simplistic assumptions and hypotheses that do not stand up to the test of empirical verification. We can criticize the population trap theory on two major grounds.

2. Criticisms of the model

First, and most important, the model (and, indeed, Malthus) assumes away or does not take into account the enormous impact of technological progress in offsetting the inhibiting forces of rapid population growth. As we discovered in Chapter 4, the history of modern economic growth has been most closely associated with rapid technological progress in the form of a continuous series of scientific, technological and social inventions and innovations. 'Increasing' rather than 'decreasing' returns to scale have been a distinguishing feature of the modern growth epoch. While Malthus was basically correct in assuming a limited supply of land, he did not and, in fairness could not at that time anticipate the manner in which technological progress could 'augment' the availability of land by raising its quality (i.e. productivity) even though its quantity might remain roughly the same.

In terms of the 'population trap' diagram, rapid and continuing technological progress can be represented by an upward shift of the income growth (total product) curve so that *at all levels of per capita income* it is vertically higher than the population growth curve. This is shown in Fig. 7.4. As a result, per capita income will grow steadily over time. All countries, therefore, have the potential of escaping the Malthusian population trap.

A second basic criticism of the trap model is its assumption that national rates of population increase are directly (positively) related to the level of national per capita income. At relatively low levels of per

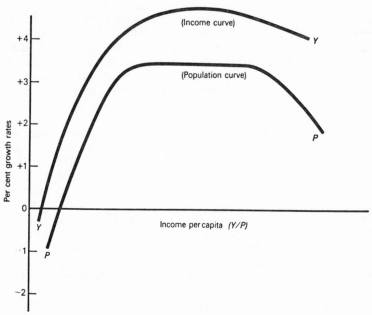

Fig 7.4
Technological (and social) progress
allows nations to avoid the
population trap

capita income, therefore, we should expect to find that population growth rates increase with increasing per capita incomes. However, as we discovered in the preceding chapter, there appears to be *no* clear correlation between population growth rates and levels of per capita income among Third World nations. As a result of modern medicine and public health programs, death rates have fallen rapidly and have become less dependent on the level of per capita income in most Third World nations. On the other hand, as we discovered in Fig. 6.2(a), birth rates seem to show no definable relationship with per capita income levels. Our conclusion, therefore, is that it is not so much the *aggregate* level of per capita income that matters for population growth but, rather, how that income is *distributed*. The social and economic institutions of a nation and its philosophy of development are probably greater determinants of population growth rates than are aggregate economic variables and simplistic models of macro-economic growth.

We can thus largely reject the Malthusian and Neo-Malthusian theories as applied to contemporary Third World nations on the grounds that:

1. they do not take adequate account of the role and impact of technological progress;
2. they are based on an hypothesis about a 'macro' relationship between population growth and levels of per capita income which does not stand up to empirical testing;
3. they focus on the *wrong* variable, per capita income, as the principal determinant of population growth rates. A much better and more valid approach to the question of population and development centers on the 'micro' economics of family size decision making in which individual, and not aggregate, levels of living become the principal determinant of a family's decision to have more or fewer children.

7.3 The micro-economic theory of fertility

In recent years economists have begun to look more closely at the **1. General considerations**
'micro'-economic determinants of family fertility in an attempt to
provide a better theoretical and empirical explanation of the observed
falling birth rates associated with Stage III of the demographic transition. In doing this, they have drawn upon the traditional 'neo-classical'
theory of household or consumer behavior for their basic analytical
model, and have utilized the principles of 'economy' and 'optimization' to explain family size decisions.

The conventional theory of consumer behavior assumes that an
individual with a given set of tastes or preferences for a range of goods
(i.e. a 'utility function') tries to maximize the satisfaction derived from
consuming these goods subject to his own income constraint and the
relative prices of all goods. In the application of this theory to fertility
analysis, children are considered as a special kind of consumption (and
in LDCs, investment) good so that fertility becomes a rational
economic response to the consumer's (family's) demand for children
relative to other goods. The usual income and substitution effects are
assumed to apply – that is, other factors held constant, the desired
number of children can be expected to vary directly with household
income (this direct relationship may not hold for poor societies; it
depends upon the strength of demand for children relative to other
consumer goods and to the sources of increased income, e.g. female
employment, see below), inversely with the price (cost) of children and
inversely with the strength of tastes for goods relative to children.
Mathematically, these relationships can be expressed as follows:

$$C_d = f(Y, P_c, P_x, t_x) \qquad x = 1, \ldots, n$$

where

C_d is the demand for surviving children (an important consideration in
   low income societies where infant mortality rates are high)

Y is the given level of household income

P_c is the 'net' price of children (i.e., the difference between anticipated
   'costs', mostly the 'opportunity cost' of a mother's time, and
   benefits', potential child income and old age support; see below)

P_x are the prices of all other goods, and

t_x are the tastes for goods relative to children.

Under normal (i.e. neo-classical) conditions we would expect that:

$\dfrac{\partial C_d}{\partial Y} > 0$; the higher the household income, the greater the demand for
   children (since the 'partial' derivative of C_d with respect to Y,
   $\partial C_d / \partial Y$, is *positive*),

$\dfrac{\partial C_d}{\partial P_c} < 0$; the higher the net price of children, the lower the quantity
   demanded (since the partial derivative of C_d with respect to
   P_c is *negative*),

$\dfrac{\partial C_d}{\partial P_x} > 0$; the higher the prices of all other goods relative to children,
   the greater the quantity of children demanded, and

$\dfrac{\partial C_d}{\partial t_x} < 0$; the greater the strength of tastes for goods relative to children,
   the fewer children demanded.

Figure 7.5 provides a simplified diagrammatic presentation of the economic theory of fertility. The number of desired (surviving) children, C_d, is measured along the horizontal axis and the total quantity of goods consumed by the parents, G_p, is measured on the vertical axis.

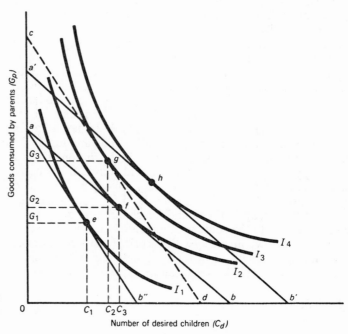

Fig 7.5
Microeconomic theory of fertility: An illustration

Household desires for children are expressed in terms of an indifference map representing the subjective degree of satisfaction derived by the parents for all possible combinations of commodities and children. Each individual indifference curve portrays a locus of commodity/children combinations that yield the same amount of satisfaction. Any point (or combination of goods and children) on a 'higher' indifference curve – that is, on a curve farther out from the origin – represents a higher level of satisfaction compared with any point on a lower indifference curve. But each indifference curve is a 'constant satisfaction' locus.

In Fig. 7.5 only four indifference curves, I_1 to I_4, are shown; in theory, an entire set of such curves filling the whole quadrant and covering all possible commodity/children combinations would exist. The household's ability to 'purchase' alternative combinations of goods and children is shown by the budget constraint line, *a–b*. Thus, all combinations on or below line *a–b* (i.e., within the triangular area *oab*) are financially attainable by the household on the basis of its perceived income prospects and the relative prices of children and goods, as represented by the slope of the *ab* budget constraint. The steeper the slope of the budget line, the higher the price of children relative to goods.

According to the demand-based theory of fertility, the household chooses from among all attainable combinations that one combination of goods and children which maximizes family satisfaction on the basis of its subjectively determined preferences. Diagrammatically, this optimal combination is represented by point f, the tangency point between the budget constraint, *ab,* and indifference curve, $I_2[2]$. C_3 children and G_2 goods will therefore be demanded.

A rise in family income, represented in Fig. 7.5 by the parallel outward shift of the budget line from *ab* to *a'b'*, enables the household to attain a higher level of satisfaction (point h on curve I_4) by consuming more of *both* commodities and children – that is, if children, like most commodities, are assumed to be 'normal' goods, an important 'if' in low-income countries where children are often demanded primarily as a source of future financial security (see below).

Similarly, an increase in the price (opportunity cost) of children relative to other goods will cause households to substitute commodities for children. Other factors (namely, income and tastes) being constant, a rise in the relative price of children causes the household utility maximizing consumption combination to occur on a lower indifference curve, as shown by the movement of the equilibrium point from f to e when the budget line rotates around point a to a–b''.

Note, finally, that if there is a simultaneous increase in household income and net child price as a result, say, of expanding female employment opportunities and/or a rise in wages coupled with a tax on children beyond a certain number per family, there will be *both* an outward shift and a downward rotation of the budget constraint line of Fig. 7.5 to, say, dashed line c–d. The result is a new utility maximizing combination that includes fewer children per family (point g compared with point f). In other words, higher levels of living for low-income families in combination with a relative increase in the price of children (whether brought about directly by fiscal measures or indirectly by expanded female employment opportunities) will *motivate* households to have fewer children while still improving their welfare. This is just one example of how the economic theory of fertility can shed light on the relationship between economic development and population growth as well as suggest possible lines of policy.

2. The demand for children in developing countries

As we have seen, the economic theory of fertility assumes that the household demand for children is determined by family preferences for a certain number of surviving (usually male) children (i.e. in regions of high mortality, parents may produce more children than they actually *desire* in the expectation that some will not survive), by the price or 'opportunity cost' of rearing these children and by levels of family income. Children, especially in poor societies, are seen partially as economic investment goods to the extent that there is an 'expected return' in the form of child labor and the provision of financial support for parents in old age when these children reach adulthood and earn a living. As Professor Kuznets has noted in a recent exhaustive empirical study,[3]

they (the LDCs) are prolific because under their economic and social conditions large proportions of the population see their economic and social interests in more children as a supply of family labor, as a pool for a genetic lottery, and as a matter of economic and social security in a wealthy organized, non-protecting society.

On the other hand, it is recognized that in many developing countries there is a strong intrinsic psychological and cultural determinant of family size so that the first two or three children should be viewed as 'consumer' goods for whom demand may not be very responsive to relative price changes in their parents' decision-making process.

The choice mechanism in the economic theory of fertility as applied to LDCs is assumed, therefore, to exist primarily with regard to the additional or marginal children who are considered as investments. In deciding whether or not to have *additional* children, parents are assumed to weigh economic benefits against costs, where the principal benefits are, as we have seen, the expected income from child labor, usually on the farm, and their financial support for elderly parents. Balanced against these benefits are the two principal elements of 'cost':

1. The 'opportunity cost' of the mother's time, i.e. the income she could earn if she were not at home caring for her children.
2. The cost (both opportunity and actual) of educating children, i.e. the financial 'trade-off' between having fewer 'high-quality', high-cost, educated children with high income-earning potentials versus more 'low-quality', low-cost, uneducated children with much lower earning prospects.

Using the same 'thought processes' as in the traditional theory of consumer behavior, the theory of family fertility as applied to LDCs concludes that when the 'price' or 'cost' of children rises as a result, say, of increased educational and employment opportunities for women, or a rise in school fees, or the establishment of minimum age child labor laws, or the provision of publically financed old age social security schemes and so on, parents will demand *fewer* 'additional' children substituting perhaps quality for quantity or a mother's employment income for her child-rearing activities. It follows that one way to induce families to desire fewer children is to raise the 'price' of child rearing, by say, providing greater educational opportunities and a wider range of higher paying jobs for young women.

3. Some empirical evidence Recent statistical studies in countries like Chile, the Philippines, Taiwan and Thailand have given a certain credence to the economic theory of fertility. For example, it has been found that high female employment opportunities outside the home and greater female and male school attendance especially at the primary and early years of secondary schooling were associated with lower levels of fertility[4]. As women become better educated, they tend to earn a larger share of household income and to produce fewer children. Moreover, these studies have confirmed the strong association between declines in child mortality and the subsequent decline in fertility. Assuming that households desire a *target* number of surviving children, increased incomes and levels of living can decrease child mortality and therefore increase the chances that the first born will survive. As a result, fewer births may be necessary to attain the same number of surviving children. This fact alone underlines the importance of improved public health and child nutrition programs in ultimately reducing Third World fertility levels.

Finally, while increased income may enable the family to support more children, the evidence seems to show that with higher incomes parents will tend to *substitute* child 'quality' for 'quantity' by investing in fewer, more educated children whose eventual earning capacity will be much higher. Additionally, it is argued that more income may also tend to lower fertility because the *status* effect of increased incomes raises the relative desire for material goods, especially among low income groups whose budget constraints previously precluded the purchase of these goods. In other words, additional children beyond a socially accepted or minimum desired number may be 'inferior goods' in low income-countries, that is, above some threshold subsistence level, higher incomes may induce families to desire fewer children.

All the above can be summarized by saying that *the effect of social and economic progress in lowering fertility in developing countries will be the greatest where the majority of the population and especially the very poor share in its benefits.* Specifically, birth rates among the very poor are likely to fall where there is:

4. The implications for 'development' and 'fertility'

(a) an increase in the education of women and a consequent change in their role and values;
(b) an increase in female non-agricultural wage employment opportunities which raises the price or 'cost' of their traditional child rearing activities;
(c) a rise in family income levels through the increased direct employment and earnings of husband and wife and/or through the redistribution of income and assets from rich to poor;
(d) a reduction in infant mortality through expanded public health programs and better nutritional status for both parent and child;
(e) the development of old age and other social security systems outside the extended family network to bridge the economic dependence of parents on their offspring.

In short, expanded efforts to make jobs, education and health more broadly available to poverty groups in Third World countries will not only contribute to their economic and psychic well-being (i.e. to their 'development'), but it also can contribute substantially to their *motivation* for smaller families (i.e. their 'freedom to choose') which is vital to reducing population growth rates. The provision of well-executed family planning programs can then give effect to these desires for smaller families by maximizing their realization in the shortest possible time.

7.4 Some policy approaches

In light of the above analysis and in terms of the broad goals and objectives discussed in Chapter 6, what kinds of economic and social policies might developing and developed country governments and international assistance agencies consider in order to bring about a reduction in the overall rate of world population growth? There are *three areas of policy* which can have important direct and indirect influences on the well-being of present and future world populations:

1. Those general and specific policies which developing country governments can initiate to influence and perhaps even 'control' their population growth and distribution.
2. Those general and specific policies which *developed country* governments can initiate in their own countries to lessen their disproportionate consumption of limited world resources and to promote a more equitable distribution of the benefits of global economic progress.
3. Those specific ways in which developed country governments and international assistance agencies can assist developing countries to

achieve their population policy objectives, whatever they may be, in shorter periods of time.

Let us deal with each of these in turn.

1. What developing countries can do As we have seen from both the cross-country data presented in Chapter 6 and the analytical and empirical content of the micro-economic theory of fertility, the principal variables influencing the demand for children at the family level are those which are most closely associated with the concept of 'development' as we have defined it in Part I of this book. Thus, certain development policies are particularly crucial in the transition from a high growth to a low growth population. These policies aim at eliminating absolute poverty, lessening income inequalities, expanding educational opportunities especially for women, providing increased job opportunities for both men and women, bringing the benefits of modern preventive medicine and public health programs, especially the provision of clean water and sanitation to the rural and urban poor, improving maternal and child health through more food, better diets, and improved nutrition so as to lower infant mortality, and finally, creating a more equitable provision of other social services to wider segments of the population. Again, it is not numbers *per se* nor parental irrationality which is at the root cause of the LDC 'population problem'. Rather, it is the pervasiveness of absolute poverty and low levels of living that provides the economic rationale for large families and burgeoning populations.

While such broad long-run development policies are essential to ultimate population stabilization, there are some specific policies that LDC governments might try to lower birth rates in the short run. Basically, governments can attempt to 'control' fertility in five ways:

1. They can try to persuade people to have smaller families through the *communications media* and the *educational process,* both formal (school system) and informal (adult education).

2. They can establish *family planning programs* to provide health and contraceptive services in order to encourage the desired behavior. Such publicly sponsored or officially supported programs now exist in some sixty Third World countries covering almost 87 per cent of LDC populations. Today only a few large countries such as Brazil, Burma, Ethiopia, and Peru do not have such publicly sponsored or officially endorsed family planning programs.

3. They can deliberately *manipulate economic incentives and disincentives* to have children, for example, through the elimination or reduction of maternity leaves and benefits, the reduction or elimination and/or the imposition of financial penalties for having children beyond a certain number, the establishment of old age social security provisions and minimum age child labor laws, the raising of school fees and the elimination of heavy public subsidies for secondary and higher education, and finally, the subsidization of smaller families through direct money payments. Singapore, India and Taiwan are all currently conducting social experiments to influence family size through alternative incentive/disincentive policies. For example, Singapore is assigning scarce public housing without giving preference to family size. It is also limiting paid maternity leave to a maximum of two children, scaling the delivery fee according to child numbers, and reducing income tax relief from five to three children. In India, a tea estate is at present experimenting with financial deposits into individual female worker savings accounts

during their periods of non-pregnancy. The deposits are scaled according to the number of children and the whole account can be cancelled if a woman bears too many children. These accumulated savings are then paid out when the woman reaches the age of 45, as a form of social security in the place of children. Finally, in Taiwan there is an experiment in a rural township in which the local government is depositing funds into bank accounts for young couples to cover the costs of educating their first two children. However, if the couple has a third child, part of this money is forfeited and it is all forfeited at the birth of the fourth child. The program is expressly designed to encourage families to have fewer, but more educated children. Early results indicate that both the India and Taiwan experiments seem to be achieving their goals. India currently also has a major vasectomy program under way in which men are given a direct cash payment, transistor radios or even free tickets to championship football matches if they agree to undergo 'voluntary' sterilization. However, the government of India has recently been seriously debating the question of forced sterilization for certain categories of families.

4. They can attempt to *redirect the distribution of their populations* away from the rapidly growing urban areas as a result of massive rural–urban internal migration by eliminating the current imbalance in economic and social opportunities in urban as compared to rural areas. As we shall see in Chapter 10, rural development programs are increasingly being emphasized in contemporary Third World development strategies, in part to stem the rising tide of rural–urban population movements and thus to promote a more geographically balanced distribution of the population.

5. Finally, governments can attempt directly *to 'coerce' people* into having smaller families through the power of state legislation and penalties. For obvious reasons, few governments would attempt to engage in such coercion, especially since it is not only morally repugnant and politically unacceptable, but also because it is almost always impossible to administer. The defeat of Mrs. Gandhi's government in the Indian elections of March 1977 was in part due to the popular backlash against the government's forced sterilization program.

2. What the developed nations can do in their own countries

When we view the problems of population in terms of a global perspective, as we should, the question of the relationship between population size and distribution and the depletion of many non-renewable resources in developed and underdeveloped countries assumes major importance. In a world where 6 per cent of the people in one country, the United States, account for 40 per cent of annual world resource use and where slightly over 30 per cent of the world's population accounts for 80 per cent of its annual resource utilization, then clearly we are not dealing only or even primarily with a problem of numbers. We must also be concerned with the impact of rising affluence and the very unequal world-wide distribution of incomes on the depletion of many non-renewable resources such as petroleum, certain basic metals and other raw materials essential for economic growth.

In terms of food consumption, basic grains like wheat, corn, rice, etc. are by far the most important source of man's *direct* food energy supply (52 per cent). Consumed *indirectly* (e.g. grain fed to livestock which are then consumed as beef, poultry, pork and lamb or indirectly as milk, cheese and eggs) they make up a significant share of the remainder. In resource terms, more than 70 per cent of the world's cropland goes into grain production. And yet, the average North American directly and indirectly consumes five times as much grain and the corresponding agricultural resources – land, fertilizer, water, etc. – as his counterpart in India, Nigeria or Colombia. With regard to energy, probably the second most essential resource to modern society, consumption of energy fuels (fossil-oil and coal, nuclear and hydro-electric) by the average American in 1976 was 25 times the average Brazilian, 60 times the average Indian, 191 times the average Nigerian, and 351 times the average Ethiopian consumption level! The use of this energy to power private automobiles, operate home and office air-conditioners and activate electric toothbrushes in the developed nations means that there is potentially that much less to, say, fertilize small family farms in the less developed nations. Alternatively, it means that poor families will have to pay more to obtain these valuable resource inputs.

Many other similar examples could be given of the gross inequalities in resource use. Perhaps more importantly, one could cite innumerable instances of the unnecessary and costly wastage of many scarce and non-renewable resources by the affluent developed nations. The point, therefore, is that *any world-wide program designed to engender a better balance between resources and people by limiting Third World population growth through social intervention and family planning must also include the responsibility of rich nations systematically to simplify their own consumption demands and life styles.* Only then will needed resources be freed which could be used by poor nations to generate the social and economic development essential to slower population growth.

For example, a 10 per cent reduction in beef consumption by North Americans (a reduction which on the whole would probably be healthy for them) would free many million tons of grain to feed the hungry in poor nations. At the very least, such a demand reduction would alleviate the upward pressure on world grain prices. More hopefully, massive food aid programs to the 'least developed' nations could then become more feasible. A similar reduction in energy consumption would greatly reduce current pressures on world petroleum supplies. This would make it easier for food-deficit nations in Asia and Africa to obtain more cheaply the necessary supplies of energy and fertilizer to expand their agricultural output. It is difficult and somewhat ironic for rich nations to preach moderation in family size to poor countries when they themselves refuse to moderate their enormously disproportionate and wasteful use of world food and energy resources. (Of course, there is the counter-argument that curtailing consumption in rich nations will have short-term harmful effects on poor nation economic growth as a result of an immediate decline in the latter's exports of raw materials. It is for this reason that a cutback in excessive rich country consumption needs to be accompanied by a large-scale increase in resource transfers to developing nations.)

In addition to simplifying life styles and consumption habits, one other very positive but unlikely internal policy which rich nations could adopt to mitigate current world population problems would be to liberalize the legal conditions for the international emigration of poor, unskilled workers and their families from Africa, Asia and Latin America to North America, Europe and Australia. The international migration of peasants from western and southern Europe to North America, Australia and New Zealand in the nineteenth and early twentieth centuries was a major factor in moderating the problems of underdevelopment and population pressure in European countries. No such 'safety valve' or outlet exists today for Third World countries. But, clearly, there are many underpopulated regions of the world and many labor-scarce societies which could benefit economically from international migration.

There are also a number of ways in which the governments of rich countries and multilateral donor agencies can assist the governments of developing countries to achieve their population policy objectives in shorter periods of time. The most important of these concerns the willingness of rich countries (including now the wealthy Arab oil states) to be of genuine assistance to poor countries in their development efforts. Such genuine support would consist not only of expanded public and private financial assistance but also of improved trade relations, more appropriate technological transfers, assistance in developing indigenous scientific research capacities, better international commodity pricing policies and a more equitable sharing of the world's scarce natural resources. (These and other areas of international economic relations between rich and poor countries will be examined in Parts III and IV.) **3. How developed countries can assist developing countries in their varied population programs**

There are two other activities more directly related to fertility moderation where rich country governments and international donor agencies can play an important assisting role. The first of these is the whole area of research into the technology of fertility control, the contraceptive pill, modern interuterine devices (IUDs), voluntary sterilization procedures, etc. Research has been going on in this area for a number of years, almost all of it financed by international donor organizations, private foundations and aid agencies of developed countries. Further efforts to improve the effectiveness of this contraceptive technology while minimizing the health risks need to be encouraged.

The second area includes financial assistance from developed countries for family planning programs, public education and national population policy research activities in the developing countries. This has been the traditional and principal area of developed country assistance in the field of population. Total resources devoted to these activities have risen dramatically from around $2 million in 1960 to almost $3,000 million by the mid 1970s. It is a moot point, however, whether such resources (especially those allocated to premature family planning programs) might not have been more effectively used to achieve their fertility goals had they instead been devoted directly to assisting LDCs to raise the levels of living of their poorest peoples. As we have seen, it is of little value to have sophisticated family planning programs where the people are not motivated to reduce family size.

7.5 Conflicts, 'trade-offs' and choices among alternative policies and competing objectives: some final observations

Our discussion of possible policy options for curtailing population growth in Third World countries and freeing scarce world resources for development activities on the part of rich countries was intended principally to illustrate the range of alternatives which might be followed in light of stated objectives. However, diverse policies need to be weighed against alternative and often conflicting goals. For example, two common population objectives are the lowering of fertility in order to slow down overall population growth and the reduction of rural–urban migration to avoid excessive urban concentrations and to improve the spatial distribution of a given population. It turns out however, as we shall show in Chapter 9, that one of the principal strategies for lowering fertility – i.e., more education especially for women – happens to be an important factor stimulating the movement of people from rural to urban areas. Thus, while more education might decrease family size, it might also increase rural–urban migration and urban population congestion with its attendant social, physical and psychological problems. In such a situation a simultaneous policy to develop rural areas would be needed. This would provide expanded rural job opportunities in addition to improved health, cultural and social amenities so that more educated men and women will remain in rural areas adding to total production and having fewer children as their levels of living increase.

In addition to analyzing possible goal conflicts and trade-offs, policy-makers in developing countries, even more so than in developed nations, are faced with severe budgetary constraints. They, therefore, have to choose among alternative policies in terms of some social benefit/cost framework. Would an extra rupee, bhat, or shilling of expenditure be more effective in lowering fertility if it went towards family planning programs, nutritional supplementation projects, educational expansion, employment creation or direct incentive and disincentive schemes? Unfortunately, the problem does not end here for there are many *other* goals and objectives of development which may take precedence over fertility reduction. Choices always have to be made not only on the basis of fundamental economic concepts such as the principles of 'economy' and 'optimization', but also in terms of explicit 'value judgements' about what is desirable and what are the priorities among alternative goals.

While it might be an important objective in certain densely populated Third World nations, we believe that direct attempts to reduce population growth rates, for example, through massive expenditures on sophisticated family planning programs, need not be a primary development objective. A decrease in population growth is more likely to be the natural consequence of policies directly designed to raise levels of living among the poverty-stricken masses of Asia, Africa and Latin America. True 'development' will normally motivate people to have fewer children. Well-conceived and well-executed family planning and other direct population policy programs can *then* play an important and useful role. But we suggest that their widespread success can *only* occur within the context of a successful poverty-focused strategy of national and regional development. Not only does this seem to be the consensus opinion among development economists, but it also represents the *unanimous* position of the more than 100 nations that participated in the First World Population Conference in Bucharest when they asserted that 'the basis for an effective solution of population problems is, above all, socio-economic transformation'[5].

Notes

1. A geometric progression is simply a doubling or some other multiple of each previous number, like 1, 2, 4, 8, 16, 32, 64, 128, 256, 512, 1,024 . . . etc. Like compound interest, geometric progressions have a way of attaining large numbers very rapidly.
2. At point f and only at point f will the marginal utility per last unit of expenditure on goods and children be equal – the condition for utility maximization in the traditional theory of consumer behavior. See, among other texts, P. W. Bell and M. P. Todaro, *Economic Theory*, Oxford U.P., Nairobi (1969), 41–55.
3. Simon Kuznets, 'Fertility differentials between less developed and developed regions: components and implications', *Discussion Paper No. 217*, Economic Growth Center, Yale University, November 1974, 87–8.
4. See T. Paul Schultz, '*Fertility Determinants: A Theory, Evidence and Application to Policy Evaluation*', Rand Corporation, Santa Monica, California, Jan. 1974.
5. *World Population Plan of Action*, Bucharest, August 1974, paragraph A.I.

Concepts for review

family planning programs
demographic transition
'Macro' population-development relationship
marginal utility
micro-economic theory of fertility
'population trap'
'opportunity cost' of a woman's time
economic incentives and disincentives for fertility reduction
private versus social benefits and costs of fertility reduction
education and fertility relationship
'investment' in children

Questions for discussion

1. Describe briefly the theory of the demographic transition. At what stage in this transition do most developing countries seem to be? Explain.
2. How does the so-called 'household' or micro-economics of fertility relate to the theory of consumer choice? Do you think that economic incentives and disincentives do influence family size decisions? Explain your answer giving some specific examples of such incentives and disincentives.
3. 'The world population problem is not just a matter of expanding numbers but also one of rising affluence and limited resources. It is as much a problem caused by developed nations as it is one deriving from Third World countries.' Comment on this statement.
4. Outline and comment briefly on the various policy options available to Third World governments in their attempt to modify or limit the rate of population growth.

Further readings

1. On the general relationship between population growth and economic development broadly defined see: (*a*) Simon Kuznets, 'Population trends and modern economic growth: notes toward an historical perspective', *Discussion Paper No. 191*, Yale Economic Growth Center, Nov, 1973; (*b*) Simon Kuznets, 'Fertility differentials between less developed and developed regions: components and implications', *Discussion Paper No. 217*, Yale Economic Growth Center, Nov. 1974; (*c*) Derek T. Healey, 'Population Growth and Real Output Growth in Developing Countries: A Survey and Analysis', University of Adelaide (mimeo.) (1974); (*d*) William Rich, *Smaller Families Through Social and Economic Progress, Monograph No. 7*, Overseas Development Council, Jan. 1973; (*e*) Léon Tabah (ed.), *Population Growth and Economic Development in the Third World*, Ordina, Belgium (1976).
2. On the new 'micro-economics' of fertility, see: (*a*) Harvey Leibenstein, 'An interpretation of the economic theory of fertility: promising path of blind alley?', *Journal of Economic Literature*, XII, No. 2 (1974); (*b*) T. Paul Schultz, 'Fertility determinants: a theory, evidence, and an application to policy evaluation', *Rand Corporation Monograph R–106*, Jan. 1974; (*c*) Richard A. Easterlin, 'An economic framework for fertility analysis', *Studies in Family Planning*, The Population Council, March 1975; (*d*) Marc Nerlove, 'Household and economy: toward a new theory of population and economic growth', *Journal of Political Economy*, **82**, No. 2, Pt 2 (1974); (*e*) Susan H. Cochrane 'A review of some micro-economic models of fertility', *Population Studies*, **29**, No. 3 (1975).
3. Finally, an excellent comprehensive survey of population policies in developing countries can be found in Timothy King *et al.*, *Population Policies and Economic Development*, Johns Hopkins U.P., Baltimore and London (1974).

Chapter 8

Unemployment: Issues, dimensions and analyses

The cities are filling up and urban unemployment steadily grows . . . the 'marginal men', the wretched strugglers for survival on the fringes of farm and city, may already number more than half a billion, by 1990 two billion. Can we imagine any human order surviving with so gross a mass of misery piling up at its base?
Robert McNamara, President of World Bank

Introduction: the employment problem: some basic issues

Historically, the economic development of Western Europe and North America has often been described in terms of the continuous transfer of economic activity and people from rural to urban areas, both within and between countries. As urban industries expanded, new employment opportunities were created while labor-saving technological progress in agriculture reduced rural manpower needs. The combination of these two phenomena made it possible for Western nations to undergo an orderly and effective rural to urban transfer of their human resources.

On the basis of this shared experience, many economists concluded that economic development in the Third World, too, necessitated a concerted effort to promote rapid urban industrial growth. They tended to view cities, therefore, as the 'growth centres' and focal points of an expanding economy. Unfortunately, this strategy of rapid industrialization has, in most instances, failed to bring about the desired results predicted by historical experience.

Today, many developing countries are plagued by an historically unique combination of massive rural to urban population movements, stagnating agricultural productivity and growing urban and rural unemployment and underemployment. Substantial unemployment in LDC economies is probably one of the most striking symptoms of their inadequate development. In a wide spectrum of poor countries, open unemployment especially in urban areas now affects 10 to 20 per cent of their labor forces. The incidence of unemployment is much higher among the young and increasingly more educated in the 15- to 24-year age bracket. Even larger fractions of *both* urban and rural labor forces are 'underemployed' (see Table 8.1). They neither have the complementary resources (if they are working full-time) nor the opportunities (if they work only part-time) for increasing their very low incomes to levels comparable with those in the modern manufacturing, commerce and service sectors. It is because of its relationship to the problem of Third World poverty, therefore, that the employment issue occupies such a central place in the study of underdevelopment.

But the dimensions of the employment problem go beyond the simple shortage of work opportunities or the underutilization and low productivity of those who do work long hours. It also includes the growing divergence between inflated attitudes and job expectations, especially among the educated youth, and the actual jobs available in urban and rural areas. In particular, the growing aversion to manual and agricultural work fostered in urban and 'white-collar' oriented educational systems creates severe strains for poor societies attempting to accelerate national development.

The employment problem in Third World countries, therefore, has a number of facets that make it both historically unique and thus subject to a variety of unconventional economic analyses. There are three major reasons for this:

1. Unemployment and underemployment regularly and chronically affect much larger proportions of LDC labor forces in a variety of different ways than did open unemployment in the industrialized countries, even during the worst years of the Great Depression.
2. The causes of Third World employment problems are much more complex than those in the developed countries. They, therefore, require a variety of policy approaches that go far beyond simple 'Keynesian' type policies to expand aggregate demand.
3. It is important to bear in mind that whatever the dimensions and the causes of unemployment in Third World nations, the human circumstances of abject poverty and low levels of living associated with this lack of productive work are such as have rarely been experienced in the now developed countries. There is an urgent need, therefore, for concerted policy action by *both* the less developed and the more developed nations. As we see, the LDCs need to readjust domestic policies to include employment creation as a major social and economic objective, while the developed countries need to review and readjust their traditional economic policies vis-à-vis the Third World, especially in the areas of trade, aid and technology transfer.

Since it is impossible to do justice to the many complexities and nuances of employment problems in diverse Third World countries, our focus in this and the next chapter will be on two major questions that face almost all LDCs:

1. Why has rapid industrial growth failed to generate substantial new employment opportunities in many developing countries?
2. Why do great numbers of people continue to migrate from diverse rural areas into the crowded and congested cities in spite of high and rising levels of urban unemployment?

In investigating these two issues, we show why the urbanization process in less developed countries has differed so markedly from the historical experience of the now developed countries, and why growing unemployment and underemployment are not, as many economists in the 1950s and 1960s believed, merely self-correcting 'transitory' phenomena in the early stages of economic growth. Rather, they will be seen as symptoms of more far-reaching economic and social disturbances both within LDCs and in their relationship with developed countries.

Our purpose in this chapter is to examine the dimensions as well as the analytics of the employment problem in developing nations. The chapter begins with a quantitative profile of employment and unemployment, urbanization, and labor force growth past, present, and prospective in a large sample of developing countries. We then discuss the nature and dimensions of the employment problem and the linkages between unemployment, poverty and income distribution. Unemployment in its simplest context is due to a relatively slow growth of labor *demand* in both the modern, industrial sector and in traditional agriculture combined with a rapidly growing labor *supply,* especially as a result of accelerated population growth and high levels of rural to urban migration. Demand factors are examined in this chapter in the form of both traditional and contemporary models of employment determination, while the supply factors are analyzed in Chapter 9 where we look at the economics of rural–urban migration. Chapter 9 then concludes with an analysis of alternative policy approaches to cope with diverse LDC employment problems.

8.1 Dimensions of Third World unemployment: evidence and concepts

First let us look at some of the quantitative and qualitative dimensions of the unemployment problem in developing nations, especially with regard to the growth of urban unemployment.

1. Employment and unemployment: trends and projections During the 1970s, increased interest in the widespread and growing problem of Third World unemployment and underemployment among individual development economists, national planning authorities and international assistance agencies has resulted in a much broader and more precise picture of the quantitative dimensions of the problem than was available only a decade ago. In particular, the International Labour Organization (ILO) launched its ambitious 'World Employment Programme' at the beginning of the 1970s with a series of detailed case studies of the employment problem in such diverse countries as Colombia, Kenya, Sri Lanka, Iran and the Philippines. These and similar studies in other countries have clearly documented the seriousness of the existing problem and the likelihood that it will worsen over the coming years.

Table 8.1 provides a summary picture of employment and unemployment trends since 1960 with projections to the year 1990 for all developing countries as well as for Africa, Asia and Latin America. We see first that unemployment grew from approximately 36·5 million in 1960 to over 54 million workers in 1973, an increase of 46 per cent. This averages out to an annual rate of increase of 3 per cent which is higher than the annual rate of employment growth during this same period. Thus, unemployment has been growing faster than employment in the developing world as a whole.

When we also consider that the 'underemployed' in 1973 comprised approximately an additional 250 million people, then the combined unemployment and underemployment rate reaches a staggering 29 per cent for all developing countries with Africa experiencing a labor underutilization rate of 38 per cent. Moreover, with rapid labor force growth (see below), the marginal unemployment rate (that is, the proportion of new labor force entrants unable to find regular jobs) is likely to be even higher than the average figures shown in Table 8.1. Although the extent of labor underutilization is lower in Asia and Latin America, the quantitative and qualitative dimensions of the problem are just as serious as in Africa. For example, even though Asia may have a lower rate of unemployment than Africa, the absolute numbers involved are many times larger (34·4 million in 1973 compared with 13·9 million for Africa).

Projections to 1990 indicate that the rate of Third World unemployment will rise steadily and that the total numbers unemployed may reach 65 million by 1980 and almost 90 million by 1990. Adding projections for the underemployed could give a figure as high as 500 million workers who are either unemployed, employed part time or whose productivity is very low. Although these figures are only rough estimates, they do strikingly underline the seriousness of the problem. In particular, the growth of urban unemployment and underemployment has been especially alarming and a cause of growing concern to most Third World nations. We turn now to an examination of this issue.

In Chapter 6, we documented the extraordinary increase in world and especially Third World, population growth over the past few decades.

2. Urban population growth

Indicator	1960	1970	1973	1980	1990
All developing countries*					
Employment (000)†	507,416	617,244	658,000	773,110	991,600
Unemployment (000)	36,466	48,798	54,130	65,620	88,693
Unemployment rate (%)	6·7	7·4	7·6	7·8	8·2
Combined unemployment and underemployment					
rate(%)‡	25	27	29		
Africa	31	39	38		
Asia	24	26	28		
Latin America	18	20	25		
All Africa					
Employment (000)†	100,412	119,633	127,490	149,390	191,180
Unemployment (000)	8,416	12,831	13,890	15,973	21,105
Unemployment rate (%)	7·7	9·6	9·8	9·8	9·9
All Asia*					
Employment (000)†	340,211	413,991	441,330	516,800	660,300
Unemployment (000)	24,792	31,440	34,420	43,029	59,485
Unemployment rate (%)	6·8	7·1	7·2	7·7	8·3
All Latin America					
Employment (000)†	66,793	83,620	89,180	106,920	140,120
Unemployment (000)	3,258	4,527	5,820	6,618	8,103
Unemployment (%)	4·7	5·1	6·1	5·8	5·5

Table 8.1 Employment and unemployment in developing countries, 1960–1990

Source: Yves Sabolo, 'Employment and unemployment, 1960–90', *International Labour Review,* **112**, No. 6 (1975), Table 3 and Appendix.
  * excluding China.
  † Including underemployment.
  ‡ Not calculated for 1980 and 1990.

By the year 2000 world population could range from 6 to 9 billion people. But, whatever the figure eventually reached, one thing is clear: *nowhere will population growth be more dramatic than in the major cities of the developing world.* In the second half of this century the number of people living in cities and towns throughout the world as a whole will double. In developing countries, the urban population will more than quadruple as rural peasants flood into the cities in search of elusive, and often non-existent modern-sector jobs.

Current rates of urban population growth range from under 1 per cent per annum in two of the world's largest cities, New York and London, to over 6 to 7 per cent in most African countries, with Asian and Latin American cities growing at annual rates of 4 to 6 per cent. As Table 8.2. dramatically illustrates, the world's twelve fastest growing cities are all located in developing nations. Each is expected to double in size over the 15-year period from 1970 to 1985. Some like Bandung, Lagos and Karachi are projected to increase even more substantially in this short time period than have any cities in history over a similar time span. The major cause of this urban growth will *not* be national population increase but the immigration of rural people. Almost 60 per cent of LDC urban growth is due to rural–urban migration. How Third World governments plan to cope economically, politically and socially with such phenomenal urban population growth is crucial to the success or failure of their long-run development strategies.

3. Labor force: present and projected   The number of people searching for work in a less developed country depends primarily on the size and age composition of its population. Among the numerous processes relating trends in overall population growth to the growth of indigenous labor forces, two are of particular interest. First, whatever the overall magnitude of the population growth rate, its fertility and mortality components have a *separate* significance. A 3 per cent (or 30 per 1,000) natural growth rate when crude birth and death rates are 50 and 20 has different labor force implications from a birth and death rate combination of 40 and 10. This is because the *age structure* of the population will be different for a high birth and death rate economy than for a low birth and death rate one, even though the natural rate of increase is the same for both. Since birth rates obviously affect only the numbers of newly born while death rates affect (although unevenly) all age groups, a high birth and death rate economy will have a greater percentage of the total population in the dependent age group (i.e. 1–15 year) than will a low birth–death rate economy. The rapid reductions in death rates recently experienced by most LDCs, therefore, have expanded the size of their present labor forces, while continuous high birth rates create high present dependency ratios and rapidly expanding future labor forces.

Second, the impact of fertility decline on labor force size and age structures operates only very long lags, even when the decline is rapid. The reason is the phenomenon of population 'momentum' described in Chapter 7. For example, a sudden halving of LDC fertility rates by 1980 would reduce the male labor force by only 13 per cent by the end of the century, a reduction from about 1·27 billion to 1·11 billion workers. This is certainly not a trivial reduction and its long-run impact would clearly be substantial. Nevertheless, the essential fact remains that over the next 15 years those who will enter the labor force have *already been born* while the size of the labor force over the next quarter century is determined by current fertility and mortality rates.

Present labor force projections suggest annual increases of the order of 2·1 per cent for all less developed regions during the present decade and approximately 2·4 per cent and 2·6 to 2·8 per cent for the 1980s and 1990s respectively (see Table 8.3). But within the Third World, Latin American countries are likely to experience the greatest rates of labor force growth over the next 25 years while Asian and African countries follow close behind. In terms of actual numbers, however, which demonstrates the prospective magnitude of the LDC employment problem more dramatically than percentage rates of growth, reasonable projections for the year 2000 indicate that there will be

City	1970 population in millions	1985 projected population in millions	Overall growth rate (%)
1. Bandung, Indonesia	1·2	4·1	242
2. Lagos, Nigeria	1·4	4·0	186
3. Karachi, Pakistan	3·5	9·2	163
4. Bogota, Colombia	2·6	6·4	146
5. Baghdad, Iraq	2·0	4·9	145
6. Bangkok, Thailand	3·0	7·1	137
7. Tehran, Iran	3·4	7·9	132
8. Seoul, South Korea	4·6	10·3	124
9. Lima, Peru	2·8	6·2	121
10. Sao Paulo, Brazil	7·8	16·8	115
11. Mexico City, Mexico	8·4	17·9	113
12. Bombay, India	5·8	12·1	109

Table 8.2
The world's fastest growing cities

	Labor force growth rate (%)		
	1970–80	1980–90	1990–2000
Developed countries	1·1	0·9	0·9
Less developed countries	2·1	2·2	2·2
Regions			
South Asia	2·3	2·5	2·5
East Asia	1·6	1·6	1·5
Africa	2·2	2·5	2·7
Latin America	2·7	2·9	2·9

Table 8.3
Annual rates of labor force growth, 1970–2000

Source: International Labour Office, *Bulletin of Labour Statistics: Labour Force and World Population Growth, 1974 Special Edition,* Geneva (1974), Table 8, p. 69.

	Labor force in millions (and per cent of total)			
	1970	1980	1990	2000
Developed countries	488 (32·5)	542 (30·4)	593 (26·6)	649 (25·1)
Less developed countries	1,012 (67·5)	1,239 (69·6)	1,547 (72·4)	1,933 (74·9)
Regions				
South Asia	429 (42·3)	537 (43·2)	691 (44·5)	886 (45·6)
East Asia	376 (37·1)	440 (35·4)	519 (33·4)	602 (31·0)
Africa	132 (13·1)	165 (13·3)	212 (13·7)	277 (14·3)
Latin America	74 (7·3)	97 (7·8)	129 (8·3)	172 (8·9)

Table 8.4
Labor force projections, 1970–2000

Source: International Labour Office, op. cit., Table 3A, p. 64.

over 920 million more job seekers than in 1970 with nearly 50 per cent of these concentrated in South Asia and 25 per cent in East Asia (Table 8.4).

4. The magnitude and age-structure of urban unemployment
Given rapid rates of urban labor force growth in the range of 4 to 7 per cent per annum and the relatively slower growth of urban employment opportunities (averaging about $2 \cdot 5$ per cent, see below), the problem of urban unemployment has attained very serious and, in some cases, crisis proportions in many developing nations. Current rates of open unemployment (people without any regular or part-time job) in the cities of Africa, Asia and Latin America average about 10 per cent of the urban labor force, or approximately 34 million people. But the problem is considerably more serious for those between the ages of 15 and 24, many of whom have had significant amounts of schooling. Table 8.5 shows that in almost all LDC urban centres, rates of unemployment in this age bracket are almost double the recorded rates of unemployment for the urban labor force as a whole.

Rates of 'open' urban unemployment, however, only reveal the visible aspects of the employment problem in Third World nations, the tip of an enormous iceberg. The actual underutilization of labor takes many other forms including various manifestations of under-employment and hidden unemployment. Although data on the various forms of underemployment in LDC cities are scarce, recent studies of countries like Colombia, Kenya, Sri Lanka and the Philippines indicate that as much as 30 per cent or over 100 million people in Third World urban areas may be counted as being heavily underutilized.

5. Labor underutilization: some definitional distinctions
To get a full understanding of the significance of the urban employment problem, we must also take into account, in addition to the openly unemployed, those larger numbers of workers who may be visibly active, but in an economic sense are grossly underutilized. As Professor Edgar O. Edwards has correctly pointed out in his comprehensive survey of employment problems in developing countries[1]:

In addition to the numbers of people unemployed, many of whom may receive minimal incomes through the extended family system, it is also necessary to consider the dimensions of (1) time (many of those employed would like to work more hours per day, per week or per year), (2) intensity of work (which brings in considerations of health and nutrition), and (3) productivity (lack of which can often be attributed to inadequate, complementary resources with which to work). Even these are only the most obvious dimensions of effective work, and factors such as motivation, attitudes, and cultural inhibitions (as against women, for example) must also be considered.

Edwards, therefore, distinguishes among the following five forms of underutilization of labor[2]:

1. *Open unemployment:* both voluntary (people who exclude from consideration some jobs for which they could qualify, implying some means of support other than employment) and involuntary.
2. *Underemployment:* those working less (daily, weekly, or seasonally) than they would like to work.
3. *The visibly active but underutilized:* those who would not normally be classified as either unemployed or underemployed by the above definitions, but who in fact have found alternative means of 'marking time', including,

	15–24	15 and over	
Ghana, 1960, large towns	21·9	11·6	
Bogota, Colombia, 1968	23·1	13·6	
Buenos Aires, Argentina, 1965	6·3	4·2	
Chile, 1968 urban areas	12·0	6·0	
Caracas, 1966	37·7	18·8	
Panama, 1963–4, urban areas	17·9	10·4	
Uruguay, 1963, mainly urban	18·5	11·8	
Venezuela, 1969, urban areas	14·8	7·9	
Bangkok, Thailand, 1966	7·7	3·4	
Ceylon, 1968, urban areas	39·0	15·0	
India, 1961–2, urban areas	8·0	3·2	
Korea, 1966	23·6	12·6	
Malaya, 1965, urban areas	21·0	9·8	
Philippines, 1965, urban areas	20·6	11·6	**Table 8.5**
Singapore, 1966	15·7	9·2	Rates of urban unemployment by
Tehran City, Iran, 1966	9·4	4·6	age

Source: David Turnham and Ian Jaeger, *The Employment Problem in Less Developed Countries*, OECD, June 1970.

(a) *Disguised underemployment.* Many people seem occupied on farms or employed in government on a full-time basis even though the services they render may actually require much less than full time. Social pressures on private industry may result also in substantial amounts of disguised underemployment. If available work is openly shared among those employed, the disguise disappears and underemployment becomes explicit.

(b) *Hidden unemployment.* Those who are engaged in 'second choice' nonemployment activities, perhaps notably education and household chores, primarily because job opportunities are not available (i) at the levels of education already attained, or (ii) for women, given social mores. Thus, educational institutions and households become 'employers of last resort'. Moreover, many of those enrolled for further education may be among the less able as indicated by their inability to compete successfully for jobs before pursuing further education.

(c) *The prematurely retired.* This phenomenon is especially evident, and apparently growing, in the civil service. In many countries, retirement ages are falling at the same time that longevity is increasing, primarily as a means of creating promotion opportunities for some of the large numbers pressing up from below.

4. *The impaired:* those who may work full time but whose intensity of effort is seriously impaired through malnutrition or lack of common preventive medicine.

5. *The unproductive:* those who can provide the human resources necessary for productive work but who struggle long hours with inadequate complementary resources to make their inputs yield even the essentials of life.

Although all of the above manifestations of the underutilization of labor in LDCs are highly interrelated, and each in its own way is of considerable significance, we shall for convenience limit our discussion throughout the remainder of this chapter to the specific problem of unemployment and underemployment.

There is a close relationship between high levels of unemployment and underemployment, widespread poverty and unequal distributions of income. For the most part, those without regular employment or with

6. Linkages between unemployment, poverty and income distribution

only scattered part-time employment are also among the very poor. Those with regular paid employment in the public and private sector are typically among the middle- to upper-income groups. But it would be wrong to assume that everyone who does not have a job is necessarily poor, while those who work full time are relatively well off. This is because there may be unemployed urban workers who are 'voluntarily' unemployed in the sense that they are searching for a specific type of job, perhaps because of high expectations based on their presumed educational or skill qualifications. They refuse to accept jobs which they feel to be inferior and are able to do this because they have outside sources of financial support (e.g. relatives, friends, or local money lenders). Such people are unemployed by definition, but they may not be poor.

Similarly, there are many individuals who may work full time in terms of hours per day but may, nevertheless, earn very little income. Many self-employed workers in the so-called urban 'informal' sector (e.g. traders, hawkers, petty service providers, workers in repair shops, etc.) may be so classified. Such people are by definition fully employed, but often they are still very poor.

In spite of the above reservations about a too literal linkage between unemployment and poverty, it still remains true that one of the major mechanisms for reducing poverty and inequality in less developed nations is the provision of adequate paying, productive employment opportunities for the very poor. As we have seen in Chapter 5, the creation of more employment opportunities should not be regarded as the sole solution to the poverty problem. More far reaching economic and social measures are needed. But the provision of more work and the wider sharing of the work that is available would certainly go a long way towards solving the problem. Employment, therefore, must be an essential ingredient in any poverty-focused development strategy.

7. The lag between industrial output and employment growth: the misplaced emphasis of the 1950s and 1960s

During the 1950s and early 1960s one of the major doctrines of the development literature was that successful economic development could be realized only through the twin forces of substantial capital accumulation and rapid industrial growth. By concentrating their efforts on the development of a modern industrial sector to serve the domestic market and to facilitate the absorption of 'redundant' or 'surplus' rural laborers in the urban economy, less developed countries, it was argued, could proceed most rapidly toward the achievement of considerable economic self-sufficiency. An inevitable consequence of this has been the extraordinary growth of urban centers resulting from an accelerated influx of rural, unskilled workers in search of scarce urban jobs.

Unfortunately, optimistic predictions regarding the ability of the modern industrial sector to absorb these migrants have not been realized. In fact, the failure of modern urban industries to generate a significant number of employment opportunities is one of the most obvious failures of the development process over the past two decades. For example, Table 8.6 shows that for many developing countries the growth of manufacturing output has exceeded the growth of employment by a factor of three or four to one.

Too much emphasis, however, cannot be placed on the expansion of the modern industrial sector to solve the urban unemployment problem. The reason is that in most Third World countries it employs only 10 to 20 per cent of the total labor force. For example, if the manufac-

Region/countries	Manufacturing annual output growth (1963–9)	Manufacturing employment growth (1963–9)
Africa		
Ethiopia	12·8	6·4
Kenya	6·4	4·3
Nigeria	14·1	5·3
Egypt (UAR)	11·2	0·7
Asia		
India	5·9	5·3
Pakistan	12·3	2·6
Philippines	6·1	4·8
Thailand	10·7	−12·0
Latin America		
Brazil	6·5	1·1
Colombia	5·9	2·8
Costa Rica	8·9	2·8
Dominican Republic	1·7	−3·3
Ecuador	11·4	6·0
Panama	12·9	7·4

Table 8.6
Industrialization and employment in developing countries

Source: David Morawetz, 'Employment implications of industrialization in developing countries', *Economic Journal,* 84, Sept. 1974.

turing sector employs, say, 20 per cent of the country's labor force, it would need to increase employment by 15 per cent per year just to absorb the increase in a total work force growing at 3 per cent per year (i.e. $0·2 \times 0·15 = 0·03$). None of the countries in Table 8.6 have been able to achieve such a high rate of employment growth in their manufacturing sectors. In fact, such industrial employment growth is virtually impossible to achieve in any economy.

Again the contrast between the present urban situation in LDCs and the historical situation in the now more developed countries is worth noting. In nineteenth-century Western Europe, the pace of industrialization was much faster than that of urbanization. The percentage of the working force in industry was always higher than that of the population living in cities. For example, in France in 1856 only 10 per cent of the total population lived in cities of 20,000 inhabitants and over, while 29 per cent of the working force was engaged in manufacturing. In Germany in 1870 the comparative figures were 12 per cent urbanization and 30 per cent engaged in manufacturing. Since the labor forces of both France and Germany were growing at no more than 1 per cent per annum over this period, the manufacturing sector needed to grow at a rate of only 3·3 per cent to absorb the *total* yearly labor force increases.

By contrast, the pace of industrialization in less developed countries has been much slower than that of urbanization. In almost all Third World countries the percentage of populations living in cities greatly *exceeds* the proportion engaged in manufacturing. For example, in 1970 Brazil had over 40 per cent of its population living in urban areas of 20,000 or more while only 18 per cent were engaged in manufacturing. Colombia had an urbanization rate of almost 48 per cent with only 12·5 per cent engaged in manufacturing. Given these very different demographic and structural economic circumstances, it would be totally unrealistic to rely solely on accelerated modern sector industrial growth to solve the problems of growing urban unemployment, even if such growth could have a substantial labor-using bias, which it usually doesn't.

8.2 Economic models of employment determination

Over the years economists have formulated a number of economic models of employment determination. The majority of these models have focused on or been derived from the social, economic and institutional circumstances of the developed nations. They have, nevertheless, often been uncritically and inappropriately applied to the unique circumstances of employment problems in developing countries. In recent years, however, more relevant and realistic models of employment and development have often led to policy conclusions diametrically opposite to those of the traditional theories.

In this section we review four major economic models of employment determination. The first two, the 'classical' and 'Keynesian' models, form the substance of the traditional theory of employment. Neither has much relevance for understanding the particular employment problems of developing countries. The third and fourth models, like the Keynesian model, grow out of the more recent 'neo-classical' tradition of economics. The first, the output/employment macro-model, focuses on the relationship between capital accumulation, industrial output growth and employment generation, while the second, the price-incentive micro-model, considers the impact of distorted factor prices on resource (especially labor) utilization. Both the output/employment and price incentive models, again like the Keynesian model, concentrate exclusively on the demand side of the employment equation: that is, they focus on policies to increase labor demand. A fifth model or group of models, which we designate as 'two-sector labor transfer' or rural–urban migration models, focus on the determinants of both demand and supply. These will be the subject of Chapter 9. Even more than the neo-classical models (although still in the same tradition) the labor transfer migration models seek to take purposeful account of the institutional and economic realities of Third World nations.

We conclude this chapter, therefore, by examining the first four of the above five models of employment determination and then devote some considerable space in the next chapter to the fifth.

1. The traditional competitive free market model

A. Flexible wages and full employment

In traditional 'Western' economics characterized by consumer sovereignty, individual utility and profit maximization, perfect competition and economic efficiency with very many 'atomistic' producers and consumers, none of whom is large enough to influence prices or wages, the level of employment and the 'wage rate' are determined simultaneously with all other prices and factor uses in the economy by the forces of demand and supply. Producers demand more workers as long as the value of the marginal product produced by an additional worker (i.e. his physical marginal product multiplied by the market price of the product he produces) exceeds his cost (i.e. the going wage rate). Since the law of diminishing marginal product is assumed to apply and since product prices are fixed by the market, the value of labor's marginal product and thus the demand curve for labor will be negatively sloped as shown in Fig. 8.1. More workers will be hired only at successively lower wage rates.

On the supply side, individuals are assumed to operate on the principle of utility maximization. They will therefore divide their time between work and leisure in accordance with the relative marginal utility of each. A rise in wage rates is equivalent to an increase in the price (or opportunity cost) of leisure. When the price of any item rises, in general its quantity demanded will decrease and other items will be substituted. It follows that more labor services will be supplied at successively higher wage rates, so that the aggregate supply curve of labor will be positively sloped. (In the next chapter we will analyze an alternative labor supply curve claimed to be more representative of labor markets in developing countries.) This supply curve is also depicted in Fig. 8.1.

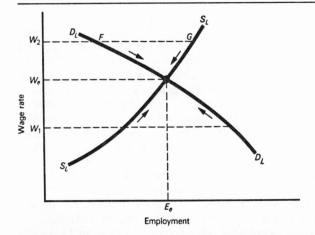

Fig 8.1
Wage and employment determination by demand and supply: The traditional approach

We see from Fig. 8.1 that only at one point, the 'equilibrium' wage rate W_e, will the amount of work that individuals are *willing* to supply just equal the amount that employers will demand. At any higher wage like W_2 the supply of labour will exceed its demand and competitive pressures among workers will force the wage rate down to W_e. At any lower price like W_1, the labor quantity demanded will exceed the quantity supplied and competition among producers will drive the wage rate up until it reaches its equilibrium level at W_e. At W_e total employment will be E_e on the horizontal axis. *By definition, this will be full employment* – i.e. at the equilibrium wage and only at this wage will all those willing to work be able to obtain jobs so that there is no 'involuntary' unemployment. In other words, in the idealized flexible wages world of traditional economics, there can never be unemployment!

ha, ha!,

B. Limitations of the competitive model for developing countries

The traditional competitive model offers little insight into the realities of wage and employment determination of Third World countries. Wage rates are typically not flexible downward since they are largely determined by 'institutional' forces including trade union pressures, legislated government salary scales and multinational corporation hiring practices. There are many more laborers seeking employment at the going wage than there are jobs available. Involuntary unemployment (and, especially, underemployment) is pervasive. For example, if the wage were institutionally set at W_2 in Fig. 8.1, there would be an *excess* supply of labor equal to line *FG*. But, as we show below and in later chapters, the concept of the 'shadow price' for a factor of production such as labor, even though it may differ from actual factor prices, still has important analytical meaning for development policy. The classical model, therefore, is useful to the extent that it gives comparative baselines for examining price distortions that can cause unemployment in developing countries[3].

2. The Keynesian model

A. Insufficient demand and the 'employment gap' – the simple model

The 1930s ushered in a Great Depression in the Western World, the like of which had not been experienced by the developed countries during their entire modern growth era. Widespread and seemingly chronic unemployment and low levels of national output shook economists out of the complacency of their idealized classical world. Clearly, there was something very inadequate about the traditional theory of wage and employment determination.

Two major theoretical responses emerged to explain what apparently was going on. At the 'micro' level, the theory of 'imperfect competition' associated with Professors Joan Robinson of England and Edward H. Chamberlain of the United States, was developed to explain the nature and implications of markets which were dominated by one (monopoly) or a few sellers of products (oligopoly) or by one or more purchasers of resources (monopsony and oligopsony). In each of these cases of imperfect competition, it was demonstrated that resources (including labor) would be underutilized and total production would be less than what would occur if product and resource markets were characterized by perfect competition. Such 'market failures' often provided the theoretical justification and economic rationale for increased government intervention in the economic system to offset the negative output and employment effects of monopoly and other forms of concentrated selling power. In Chapter 15 we will discuss in more detail the market failure argument, among others, as a basis for 'development planning' in Third World nations.

The other and by far the more influential theory which emerged in response to the harsh economic realities of the Great Depression was 'macro' oriented. This is the famous Keynesian 'general' theory of income and employment determination. What may have appeared to be a 'general theory' of employment at the time, however, has now been recognized, especially in the less developed countries, as a 'special' theory of unemployment for the developed countries[4]. Let us briefly review the simple Keynesian model to see why this is so.

Basically, Keynesian theory explains the determination of national output and employment in terms of the level of 'aggregate demand' in relation to an economy's 'potential output' – what it could produce if resources were fully and efficiently utilized given the prevailing technology. In its simplest form aggregate demand for a 'closed' economy consists of three fundamental components: (1) the total demand for all goods and services by private consumers (*C* for consumption); (2) the total demand for investment goods by private industry (*I* for investment) and (3) the demand for goods and services, both consumption and investment, by the government (*G* for government). The level of National Income or GNP (*Y*) is then defined simply as:

National income (*Y*) = Consumption (*C*) + Investment (*I*) + Government expenditure (*G*)

or, simply $Y = C + I + G$ (1)

For an 'open economy' with foreign trade, one would need to add expressions for Exports (*X*) and Imports (*M*), the difference constituting a 'surplus' balance of trade (i.e. $X - M > O$) and thus an additional positive component of aggregate demand, or a 'deficit' trade balance ($X - M < 0$) which would lower national income. Thus, for an open economy, equation (1) would be written as:

$$Y = C + I + G + (X - M) \tag{2}$$

Finally, since governments need to collect taxes (T) to finance some or all of their expenditures, the 'net' impact of government activity is $G - T$ (if G is greater than T, the government is operating at a 'deficit'; T greater than G would imply a 'surplus'). Equation (2), therefore, becomes:

$$Y = C + I + (G - T) + (X - M) \tag{3}$$

For illustrative purposes, however, let's use only equation (1). National income and/or expenditure (Y) is determined by the level of aggregate demand (i.e. $C + I + G$). This level of national output is assumed to be uniquely associated with a level of national employment (N) as expressed, for example, in a national production function, $Y = f(N, \bar{K}, t)$ where $f'_N > 0$ and $f''_N < 0$. For any given technology (t) and stock of fixed land and capital ($\bar{K}$), total national output (real GNP) will be uniquely and positively associated with different levels of employment – i.e. higher levels of national output (Y) are associated with higher levels of employment (N). But since for any given society total employment is limited by the size of the active labor force, there will be some unique level of *maximum national output* which can be achieved only at full employment. This full employment level of national income, sometimes called 'potential output', may be denoted Y_F.

The main thrust of Keynesian theory and the factor which distinguished it from the classical model, was the contention that there was nothing inherent in a market economy which would *guarantee* that the *actual* level of national income (Y) would be exactly equal to the potential, full-employment level (Y_F). Everything depends on the level of total aggregate demand ($C + I + G$). This is shown in Fig. 8.2. In diagram (a) the combined sums of C plus I plus G yields a level of national output (Y_1) that is *less* than the potential full employment output level (Y_F). As a result, the level of unemployment will be given by the 'gap' between N_F and N_1 in the aggregate production function of diagram (b). It follows, therefore, that if consumption and investment are already determined by the existing level of national income, the only way that aggregate demand can be increased is for the government to increase its level of total expenditure from G to G'. Government 'deficit' expenditure (i.e. $G - T > 0$) thus becomes necessary to fill in the 'gap' between actual and potential GNP so as to increase the level of national output and consequently eliminate unemployment.

The Keynesian prescription for reducing or eradicating unemployment is therefore quite simple: increase aggregate total demand through direct increases in government expenditure or by government policies that indirectly encourage more private investment (e.g. low interest rates on business loans, tax allowances, investment subsidies, etc.). As long as there is unemployment and excess capacity in the economy, the supply of goods and services will respond automatically to this higher demand. A new equilibrium will be established with more income and higher levels of employment.

Without enumerating all the shortcomings of the Keynesian model as applied to the economies of Third World nations, we must draw attention to two major deficiencies. First, since the model is derived

B. Limitations of the model in the development context

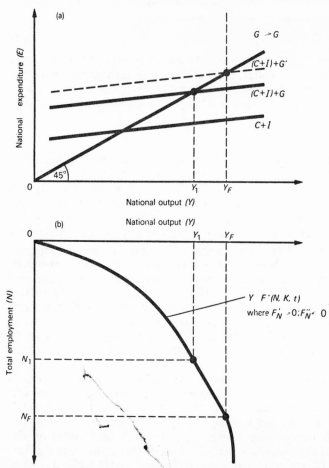

Fig 8.2
The simple Keynesian model of
employment determination

from advanced country economies, it is implicitly based on the institutional and structural assumption of well functioning product, factor and money markets that characterize these countries. Specifically, it is based on the assumption, correct for developed nations but not for LDCs, that firms and farms can respond quickly and effectively to increases in the demand for their products by rapidly expanding output and employment. But in most Third World countries, the major bottleneck to higher output and employment levels typically is not insufficient demand but structural and institutional constraints on the supply side. Shortages of capital, raw materials, intermediate products, skilled and managerial human resources, combined with poorly functioning and inefficiently organized commodity and loan markets, poor transport and communications, shortages of foreign exchange and import-dominated consumption patterns among the rich – all of these, and many other structural and institutional factors, militate against the simple notion that expanded government and private demand will be effective measures to solve employment (and poverty) problems in most Third World countries. In fact, under conditions of severe constraints on the supply side (i.e. where the aggregate supply curve of national output is price 'inelastic'), expanding aggregate demand through deficit-financed government expenditure may merely result in higher prices and chronic inflation. This was the common experience of many Latin American countries during the 1950s and 1960s. The worldwide inflation of the 1970s can also be attributed largely to supply constraints especially in the area of raw materials, energy resources and food products (see Chapter 17).

The second major limitation of the Keynesian model for most LDCs relates also to conditions of supply in developing countries, this time to the supply of *labor* to the urban industrial sector. As we show in Chapter 9 when we discuss the economics of rural–urban migration, the creation of additional modern sector urban jobs through increased aggregate demand is likely to attract many more additional migrants from rural areas. Since urban wages are typically much higher than average rural incomes, every urban job created may induce three or four new job seekers to migrate from the countryside. The net result may be that the creation of additional urban jobs through traditional Keynesian demand-oriented policies designed to reduce unemployment may in fact cause urban unemployment to rise! Moreover, since many of the rural migrants were productive farmers or low-paid farm workers, *the overall level of national employment and output may be reduced by Keynesian policies designed to increase employment and output!*

We may conclude that for many reasons, but especially because of structural and institutional supply constraints and the phenomenon of induced rural–urban migration, the Keynesian macro-model of employment determination has limited analytical relevance for understanding and dealing with employment problems in developing nations.

3. Output and employment growth: conflict or congruence?

A. Growth models and employment levels: the conflict argument

A natural extension of the Keynesian model which dominated many theories of development in the 1950s and 1960s focused on policies to increase the levels of national output rapidly through accelerated capital formation. Since the 'static' Keynesian model associated levels of employment uniquely with levels of GNP, it followed that by maximizing the rate of growth of GNP, Third World countries could also maximize their rate of labor absorption. The principal theoretical tool used to describe the growth process was the simple Harrod–Domar model described in Chapter 3. Although many sophisticated variants of this model appeared later, the basic idea remained the same. Economic growth is explained as the combined result of the rate of saving and the resultant physical capital accumulation on the one hand, and the capital/output ratio (i.e. the physical productivity of new investment) on the other. For a given aggregate capital/output ratio, therefore, the rate of national output and employment growth could be maximized by maximizing the rate of saving and investment. A natural and inevitable outgrowth of this neo-Keynesian view was the emphasis on generating domestic savings and foreign exchange to make possible heavy capital investments in the growing urban industrial sector. The 'big push' for rapid industrialization thus became the code-word for development and growth.

But as we saw in Table 8.5, in spite of relatively impressive rates of industrial output growth in many less developed countries, the rate of employment growth has lagged significantly behind. In a number of cases, it has even stagnated. Why has rapid industrial output growth failed to generate correspondingly rapid rates of employment growth?

Basically, the reason is due to the growth in labor productivity. By definition, the rate of growth in output less the rate of growth in labor productivity approximately equals the rate of growth of employment, that is,

$$\frac{dQ}{Q} - \frac{d(Q/N)}{Q/N} = \frac{dN}{N} \ .$$

It follows that if output is growing at 8 per cent per year while employment is expanding by only 3 per cent, the difference is due to the rise in labor productivity. The original Harrod–Domar model did not specifically incorporate technological change although later modifications did. It was a 'fixed coefficient' model, i.e. it assumed a fixed relationship between changes in output levels and changes in the capital stock. This constant capital/output ratio was then paralleled in early versions of the model by a constant output/labor ratio (i.e. a fixed labor coefficient). It follows from this constant labor productivity assumption that a 10 per cent increase in national output (GNP) will always be accompanied by a 10 per cent increase in employment. But, if labor productivity is rising so that fewer workers are required to produce any given level of total output, a 10 per cent output growth may only result in say a 3 per cent increase in employment.

The phenomenon of rising labor productivity associated with higher capital/labor ratios can be explained better (at least, 'theoretically' better) with the aid of a variable proportions neo-classical growth model like the one described in Appendix 5.1 (Ch. 5). Recall that this model of savings, capital accumulation and economic development – the latter term defined simply as maximum output growth – purports to demonstrate that higher capital/labor ratios (i.e. more capital-intensive production methods) will generate larger profit shares, higher savings rates and thus higher rates of growth. The 'optimal' savings rate – that is, the one which leads to maximum output growth – can only be generated by relatively capital intensive methods of production. Maximum output and maximum employment growth are, therefore, seen as 'conflicting' objectives.

B. Growth and employment: the congruence argument

In general, increases in labor productivity are desirable. But what is really desirable are increases in 'total' factor productivity: output per unit of *all* resources. The productivity of labor can increase for a variety of reasons; some good and some not so good. Improved education, better training and better management are all desirable forms of human resource growth. But increases in labor productivity as a result of the substitution of capital for labor in production processes or as a result of the importation of sophisticated and expensive labor-saving machinery and equipment (e.g. tractors, power tools, fully-automated textile machinery, heavy construction equipment, etc.) may be less satisfactory in heavily populated nations. Not only can such capital accumulation waste valuable domestic financial resources and foreign exchange, it can also curtail the growth of new employment opportunities. Moreover, the importation of inappropriate and expensive labor-saving capital equipment may, in fact, *reduce* total factor productivity and thereby *increase* average costs of production even though it increases labor productivity. In other words, the average total costs of production may rise even though average labor costs fall as a result of the underutilized productive capacity that often ensues when expensive mechanical equipment designed for large-scale production in developed countries is imported into less developed countries where the local market is too small for the efficient utilization of this sophisticated equipment.

Our conclusion, therefore, is that typical Harrod–Domar and neo-classical type models of capital accumulation and economic growth, and the kinds of economic policies which they imply, can and often do lead to rapid output growth but with lagging employment creation. If the overriding development objective is to maximize the rate of GNP growth, these approaches may be the right ones. But if it is equally or more important to create jobs, then different policies (e.g. focusing on the promotion of labor-intensive industries, such as small-scale agriculture and manufacturing) may be better.

Moreover, it is far from self-evident that higher levels of employment must necessarily be achieved *at the expense of* output growth. Just as the conventional wisdom of the 1950s and 1960s, which assumed that income growth and more equitable distributions of that income were mutually exclusive objectives, has recently been widely challenged, so too many economists are now convinced that an employment-oriented (and therefore, indirectly, a poverty-oriented) development strategy is likely also to be one which *accelerates* rather than retards overall economic progress[5]. This is especially true with regard to the growth and development of the rural and small-scale urban sectors. More employment means more income for the poor, which in turn implies a greater demand for locally produced basic consumption goods. Since these products tend to be more labor-intensive than many of those produced by large-scale industry, both domestic and foreign, it follows that more jobs and higher incomes can become self-reinforcing phenomena. They ultimately lead to higher growth rates of both national output *and* aggregate employment. But in order to achieve this dual objective, a complementary policy of removing factor–price distortions and promoting labor-intensive technologies of production may be required. This leads us to the fourth model of employment determination.

4. Appropriate technology and employment generation: the price incentive model

We briefly discussed the question of factor price distortions and their impact on poverty and employment in Chapter 5 and at other points in earlier chapters. However, since the 'neo-classical price incentive' school of thought has occupied such a prominent place in the debate about employment problems in developing countries, it is important to recall it here.

A. Choice of techniques: an illustration

The basic proposition of the price incentive model is quite simple and in the best tradition of the neo-classical theory of the firm. Following the principle of economy, producers (firms and farms) are assumed to face a given set of relative factor prices (e.g. of capital and labor) and to utilize that combination of capital and labor which minimizes the cost of producing a desired level of output. They are further assumed to be capable of producing that output with a variety of technological production processes, ranging from highly labor-intensive to highly capital-intensive methods. Thus, if the price of capital is very expensive relative to the price of labor, a relatively labor-intensive process will be chosen. On the other hand, if labor is relatively expensive, our economizing firm or farm will utilize a more capital-intensive method of production – i.e. it will economize on the use of the expensive factor which in this case is labor.

The conventional economics of technical choice are portrayed in Fig. 8.3. Assume that the firm, farm, industry or economy in question has only two techniques of production from which to choose: technique or process $0A$ which requires larger inputs of (homogeneous)

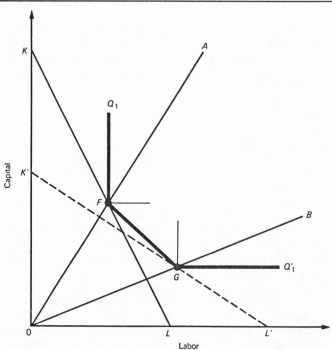

Fig 8.3
Choice of techniques: The price
incentive model

capital relative to (homogeneous) labor, and technique or process $0B$
which is relatively labor-intensive. Points F and G represent *unit*
output levels for each process and the line $Q_1FGQ'_1$ connecting F and
G is, therefore, a unit-output isoquant. (Note that in the traditional
neo-classical model, an infinite number of such techniques or processes are assumed so that the isoquant takes on its typical convex curvature, as for example in Fig. 4.5.)

According to this theory, optimum (least cost) capital–labor combinations (i.e. efficient or 'appropriate' technologies) are determined by
relative factor prices. Assuming for the moment that market prices of
capital and labor reflect their true scarcity or 'shadow' values, and that
the desired output level is Q_1 in Fig. 8.3, if capital is cheap relative to
labor (price line KL), production will occur at point F using capital-
intensive process $0A$. Alternatively, if the market prices of labor and
capital are such that labor is the relatively cheap (abundant) factor
(dashed line $K'L'$), optimal production will occur at point G with the
labor-intensive technique, $0B$, chosen. It follows that for any technique of production currently in use, a fall in the relative price of labor,
ceteris paribus, will lead to a substitution of labor for capital in an
optimal production strategy. (Note that if capital intensive process $0A$
'dominates' labor-intensive process $0B$ – that is, if technology $0A$
requires less labor *and* less capital than $0B$ *for all levels of output* – then
for any factor price ratio, the capital-intensive technique will be chosen. See Section C below for further discussion.)

B. Factor–price distortions   Given that most Third World countries are endowed with abundant
and appropriate technology supplies of labor but possess very little capital, either financial or
physical, one would naturally expect production methods to be rela-
tively labor-intensive. But, in fact, one often finds production techniques in *both* agriculture and industry to be heavily mechanized and

capital-intensive. Large tractors and combines dot the rural landscape of Asia, Africa and Latin America while people watch idly by. Gleaming new factories with the most modern and sophisticated automated machinery and equipment are a common feature of urban industries while idle workers congregate outside the factory gates. Surely, this phenomenon could not be the result of a lesser degree of economic rationality on the part of Third World farmers and manufacturers.

The explanation, according to the price incentive school, is simple. Because of a variety of structural, institutional and political factors, the actual 'market' price of labor is higher and that of capital lower than each of their true scarcity or 'shadow' values would dictate. In Fig. 8.3 the 'shadow' price ratio would be given by dashed line $K'L'$ whereas the actual (distorted) market price ratio is shown by line KL. Market wage structures are relatively high because of trade-union pressure, politically inspired minimum wage laws, an increasing range of employee fringe benefits and the high wage policies of multinational corporations. In former colonial nations high wage structures are often relics of expatriate remuneration scales based on European levels of living and 'hardship' premiums. On the other hand, the price of (scarce) capital is kept artificially low by a combination of liberal capital depreciation allowances, low interest rates, low or negative effective rates of protection (see Ch. 13), on capital good imports, tax rebates, overvalued exchange rates (see also Ch. 13), etc.

The net result of these 'distorted' factor prices is the encouragement of 'inappropriate' capital-intensive methods of production in both agriculture and manufacturing. Note that from the 'private' cost-minimizing viewpoint of individual firms and farms, the choice of a capital-intensive technique is correct. They are only rationally responding to the existing structure of price signals in the market for factors of production. However, from the viewpoint of society as a whole, the 'social' cost of underutilized capital and, especially, labor can be very substantial. Government policies designed to 'get the prices right' – that is, to remove factor–price distortions – would contribute not only to more employment but also to a better overall utilization of scarce capital resources through the adoption of more 'appropriate' technologies of production.

The actual employment impact of removing factor price distortions will depend, however, on the degree to which labor can be substituted for capital in the production processes of various Third World industries. Economists refer to this as the 'elasticity of substitution' and define it roughly as the ratio of the percentage change in the proportion of labor used relative to capital (i.e. the labor–capital or L/K ratio) compared to a given percentage change in the price of capital relative to labor (i.e. P_k/P_L). Algebraically, the elasticity of substitution can be defined as:

C. The possibilities of labor–capital substitution

$$\eta_{LK} = -\ \mathrm{d}\left(\frac{L}{K}\right)\Big/\frac{L}{K} \div \left(\mathrm{d}\left(\frac{P_K}{P_L}\right)\Big/\frac{P_K}{P_L}\right)$$

For example, if the relative price of capital rises by one per cent in the manufacturing sector and the labor/capital ratio rises as a result by, say, $1\cdot5$ per cent, the elasticity of substitution in the manufacturing industry will be equal to $1\cdot5$. If P_k/P_L falls by say 10 per cent while L/K

falls by only 6 per cent, then the elasticity of substitution for that industry would be 0·6. Relatively high elasticities of substitution (e.g. ratios greater than say 0·7) are indicative that factor price adjustments can have a substantial impact on levels and combinations of factor utilization. In such cases, factor price modifications may be an important means of generating more employment opportunities.

In general, most empirical studies of the elasticity of substitution for manufacturing industries in less developed countries reveal coefficients in the range of 0·5 to 1·0[7]. These results indicate that a relative reduction in wages (either directly or by holding wages constant while letting the price of capital rise) of say 10 per cent will lead to a 5 to 10 per cent increase in employment. But, given the fact that the organized wage and manufacturing sector in most LDCs employs only a small proportion of the total labor force, the *total* impact of even a 10 per cent increase in industrial employment will not be sufficient to *solve* the employment problem. Nevertheless, it can make a contribution to the ultimate solution. Policies to eliminate factor price distortions, therefore, do have an important role to play in any overall employment-oriented development strategy.

Notes

1. Edgar O. Edwards, *Employment in Developing Countries: Report on a Ford Foundation Study,* Columbia U.P., New York (1974), 10.
2. Ibid., pp. 10–11.
3. There are many who would also argue that the flexible wages model provides a useful depiction of LDC labor market interactions in small-scale industry (the so-called urban 'informal' sector) and agriculture. While it is true that wages are more flexible and competitively determined in urban and rural traditional industry, the classical concept of full employment is hardly adequate for these purposes.
4. See, for example, Dudley Seers, 'The limitations of the special cost', *Bulletin of the Oxford Institute of Economics and Statistics,* May 1965.
5. For one of the most well-known arguments that output growth and employment creation are congruent rather than conflicting development objectives, see P. Streeten and F. Stewart, 'Conflicts between output and employment objectives in developing countries', *Oxford Economic Papers,* July 1971, 145–68.
6. This argument as applied to LDCs was first expounded in R. S. Eckaus's seminal article, 'The factor proportions problem in underdeveloped areas', *American Economic Review,* Sept. 1955.
7. For a useful summary of evidence on this issue, see David Morawetz, 'Employment implications of industrialization in developing countries', *Economic Journal,* Sept. 1974.

Concepts for review

complementary resources	output-employment 'lag'
urbanization	'classical' model
labor-force	'equilibrium' wage rate
underutilization of labor	flexible wages
open unemployment	'shadow' price
underemployment	Keynesian employment model
disguised underemployment	aggregate demand
hidden unemployment	full employment
voluntary unemployment	'potential' output
'informal' sector	deficit expenditure
industrialization	'fixed' input coefficients
employment 'gap'	'Big Push' theory of

'total' factor
  productivity
small-scale industry
'neo-classical' price
  incentive model

development
elasticity of (factor)
  substitution
appropriate technology

1. Discuss the nature of the 'employment problem' in Third World countries. Include in your discussion a review of the various manifestations of the underutilization of labor.
2. Why should we be so concerned with unemployment and underemployment? Why is it a serious development problem?
3. Compare and contrast the contemporary urbanization process in Third World countries with the historical experience of Western Europe and North America. What are the major differences and how did they arise?
4. What is the relationship, if any, between unemployment (and underemployment) and the problems of poverty and inequality?
5. What are the principal economic reasons for the widespread failure of rapid LDC industrial growth to generate equally rapid employment growth? Is such a large 'output-employment lag' an 'inevitable' result of the process of modern industrial growth? Explain your answer.
6. The Keynesian model of employment determination seems to offer some simple policy prescriptions for generating full employment which, by and large, have proven successful over the past 25 years in the industrially developed countries. What are the principal limitations of utilizing this same approach for solving Third World employment problems? Is it possible that Keynesian policy prescriptions could actually *worsen* the problem of urban unemployment? Explain the meaning behind your answer.

1. The literature on Third World employment problems has grown to voluminous proportions over the past few years. Out of many excellent surveys, the following are perhaps the best: (*a*) Edgar O. Edwards (ed.), *Employment in Developing Nations,* Columbia U.P., New York (1974);   (*b*) David Turnham and Ian Jaeger, *The Employment Problem in Less Developed Countries,* OECD, Paris, June 1970;   (*c*) Richard Jolly, *et al.* (eds), *Third World Employment: Problems and Strategy,* Penquin Modern Economics Readings, Middlesex, England (1973);   (*d*) International Labour Office, *Employment in Africa: Some Critical Issues,* Geneva (1974);   (*e*) Paul Bairoch, *Urban Unemployment in Developing Countries,* ILO, Geneva (1973).
2. For comparative and comprehensive 'country' studies of Colombia, Kenya, Sri Lanka and the Philippines, see the various ILO expert mission reports available from the International Labour Office in Geneva and its various UN distributional outlets in Africa, Asia and Latin America.
3. On the question of technology and employment, see especially: (*a*) Frances Stewart, 'Technology and employment in LDCs', in Edwards, *op. cit.,* pp. 83–132;   (*b*) Amartya Sen, *Employment, Technology and Development,* Oxford U.P., London (1975).

Chapter 9	# Rural – urban migration: Theory and policy

We are firmly persuaded that the most fundamental and promising attack on employment problems in developing countries is in efforts to redress the present urban bias in development strategies.
Edgar O. Edwards, Report on Employment in Developing Countries

Introduction

In this chapter we focus on one of the most perplexing dilemmas of the development experience. This is the phenomenon of massive and historically unprecedented movements of people from the rural countrysides to the burgeoning cities of Africa, Asia and Latin America. Two major theoretical approaches to the problem of rural urban labor transfer will be discussed in the first part of the chapter. We conclude by examining a range of alternative public policies designed to curtail the excessive flow of rural to urban migration and to deal with the pervasive urban unemployment problems that continue to plague the vast majority of Third World countries.

9.1 Migration and development

Only a few years ago, rural–urban migration was viewed favorably in the economic development literature. Internal migration was thought to be a natural process in which surplus labor was gradually withdrawn from the rural sector to provide needed manpower for urban industrial growth. The process was deemed socially beneficial since human resources were being shifted from locations where their social marginal products were often assumed to be zero to places where this marginal product was not only positive but also rapidly growing as a result of capital accumulation and technological progress. As Richard Jolly, Director of the Institute of Development Studies at the University of Sussex, has noted, 'Far from being concerned with measures to stem the flow, the major interest of these economists (i.e. those who stressed the importance of labor transfer) was with policies that would *release* labor to *increase* the flow. Indeed, one of the reasons given for trying to increase productivity in the agricultural sector was to release *sufficient* labor for urban industrialization. How irrelevant most of this concern looks today![1]'

In contrast to this viewpoint, it is now abundantly clear from recent LDC experience that rates of rural–urban migration continue to exceed rates of urban job creation and to surpass greatly the capacity of both industry and urban social services effectively to absorb this labor. No longer is migration viewed by economists as a beneficent process necessary to solve problems of growing urban labor demand. On the contrary, migration today must be seen as the major contributing factor to the ubiquitous phenomenon of urban surplus labor and a force which continues to exacerbate already serious urban unemployment problems caused by growing economic and structural imbalances between urban and rural areas.

Migration exacerbates these rural–urban structural imbalances in two direct ways. First, on the supply side, internal migration disproportionately increases the growth rate of urban job seekers relative to urban population growth, which itself is at historically unprecedented levels, because of the high proportions of well-educated young people who dominate the migrant stream. Their presence tends to swell the growth of urban labor supply while depleting the rural countryside of valuable human capital. Second, on the demand side, most urban job creation is more difficult and costly to accomplish than rural employment creation because of the need for substantial complementary resource inputs for most jobs in the industrial sector. Moreover, the pressures of rising urban wages and compulsory employee fringe benefits in combination with the unavailability of 'appropriate' more labor-intensive production technologies means that a rising share of modern sector output growth is accounted for by increases in labor productivity. Together this rapid supply increase and lagging demand growth tend to convert a short-run problem of manpower imbalances into a long-run situation of chronic and rising urban surplus labor.

But the impact of migration on the development process is much more pervasive than its obvious exacerbation of urban unemployment and underemployment. In fact, the significance of the migration phenomenon in most developing countries is not necessarily in the process itself or even in its impact on the sectoral allocation of human resources. It is in the context of its implications for economic growth in general and for the 'character' of that growth, particularly its distributional manifestations, that migration research has assumed growing importance in recent years.

We must recognize at the outset, therefore, that migration in excess of job opportunities is both a symptom of and contributing factor to Third World underdevelopment. Understanding the causes, determinants and consequences of internal and international migration is thus central to a better understanding of the nature and character of the development process and for formulating appropriate policies to influence the nature and character of this process in socially desirable ways. A simple yet crucial step in underlining the centrality of the migration phenomenon is to recognize that *any economic and social policy that affects rural and urban real incomes will directly and/or indirectly influence the migration process. This process in turn will itself tend to alter the pattern of sectoral and geographic economic activity, income distribution and even population growth.* Since all economic policies have direct and indirect effects on the level and growth of *either* urban or rural incomes or of *both,* they *all* will have a tendency to influence the nature and magnitude of the migration stream. Although some policies may have a more direct and immediate impact (e.g. wages and income policies, and employment promotion programs, etc.), there are many others which, though less obvious, may in the long run be no less important. Included among these policies, for example, would be land tenure arrangements, commodity pricing, credit allocation, taxation, export promotion, import substitution, commercial and exchange rate policies, the geographic distribution of social services, the nature of public investment programs, attitudes towards private foreign investors, the organization of population and family planning programs, the structure, content and orientation of the educational system, the functioning of labor markets, and the nature of public policies towards international technological transfer and the location of new industries. There is thus a clear need to recognize the central importance of internal and, for many countries, even international migration and to integrate the two-way relationship between migration and population distribution on the one hand and economic variables on the other into a more comprehensive framework designed to improve development policy formulation.

In addition, we need to understand better not only why people move and what factors are most important in their decision-making process but also what are the *consequences* of migration for rural and urban economic and social development. If all development policies affect and are affected by migration, which are the most significant and why? What are the policy options and trade-offs among different and sometimes competing objectives (e.g., curtailing internal migration and expanding educational opportunities in rural areas)? Part of our task in this chapter will be to seek answers to these and other questions relating to migration, unemployment and development. But first let us examine one of the most well-known theories of development dealing with the sectoral allocation of labor.

9.2 The Lewis–Fei–Ranis theory of development

1. The basic model   The first and most well-known model of development which at least implicitly considered the process of rural–urban labor transfer was that developed by Sir W. Arthur Lewis and later formalized and extended by John Fei and Gustav Ranis[2]. The Lewis–Fei–Ranis (L–F–R) model became the received 'general' theory of the development process in 'labor surplus' Third World nations during most of the late 1950s and 1960s. In the L–F–R model, the economy consists of two sectors: (*a*) a traditional, *rural subsistence sector* characterized by zero or very low productivity 'surplus' labor and (*b*) a high productivity modern *urban industrial sector* into which labor from the subsistence sector is gradually transferred. The primary focus of the model is both on the process of labor transfer and on the growth of employment in the modern sector. Both labor transfer and urban employment growth are brought about by output expansion in the modern sector. The speed with which they occur is given by the rate of industrial capital accumulation in the modern sector. Such investment is made possible

by the excess of modern sector profits over wages on the assumption that 'capitalists' reinvest all of their profits. Finally, the level of wages in the urban industrial sector is assumed to be constant and determined as a fixed premium over a constant subsistence level of wages in the traditional agricultural sector (Lewis assumed that urban wages would have to be at least 30 per cent higher than average rural income to induce workers to migrate from their home areas). However, at the constant urban wage, the supply of rural labor was considered to be perfectly elastic.

The following provides a simple illustration of the Lewis–Fei–Ranis model. The process of modern sector growth is depicted in Fig. 9.1. On the vertical axis we have the real wage and the marginal product of labor (assumed to be equalized in the competitive modern sector) and on the horizontal axis the quantity of labor.

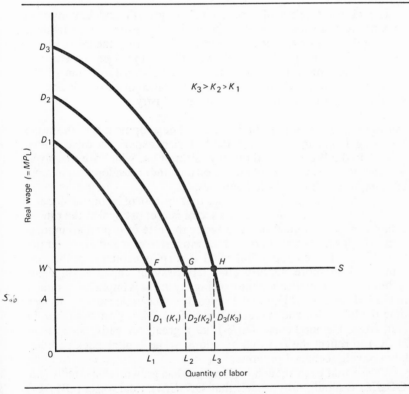

$K_3 > K_2 > K_1$

Fig 9.1
The Lewis model of growth and employment in a dual labor surplus economy

OA represents the average level of real subsistence income in the traditional rural sector. OW, therefore, is the real wage in the capitalist sector. At this wage, the supply of rural labor is assumed to be 'unlimited' or perfectly elastic, as shown by the horizontal labor supply curve WS. Given a fixed supply of capital, K_1, in the initial stage of modern sector growth, the demand curve for labor is determined by labor's declining marginal product and is shown by curve $D_1(K_1)$. Since profit maximizing modern sector employers are assumed to hire laborers up to the point where their marginal physical product is equal to the real wage (i.e. the point F of intersection between the labor demand and supply curves), total modern sector employment will be equal to OL_1. Total modern sector output would be given by the area bounded by points OD_1FL_1. The share of this total output which is paid to workers in the form of wages would be equal, therefore, to the area of the rectangle $OWFL_1$. The surplus output shown by the area WD_1F would be the total profits that accrue to the capitalists. Since it is assumed that all of these profits are re-invested, the total capital stock in the modern sector will rise from K_1 to K_2. This larger capital stock causes the total product curve of the modern sector to rise which in turn induces a rise in the marginal product or demand curve for labor. This outward shift in the labor demand curve is shown by line $D_2(K_2)$ in the figure. A new equilibrium urban employment level will be established at point G with OL_2 workers now employed. Total output rises to OD_2GL_2 while total wages and profits increase to $OWGL_2$ and WD_2G respectively. Once again, these larger (WD_2G) profits are reinvested, increasing the total capital stock to K_3, shifting the labor demand curve to $D_3(K_3)$ and raising the level of modern sector employment to L_3.

The above process of modern sector growth and employment expansion is assumed to continue until all 'surplus' rural labor is absorbed in the urban industrial sector. Thereafter, the labor supply curve becomes positively sloped and both urban wages and employment will continue to grow. The structural transformation of the economy will have taken place with the balance of economic activity shifting from rural agriculture to urban industry.

2. Criticisms of the L–F–R model

Although the Lewis–Fei–Ranis model of development is both simple and roughly in conformity with the historical experience of economic growth in the West, it has three key assumptions which are sharply at variance with the realities of migration and underdevelopment in most contemporary Third World countries.

First, the model implicitly assumes that the rate of labor transfer and employment creation in the urban sector is proportional to the rate of urban capital accumulation. The faster the rate of capital accumulation, the higher the growth rate of the modern sector and the faster the rate of new job creation. But what if surplus capitalist profits are reinvested in more sophisticated labor-saving capital equipment rather than just duplicating the existing capital as is implicitly assumed in the L–F–R model? Figure 9.2 reproduces the basic model, only this time the labor demand curves do not shift uniformly outward, but, in fact, cross. Demand curve $D_2(K_2)$ has a greater negative slope than $D_1(K_1)$ to reflect the fact that additions to the capital stock embody labor-saving technical progress.

We see that even though total output has grown substantially (i.e. OD_2EL_1 is significantly greater than OD_1EL_1), total wages ($OWEL_1$) and employment (OL_1) remain unchanged. All of the extra output accrues to capitalists in the form of excess profits. Figure 9.2, therefore, provides an illustration of what some might call 'antidevelopmental' economic growth – i.e. *all* the extra income and output growth is distributed to the few owners of capital while income levels of the masses of workers remain largely unchanged. Although total GNP would rise, a poverty-weighted index of development like that described in Chapter 5 would show no improvement in aggregate social welfare.

The second key assumption of the model at variance with reality is the assumption, again implicit, that 'surplus' labor exists in rural areas while there is *full employment in the urban areas*. Most contemporary research indicates that almost exactly the reverse is true in most Third

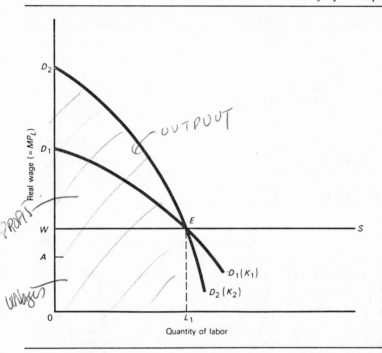

Fig 9.2
Labor saving capital accumulation
modifies the employment
implications of the Lewis model

World countries, i.e. there is substantial open unemployment in urban
areas but little general surplus labor in rural locations. True, there are
both seasonal and geographic exceptions to this rule (e.g. parts of the
Asian subcontinent and isolated regions of Latin America where land
ownership is very unequal) but, by and large, most development
economists seem to agree that the assumption of urban surplus labor is
empirically more valid than the opposite L–F–R assumption of a
general rural surplus labor.

The third unreal assumption is the notion of the continued existence
of constant real urban wages until the point where the supply of rural
surplus labor is exhausted. One of the most striking features of urban
labor markets and wage determination in almost all developing countries has been the tendency for these wages to rise substantially over
time, both in absolute terms and relative to average rural incomes,
even in the presence of rising levels of open unemployment.

We conclude, therefore, that when one takes into account the
labor-saving bias of most modern technological transfer, the widespread non-existence of rural surplus labor, the growing prevalence of
'urban surplus' labor, and the tendency for urban wages to rise rapidly
even where substantial urban open unemployment exists, then the
Lewis–Fei–Ranis model can be seen to offer little analytical and policy
guidance for solving Third World employment and migration problems. Nevertheless, the model does have some redeeming analytical
value in that it does at least emphasize two major elements of the
employment problem: the structural and economic differences between the rural and the urban sectors, and the central importance of
the process of labor transfer which links them together. With these two
elements in mind, we now turn to a more specific analysis of rural
–urban migration and urban unemployment in developing countries.

9.3 Migration in developing nations: some general facts

An understanding of the causes and determinants of rural–urban migration and the relationship between migration and relative economic opportunities in urban and rural areas is central to any analysis of Third World employment problems. Since migrants comprise the majority of the urban labor force in developing nations, the magnitude of rural–urban migration has been and will continue to be the principal determinant of the supply of new job seekers. And, if migration is the key determinant of the urban labor supply, then the migration process must be understood before the nature and causes of urban unemployment can be understood in their turn. Government policies to ameliorate the urban unemployment problem must be based, in the first instance, on knowledge of who comes to town and why.

1. The migration process The factors influencing the decision to migrate are varied and complex. Since migration is a *selective process* affecting individuals with certain economic, social, educational and demographic characteristics, the relative influence of economic and non-economic factors may vary not only between nations and regions but also within defined geographic areas and populations. Much of the early research on migration tended to focus on social, cultural, and psychological factors while recognizing, but not carefully evaluating, the importance of economic variables. Emphasis has variously been placed, for example on:

(a) *Social factors* including the desire of migrants to break away from traditional constraints of social organizations;

(b) *Physical factors* including climate and meteorological disasters like floods and droughts;

(c) *Demographic factors* including the reduction in mortality rates and the concomitant high rates of rural population growth;

(d) *Cultural factors* including the security of urban 'extended family' relationships and the allurement of the so-called 'bright city lights'; and,

(e) *Communication factors* resulting from improved transportation, urban-oriented educational systems and the 'modernizing' impact of the introduction of radio, television and the cinema.

All these 'non-economic' factors are of course relevant. However, there now seems to be widespread agreement among economists and non-economists alike that *rural–urban migration can be explained primarily by the influence of economic factors*. These include not only the standard 'push' from subsistence agriculture and 'pull' of relatively high urban wages, but also the potential 'push-back' towards rural areas as a result of high urban unemployment.

2. Migrant characteristics It is convenient to divide the main characteristics of migrants into three broad categories: demographic, educational, and economic.

1. Demographic characteristics Urban migrants in Third World countries tend to be young males between the ages of 15 and 24. Various studies in Africa and Asia have provided quantitative evidence of this phenomenon in countries such as Kenya, Tanzania, Ghana, Nigeria, India, Thailand, Korea and the Philippines. However, the proportion of migrating women also seems to be on the increase as their educational opportunities expand. In Latin America a review of rural–urban migration indicates that women now apparently constitute the majority in the migration stream, probably as a result of Latin America's relatively advanced state of urbanization compared with other developing continents[3].

One of the most consistent findings of rural–urban migration studies is the positive correlation between educational attainment and migration. There seems to be a clear association between the level of completed education and the propensity to migrate – those with more years of schooling, everything else being equal, are more likely to migrate than those with less. In a comprehensive study of migration in Tanzania, for example, the relationship between education and migration is clearly documented, especially in terms of the impact of declining urban employment opportunities on the educational characteristics of migrants[4]. Tanzanian secondary-school leavers were found to constitute a rising proportion of the migration stream. The explanation offered by Barnum and Sabot is that limited urban employment opportunities were being rationed by educational levels and only those workers with some secondary education had a chance of finding a job. Those with only some primary school education found it very difficult to secure employment. Their proportionate numbers in the 'migrant stream', therefore, have begun to decline.

2. Educational characteristics

For many years the largest percentage of urban migrants were those poor, landless, unskilled individuals whose rural opportunities were for the most part nonexistent. In colonial Africa, seasonal migration was predominant with migrants from various income levels seeking short-term urban jobs. Recently, however, with the emergence of a stabilized, modern industrial sector in most urban areas of the less developed countries, the financial assets of migrants from rural areas have become important only to the extent that individuals with larger financial resources can survive longer while searching for the elusive urban job. In short, migrants seem to come from all socio-economic strata with the vast majority being very poor only because most rural inhabitants are poor.

3. Economic characteristics

9.4 Towards an economic theory of rural–urban migration

As we discovered in Chapter 4, the historical economic development of Western Europe and the United States was closely associated with, and in fact often defined in terms of, the movement of labor from rural to urban areas. For the most part, with a rural sector dominated by agricultural activities and an urban sector focusing on industrialization, overall economic development was characterized by the gradual reallocation of labor out of agriculture and into industry through rural–urban migration, both internal and international. Urbanization and industrialization, therefore, became synonymous. This historical model served as a blueprint for the development of Third World nations, as evidenced, for example, by the Lewis–Fei–Ranis theory of labor transfer.

But the overwhelming evidence of the 1960s when Third World nations witnessed a massive migration of their rural populations into urban areas in spite of rising levels of urban unemployment and underemployment lessens the validity of the Lewis–Fei–Ranis model of development. In a series of articles, the present author has sought to develop a theory of rural–urban migration to explain the apparently paradoxical relationship (at least to economists) of accelerated rural–urban migration in the context of rising urban unemployment[5].

1. A verbal description of the Todaro model

Starting from the assumption that migration is primarily an economic phenomenon which for the individual migrant can be a quite rational decision despite the existence of urban unemployment, the Todaro model postulates that migration proceeds in response to urban–rural differences in *expected rather than actual earnings*. The fundamental premise is that migrants consider the various labor market opportunities available to them as between the rural and urban sectors and choose the one which maximizes their 'expected' gains from migration. Expected gains are measured by the *difference in real incomes between rural and urban work* and the *probability of a new migrant obtaining an urban job*. A schematic framework showing how the varying factors affecting the migration decision interact is portrayed in Fig. 9.3.

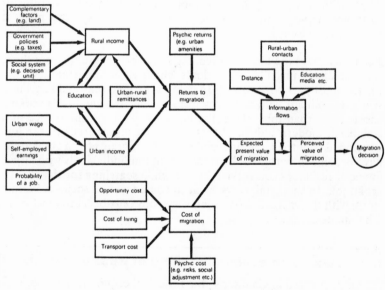

Fig 9.3
A schematic framework for the analysis of the migration decision
source: Byerlee (1974)

In essence, the theory assumes that members of the labor force, both actual and potential, compare their 'expected' incomes for a given time horizon in the urban sector (i.e. the difference between returns and costs of migration) with prevailing average rural incomes and migrate if the former exceeds the latter.

Consider the following illustration. Suppose the average unskilled or semi-skilled rural worker has a choice between being a farm laborer (or working his own land) for an annual average real income of, say, 50 units, or migrating to the city where a worker with his skill or educational background can obtain wage employment yielding an annual real income of 100 units. The more commonly used economic models of migration which place exclusive emphasis on the income differential factor as the determinant of the decision to migrate would indicate a clear choice in this situation. The worker should seek the higher-paying urban job. It is important to recognize, however, that these migration models were developed largely in the context of advanced industrial economies and, as such, implicitly assume the existence of full or near-full employment. In a full employment environment the decision to migrate can be based solely on the desire to secure the highest paid job wherever it becomes available. Simple economic theory would then indicate that such migration should lead to a reduction in wage differentials through the interaction of the forces of supply and demand, both in areas of emigration and in points of immigration.

Unfortunately, such an analysis is not realistic in the context of the institutional and economic framework of most of Third World nations. First of all, these countries are beset by a chronic and serious unemployment problem with the result that a typical migrant cannot expect to secure a high-paying urban job immediately. In fact, it is much more likely that upon entering the urban labor market many migrants will either become totally unemployed or will seek casual and part-time employment in the urban 'traditional' or 'informal' sector. Consequently, in his decision to migrate the individual must balance the probabilities and risks of being unemployed or underemployed for a considerable period of time against the positive urban–rural real income differential. The fact that a typical migrant can expect to earn twice the annual real income in an urban area than in a rural environment may be of little consequence if the actual 'probability' of his securing the higher-paying job within, say, a 1-year period is one chance in five. Thus, the actual probability of his being successful in securing the higher-paying urban job is 20 per cent and therefore his 'expected' urban income for the 1-year period is in fact 20 units and not the 100 units that an urban worker in a full-employment environment would expect to receive. So with a one-period time horizon and a probability of success of 20 per cent it would be irrational for this migrant to seek an urban job even though the differential between urban and rural earnings capacity is 100 per cent. On the other hand, if the probability of success were, say, 60 per cent so that the expected urban income is 60 units, it would be entirely rational for our migrant with his one-period time horizon to try his luck in the urban area even though urban unemployment may be extremely high.

If we now approach the situation more realistically by assuming a considerably longer time horizon, especially in view of the fact that the vast majority of migrants are between the ages of 15 and 24 years, the decision to migrate should be represented on the basis of a longer-term, more 'permanent' income calculation. If the migrant anticipates a relatively low probability of finding regular wage employment in the initial period but expects this probability to increase over time as he is able to broaden his urban contacts, it would still be rational for him to migrate even though expected urban income during the initial period or periods might be lower than expected rural income. As long as the 'present value' of the net stream of expected urban incomes over the migrant's planning horizon exceeds that of the expected rural income, the decision to migrate is justifiable. This, in essence, is the process portrayed in Fig. 9.3.

Rather than equalizing urban and rural wage rates as would be the case in a competitive model, we see that rural–urban migration in our model acts as an equilibrating force which equates rural and urban *expected* incomes. For example, if average rural income is 60 and urban income is 120, then a 50 per cent urban unemployment rate would be necessary before further migration would no longer be profitable. Since expected incomes are defined in terms of *both* wages and employment probabilities, it is possible to have continued migration in spite of the existence of sizable rates of urban unemployment. In the above numerical example, migration would continue even if the urban unemployment rate were 30 or 40 per cent.

To sum up, the Todaro migration model has four basic characteristics:

1. *Migration is stimulated primarily by rational economic considerations* of relative benefits and costs, mostly financial but also psychological;
2. *The decision to migrate depends on 'expected' rather than actual urban-rural real wage differentials* where the 'expected' differential is determined by the interaction of two variables, the actual urban–rural wage differential *and* the probability of successfully obtaining employment in the urban sector;
3. *The probability of obtaining an urban job is inversely related to the urban unemployment rate;*
4. *Migration rates in excess of urban job opportunity growth rates are not only possible but rational* and even likely in the face of wide urban–rural *expected* income differentials. High rates of urban unemployment are therefore inevitable outcomes of the serious *imbalance* of economic opportunities between urban and rural areas of most underdeveloped countries. (For a mathematical presentation of the Todaro model, see Appendix 9.1.)

2. Some policy implications While the above theory might at first seem to devalue the critical importance of rural–urban migration by portraying it as an adjustment mechanism by which workers allocate themselves between rural and urban labor markets, it does have important policy implications for development strategy with regard to wages and incomes, rural development, and industrialization. These include the following:

A. The need to reduce imbalances in urban–rural employment opportunities Since migrants are assumed to respond to differentials in expected incomes, it is vitally important that imbalances between economic opportunities in rural and urban sectors be minimized. Permitting urban wage rates to grow at a greater pace than average rural incomes will stimulate further rural–urban migration in spite of rising levels of urban unemployment. This heavy influx of people into urban areas gives rise not only to socio-economic problems in the cities, but it may also eventually create problems of labor shortages in rural areas, especially during the busy seasons.

B. Urban job creation is an insufficient solution for the urban unemployment problem The traditional (Keynesian) economic solution to urban unemployment, i.e. the creation of more urban jobs without simultaneous attempts to improve rural incomes and employment opportunities, can lead to the paradoxical situation where more urban *employment* leads to higher levels of urban and rural *unemployment*! Once again, the imbalance in 'expected' income earning opportunities is the crucial concept. Since migration rates are assumed to respond positively to *both* higher urban wages and higher urban employment opportunities (or probabilities), it follows that for any given positive urban–rural wage differential (in most LDCs urban wages are typically three to four times as large as rural wages), higher urban employment rates will widen the expected differential and induce even higher rates of rural–urban migration. For every new job created, two or three migrants who were productively occupied in rural areas may come to the city. Thus, if 100 new jobs are created, there may be as many as 300 new migrants and, therefore, 200 more urban unemployed. A policy designed to reduce urban unemployment, therefore, may lead not only to the higher levels of urban unemployment but also to lower levels of agricultural output and employment.

The Todaro model also has important policy implications for curtailing investment in excessive educational expansion, especially at the higher levels. The heavy influx of rural migrants into urban areas at rates much in excess of new employment opportunities has necessitated a rationing device in the selection of new employees. Although within each educational group such selection may be largely random, many observers have noted that employers tend to use educational attainment or number of years of completed schooling as the typical rationing device. For the same wage, they will hire those with more education in preference to those with less even though extra education may not contribute to better job performance. Jobs which could formerly be filled by those with primary education (sweepers, messengers, filing clerks, etc.) now require secondary training; those formerly requiring a secondary certificate (clerks, typists, bookkeepers, etc.) now necessitate a university degree. It follows that for any given urban wage, if the probability of success in securing a modern sector job is higher for those with more education, their 'expected' income differential will also be higher and the more likely they will be to migrate to the cities. The basic Todaro model, therefore, provides an economic rationale for the observed fact in most LDCs that rural inhabitants with more education are more likely to migrate than those with less.

From the viewpoint of educational policy, it is safe to predict that as job opportunities become scarce in relation to the number of applicants, students will experience increasing pressure to proceed further up the educational ladder. The private demand for education, which in many ways is a 'derived demand' for urban jobs, will continue to exert tremendous pressure on governments to invest in post-primary school facilities. But for many of these students, the spectre of joining the ranks of the 'educated unemployed' becomes more of a reality with each passing year. Government over-investment in post-primary educational facilities thus often turns out to be an investment in idle human resources. Chapter 11 will focus on this and other issues related to the economics of education in greater detail.

As we have seen in Chapter 8, a standard economic policy prescription for generating urban employment opportunities is to eliminate factor–price distortions by using 'correct' prices perhaps implemented by wage subsidies (i.e. fixed government subsidies to employers for each worker employed) or direct government hiring. Since actual urban wages generally exceed the market or 'correct' wage as a result of a variety of institutional factors, it is often correctly argued that the elimination of wage distortions through price adjustments or a subsidy system will encourage more labor-intensive modes of production. While such policies can generate more urban *employment* opportunities, they can also lead to higher levels of *unemployment* in accordance with the argument above about induced migration. The overall welfare impact of a wage subsidy policy when both the rural and urban sectors are taken into account is not immediately clear. Much will

C. Indiscriminate educational expansion will lead to further migration and unemployment

D. Wage subsidies and traditional scarcity factor pricing can be counterproductive

depend on the level of urban unemployment, the size of the urban–rural expected income differential, and the magnitude of induced migration as more urban jobs are created.

E. Programs of integrated rural development should be encouraged

Policies which operate only on the demand side of the urban employ-ment picture such as wage subsidies, direct government hiring, elimi-nation of factor–price distortions and employer tax incentives are probably far less effective in the long run in alleviating the *unemploy-ment* problem than are policies designed directly to regulate the supply of labor to urban areas. Clearly, however, some combination of both policies is most desirable.

Policies of rural development are crucial to this aim. Many informed observers of Third World development agree on the central impor-tance of rural and agricultural development if the urban unemploy-ment problem is to be solved. Most proposals call for the restoration of a proper balance between rural and urban incomes and the moderation of government policies which give development programs a partial bias towards the urban industrial sector (e.g. in the provision of health, educational and other social services).

Given the political difficulties of reducing urban wage rates, the need continuously to expand urban employment opportunities through judicious investments in small- and medium-scale labor-intensive industries, and the inevitable growth of the urban industrial sector, every effort must be made to broaden the economic base of the rural economy at the same time. The present unnecessary economic incentives for rural–urban migration need to be minimized through creative and well-designed programs of integrated rural development. These should focus on income generation, both farm and non-farm, employment growth, health delivery, educational improvement, infrastructure development (electricity, water, roads, etc.) and the provision of other rural amenities. Successful rural development prog-rams adapted to the socio-economic and environmental needs of particular countries and regions seem to offer the only viable long-run solution to the problem of excessive rural–urban migration.

To assert, however, that there is an urgent need for policies designed to curb the excessive influx of rural migrants is not to imply an attempt to reverse what some have called 'inevitable historical trends'. Rather, the implication of the Todaro migration model is that there is a growing need for a 'policy package' that does not *exacerbate* these historical trends towards urbanization by *artificially* creating serious imbalances in economic opportunities between urban and rural areas.

9.5 Summary and conclusions: the shape of a comprehensive employment strategy

At various points throughout this and the previous chapter, we have mentioned possible policy approaches designed to improve the very serious employment situation in many Third World countries. We conclude by summarizing what we believe is the 'consensus' opinion of most economists on the shape of a comprehensive employment strategy[6]. This would appear to have *five key elements*:

1. *Creating an appropriate rural–urban economic balance.* A more appropriate balance between rural and urban economic oppor-tunities appears to be indispensable to ameliorating urban unemp-loyment problems in most developing countries. The main thrust of

this activity should be in the integrated development of the rural sector, the spread of small-scale industries throughout the countryside and the reorientation of economic activity and social investments towards the rural areas.

2. *Expansion of small-scale, labor-intensive industries.* The composition or 'product mix' of output has obvious effects on the magnitude of employment since some products (often basic consumer goods) require more labor per unit of output and per unit of capital than others. Efforts to expand these, mostly small-scale, labor-intensive industries can be accomplished in two ways: *directly* through government investment and incentives, and *indirectly* through income redistribution (either directly or from future growth) to the poor whose structure of consumer demand is both less import-intensive and more labor-intensive than the rich.

[handwritten margin note: Small is beautiful]

3. *Elimination of factor–price distortions.* There is ample evidence to demonstrate that correcting factor price distortions primarily through the elimination of various capital subsidies and curtailing the growth of urban wages would undoubtedly increase employment opportunities and make better use of scarce capital resources. But by how much and how quickly these policies would work is not clear. Surely correct pricing policies by themselves are insufficient to alter significantly the present employment situation for the reasons described in Chapter 8.

4. *Choosing 'appropriate' labor-intensive technologies of production.* One of the principal inhibiting factors to the success of any long-run program of employment creation both in urban industry and rural agriculture is the almost complete technological dependence of Third World nations on imported (typically labor-saving) machinery and equipment from the developed countries. Both domestic and international efforts must be made to reduce this dependence by developing indigenous technological research and adaptation capacities in the developing countries themselves. Such efforts might first be linked to the development of small-scale, labour-intensive rural and urban enterprises. They could also focus on the development of low-cost, labor-intensive methods of providing rural infrastructure needs including roads, irrigation and drainage systems, and essential health and educational services. Clearly, this is an area where scientific and technological assistance from the developed countries could be most fruitful.

[handwritten margin note: = "rural technocrats"]

5. *Modifying the direct linkage between education and employment.* The emergence of the phenomenon of the 'educated unemployed' in many developing countries is calling into question the appropriateness of massive quantitative expansion of educational systems especially at the higher levels. Formal education has become the rationing tunnel through which all prospective job holders must pass. As modern sector jobs multiply more slowly than the numbers leaving the educational tunnel, it becomes necessary to extend the length of the tunnel and to narrow its exit. While a full discussion of educational problems and policies must await Chapter 11, we may point out that one way to moderate the excessive demand for additional years of schooling (which in reality is a demand for modern sector jobs) would be for governments, often the largest employers, to base their hiring practices and their wage structures on other criteria. Moreover, by creating attractive economic opportunities in rural areas, it will become more easy to redirect educa-

tional systems toward the needs of rural development. It is ironic that many Third World educational systems, being transplants of Western systems, are oriented towards preparing students to function in a small modern sector employing at the most 20 to 30 per cent of the labour force. Many of the necessary skills for development, therefore, remain largely neglected.

A final comment on population The reader may have noted that we have not specifically mentioned an active population policy as one of our major employment-oriented strategies. Reducing excessive population growth rates is undoubtedly critical to the ultimate amelioration of the employment problem, for the simple reason that it would reduce the future size and growth of new job seekers. However, we know that for the next 15 to 25 years the size of the labor force has already been determined by existing fertility rates. This does not negate the need to lower fertility rates as soon as possible, especially in heavily populated developing nations. The reason why we have not included an active, government-sponsored family planning program among our five 'priority' policy areas is simply that, as stressed in Chapter 7, each of the five policies suggested above will contribute indirectly to lowering levels of fertility by raising living standards for the very poor, especially in rural areas.

Notes

1. Richard Jolly, 'Rural–urban migration: dimensions, causes, issues and policies', Conference on *Prospects for Employment Opportunities in the Nineteen Seventies,* Cambridge U.P. (1970), 4.
2. W. A. Lewis, 'Economic development with unlimited supplies of labour', *Manchester School* (1954), and J. C. H. Fei and G. Ranis, 'A theory of economic development', *American Economic Review,* 1961.
3. Pamela Brigg, 'Migration to urban areas', *World Bank Staff Working Paper No. 107,* 1971.
4. H. N. Barnum and R. H. Sabot, *Migration, Education and Urban Surplus Labour,* OECD Development Center Employment Series Monograph, October 1975 (mimeo.).
5. See, for example, Michael P. Todaro, 'An analysis of industrialization: employment and unemployment in LDCs', *Yale Economic Essays,* **8**(2), (1968), 329–492 and 'A model of labor migration and urban unemployment in less developed countries', *American Economic Review,* **59**(1) (1969), 138–48.
6. See, for example, Edgar O. Edwards (ed.), *Employment in Developing Nations,* Report on a Ford Foundation Study, New York (1974), 1–46.

Concepts for review
two-sector models
modern sector
labour-saving capital
  accumulation
'push' and 'pull' migration
  factors
job probabilities
migrant time horizon
'institutional' urban wage
wage subsidy

'unlimited' supplies of
  labor
demand curve for labor
extended family system
'expected' income
present values
income differentials
urban–rural economic imbalances
induced migration
school leaver problem
economic and social 'infrastructure'

Questions for discussion 1. Describe briefly the essential assumptions and features of the Lewis–Fei–Ranis surplus labor model of development. What are the major strengths and weaknesses of this two-sector model for analysing the actual process of rural–urban labor transfer in most Third World countries?

2. Describe briefly the essential assumptions and major features of the Todaro model of rural–urban migration. One of the most significant implications of this model is the paradoxical conclusion that government policies designed to create more urban employment may in fact lead to more urban unemployment! Explain the reasons why such a paradoxical result might be forthcoming.
3. 'The key to solving the serious problem of excessive rural–urban migration and rising urban unemployment and underemployment in Third World countries is to restore a proper balance between urban and rural economic and social opportunities.' Discuss the reasoning behind this statement and give a few specific examples of government policies which will promote a better 'balance' between urban and rural economic and social opportunities.
4. For many years the 'convention wisdom' of development economics assumed that there existed an inherent *conflict* between the objective of maximizing output growth and promoting rapid industrial employment growth. Why might these two objectives be mutually supportive rather than conflicting? Explain.
5. What is meant by the expression 'getting prices right'? Under what conditions will eliminating factor price distortions generate substantial new employment opportunities? Be sure to include in your discussion a brief definition of what is meant by 'factor–price destortions'.

1. The Lewis and Fei–Ranis models of development in labor-surplus economies are best described in the following original papers by these well-known development economists: (*a*) W. A. Lewis, 'Economic development with unlimited supplies of labour', *Manchester School,* 1954; (*b*) J. C. H. Fei and G. Ranis, 'A theory of economic development', *American Economic Review,* **51,** no. 3, 1961.
2. Among the many readings on the critical problem of rural–urban migration in developing countries, the following are perhaps the most comprehensive: (*a*) D. Byerlee, 'Rural–urban migration in Africa: theory, policy and research implications', *International Migration Review,* 1974; (*b*) P. Brigg, 'Migration to urban areas: a survey', *IBRD Staff Working Paper No. 107,* 1971; (*c*) N. Carynnyk-Sinclair, 'Rural to urban migration in developing countries, 1950–1970: a survey of the literature', *Working Paper, WEP2–19,* International Labour Organization, February 1974; (*d*) J. R. Harris and M. P. Todaro, 'Migration, unemployment and development: a two-sector analysis', *American Economic Review,* March 1970; (*e*) M. P. Todaro, *Internal Migration in Developing Countries: A Review of Theory, Evidence, Methodology and Research Priorities,* International Labour Organization, Geneva (1976).
3. For a suggested national and international strategy to combat Third World poverty and unemployment, see ILO, *Employment, Growth and Basic Needs: A One-World Problem,* Geneva (1976).

Appendix 9.1

Consider the following mathematical formulation of the basic Todaro model discussed in this chapter. Individuals are assumed to base their decision to migrate on considerations of income maximization and what they perceive to be their expected income streams in urban and rural areas. It is further assumed that the individual who chooses to migrate is attempting to achieve the prevailing average income for his level of education or skill attainment in the urban centre of his choice. Nevertheless, he is assumed to be aware of his limited chances of immediately securing wage employment and the likelihood that he will be unemployed or underemployed for a certain period of time. It follows that the migrant's expected income stream is determined both by the prevailing income in the modern sector and the probability of being employed there, rather than being underemployed in the traditional sector or totally unemployed.

If we let $V(0)$ be the discounted present value of the expected 'net' urban–rural income stream over the migrant's time horizon; Y_u, $Y_r(t)$ the average real incomes of individuals employed in the urban and the rural economy; n the number of time periods in the migrant's planning horizon; and r the discount rate reflecting the migrant's degree of time preference, then the decision to migrate or not will depend on whether

$$V(0) = \int_{t=0}^{n} [p(t)Y_u(t) - Y_r(t)]e^{-rt}\,\mathrm{d}t - C(0)$$

is positive or negative, where
   $C(0)$ represents the cost of migration, and
   $p(t)$ is the probability that a migrant will have secured an urban job at the average income level in period t.

In any one time period, the probability of being employed in the modern sector, $p(t)$, will be directly related to the probability π of having been selected in that or any previous period from a given stock of unemployed or underemployed job seekers. If we assume that for most migrants the selection procedure is random, then the probability of having a job in the modern sector within x periods after migration, $p(x)$, is:

$$p(1) = \pi(1)$$

and

$$p(2) = \pi(1) + [1 - \pi(1)]\pi(2)$$

so that

$$p(x) = p(x-1) + [1 - p(x-1)]\pi(x)$$

or

$$p(x) = \pi(1) + \sum_{t=2}^{x} \pi(t) \prod_{s=1}^{t-1} [1 - \pi(s)]$$

where
$\pi(t)$ equals the ratio of new job openings relative to the number of accumulated job aspirants in period t.

It follows from this probability formulation that for any given level of $Y_u(t)$ and $Y_r(t)$, the longer the migrant has been in the city the higher his probability p of having a job and the higher, therefore, is his expected income in that period.

Formulating the probability variable in this way has two advantages:

1. It avoids the 'all or nothing' problem of having to assume that the migrant either earns the average income or earns nothing in the periods immediately following migration: consequently, it reflects the fact that many underemployed migrants will be able to generate some income in the urban traditional sector while searching for a regular job.
2. It modifies somewhat the assumption of random selection since the probability of a migrant having been selected varies directly with the time he has been in the city. This permits adjustments for the fact that longer-term migrants usually have more contacts and better information systems so that their expected incomes should be higher than those of newly arrived migrants with similar skills.

Suppose we now incorporate this behavioristic theory of migration into a simple aggregate dynamic equilibrium model of urban labor demand and supply in the following manner. We once again define the probability π of obtaining a job in the urban sector in any one time period as being directly related to the rate of new employment creation and inversely related to the ratio of unemployed job seekers to the number of existing job opportunities, that is:

$$\pi = \frac{\lambda N}{S - N} \tag{A9.1}$$

where λ is the net rate of urban new job creation, N is the level of urban employment and S is the total urban labor force.

If w is the urban real wage rate and r represents average rural real income, then the 'expected' urban–rural real income differential d is:

$$d = w \cdot \pi - r \tag{A9.2}$$

or, substituting (A9.1) into (A9.2),

$$d = w \cdot \frac{\lambda N}{S - N} - r \tag{A9.3}$$

The basic assumption of our model once again is that the supply of labour to the urban sector is a function of the urban–rural *expected* real income differential, i.e.:

$$S = f_s(d) \tag{A9.4}$$

If the rate of urban job creation is a function of the urban wage w and a policy parameter a, e.g. a concentrated governmental effort to increase employment through a program of import substitution, both of which operate on labor demand, we have:

$$\lambda = f_d(w; a) \tag{A9.5}$$

where it is assumed that $\frac{\partial \lambda}{\partial a} > 0$. If the growth in the urban labor demand is increased as a result of the governmental policy shift, the increase in the urban labor supply is:

$$\frac{\partial S}{\partial a} = \frac{\partial S}{\partial d} \frac{\partial d}{\partial \lambda} \frac{\partial \lambda}{\partial a} \tag{A9.6}$$

Differentiating (A9.3) and substituting into (A9.6), we obtain,

$$\frac{\partial S}{\partial a} = \frac{\partial S}{\partial d} w \frac{N}{S-N} \cdot \frac{\partial \lambda}{\partial a} \tag{A9.7}$$

The absolute number of urban employed will increase if the increase in labor supply exceeds the increase in the number of new jobs created, i.e. if:

$$\frac{\partial S}{\partial a} > \frac{\partial(\lambda N)}{\partial a} = \frac{N\partial \lambda}{\partial a} \tag{A9.8}$$

Combining (A9.7) and (A9.8), we get,

$$\frac{\partial S}{\partial d} w \frac{N}{S-N} \cdot \frac{\partial \lambda}{\partial a} > \frac{N\partial \lambda}{\partial a} \tag{A9.9}$$

or,

$$\frac{\partial S/S}{\partial d/d} > \frac{d}{w} \cdot \frac{(S-N)}{S} \tag{A9.10}$$

or, finally, substituting for d:

$$\frac{\partial S/S}{\partial d/d} > \frac{w \cdot \pi - r}{w} \cdot \frac{(S-N)}{S} \tag{A9.11}$$

Expression (A9.11) reveals that the absolute level of unemployment will rise if the elasticity of urban labor supply with respect to the expected urban–rural income differential $\frac{\partial S/S}{\partial d/d}$ (what has been called elsewhere the 'migration response function'), exceeds the urban–rural differential as a proportion of the urban wage times the unemployment rate, $S-N/S$. Alternatively, equation (A9.11) shows that the higher the unemployment rate, the higher must be the elasticity to increase the level of unemployment for any expected real income differential. But note that in most developing nations the inequality (A9.11) will be satisfied by a very low elasticity of supply when realistic figures are used. For example, if the urban real wage is 60, average rural real income is 20, the probability of getting a job is 0·50 and the unemployment rate is 20 per cent, then the level of unemployment will increase if the elasticity of urban labor supply is greater than 0·033, i.e. substituting into (A9.11) we get:

$$\frac{\partial S/S}{\partial d/d} = \frac{0.50 \times 60 - 20}{60} \times 0.20 = 0.033$$

Much more needs to be known about the empirical value of this elasticity coefficient in different developing nations before one can realistically predict what the impact of a policy to generate more urban *employment* will be on the over-all level of urban *unemployment*.

Chapter 10	# Agricultural transformation and rural development

It is in the agricultural sector that the battle for long term economic development will be won or lost.
  Gunnar Myrdal, 1968

The main burden of development and employment creation will have to be borne by the part of the economy in which agriculture is the predominant activity: that is, the rural sector.
  Francis Blanchard, Director-General of the International Labour Organization (ILO), 1975

Introduction: the imperative of agricultural progress and rural development

If migration to the cities in Africa, Asia and Latin America is proceeding at historically unprecedented rates, a large part of the explanation can be found in the economic stagnation of the outlying rural areas. This is where the people are. Over 1½ billion people in the Third World grind out a meager and often inadequate existence in agricultural pursuits. Over 2 billion people lived in rural areas in the mid-1970s. Estimates indicate that this figure will rise to almost 2·8 billion by the year 2000. People living in the countryside of Latin America and Asia comprise considerably more than half the total populations of such diverse nations as Brazil, Peru, India, Indonesia, Burma, Bolivia, Sri Lanka, Pakistan and the Philippines. In Africa, the ratios are much higher with almost every country having rural dwellers in excess of three-quarters of the total population. In spite of the massive migration to the cities, the absolute population *increase* in rural areas of most Third World nations will continue to be greater than that of urban areas for at least the next decade.

Of greater importance than sheer numbers is the fact that the vast majority (almost 70 per cent) of the world's poorest people are also located in rural areas and engaged primarily in subsistence agriculture. Their basic concern is survival. These are the many hundreds of millions of people who have been bypassed by whatever economic 'progress' has been attained. In their daily struggle to subsist, their behavior may often appear irrational to Western economists who have little comprehension of the precarious nature of subsistence living. If 'development' is to take place and become self-sustaining, it will have to start in the rural areas in general and the agricultural sector in particular. The core problems of widespread poverty, growing inequality, rapid population growth and rising unemployment which we have examined in previous chapters all find their origins in the stagnation and often retrogression of economic life in rural areas.

Traditionally, the role of agriculture in economic development has been viewed as largely passive and supportive. Based on the historical experience of Western countries, economic development was seen to require a rapid structural transformation of the economy from one predominantly focused on agricultural activities to a more complex, modern industrial and service society. As a result, agriculture's primary role was to provide sufficient low priced food and manpower to the expanding industrial economy which was thought to be the dynamic, 'leading sector' in any overall strategy of economic development. Among others, Arthur Lewis's famous two-sector model discussed in the preceding chapter is an outstanding example of a theory of development which places heavy emphasis on rapid industrial growth with an agricultural sector fuelling this industrial expansion with its cheap food and surplus labor.

Today, as we have seen, development economists are less sanguine about the desirability of placing such heavy emphasis on rapid industrialization. Perhaps more importantly, they have come to realize that, far from being a passive supporting sector in the process of economic development and the handmaiden of industry, the agricultural sector in particular and the rural economy in general need to be viewed as the dynamic and leading elements in any overall strategy – at least for the vast majority of contemporary Third World countries. To a large extent, therefore, the 1970s have witnessed a remarkable transition in development thinking – one in which agricultural and rural development is now seen by many as the *sine qua non* of national development. Without such agricultural and rural development, industrial growth will either be stultified or, if it succeeds, will create such severe internal imbalances in the economy that the problems of widespread poverty, inequality and unemployment which we analyzed in previous chapters will become even more pronounced.

Five main questions, therefore, need to be asked about Third World agriculture and rural development as these relate to overall national development:

1. How can total agricultural output and productivity per capita be substantially increased in a manner that will directly benefit the average small farmer and the landless rural dweller while still providing a sufficient food surplus to support a growing urban, industrial sector?
2. What is the process by which traditional low productivity subsistence farms are transformed into high productivity commercial enterprises?
3. Do traditional small farmers and peasant cultivators stubbornly resist change or are they acting rationally within the context of their particular environment?
4. Are economic incentives sufficient to elicit output increases among peasant agriculturalists or are institutional and structural changes in rural farming 'systems' also required?

5. Is raising agricultural productivity sufficient to improve rural life or must there be concomitant improvements in educational, medical and other social services? In other words, what do we mean by 'rural development' and how can it be achieved?

Our approach in this chapter is to start with a brief factual account of the relative stagnation of the agricultural sector in most Third World nations over the past two decades. Next, we describe and analyze the basic characteristics of agrarian systems in Latin America, Asia and Africa to see if we can identify some important similarities and differences. We then look at the economics of subsistence agriculture and discuss the stages of transition from subsistence to commercial farming in Third World Nations. Our focus here is not only on the economic factors but also the social, institutional and structural requirements of small-farm modernization. We then explore the meaning of 'rural development' and review alternative policies designed to raise levels of living in Third World rural areas. A brief look at the Chinese experience with rural development and the lessons, if any, which this experience affords to other developing nations concludes the chapter.

10.1 Agricultural stagnation in the 'development decade'

We have seen that many developing countries experienced respectable rates of GNP growth during the 1960s. The greatest proportionate share of this overall growth, however, occurred in the manufacturing and commerce sectors where recorded rates of annual output growth often exceeded 10 per cent. In contrast, agricultural output growth for most developing regions remained stagnant during the 1960s (the so-called 'Development Decade'), so that the share of agricultural output in total GNP declined. Table 10.1 reveals that in spite of the fact that the agricultural sector accounts for most of the employment in developing countries, it accounts for a much lower share of the output. In fact, in no Third World region does agricultural production constitute even half of the total national product. This is in marked contrast to the historical experience of advanced countries where agricultural output in their early stages of growth always contributed at least as much to total output as the share of the labour force engaged in these activities. The fact that contemporary Third World agricultural *employment* is typically twice as large in proportion to the total as is agricultural *output* simply reflects the relatively low levels of agricultural labor productivity compared with that in manufacturing and commerce.

	Third World region	Per cent of labor force in agriculture	Output of agriculture, forestry and fishing as per cent of GNP
	South Asia	71	>40
Table 10.1	East Asia	64	33
Output and employment in Third	Latin America	49	21
World agriculture	Africa	79	44

The data in Table 10.1 and especially in Chapter 5, where we discussed the sectoral location of absolute poverty, strongly suggest that a direct attack on rural poverty through accelerated agricultural development is necessary to raise rural living standards. Mere concern with maximizing GNP growth is not enough. Unfortunately, the record of the past two decades offers little hope, as can be seen from Table 10.2.

Over the two decades which ended in 1970, per capita food production and per capita agricultural production (which includes not only food but also non-edible agricultural products like cotton, sisal, rubber, etc.) each increased less than 1 per cent per year in the Third World as a whole. Moreover, Table 10.2 shows that the rates of growth of both of these measures of agricultural performance were much slower in the 1960s than in the 1950s. In fact, the agricultural sector in many developing countries completely stagnated in the 1960s. People on the whole were little or no better off in terms of the *per capita* availability of food at the end of the decade than they were at the beginning. In contrast, in the more developed countries per capita food production continued to rise at an annual rate nine times higher.

Looking at each major region within the Third World, we can also see from Table 10.2 that the same broad tendencies were at work. In Latin America there was some increase in the growth of per capita food production, but agricultural production as a whole showed no such increase. The picture for Africa is even more dismal. Per capita food *and* agricultural production declined sharply in the 1960s. This suggests that the average African suffered a *fall* in his level of food consumption during the decade. Since food consumption constitutes by far the largest component in a typical African's standard of living, the total decline of almost 10 per cent in per capita food consumption meant that the region as a whole was becoming even more underdeveloped during the 1960s.

The agricultural performance in Asia was only slightly better. In the Near East there was a decline in the rate of growth compared to the pre-1960 period. During the 1960–70 decade both per capita food and agricultural production tended to stagnate. Rates of growth also fell in the Far East though production per capita did increase at about $0 \cdot 3$ per cent per annum.

Region	Per capita food production		Per capita agricultural production	
	1948/52–70	1960–70	1948/52–70	1960–70
Latin America	0·4	0·6	0·2	0·0
Far East (excl. Japan)	0·8	0·3	0·7	0·3
Near East (excl. Israel)	0·7	0·0	0·8	0·0
Africa (excl. South Africa)	0·0	−0·7	0·3	−0·5
All underdeveloped countries	0·6	0·1	0·6	0·0
Developed capitalist countries	1·1	0·9	1·0	0·6

Table **10.2**
The growth (and stagnation) of per capita food and agricultural output in Third World regions

Source: K. Griffen, 'Agrarian policy: the political and economic context', *World Development*, **1**, No. 11 (1973), 3.

We may conclude that in spite of some impressive rates of per capita GNP growth recorded in Third World regions during the 1960s, the agricultural sector not only showed negligible progress as a whole but it even showed a sharp decline when compared with the previous decade. Since the vast majority of people in developing countries seek their livelihoods in this sector, the data of Table 10.2 confirms what we discovered in Chapter 5; that the magnitude and extent of Third World poverty has probably worsened over the past 10 to 15 years. This is especially so when one realizes once again that per capita aggregates for food consumption mask the inherently unequal distribution of that consumption just as per capita GNP figures fail to give any indication of the magnitude of absolute poverty. If the distribution of limited food supplies is at all analogous to the highly unequal distribution of income in many LDCs, then the deteriorating food situation for many hundreds of millions of people was even worse during the 1960s than the data in Table 10.2 reveal.

Finally, if we look at the experience of the early 1970s as shown in Table 10.3, the per capita food production picture for the Third World shows only a very negligible improvement in 1973 compared with the 1961–5 period, and an actual further deterioration since 1970. Compounding this production problem along with the persistence of severe droughts and famines in many parts of central Africa and South Asia was the unprecedented rise in world food and fertilizer prices during the first half of the 1970s. The combination of growing resource scarcities and rapidly rising food prices has undoubtedly meant a marked deterioration in levels of living for that sizable segment of mankind that spends 80 per cent of its income on food. A doubling in the price of wheat, maize or rice (as occurred in the early 1970s) cannot possibly be offset by increased expenditures for these already impoverished people. It can only drive a subsistence diet below the subsistence and survival level.

	World*	Developed countries†	Third World countries‡
1961–5	100	100	100
1966	102	106	97
1967	104	108	100
1968	105	111	101
1969	104	109	102
1970	105	110	103
Table 10.3 1971	107	113	103
Indices of per capita agricultural 1972	104	112	99
production 1973	108	117	102

Source: Overseas Development Council, *Agenda for Action, 1974,* Praeger, Washington D.C. (1974).
* Excludes Communist Asia.
† North America, Europe, USSR, Japan, Republic of South Africa, Australia and New Zealand.
‡ Latin America, Asia (except Japan and Communist Asia), Africa (except Republic of South Africa).

A major reason for the relatively poor performance of Third World agriculture has been the relative neglect of this sector in the development priorities of the 1950s and 1960s. This neglect of agriculture and the accompanying bias towards investment in the urban industrial sector in turn can be traced largely to the misplaced emphasis on rapid industrialization which permeated development thinking and strategy during the past two decades. For example, during the 1950s and throughout most of the 1960s the share of total national investment allocated towards the agricultural sector in a sample of eighteen LDCs was approximately 12 per cent even though agricultural output in these countries constituted almost 30 per cent of their GNPs and more than 60 per cent of their total employment[1]. As we saw in Chapter 9, one significant manifestation of this rural neglect and the corresponding emphasis on urban growth has been the massive migration of rural peasants into the teeming cities of Third World nations.

As a result of the disappointing experience of the 1960s and the realization that the future of most underdeveloped countries will depend to a large extent on what happens to their agriculture, there has been a marked shift over the past few years in development thinking and policy-making. This shift has been away from the almost exclusive emphasis on rapid industrialization and towards a more realistic appreciation of the overwhelming importance of agricultural and rural development for the ultimate realization of national development. A first essential towards understanding what is needed for agricultural and rural development, however, must be an understanding of the nature of agricultural systems in diverse Third World regions in general, and the economic aspects of the transition from subsistence to commercial agriculture in particular.

10.2 The structure of Third World agrarian systems

When we look at the state of contemporary agriculture in most poor countries, we realize the enormity of the task that lies ahead. A brief comparison between agricultural productivity in the developed nations with that of underdeveloped nations makes this clear[2]. World agriculture, in fact, comprises two very distinct types of farming: (1) the *highly efficient agriculture of the developed countries* where substantial productive capacity and high output per worker permits a very small number of farmers to feed entire nations; and (2) the *inefficient and low productivity agriculture* of developing countries, where in many instances the agricultural sector can barely sustain the farm population, let alone the burgeoning urban population, even at a minimum level of subsistence.

1. Two kinds of world agriculture

The gap between the two kinds of agriculture is immense. This is best illustrated by the disparities in labor productivity, shown in Table 10.4. In 1960 the agricultural population of the developed nations totalled about 115 million people. They produced a total output amounting to $78 billion, or about $680 per capita of their agricultural population. In contrast, we see from Table 10.4 that the per capita product of the agricultural population in the underdeveloped countries in 1960 was only $52. In other words, agricultural labor productivity in developed countries was more than thirteen times as large as that in the less developed countries. Projections for 1980 and the end of the century show this productivity gap widening to 25 and eventually 40 to 1.

In the developed countries, the steady growth of agriculture has been occurring since the mid-eighteenth century. It has benefited primarily from technological and biological improvements that have resulted in even higher levels of labor and land productivity. This growth rate accelerated after the First World War and particularly after the Second World War. As a result, fewer farmers have been able to produce more food. This is especially the case in the United States where less than 6 per cent of the total work force is agricultural compared with more than 70 per cent in the early nineteenth century. For example, in 1820 the American farmer could produce only four times his own consumption. One hundred years later in 1920, his productivity had doubled and he could provide enough for eight per-

sons. It took only another 32 years for this productivity to double again
and then only 12 more years for it to double once more. By 1974 a
single American farmer could provide enough food to feed almost 65
people. Moreover, during the entire period average farm incomes in
North America were steadily rising[3].

	1960		1980		2000	
	Developed nations	LDCs	Developed nations	LDCs	Developed nations	LDCs
Agricultural population (millions)	115	850	75	1,230	50	1,480
Agricultural production total (billions)	$78	$43	$125	$77	$186	$135
Per capita (agricultural population	$680	$52	$1,660	$63	$3,720	$91

Table 10.4
Agricultural population and
production in developed and less
developed countries: 1960, 1980 and
2000

Source: R. Weitz, *From Peasant to Farmer: A Revolutionary Strategy for Development*,
Columbia U.P. (1971), 7.

The picture is entirely different when we turn to the agricultural
production experience of Third World nations. In many poor countries
agricultural production methods have changed relatively slowly over
time. Later in this chapter, we discover that much of this technological
stagnation can be traced to the special circumstances of subsistence
agriculture with its high risks and uncertain rewards. Rapid rural
population growth has compounded the problem by causing great
pressure to be exerted on existing resources. Where fertile land is
scarce, especially throughout South and Southeast Asia but also in
many parts of Latin America and Africa, rapid population growth has
led to an increase in the number of people living on each unit of land.
Given the same farming technology and the use of traditional non-
labour inputs (e.g. simple tools, animal power, traditional seeds, etc.),
we know from the principle of diminishing returns that as more and
more people are forced to work on a given piece of land, their marginal
(and average) productivity will decline. The net result is a continuous
deterioration in real living standards for rural peasants.

As an extreme example of this situation, consider the case of India.
At the end of the nineteenth century, food consumption was only
slightly above the minimum regarded as necessary for survival. Today
many believe that it is below that standard with hundreds of thousands
of people on the verge of starvation. In recent years the volume of
production has been expanding, but not fast enough to keep up with
the rapid increases in human numbers. As a result, farm labor productivity hardly changed during the 1950s and 1960s. The experience of
many other developing countries has been similar.

In order to avert massive starvation and to raise levels of living for
the average rural dweller, agricultural production and the productivity
of both labor *and* land must be rapidly increased throughout Asia,
Africa and Latin America. Third World nations need to become more
self-sufficient in their food production. But unless some major
economic, institutional and structural changes are made, their dependence especially on North American food supplies will increase over
the coming decades.

In many developing countries, various historical circumstances have led to a concentration of large areas of land in the possession of a small class of powerful land owners. This is especially true in Latin America and parts of the Asian subcontinent. In Africa, both historical circumstances and the availability of relatively more unused land has resulted in a different pattern and structure of agricultural activity; although in terms of levels of farm productivity, there is little to distinguish between the three regions.

2. Peasant agriculture in Latin America, Asia and Africa

A common characteristic of agriculture in all three regions, and for that matter in many developed countries as well, is the position of the family farm as the basic unit of production. As Professor Weitz points out[4]:

For the vast number of farm families, whose members constitute the main agricultural work force, agriculture is not merely an occupation or a source of income; it is a way of life. This is particularly evident in traditional societies, where farmers are closely attached to their land and devote long, arduous days to its cultivation. Any change in farming methods perforce brings with it changes in the farmer's way of life. The introduction of biological and technical innovations must therefore be adapted not only to the natural and economic conditions, but perhaps even more to the attitudes, values and abilities of the mass of producers, who must understand the suggested changes, must be willing to accept them, and must be capable of carrying them out.

In spite of the very obvious difference between agricultural systems in Asia, Latin America and Africa and among individual nations within each region, certain broad similarities enable us to make some generalizations and comparisons. In particular, agrarian systems in many parts of Asia and Latin America show more structural and institutional similarities than differences, while African subsistence farmers exhibit many economic behaviour patterns similar to those of their counterparts in the other two regions. We examine first the major features of agricultural systems in Latin America and Asia.

Although the heritage and culture in these two regions are quite distinct, they have some characteristics of peasant life in common. Francis Foland has succinctly described these in the following passage:[5]

A. Latin America and Asia: similarities and differences

Both the Latin American and Asian peasant is a rural cultivator whose prime concern is survival. Subsistence defines his concept of life. He may strive to obtain his and his family's minimal needs by tilling an inadequate piece of land which is his own or, more often, which is rented from or pawned to a landlord or money lender, or by selling his labour for substandard wages to a commercial agricultural enterprise. Profits which might come to him through the fortunes of weather or market are windfalls, not preconceived goals. Debt rather than profit is his normal fate, and, therefore, his farming techniques are rationally scaled to his level of disposable capital; human and animal power rather than mechanized equipment; excrement rather than chemical fertilizers; traditional crops and seeds rather than experimental cultivations.

No effective social security, unemployment insurance, or minimum-wage law ease his plight. His every decision and act impinge directly upon his struggle for physical survival. In countries with a high proportion of peasantry, traditional food crops which a rural family can itself convert readily into the daily fare for its grain – or tuber-based diet dominate the agriculture; corn in Mexico, rice in Indonesia, mandioca in Brazil, soybeans in China. India's is typical of peasant agriculture with seventy-five per cent of the cropped land devoted to food grains such as rice, wheat, millets, barley and lentils. When these fail, as in Maharashtra in 1972, a peasant is reduced to trading his bullocks for a few bananas.

Although the day-to-day struggle for survival permeates the lives and attitudes of peasants in both Latin America and Asia (and, also, Africa – although the rural structure and institutions are considerably different), the structural nature of their agrarian existence differs markedly. In Latin America, the peasant's plague is the *latifundio–minifundio* system. In Asia, it is the fragmented and heavily congested dwarf parcels of land.

B. The *latifundio–minifundio* pattern and resource underutilization in Latin America In Latin America, as indeed in Asia and Africa, agrarian structures are not only part of the production system but also a basic feature of the entire economic, social and political organization of rural life. The type of agrarian structure which has prevailed in Latin America since colonial times and which provides much of the region with its social organization is the pattern of agricultural dualism known as *latifundio–minifundio*. Basically, *latifundios* are very large land holdings. They are defined in Latin America as those farms large enough to provide employment for over twelve people. In contrast *minifundios* are the smallest farms. They are defined as those farms which are too small to provide employment for a single family (two workers) with the typical incomes markets and level of technology and capital prevailing in each country or region.

According to the United Nations Food and Agricultural Organization (FAO), $1 \cdot 3$ per cent of landowners in Latin America hold $71 \cdot 6$ per cent of the entire area of land under cultivation. If we exclude those countries that have carried out drastic land reforms during the last 60 years (Mexico, Bolivia and Cuba), Latin America's agrarian structure seems to follow a uniform pattern. This pattern is basically one in which a small number of *latifundios* control a very large proportion of the agricultural land while a vast number of *minifundios* must scratch a survival existence on a meager fraction of the occupied land. Moreover, they must be ready to provide unpaid seasonal labour to the *latifundios*.

Table 10.5 provides a dramatic picture of this very unequal distribution of land holdings in seven Latin American countries. In no case do *minifundios,* which comprise up to 90 per cent of the total farms, occupy more than 17 per cent of the total agricultural land. In those countries with very dense indigenous populations like Ecuador, Guatemala and Peru, *minifundios* are much more widespread. The *latifundios* on the other hand comprise less than 7 per cent of the total farms in these countries. Yet they occupy as much as 82 per cent of the agricultural land. The average size of the *latifundios* in Argentina is 270 times that of the minifundios in Guatemala, the *latifundio* is often as much as 1,732 times the size of the *minifundio*. Countries like Guatemala with large and rapidly growing indigenous populations crowded on to shrinking areas of poor land have even evolved what has come to be known as 'microfundios' as a major form of land tenure. For example, there are presently 75,000 *microfundios* in Guatemala yielding an average income that is is less than one third of that provided by its 'minifundios' and about one-thousandth of the average incomes realized on its *latifundios*[6]. *Microfundio* peasants cannot even meet their subsistence requirements; they are thus forced to sell their labour at pitiful wages in order to secure a minimum diet for their families.

	Minifundios		*Latifundios*	
	Per cent of farms	Per cent of occupied land	Per cent of farms	Per cent of occupied land
Argentina	43·2	3·4	0·8	36·9
Brazil	22·5	0·5	4·7	59·5
Colombia	64·0	4·9	1·3	49·5
Chile	36·9	0·2	6·9	81·3
Ecuador	89·9	16·6	0·4	45·1
Guatamala	88·4	14·3	0·1	40·8
Peru	88·0	7·4	1·1	82·4

Table 10.5
Minifundios and *Latifundios* in the agrarian structure of selected Latin American countries

Source: Celso Furtado, *Economic Development in Latin America,* Cambridge U.P. (1970), 54.

But *latifundios* and *minifundios* do not constitute the entire gamut of Latin American agricultural landholdings. A considerable amount of production is also earned on what are known as 'family' farms and 'medium-sized' farms. The former provides work for two to four people (recall the *minifundio* could only provide work for less than two people) while the latter, also sometimes known as 'multi-family' farms, employ four to twelve workers (just below the *latifundio*). We see from Table 10.6 that in Argentina, Brazil and Colombia, these intermediate forms of farm organization account for over 60 per cent of total agricultural output and employ similar proportions of agricultural labour.

The economic and social ramifications of heavy land concentration in the hands of a very few large landowners are compounded by the relative inefficiency of *latifundios* in comparison with other types of Latin American farm organizations. Economists normally assume that large farms (or firms) use productive resources more efficiently than small ones on the grounds that large enterprises can take advantage of 'economies of large scale production' and thereby lower costs. In terms of agriculture, the efficient utilization of large tractors and combine harvesters requires large tracts of land – otherwise, this capital equipment will be grossly underutilized. The evidence from a wide range of Third World countries, however, indicates, that small farms are more efficient – i.e. lower cost – producers of most agricultural commodities[7]. For example, *minifundios* in Argentina, Brazil and Chile yield more than twice the value of output per hectare under cultivation than do the *latifundios* and more than ten times the value per hectare of total farmland[8]. This finding does not contradict the theory since most large farms in developed countries are lower cost producers compared with small family farms. Rather, the reason is to be found in the poor utilization of productive farm resources in developing nations – especially land resources on *latifundios* in Latin America. In terms of farm yields per unit of land actually under cultivation, the *latifundios* of Argentina, Brazil, Colombia, Chile and Guatemala are all below not only the *minifundios* but also the medium-sized family farms[9]. Moreover, in Brazil it has been estimated that the *latifundios* with an average area 31·6 times larger than that of the family farm invest only eleven times as much. A considerable portion of the arable *latifundio* land is thus left idle. The net result is that *total factor productivity* on family farms was twice as high (and, therefore, unit costs twice as low) as on the large *latifundio* tracts of land. It follows that a redistribution of these large unused arable lands to family farms would probably raise national agricultural output and productivity. In terms of simple economic efficiency criteria, the above argument is straightforward. However, the pattern of land ownership and control in Latin America is based on much more than economic criteria. It touches the whole social and political fabric of Latin American societies.

	Minifundios	Family farms	Medium-sized farms	Latifundios
Argentina				
Total farmland (%)	3	46	15	36
Value of agricultural product (%)	12	47	26	15
Labour employed (%)	30	49	15	6
Brazil				
Total farmland (%)	—	6	34	60
Value of agricultural product (%)	3	18	43	36
Labour employed (%)	11	26	42	21
Chile				
Total farmland (%)	—	8	13	79
Value of agricultural product (%)	4	16	23	57
Labour employed (%)	13	28	21	38
Colombia				
Total farmland (%)	5	25	25	45
Value of agricultural product (%)	21	45	19	15
Labour employed (%)	58	31	7	4
Guatemala				
Total farmland (%)	14	13	32	41
Value of agricultural product (%)	30	13	36	21
Labour employed (%)	68	13	12	7

Table 10.6 Agrarian structure indicators in selected Latin American countries

Source: Furtado, op. cit., p. 55.

Such a concentrated distribution of land ownership is typically accompanied in Latin America, as it is in many parts of Asia, by a feudal-type social system in which the masses of small producers are dependent upon the benevolence and good will of the large landowner. He has the power backed by local social and political institutions to permit them to make a meagre living off his land or to deny them even this opportunity, in which case they have no means of subsistence. Small producers pay for this privilege either by giving up to the landowner large proportions of their output (sometimes as much as 80 per cent) or by working his land for nothing at different times of the year. In some cases, these tenant farmers must provide *both* output and free labour to the *patron*. Under such a system, land ownership provides not only economic benefits but also, and often more importantly, social status and political power.

In short, a major explanation for the relative economic inefficiency and misuse of fertile land on the *latifundios* in Latin America is simply that the landowners often value these holdings not for their potential contributions to national agricultural output, but rather because of the considerable power and prestige that large landownership brings in many Latin American regions. It follows, and we discuss this issue later in the chapter, that raising agricultural production and improving the efficiency of Latin American agrarian systems will require much more than direct economic policies that lead to the provision of better seeds, more fertilizer, less 'distorted' factor prices, higher output prices and improved marketing facilities. It will also require a reorganization of rural social and institutional structures to provide the Latin American peasant, who now constitutes almost 70 per cent of the total rural population, a real opportunity to rise out of his present state of economic subsistence and social subservience.

If the major agrarian problem of Latin America can be identified as too much land under the control of too few people, the basic problem in Asia is one of too many people crowded on too little land. For example, the per capita availability of arable land in India is $0 \cdot 29$ hectares while in the People's Republic of China and Japan the figures are $0 \cdot 20$ and $0 \cdot 07$ hectares respectively. Central Java in Indonesia most exemplifies the pressure of population on limited land that characterizes the Asian agrarian scene. It has the dubious distinction of possessing the world's record population density – over 1,500 persons per square km[10].

C. The fragmentation and subdivision of peasant land in Asia

Throughout the twentieth century rural conditions in Asia have deteriorated significantly. Professor Myrdal has identified three major and interrelated forces which have moulded the traditional pattern of land ownership into its present fragmented condition: (*a*) the intervention of European rule; (*b*) the progressive introduction of monetized transactions and the rise in power of the moneylender; and (*c*) the rapid growth of Asian populations[11].

Briefly, the traditional Asian agrarian structure before European colonization was organized around the village community. Local chiefs and peasant families each provided goods and services – produce and labour from the peasants to the chief in return for protection, rights to use community land and the provision of public services from the chiefs to the peasants. Decisions on the allocation, disposition and use of the village's most valuable resource – land – belonged to the tribe or village community, either as a body or through its chief. Land could be redistributed among village members either as a result of population increase or natural calamities like droughts, floods, famines, war or disease. Within the community, families had a basic right to cultivate land for their own use and they could be evicted from their land only after a decision by the village community.

With the arrival of the Europeans, mainly in the form of British, French and Dutch colonists, major changes in the traditional agrarian structure occurred (some of which had already begun). As Myrdal[12] points out, 'Colonial rule acted as an important catalyst to change, both directly through its effects on property rights and indirectly through its effects on the pace of monetization on the indigenous economy and on the growth of population'. In the area of property rights, European land tenure systems of private property ownership were both encouraged and reinforced by law. One of the major social consequences of the imposition of European private property land tenure systems was, as Mydral[13] says, the

'breakdown of much of the earlier cohesion of village life with its often elaborate, though informal, structure of rights and obligations. The landlord was given unrestricted rights to dispose of the land and to raise

the tribute from its customary level to whatever amount he was able to extract. He was usually relieved of the obligation to supply security and public amenities because these functions were taken over by the government. Thus his status was transformed from that of a tribute receiver with responsibilities to the community to that of an absolute owner unencumbered by obligations towards the peasants and the public, other than the payment of land taxes.'

Contemporary landlords in India and Pakistan are able to avoid much of the taxation on income derived from their ownership of land. Today, the typical landlord in South Asia is an absentee owner who lives in the town and turns over the working of the land to share-croppers and tenant farmers. In many respects, therefore, his position of power in the economic, political and social structure of the rural community is analogous to that of the Latin American *patron* – the only difference being that the former is an absentee owner while the latter often lives on his *latifundio*.

The creation of individual titles to land enabled another dubious 'agent of change' in Asian rural socio-economic structures to rise to power – the moneylender. Once private property came into effect, land became a negotiable asset that could be offered by peasants as security for loans, and in the case of default could be forfeited and transferred to the often unscrupulous moneylender. At the same time Asian agriculture was being transformed from a subsistence to a commercial orientation both as a result of rising local demand in new towns and, more importantly, in response to external food demands of colonial European countries.

With the transition from subsistence to commercial production, the role of the moneylender changed drastically. In the subsistence economy, his activities were restricted to supplying the peasant with money to tide him over a crop failure or to cover extraordinary ceremonial expenditures such as family weddings or funerals. Most of these loans were paid in kind (i.e. in the form of food) at very high rates of interest. With the development of commercial farming, however, the peasant's cash needs grew significantly. Money was needed for seeds, fertilizer and other inputs. It was also needed to cover his food requirements if he shifted to the production of cash crops such as tea, rubber or jute. Often moneylenders were more interested in acquiring peasant lands as a result of loan defaults than they were in extracting high rates of interest. By charging exorbitant interest rates or inducing peasants to secure larger credits than they could manage, moneylenders were able to drive the peasants off their land. They could then reap the profits of land speculation by selling this farmland to rich and acquisitive landlords. Alternatively, they often became powerful landlords themselves. At any rate, as a consequence of the moneylender's influence, Asian peasant cultivators have seen their economic status deteriorate steadily over time.

The final major force altering the traditional agrarian structure in Asia has been the rapid rate of population growth, especially over the past 30 years. Myrdal[14] notes in reference to the population phenomenon that

When and where expansion in the cultivated area was not a feasible alternative – whether for physical, technical, social, economic, or institutional reasons – population growth was reflected, in the first instance, in the cumulative subdivision and fragmentation of the acreages already

under cultivation. Later this process, in combination with the emergence of private property and the rise of commercial agriculture and money-lending often contributed to the rise of large landowners, the demise of small peasant proprietors, and the increase of the landless.

The ultimate impoverishment of the peasantry was the inevitable consequence of this process of fragmentation, economic vulnerability and loss of land to rich and powerful landlords.

To give a dramatic example of the deterioration of rural conditions in some Asian countries during this century, consider the cases of India, Indonesia and the Philippines. In 1901 there were 286 million Indians. Now there are more than twice that number. The Indonesian population grew from 28·4 million in 1900 to its present level of over 125 million. The population of Central Luzoa in the Philippines has increased almost five-fold from its level of 1 million in 1903. In each case, severe fragmentation of landholdings inevitably followed so that today average peasant holdings in many areas of these countries is less than 1 hectare.

As these holdings shrink even further, production falls below the subsistence level and chronic poverty becomes a way of life. Peasants are forced to borrow even more from the moneylender at interest rates of 50 to 200 per cent. Most cannot repay these loans. They are compelled to sell their land and become tenants with large debts. Since land is scarce, they are forced to pay high rents. If they are share-croppers, they typically have to give the landlord 50 to 80 per cent of their crop. Since labour is abundant, wages are extremely low. Peasants, therefore, have no source of external income. They are trapped in a vice of chronic poverty from which there is no escape short of major rural reconstruction and reform. They thus share a common experience with their Latin American counterparts in the sense that both are gradually being transformed from small proprietors to tenant farmers and sharecroppers, then landless rural laborers, then jobless vagrants and finally migrant slum-dwellers on the fringes of modern urban areas. Not only have their levels of living deteriorated but their sense of self-esteem and freedom from exploitation, which may have been relatively high in spite of low incomes in the past, have also vanished. These many hundreds of millions of people in Asia and Latin America are thus caught in a downward spiral of underdevelopment, instead of an upward thrust towards real economic development and social progress.

As in Asia and Latin America, subsistence agriculture on small plots of land is the way of life for the vast majority of African people. However, the organization and structure of African agricultural systems differs markedly from those found in contemporary Asia or Latin America. Except in former colonial settlement areas like 'White Highlands' of Kenya and some of the large sugar, cocoa and coffee plantations of East and West Africa, the great majority of farm families in tropical Africa still plan their output primarily for their own subsistence. Since the basic variable input in African agriculture is farm family and village labour, African agricultural systems are dominated by three major characteristics: (*a*) the importance of subsistence farming in the village community, (*b*) the existence of land in excess of immediate require-ments which permits a general practice of shifting cultivation and diminishes the value of land ownership as an instrument of economic

D. Subsistence agriculture and extensive cultivation in Africa

and political power, and (c) the rights of each family (both nuclear and extended) in a village to have access to land and water in the immediate territorial vicinity, excluding from such access use by those families that do not 'belong' to the community even though they may be of the same tribe.

Low productivity subsistence farming characteristic of most traditional types of African agriculture results from a combination of three forces restricting the growth of output:

1. In spite of the existence of some unused and potentially cultivable land, only small areas can be planted and weeded by the farm family at a time when it uses only traditional tools such as the short-handled hoe, the axe and the long-handled knife or panga. Prevented in some countries from using animals by the notorious tsetse fly or by a lack of fodder in the long dry seasons, traditional African farming practices must rely to a great extent on the application of human labour to small parcels of land.

2. Second, given the limited amount of land that a farm family can cultivate in the context of a traditional technology and the use of primitive tools, these small areas tend to be intensively cultivated. As a result, they are subject to rapidly diminishing returns to increased labour inputs. In such conditions, *shifting cultivation* is the most economic method of using limited supplies of labor on extensive tracts of land. Under shifting cultivation, once the minerals are drawn out of the soil as a result of numerous croppings, new land is cleared and the process of planting and weeding is repeated. In the meantime, the fertility is restored to formerly cropped land until eventually it can be used again. Under such a process, manure and chemical fertilizers are unnecessary, although in most African villages some form of manure (mostly animal waste) is applied to nearby plots that are intensively cultivated in order to extend their period of fertility.

3. The third major factor curtailing output increases in traditional African agriculture is the scarcity of labor available during the busiest part of the growing season – namely for planting and weeding. At other times much of the labor is underemployed. Since the time of planting is determined by the onset of the rains and since much of Africa experiences only one extended rainy season, the demand for workers at times of planting and weeding during the early weeks of the rainy season usually exceeds all available rural labor supplies.

The net result of these three forces has been a relatively constant level of agricultural total output and labor productivity throughout much of Africa. As long as population size remained relatively stable, the pattern of low productivity and shifting cultivation enabled most African tribes to meet their subsistence food requirements (that is, with the obvious exception of climatic uncertainties in the form of severe and prolonged draughts such as that experienced in much of the Sahalian regions of Africa during the early 1970s). But the feasibility of shifting cultivation breaks down as population densities increase, as they have during the past two decades. It tends to be replaced by sedentary cultivation on small-owner-occupied plots of land. As a result, the need for other non-human productive inputs grows, especially in the more densely populated agricultural regions of Kenya, Nigeria, Ghana and Uganda. Moreover, with the growth of towns, the penetration of the monetary economy and the introduction of land taxes, purely subsistence agricultural practices are no longer viable. Mixed and exclusively commercial farming begins to appear.

We may conclude our analysis by noting that although both resource E. Conclusions
endowments and the traditional African communal social systems differ markedly from those agrarian structures prevalent throughout much of Asia and Latin America, the contemporary economic status of the small farmer is not very different among the three regions. *Achieving subsistence is still the major objective of Third World peasant agriculture.* Even though the small African farmer may appear to have more room to manoeuvre than his typical Asian or Latin American counterpart, the rapid growth of rural populations in countries like Nigeria, Kenya and Uganda threatens to create mounting pressures for the further fragmentation of smallholder agriculture. Unless low productivity peasant agriculture can be transformed rapidly into higher productivity farming in Asia and Latin America (primarily through judicious land reform accompanied by concomitant structural changes in socio-economic institutions) and Africa (basically through improved farming practices), the masses of impoverished rural dwellers face an even more precarious existence in the years immediately ahead.

10.3 The economics of small-scale agricultural development: transition from subsistence to specialized farming

There are three major stages in the evolution of agricultural production[15]. The first and most primitive is the pure, low productivity, subsistence farm. The second stage might be called 'diversified' or 'mixed' agriculture where part of the produce is grown for self consumption and part for sale to the commercial sector. Finally, the third stage represents the 'modern' farm which is exclusively engaged in high productivity, 'specialized' agriculture catering entirely for the commercial market.

Agricultural modernization in mixed-market developing economies may be described in terms of the gradual but sustained transition from subsistence to specialized production. But such a transition involves much more than reorganizing the structure of the farm economy or the application of new agricultural technologies. We have seen that in most traditional societies agriculture is not just an economic activity; it is a way of life. Any government attempting to transform this traditional agriculture must recognize that in addition to adapting the farm structure to meet the demand for increased agricultural production, profound changes affecting the entire social, political and institutional structure of rural societies will often be necessary. Without such changes, agricultural development will either never get started or, more likely, will simply widen the already sizeable gap between the few wealthy large landholders and the masses of impoverished tenant farmers, smallholders and landless laborers.

Before analyzing the economics of agricultural and rural development, therefore, we need to understand the evolutionary process by which traditional subsistence farms are transformed into modern specialized commercial farms both through the farm family's own efforts and also through supporting activities of governments and local institutions. These three stages are outlined below:

1. Stage 1: subsistence
farming: risk, uncertainty
and survival

In the traditional subsistence farm, output and consumption are identical and one or two stable crops (usually wheat, barley, sorghum, rice or corn) are the chief sources of food intake. Output and productivity are low and only the simplest tools are used. Capital investment is minimal while land and labor are the principal factors of production. The law of diminishing returns is in operation as more labor is applied to shrinking (or shifting) parcels of land. The failure of the rains, the appropriation of his land or the appearance of the exploiting moneylender to collect outstanding debts are the bane of the peasant's existence and the source of fear for his survival. Labor is underemployed for most of the year, although workers may be fully occupied at seasonal peak periods such as planting and harvesting. The peasant usually cultivates only as much land as his family can manage without the need for hired labor; although many peasant farmers do intermittently employ one or two landless laborers. The environment is harsh and static. Technological limitations, rigid social institutions and fragmented markets and communication networks between rural areas and urban centers tend to discourage higher levels of production.

Throughout much of the Third World agriculture is still in this subsistence stage. But in spite of the relative backwardness of production technologies and the misguided convictions of some foreigners who attribute the peasants' resistance to change as a sign of incompetence or irrationality, the fact remains that given the static nature of the peasant's environment, the uncertainties which surround him, the need to meet minimum survival levels of output and the rigid social institutions into which he is locked, most peasants behave in an economically rational manner when confronted with alternative opportunities. As one informed observer[16] has noted about peasant agricultural systems:

Despite the almost infinite variety of village-level institutions and processes to be found around the world, they have three common characteristics which are pertinent to change: 1, they have historically proven to be successful, i.e. the members have survived; 2, they are relatively static, at least the general pace of change is below that which is considered desirable today; and 3, attempts at change are frequently resisted, both because these institutions and processes have proven dependable and because the various elements constitute something akin to an ecological unity in the human realm.

The traditional two-factor neo-classical theory of production where land (and perhaps capital) is fixed and labor is the only variable input provides some insight into the economics of subsistence agriculture. Specifically, it provides an economic rationale for the observed low productivity of traditional agriculture in the form of the 'law' of diminishing marginal productivity.

Unfortunately, this same traditional theory of production does not satisfactorily explain why peasant agriculturalists are often very resistant to technological innovation in farming techniques or to the introduction of new seeds or different cash crops. According to the standard theory a rational income or profit-maximizing farm or firm will always choose a method of production which will increase output for a given cost (in this case, the available labor time) or lower costs for a given output level. But the theory is based on the crucial assumption that farmers possess 'perfect knowledge' of all input–output relationships in the form of a technological production function for their crop. This is the point at which the theory loses a good deal of its validity when applied to the environment of subsistence agriculture in much of Asia, Africa and Latin America.

Subsistence agriculture is a highly *risky* and *uncertain* venture. It is made even more so by the fact that human lives are at stake. In regions where farms are extremely small and cultivation is dependent upon the uncertainties of a highly variable rainfall, average output will be low and in-poor years the peasant and his family will be exposed to the very real danger of starvation. In such circumstances, the main motivating force in the peasant's life may be the maximization *not* of income, but rather *of his family's chances of survival.* Accordingly, when risk and uncertainty are high, a small farmer may be very reluctant to shift from a traditional technology and crop pattern which over the years he has come to know and understand to a new one which promises higher yields but may entail greater risks of crop failure. When sheer survival is at stake, it is more important to avoid a 'bad' year' (i.e. total crop failure) than it is to maximize the output in better years. In the jargon of economic statistics, 'risk-avoiding' peasant farmers are likely to prefer a technology of food production which combines a low 'mean' per hectare yield with low 'variance' (i.e. less fluctuations around the average) to alternative technologies and crops which may promise a higher mean yield but also present the risk of a greater variance.

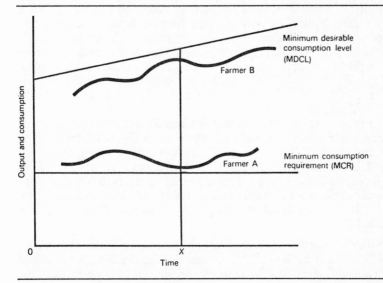

Fig 10.1
Small farmer attitudes towards risk: Why it sometimes is rational to resist innovation and change

Figure 10.1 provides a simple illustration of how attitudes towards risk among small farmers may militate against apparently economically justified innovations[17].

In Fig. 10.1 we measure levels of output and consumption on the vertical axis and time on the horizontal axis. We then draw two straight lines. The lower horizontal line measures the minimum physiological consumption requirements (MCR) necessary for the farm family's physical survival. This may be taken as the starvation minimum that is fixed by nature: any output below this level would be catastrophic for the peasant and his family. The upper positively sloped straight line represents the minimum level of food consumption that would be *desirable* (MDCL) in terms of the prevailing cultural factors affecting village consumption standards. It is assumed that MDCL rises over time to reflect rising expectations as traditional societies are opened up to external influences. The producer's attitude toward risk will be largely conditioned by his historic output performance relative to these two standards of reference.

Looking at Fig. 10.1, we see that at the moment of time X, Farmer A's output levels over the past few years have been very close to the family's minimum consumption requirement (MCR). He is barely getting by and cannot take a chance of falling below MCR. He will therefore have a greater incentive to minimize risk than will Farmer B, whose output performance over recent years has been well above the minimum subsistence level and is close to the culturally determined desirable consumption standard (MDCL). Farmer B will, therefore, be more likely to innovate and change than will Farmer A.

Many programs to raise agricultural productivity among small farmers have suffered because of failure to provide adequate insurance (both financial credit and physical 'buffer' stocks) against the risks of crop shortfalls, whether these risks are real or imagined in the peasant's mind. An understanding of the major role which risk and uncertainty play in the economics of subsistence agriculture would have prevented early and unfortunate characterizations of subsistence or traditional farmers as technologically backward, irrational producers with limited aspirations, or just plain 'lazy natives' as in the colonial stereotype. Moreover, in many parts of Asia and Latin America, a closer examination of why peasant farmers have apparently not responded to an 'obvious' economic opportunity will often reveal that (a) the landlord secured all the gain, or (b) the moneylender captured all the profits, or (c) the government 'guaranteed' price was never paid, or (d) complementary inputs, fertilizer, pesticides, assured supplies of water, adequate non-usurous credit, etc., were never made available to the small farmer.

We may conclude that peasant farmers *do* act rationally and are responsive to economic incentives and opportunities. Where innovation and change fail to occur, we should not assume that peasants are stupid, irrational or conservative; instead we should examine carefully the environment in which the small farmer operates to search for the particular institutional or commercial obstacles which may be blocking or frustrating constructive change. As Professor Griffen[18] has pointed out,

If peasants sometimes appear to be unresponsive or hostile to proposed technical changes it is probably because the risks are high, the returns to the cultivator are low – for example, because of local custom or land tenure conditions, or because credit facilities and marketing outlets are inadequate and the necessary inputs – including knowledge – are missing.

Efforts to minimize risk and remove commercial and institutional obstacles to small farmer innovation are, therefore, essential requirements of agricultural and rural development.

2. Stage II: the transition to mixed and diversified farming
It is unrealistic to think in terms of instantly transforming a traditional agrarian system which has prevailed for many generations into a highly specialized commercial farming system. Attempts to introduce cash crops indiscriminately in subsistence farms have more often than not resulted in the peasant's loss of land to moneylenders or landlords. Subsistence living is merely substituted for subsistence production.

Exclusive reliance on cash crops for small farmers can be more precarious than pure subsistence agriculture since risks of price fluctuations are added to the uncertainty of nature.

Diversified or *mixed farming,* therefore, represents a logical first step in the transition from subsistence to specialized production. In this stage the staple crop no longer dominates farm output since new cash crops such as fruits, vegetables, coffee, tea, pyrethrum, etc. are established, together with simple animal husbandry. These new activities can take up the normal slack in farm workloads during times of the year when 'disguised unemployment' is prevalent. This is especially desirable in most Third World nations where rural labor is abundantly available for better and more efficient utilization.

For example, if the staple crop occupies the land during only parts of the year, new crops can be introduced in the slack season to take advantage of both idle land and family labor. Alternatively, in many parts of Africa where labor is in short supply during peak planting seasons, simple labor-saving devices (such as small tractors, mechanical seeders or animal-operated steel ploughs) can be introduced to free labor for other farm activities. Finally, the use of better seeds, fertilizer and simple irrigation to increase yields of staple crops like wheat, maize and rice can free part of the land for cash crop cultivation while still assuring an adequate supply of the staple food. The farm operator can thus have a marketable surplus which he can sell to raise his family's consumption standards and/or invest in farm improvements. Diversified farming can also minimize the impact of staple crop failure and provide a security of income previously unavailable.

The success or failure of such efforts to transform traditional agriculture will depend not only on the farmer's ability and skill in raising his productivity but even more importantly on the social, commercial and institutional conditions under which he must function. Specifically, if he can have a reasonable and reliable access to credit, fertilizer, water, crop information, marketing facilities, etc., *and* if he can feel secure that he and his family will be the primary beneficiaries of any improvements, then there is no reason to assume that traditional farmers will not respond to economic incentives and new opportunities to improve their standard of living. Evidence from such diverse countries as Colombia, Mexico, Nigeria, Ghana, Kenya, India, Pakistan, Thailand and the Philippines show that under proper conditions small farmers are responsive to incentives and opportunities and will make radical changes in what and how they produce. Lack of innovation in agriculture, as we have seen, is usually due not to poor motivation or fear of change *per se,* but to inadequate or unprofitable opportunities.

3. Stage III: from divergence to specialization – modern commercial farming

The specialized farm represents the final and most advanced stage of individual holding in a mixed, market economy. It is the most prevalent type of farming in advanced industrial nations. It has evolved in response to and parallel with the overall development in other areas of the national economy. General rises in living standards, biological and technical progress and the expansion of national and international markets have provided the main impetus for its emergence and growth.

On specialized farms, the provision of food for the family with some marketable surplus no longer provides the basic motivational objective. Pure commercial 'profit' becomes the criterion of success and maximum per hectare yields derived from man-made (irrigation, fertilizer, pesticides, hybrid seeds, etc.) and natural resources become the object of farm activity. Production is entirely for the market. Economic concepts such as fixed and variable costs, saving, investment and rates of return, optimal factor combinations, maximum production possibilities, market prices and price supports, etc., take on quantitative and qualitative significance. The emphasis in resource utilization is no longer on land, water and labor as in subsistence and often mixed farming. Instead, capital formation, technological progress and scientific research and development play a major role in stimulating higher levels of output and productivity.

Specialized farms may vary in both size and function. They may range from intensively cultivated fruit and vegetable farms to the vast wheat and corn fields of North America. In most cases, sophisticated labour-saving mechanical equipment ranging from huge tractors and combine harvesters to airborne spraying techniques permit a single family to cultivate many thousands of acres of land.

Characteristic	Subsistence	Mixed	Specialized
Composition of output	One dominant staple crop and auxiliary crops	Diversified	One dominant cash crop and auxiliary crops
Purpose of production	Domestic supply	Domestic and market supply	Market only
Work schedule	Seasonal	Balanced	Seasonal
Capital investment	Low	Medium	High
Income	Low	Medium	High
Income security	Low	High	Medium (price fluctuations)
Ratio of income to value of output	High	Approximately half	Low
Farmer's professional know-how	Specialized	Diverse	Specialized
Dependence on a supporting system	None	Partial	Full

Table 10.7
Distinguishing characteristics of the three stages of farm evolution

Source: Weitz, op. cit., p. 20.

The common feature of all specialized farms, therefore, is the emphasis on the cultivation of one particular crop, the use of capital-intensive and, in many cases, labor saving techniques of production and the reliance on 'economies of scale' to reduce unit costs and maximize profits. For all practical purposes, specialized farming is no different in concept or operation from large industrial enterprises. In fact, some of the largest specialized farming operations in both the developed and especially the less developed nations are owned and managed by large 'agrobusiness' multinational corporate enterprises.

4. Stages of farm evolution: a summary Table 10.7 summarizes the basic characteristics of the three stages of farm evolution, subsistence, mixed and specialized, that parallel the broad stages of national economic growth. Most Third World nations are in the process of transition from subsistence to mixed farming (excluding, of course, the scattered enclaves of large and often foreign-owned specialized plantation agriculture). The further transition from mixed to widespread specialized farming may or may not be an ultimate national goal, especially in view of the serious nature of rural and urban unemployment problems. Moreover, the predominance of specialized farming in developing nations is a very tentative future aspiration. Its ultimate emergence depends upon the solution of many other short- and intermediate-term problems. The improvement of small-scale, mixed farming practices that will not only raise farm incomes and average yields but will also effectively absorb presently underutilized rural labor through the adoption of effective labor-intensive farming practices offer the major immediate avenue towards the achievement of real people-oriented rural development.

10.4 Towards a strategy of agricultural and rural development: some main requirements

If the major objective of agricultural and rural development in Third World nations is the progressive improvement in rural levels of living achieved primarily through increases in small-farm incomes, output and productivity, it is important to identify the principal sources of agricultural progress and the basic conditions essential to its achievement. These are necessarily interrelated. But for purposes of description we may separate each into three components:

Sources of small-scale
agricultural progress
1. Technical change and innovation

2. Appropriate government economic policies
3. Supportive social institutions

Conditions of general
rural advancement
1. Modernizing farm structures to meet rising food demands
2. Creating an effective supporting system
3. Changing the rural environment to improve levels of living

Each of these six interrelated components of agricultural and rural development are discussed briefly in turn.

1. Improving small-scale agriculture

A. Technology and innovation

In most developing countries new agricultural technologies and innovations in farm practices are preconditions for sustained improvements in levels of output and productivity. In many parts of Africa and Latin America, however, increased output has been achieved without the need for new technology simply by extending cultivation into unused but potentially productive lands. Most of these opportunities have by now been exploited and there is not much scope for further significant improvement.

Two major sources of technological innovation can increase farm yields. Unfortunately they have very different implications for Third World agricultural development. The first is the introduction of 'mechanized' agriculture to replace human labor. The introduction of such labor-saving machinery (e.g. large tractors) can have a dramatic effect on the volume of output per worker, especially where land is extensively cultivated and labor is scarce. For example, one man operating a huge combine-harvester can accomplish in a single hour the equivalent of a thousand workers using traditional methods.

But in the rural areas of most developing nations where land parcels are small, capital is scarce and labor is abundant, the introduction of heavily mechanized techniques is not only often ill-suited to the physical environment but, more important, often has the effect of creating more rural unemployment without necessarily lowering per unit costs of food production[19]. Importation of such machinery can, therefore, be 'anti-developmental' since its efficient deployment requires large tracts of land (and thus the expropriation of small holdings by land-lords and moneylenders) and it tends to exacerbate the already serious problems of rural poverty and unemployment.

By contrast, biological (hybrid seeds) and chemical (fertilizer, pes-ticides, insecticides, etc.) innovations are land-augmenting, that is, they improve the quality of existing land by raising yields per hectare. Only indirectly do they increase output per worker. Improved seeds, advanced techniques of irrigation and crop rotation, the increasing use of fertilizers, pesticides and herbicides, and new developments in veterinary medicine and animal nutrition represent major scientific advances in modern agricultures. These measures are technologically 'scale-neutral' that is, theoretically they can be applied equally effec-tively on large and small farms. They do not necessarily require large capital inputs or mechanized equipment. They are, therefore, particu-larly well suited for tropical and subtropical regions and offer an enormous *potential* for raising agricultural output in Third World nations.

B. Policies and institutions Unfortunately, although the new hybrid seed varieties of wheat, corn and rice (often collectively referred to as the 'miracle seeds' or the basis of the 'Green Revolution') are scale neutral and thus offer the potential for small-farm progress, the 'institutions' and 'government policies' that accompany their introduction into the rural economy often are *not* scale neutral. On the contrary, they often merely serve the needs and vested interests of the wealthy landowners. Since the new hybrid seeds need access to complementary inputs like irrigation, fertilizer, insecticides, credit and agricultural extension services, if these are provided only to a small minority of large landowners, then the effective impact of the Green Revolution can be and has been in parts of South Asia and Mexico the further impoverishment of the masses of rural peasants. Large landowners with their disproportion-ate access to these complementary inputs and support services are able to gain a 'competitive' advantage over smallholders and eventually drive them out of the market. Large-scale farmers obtain access to low-interest government credit, while smallholders are forced to turn to the moneylender. The inevitable result is the further widening of the gap between rich and poor and the increased consolidation of agricul-tural land in the hands of a very few so-called 'progressive' farmers. A 'developmental' innovation with great potential for alleviating rural poverty and raising agricultural output thus becomes a further instru-ment for the impoverishment of the rural peasant class. What was designed to be developmental can thus turn out to be 'anti-developmental' if public policies and social institutions (e.g. land tenure and credit arrangements) militate against the active participa-tion of the small farmer in the evolving agrarian structure[20].

2. Three conditions for rural-development Let us now collect what has already been said to formulate three propositions which we believe constitute the necessary conditions for the realization of a people-oriented agricultural and rural develop-ment strategy.

A. Land reform Proposition I: *Farm structures and land tenure patterns need to be adapted to the dual objectives of increasing food production and prom-oting a wider distribution of the benefits of agrarian progress.*
Agricultural and rural development which benefits the masses of peo-

ple can only succeed through a joint effort by the government and *all* the farmers, not just the 'large' farmers. A first step in any such effort, especially in Latin America but also in parts of Asia, is the provision of secured tenure rights to the individual farmer. A small farmer's attachment to his land is very profound. It is closely bound up with his innermost sense of self-esteem and freedom from coercion. When he is driven off his land or is gradually impoverished through accumulated debts, not only is his material well-being damaged but, more important, his sense of self-worth and his desire for self and family improvement can be permanently destroyed.

It is for these human reasons as well as for reasons of greater agricultural output that 'land reform' is often proposed as a necessary first condition for agricultural development in many LDCs. *In most countries the highly unequal structure of the land ownership is probably the single most important determinant of the existing highly inequitable distribution of rural income and wealth.* It is also the basis for the character of agricultural development. When land is very unevenly distributed, rural peasants can have little hope for economic advancement.

Land reform usually entails a redistribution of the rights of ownership and/or use of land away from large landowners and in favor of cultivators with very limited or no landholdings. It can take on many forms: the transfer of ownership to tenants who already work the land (as in Cuba, Ethiopia, Japan and Taiwan); transfer of land from large estates to small farms (as in Mexico); the appropriation of large estates for new settlement (as in Kenya); and the improvement or irrigation and subsequent development of large private or state-owned lands into farmer cooperatives (as in China and Tanzania). All go under the heading of land reform and are designed to fulfill one central function: *the transfer of land ownership or control directly or indirectly to those who actually work the land.*

There is widespread agreement among economists and other development specialists on the need for land reform. To Myrdal, land reform holds the key to agricultural development in Asia. The Economic Commission for Latin America (ECLA) has repeatedly identified land reform as a necessary precondition for agricultural and rural progress. A 1971 Food and Agricultural Organization (FAO) report concluded that in many Third World regions land reform remains a prerequisite for development. The report argued that such reform was more urgent today than ever before, primarily because (*a*) income inequalities and unemployment in rural areas have worsened; (*b*) rapid population growth threatens further to worsen existing inequalities; and (*c*) recent and potential technological breakthroughs in agriculture (the Green Revolution) will be exploited primarily by large and powerful rural landholders and, as a consequence of the already highly unequal agrarian structure, will result in an increase in their power, wealth and capacity to resist future reform.

If programs of land reform can be legislated and *effectively implemented by the government,* a major problem with many such efforts in Asia and Latin America, then the basis for the transition from subsistence to mixed farming with improved output levels and higher standards of living for rural peasants will be established. But the mere enactment and enforcement of an egalitarian land reform program is no guarantee of successful agricultural and rural development, if such reforms are not accompanied by complementary government programs to transform the potentiality for improvement into an actuality. This leads to our second proposition:

B. Supportive policies Proposition II: *The full benefits of smale-scale agricultural development cannot be realized unless government support systems are created which provide the necessary incentives, economic opportunities and access to needed inputs to enable small cultivators to expand their output and raise their productivity.*

While land reform is essential in many parts of Asia and Latin America, it is likely to be ineffective and perhaps even counterproductive unless there is a corresponding change in rural institutions that control production (e.g. banks, moneylenders, seed and fertilizer distributors, etc.), supporting government services (technical and educational extension services, public credit agencies, storage and marketing facilities, rural transport and feeder roads, etc.), and government pricing policies with regard to both inputs (e.g. removing factor price distortions) and outputs. Even where land reform is not necessary but where productivity and incomes are low (as in the whole of Africa and much of Southeast Asia), this broad network of external support services along with appropriate governmental pricing policies related to both farm inputs and outputs is an essential condition of sustained agricultural progress.

C. Integrated development objectives Proposition III: *Rural development, while dependent primarily on small-farmer agricultural progress, implies much more. It encompasses (a) improvement in 'levels of living' including income, employment, education, health and nutrition, housing and a variety of related social services; (b) a decreasing inequality in the distribution of rural incomes and in urban–rural imbalances in incomes and economic opportunities; and (c) the capacity of the rural sector to sustain and accelerate the pace of these improvements over time.*

The proposition is self-explanatory. We need only add that the achievement of its three objectives is vital to national development. This is not only because the majority of Third World populations are located in rural areas but because the burgeoning problems of urban unemployment and population congestion must find their ultimate solution in the improvement of the rural environment. By restoring a proper balance between urban and rural economic opportunities and by creating the conditions for the broad popular participation in national development efforts and rewards, developing nations will have taken a giant step towards the realization of the true meaning of 'development'.

With these thoughts in mind, let us now conclude with a brief look at one unique approach to rural development which in the past few years has attracted considerable attention.

10.5 Rural development in China: a unique approach[21]

Since the opening up of the People's Republic of China to foreign visitors in the early 1970s, there has been widespread interest in the Chinese model of rural development. The question most often asked is: of what relevance is it to other Third World nations in their attempt to eliminate mass poverty and build a unified and largely self-sufficient social and economic system? We can only hint at the range of possible answers in this brief section, but according to Dr Aziz[22] 'the Chinese experiment in rural development has already thrown up some very important truths and principles which every policy-maker or social scientist concerned with rural development should at least begin to think about'.

Rural development in China is based on the people's commune, a **1. The people's commune** 'multi-purpose political, administrative and organizational unit covering the full range of economic, social and administrative activities necessary and feasible in a rural community'[23]. The contemporary people's commune introduced in 1958 represents the fourth stage in the evolution of China's programme of agrarian reform. The first stage was characterized by China's traditional feudal system of land tenure in which 10 per cent of the rural population (landlords and rich peasants) owned 70 to 75 per cent of the land. This land was confiscated during the Chinese revolution of 1949 and distributed to the poor and landless peasants who nevertheless found it very difficult to cultivate the land economically on an individual basis without supporting commercial and social services. As a result, 'mutual aid teams' were formed during the second stage of agrarian reform between 1949 and 1952. These groups were still too small to be effective both in terms of their purchase of inputs and their efficiency in producing outputs. Thus, the third stage appeared in 1955–6. It was characterized by the formation of agricultural producers cooperatives and then by advanced cooperatives ranging from 100 to 500 hectares. Such cooperatives were able to pool their resources effectively and consequently to raise agricultural yields. But they were not equipped to carry out the diverse economic, political and administrative functions required for sustained progress. As a result, in 1958 the fourth and final stage of agrarian reform was introduced 'by converting and regrouping all the Advanced Cooperatives into People's Agricultural Communes and abolishing whatever individual ownership of land still existed in favour of communal ownership'[24]. Communal ownership includes all land in rural communities, all means of agricultural production and commune-owned industries.

Organizationally, each commune is divided into production 'brigades' and each brigade into a number of basic units known as 'work teams'. Each work team is equal to a village of about twenty-five to thirty families. It produces both to meet its own needs and to meet quotas allotted to it by the commune. The total land and population in a commune can vary anywhere from 3,000 to 12,000 hectares and from 9,000 to 50,000 people. There are reported to be about 26,000 communes in present-day China[25].

Apparently, China has been able to abolish poverty by providing **2. Poverty, employment** minimum levels of living for all its people, to eliminate unemployment **and income distribution** by mobilizing all available human resources into production brigades and work teams and greatly to reduce disparities in the distribution of personal income and wealth through the abolition of private assets and the introduction of a system of fixed wages and prices. Average 'real' income levels of Chinese farmers appear to be two or three times those in India and Pakistan and 50 to 100 per cent higher than in Thailand, Indonesia and the Philippines. More significantly, this average is relatively evenly distributed with the highest income levels said to be only twice as large as the lowest. As we have seen, average income levels in other Third World countries often mask great differences between wealthy landowners and poor subsistence farmers. But, at an even more basic level, Chinese officials are quick to assert that 'The days in which the Chinese were without food and clothing are gone forever. There is no Chinese man or woman today whose basic needs of food, clothing, shelter, education and medical facilities are not met.'[26] If this statement is true, then there are few countries in the world, including the most developed, which can make a similar claim.

3. How the Chinese system works: six important factors According to Dr Aziz, there are six central attributes of the Chinese commune system. The first and historically most important factor in the system was its ability to *mobilize the unemployed labor force* for land improvements, building dams and dikes, digging irrigation channels, constructing roads and cultivating existing land more intensively. As a result, average Chinese farm yields are twice those in India and Pakistan. Chinese food grain production increased from 108 million tons in 1949 to 246 million tons in the early 1970s. China is now and has been for several years more than self-sufficient in food production in spite of its enormous population of over 800 million.

The second important factor about the Chinese commune has been its ability to *diversify its rural economic activity* from agriculture to forestry, fisheries and finally small industries. This was done only after a satisfactory base had been established within the agricultural sector itself. According to Aziz[27], 'this continuing diversification in economic activities can be regarded as the most important factor in tackling the problem of rural employment by absorbing the internal additions to the labour force and workers rendered potentially surplus by increasing productivity in agriculture'.

The third major element of the system is its ability to *generate rural capital formation and industrialization* through a system of transfers of 15 to 20 per cent of total commune revenue into an accumulation fund. These funds are then used to invest in productive improvements in commune industries, especially in the form of capital construction but increasingly also in mechanized farm equipment. Of perhaps even greater importance from the viewpoint of economic incentives have been the Chinese government's deliberate attempts to improve rural standards of living by consciously raising the price of agricultural goods relative to that of industrial goods (i.e. the 'terms of trade' between agriculture and industry). As table 10.8 reveals, between 1950 and 1970 the quantity of industrial goods that a *given* amount of agricultural produce could purchase increased by almost 67 per cent.

A fourth significant aspect of the Chinese system is the commune's role in *providing essential social services to all rural people* particularly in the field of education and health. Schools and hospitals are provided out of the commune's own savings. The people are therefore able to realize the direct social benefits of their labor.

The unique system of Chinese *decentralized rural planning* with its emphasis on the maximum exploitation of local resources to meet local needs is the fifth strategic aspect of the commune system. Chinese planning differs from that of most other countries by its emphasis on mass participation in the planning process rather than production targets and industrial or regional preferences being decided in the urban offices of some out-of-touch central planners.

Sixth, and probably most important, is the strategic position of the commune in *the political and ideological system* of China. Again, we quote Dr Aziz[28]:

The most important factor in the system of the Chinese Commune is its place in the ideological and political system of China. The main objective of the Chinese society is not the most rapid material progress or the creation of a consumer society but the evolution of a classless society in which social inequalities are reduced to the minimum, and where there is a high level of political and ideological consciousness and a pronounced concern for the well-being of every citizen. These goals are radically different from the implicit or express objectives of many other developing countries, where in the name of economic growth or economic development the main pursuits are essentially material in nature and the end result is generally the enrichment of a privileged minority or 'a consumer society but without anything to consume'. Pecuniary incentives are not absent in China – they have sought to meet everyone's basic needs and provide for a steady increase in real income – but the desire for a larger monetary reward is not the prime mover of the system: it is ideology plus organization.

	(1) Agricultural purchase price index	(2) Industrial retail prices in rural areas index	(3) Ratio of (1) to (2)
1950	100·0	100·0	100·0
1951	119·6	110·2	108·5
1952	121·6	109·7	110·8
1953	132·5	108·2	122·4
1954	136·7	110·3	123·9
1955	135·1	111·9	120·7
1956	139·2	110·8	125·6
1957	146·2	112·1	130·4
1958	149·5	111·2	134·4
1970	n.a.	n.a.	166·7

Table **10.8**
Terms of trade between agriculture and industry, Peoples Republic of China 1950–70

Source: John G. Gurley, 'Rural development in China: 1949–1972 and the lessons to be learned from it', in E. O. Edwards (ed.), *Employment in Developing Nations,* Columbia U.P., New York (1974), 396.

Since their formation in 1958, the Chinese rural communes have apparently made remarkable economic and social strides among which the following are most significant:

4. Implications for rural development in other Third World nations

1. the transformation of an impoverished and stratified rural society into viable production units capable of meeting the food and basic material needs of the world's largest population;
2. the transformation of the rural economy into a diversified economic system with labour-intensive, small-scale industry functioning in conjunction with labour-intensive agriculture;
3. the creation of a social system founded on principles of equality and social justice; and
4. the development of a decentralized administrative and planning system that is close to the people and based on their perceived needs and requirements.

If all reports are correct, in the short period since the 1949 Chinese revolution, China, which effectively isolated itself from the rest of the world, has 'already abolished absolute poverty; there is no unemployment in China and no inflation – the three problems which most other developing countries of Asia, Africa and Latin America have failed to solve so far'[29]. We might add that absolute poverty, unemployment, and inflation are not unknown phenomena in countries like the United States and Western Europe as well.

But the tough questions still remain. Of what relevance is the Chinese experience – assuming that those like Dr. Aziz and Professor Gurley who have visited and written about China are accurately reflecting the prevailing situation – for other Third World nations? Specifically, without the powerful and massively supported political and ideological basis of Chinese society, can other LDCs develop effective rural cooperative efforts on a basis other than private property? Can they eliminate wide disparities in the distribution of wealth and income? Can they content the majority of their populations with only basic necessities such as food, clothing and shelter plus a few minor luxuries such as bicycles, radios and clocks when both their leaders and their people are continually exposed to the 'demonstration effects' of mass consumption items like cars, fashionable clothes, TV sets, refrigerators and other luxury goods of developed countries? Is it possible for resource-deficient small countries like most of those in Asia, Africa and Latin America to shut themselves off from the rest of the world and become totally self-reliant? And finally, can the sense of security and prestige derived from private land ownership – a sense so central to the societies of Asia and Latin America and increasingly so in Africa – be replaced by a sense of communal commitment and motivation based on a political ideology of equality and social justice?

These are not easy questions to answer without reference to particular nations and societies. Moreover, the real material benefit which the average Chinese rural dweller has obtained over the past quarter of a century is not without its price; his limited private freedom to choose a way of life that may not be in tune with the prevailing ideology. Freedom of choice may be relatively unimportant when sheer survival is the major concern, but it tends to assume greater importance as basic material needs become satisfied. In other words, how long will the present ideological and economic system in China be able to be sustained as it opens itself and its peoples to outside influences.

Even if for most underdeveloped countries the answer to many of the above questions would be negative, there is still much to be learned from the Chinese experience. Perhaps most important is the lesson it provides about agricultural output and promoting rural industries through small-scale, labor-intensive activities supported by publicly provided economic and social services. While the Chinese model may not provide a blueprint for other less well-endowed or less culturally homogeneous Third World nations, it does provide a rough sketch of how it can be done. Perhaps, more important, it shows that it *can* be done, even for a country with 800 million people.

Notes

1. E. F. Szcepanik, 'Agricultural capital formation in selected developing countries', *Agricultural Planning Studies,* No. 11, FAO, 1970.
2. See Raanan Weitz, *From Peasant to Farmer: A Revolutionary Strategy for Development,* Columbia U.P. (1971), 6–9. Much of the following analysis is drawn from this very informative and thoughtful book.
3. Ibid., pp. 7–8.
4. Ibid., p. 9.
5. Frances M. Foland, 'Agrarian unrest in Asia and Latin America', *World Development,* **2,** no. 4 and 5 (1974), 56.
6. Celso Furtado, *Economic Development in Latin America,* Cambridge U.P. (1970), 54.

7. For a summary of Asian evidence on this point see Keith Griffen, *The Political Economy of Agrarian Change,* Macmillan, London (1974).
8. Furtado, op. cit., p. 56.
9. Ibid., pp. 57–8.
10. Foland, op. cit., p. 57.
11. G. Myrdal, *Asian Drama,* Pantheon (1968), 1033–52.
12. Ibid., p. 1035.
13. Ibid., p. 1035.
14. Ibid., p. 1048.
15. See Weitz, op. cit., pp. 15–28.
16. Clifton R. Wharton, Jr. 'Risk, uncertainty, and the subsistence farmer', *Development Digest,* VII, no. 2 (1969), 3.
17. See Marvin P. Miracle, 'Subsistence agriculture: analytical problems and alternative concepts', *American Journal of Agricultural Economics,* May 1968, 292–310.
18. K. Griffen, 'Agrarian policy: the political and economic context', *World Development,* **1,** no. 11 (1973), 6.
19. For an extensive analysis of this phenomenon, see Montague Yudelman *et al., 'Technological Change in Agriculture and Employment in Developing Countries,* Development Centre, OECD, Paris, 1971.
20. For an analysis of the impact of the 'Green Revolution' in the developing world, see Keith Griffen, *The Political Economy of Agrarian Change,* Macmillan, London (1974).
21. Given the author's lack of first-hand familiarity with the economy of China, much of the information in this section is derived from Sartaj Aziz, 'The Chinese approach to rural development', *World Development,* **2,** no. 2 (1974), 87–91 and John G. Gurley, 'Rural development in China, 1949–1972 and the lessons to be learned from it', in E. O. Edwards (ed.), *Employment in Developing Nations,* Columbia U.P., New York (1974), 383–403.
22. S. Aziz, op. cit., p. 87.
23. Ibid., p. 88.
24. Ibid., p. 88.
25. Gurley, op. cit., p. 391.
26. As quoted in Aziz, op. cit., p. 88.
27. Ibid., p. 89.
28. Ibid., p. 90.
29. Ibid., p. 91.

Concepts for review

per capita food production
staple foods
the productivity gap
farm yields
agrarian systems
latifundio
minifundio
microfundio
small farmer (family farm)
landlord
tenant farmer
sharecropper
moneylender
land tenure systems
shifting cultivation
integrated rural development

subsistence farming
'mixed' commercial farming
mechanization
demonstration effects
population density
land reform
hybrid seeds
'scale neutral' technological progress
agricultural extension services
Green Revolution
farmer cooperatives
government support systems
Chinese Peoples commune
risk and uncertainty
cash crops

Questions for discussion

1. Why should any analysis of Third World development problems place heavy emphasis on the study of agricultural systems, especially peasant agriculture, and the rural sector?
2. What were the principal reasons for the relative stagnation of Third World agriculture during the so-called 'development decade' of the 1960s? How can this disappointing performance be improved upon in the future? Explain.
3. It is sometimes said that the world consists of 'two kinds' of agriculture. What is meant by this statement and how might it be illustrated both between and within countries?

4. Compare and contrast the nature of peasant or small-scale agriculture in Asia, Africa and Latin America. How do overall agricultural systems differ among these three regions? What are the common characteristics?
5. Explain the meaning of Professor Myrdal's quote at the beginning of this chapter, i.e. 'it is in the agricultural sector that the battle for long-term economic development will be won or lost'.
6. It is sometimes asserted that small peasant farmers are backward and ignorant because they sometimes seem to resist agricultural innovations that could raise farm yields substantially. Is this resistance due to an inherent 'irrationality' on their part or might it be due to some other factors often overlooked by Western economists? Explain your answer.
7. In the chapter we described three stages in the transition from subsistence to 'modern' agriculture. What are the principal characteristics of these stages?
8. There appears to be widespread agreement that in those regions where the distribution of land ownership is highly unequal (e.g. mainly Latin America but also parts of Asia), land reform is a *necessary* but not sufficient condition for promoting and improving small-scale agriculture. What is meant by this statement and by the concept of land reform? Will the mere redistribution of land guarantee rural economic and social progress or are other policy measures necessary? Explain, giving specific examples of such supportive policies.
9. What is meant by comprehensive or 'integrated' rural development? What criteria would you use to decide whether or not such integrated rural development was or was not taking place?
10. The People's Republic of China has apparently evolved an unique approach to promoting rural development. What are the main characteristics of this approach and what have been its supposed achievements?
11. A crucial issue in the debate on development is whether or not the Chinese experiment in rural development offers any lessons or strategies that can be adopted in other Third World nations. What relevance, if any, do you think the Chinese experience offers?

Further readings 1. For specific studies of agriculture and agrarian systems in Third World regions, see: For Africa: P. Robson and D. A. Lury (eds), *The Economies of Africa,* Allen and Unwin, London (1969); For Asia: Gunnar Myrdal, *Asian Drama,* Pantheon, New York (1968), Ch. 22, 23, and 26; For Latin America: Rodolfo Stavenhagen (ed), *Agrarian Problems and Peasant Movements in Latin America,* Doubleday, New York (1970); Celso Furtado, *Economic Development in Latin America,* Cambridge U.P., London (1970), Ch. 7 and 14; and, especially, Solon Barraclough, *Agrarian Structure in Latin America,* Lexington Books (1973).
2. Three outstanding comparative studies of Third World Agrarian systems are: Guy Hunter, *Modernizing Peasant Societies: A Comparative Study of Asia and Africa,* Oxford U.P., London and New York (1969); Keith Griffen, *The Political Economy of Agrarian Change,* Macmillan, London (1974) and especially Bruce F. Johnston and Peter Kilby, *Agriculture and Structural Transformation: Economic Strategies in Late Developing Countries,* Oxford U.P., London and New York (1975).
3. For a general introduction to the economics of agricultural and rural development in Third World countries see: (a) Erik Thorbecke (ed.), *The Role of Agriculture in Economic Development,* Columbia U.P., New York (1969); (b) Raanan Weitz, *From Peasant to Farmer: A Revolutionary Strategy for Development,* Columbia U.P., New York and London, 1971; (c) Bruce F. Johnston, 'Agriculture and structural transformation in developing countries: a survey of research', *Journal of Economic Literature,* VIII, No. 2 (1970); (d) John Mellor, *The Economics of Agricultural Development,* Cornell U.P., Ithaca, 1966; (e) A. T. Mosher, *Creating A Progressive Rural Structure,* Agricultural Development Council, New York (1969); (f) T. W. Schultz, *Transforming Traditional Agriculture,* Yale U.P., New Haven, 1964; (g) Robert d'A. Shaw, *Jobs and Agricultural Development,* Overseas Development Council, Washington (1970); (h) Nural Islam (ed.), *Agricultural Policy in Developing Countries,* Halsted Press, New York (1974); (i) World Bank, *Rural Development: Sector Policy Paper. World Bank, Washington DC (1975).*
4. *In addition to the Aziz article in World Development,* Feb. 1974, another excellent survey article on Chinese rural development is that of John G. Gurley, 'Rural development in China, 1949–1972 and the lessons to be learned from it', in E. O. Edwards (ed.), *Employment in Developing Nations,* Columbia U.P., New York and London (1974), 383–403. See also: Carl Riskin, 'Small industry and the Chinese model of development', *The China Quarterly,* April–June 1971, 245–73; Keith Buchanan, *The Transformation of the Chinese Earth,* Praeger, New York (1970); and Lloyd G. Reynolds, 'China as a less developed economy', *American Economic Review,* **65,** No. 3 (1975), 418–28.

Education and development | Chapter 11

The school in many underdeveloped countries is a reflection and a fruit of the surrounding underdevelopment, from which arises its deficiency, its quantitative and qualitative poverty. But little by little, and there lies the really serious risk, the school in these underdeveloped countries risks becoming in turn a factor of underdevelopment.
Joseph KiZerbo, former Minister of Education, Upper Volta.

Virtually every serious commentator agrees that major reform within Third World education is long overdue.
Richard Jolly, Director, Institute of Development Studies, University of Sussex, England.

Introduction: education and human resources

Most economists would probably agree that it is the 'human resources' of a nation, not its capital, nor its material resources, that ultimately determine the character and pace of its economic and social development. For example, according to Professor Frederick Harbison[1] of Princeton University:

human resources . . . constitute the ultimate basis for wealth of nations. Capital and natural resources are passive factors of production; human beings are the active agents who accumulate capital, exploit natural resources, build social, economic and political organizations, and carry forward national development. Clearly, a country which is unable to develop the skills and knowledge of its people and to utilize them effectively in the national economy will be unable to develop anything else.

The principal institutional mechanism for developing human skills and knowledge is the formal educational system. Most Third World nations have been led to believe or have wanted to believe that it is the rapid *quantitative* expansion of educational opportunities which holds the basic key to national development. The more education, the more rapid the anticipated development. All countries have committed themselves, therefore, to the goal of 'universal' primary education in the shortest possible time. This quest has become a politically very sensitive, but often economically costly, 'sacred cow'. Until recently few politicians, statesmen, economists or educational planners inside or outside of the Third World would have dared publicly to challenge the cult of formal education.

Nevertheless, the challenge is gathering momentum, and it comes from many sources. It can be found most clearly in the character and results of the development process itself. After almost three decades of rapidly expanding enrolments and hundreds of billions of dollars of educational expenditure, the plight of the average citizen of Asia, Africa and Latin America seems little improved. Absolute poverty is chronic and pervasive. Economic disparities between rich and poor widen with each passing year. Unemployment and underemployment have reached staggering proportions with the 'educated' increasingly swelling the ranks of those without jobs.

It would be foolish and naive to blame these problems exclusively on the failures of the formal educational system. At the same time, however, one must recognize that many of the early claims made on behalf of the unfettered quantitative expansion of educational opportunities – that it would accelerate economic growth; that it would raise levels of living especially for the poor; that it would generate widespread and equal employment opportunities for all; that it would acculturate diverse ethnic or tribal groups; and that it would encourage 'modern' attitudes – have been shown to be greatly exaggerated and, in many instances, simply false.

As a result there has been a growing awareness in many developing nations that the expansion of formal schooling is not always to be equated with the spread of learning; that the student's and teacher's exclusive concern with the acquisition of school certificates and higher degrees should not necessarily be associated with the former's improved ability to undertake productive work; that education which is almost entirely oriented towards preparation for work in the modern urban sector can greatly distort student aspirations; and that too much investment in formal schooling, especially at the secondary and higher levels, can divert scarce resources from more socially productive activities (e.g. direct employment creation) and thus be a drag rather than a stimulus to national development.

The educational systems of Third World nations strongly influence and are influenced by the whole nature, magnitude and character of their development process. Formal education not only attempts to impart knowledge and skills to individuals to enable them to function as economic change agents in their societies. It also imparts values, ideas, attitudes and aspirations which may or may not be in the nation's best 'developmental' interests. Education absorbs the greatest share of LDC recurrent government expenditures, occupies the time and activities of the greatest number of adults and children (almost 30 per cent of Third World populations) and carries the greatest psychological burden of development aspirations. We must therefore examine its fundamental economic basis in developing countries and also its social and institutional ramifications.

The 'economics' of education is a vital yet somewhat amorphous component of the economics of development. It is a young subject having emerged as a separate branch of economics only in the early 1960s. Yet when we recognize the principal motivation or 'demand' for education in Third World countries as a desire for economic improvement by means of better access to highly paid jobs, we must understand the economic processes through which such aspirations are either realized or frustrated.

Our purpose in this chapter is to explore the relationship (both positive and negative) between quantitative and qualitative educational expansion and 'development' in terms of six basic issues that grow directly out of the discussions of previous chapters:

1. How does education influence the rate, structure and character of economic growth? Conversely, how does the rate, structure and character of economic growth influence the nature of the educational system?
2. Do education in general and the structure of Third World educational systems in particular contribute to or retard the growth of domestic inequality and poverty?
3. What is the relationship between education, rural–urban migration and urban unemployment? Are rising levels of the 'educated unemployed' a temporary or chronic phenomenon?
4. Is there a relationship between the education of women and their desired family size?
5. Do contemporary Third World formal educational systems tend to promote or retard agricultural and rural development?
6. What is the relationship, if any, between Third World educational systems, developed country educational systems and the international migration of highly educated professional and technical manpower from the less developed to the more developed nations?

We begin this chapter with a brief profile of the status of education in a range of Third World countries. First we focus on public expenditure levels, enrolment ratios, literacy levels, dropout rates, costs and earnings differentials. After discussing the principal economic and environmental factors affecting the ability to learn, we review some basic concepts in the 'economics of education' including the determinants of the demand for and supply of school places and the distinction between private and social benefits and costs of investment in education. We then examine in detail the above six issues to see if we can reach any conclusions about the relationship between education and various key components of the development process. Finally, we conclude with a review of alternative policy options open to Third World governments in their attempt to evolve an educational system which will serve the needs and aspirations of all of their people more efficiently.

11.1 A profile of education in developing regions

In many developing countries formal education is the largest 'industry' and the greatest consumer of public revenues. Poor nations have invested huge sums of money in education. The reasons are numerous. Literate farmers with at least a primary education are thought to be more productive and more responsive to new agricultural technologies than illiterate farmers. Specially trained craftsmen and mechanics who can read and write are assumed to be better able to keep up to date with changing products and materials. Secondary school graduates with arithmetic and clerical efficiency are needed to perform technical and administrative functions in a growing public and private bureaucracy. In former colonial countries many of them were also needed in large quantities to replace departing expatriates. University graduates with advanced training are needed to provide essential professional and managerial skills necessary for a modernized public and private sector.

1. Public educational expenditure

In addition to these obvious 'manpower planning' needs, the people themselves, both rich and poor, have exerted tremendous political pressure for the expansion of school places in developing countries. Parents quickly realized that in an era of scarce skilled manpower, the more schooling and certificates their children could accumulate the better would be their chances of getting secure and well-paid jobs. For the poor especially, more years of schooling were perceived to be the only avenue of hope for their children to escape from poverty.

As a result of these forces on both demand and supply, there has been a tremendous acceleration in LDC public expenditures on education during the last two decades. Both the proportion of national income and of national budgets spent on education has increased rapidly. In Asia total public expenditures tripled during the 1960s. In Africa and Latin America, public educational expenditures more than doubled. In fact, the increase in public expenditure on education during the 1960s was more pronounced than for any other sector of the economy. By the mid-1970s educational budgets in many Third World nations were absorbing anywhere from 20 to 35 per cent of total government recurrent expenditure.

2. Enrolments Between 1960 and 1975 the total number of persons enrolled in the three main levels of education in Africa, Asia, the Middle East and Latin America rose from 163 million to 370 million – an average annual increase of 6 per cent. Although the largest part of this increase has been in primary education, it is in the second and third levels that the greatest proportionate increases have occurred – 12·7 per cent and 14·5 per cent per annum respectively compared with approximately 8 per cent per annum for primary enrolment. Nevertheless, primary enrolment still accounted for nearly 80 per cent of the total LDC school enrolment in the 1970s.

In terms of the proportion of children of school age actually attending school at the primary, secondary and tertiary level, the differential between the developed and the less developed regions and among Third World regions themselves is substantial. Africa lags behind at all levels with only 40 per cent of its primary school age children actually enrolled in a primary school. Finally, average annual rates of growth have typically been highest for higher eduation, followed by secondary and primary enrolments.

3. Drop-outs One of the major educational problems of developing nations is the very high percentage of students who drop out before completing a particular cycle. For example, it has been estimated that in Latin America 60 out of every 100 students who enter primary school drop out before completion. In some Latin American countries, the primary school drop-out rate is as high as 75 per cent. In Africa and Asia the median drop-out rates are approximately 54 per cent and 20 per cent respectively. But here too the variation among countries has been very wide with drop-out rates as high as 81 per cent and 64 per cent respectively in certain African and Asian nations.

At the secondary level, median drop-out rates for those entering in 1960 were 41·9 per cent in Africa and 18 per cent in Latin America and Asia. In Europe the rate was approximately 11·4 per cent. One consequence of this, particularly for Africa, is the serious and growing problem of the secondary school leaver who joins the ranks of the educated unemployed.

The percentage of adults, persons aged 15 and over, who are illiterate has fallen since 1960 from 39 to 34 per cent of the adult population in developing countries. However, due to rapid population growth, the actual number of adult illiterates has risen since then by nearly 70 million to an estimated total of over 800 million by 1975. The highest illiteracy rates are found in Africa (73·7) and the Arab States (73·0), followed by Asia (46·8) and Latin America (23·6). In North America and Europe, illiteracy rates are a mere 1·5 and 3·6 per cent respectively. **4. Literacy**

Criticism has intensified in recent years of the very serious disproportionate per pupil costs of education at various levels in the LDCs. This is especially true when one compares secondary and higher educational costs with primary level costs. While much of this criticism in the past has been based on scattered *ad hoc* empirical and interpretative information, a recently published international comparative study provides detailed data on the magnitude of these cost divergences[2]. **5. Costs and earnings**

Groups of countries	Relative cost		
	Secondary/primary	Higher/primary	
USA, Great Britain, New Zealand	6·6	17·6	**Table 11.1**
Malaysia, Ghana, South Korea,	11·9	87·9	Ratios of total costs by educational
Kenya, Uganda, Nigeria, India			level per student year

Source: G. Psacharopoulos, *The Returns to Education: An International Comparison,* (Elsevier, 1972), Table 8.2.

Groups of countries	Relative earnings		
	Secondary/primary	Higher/primary	
USA, Canada, Great Britain	1·4	2·4	**Table 11.2**
Malaysia, Ghana, South Korea,	2·4	6·4	Ratios of average annual earnings of
Kenya, Uganda, Nigeria, India			labor by educational level

Source: G. Psacharopoulos, op. cit., Table 8.4.

Table 11.1 compares the ratio of total costs per student year by educational level for a group of developed and less developed countries. The data reveals that whereas in the three developed countries shown the ratio of total per pupil costs of secondary to primary education is 6·6 to 1 and that of higher to primary education is 17·6 to 1, in the seven LDCs shown these relative costs are 11·9 and 87·9 to 1 respectively. In other words, taking the 87·9 figure, for the equivalent cost of educating one LDC university student for 1 year, eighty-eight primary school children could have received a year of schooling. In many African countries (e.g. Sierre Leone, Malawi, Kenya and Tanzania) cost ratios per pupil between higher and primary education range as high as 283 to 1. Since in over half of the world's developing countries the ratio of pupils in primary schools to students in higher education is above 100 to 1 (as compared, for example, to ratios of less than 10 to 1 in the developed countries), it follows that LDCs spend large proportions of their educational budgets on a very small proportion of their students enrolled in universities and professional schools.

If one then compares the data in Table 11.2, showing the relative average earnings of individuals by educational level, with those on costs, it becomes clear that relative earnings differentials by educational level are much less than unit cost differentials in the developing compared with the developed countries. For example, looking once again at the figures in the lower right corners of Tables 11.1 and 11.2, we see that while an LDC university student costs $87 \cdot 9$ times as much as a primary pupil to educate for one year, the university student on the average earned only $6 \cdot 4$ times as much as the typical primary pupil – a very high (and often artificial) differential, but not as high as the cost differential. To the extent that average relative earnings reflect average relative productivity, the wide disparity between relative earnings and relative costs of higher versus primary education implies that in the past LDC governments may have unwisely invested too much in higher education. These funds might have been more productively invested in primary school expansion. This does not necessarily imply that future relative cost/benefit ratios will continue to favor primary school expansion; much depends on the relative employment prospects of the various educational groups.

11.2 Basic problems of primary and secondary education

1. Inertia and inefficiency While the foregoing statistics provide a useful summary of enrolments, drop-outs, literacy rates, costs per student and returns to education, there are other underlying but less quantifiable problems of education in the Third World – problems sometimes serious in industrialized nations also. These are broadly referred to as the *inefficiencies* and *inertia of educational systems.*

One might start with the outdated content and dubious quality of education at all levels. As stated by a former Deputy Director-General of UNESCO

The learning techniques ... remain the same: the rote method, the technique of cramming, and, once the examination menace is passed, of forgetting all these useless impedimenta. The examination system is not an evaluation of a student's personality and intellectual equipment, his powers of thinking for himself, reflection, and reasoning. It is a challenge to resourceful deception and display of superficial cleverness ... Looked at as a business enterprise, the school and college present a woebegone spectacle. We find in education antediluvian technology which would not survive for an instant in any other economic sector. The teaching methods and learning techniques ... are rusty, cranky and antiquated.

Deficiencies of learning methods and curricula are closely related to inadequate competence and motivations of most teachers who are usually underpaid and without incentive or opportunity to learn any more themselves than they took in at their start. The situation is hardly better among educational administrators.

2. Poor management and distorted incentives Indeed problems seem most acute and difficult to remedy in the realm of educational management – its direction, organization and programing. Here are the immediate causes of perpetuating old and dysfunctional patterns. Rigidity persists along with a lack of requisite information of the society's needs, conditions and developmental possibilities, and a lack of practically oriented research, experimentation and evaluation.

These problems of education result in part because socially perceived needs within the educational system vastly exceed available
funds and other resources. But they also result from demands, pricing
and financial and non-financial *incentives* in the society at large, *outside*
the educational system. What society and individuals want of education are often impossible dreams, demands frequently out of line with
priorities of national development, indeed, often running against those
priorities.

These demands sometimes also take the form of political interference in the educational system and distortion of its governing policies.
Political pressures intrude at all levels in education, forcing the system
to respond, but such pressures may have little to do with primary goals
of national development or with real changing needs in the society as a
whole.

Nowhere is the maladjustment of the educational system to needs of **3. Maladjustment to social**
national development more evident than in rural primary schools. **needs at the primary level**
Primary education receives the lion's share of Third World expendi-
tures. More than 50 per cent of all educational expenditure and almost
10 per cent of governmental recurrent expenditure is allocated to
primary education. Primary education received approximately 3·8 per
cent of the total GNP of LDCs in 1970, over 43 billion dollars.

Given the tremendous importance of primary education for national
development and the distinctive economic, social and cultural conditions of less developed nations, one must seriously question the
advisability and utility of a system which for all practical purposes is no
different in structure and content from its counterpart in the advanced
nations.

The basic problems of rural primary education and the reasons why
it is often out of tune with the real needs of poor societies can best be
summarized as follows:
1. Over 70 per cent of the children in LDCs live and attend school in
   rural areas.
2. Over 80 per cent of these children are likely to spend their lives
   earning a living either directly from the land or from unskilled paid
   employment in rural areas. Yet primary schools spend very little
   time giving these students the knowledge, skills and new ideas
   necessary to function efficiently in their rural environment (e.g.
   farming practices and management, hygiene, nutrition, community
   development, etc.).
3. Primary schools typically attempt to prepare students for secondary
   school with training in literacy, numeracy and foreign languages
   receiving highest priority. The training, moreover, usually consists
   of recitation, repetition and drill learning rather than thinking and
   problem solving.
4. In those developed nations in which the vast majority of primary
   school entrants proceed to secondary school which in turn tends to
   concentrate on college preparatory education, the heavy emphasis
   on literacy, numeracy and foreign languages might be less questionable. But it has been estimated that it takes approximately 5
   years (depending on age of entry) for a child to achieve literacy and
   even longer to master numeracy and foreign languages (even if the
   latter were really relevant).
5. The problem with this approach to primary and secondary education – i.e., structuring the primary school curriculum solely as a

preparation for secondary school – in the LDCs is that:

(a) For a variety of economic and social reasons, over 15 per cent of the children who enter primary school will drop out after the first year, with an additional 10 per cent dropping out the following year.

(b) Approximately 50 per cent of those who enter the first class of primary school are unlikely to complete 4 years.

(c) Less than 10 per cent of those who enter primary school are likely to succeed in reaching secondary school, even though 25 to 30 per cent of the original entrants might complete the primary cycle.

(d) Of those who do get to secondary school, less than 60 per cent are likely to complete the course (the ratio is much lower in Africa) and only about 20 per cent will proceed to a university.

(e) Of those who do make it through secondary school but do not obtain a place in a university, the probability of their finding a job in the modern sector (towards which their secondary education has been oriented) gets lower with each passing year.

Clearly something is seriously wrong with a primary and secondary educational system modelled upon its counterpart in economically advanced societies and transferred to an environment to which it has little if any relevance (we deal with the problems of university education in the next section). But to document these problems is not to answer them. What is urgently needed are detailed studies and well-conceived experiments to answer such critical questions as the following:[3]

1. At what age should a child, who is going to have only a few years of primary education, enter school?

2. Should primary education in a rural community in a developing country be full-time or part-time?

3. Given some type of formal education for children, do literacy and numeracy constitute the highest priority areas of instruction for those destined to spend their lives in a rural zone?

4. Given that the medium of instruction in higher and secondary education is in a langugage other than the mother tongue, is it necessary to teach this language in primary school?

5. Given that for financial reasons it is not possible to lengthen the training of teachers (salaries are usually directly related to length of training), can the type of training given to teachers be changed and the curriculum and inspection system altered, so that the teacher becomes more effective?

6. If children are given certain ideas which they forget because they have no possibility of practising them, are they more or less likely to accept and practise these ideas again when they are reintroduced later in adult life?

7. Have the children who drop out of primary school after 1, 2 or 3 years gained much, if anything? If not, can a curriculum be designed so that they would benefit more?

8. Are the highest priority areas of instruction the same for (a) those children proceeding to secondary education; (b) those children getting paid employment in the modern sector; (c) those children remaining in the rural areas? If not, is it possible to structure the system in such a way as to provide both some equality of opportunity, and to fulfil their differing requirements?

9. Related to 8 above, is it possible to design a reasonably just and

incorruptible selection procedure which does not over-influence
what is taught in the schools?
10. Should the school and community be integrated? Should adult
and child education be integrated? Should mass education (or
community development) be designed to solve particular
developmental problems? If so, how?
These and other questions of great significance to the nation-building
aspirations of Third World countries need to be answered if their
primary (and secondary) educational systems are to make maximum
contributions to development.

11.3 Problems of higher education

President Julius Nyerere of Tanzania perhaps best summed up the role
of universities in developing societies when he said:[4]

*The University in a developing society must put the emphasis of its work
on subjects of immediate moment to the nation in which it exists, and it
must be committed to the people of that nation and their humanistic
goals . . . We in poor societies can only justify expenditure on a University – of any type – if it promotes real development of our people . . . The
role of a University in a developing nation is to contribute; to give ideas,
manpower, and service for the furtherance of human equality, human
dignity and human development.*

Higher education in the LDCs is a very much smaller world than that
of primary and secondary levels. The proportion of enrolled students
in higher education is less than 3 per cent of all students, while the
proportion of teachers in higher education is less than 8 per cent of the
total. Although there are a considerable variety of institutions in
higher education (e.g. colleges and professional schools) the university
is generally identified as the most important and apex institution. Yet
Third World universities have been found by practically all informed
observers to be as maladjusted and out of step with the real needs of
development as the educational institutions in lower levels. Many of
the problems basic to primary and secondary education already discussed recur in more or less aggravated form in universities.
The basic causes of university defects have been examined in what is
now a substantial literature, and are generally agreed on. Most Third
World universities have been modelled in structure and function upon
the older institutions in the industrialized societies. In the last 20 years
many national programs of university development have resulted in
(even where it was not the primary intention) patterning university
additions and changes in LDCs to resemble practices established in the
United States, France, Great Britain and other developed countries.
By long and powerful tradition the universities of the Western world
are structured by professional disciplines, as they have been since the
medieval period. This structure, departments (discipline) and their
grouping (faculty) was exported on a large scale to universities in the
LDCs. Little thought or effort was given to questions of how this mode
of academic organization would serve existing Third World conditions
and problems. 'Excellence' continued to be measured in terms of
international academic standards rather than contributions to national
development. But the pressures of expanding enrolments, tight
budgets and, most important, student demands for relevant and meaningful curricula have recently caused many Third World university

leaders to rethink their role and mission and to begin to heed the perceptive advice of thoughtful statesmen like President Nyerere of Tanzania[5].

11.4 Factors affecting the ability to learn: some causes and consequences

Recent evidence from a wide range of countries, both developed and less developed, has convincingly demonstrated that early factors in the life of a child – the health and feeding habits of mothers during pregnancy, the child's own health and nutritional status during his or her first few years of life, the family's income and living conditions, etc. – can determine whether or not the child will perform well in school and in later life[6]. Figure 11.1 portrays the influence of these early factors (individual, family and non-family environment) not only on school performance ('later factors') but also on individual capacities for behavioral change and the private and social benefits that are derived from such change, mainly in the form of wage or self-employment.

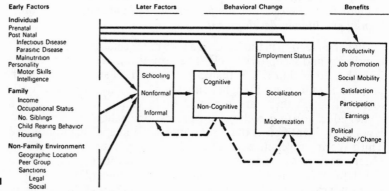

Fig 11.1
The learning system: Causes, consequences and interactions

N.B. Other arrows are omitted to maintain the clarity of the diagram. For example, Family and Non-family Environment should have dotted lines to Later Factors and Behavioral Change.

Source: John Simmons, 'Investment in education for developing countries: national strategy options', IBRD, Washington (Feb. 1976), 196.

For example, we see from Fig. 11.1 that early malnutrition and disease can not only adversely affect a child's ability to read, write, perform arithmetic operations and to think clearly and logically in school (his 'cognitive' abilities). They also can adversely affect his chances of obtaining and/or holding a job (employment status) and lower his productivity and general performance in that job. Thus family and child health are important determinants of both school performance and the physical and mental ability of an individual to function effectively in later life.

Children from poor families with low levels of living are, therefore, often placed at a competitive disadvantage vis-à-vis the economically better off child in school activities. For example, most studies of school performance reveal that the four most important factors in the determination of a child's capacity to learn are:

1. *Family environment* including income levels, parent's education, housing conditions, number of children in household, etc.;
2. *Peer group interactions* – i.e. the type of children with whom an individual child associates;
3. *Personality* – i.e. the child's inherited intelligence and abilities; and
4. *Early nutrition and health.*

If a child enters school deficient in all four of the above factors, as many very poor children do, the educational process may have little effect on his capacity for self-improvement and economic advancement. In fact, he is very likely to be among the 50 per cent of primary school students who drop out before completing 4 years. Equality of educational opportunity – a social goal professed by all nations – can thus have little meaning in societies where children come from very unequal backgrounds.

11.5 The economics of education and employment

Much of the literature and public discussion about education and economic development in general, and education and employment in particular revolves around two fundamental economic processes, (1) the interaction between economically motivated *demands* with politically responsive *supplies* in the determinants of how many school places are provided, what kind of instruction is promoted, and who gets access to these places; and (2) the important distinction between 'social' versus 'private' *benefits* and *costs* of different levels of education, and the implications of these differentials for educational investment strategy.

1. Educational supply and demand: the relationship between employment opportunities and educational demands[7]

The amount of schooling received by an individual, although affected by many non-market factors, can be regarded as largely determined by demand and supply, just as for any other commodity or service. However, since most education is publicly provided in less developed countries, the determinants of demand turn out to be much more important than the determinants of supply. On the demand side the two principal influences on the amount of schooling desired are: (*a*) a more educated student's prospects of earning considerably more income through future modern sector employment, i.e. his or his family's 'private benefits' of education; and (*b*) the educational 'costs' both direct and indirect which a student and/or his or her family must bear. The 'demand' for education is thus in reality a 'derived demand' for high wage employment opportunities in the modern sector. This is because access to such jobs is largely determined by an individual's education. Most people (especially the poor) in less developed nations do not demand education for its intrinsic non-economic benefits but simply because it is the only means of securing modern-sector employment. These derived benefits must in turn be weighed against the costs of education.

On the supply side, the quantity of school places at the primary, secondary and university levels is determined largely by political processes, often unrelated to economic criteria. Because of mounting political pressure for greater numbers of school places throughout the Third World, we can for convenience assume that the public supply of these places is fixed by the level of government educational expenditures. These in turn are influenced by the level of aggregate private demand for education.

Since it is the demand for education which largely determines the supply (within the limits of government financial feasibility), let us look more closely at the economic (employment-oriented) determinants of this derived demand.

The *demand* for an education sufficient to qualify an individual for entry into modern-sector employment opportunities appears to be related to or determined by the combined influence of the following four variables.

1. The wage and/or income differential This is the wage differential between jobs in the 'modern' sector and those outside it (family farming, rural and urban self-employment, etc.) which for simplicity we can designate as the 'traditional' sector. Entry into modern-sector jobs depends initially on the level of completed education, whereas income-earning opportunities in the traditional sector have no fixed educational requirements. The greater the modern-sector/traditional-sector income differential, the greater will be the demand for education. Thus, *our first relationship states that the demand for education is positively related to the modern–traditional sector wage differential.* Since we know from empirical studies that these differentials can be considerable in developing nations, we might expect the demand for education to be greater than if differentials were smaller.

2. The probability of success in finding modern sector employment An individual who successfully completes the necessary schooling for entry into the modern-sector labor market has a higher 'probability' of getting that well-paid urban job than someone who does not. Clearly, if urban unemployment rates among the educated are growing and/or if the supply of, say, secondary-school graduates continually exceeds the number of new job openings for which a secondary graduate can qualify, then we need to modify the 'actual' wage differential and instead speak once again about an 'expected' income differential (see Ch. 9). Since the probability of success is inversely related to the unemployment rate – that is, the more people with appropriate qualifications who seek a particular job, the lower will be the probability that any one of them will be successful – we can argue that the demand for education through, say, the secondary level will be *inversely* related to the current unemployment rate among secondary school graduates[8].

3. The direct private costs of education We refer here to the current out-of-pocket expenses of financing a child's education. These expenses include school fees, books, clothing and related costs. We would expect that *the demand for education would be inversely related to these direct costs* – that is, the higher the school fees and associated costs, the lower would be the private demand for education, everything else being equal.

4. The indirect or 'opportunity costs' of education An investment in a child's education involves more than just the direct, out-of-pocket costs of that education, especially when the child passes the age at which he can make a productive contribution to family income, whether in 'kind' or in money. For example, by continuing his education at secondary school, a child who has completed his primary schooling is in effect forgoing the income which he could expect to earn during the years he spends receiving a secondary education. This 'opportunity cost' of education must also be included as a variable affecting its demand. One would expect the relationship between opportunity costs and demand to be *inverse* – that is, the *greater are the opportunity costs, the lower will be the demand for education.*

Although several other important variables, many of which are non-economic, including cultural traditions, social status, education of parents and size of family certainly influence the demand for education, we believe that by concentrating on the four variables described above, important insights can be gained on the relationship between the demand for education and the supply of employment opportunities.

To give an example, suppose we have a situation in an LDC where the following conditions prevail – a typical scenario.

(a) The modern–traditional or urban–rural wage gap is of the magnitude of, say, 100 per cent for primary versus non-primary school graduates.

(b) The rate of increase in modern-sector employment opportunities for primary-school leavers is slower than the rate at which new primary school leavers enter the labor force. The same may be true at the secondary level and even the university level in countries such as India, Mexico, Egypt, Pakistan, and more recently, Ghana, Nigeria and Kenya.

(c) Employers, faced with an excess of applicants, tend to select by level of education. They will choose candidates with secondary rather than primary education even though satisfactory job performance may require no more than a primary education.

(d) Trade unions, supported by the political pressure of the educated, tend to bind the going wage to the level of educational attainment of job holders rather than to the minimum educational qualification required for the job.

(e) School fees are often nominal or even non-existent. Moreover, in many cases, the state bears a larger proportion of the student's costs at successively higher levels.

Under the above conditions, which conform closely to the realities of the employment and education situation in many developing nations, we would expect the demand for education to be substantial. This is because the anticipated 'private' *benefits* of more schooling would be large compared to the alternative of little or no schooling, while the direct and indirect private educational *costs* are relatively low. Over time, as job opportunities for the uneducated diminish, individuals must safeguard their position by acquiring a complete primary education. This may suffice for a while but the internal dynamics of the employment demand/supply process eventually leads to a situation in which job prospects for those with only primary education begin to decline. This in turn creates a growing demand for secondary education. But the demand for primary education must increase concurrently since some who were previously content with no education are now being 'squeezed' out of the labor market.

The irony is that *the more unprofitable a given level of education becomes as a terminal point, the more demand for it increases as an intermediate stage or precondition to the next level of education!* This puts great pressure on the government to expand educational facilities at *all* levels to meet the growing demand. If they cannot respond fast enough, the people may do so on their own, as evidenced, for example, by the 'Harambee' school self-help movement in Kenya where private secondary schools were built throughout the country to be taken over later by the government.

The upshot of all this is the chronic tendency for developing nations to expand their educational facilities at a rate which is extremely difficult to justify either socially or financially in terms of optimal resource allocation. Each worsening of the employment situation calls forth an increased demand for (and supply of) more formal education at *all* levels. Initially the uneducated swell the ranks of the unemployed. However, over time there is an inexorable tendency for the average educational level among the unemployed to rise as the supply of school graduates continues to exceed the demand for middle and high level manpower. The better educated must, after varying periods of unemployment during which aspirations are scaled downward, take jobs requiring lower levels of education. The diploma and degree thus become requirements for employment, not the education they were intended to signify.

Governments and private employers in many LDCs tend to strengthen this trend by continuously upgrading formal educational entry requirements for jobs which were previously filled by those less educated. Excess educational qualification becomes formalized and may resist downward adjustment. Moreover, to the extent that trade unions succeed in binding going wages to the educational attainments of job holders, the going wage for each job will tend to rise (even though worker productivity in that job has not significantly increased). Existing distortions in wage differentials will be magnified, thus stimulating the demand for education even further.

As a result of this 'educational displacement phenomenon', those who for some reason (mostly their poverty) are unable to continue their education will fall by the wayside as unemployed school leavers. At the same time, the more affluent continue to over-qualify themselves through more years of education. In the extreme case, one gets a situation like that of contemporary India where the higher education system is in effect an 'absorber of last resort' for the great numbers of educated unemployed. This is a terribly expensive form of unemployment compensation. Moreover, since people cannot remain students until they retire, these great masses will eventually have to emerge from behind the walls of academia into a world of tight labor markets. The result will be a more visible unemployment among those who are both highly educated and highly vocal[9].

Finally, it should be pointed out that many individuals tend to resist what they see as a down-grading of their job qualifications. Consequently, even though on the demand-for-labor side employers will attempt to substitute the more educated for the less educated for a given job, on the supply side there will be many job seekers whose expectations exceed the emerging realities of the labor market. They might prefer to remain unemployed for some time rather than accept a job which they feel is 'beneath' them. It follows that as result of these 'frictional' effects and 'lags' in adjustment on the supply side, unemployment will exist at all levels of education even though it is concentrated at lower levels and, in general, is inversely related to educational attainment.

2. Social versus private benefits and costs The inexorable attraction of ever higher levels of education is even more costly than this simple picture suggests. Typically in developing countries, the 'social' cost of education – i.e. the opportunity cost to society as a whole resulting from the need to finance costly educational expansion at higher levels when these limited funds might be more productively used in other sectors of the economy – increases rapidly as students climb the educational ladder. The 'private' costs (those borne by the student himself) increase more slowly or indeed may decline.

This widening gap between social and private costs provides an even greater stimulus to the demand for higher education than it does for lower levels. Educational demand, therefore, becomes increasingly exaggerated at the higher (post secondary) levels. But educational opportunities can be accommodated to these distorted demands only at full social cost. As demands are generated progressively through the system, the social cost of accommodation grows much more rapidly than the places provided. More and more resources, therefore, may be misallocated to educational expansion in terms of social costs, and the potential for creating new jobs will consequently diminish for lack of public financial resources.

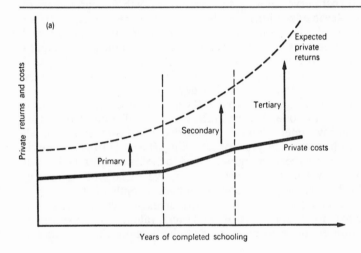

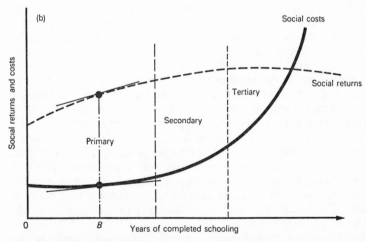

Fig 11.2
Private versus social benefits and costs of education: An illustration

Figure 11.2 provides an illustration of this divergence between private versus social benefits and costs. It also demonstrates how this divergence can lead to a misallocation of resources when private interests supersede social investment criteria. In Fig. 11.2(a) expected private returns to years of completed schooling are plotted against actual private costs. As a student completes more and more years of schooling his expected private returns grow at a much faster rate than his private costs for reasons explained earlier. In order to maximize the difference between expected benefits and costs (and thereby the private 'rate of return' to investment in education), the optimal strategy for a student would be to secure as much schooling as possible.

Consider now Fig. 11.2(b) where social returns and social costs are plotted against years of schooling. The social benefits curve rises sharply at first, reflecting the improved levels of productivity of, say, small farmers and the self-employed that result from receipt of a 'basic education' and the attainment of literacy, numeracy and elementary vocational skills. Thereafter, the 'marginal' social benefit of additional years of schooling increases but at a decreasing rate – thus the reason for the declining slope of the social returns curve. On the other hand, the social cost curve shows a slow rate of growth for early years of schooling (basic education) and then a much more rapid growth for higher levels of education. This rapid increase in the marginal social costs of post primary education is due both to the much more expensive capital and recurrent costs of higher education (i.e. buildings and equipment) and, more important, to the fact that much post primary education in developing countries is heavily subsidized.

It follows from Figure 11.2(b) that the *optimal* strategy from a social viewpoint, i.e. the one that maximizes the 'social' rate of return to educational investment, would be one that focuses on providing all students with at least OB years of schooling. Beyond OB years marginal social costs exceed marginal social benefits so that additional educational investment will yield a negative social rate of return. Figure 11.2, therefore, illustrates the inherent conflict between optimal private and social investment strategies – a conflict that will continue to exist as long as private and social valuations of investment in education continue to diverge as students climb the educational ladder.

To a large degree, therefore, the problem of divergent social versus private benefits and costs has been 'artificially' created by inappropriate public and private policies with regard to wage differentials, educational selectivity and the pricing of educational services. As a result, private perceptions of the value of education exceed its social value, which must take account of rising unemployment. As long as artificial and non-market incentives in the form of disproportionate expected benefits and subsidized costs continue to exist and place a premium on the number of years one spends 'getting an education', the individual will decide that it is in his best private interests to pursue a lengthy formal education process even though he may be aware that modern-sector jobs are becoming more scarce and unemployment rates are rising. Unless these several price 'signals' are made to conform more closely to social realities, the misallocation of national resources (in this case too much expenditure on formal education) will persist and possibly increase.

What is needed, therefore, is a proper functioning reward- and cost-structure which develops and allocates human resources in accordance with requirements and opportunities in various segments of the economy. Where this is absent (i.e. where the very high wage premiums paid to workers in the modern urban sector are complemented by the allocation of scarce jobs on the basis of ever increasing educational 'credentials') two obvious misallocations of human resources are likely to follow. First, with the output of the educational system greatly in excess of that which the economy can absorb, many students will emerge seeking jobs for which they may be educationally qualified but which have been pre-empted by others with even more education. They become temporarily unemployed for as long as it takes for their aspirations and status requirements, partly perhaps instilled in them by the educational system itself, to adjust to the stinging realities of unemployment in the modern sector.

Second, those who adjust their sights downward and secure modern-sector employment normally have to take jobs for which they are 'overeducated' in terms of the number of years spent in school. Those who fail to get modern-sector jobs at all swell the ranks of the permanently unemployed or become self-employed in the traditional sector. They are thus denied the opportunity to contribute productively to the society which invested so heavily in their education. The combined effect of the overpaid and, in many cases, over-educated employed and the impoverished and unproductive 'educated unemployed' reflects a serious misallocation of scarce national resources. The resources that were allocated to the expansion of the educational system might alternatively have been spent on, say, needed rural public works projects. Such investment would provide emergency employment opportunities for school leavers as well as for those with less education.

The imbalance between educational demands and productive job opportunities is not likely to be rectified in the manipulation of the supply of school places since popular political pressures usually prevent substantial supply adjustments. Rather pressures must build until policy attention is turned to the more fundamental issues of tempering demand to more realistic proportions and generating more urban and rural employment opportunities.

3. The need to curtail artificially induced educational demands: convergent benefits and costs

To temper the demand for education toward more realistic levels, Third World governments should strive to bring the private calculations of the benefits and costs associated with education closer to the social valuations by:

1. *Making the beneficiary (as opposed to his family or society as a whole) bear a larger and rising proportion of his educational costs as he proceeds through the system (with appropriate subsidies for the able poor at low levels of education and through loan programs at higher levels).*

There are three principles in this policy recommendation. First, the share of educational costs borne privately should be substantially larger than they typically are in many developing countries. This would reduce the demand for education beyond literacy. Second, the rate of educational subsidy should decline as an individual advances in the educational system. As a result, the private demand for education would be curtailed more at high levels where it is socially most expensive and where most of the overeducation in terms of educational requirements for jobs takes place. A policy of declining subsidies would also respond to the valid criticism that current programs involving rising subsidies are anti-egalitarian and in fact represent a subsidy to the rich by the poor. Third, the private share of educational costs should, insofar as possible, fall on the beneficiary, not on his family or friends. It is his or her future earnings which will be increased although the extended family is likely to share in the benefits. Ideally, he should pay for his education out of those future earnings. This suggests, of course, that private educational costs should be financed directly out of a student's own resources or indirectly through loans repaid either by financial levies against his future income or by social contributions of his expertise, such as national service in rural areas. Such arrangements appear especially desirable and feasible at all levels of education beyond secondary. Below those levels the burden of private costs would probably continue to fall on the family and would necessitate a system of subsidizing the able poor.

2. *Reducing income differentials between the modern and traditional sectors and within the modern sector to ensure a more realistic appraisal of the prospective benefits of education.*

It would carry us too far from the field of education to consider means in detail here (but see the policy recommendations for promoting rural development (in Ch. 10) and for reducing internal migration (Ch. 9)). We note only that these means are much more extensive than direct, sharp and unrealistic cuts in modern-sector money wages. They include more time-consuming processes of holding the line on average and minimum wages in the modern sector while rural productivity and prices are adjusted upward.

3. *Ensuring that minimum job specifications do not overvalue education.*

Students should not be encouraged to seek levels of education which overqualify them for the jobs they can realistically expect to obtain. It is essential for that purpose that the economic system should not exaggerate educational prerequisites to employment. Governments can take direct action on this matter by eliminating allocation of jobs by credentialization within the civil service where a large share of modern-sector employment is to be found.

4. *Ensuring that wages are related to jobs and not to educational attainments.*

If the other policies are effective, this becomes essentially an interim measure. So long as over-education is increasing and those emerging from the system must accept jobs which realistically require progressively lower educational qualifications, the tendency, particularly in teaching and the civil service, to tie salaries to levels of education simply increases rates of overpayment. This eventually induces even more students to follow the same privately profitable, but socially costly, path.

To increase the supply of urban and rural job opportunities, we have suggested in previous chapters that governments should:

(a) reduce factor–price distortions to the extent that these enter into employment decisions in both the public and private sectors;

(b) give more careful consideration to improving rural infrastructure and to the possible location of new modern-sector activities in areas where wages have not yet reached the distorted levels typical of established urban centers;

(c) allocate a larger share of public budgets to productive employment-creating activities and less to educational expansion than has been the pattern in the last decade.

This is not to say that funds spent on education do not also create employment: they do. Our point is simply that some of the funds so spent in the past might have been more usefully allocated to other more productive, labour-intensive activities, including the provision of complementary resources for the productive employment of the already educated. Education beyond literacy should compete for funds on these social benefit/cost criteria, not on the notion that it is a privileged activity exempt from such social and economic considerations.

11.6 Education, society and development: some issues

One cannot discuss the relationship between education and development without explicitly linking the structure of the educational system to the economic and social character of the Third World society in which it is contained. Educational systems more often than not reflect the essential nature of that society. For example, if the society is very inegalitarian in economic and social structure, the educational system will probably reflect that bias in terms of who is able to proceed through the system. At the same time education *can* influence the future shape and direction of society in a number of ways. Thus the linkage between education and development is a two-way process. By reflecting the socio-economic structures of the societies in which they function (whether egalitarian or not), educational systems tend to perpetuate, reinforce and reproduce that economic and social structure. On the other hand, educational reform, whether introduced from within or outside the system, has the great potential for inducing corresponding social and economic reform in the nation as a whole.

With these general observations in mind, let us look at six specific economic components of the 'development' question – growth, inequality and poverty, population and fertility, internal migration, rural development and external migration – to see in what way they influence or are influenced by most LDC educational systems. Such an examination will demonstrate the important two-way relationship that exists between education and development. It should also provide us with an even broader understanding of the development problems and issues which have been discussed in previous chapters.

1. Education and economic growth

For many years the proposition that educational expansion promoted and in some cases even determined the rate of overall GNP growth remained unquestioned. The logic seemed fairly straightforward. Third World nations were very deficient in their supply of semi-skilled and skilled manpower. Without such manpower, which it was assumed could be created only through the formal educational system, development leadership in both the public and private sectors would be woefully lacking and retarded.

Impressive statistics and numerous quantitative studies of the 'sources of economic growth' in the West were paraded out to demonstrate that it was not the growth of physical capital but that of 'human capital' (the 'residual' in econometric production function estimates) which was the principal source of economic progress in the developed nations[10]. Clearly, in the newly independent nations of Africa and Asia, there was an immediate need to build up the 'human' as well as physical capital infrastructure in order to provide indigenous leadership for the major tasks of development. Rapid quantitative expansion of enrolments, therefore, appeared justified in light of the substantial manpower scarcities of the 1950s and 1960s. And, although it is extremely difficult to document statistically, it seems clear that the expansion of educational opportunities at all levels has probably contributed to *aggregate economic growth* by (*a*) creating a more productive labor force and endowing it with increased knowledge and skills; (*b*) providing widespread employment and income earning opportunities for teachers, school and construction workers, textbook and paper printers, school uniform manufacturers, etc; (*c*) creating a class of educated leaders to fill vacancies left by departing expatriates or otherwise vacant positions in governmental services, public corporations, private businesses and professions; and (*d*) presumably providing the kind of training and education that would promote literacy, numeracy and basic skills while encouraging 'modern' attitudes on the part of diverse segments of the population. Whether a social benefit▸ cost comparison of alternative investments in the economy would have generated even more economic growth, even if such calculations could be made, would not detract from the important contributions, noneconomic as well as economic, which education can make and has made to promoting aggregate economic growth. That an educated and skilled labor force is a necessary condition of sustained economic growth cannot be denied.

On the other hand, however, any evaluation of the role of education in the process of economic development should go beyond the analysis of a single statistic of aggregate growth. One must also consider the *structure* and *pattern* of that economic growth and its *distributed implications* – i.e., who benefits.

2. Education, inequality and poverty

Until recently, most of the work on the economics of education in both developed and developing nations focused on the linkages between education, labor productivity and output growth. This is not surprising since, as we have seen, the principal objective of development during the 1950s and 1960s was the maximization of aggregate rates of output growth. As a result, the impact of education on the distribution of income and the elimination of absolute poverty was largely neglected. Recent studies, however, have demonstrated that rather than being a general force for equality, *the educational systems of most developing nations act to increase rather than to decrease these income inequalities*[11].

The basic reason for this perverse effect of formal education on income distribution is the positive correlation between a person's level of education and his level of lifetime earnings. This is especially true for those who are able to complete secondary and university education where income differentials over workers who have only completed part or all of their primary education can be of the order of 300 to 800 per cent. Since levels of earned income are so clearly dependent on years of completed schooling, it follows that large income inequalities will be reinforced and the magnitude of poverty perpetuated if students from middle and upper income brackets are represented disproportionately in secondary and university enrolments. If for financial and/or other reasons the poor are effectively denied access to secondary and higher educational opportunities, then the educational system can actually perpetuate and even increase inequality in Third World nations.

World Bank educational economist John Simmons, for example, gives the following sketch of how the poor are beginning to regard education[12]:

Schooling, the poor quickly learn, in most countries, is an escape from poverty for only a few. The poor are the first to drop out because they need to work, the first to be pushed out because they fall asleep in class as one result of malnourishment, and the first to fail their French or English tests because upper income children have had better opportunities at home. The hope brought to village parents by the construction of the primary school soon fades. Enough schooling to secure a steady, even menial job for their son, let alone for their daughter, seems just beyond their grasp. Before . . . any schooling would have done to achieve their aspiration. Now a primary school certificate is needed, and some are saying that even students with some secondary schooling cannot get a steady job; and they could never afford to send their son away to town for secondary schooling.

There are two fundamental economic reasons why one might suspect that many LDC educational systems are inherently inegalitarian, in the sense that poor students have less chance of completing any given educational cycle than relatively rich students. First, the private *'costs'* of primary education, especially the 'opportunity cost' of a child's labour to poor families, is higher for poor students than for rich students. Second, the expected 'benefits' of primary education are lower for poor students than for rich students. Together the high costs and lower expected benefits of education mean that a family's 'rate of return' from investment in a child's education is lower for the relatively poor than for the relatively rich. The poor are, therefore, more likely to 'drop out' during early years of schooling. Let's briefly examine why 'costs' might be relatively higher and benefits relatively lower for a poor child.

First, the higher opportunity cost of labor to poor families means that even if the first few years of education are 'free' for their children, they are not without cost to the family. Children of primary school age typically are needed to work on family farms – often at the same time they are required to be at school. If a child cannot work because he is at school, the family will either suffer a loss of valuable subsistence output or be required to hire paid labor to replace the absent child. In any case there is a real cost to a poor family of having an able-bodied child attend school when there is productive work to be done on the farm – a cost which is not reflected in school fees and one which is of much less significance to higher income families, many of whom may live in the urban areas anyway.

As a result of these higher opportunity costs, school attendance and therefore school performance tend to be much lower for children of poor families than for those from relatively higher income backgrounds. Thus, in spite of the existence of free and universal primary education in many LDCs (which even when it exists typically covers only the first few years of schooling), children of the poor, especially in rural areas, are seldom able to proceed beyond the first few years of their education. Their relatively poor school performance may have nothing to do with a lack of cognitive abilities. On the contrary, it may merely reflect their disadvantaged economic circumstances.

This financial process of eliminating the relatively poor during their first few years of schooling is often compounded by the substantial school fees charged at the secondary level. In many developing countries these yearly fees may be the equivalent of the level of per capita income for the country as a whole. They therefore become prohibitive to lower income families. This in effect amounts to a system of educational advancement and selection based not on any criteria of merit but strictly on the basis of family income levels. It thus leads to a concentration of income in the succeeding generations within the same population groups which receive disproportionately high incomes in the present generation. It also eventually leads to a concentration of 'earned income' among that group which already possesses the bulk of 'unearned' income and wealth, those whose physical and financial assets already place them in the upper deciles of the personal income distribution scale.

The inegalitarian nature of many Third World educational systems is compounded even further at the university level where the government may pay the full cost of tuition and fees as well as provide university students with income.grants in the form of bursaries. Since most university students already come from upper-income brackets (and were so selected at the secondary level), highly subsidized university education utilizing public funds extracted from the taxation of the poor often represents in fact a subsidy or transfer payment from the poor to the wealthy – in the name of 'free' higher education!

On the benefit side, the poor are also at a disadvantage vis-à-vis the rich. Even if they are able to complete their primary education, the poor typically have more difficulty competing for rural and urban jobs with the relatively rich because of the latter's greater range of contacts and influences. In other words, for any given level of completed education (except perhaps university level education) the poor student will tend to be less likely to be selected for a job requiring that educational certification than the rich student. Even in agriculture one could argue that although education may raise farm labor productivity, the benefits of this will accrue disproportionately to those farm families who own their land and also have the complementary financial resources to modernize their agricultural techniques, i.e. the well-to-do, large-scale farmer. In the extreme case of landless rural laborers, the greatest proportion of the benefits of their limited education and higher productivity may accrue largely to the rich landlord on whose farm they work.

It follows that in Third World countries characterized by highly unequal distributions of personal income, sizable secondary school fees and subsidized higher education, the educational system, especially at the secondary and higher levels, probably operates to *increase* inequality and perpetuate poverty. It should be stressed, however, that this outcome is not inherently the result of the educational system *per se* but the institutional and social structure within which that system must function. Specifically, as long as wage differentials between different educational categories are kept artificially wide in spite of rising levels of educated unemployment; as long as access to jobs is based almost exclusively on educational credentials irrespective of the relationship between years of schooling and job performance; and, as long as a family's income serves as the basic criterion of who is able to proceed up the educational ladder to highly paid jobs, then publicly supported educational systems will merely serve to reproduce the inegalitarian social and economic structure that, at least in theory, they were devised to combat. *Equality of educational opportunity can have little meaning if financial assets and income earning opportunities are very unequally distributed.*

Finally, we should point out that even if all of the above cost and benefit distributions in favor of the rich were removed (e.g. by taxing higher incomes at higher rates, subsidizing the education of the poor, broadening employment opportunities for all, making the rich bear the full costs of their education, etc.) so as to make progress in the educational system strictly a function of merit and school performance, the poor would nevertheless *still* be at a competitive disadvantage. As we saw earlier in the chapter, an early childhood characterized by poor nutrition and a congested and illiterate home environment has negative mental effects.

We are therefore compelled to conclude that as in the case of the population problem where family planning programs are most effective in the context of an economic motivation for smaller families based on improved levels of living, the problems of inequality and poverty depend ultimately on the direct measures aimed at eliminating them and only partially on indirect measures such as universal education. As long as the institutional, social and economic structures of Third World nations cater primarily for the needs and desires of upper-income groups, an educational system which in principle at least is open to all classes, tribes and castes and which is considered socially progressive, a matter of national pride and an instrument of egalitarianism, can in reality merely provide short-term cover for the further widening of the gap between rich and poor. But with rising unemployment, greater inequality and the chronic persistence of absolute poverty, the political cover provided by thinly disguised inegalitarian systems of Third World education becomes ever more difficult to maintain. Ironically, it is typically the middle and upper-class students themselves, especially at the university level, who are often in the vanguard of economic and social reform. There have recently been economic and social reforms arising out of such student-led movements in Thailand, Ethiopia, Sri Lanka, Colombia, Pakistan and the Philippines, to name just a few.

3. Education, internal migration and fertility

Education appears to be an important factor influencing both rural–urban migration and levels of fertility. The relationship between education and migration, however, appears to be more powerful than that between education and fertility. Moreover, existing empirical evidence reveals that education influences labor mobility even more directly (i.e. through its impact on higher income expectations) than fertility.

Numerous studies of migration in diverse countries have documented the positive relationship between the educational attainment of an individual and his propensity to migrate from rural to urban areas. Basically, individuals with higher levels of education face wider urban–rural real income differentials and higher probabilities of obtaining modern-sector jobs than those with lower levels of education (recall from Chapter 9 how income differentials and job probabilities interact to determine migration patterns). The probability variable in particular accounts for the growing proportion of the more educated rural migrants in the face of rising levels of urban unemployment among the less educated[13].

With regard to the education and fertility relationship, the evidence is less clear. While most studies reveal an inverse relationship between the education of women and their size of family, particularly at lower levels of education, the mechanism through which education *per se* influences decisions regarding family size is still subject to considerable speculation.

Assuming that lower levels of urban unemployment (especially among the educated) and lower levels of fertility are important policy objectives for Third World governments, the basic issue is whether or not the continued rapid quantitative expansion of the formal educational system (and the resource allocation decisions implicit therein) will ameliorate or exacerbate the twin problems of accelerating internal migration and rapid population growth. The evidence as well as the theory seems to indicate once again that given limited government resources, the further excessive quantitative expansion of school places beyond perhaps basic education is both undesirable and unwise. There are two main reasons for this contention:

First, as we discovered earlier in the chapter, any rapid expansion of the formal primary system creates inexorable pressures on the demand side for the expansion of secondary and tertiary school places. The net result is the widespread phenomenon of excessive expansion of school places in terms of real resource needs in many LDCs and the associated dilemma of rising levels of rural–urban migration and urban unemployment among a cadre of increasingly more educated and more politically vocal migrants.

Secondly, if as many have argued, the education of women does affect their fertility behavior primarily through the mechanism of raising the opportunity cost of their time in child-rearing activities (see Ch. 7), then it follows that unless sufficient employment opportunities for women (as well as for men) can be created, the reliance on educational expansion as a policy instrument for lowering fertility will be weak, if not totally ineffective.

4. Education and rural development In Chapter 10 we argued that if national development is to become a reality in Third World nations, there needs to be a better balance between rural and urban development. Since most of the priority projects of the 1950s and 1960s focused on the modernization and development of the urban sector, much more emphasis needs to be placed in future years on expanding economic and social opportunities in rural areas. While agricultural development represents the main component of any successful rural development program simply because of 80 per cent of Third World rural populations are engaged directly or indirectly in agricultural activities, rural development nevertheless must be viewed in a broader perspective.

First and foremost, it needs to be viewed in the context of far-reaching transformations of economic and social structures, institutions, relationships and processes in rural areas. The goals of rural development cannot simply be restricted to agricultural and economic growth. Rather, they must be viewed in terms of a 'balanced' economic and social development with emphasis on the *equitable distribution* as well as the rapid generation of the benefits of higher levels of living. Among these broader goals, therefore, are the creation of more numbers of employment opportunities both on and off the farm; more equitable access to arable land; more equitable distribution of rural income; more widely distributed improvements in health, nutrition and housing; and, finally, a broadened access to the kind of formal (in-school) and non-formal (out-of-school) education for adults as well as children that will have *direct relevance* to the needs and aspirations of rural dwellers.

How do present Third World systems of education fit into this holistic view of the meaning of rural development? Basically, not very well. As we saw, earlier in the chapter, the formal primary school system in most LDCs is with minor modifications a direct transplant of the system in developed countries. The overriding goal is to prepare all children to pass standard qualifying examinations for secondary schools so that the curricula have a very strong urban bias. The priority needs of that greatest proportion of students – those who are destined to spend their lives living and working in rural areas – are given minimal attention. Major groups with important rural training needs such as out-of-school children and youth, women and small subsistence farmers are largely neglected by organized educational programs, both formal and non-formal. As a result, much of the primary education in the rural communities of developing nations contributes little to improving levels of agricultural productivity or towards assisting the student to function more effectively in his or her rural environment.

What then might be the real and lasting educational needs for rural development? Philip H. Coombs, a noted educational economist, has provided one very appealing typology[14]. He groups these educational needs for both young people and adults, male and female, under four main headings:

1. *General or basic education:* literacy, numeracy and elementary understanding of science and one's environment, etc. – what most primary and secondary schools now seek to achieve.
2. *Family improvement education,* designed primarily to impart knowledge, skills and attitudes, useful in improving the quality of family life, on such subjects as health and nutrition, homemaking and child care, home repairs and improvements, family planning and so on.
3. *Community improvement education,* designed to strengthen local and national institutions and processes through instruction in such matters as local and national government, cooperatives, community projects and the like.
4. *Occupational education,* designed to develop particular knowledge and skills associated with various economic activities and useful in making a living.

For the most part only category 1 – general education – has been emphasized in most developing countries. But the types of learning needs required for the three principal occupational subgroups of rural areas – farmers and farm workers, persons engaged in non-farm rural enterprises and rural general personnel – are likely to be very different from that currently provided by most formal educational curricula. Table 11.3 shows how these learning needs vary from group to group within the rural environment. Effective and well-designed educational programs catering for *each* of these three diverse occupational groups are needed if education is to make its essential contribution to rural development.

5. Education and international migration: intellectual 'dependence' and the 'brain drain'

In addition to the transfer of production and consumption technology (i.e. production processes and consumer tastes), a major aspect of the international transfer of institutional technology lies in the area of transplanted formal educational systems. But, just as the international transfer of techniques of production may be ill-suited to the factor endowments and output priorities of developing nations, so too the human resource needs of agrarian societies attempting to modernize may be and usually are quite different from those catered for by the formal educational systems of highly industrialized, highly urbanized

Groups	Types of Learning Needs (at varying levels of sophistication and specialization)
A. Persons directly engaged in agriculture 1. Commercial farmers 2. Small subsistence and semi-subsistence farm families 3. Landless farm workers	• Farm planning and management; rational decision-making; record keeping; cost and revenue computations; use of credit • Application of new inputs, varieties, improved farm practices • Storage, processing, food preservation • Supplementary skills for farm maintenance and improvement, and sideline jobs for extra income • Knowledge of government services, policies, programs, targets • Knowledge and skills for family improvement (e.g., health, nutrition, home economics, child care, family planning) • Civic skills (e.g., knowledge of how cooperatives, local government, national government function)
B. Persons engaged in off-farm commercial activities 1. Retailers and wholesalers of farm supplies and equipment, consumer goods and other times 2. Suppliers of repair and maintenance services 3. Processors, storers and shippers of agricultural commodities 4. Suppliers of banking and credit services 5. Construction and other artisans 6. Suppliers of general transport services 7. Small manufacturers	• New and improved technical skills applicable to particular goods and services • Quality control • Technical knowledge of goods handled sufficient to advise customers on their use, maintenance, etc. • Management skills (business planning; record keeping and cost accounting; procurement and inventory control; market analysis and sales methods; customer and employee relations; knowledge of government services, regulations, taxes; use of credit)
C. General services personnel: rural administrators, planners, technical experts 1. General public administrators, broad-gauged analysts and planners at sub-national levels 2. Managers, planners, technicians, and trainers for specific public services (e.g., agriculture, transport, irrigation, health, small industry, education, family services, local government, etc.) 3. Managers of cooperatives and other farmer associations 4. Managers and other personnel of credit services	• General skills for administration, planning, implementation, information flows, promotional activities • Technical and management skills applying to particular specialties • Leadership skills for generating community enthusiasm and collective action, staff team work and support from higher echelons

Table 11.3
Illustrative rural occupational groups
and their learning needs

Source: P. H. Coombs and Munzoor Ahmed, *Attacking Rural Poverty: How Nonconformal Education Can Help,* Johns Hopkins U.P. (1974), 17.

and technologically sophisticated nations of the West. The inherently dysfunctional nature of such systems of formal education for Third World rural areas was portrayed in the previous and earlier sections.

But in addition to rich-country dominance in the international development and transfer of physical and intellectual technology, there is also the problem of the international migration of high-level educated manpower – the so-called 'brain drain' – from poor to rich countries. This is particularly true in the case of scientists, engineers, academics and doctors, many thousands of whom have been trained in home country institutions at considerable social cost only to reap the benefits from and contribute to the further economic growth of the already affluent nations. Table 11.4 reveals the annual magnitude of the professional and technical brain drain from the developing nations to North America and the United Kingdom for the period 1962 to 1973. Note particularly the rapid jump in US immigration following the liberalization of US immigration laws in 1966.

The international brain drain deserves mention, however, not only because of its effects on the rate and structure of LDC economic growth, but also because of its impact on the style and approach of Third World educational systems. Thus, the brain drain has not merely reduced the supply of vital professional people available within developing countries. Perhaps even more seriously, it has diverted the attention of *local* scientists, doctors, architects, engineers and academics away from important problems. These include the development of 'appropriate' technology, the promotion of low-cost preventive health care, the construction of low-cost housing, hospitals, schools and other service facilities, the design and building of functional yet inexpensive, labor-intensive roads, bridges and machinery, and the development of relevant university teaching materials such as

Year	United States	Canada	United Kingdom	3-country sum
1962	9,024	1,381	—	—
1963	11,029	1,525	4,600	17,154
1964	11,418	1,873	—	—
1965	11,001	3,707	3,230	17,938
1966	13,986	5,548	—	—
1967	23,361	7,897	2,900	34,158
1968	28,511	6,930	2,420	37,861
1969	27,536	7,585	1,720	36,841
1970	33,796	6,118	1,000	40,914
1971	38,647	5,184	1,270	45,101
1972	39,106	5,360	377	44,843
1973	31,939	—	—	—

Table 11.4
Gross immigration of professional and technical personnel from less developed countries into the United States, Canada and United Kingdom, 1962–73

Source: Edwin P. Reubens, 'Professional migration from the less developed countries', Feb. 1975 (mimeo.), 42.

Note: Coverage of 'less developed countries' comprises all countries in Africa, Asia, North America (excluding Canada and USA) and South America. Coverage of 'Professional and technical personnel' is based on 'Professional, technical, and kindred workers' in the usage of the United States Immigration and Naturalization Service, *Annual Reports*, Table 8; data refer to fiscal years (ending 30 June of year shown), and immigrants' country of birth. Data for Canada are taken from the closest corresponding occupational categories as reported by Department of Manpower and Immigration, annual *Immigration Statistics*, Table 11, categories 2–48 inclusive; data refer to calendar years, and country of former residence. Figures for United Kingdom are enlarged (at ratio of 100:85) from Commonwealth immigration data, according to country of citizenship, in E. J. B. Rose *et al., Colour and Citizenship,* pp. 83, 86, for the period 1962–66, and from Home Office, *Commonwealth Immigrants Statistics,* annual reports for period 1967–72, Table 9 covering arrivals of holders of 'Category B vouchers' (excluding those from Australia, Canada and New Zealand); calendar years.

Listing of persons by occupation is generally based on the immigrant's own declaration.

'appropriate' introductory economics texts and the promotion of problem-oriented research on vital domestic development issues. Instead, dominated by rich-country ideas as to what represents true international and professional 'excellence', those highly educated and highly skilled Third World professionals who do not 'physically' migrate to the developed nations, nevertheless, migrate 'intellectually' to these countries in terms of the orientation of their activities. This 'internal' brain drain is much more serious than the 'external' one.

For example, one constantly finds developing nations with doctors specializing in diseases of the heart, while preventive 'tropical medicine' is considered to be a second-rate 'speciality'. Architects are concerned with the design of national monuments and 'modern' public buildings, while low-cost housing, schools and clinics remain an area of remote concern. Engineers and scientists concentrate on the newest and most modern electronic equipment, while simple machine tools, hand- or animal-operated farm equipment, basic sanitation and water-purifying systems and labor-intensive mechanical processes are relegated to the attention of 'foreign experts'. Finally, some academic economists teach and do research on totally irrelevant, 'sophisticated' mathematical models of non-existent competitive economies, while problems of poverty, unemployment, rural development and education are considered less intellectually 'interesting'.

In all these diverse professional activities, performance criteria are based not on contributions to national development but rather on praise from the 'international community' (i.e. professional mentors in the developed nations). For example, the acceptance of an LDC scholar's publication in international professional journals or the receipt of an invitation to attend a professional meeting in London, Paris, New York or Moscow is often deemed more important than finding a solution to a local technological, agricultural, medical or economic problem.

The 'anti-developmental' effects of such an international dominance of professional attitudes and orientations in developing nations (especially in former colonial countries) for a while tended to permeate the whole educational and intellectual establishment. While difficult to quantify in terms of rates of economic growth and levels of poverty, the combined 'brain drain' and 'outward-looking' orientation of many LDC professionals has no doubt been an important contributing factor to the perpetuation of conditions of underdevelopment in Africa, Asia and Latin America. Recent student and faculty calls for more relevant curricula, teaching materials and research activities, however, attest to the emergence of a new spirit of nationalism and collective self-reliance which appears to be gathering momentum among Third World intellectuals. If a good university is to be more than 'just a collection of books' as the philosopher Thomas Carlyle once remarked, Third World universities and professional schools have a vital role to play in making higher education more tuned to the real needs of social and economic development. Perhaps 10 years from now a section entitled 'intellectual dependence and the brain drain' will no longer be necessary in a book such as this. Let us hope so.

11.7 Summary and conclusions: major educational policy options[15]

Developing nations are confronted with two basic alternatives in their policy approaches to problems of education. They can continue as in the past to expand formal systems quantitatively with minor modifications in curricula, teaching methods and examinations while retaining the same institutional labor market structures and educational costing policies. Or they can attempt to reform the overall educational system by modifying both the conditions of demand for and the supply of educational opportunities and by reorienting curricula in accordance with the real resource needs of the nation. We believe that the first alternative can only exacerbate the problems of unemployment, poverty, inequality, rural stagnation and international intellectual dominance that now define the very conditions of underdevelopment in much of Africa, Asia and Latin America and that, therefore, the second alternative needs to be pursued.

Since educational systems largely reflect and reproduce rather than alter the economic and social structures of the societies in which they exist, any program or set of policies designed to make education more relevant for development needs must, therefore, operate simultaneously on *two levels*:

1. Modifying the economic and social signals and incentives *outside* the educational system which largely determine the magnitude, structure and orientation of the aggregate private demand for education and consequently the political response in the form of the public supply of school places; and

2. Modifying the *internal* effectiveness and equity of educational systems by appropriate changes in course content especially for rural areas, structures of public versus private financing, methods of selection and promotion, and procedures for occupational certification by educational level.

Only by policies designed *simultaneously* to achieve these two objectives can the real positive links between education and development be successfully forged. We conclude, therefore, with a brief review of what these external and internal policies might specifically encompass.

1. Policies largely external to educational systems

A. Adjusting imbalances, signals and incentives

Policies which tend to remedy major economic imbalances and incentive distortions (e.g. in income and wage differentials) and to alleviate social and political constraints on upward mobility can have the multiple beneficial effect of increasing job opportunities, modifying the accelerated rate of rural–urban migration and facilitating development-related modifications of educational systems.

B. Modifying job-rationing by educational certification

In order to break the vicious circle in which overstated job specifications make overeducation necessary for employment, policies are needed which will induce or require both public and private employers to seek realistic qualifications even though the task of job rationing may be made somewhat more difficult as a result. Basic to this procedure would be the elimination of school certificates for many of the jobs, especially in the public sector (janitors, messengers, file clerks, etc.), which tend to set the pattern for the whole private sector.

C. Curbing the brain drain

Controlling or taxing the international migration of indigenously trained high-level professional manpower is a very sensitive area. It can potentially infringe on the basic human right and freedom to choose both the nature and location of one's work. In a repressive regime, such a restrictive policy can be morally repugnant. On the other hand, when a nation invests scarce public financial resources in the education and training of its people only then to forgo the social returns on that investment as a result of international migration, it seems both economically and morally justifiable to seek either to restrict that movement in the national interest, or better, to tax if possible the overseas earnings of professional migrants and reinvest these revenues in programs of national development. Such a tax on overseas earnings would act as a financial disincentive to migrate. Its implementation, however, would require the cooperation and assistance of the governments of countries to which these professionals migrate[16].

2. Policies internal to educational systems
A. Educational budgets

Where politically feasible, educational budgets should grow more slowly than in the past to permit more revenue to be used for the creation of rural and urban employment opportunities. Moreover, a larger share of educational budgets should be allocated to the development of primary as opposed to secondary and higher education as a basis for self-education and rural work-related learning experiences.

B. Subsidies

Subsidies for the higher levels of education should be reduced as a means of overcoming distortions in the aggregate private demand for education. Policies should be promoted by which the beneficiary of education (as opposed to his family or society as a whole) would bear a larger and rising proportion of his educational costs as he proceeds through the system. This should be done either directly, through loan repayments, or by service in rural areas. At the same time low-income groups should be provided with sufficient subsidies to permit them to overcome the sizable private costs (including 'opportunity costs') of schooling.

C. Primary school curricula in relation to rural needs

In order to maximize the productivity of rural human resources, primary school curricula as well as 'non-formal' educational opportunities for school drop-outs and adults need to be directed more towards the occupational requirements of rural inhabitants whether in small-farm agriculture, non-farm artisan and entrepreneurial activities, or in rural public and commercial services. Such curricula and task-related reorientations of rural learning systems, however, will not be effective in eliciting popular support unless *rural economic opportunities* are created through which small farmers, artisans and entrepreneurs can take advantage of their vocational knowledge and training. Without these incentives, people will justifiably view such formal and non-formal occupational training programs with considerable scepticism. They would probably rather pursue the formal school certificate and take their chances in the urban job lottery.

D. Quotas

To compensate for the inequality effects of most existing formal school systems some form of quotas may be required to ensure that the proportion of low-income students at secondary or higher educational levels at least approximate their proportions in the overall population. Under present systems 'indirect' quotas by income status often determine which students proceed through the educational system. Replacing this *de facto* quota system by an alternative which ensures that capable low-income students will be able to improve their own and their family's well-being by overcoming the financial barriers to educational advancement would go a long way to making educational systems true vehicles of economic and social equality. The nature of such quota systems will obviously vary from country to country. But there is no *a priori* basis for assuming that such a quota-by-income level system will be any less efficient or socially productive for both growth and equity than the present system which tends to perpetuate poverty and inequality while having a dubious impact on the overall rate of economic growth.

Notes

1. Frederick H. Harbinson, *Human Resources as the Wealth of Nations*, Oxford U.P. (1973), 3.
2. G. Psacharopoulos, *The Returns to Education: An International Comparison*, Elsevier, London (1972).
3. Nicholas Bennett, *'Primary education in rural communities: An investment in ignor-nance'*, International Institute for Educational Planning, Paris (1972), 5–6 (mimeo).
4. Julius Nyerere, 'The University's Role in the Development of New Countries', World University Service Assembly, Dar es Salaam, Tanzania, June 27 1966.
5. See, for example, *Education in the Nation's Service: Experiments in Higher Education for Development*, Prepared by International Council for Educational Development, New York, May 1975.
6. For a review of the evidence for both developed and less developed nations see J. Simmons and L. Alexander, 'The determinents of school achievement: education production function analysis', IBRD, Washington DC, June 1974.
7. Much of the material in this section is drawn from the author's joint paper with E. O. Edwards, 'Educational demand and supply in the context of growing unemployment in less developed countries', *World Development*, **1**, nos. 3 and 4 (1973).
8. In fact, since most expectations for the future tend to be based on a 'static' picture of the employment situation that now prevails, we might anticipate that with a worsening employment picture individuals will tend to overestimate their expected incomes and demand even more education than is justified even in terms of 'correct' private calculations of benefits and costs.
9. For a penetrating analysis of the Indian educational/employment problem, see Marc Blaug, *et al. Causes of Graduate Unemployment in India*, Allen Lane, The Penguin Press, London (1967).
10. See, for example, Edward F. Denison, *The Sources of Economic Growth in the United States*, NBER, New York (1962), and Robert Solow, 'Technical change and the aggregate production function', *Review of Economics and Statistics*, August, 1957.
11. See, for example, Jagdish Bhagwati, 'Education, class structure and income equality', *World Development*, **1**, no. 5 (1973).
12. John Simmons, 'Education, poverty and development', *World Bank Staff Working Paper*, no. 188, (1974), 32.
13. For evidence of this in the case of Tanzania see Barnum and Sabot, op. cit. Ch. 9.
14. Philip H. Coombs and Manzoor Ahmed, *Attacking Rural Poverty: How Nonformal Education Can Help*, Johns Hopkins U.P. (1974), 15.
15. As in other chapters, the policies put forward here are designed primarily to stimulate group discussion and individual analysis. We believe that they are sensible policies with a solid economic rationale, but they should not be viewed as absolute and/or immutable.
16. For an analysis of the problem, see Jagdish Bhagwati and William Dellalfar, 'The brain drain and income taxation', *World Development*, **1**, nos. 1 and 2 (1973), 94–101: see also the entire September 1975 issue of the *Journal of Development Economics* which is devoted to the subject of the international brain drain.

human resources
schooling
'formal' educational system
'non-formal' education
manpower planning
universal education

private versus social benefits
  of education
private versus social costs
  of education
economic 'signals' and
  'incentives'

Concepts for review

Concepts for review

enrolment ratios
drop-out (or wastage) rates
literacy
cognitive skills
derived demand
educational 'rates of
  return'
'opportunity costs' of
  education
educational 'certification'
'basic' education
'family improvement' education
International brain drain
socio-political constraints
  on educational mobility
educational job displacement
  phenomenon

overeducation
job rationing by education
on-the-job training
high-level manpower
equal educational opportunity
pre-school environmental effects
  on ability to learn
modern sector or urban 'bias'
  of educational systems
internal effectiveness of
  educational systems
'community improvement' education
'occupational' education
'internal' brain drain
educational subsidies
quota systems

Questions for discussion

1. What reasons would you give for the rather sizeable school drop-out rates in Third World countries? What might be done to lower these dropout or school 'wastages' rates.

2. What are the differences between 'formal' and 'non-formal' education? Give some examples of each.

3. It is often asserted that Third World educational systems especially in rural areas are 'dysfuntional' – that is, they are not suited to the real social and economic needs of development. Do you agree or disagree with this statement? Explain your reasoning.

4. How would you explain the fact that relative 'costs' of and 'returns to' higher education are so much higher in LDCs than in developed countries?

5. What is the supposed rationale for subsidizing higher education in many Third World countries? Do you think that it is a legitimate rationale from an economic viewpoint? Explain.

6. 'Pre-school' environmental factors are said to be important determinants of school performance. What are some of these pre-school factors, how important do you think they are and what might be done to minimize their incidence among the population?

7. What do we mean by 'the economics of education'. To what extent do you think educational planning and policy decisions ought to be guided by economic considerations? Explain, giving hypothetical or actual examples.

8. What is meant by the statement 'the demand for education is a "derived demand" for high paying modern sector job opportunities'? Many educational specialists claim that families and children in LDCs demand education not so much as an 'investment' good but as a 'consumption' good. What do you think is the meaning of this statement and what do you think is the relative importance of the 'consumption' demand for education in your own country?

9. What are the linkages between educational systems, labor markets and employment determination in many Third World countries? Describe the process of 'educational job displacement'.

10. Distinguish carefully between 'private' and 'social' benefits and costs of education. What economic factors give rise to the wide divergence between private and social benefit/cost valuations in most developing countries? Should governments attempt through their educational and economic policies to narrow the gap between private and social valuations? Explain.

11. Describe and comment on each of the following education-development relationships:
    (a) Education and economic growth: does education promote growth? How?
    (b) Education, inequality and poverty: do educational systems typical of most LDCs tend to reduce, exacerbate or have no effect on inequality and poverty? Explain with specific reference to your own country.
    (c) Education and migration: does education stimulate rural–urban migration? Why?
    (d) Education and fertility: does the education of women tend to reduce their fertility? Why and how?
    (e) Education and rural development: do most LDC formal educational systems contribute substantially to the promotion of rural development? Explain.
    (f) Education and the brain drain: what factors cause the international migration of high-level educated manpower from LDCs to developed countries? What do we mean by the 'internal' brain drain? Explain, giving examples.

12. Governments can influence the character, quality and content of their educational systems by manipulating important economic and non-economic factors or variables both outside of and within educational systems. What are some of these 'external' and 'internal' factors and how can government policies make education more relevant to the real meaning of development?

For an informative, general approach to the study of education and human resource development, see Frederick H. Harbison, *Human Resources as the Wealth of Nations,* Oxford U.P., New York (1973). Suggested readings

An excellent survey of current economic issues relating education to development can be found in: (*a*) John Simmons (ed.), 'Investment in education: national strategy options for developing countries', IBRD, Working Paper, October 1973;   (*b*) M. Blaug, *An Introduction to the Economics of Education,* Penguin Press, London (1970).

For a broad analysis of how education can promote rural development, see Philip H. Coombs and Manzoor Ahmed, *Attacking Rural Poverty: How Nonformal Education Can Help,* Johns Hopkins U.P., Baltimore (1974).

A challenging and critical view of the role of education in society can be found in Ivan Illich, *Deschooling Society,* Harper and Row, World Perspective, New York (1970).

A good summary of the issues involved in the question of education and inequality can be obtained from Jagdish Bhagwati, 'Education, class structure and income equality', *World Development,* **1,** no. 5, (1973).

Finally, a multidisciplinary approach to education and development well worth reading can be found in F. Champion Ward (ed.), *Education and Development Reconsidered,* Praeger, New York (1974).

Problems and policies
International

Part III

Chapter 12	**Trade theory and development experience**

The opening of a foreign trade . . . sometimes works a sort of industrial revolution in a country whose resources were previously underdeveloped.
John Stuart Mill, 1846

For unto everyone that hath shall be given, and he shall have abundance; but for him that hath not shall be taken away, even that which he hath.
Matthew 25:29; cf. 13:12

Introduction: the importance of international trade and finance

International trade has often played a crucial though not necessarily a benign role in the historical development of the Third World. Throughout Africa, Asia, the Middle East and Latin America, primary product exports have traditionally accounted for a sizable proportion of individual Gross National Products. In some of the smaller countries almost 25 to 30 per cent of the monetary GNP is derived from the overseas sale of agricultural commodities such as coffee, tea, cotton, cocoa and sugar. In the special circumstances of the oil-producing nations in Persian Gulf, the sale of unrefined and refined petroleum products to countries throughout the world accounts for over 90 per cent of their national incomes. But, unlike the oil-producing states, most developing countries must depend on non-mineral primary product exports for the vast majority of their foreign exchange earnings. Since the markets for these exports are often very unstable, primary product export dependence carries with it a degree of risk and uncertainty which few nations desire.

In addition to their export dependence, many developing countries rely even more on the importation of raw materials, machinery, capital goods, intermediate producer goods and consumer products both to fuel their industrial expansion and to satisfy the rising consumption aspirations of their people. For most non-petroleum-rich developing nations, import demands have exceeded the capacity to generate sufficient revenues from the sale of exports. This has led to chronic 'deficits' on their balance-of-payments position vis-à-vis the rest of the world. While such deficits on the 'current account' – i.e. an excess of import *payments* over export *receipts* for goods and services – were often more than compensated for by a 'surplus' on the 'capital account' of their balance-of-payments table – i.e. a receipt of foreign private and public lending and investment in excess of repayment of principal and interest on former loans and investments – in recent years the 'debt burden' of repaying earlier international loans and investments has become increasingly acute. In a number of LDCs severe deficits on both current and capital accounts therefore have led to a rapid depletion of their international monetary 'reserves'. We explain the precise meaning of these and other concepts of international economics in this chapter and the next. Now we merely point out that a chronic excess of foreign expenditures over receipts (which incidentally may have nothing to do with an LDC's inability to handle its financial affairs but may rather be related to its vulnerability to global economic disturbances) can not only retard development efforts. It can also greatly limit a poor nation's ability to decide the most desirable development strategies for itself.

But international trade and finance must be understood in a much broader perspective than simply the inter-country flow of commodities and financial resources. By 'opening' their economies and societies to world trade and commerce and by 'looking outward' to the rest of the world, Third World countries invite not only the international transfer of goods, services and financial resources, but also the 'developmental' or 'anti-developmental' influences of the transfer of production technologies, consumption patterns, institutional and organizational arrangements, educational, health and social systems, and the more general values, ideals and lifestyles of the developed nations of the world, both capitalist and socialist. The impact of such technological, economic, social and cultural transfers on the character of the development process can be either benign or malevolent. Much will depend on the nature of the political, social and institutional structure of the recipient country and its development priorities. Whether it is best for LDCs to 'look outward' as the free traders and cultural internationalists advocate, or to 'look inward' as the protectionists and cultural nationalists propose, or to be *both* simultaneously and strategically outward- *and* inward-looking in its international economic policies as suggested by many middle-of-the-road economists, developing nations need to appraise their present and prospective situation in the world community realistically in the light of their specific development objectives. Only thus can they judge how much to expose themselves, if at all, to both the obvious benefits and the many dangers of international commerce.

Unfortunately, many small and very poor countries (and these constitute well over half the total of 118 Third World nations) may have little choice whether to 'opt out' or not. Even in these extreme cases the choice might not be simply one of looking 'outward' to the developed world for assistance or turning 'inward' in an attempt to become more self-reliant. As we shall see, a more promising strategy, especially for the smaller LDCs, may be to look *both* outward but in a different direction (towards cooperation with other LDCs) and inward towards each other as members of a group of nations trying to integrate their economies and coordinate their joint development strategies in an effort to achieve 'collective' self-reliance.

The study of foreign trade and international finance is among the oldest and most controversial branches of the discipline of economics. It dates back to the sixteenth century and Europe's mercantilist passion for Spanish gold. It flowered in the eighteenth and nineteenth centuries as modern economic growth was fuelled and propelled by the 'engine' of international trade. The greatest minds in economics – Adam Smith, David Ricardo and John Stuart Mill – provided the basic concepts and insights which to this day still endure. A deep and abiding concern with global international relations flourishes even more today not only because of the still bitter controversies between those who champion more trade and those who advocate less, especially in the context of development, but also because modern transport and communications are rapidly shrinking the world to the point where some even refer to it as a 'global village'. It is for these and the other reasons mentioned above that we now approach, rather cautiously, this very important and still very controversial area of economic analyses and policy.

12.1 Five basic questions about trade and development

In order to give our discussion contemporary relevance, our objective in this chapter is to expound the main traditional analytical approaches to the subject in the context of *five* basic themes or questions of particular current importance to developing nations – individually and as a whole.

1. How does international trade affect the rate, structure and character of LDC economic growth? This is the traditional 'trade-as-an-engine-of-growth' controversy but set in terms of contemporary development aspirations.
2. How does trade alter the distribution of income and wealth within a country and among different countries or groups of countries? Is trade a force for international and domestic equality or inequality? In other words, how are the gains and losses distributed and who benefits at whose expense (for every 'winner' must there be at least one or, more likely, very many 'losers')?
3. Under what conditions can trade help LDCs achieve their development objectives?
4. Can LDCs by their own actions determine how much they trade?
5. In light of past experience and prospective judgement, should LDCs adopt an 'outward looking' (freer trade, expanded flows of capital and human resources, ideas and technology, etc.) or an 'inward looking' (protectionism in the interest of self-reliance) policy or should they pursue some combination of both, for example, in the form of regional economic cooperation? What are the arguments for and against these alternative trade strategies for development?

Clearly, the answers or suggested answers to these five questions will not be uniform throughout the diverse economies of the Third World. The whole economic basis for international trade rests on the fact that *countries do differ* in their resource endowments, their economic and social institutions and their capacities for growth and development. Developing countries are no exception to this rule. Some are very populous yet deficient in natural resources and human skills. Others are sparsely populated yet endowed with abundant mineral and raw material resources. Still others – the majority – are small and economically weak, having at present neither the human nor the material resources on which to base a sustained and largely self-sufficient strategy of economic and social development. Yet, with the notable exception of the now very wealthy oil nations of the Middle East and a few other countries rich in internationally demanded mineral resources, most developing nations face similar issues and choices in their international relations with both the developed countries and with each other. Consequently, while we shall try to place our generalizations about LDC trade prospects and policy alternatives in the context of a broad typology of Third World nations, our attempt to be catholic in coverage will necessitate a number of sweeping generalizations, many of which may not hold for a particular country at a particular time. On balance, however, we feel that the 'social benefits' of this broad Third World perspective outweigh the 'social costs' of our having to make some analytical and policy generalizations.

Accordingly, we begin with a statistical summary of recent Third World trade performance and patterns. A simplified presentation follows of the classical and more recent theories of international trade and its effect on efficiency, equity, stability and growth (four basic economic concepts related to the central questions outlined above). We then present an extensive critique of 'free trade' theories in light of both historical experience and the contemporary conditions and strategies of economic development. In succeeding chapters, some alternative trade and commercial policies for development are surveyed and the controversies surrounding each summarized.

12.2 The importance of trade for development: a statistical review

The export of commodities, of which primary products (food, food products, raw materials, minerals and fossil fuels) constitute over three-quarters of the total, provides by far the most important source of foreign exchange earnings for the developing world. We see from Table 12.1, for example, that over the period from 1960 to 1972 receipts from commodity exports amounted to almost 80 per cent of the total balance-of-payments receipts of all developing countries.

1. Commodity exports

	1960	1970	1972	
Receipts or sources of funds				
Commodity exports	26·0	63·0	79·9	
Official flows (gross)	4·8	9·9	13·2	
Private investment	3·5	8·2	11·0	
Private transfer payment (gross)	0·6	2·2	2·9	
Allocation of special drawing rights*	—	0·8	0·7	
Total sources	34·7	84·1	107·7	
Uses of funds				
Commodity imports	29·5	64·8	79·1	
Debt service	2·0	5·4	7·3	
Other investment payments	3·0	7·6	10·0	Table **12.1**
Changes in reserves	− 0·1	+ 3·0	+ 8·3	Major components of the balance of
Miscellaneous	0·3	3·3	3·0	payments of Third World nations as a
Total uses	34·7	84·1	107·7	whole, 1960–72

Source: Adapted from ODC, op. cit., 1974, Table B–1.
    * See Chapter 14 for an explanation of the nature and function of Special Drawing Rights (SDRs)

They were more than six times as large as the value of official capital flows (foreign aid) to these countries in 1972. In other words, over the period from 1960 to 1972 the sale of commodities in foreign markets provided steadily greater amounts of foreign exchange than 'bilateral' grants and loans (those provided by one government to another) and 'multilateral' grants and loans (those from a variety of countries channelled through international organizations like the World Bank, the International Monetary Fund and the various regional development banks) combined.

Table 12.1 however conceals the fact that for most LDCs the value of commodity exports over this period did not expand as fast as commodity imports. This is because the table includes the export earnings of major oil-producing countries. If for example these earnings are excluded from the 1972 figures, the total value of Third World commodity exports would amount to 44·6 billion dollars compared to commodity imports totalling 54·7 billion dollars – a negative trade gap or deficit of over $10 billion. By the end of 1975 this gap between import expenditures and export receipts of all non-oil-exporting developing nations had more than quadrupled from 10 to 42 billion dollars largely as a result of the quadrupling of international petroleum prices, the sharp rise in prices of imported manufactured products and the rapid deterioration after 1974 of Third World commodity prices. This increased trade deficit alone exceeded the *total* annual flow of private foreign investments and public development assistance to *all* developing nations over the same period! Trade prospects for most of the non-oil-exporting developing countries for the remainder of the decade remain bleak.

If we look specifically at the annual growth rate in the value of exports for the world as a whole and for its three subcomponents (the 'First World' of developed market economies, the 'Second World' of developed socialist economies and the 'Third World' of developing countries) over the period 1950 to 1972, we find that between 1950 and 1967 First, Second and Third World exports grew at 7·6, 9·2 and 4·1 per cent annually. During the 1967 to 1972 period, however, the rates were 14·5, 11·6 and 11·6 respectively. These data are shown in Table 12.2.

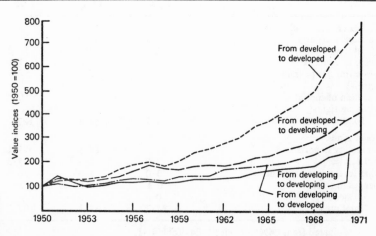

Fig 12.1
Value indices of exports from developed and developing countries 1950–71

Source: World Bank Group, *Trends in Developing Countries, 1973,* Chart 5.5.

As a result of the more rapid growth rates in the value of developed country (both capitalist and socialist) exports, their share of total world trade rose from 68·8 per cent in 1950 to 81·2 per cent during the 1967–72 period. Again, if we exclude the major oil-exporting countries from Third World figures, we discover that the remaining less developed countries have been *losing ground* in terms of their proportionate share of total world trade in *every year* from 1950 to the mid-1970s. This is an important indicator of their relatively weakened international trade position. The main reason for this deteriorating position is that developed nations have been able to increase their share of world trade by annually exporting more to each other and to the Third World than the Third World countries have been able to export either to the developed nations or to themselves. These trends are shown clearly in Figure 12.1.

Moreover, during the past decade and a half the developing countries have been doing proportionately less trade with each other. The percentage of total exports going to each other dropped from 23 per cent in 1960 to under 20 per cent by the mid-1970s. In other words, Third World countries became even more dependent on rich countries for the sale of their products, while their own share of world trade was declining.

	1950–67	1960–6	1967–72	
World	6·9	8·0	13·6	
Developed 'Market' countries	7·6	8·7	14·5	**Table 12.2**
Developed 'Socialist' countries	9·2	7·5	11·5	Annual average growth rates of the
Less developed countries	4·1	6·0	11·5	value of exports

Sources: Handbook of International Trade and Development Statistics, 1969, U.N.

While overall Third World figures for export growth rates and shares of total world exports are important indicators of patterns of trade for the group as a whole, the varying importance of exports and imports to the economic well-being of individual nations is masked by these aggregate statistics. In order, therefore, to provide a capsule picture on the relative importance of commodity export earnings to various developing nations of different sizes and in different regions, Table

2. Importance of exports to different developing nations

Country	Ratio of total exports to GNP	
Ghana	18·9	
Kenya	16·3	
India	8·0	
Sri Lanka	24·4	
Zaire	39·6	
Brazil	9·2	
Colombia	13·0	
Nicaragua	26·6	
Philippines	16·0	
Taiwan	47·0	
Nigeria*	25·6	**Table 12.3**
USA	4·9	Export earnings as percentage of
USSR	4·1	GNP in selected Third World
France	13·5	countries: 1972

Source: Calculated from ODC, op. cit., 1974, Table A–4.
   * Note that the Nigerian figure jumped from an average of around 25 per cent in the 1960s and early 1970s to over 85 per cent by the mid-1970s as a direct result of the oil price and export boom of 1974.

12.3 has been compiled. Comparisons with key developed countries are given at the bottom of the table.

We see that large countries like Brazil and India tend to be less dependent on foreign trade in terms of national income than relatively small countries like those in tropical Africa and Central America. As a group, however, less developed nations are more dependent on foreign trade in terms of its share in national income than are the very highly developed countries. This is shown clearly in the US and USSR, both of whose exports amount to less than 5 per cent of their respective GNPs

3. The composition of trade   Another critical dimension of the trade characteristics of Third World countries can be gleaned from analysis of the commodity composition of their exports and imports. As Table 12.4 shows, LDCs depend heavily upon their exports of raw materials and primary products while the developed nations export primarily manufactured goods. (In spite of the preponderance of manufactured exports, however, the United States and Canada still dominate world exports of the principal cereals such as wheat, corn and rice. We discuss the economic and political implications of this North American dominance of world food exports in Chapter 17.)

We have an important clue here to why LDC export performance has been relatively weak compared with the export performance of rich countries. It relates to the concept of elasticity of demand. Most statistical studies of world demand patterns for different commodity groups tend to demonstrate that in the case of primary products the 'income elasticity of demand' is relatively low – that is, the percentage increase in quantity demanded will rise by less than the percentage increase in national income. On the other hand for fuels, certain raw materials and manufactured goods, the income elasticity is relatively high. For example, it has been estimated that a 1 per cent increase in developed-country incomes will normally raise their import of food-stuffs from less developed countries by $0 \cdot 6$ per cent, agricultural raw materials such as rubber and vegetable oils by $0 \cdot 5$ per cent, petroleum products and other fuels by $2 \cdot 4$ per cent and manufactures by about $1 \cdot 9$ per cent. Consequently, when incomes rise in rich countries their demand for food, food products and raw materials from the Third World nations goes up relatively slowly while the worldwide demand for manufactures, the production of which is dominated by the developed countries, goes up very rapidly.

Category	Less developed countries	Developed countries
Primary commodities		
Food, food products and raw materials	39	18
Fuels	39	4
Manufactures		
Chemicals	2	9
Engineering products	2	36
Manufactures (non-metallic mineral and others)	17	31
Unspecified	1	2
Total	100	100

Table 12.4 Commodity composition of exports, 1971

Source: ODC, op. cit., 1974, Table B–7.

Finally, the concentration of export production on a relatively few major non-cereal primary commodities such as cocoa, tea, sugar and coffee renders certain LDCs very vulnerable to market fluctuations in specific products. For example, nearly half the Third World countries earn over 50 per cent of their export receipts from a single primary commodity, such as coffee, cocoa or bananas. Moreover, about 75 per cent of these nations earn 60 per cent or more of their foreign exchange receipts from no more than three primary products. Significant price variations, therefore, for these commodities can render development strategies highly uncertain. It is for this reason that international commodity agreements (such as those for coffee, cocoa and sugar) among primary producing nations exporting the same commodity have come into being in recent years.

The question of changing relative price levels for different com-   **4. The terms of trade**
modities brings us to another important quantitative dimension of the trade problems historically faced by Third World nations. The total value of export earnings depends not only on the *volume* of these exports sold abroad but also on the *price* paid for them. If export prices decline, a greater volume of exports will have to be sold merely to keep total earnings constant. Similarly, on the import side, the total foreign exchange expended depends on both the quantity and price of imports.

Clearly, if the price of a country's exports is falling *relative* to the prices of the products it imports, it will have to sell that much more of its export product and enlist so much more of its scarce productive resources merely to secure the same level of imported goods that it purchased in previous years. In other words, the 'real' or 'social' opportunity costs of a unit of imports will rise for a country when its export prices decline relative to its import prices.

Economists have a special name for the relationship or ratio between the price of a typical unit of exports and the price of a typical unit of imports. It is called the *commodity terms of trade* and it is expressed as P_x/P_m, where P_x and P_m represent export and import price indices calculated on the same base period (e.g. 1955 = 100). The terms of trade are said to 'deteriorate' for a country if P_x/P_m falls, that is, if export prices decline relative to import prices, even though both may rise. Historically, the prices of primary commodities (the exports of most LDCs) have declined relative to manufactured goods (the principal exports of developed nations). As a result, the terms of trade have on the average tended to worsen for Third World countries (excluding the major oil producers during the 1970s) while they improved for the developed countries. For example, between 1955 and 1970 the terms of trade for developed countries rose by over 10 per cent while that of the Third World fell by over 7 per cent. The LDCs therefore had to sell greater quantities of their primary products (the international demand for which, as we have seen, is relatively 'income inelastic') in order to purchase a given quantity of manufactured imports. One estimate has placed the extra costs of deteriorating terms of trade for the LDCs at over $2·5 billion per year during the last decade.

A good deal of the argument against primary product export expansion and in favor of diversification into manufactured exports for developing countries during the 1950s and 1960s was based on this secular deterioration of their commodity terms of trade. But since past commodity price trends are no indication of what future prices will be (witness the dramatic rise and then fall in world food grain, raw material, and other primary product prices during the 1973–7 period) and since the international economic vulnerability of developing nations is not confined solely to adverse movements in commodity terms of trade (how are these prices determined anyway?), it is important to understand both the broader theory and the practice of international economics lest we lose sight of the forest by focusing on a single tree. Let us, therefore, first review the traditional theory of international trade and then look at the factors that determine the actual trade patterns and performances of developing nations.

12.3 The traditional theory of international trade

1. Specialization and the principle of comparative advantage: the classical labor–cost model

The phenomenon of transactions and exchange is a basic component of human activity throughout the world. Even in the remotest villages of Africa, people regularly meet in the village market to exchange goods, sometimes for money, but mostly for other goods through simple 'barter' transactions. A transaction is an exchange of two things – something is given up in return for something else. In an African village, women may barter food such as cassava for cloth or simple jewellery for clay pots. Implicit in all transactions is a 'price'. For example, if twenty cassavas are traded for a metre of bark cloth, the implicit price (or 'terms of trade') of the bark cloth is twenty cassavas. If in turn twenty cassavas can be exchanged in the same market for one small clay pot, it follows that clay pots and pieces of bark cloth can be exchanged on a one-to-one basis. A price system is already in the making.

Why do people trade? Basically, because it is profitable to do so. Different people possess different abilities and resources and may want to consume goods in different proportions. Diverse preferences as well as varied physical and financial endowments open up the possibility of profitable trade. People usually find it profitable to trade the things they possess in large quantities (i.e. relative to their tastes and or needs) in return for things they want more urgently. Since it is virtually impossible for each individual or family to provide itself with all the consumption requirements of even the simplest life, they usually find it profitable to engage in those activities for which they are best suited or have a 'comparative advantage' in terms of their natural abilities and/or resource endowments. They can then exchange any surplus of these home-produced commodities for products which others may be relatively more suited to produce. The phenomenon of specialization based on comparative advantage arises, therefore, to some extent in even the most primitive of subsistence economies.

These same principles of specialization and comparative advantages have long been applied by economists to the exchange of goods between individual nations. In answer to the question of what determines which goods are traded and why some countries produce some things while others produce different things, economists since the time of Adam Smith have sought the answer in terms of *international differences in costs of production and prices of different products*. Countries, like people, specialize in a limited range of production activities because it is to their advantage to do so. They specialize in those activities where the gains from specialization are likely to be the largest.

But why, in the case of international trade, should costs differ from country to country? For example, how can, say, Germany produce cameras, electrical appliances and automobiles cheaper than, say, Kenya and exchange these manufactured goods for Kenya's relatively cheaper agricultural produce (fruits, vegetables, coffee and tea)? Again, the answer is to be found in international differences in the structure of costs and prices. Some things (basically manufactured goods) are relatively cheaper to produce in Germany and can profitably be exported to other countries like Kenya; other things (e.g. agricultural goods) can be produced in Kenya at a lower relative cost and are therefore imported into Germany in exchange for its manufactures.

The concept of *relative* cost and price differences is basic to the theory of international trade. It is known as the principle of 'comparative advantage' and it asserts that a country will specialize in the export of these products which it can produce at the lowest *relative* cost. Germany may be able to produce cameras and cars as well as fruits and vegetables at lower *absolute* unit costs than Kenya, but since the commodity cost differences between countries are greater for the manufactured goods than for agricultural products, it will be to the advantage of Germany to specialize in the production of manufactured goods and exchange them for Kenya's agricultural produce. Thus, while Germany may have an *absolute* cost advantage in both commodities, its *comparative* cost advantage lies in manufactured goods. Conversely, Kenya may be at an absolute disadvantage vis-à-vis Germany in *both* manufacturing and agriculture in that its absolute units costs of production are higher for both types of products. It can nevertheless still engage in profitable trade because it has a 'comparative' advantage in agricultural specialization (or, alternatively, because its absolute disadvantage is less in agriculture). It is this phenomenon of differences in comparative advantage, therefore, that gives rise to profitable trade even amongst the most unequal of trading partners.

Free trade, based on the principle of comparative advantage, has two major theoretical benefits. The first is that *trade enables all countries to escape from the confines of their resource endowments and consume commodities in combinations that lie outside their production possibility frontiers*. Thus, free international trade will benefit *all* nations of the world, even though the benefits may be disproportionately distributed depending on world demand conditions and cost differences for different commodities in different countries. The second major implication of the classical theory is that *free trade will maximize global output* by permitting every country to specialize in what it does best – i.e. by focusing on the production of those goods in which it has a 'comparative advantage'. Specialization and trade can therefore lead to world output increases for *all* traded commodities. Note finally that commodity trade is *balanced* in the sense that the value of exports equals the value of imports in both regions. This is an important assumption of classical trade theory.

2. Relative factor endowments and international specialization: the neo-classical model

Classical trade theory is based on a static one-variable-factor, labor cost, complete specialization approach to demonstrating the gains from trade. This nineteenth-century free trade model, primarily associated with David Ricardo and John Stuart Mill, was modified and refined in the twentieth century by two Swedish economists, Eli Heckscher and Bertil Ohlin, to take into account differences in factor supplies (mainly land, labor and capital) on international specialization. The Hecksher–Ohlin neo-classical (i.e. variable proportions) factor endowment approach also enables one to describe analytically the impact of economic growth on trade patterns and the impact of trade on the structure of national economies and on the differential returns or payments to various factors of production.

Unlike the classical labor–cost model, however, where trade arises because of fixed but differing labor productivities for different commodities in different countries, the factor endowment model assumes away inherent differences in relative labor productivity by postulating that *all countries have access to the same technological possibilities for all commodities*. If domestic factor prices were the same, all countries would use identical methods of production and therefore have the same relative domestic product price ratios and factor productivities. The basis for trade arises, therefore, not because of inherent technological differences in labor productivity for different commodities between different countries but because *countries are endowed with different factor supplies*. Given different factor supplies, relative factor prices will differ (e.g. labor will be relatively cheap in labor-abundant countries) and so too will domestic commodity price ratios and factor combinations. Countries with cheap labor will have a relative cost and price advantage over countries with relatively expensive labor in those commodities which make abundant use of labor (e.g. primary products). They should therefore focus on the production of these labor-intensive products and export the surplus in return for imports of capital intensive goods.

On the other hand, countries well endowed with capital will have a relative cost and price advantage in the production of manufactured goods which tend to require relatively large inputs of capital compared with labor. They can then benefit from specialization and export of their capital intensive manufactures in return for imports of labor-intensive products from labor-abundant countries. Trade, therefore, serves as a vehicle for a nation to capitalize on its abundant resources through more intensive production and export of those commodities that require large inputs of those resources while relieving its factor shortage through the importation of commodities that utilize large amounts of its relatively scarce resources.

To sum up, the factor endowment theory is based on two crucial propositions:

1. *Different products require productive factors in different relative proportions.* For example, agricultural products generally require relatively greater proportions of labor per unit of capital than manufactured goods which require more machine-time (capital) per worker than most primary products. The proportions in which factors are actually used to produce different goods will depend on their relative prices. But, no matter what factor prices may be, the factor-endowment model assumes that certain products will *always* be relatively more capital intensive while others will always be relatively more labor intensive. Moreover, it is assumed that these relative factor intensities will be no different in India from those in the United States; primary products will be the relatively labor-intensive commodity compared with say secondary manufactured goods in both India and the US.

2. *Countries have different endowments of factors of production.* Some countries like the United States have large amounts of capital per worker and are thus designated as 'capital-abundant' countries while others like India, Egypt or Colombia have little capital and

much labor. They are thus designated as 'labor-abundant' nations. In general, developed countries are assumed to be relatively capital abundant (one could also add that they are well endowed with skilled labor) while, for the most part, Third World countries have little capital and much unskilled labor – i.e. they are labor-abundant countries.

The factor-endowments theory goes on to argue that capital-abundant countries will specialize in such products as automobiles, aircraft, machinery and equipment, sophisticated electronic communication goods, computers, etc., which utilize capital intensively in their technology of production. They will export some of these capital-intensive products in exchange for those labor- or land-intensive products like food, raw materials and minerals which can best be produced by those countries that are relatively well endowed with labor and/or land.

This theory, described in much of the early literature on trade and development, encouraged Third World countries to focus on their labor- and land-intensive primary product exports. It was argued that by trading these primary commodities for the manufactured goods that developed countries were 'best suited' to produce developing nations could best realize the enormous potential benefit from free trade with the richer nations of the world. This free trade doctrine also served the political interests of colonizing nations searching for raw materials to feed their industrial expansion and for market outlets for their manufactured goods.

The factor endowment model leads to the same basic conclusions as the labor–cost theory: free trade maximizes world output with all participating countries sharing in the gains from trade. However, in addition to these two basic conclusions, there are several others. First, due to increasing opportunity costs associated with resource shifting among commodities with different factor intensities of production, complete or nearly complete specialization will not occur as in the simple labor–cost model. Countries will tend to specialize in these products which utilize their abundant resources intensively. They will compensate for their scarce resources by importing those products which utilize these scarce resources most intensively. But rising domestic costs and, therefore, prices in excess of world prices will prevent complete specialization from occurring.

Second, given identical technologies of production throughout the world, the equalization of domestic product price ratios with the international free trade price ratio *will tend to equalize factor prices across trading countries*. Wage rates, for example, will rise in the labor-abundant Third World as a result of the more intensive use of human resources in the production of additional agricultural output. On the other hand, the price of scarce capital will decline owing to the diminished production of manufactured goods which are heavy users of capital. In the rest of developed world, the price of its abundant capital will rise relative to its scarce labor as more emphasis is placed on the production of capital-intensive manufactured goods and less on labor-intensive agriculture. The factor endowment, variable factor proportions theory, therefore, makes the important prediction that over time international real wage rates and capital costs will tend towards equalization[1]. This is also one of its greatest defects since we know that in the real world just the opposite is happening; international income inequalities increase with each passing year. We shall see below how the restrictive and unreal assumptions of both the labor cost and factor endowment theories can often lead to erroneous conclusions about the actual structure of world trade and the distribution of its benefits.

Third, within countries the factor-endowment theory of trade predicts that the economic return to owners of the abundant resources will rise in relation to owners of scarce resources as the abundant factor is more intensively utilized. In Third World countries this in general would mean a rise in the share of national income going to labor. In the absence of trade, labor's share might be smaller. Thus trade tends to promote more equality in domestic income distributions.

Finally, by enabling countries to move outside of their production possibility frontiers and secure capital as well as consumption goods from other parts of the world, trade is assumed to stimulate or be an 'engine' of economic growth. It also enables a nation to obtain those domestically expensive raw materials and other products (as well as knowledge, ideas, new technologies, etc.) with which it is relatively less well endowed at lower world market prices. It thus can create the conditions for a more broadly based and self-sustaining growth of a nation's industrial output.

3. Trade theory and development: the traditional arguments

The 'classical' labor–cost and the more recent 'neo-classical' factor-endowment theories of international trade provide the following theoretical answers to our five basic questions about trade and development.

1. *Trade is an important stimulator of economic growth.* It enlarges a country's consumption capacities, increases world output and provides access to scarce resources and worldwide markets for products without which poor countries would be unable to grow.
2. *Trade tends to promote greater international and domestic equality* by equalizing factor prices, raising real incomes of trading countries and making efficient use of each nation's and the world's resource endowments – e.g. raising relative wages in labor-abundant countries and lowering them in labor scarce nations.
3. *Trade helps countries to achieve development* by promoting and rewarding those sectors of the economy where individual countries possess a comparative advantage whether in terms of labor efficiency or factor endowments.
4. In a world of free trade, *international prices and costs of production determine how much a country should trade in* order to maximize its national welfare. Countries should follow the dictates of the principle of comparative advantage and not try to interfere with the free workings of the market.
5. Finally, in order to promote growth and development, an *'outward looking' internationalist policy is required.* In all cases, self-reliance and autarchy based on isolation are asserted to be economically inferior to participation in a world of free and unlimited trade.

12.4 Some criticisms of traditional free trade theories in the context of Third World experience

The labor–cost and factor endowment theories of international trade are both based on a number of explicit and implicit assumptions which in many ways are grossly contrary to the reality of contemporary international economic relations. These theories, therefore, often lead to conclusions foreign to both the historical and contemporary trade experience of many developing nations. This is not to deny the real 'potential' benefits of a world of free trade, but rather to recognize that free trade exists mostly in the diagrams and models of economists, whereas the real world is beset by all varieties of national protection and international non-competitive pricing policies.

What are the major and crucial assumptions of the traditional theories of international trade, and how are these assumptions violated in the real world? What are the implications for the trade and financial prospects of developing nations when a more realistic assessment of the actual mechanism of international economic and political relations is made?

There are six basic assumptions of the classical and neo-classical trade models.

1. All productive resources are fixed in quantity and constant in quality across nations. They are fully employed and there is no international mobility of productive factors.
2. The technology of production is fixed (classical model) or similar and freely available (factor endowment model) to all nations. The spread of such technology works to the benefit of every nation. Consumer tastes are also fixed and independent of the influence of producers – i.e. international consumer sovereignty prevails.
3. Within nations, factors of production are perfectly mobile between different production activities and the economy as a whole is characterized by the existence of perfect competition. There are no risks and uncertainties.
4. The national government plays no role in international economic relations so that trade is strictly carried out among many atomistic and anonymous producers seeking to minimize costs and maximize profits. International prices are, therefore, set by the forces of supply and demand.
5. Trade is balanced for each country at any moment of time and all economies are readily able to adjust to changes in the international prices with a minimum of dislocation.
6. The gains from trade that accrue to any country benefit the nationals of that country.

We can now take a critical look at each of these assumptions in the context of the contemporary position of Third World countries in the international economic system.

1. Fixed resources, full employment and the international immobility of capital and skilled labor

A. Trade and resource growth

This initial assumption about the static nature of international exchange – i.e. that resources are fixed, fully utilized and internationally immobile – is central to the whole traditional theory of trade and finance. In reality the world economy is characterized by rapid change and factors of production are fixed neither in quantity nor quality. Not only does capital accumulation and human resource development take place all the time, but trade has always been and will continue to be one of the main *determinants* of the unequal *growth* of productive resources in different nations. This is especially true with respect to those resources most crucial to growth and development such as physical capital, entrepreneurial abilities, scientific capacities, the ability to carry out technological research and development and the upgrading of technical skills in the labor force.

It follows, therefore, that relative factor endowments and comparative costs are *not* given but are in a state of constant change. Moreover, they are often determined by, rather than determining the, nature and character of international specialization. In the context of unequal trade between rich and poor nations, this means that *any initial state of unequal resource endowments will tend to be reinforced and exacerbated by the very trade which these differing resource endowments were supposed to justify.* Specifically, if rich nations as a result of historical forces are relatively 'well endowed' with the vital resources of capital, entrepreneurial ability and skilled labor, their continued specialization in products and processes which intensively utilize these resources will create the necessary conditions for their further growth. On the other hand, Third World countries, 'endowed' with abundant supplies of unskilled labor, by specializing in products which intensively utilize unskilled labor, and whose world demand prospects and terms of trade may be very unfavorable, often find themselves locked in to a stagnant situation which perpetuates their 'comparative advantage' in unskilled productive activities. This in turn will inhibit the domestic growth of needed capital, entrepreneurship and technical skills.

A cumulative process is therefore set in motion in which trade exacerbates already unequal trading relationships, distributes the benefits largely to those who already 'have', and perpetuates the physical and human resource underdevelopment that characterizes Third World nations. No country likes to think of itself specializing in unskilled labor activities while letting foreigners reap the rewards of higher skills, technology and capital. By pursuing the theoretical dictates of their factor endowments, less developed countries may lock themselves into a domestic economic structure that reinforces such relatively poor endowments and is inimical to their long-run development aspirations.

B. Unemployment, resource underutilization and the 'vent-for-surplus' theory of trade

The assumption of full employment in traditional trade models, like that of the standard perfectly competitive equilibrium model of micro-economic theory, also violates the reality of unemployment and underemployment in developing nations. Two conclusions may be drawn from the recognition of widespread unemployment in the Third World. First, underutilized human resources create the opportunity to expand productive capacity and GNP at little or no real cost by producing for export markets products which are not demanded locally. This is known as the '*vent-for-surplus*' theory of international trade. It was formulated first by Adam Smith but expounded more recently in the context of developing nations by the Burmese economist Hla Myint.

According to this theory, the opening of world markets to remote agrarian societies creates opportunities not to reallocate fully employed resources as in the traditional models but, rather, to make use of formerly *underemployed* land and labor resources to produce greater output for export to foreign markets. The colonial system of plantation agriculture as well as the commercialization of small-scale subsistence agriculture were made possible, according to this view, by the availability of unemployed and underemployed human resources. In terms of our production possibility analyses, the 'vent-for-surplus' argument can be represented by a shift in production from point V to point B in Fig. 12.2 with trade enlarging final domestic consumption from point V to C.

We see that before trade, the resources of this closed Third World economy were grossly underutilized with production occurring at point V, well within the confines of the production possibility frontier.

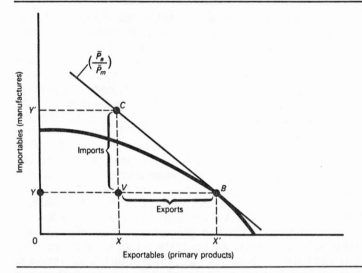

Fig 12.2
The 'vent-for-surplus' theory of trade in LDCs

Initial production and consumption situation before trade is shown by point *V*.
With opening of trade, production of primary products (exportables) shifts from *V* to *B*.
At international price ratio $(\bar{P}_a /\bar{P}_m)$, *VB* primary products can be exported for *VC* manufactured imports.
Final (after trade) consumption situation shown by point *C*. Same primary products being consumed (0*X*) as before but *Y'Y* more manufactures available as result of trade, i.e. consumption is 0*Y'* instead of 0*Y* manufactures.

0*X* primary products and 0*Y* manufactures were being produced and consumed. The 'opening up' of the nation to foreign markets (probably as a result of colonization) provides the economic impetus to utilize these idle resources (mostly excess land and labor) and expand primary product exportable production from 0*X* to 0*X'* at point *B* on the production frontier. Given the international price ratio $(\bar{P}_a /\bar{F}_m)$, *X–X'* (equal to *VB*) primary products can now be exported in exchange for *Y–Y'* (equal to *VC*) manufactures with the result that the final consumption point, *C*, is attained with the same primary products (0*X*) being consumed as before but *Y'–Y* more imported manufactures are now available.

The 'vent-for-surplus' argument does provide a more realistic analytical scenario of the historical trading experience of many LDCs than do either the classical or neo-classical models. However, it is a moot point whether LDC nationals as opposed to the colonial and expatriate entrepreneurs actually benefited from this process in the short run. In the long run the heavy structural orientation of the LDC economy towards primary product exports in many cases created an export 'enclave' situation and thus inhibited needed structural transformation towards a more diversified and self-reliant economy.

The second conclusion that one may draw from the recognition of widespread unemployment in the Third World is that the only way to create sufficient local job opportunities is to protect domestic industries (both manufacturing and agriculture) against low-cost foreign competition. This protection is accomplished through the erection of various 'trade barriers' such as tariffs or quotas. Although we discuss the pros and cons of commercial policy in the next chapter, the point is that those LDCs which place priority on employment creation may wish to pursue a protectionist policy to build up local rural and urban industries so as to absorb their surplus labor.

C. International factor mobility and multinational corporations

The third component of the crucial first assumption of traditional trade theory (the international immobility of productive factors) is, after the assumption of perfect competition, the most unrealistic of all premises of classical and neo-classical trade theory. Capital and skilled labor have always moved between nations. The nineteenth century growth experience of Western nations can largely be explained in terms of the impact of international capital movements. Perhaps the most powerful force in international economic relations during the past two decades has been the spectacular rise in power and influence of the giant multinational corporations. These international carriers of capital, technology and skilled labor with their diverse productive operations throughout the Third World greatly complicate the simple theory of international trade, especially in the context of the distribution of its benefits. Companies like IBM, Ford Motor, Exxon, Philips, Hitachi, British Petroleum, Renault, Volkswagen, Coca-Cola, etc., have so internationalized their production process that calculations of the distribution of the benefits of international production between foreigners and nationals becomes exceedingly difficult. We return to this important issue in the next chapter when we examine the pros and cons of private foreign investment. For the present, let us recognize that enormous international movements of capital and skills play a crucial role in contemporary world economic relations. To assume away their existence and their impact on the economies and economic structures of developing nations, as in the classical and factor endowment theories of trade, is to blind ourselves to one of the major realities of the contemporary world economy.

2. Fixed, freely available technology and consumer sovereignty

Just as capital resources are rapidly growing and being dispersed to maximize the returns of their owners throughout the world, so too is rapid technological change (mostly in the West) profoundly affecting world trading relationships. One of the most obvious examples of the impact of developed country technological change on Third World export earnings is the development of synthetic substitutes for many traditional primary products. Over the past 20 years, synthetic substitutes for such diverse commodities as rubber, wool, cotton, sisal, jute, hides and skins have been manufactured in increasing quantities. The Third World's market shares of these natural products in all cases has fallen steadily. For example, between 1950 and the mid-1970s the share of natural rubber in total world rubber consumption fell from 62 to 28 per cent, while cotton's share of total fiber consumption dropped from 41 to 29 per cent. Combining these technological substitution forces with those of low income and price elasticities of demand for primary products and the rise of agricultural protection in the markets of developed nations, one can see why the uncritical adherence to the theoretical dictates of 'comparative advantage' can be a risky and often unrewarding venture for many LDCs.

The assumption of fixed worldwide consumer tastes and preferences dictating production patterns to market responsive atomistic producers is another fiction of trade theory. Not only are capital and production technologies disseminated throughout the world by means of the multinational corporations often aided and abetted by their home governments, but 'consumption technologies' (i.e. consumer preferences and tastes) are often created and reinforced by the advertising campaigns of the powerful financial giants who dominate local markets. By creating demands for imported goods, market-dominating international enterprises can manufacture the conditions for their own further aggrandizement. For example, it has been estimated that over 90 per cent of all advertising in many developing nations is financed by foreign firms selling in the local market. As pointed out earlier, contemporary consumers are rarely 'sovereign' about anything, let alone what and how much major corporations are going to produce.

The traditional theory of trade assumes that nations are readily able to adjust their economic structures to the changing dictates of world prices and markets. Movements along production possibility frontiers involving the reallocation of resources from one industry to another may be easy to make on paper. But, they are extremely difficult to achieve in practice. This is especially true in Third World nations where production structures are often very rigid and factor movements largely restricted. The most obvious example of this is plantation and small-farm commercial agriculture. In those economies which have gradually become heavily dependent on their primary product exports, the whole economic and social infrastructure (roads, railways, communications, power locations, credit and marketing arrangements, etc.) may be geared to facilitate the movement of goods from production locations to shipping and storage depots for transfer to foreign markets. Cumulative investments of capital over time may have been sunk into these economic and infrastructure facilities and they cannot easily be transferred to different spatially located manufacturing activities. Thus, the more dependent less-developed nations become on a few primary product exports, the more inflexible their economic structures become and the more vulnerable they are to the unpredictabilities of international markets. It may take many years to transform an underdeveloped economy from an almost exclusive primary product, export-oriented reliance to a more diversified, multi-sector structure.

3. Internal factor mobility and 'perfect competition'

In short, the internal processes of adjustment and resource reallocation necessary to capitalize on changing world economic conditions are much more difficult for the less diversified economies of the Third World to realize than for their rich counterparts in the Northern hemisphere. And yet, curiously enough, those LDCs that can expand their capacities to produce low-cost, labor-intensive manufactured goods for export in industries such as textiles, shoes, sporting goods, handbags, processed foodstuff, wigs, rugs, etc. often find these exports blocked by the tariff and non-tariff barriers erected by developed countries to restrict the entry of such low-cost goods into their home markets. The reason usually given is that this low-cost foreign competition will create unemployment among the higher-cost domestic industries of the developed country and that the problems of internal economic adjustment are too serious to permit such unfettered foreign competition! Thus, the internal factor mobility assumption turns out to have limited applicability – whether because of real or imagined rationales – in even the most diversified economies of the developed nations.

We need not dwell on the limitations of the perfectly competitive model here since this issue was discussed in Chapter 1. Nevertheless, it is essential to point out two major limitations of the application of this model to the theory of international trade. First by assuming either fixed or diminishing returns to scale (i.e. fixed or increasing production costs as output is expanded), the labor–cost and factor endowment theories of trade neglect one of the most important phenomena in international economic relations. This is the pervasive and income-widening effect of increasing returns to scale and, therefore, decreasing costs of production. Decreasing production costs mean simply that large existing firms are able to underprice smaller or new firms and thus exert monopolistic control over world markets. Far from being a rare exception as the defenders of free trade would like to suggest, *economies of scale (increasing returns) and decreasing costs are a pervasive factor in determining trade patterns* – not the least of which is in the area of agriculture where huge agribusiness enterprises in developed countries are able to underprice the lower productivity family farm in Third World countries. Economies of large-scale production lead to monopolistic control of world supply conditions (just as they do in domestic markets) for a wide range of products. Moreover, this process of market domination and control is largely irreversible – *i.e.* poor-country industries, once behind, simply cannot compete with the giant corporations.

Monopolistic and oligopolistic market control of internationally traded commodities means that large individual corporations are able to manipulate world prices and supplies (and often demands as well) in their own private interests. *Instead of competition, one finds joint producer activities and oligopolistic bargaining among giant buyers and sellers as the most pervasive price and quantity determining force in the international economy.* But from the perspective of developing nations trying to diversify their economies and promote industrial exports in particular, the widespread phenomenon of increasing returns (decreasing costs) to large-scale production in addition to the non-economic power of large multinational corporations (i.e. their political influence with many governments) means that those who are first to industrialize (the rich nations) are able to take advantage of these economies of scale and perpetuate their dominant position in world markets. It is simply another case of the rich getting richer by holding all the economic and non-economic cards.

The second major limitation of the perfectly competitive assumption of trade models is its exclusion of *risk* and *uncertainty* in international trading arrangements. Even if one were to accept all the unreal assumptions of the traditional trade model as applied to the LDCs, it may still not be in their long-run interest to invest heavily in primary product export promotion due to the historical instability of world markets for primary commodities in comparison to manufactured goods.

As we have pointed out before, concentration on one or two vital primary exports can play havoc with LDC development plans when foreign exchange earnings are largely unpredictable from one year to the next. Thus, following the dictates of static comparative advantage even in the unreal world of traditional trade theory may not be the best policy from the perspective of a long-run development strategy.

4. The absence of national governments in trading relations In the context of domestic economies, the coexistence of rich and poor regions, of rapidly growing and stagnating industries, and of the persistent disproportionate regional distribution of the benefits of economic growth can, at least in theory, be counteracted and ameliorated by the *intervention of the state* in market forces. Thus, cumulative processes for inequality within nation-states by which 'growth poles' may enrich themselves at the expense of the regions left behind can be modified by government legislation, taxes, transfer payments, subsidies, social services, regional development programs, etc. But since there is no effective international government to modify and counter the natural tendency of the rich nations to grow often at the trading expense of the poor, not only can the highly uneven gains from trade become self-sustaining, they can also be reinforced by the uneven power of national governments to promote and protect the interests of their countries.

By focusing on the atomistic behavior of competitive firms in the context of different commodities being produced in anonymous countries, standard trade theory has ignored the crucial role which governments play in international economic affairs. They possess many instruments of commercial policy such as tariffs, import quotas, export subsidies, etc. to manipulate their trade position vis-à-vis the rest of the world. Moreover, when developed nation governments pursue restrictive economic policies designed to deal with purely domestic issues like inflation, they can have profound negative effects on the economies of poor nations.

The reverse, unfortunately, is not true. Third World domestic economic policies often have little impact on the economies of rich nations. Moreover, governments of developed countries often conspire to promote their joint interests through coordinated trade and other economic ventures. While these activities may not be intentionally designed to promote their own welfare at the expense of the welfare of poor countries, yet this is often the result. Increasingly, however, poor nations are recognizing the benefits of their own coordinated activities and are attempting to provide a united front in international bargaining arrangements, especially in the area of scarce natural resources and raw materials where some do have considerable leverage.

Our point, therefore, is quite simple. Traditional trade theories neglect the crucial role which national governments can and do play in the international economic arena. Governments often serve to reinforce the unequal distribution of resources and gains from trade by differences in their size and relative economic power. Rich country governments can influence world economic affairs by their domestic and international policies. They can resist countervailing economic pressures from weaker nations and can act collusively and often in conjunction with their powerful multinational corporations to manipulate the terms and conditions of international trade to their own national interests. There is no super agency or world government to protect and promote the interests of the weaker parties (i.e. the LDCs) in such international affairs. Trade theory makes no mention of these powerful governmental forces. Its prescriptions are therefore greatly weakened by this neglect.

5. Balanced trade and international price adjustments

The theory of international trade like other perfectly competitive 'general equilibrium' models in economics is not only a full employment model but also one in which flexible domestic and international product and resource prices always adjust instantaneously to conditions of supply and demand. In particular, the terms of trade (international commodity price ratios) adjust to equate supply and demand for a country's exportable and importable products so that trade is always balanced, that is, the value of exports (quantity times price) is always equal to the value of imports. With balanced commodity trade and no international capital movements 'balance of payments' problems never arise in the 'pure' theory of trade.

But the realities of the world economy in the 1970s, especially in the period immediately following the quadrupling of international oil prices in 1974, are such that balance of payments deficits and the consequent depletion of foreign reserves (or the need to borrow foreign funds to cover commodity deficits) are a major cause of concern for all nations, both rich and poor.

In poor nations in particular, a combination of declining terms of trade and sluggish international demands for their export products has meant chronic commodity trade deficits. The gradual drying up of bilateral and multilateral foreign assistance and the growing concern of LDCs with the 'social' costs of private foreign investment (see Ch. 14), has meant that severe balance of payments problems necessitate even further departures from relatively free trade. In addition to coping with chronic balance of payments deficits and rising debt burdens on former loans, developing nations faced a new and even more serious economic threat in the mid-1970s, the spread of worldwide inflation. All in all, gross imperfections in the international economy and the prevalence of non-market determined commodity pricing systems make the 'automatic adjustment' mechanism of traditional trade theory somewhat ludicrous.

6. Country trade gains accrue to country nationals The sixth and final major assumption of traditional trade theory, that country trade gains accrue to country nationals, is more implicit than the other five. It is rarely spelled out, nor need it be if one accepts the assumption that factors are internationally immobile. But given the gross unreality of that assumption, we need to examine the implicit notion, rarely challenged, that if developing countries do benefit from trade, it is the people of these countries who reap the benefits. The issue thus revolves around the question of who owns the land, the capital and the skills that are rewarded as a result of trade. Are they nationals or are they foreigners? If both, in what proportions are the gains distributed?

We know, for example, that in the 'enclave' Third World economies, like those with substantial foreign-owned mining and plantation operations, foreigners pay very low rents for the rights to use land, bring in their own foreign capital and skilled labor, hire local unskilled workers at subsistence wages and, in general, leave a minimal impact on the rest of the economy even though they may generate significant export revenues. While such visible enclaves are gradually disappearing in the Third World, they are often being replaced by more subtle forms of foreign domination – i.e. the economic penetrations of multinational corporations. The distinction, therefore, between Gross Domestic Product (GDP), which is a measure of the value of output generated within defined geographic boundaries, and Gross National Product (GNP), which measures the income actually earned by nationals of that country, becomes extremely important. To the extent that the export sector, or for that matter any sector of the economy, is foreign owned and operated, GDP will be that much higher than GNP and few of the benefits of trade will actually accrue to LDC nationals. It is even possible for the value of exports to be greater than GNP, that is, foreign export earnings may exceed the total value of domestically accrued income.

Our point here is an important one. With the proliferation of multinational corporations and the international ownership of the means of production in a wide range of countries, aggregate statistics for LDC export earnings may mask the fact that LDC nationals, especially those in lower income brackets, may not benefit at all from these exports. The major gains from trade may instead accrue to non-nationals who often repatriate large proportions of these earnings. In effect, the trade which is being carried out may look like trade between rich and poor nations. But in reality such trade is being conducted between rich nations and *other nationals of rich nations* operating in foreign countries! Until recently the activities of most mining and plantation operations had this characteristic. More important, much of the recent import substituting, export-oriented manufacturing activities in poor countries may merely have masked the fact that many of the benefits were still being reaped by foreign enterprises. In short, LDC export performances can be deceptive unless we analyze the character and structure of export earnings by ascertaining who owns or controls the factors of production that are rewarded as a result of export expansion.

12.5 Some conclusions: trade and economic development, the limits of theory

We can now attempt to provide some preliminary general answers to the five questions posed at the beginning of the chapter. Again, we must stress that our conclusions are highly general and set in the context of the diversity of developing nations. Many will not be valid for specific nations at different times and periods. But on the whole we believe that these conclusions represent the consensus of current economic thinking, especially among Third World economists, on the relationship between trade and 'development' as the latter term has been defined throughout this book.

First, with regard to the rate, structure and character of economic growth, our conclusion is that *trade can be an important stimulus to rapid economic growth* as the 1960s experiences of countries like Brazil, Taiwan and South Korea and the OPEC experience of the 1970s have amply demonstrated. Access to the markets of developed nations (an important 'if' for those Third World nations bent on export promotion) can provide an important stimulus for the greater utilization of idle human and capital resources. Expanded foreign exchange earnings through improved export performance also provide the wherewithal by which LDCs can augment their scarce physical and financial resources. In short, where opportunities for profitable exchange arise, foreign trade can provide an important stimulus to aggregate economic growth along the lines suggested by the traditional theory.

But, as we have seen in earlier chapters, rapid growth of national output may have little impact on 'development'. An export-oriented strategy of growth, particularly when a large proportion of export earnings accrue to foreigners, may not only bias the structure of the economy in the wrong directions (by not catering to the real needs of the people) but it may also reinforce the internal and external dualistic, and inegalitarian character of that growth. Therefore, the fact that trade may promote expanded export earnings, even increase output levels, does not mean that it is a desirable strategy for economic and social development. It all depends on the nature of the export sector, the distribution of its benefits and its linkages with the rest of the economy.

As for the distributional effects of trade, we can state almost without reservation that *the principal benefits of world trade have accrued disproportionately to rich nations and within poor nations dispropor-tionately to both foreign residents and wealthy nationals.* This should not be construed as an indictment of the inherent nature of trade *per se.* Rather, it reflects the highly inegalitarian institutional, social and economic ordering of the global system in which a few powerful nations and their multinational corporations control vast amounts of world resources. The conclusion of traditional trade theory, that free trade will tend to equalize incomes, is no more than a theoretical curiosum. *Trade, like education, tends to reinforce existing inequalities.* But it has the added defect of being conducted at the international level where the absence of a 'supranational' state eliminates the possi-bility, which at least exists in theory at the national level, of redistribut-ing the gains or investing them to promote development in disadvan-taged regions. Factors such as the widespread existence of increasing returns, the unequal international distribution of economic assets and power, the growing influence of large multinational corporations, the often blatant collusion among a few powerful governments and their giant corporations, and the combined ability of both to manipulate international prices, levels of production and patterns of demand; all these factors, assumed not to exist in the traditional theory of trade, are crucial. Together, they lead us to the general conclusion that *Third World countries have in the past benefited disproportionately less from their economic dealings with developed nations and may have in fact even suffered absolutely from this association.*

It should be apparent by now that the answer to the third question – under what conditions can trade help LDCs to achieve their develop-ment aspirations? – is to be found largely in the ability of developing nations (probably as a group) to extract favorable trade concessions from the developed nations, especially in the form of the latter's elimination of barriers to LDC exports of labor-intensive manufac-tured goods. (We discuss the economic effects of tariffs in the next chapter). Secondly, the extent to which LDC exports can efficiently utilize scarce capital resources while making maximum use of abun-dant but presently underutilized labor supplies will determine the degree to which export earnings benefit the ordinary citizen. Here linkages between export earnings and other sectors of the economy are crucial: for example, small-farm agricultural export earnings will expand the demand for domestically produced simple household goods while export earnings from capital-intensive manufacturing industries are more likely to find their way back to rich nations in payment for luxury imports. Finally, much will depend on how much LDCs can influence and control the activities of private foreign enter-prises. Their ability to deal effectively with multinational corporations in guaranteeing a fair share of the benefits to local citizens is, therefore, extremely important.

The answer to the fourth question – whether LDCs can determine how much they trade – can only be speculative. *For most small and poor countries, the option of not trading at all by closing their borders to the rest of the world is not very feasible.* Not only do they lack the resources and market-size to be self-sufficient but their very existence, especially in the area of food production, often depends on their ability to secure foreign goods and resources. Some thirty-two of the 'least developed' countries face annual threats of severe famine for which international assistance is not a choice but a necessity.

For those more fortunate developing nations which at least do not face annual fears of mass starvation, the international economic system, however unequal and biased against their long-run development interests, still offers the only real source of scarce capital and needed technological knowledge. The conditions under which such resources are obtained will greatly influence the character of the development process. As we show in the next chapter, the long-run benefits from trade among Third World countries themselves through the creation of regional trading blocs similar to the European Economic Community (EEC) may offer better prospects for a balanced and diversified development strategy than the almost exclusive reliance on the very unequal trading relations that they now individually engage in with the developed nations. Finally, for the few countries rich in mineral resources and raw materials, especially those that have been able to provide an effective international bargaining stance against the large corporations which purchase their exports (e.g. OPEC), trade has been and continues to be a vital source of development finance.

The fifth question – whether on balance it is best for Third World countries to 'look outward' towards the rest of the world or more 'inwards' towards their own internal capacities for development – turns out not to be an 'either–or' question at all. The consensus among most development economists, especially those from the Third World, is leaning in the direction of a greater degree of 'collective' self-reliance[2]. Their basic argument goes like this. Trade in the past has not been a great help to most developing nations and it has been positively harmful to some. Given the present imbalance in international power and wealth, pursuit of so-called 'free trade' policies and a more equitable distribution of the benefits of trade will more than likely be subverted by the wealthy to further their own private or national interests. Therefore, LDCs have to be very selective in their economic relations with the developed countries. They need to guard against entering into agreements and joint production ventures over which they are likely to relinquish control. While not shutting themselves off from trade with the rest of the world, developing countries should seek ways to expand their share of world trade and extend their economic ties with one another. For example, by pooling their resources, small countries can overcome the limits of their small individual markets and their serious resource constraints while still retaining an important degree of autonomy in pursuing their indvidual development aspirations. While it may not be possible for most LDCs to be self-reliant on an individual country-by-country basis, some form of trade and economic cooperation among equals is probably preferable to continued exposure to the dominating international power of rich nations and their potent multinational corporations.

A growing consensus of opinion has recently emerged stating that a 'new international economic order' needs to be established in which developing countries can begin to reap the benefits of international trade which they have long been denied. Early in 1975 a joint resolution among 150 Third World and developed countries (with only the United States casting a negative vote) was passed in Lima, Peru setting as a target a 25 per cent share of world output for the LDCs by the year 2000 as opposed to the 7 per cent now being produced. Morever, there is now widespread belief that Third World countries should begin to look *both* outward and inward – outward towards new forms of economic cooperation and trade with each other and inward to a greater degree of 'collective' self-reliance through the intelligent economic use of their own joint resources, both human and physical. The new experiment in cooperation among the five Andean nations in South America (Bolivia, Chile, Colombia, Ecuador and Peru) is a real world manifestation of this outward–inward search for collective self-reliance (in the next chapter we deal in detail with the various arguments for and against 'economic integration' among developing countries). It remains to be seen whether political obstacles will continue to inhibit such effective forms of economic cooperation as they have in the past for such regional groupings as the Latin American Free Trade Association and the East African Community, or whether the powerful economic logic of such cooperation will transcend and overcome political inhibitions.

In the absence of such political roadblocks, it seems clear that increased economic cooperation among diverse Third World nations at roughly equal stages of development offers a viable and real alternative to their present pursuit of separate and therefore very unequal trade relationships with the rest of the world. Thus, it may still be possible for LDCs to capture some of the real potential gains from specialization and trade (among themselves) without the need to expose themselves to the continued 'backwash' effects of a contemporary world economy and trading system which is dominated by a wealthy clique of rich nations and powerful multinational corporations.

Notes

1. The classic article on factor-price equalization is that of Paul A. Samuelson, 'International trade and equalization of factor prices', *Economic Journal,* June 1948, 163–84.
2. See, for example, the Santiago Declaration of Third World economists, April 1973 and the Communique of the Third World Forum, Karachi, 1975, both of which are reproduced as Appendices 17.1 and 17.2.

Concepts for review

export dependence
intermediate producer goods
primary products
commodity composition of trade
export concentration
commodity terms of trade
comparative advantage
absolute advantage
barter transactions
specialization
foreign exchange earnings
commercial policy
foreign reserves
closed versus open economy
domestic versus international price ratios
free trade
gains from trade

labor theory of value
resource endowments
factor endowment trade theory
labor versus capital abundant nations
factor price equalization
factor mobility
'vent-for-surplus' theory of trade
synthetic commodity substitutes
monopolistic and oligopolistic market control
collusion
increasing returns and decreasing costs
'growth poles'
balanced trade
'enclave' economies
'collective' self-reliance

Questions for discussion   1. The effects of international trade on a country's development are often related to four basic economic concepts: efficiency, growth, equity and stability. Briefly explain what is meant by each of these concepts as they relate to the theory of international trade.

Questions for discussion

2. Compare and contrast the classical labor–cost theory of comparative advantage with the neo-classical factor endowments theory of international trade. Be sure to include an analysis of both assumptions and conclusions.
3. Briefly summarize the major conclusions of the traditional theory of free trade with regard to its theoretical effects on world and domestic efficiency, world and domestic economic growth, world and domestic income distribution, and the pattern of world production and consumption.
4. Proponents of free trade, primarily developed country economists, argue that the liberalization of trading relationships between rich and poor countries (i.e. the removal of tariff and non-tariff barriers) would work towards the long run benefit of *all* countries. Under what conditions might the removal of all tariffs and other impediments to trade work to the best advantage of Third World countries? Explain.
5. What factors – economic, political and/or historical – do you think will determine whether or not a particular Third World nation is more or less dependent on international exchange? Explain your answer giving a few specific examples of different LDCs.
6. Explain some of the reasons why the non-oil-producing countries of Third World seem to have benefited relatively less than the developed nations over the past 25 years from their participation in international trade.
7. Traditional free trade theories are based on six crucial assumptions which may or may not be valid for Third World nations (or, for developed nations for that matter). What are these crucial assumptions and how might they be violated in the real world of international trade?
8. Traditional free trade theory is basically a *static* theory of international exchange leading to certain conclusions about the benefits likely to accrue to all participants. What *dynamic* elements in real world economies will tend to negate the widespread distribution of the benefits of free trade? Explain this dynamic process.
9. Third World critics of international trade sometimes claim that present trading relationships between developed and underdeveloped countries can be a source of 'antidevelopment' for the latter and merely serve to perpetuate their weak and dependent status. Explain the apparent meaning of this argument. Do you tend to agree or disagree and why?

Further readings

1. For an explication of the traditional classical and neo-classical theories of free trade, see: (*a*) Peter Kenen, *International Economics,* 2nd ed., Prentice-Hall, New Jersey (1967); or (*b*) Gerald M. Meier, *The International Economics of Development: Theory and Policy,* Harper and Row, New York (1968), Ch. 2.
2. A more comprehensive and slightly advanced survey of trade theory can be found in: J. Bhagwati, 'The pure theory of international trade: a survey', *Economic Journal,* March, 1964, 1–84.
3. For a critique of the traditional theory of trade as applied to underdeveloped nations, see: (*a*) H. Myint, 'The "classical theory" of international trade and underdeveloped countries', *Economic Journal,* **68** (1968); (*b*) H. Kitamura, 'Capital accumulation and the theory of international trade', *Malayan Economic Review,* **3,** no. 1 (1968); (*c*) G. Myrdal, the *Challenge of World Poverty,* Pantheon, New York (1970), Ch. 9; (*d*) H. Myint, 'International trade and the developing countries', in P. A. Samuelson (ed.), *International Economic Relations,* Macmillan, London (1969); (*e*) T. Balogh, 'Fact and fancy in international economic relations, Part I', *World Development,* **1,** nos 1 and 2 (1973).

Chapter 13	# The balance of payments and commercial policies

What the Third World must ask of the international order is protection of its
legitimate interests in the trade field, not trade concessions.
Santiago resolution of Third World Social Scientists, April 1973

Introduction: extending our analysis to commercial and financial policies

In the previous chapter we examined the scope and limitations of the
traditional theory of international trade as applied to the contemporary position of less developed nations in the world economy. Our focus
was primarily on international commodity trade in theory and practice
and its likely effects on Third World growth, efficiency, equity and
stability in comparison to the developed world. In this chapter and the
next we extend this analysis in two ways. First, in this chapter, we
examine the range of LDC commercial and financial policies – e.g.
import tariffs, physical quotas, export promotion versus import substitution, exchange rate adjustments, international commodity agreements and economic integration – within the broad framework of
'outward'- versus 'inward'-looking strategies of development. In
Chapter 14 we go beyond simple commodity trade to examine the
international flow of financial resources. Traditionally this flow has
been almost exclusively a 'north–south' phenomenon, i.e. financial
resources have been transferred from the developed to the less
developed countries. However, the need to 'recycle' the vast new Arab
oil wealth opens up new possibilities for intra-Third World resource
transfers – possibilities to be examined in the next chapter.

The flow of financial resources has two main components: the flow of
private foreign investments and other resources primarily via the car-
rier of the modern multinational corporation, and the flow of *public*

resources in the form of bilateral and multilateral *foreign aid*. Within the context of the flow of private foreign investments and public foreign aid, we review some alternative Third World policy approaches towards its financial dealings with the developed world. But first we look more closely at the nature of a country's 'balance of payments' and some of the issues surrounding various trade strategies for development.

13.1 The balance of payments

The extension of our analysis beyond simple commodity trade into the area of the international flow of financial resources permits us to examine the *balance-of-payments* position of Third World nations vis-à-vis the rest of the world. A balance-of-payments table is designed to summarize a nation's transactions with the outside world; for example, Table 12.1 showed changes over a period of time for the Third World as a whole and the 'sources' and 'uses' of funds. A more analytically convenient way to present such a table, however, is to divide it into three components. The *current account* component portrays the flow of goods and services in the form of exports and imports for a country during a given year. It allows us to analyze the impact of various commercial policies on commodity trade. The *capital account* shows the volume of private foreign investment and public grants and loans from individual nations and multilateral donor agencies such as UNDP and the World Bank. It permits us to examine the relative importance of international flows of financial resources in augmenting a nation's domestic savings. Finally, the *cash account* shows how cash balances (foreign reserves) and short-term claims have changed in response to current and capital account transactions. The cash account is thus the 'balancing' item which is lowered (i.e. a net outflow of foreign exchange) whenever total disbursements on the current and capital account exceed total receipts. In practice, the dividing line between the capital and cash accounts is arbitrarily set so that claims and debts maturing in more than a year (or those that have no fixed maturity date as in the case of grants) are listed in the 'capital' account. All other 'short-term' financial claims and debts – i.e., those that mature in one year or less – are normally included in the 'cash' account.

A balance of payments table for a hypothetical developing country is shown in Table 13.1. We see that there is a net negative balance of $15 million on current account. Commodity imports (primarily manufactured consumer, intermediate and capital goods) plus payments to foreign shipping firms exceed commodity exports (primarily agricultural and raw material products) by these $15 million. On the capital account we see that there is a net inflow of $7 million of private foreign investments (mostly from multinational corporations who build factories in the LDC). There is also a net positive $3 million inflow of public loans and grants in the form of foreign aid and multilateral donor agency assistance. Note that the gross inflow of $6 million in public loans and grants is partially offset by a $3 million capital outflow representing amortization and interest payments on former loans.

In a number of developing countries these debt service repayments on former loans are now at a point where they almost exceed new public financial inflows. If forced to repay all these loans, many poor countries may soon on balance actually be transferring financial resources to rich nations! Finally, private transfer payments of $1 million – i.e., monet-

Item		
A. Current account		
Commodity exports		+35
Primary products	25	
Manufactured goods	10	
Commodity imports		−45
Primary products	10	
Manufactured goods	35	
Services (e.g. shipping costs)		− 5
Balance on current account		−15
B. Capital account		
Private foreign investment (net)		+ 7
Government and multilateral flows (net)		+ 3
Loans	+5	
Grants	+1	
Debt repayments	−3	
Private transfer payments (net)		− 1
Balance on capital account		+ 9
Balance on current and capital accounts		− 6
C. Cash account		
Net decrease in official monetary reserves		+ 6
Balance on cash account		+ 6

Table 13.1 An hypothetical balance of payments table for a less developed nation

ary outflows of private individuals such as friends and relatives living overseas – bring the capital accounts into a net positive balance of $9 million. This means that the combined net balance on current *and* capital accounts is a negative $6 million. This amount represents the balance-of-payments 'deficit' of our hypothetical LDC. If the balance on current and capital account were positive it would be called a balance-of-payments 'surplus'.

13.2 Financing payments deficits: the international monetary system and Special Drawing Rights

In order to finance this $6 million negative balance on combined current and capital accounts, our hypothetical country will have to draw down on its Central Bank holdings of official monetary reserves. Such reserves consist of gold and a few major foreign currencies (usually the traditionally 'strong' currencies like US dollars and British pounds sterling but more recently, also German marks or Swiss francs) to the tune of $6 million or its equivalent. We see, therefore, that the balance on current account *plus* the balance on capital account must always be offset by the balance on cash account. This is shown by the net *decrease* of $6 million in official monetary reserves. If the country is very poor, it is likely to have a very limited stock of these official monetary reserves. This overall balance of payments deficit of $6 million, therefore, may pose severe strains on the economy and greatly inhibit its ability to continue importing needed capital and consumer goods. In the 'least developed' nations of the world which have to import to feed a hungry population and which possess very limited stocks of monetary reserves, such payments deficits may spell disaster for many millions of people.

Faced with existing or projected balance of payments deficits on combined current and capital accounts, developing nations have a variety of policy options. They can seek to improve the balance on current account by promoting export expansion and/or limiting imports. In the former case, there is the further choice of concentrating on primary or 'secondary' product export expansion. In the latter case, policies of 'import substitution' (i.e. the protection and stimulus of domestic industries to replace manufactured imports in the local market) and/or selective physical quotas or bans on the importation of specific consumer goods may be tried. Alternatively, they can seek to achieve both objectives simultaneously by altering their official foreign exchange rates through a currency 'devaluation'. We will examine the controversy over export promotion, import substitution and exchange rate adjustments in the next section.

A second alternative, though often not exclusive of the first, is for developing countries to try to improve the balance on their capital account by encouraging more private foreign investment and seeking more public foreign assistance. But since neither private foreign investment nor more than a minor proportion of foreign aid comes in the form of gifts (i.e. outright grants), the receipt of such loan assistance implies the necessity of future repayments of principal and interest. In the case of directly productive foreign investments in say building local factories, it also entails the potential repatriation overseas of sizeable proportions of the profits of the foreign owned enterprise. Moreover, as shown in the next chapter, the encouragement of private foreign investment has broader 'development' implications than the mere transfer of financial and/or physical capital resources.

Finally, Third World nations can seek to modify the detrimental impact of chronic balance of payments deficits by expanding their stocks of official monetary reserves. One way of doing this is through the acquisition of a greater share of a new international 'paper gold' known as Special Drawing Rights (SDRs). Traditionally, under the workings of the international monetary system, countries with deficits in their balance of payments were required to pay for these deficits by drawing down on their official reserves of the two principal international monetary assets, gold and US dollars. But, with the phenomenal growth in the volume and value of world trade, a new kind of international asset was needed to supplement the limited stock of gold and dollars. Consequently, in 1970 the International Monetary Fund (IMF) was given the authority to create $10 billion of these Special Drawing Rights. These new international assets perform many of the functions of gold and dollars in settling balance of payments accounts (see Table 13.1).

A major issue of great concern to developing countries, therefore, is the distribution of the benefits of SDRs. The present formula for distributing SDRs gives 75 per cent of the total (i.e. $7·5 billion) to the twenty-five industrial nations. This leaves only 25 per cent or $2·5 billion to be distributed among the ninety or so Third World countries who participate in the international monetary system. Dissatisfied with this situation, these countries acting as a group are now exerting pressure on the developed nations to agree to the creation of supplementary Special Drawing Rights which would be allocated in preferential amounts and/or preferential terms to developing nations. The issue of these supplementary SDRs could have greatly helped solve the short-run financial crisis faced by most Third World nations, particularly the forty or so 'least developed', as a result of the rapid rise in international oil and food prices in 1973–4[1].

More generally, Third World nations acting as a group are beginning to exert increasing pressures on the developed nations for a greater voice in the shaping and control of a reformed international monetary system. Before 1972, less developed nations had virtually no role and no voting power in the monetary system. It was run by a so-called 'Committee of Ten' which consisted of ten rich nations whose decisions rarely took into account the plight of the vast majority of the world's peoples. More recently, this committee was increased on a permanent basis to the new IMF Committee of Twenty with increased representation of developing nations. It is to be hoped future reforms of the international monetary system will increasingly reflect the needs and desires of these poor nations. At least they now have a forum to express their views and to air their grievances. Most important, however, if Third World nations can present a unified stance, they now possess the voting power to veto any monetary reform which they believe is not in their best economic interests.

Having summarized some basic balance-of-payments concepts and issues as they relate to both commodity trade and international flows of financial resources, we can now turn to the question of alternative trade policies for development.

13.3 Trade strategies for development: to look 'outward' or 'inward', or 'outward and inward'?

A convenient and instructive way to approach the complex issues of appropriate trade policies for development is to set these specific policies in the context of a broader LDC strategy of 'looking outward' or 'looking inward'[2]. In the words of Professor Streeten, outward-looking policies 'encourage not only free trade but also the free movement of capital, workers, enterprises and students, a welcome to the multinational enterprise, and an open system of communications'. On the other hand, inward-looking policies stress the need for LDCs to evolve their own style of development and to be the masters of their own fate. This means policies to encourage indigenous 'learning by doing' in manufacturing and the development of indigenous technologies appropriate to a country's resource endowment. Such greater self-reliance can be accomplished, according to proponents of inward-looking trade policies, only if 'you restrict trade, the movement of people and communications, and if you keep out the multinational enterprise, with its wrong products and wrong want-stimulation and hence its wrong technology'[3].

Within these two broad philosophical approaches to development, one can conveniently analyze specific commodity trade policies by applying the following fourfold categorization:

1. *primary outward-looking policies* (encouragement of agricultural and raw material exports);
2. *secondary outward-looking policies* (promotion of manufactured exports);
3. *primary inward-looking policies* (mainly agricultural self-sufficiency); and
4. *secondary inward-looking policies* (manufactured commodity self-sufficiency through 'import substitution').

Keeping this typology in mind, let us look at three broad areas of commercial and financial policy before examining the important question of economic integration in section 13.4.

1. export promotion;
2. import substitution;
3. exchange rate adujstments.

The promotion of LDC exports, either primary or secondary, has long **1. Export promotion:** been considered a major ingredient in any viable long-run develop- **'looking outward' and** ment strategy. The colonial territories of Africa and Asia with their **seeing trade barriers** foreign-owned mines and plantations were classic examples of primary outward-looking regions. It was partly in reaction to this 'enclave' economic structure and partly due to the industrialization bias of the 1950s and 1960s that newly independent states as well as older LDCs put great emphasis on the production of manufactured goods first for the home market (secondary inward) and then for export (secondary outward). Let us, therefore, look briefly at the scope and limitations of LDC export expansion, first with respect to primary products and then in the context of manufactured exports.

As we discovered in the previous chapter, the Third World still relies **A. Primary commodity** on primary products for over three-quarters of its export earnings. **export expansion** With the notable exception of petroleum exports and a few needed minerals, primary product exports have grown more slowly than total world trade. Moreover, the LDC share of these exports has been falling over the past two decades. Since food, food products and raw materials make up almost 40 per cent of all LDC exports and, for the vast majority of the 118 Third World nations, constitute their principal source of foreign exchange earnings, we need to examine the factors affecting the demand for and supply of primary product exports.

On the demand side there appear to be at least *five* factors working against the rapid expansion of Third World primary product, and especially agricultural, exports to the developed nations (their major markets). First, the per capita income elasticities of demand for agricultural foodstuffs and raw materials are relatively low compared with fuels, certain minerals and manufactures. For example, the income elasticities of demand for sugar, cocoa, tea, coffee and bananas have all been estimated at less than unity, with most in the range of $0 \cdot 3$ to $0 \cdot 5$[4]. This means that only a sustained high rate of per capita income growth in the developed countries can maintain even modest export growth rates of these particular commodities from the LDCs. Such high growth rates that prevailed in the 1960s have not been matched in the 1970s. Second, developed country population growth rates are now at or near the replacement level so that little expansion can be expected from this source. Third, the price elasticity of demand for most non-fuel primary commodities appears to be relatively low, although the data on this point are far from convincing. When relative agricultural prices are falling as they have during most of the last two decades, such low elasticities mean less total revenue for agricultural exporting nations; but when commodity prices are rapidly rising as they did for say sugar during the 1973–4 period, those nineteen or so LDCs which together supply 80 per cent of world sugar exports stand to gain substantial short-run revenues. Coffee exporting nations enjoyed a similar experience in 1976.

A widely used device to modify the tendency for primary product prices to decline relative to other traded goods is the establishment of *international commodity agreements*. The primary purposes of such agreements are to set overall output levels, to stabilize world prices and to assign quota shares to various producing nations for such diverse items as coffee, tea, copper, lead and sugar. Commodity agreements can also provide greater protection to individual exporting nations against excessive competition and the overexpansion of world production. Such overexpansion of supply tends to drive down prices and curtail the growth of earnings for all countries. In short, commodity agreements are intended to guarantee participating nations a relatively fixed share of world export earnings and a more stable world price for their commodity. It is for this reason that at its fourth world conference held in Nairobi in May 1976 the United Nations Committee on Trade and Development (UNCTAD) advocated the establishment of an $11 billion 'common fund' to finance 'buffer stocks' to support the prices of some nineteen primary commodities including sugar, coffee, tea, bauxite, jute, cotton, tin and vegetable oil produced by various Third World nations in order to stabilize export earnings.

The fourth and fifth factors working against the long-run expansion of LDC primary product export earnings – i.e. the development of synthetic substitutes and the growth of agricultural protection in the developed countries – are perhaps the most important. Synthetic substitutes for commodities like cotton, rubber, sisal, jute, hides and skins act both as a brake against higher commodity prices and as a direct source of competition in world export markets. As we saw in the previous chapter, the synthetic share of world market export earnings has steadily risen over time while the share of natural products has fallen.

In the case of agricultural protection, which usually takes the form of tariffs, quotas, and non-tariff barriers such as sanitary laws in developed countries against food and fibre exports of developing nations, the effects can be most devastating to Third World export earnings. The common agricultural policy of the European Economic Community, for example, is much more discriminatory against LDC food exports than that which prevailed in each individual EEC nation before the agreement to integrate their economies was finalized.

On the supply side, there are also a number of factors working against the rapid expansion of primary product export earnings. The most important, however, is the structural rigidity of many Third World rural production systems. We discussed rigidities such as limited resources, poor climate, bad soils, antiquated rural institutional, social and economic structures and non-productive patterns of land tenure in Chapter 10. Whatever the international demand situation for particular commodities (and these will certainly differ from commodity to commodity), little export expansion can be expected when rural economic and social structures militate against positive supply responses from peasant farmers who are averse to risk. Furthermore, in those developing nations with markedly dualistic farming structures (i.e. large corporate capital-intensive farms, existing side by side with thousands of fragmented low productivity peasant holdings), any growth in export earnings is likely to be distributed very unevenly among the rural population.

We may conclude therefore that the successful promotion of primary product exports first necessitates a reorganization of rural social and economic structures along the lines suggested in Chapter 10 to raise total agricultural productivity and distribute the benefits more widely. The primary objective of any Third World rural development strategy must be to provide sufficient food to feed the indigenous people of the nation *first,* and then be concerned about export expansion. But having accomplished this most difficult internal development task, LDCs may be able to realize the potential benefits of their comparative advantage in world primary commodity markets only if they can (*a*) *cooperate* with one another; (*b*) be *assisted* by developed nations in formulating and carrying out international commodity agreements; and (*c*) secure *greater access* to developed country markets. Unfortunately, given the structure of world demands for primary products, the threat of local food shortages and thus the desire for agricultural self-sufficiency, the inevitability of further technological developments of synthetic substitutes and the unlikelihood of lower levels of agricultural protection among developed nations, the real scope for primary product export expansion in individual LDCs vis-à-vis developed nations seems rather limited.

Nevertheless, such primary product export pessimism should be no cause for a retreat from emphasis on rural development. The rapid expansion of local food production is or should be a major component of any national development strategy whether or not a country seeks to export its surplus food to the rest of the world. However, for some commodities such as food grains, timber products, fish, meat and certain fruits and vegetables, world demand is better suited for rapid export expansion than for most others, since both income and price elasticities are relatively high. In the final analysis, however, one cannot really talk about primary product export expansion without reference to particular commodities and specific countries. Unfortunately, such a specific commodity and country analysis is beyond the scope of this book[5].

B. Expanding exports of manufactured goods

The expansion of Third World manufactured exports has been given great stimulus by the spectacular export performances of countries like South Korea, Singapore, Hong Kong, Taiwan and Brazil during the 1960s. For example, Taiwan's total exports grew at an annual rate of over 20 per cent during the 1960s, while exports from South Korea grew even faster. In both cases, this export growth was led by manufactured goods which contributed almost 75 per cent of both nations' foreign exchange earnings. For the Third World as a whole, manufactured exports grew from 6 per cent of their total exports in 1950 to almost 20 per cent in the mid-1970s. However, the LDC share of total world trade in manufactures has remained relatively unchanged at under 6 per cent.

The demand problems facing LDC export expansion of manufactured goods though different in basic economic content from those facing primary products are nonetheless similar in practice. Thus, although income and price elasticities of international demand for manufactured goods in the aggregate are higher than for primary commodities, they afford little relief to developing nations bent on expanding their exports. This is largely due to the growing protection in developed nations against the manufactured exports of LDCs – in part, the direct result of the successful penetration of low-cost labor-intensive manufactures from countries like Taiwan, Hong Kong and Korea during the 1960s. The Canadian economist Gerald Helleiner makes the point well when he observes that:

Of fundamental importance to the issue of Third World manufacturing export prospects are the barriers which are erected by the developed countries to restrict entry of these products to their own markets. Tariffs, quotas and other barriers in the markets of the rich constitute a major impediment to large-scale industrial exports. The tariff structures of the rich nations are such as to offer the greatest degree of effective protection to their producers in the very industries in which poor countries are most likely to be competitive – light industries relatively intensive in the use of unskilled labour such as textiles, footwear, rugs, sporting goods, handbags, processed foodstuffs, etc. This is precisely because of these industries' inability freely to compete, unskilled labour-intensity putting them at a comparative disadvantage within the context of their relatively high wage economies[6].

The growth of unemployment in developed countries, especially in traditional industries such as textiles where almost 40 per cent of Third World manufactured exports are concentrated, makes the prospects for lower trade barriers on LDC light manufactures for the remainder of the 1970s seem rather remote. Moreover, as more and more developing countries attempt to emulate the spectacular manufactured export performance of a few, the competition for access to the narrowing developed country markets is likely to lead to many unforeseen difficulties and disappointments. As in the case of agricultural production, however, this gloomy export outlook should be no cause for curtailing the needed expansion of manufacturing production to serve local LDC markets. Moreover, as we argue below, there is great scope for mutually beneficial trade in manufactures among Third World countries themselves within the context of the gradual economic integration of their national economies. Too much emphasis has been placed on the analysis of trade prospects of individual LDCs with the developed nations and not enough on the prospects for mutually beneficial trade with one another.

2. Import substitution: 'looking inward' but still paying outward
A. The strategy and results

For the past two decades, developing countries faced with declining world markets for their primary products, growing balance-of-payments deficits on current account and a general belief in the magic of industrialization decided to pursue what has come to be known as an 'import substitution' strategy of industrial development. Import substitution entails an attempt to replace commodities, usually manufactured goods which were formerly imported, with domestic sources of production and supply. The typical strategy is first to erect tariff barriers or quotas on the importation of certain commodities, then to try to set up a local industry to produce the goods that were formerly imported – items such as radios, bicycles, household electrical appliances, etc. Typically, this involves cooperation with foreign companies who are encouraged to set up their plants behind the wall of tariff protection and given all kinds of tax and investment incentives. While initial costs of production may be higher than former import prices, the economic rationale put forward for the establishment of import-substituting manufacturing operations is either that, given time, the industry will eventually be able to reap the benefits of large-scale production and lower costs (the so-called 'infant industry' argument for tariff protection), or that the balance of payments will be improved as fewer consumer goods are imported. Often a combination of both arguments is advanced. Eventually, it is hoped and, in many cases, anticipated that the infant industry will 'grow up' and be able to compete in world markets. It can then generate net foreign exchange earnings once it has lowered its average costs of production.

Most observers agree that the import-substituting strategy of industrialization in a large number of developing countries, especially those
in Latin America, has for the most part been a failure[7]. Specifically,
four undesirable outcomes have emerged. First, the main beneficiaries
of the import substitution process have been the foreign firms who
were able to locate behind tariff walls and take advantage of liberal tax
and investment incentives. After deducting interest, profits, royalty
and management fees, most of which are remitted abroad, the little
that may be left over usually accrues to the wealthy local industrialist
with whom foreign manufacturers cooperate and who provide their
political and economic cover.

Second, most import substitution has been made possible by the
heavy and often government-subsidized importation of capital goods
and intermediate products by foreign (and domestic) companies. In
the case of foreign companies many of these are purchased from their
parent and sister companies abroad, with two immediate results. First,
capital-intensive industries are set up, usually catering to the consumption habits of the rich while having a minimal employment effect.
Second, far from improving the LDCs' balance-of-payments situation,
indiscriminate import substitution often worsens it by raising the
requirements for imported capital-good inputs and intermediate products while, as we have just seen, a good part of the profits is remitted
abroad in the form of private transfer payments.

A third detrimental effect of many of the import substitution
strategies of the 1950s and 1960s was their impact on traditional
primary product exports. In order to encourage local manufacturing
through the importation of cheap capital and intermediate goods,
foreign exchange rates (i.e. the rate at which the Central Bank of a
nation is prepared to purchase foreign currencies) were often artificially 'overvalued'. This has the effect of raising the price of exports
and lowering the price of imports in terms of the local currency. For
example, if the 'appropriate' or free market exchange rate between
Pakistani rupees and US dollars were say 20 to 1 but the 'official'
exchange rate were set at 10 rupees to the dollar, an item which costs
$10 in the US could be imported into Pakistan for 100 rupees (exclud-
ing transport costs and other service charges). If the 'free market'
exchange rate prevailed (i.e. the exchange rate determined by the
supply and demand for Pakistani rupees in terms of dollars) it would
cost 200 rupees. Thus by 'overvaluing' their exchange rate, LDC
governments are able effectively to lower the domestic currency price
of their imports. At the same time, their export prices are increased –
for example, at an exchange rate of 10 to 1, US importers would have
to pay 10 cents for every one rupee item rather than 5 cents if the
hypothetical free market ratio of 20 to 1 were in effect. Table 13.2
provides rough estimates of the extent of currency overvaluation in
nine developing countries.

The net effect of overvaluing exchange rates in the context of import
substitution policies is to encourage capital-intensive production
methods still further (since the price of imported capital goods is
artificially lowered) and to penalize the traditional primary product
export sector by artificially raising the price of these exports in terms of
foreign currencies. This causes local farmers to be less competitive in
world markets. In terms of its income distribution effects, the outcome
of such government policies may be to penalize the small farmer and
the self-employed at the expense of improving the profits of the owners

of capital, both foreign and domestic. *Industrial protection thus has the effect of taxing agricultural goods in the home market as well as discouraging agricultural exports.* Import substitution policies in practice have often worsened the local distribution of income by favoring the urban sector and the higher income groups while discriminating against the rural sector and the lower income groups.

Country	Year	Domestic currency units	Units of national currency per $US		
			Official rate (c)	Degree of overvaluation (per cent)	Implied free market exchange rate
Argentina	1958	Pesos	18·0	100	36·0
Brazil	1966	Cruzeiros	2,220·0	50	3,330·0
	1966	Cruzeiros	2,220·0	27	2,819·0
Chile	1961	Pesos	1·053	68	1·769
Colombia	1968	Pesos	15·89	22	19·39
Malaya	1965	Dollars(M)	3·06	4	3·18
Mexico	1960	Pesos	12·49	15	14·36
	1960	Pesos	12·49	9	13·61
Pakistan	1963–4	Rupees	4·799	25	5·999
	1963–4	Rupees	4·799	50	7·199
Philippines	1965	Pesos	3·90	20	4·68
	1965	Pesos	3·90	15	4·49
Taiwan	1965	$NT	40·10	20	48·12

Table 13.2 Official and estimated free market exchange rates

Source: Derek Healey, 'Development policy: new thinking about an interpretation', *Journal of Economic Literature*, X, No. 3 (1972), 781.

Fourth, and finally, import substitution which may have been conceived with the idea of stimulating self-sustained industrialization by creating 'forward' and 'backward' linkages with the rest of the economy, has in practice often inhibited that industrialization. By increasing the costs of inputs to potentially 'forward' linked industries (those which purchase the output of the protected firm as inputs) or intermediate products in their own productive process, (e.g. a printer's purchase of paper from a locally protected paper mill) and by purchasing its inputs from overseas sources of supply rather than through 'backward' linkages to domestic suppliers, inefficient import substituting firms may in fact block the hoped-for process of self-reliant integrated industrialization.

All things considered, we may concur with Professor Helleiner, whose views seem to reflect a consensus among development economists, that:

It is difficult to find any rationale for the pattern of import substituting industrialization which has, whether consciously or not, actually been promoted. It has given undue emphasis to consumer goods in most countries; it has given insufficient attention to potential long-run comparative advantages, i.e. resource endowments and learning possibilities; and it has employed alien and unsuitable, i.e. capital-intensive technologies to an extraordinary and unnecessary degree. If a selective approach to import substitution is to be pursued at all, and there is a strong case to be made for a more generalized approach, the selection actually employed in recent years has left a great deal to be desired. The consequence has too frequently been the creation of an inefficient industrial sector operating far below capacity, and creating very little employment, very little foreign exchange saving, and little prospect of further productivity growth. The object of policy must now be gradually to bring incentive structures and thus the relative efficiencies of various industrial activities into some sort of balance, thereby encouraging domestic manufacture of intermediate and capital goods at the expense of importable consumer goods and the development eventually of manufacture for export[8].

Since import substitution programs are based on the protection of local industries against competing imports primarily through the use of tariffs and physical quotas, we need to analyze the role and limitations of these commercial policy instruments in developing nations. Governments impose tariffs and physical quotas on imports for a variety of reasons. For example, tariff barriers may be erected in order to raise public revenue. In fact, given administrative and political difficulties of collecting local income taxes, fixed percentage taxes on imports (*ad valorem* tariffs) collected at a relatively few ports or border posts often constitute one of the cheapest and most efficient forms of raising government revenue. In many LDCs, these foreign trade taxes constitute the major source of government income and thus provide a central feature of the overall fiscal system. On the other hand, physical quotas on certain imports like automobiles and other 'luxury' consumer goods, while more difficult to administer and more subject to delay, inefficiency and corruption (e.g. with regard to the granting of import licences), are nevertheless another effective means of restricting the entry of particularly troublesome commodities.

B. Tariff structures and effective protection

Tariffs may also be levied to restrict the importation of non-necessity products (usually expensive consumer goods) and thus improve the balance of payments. Like overvaluing the official rate of foreign exchange, tariffs may be used to improve a nation's terms of trade. However, in a small country unable to influence world prices of its exports or imports (in other words, most LDCs) this terms of trade argument for tariffs (or devaluation) has little validity. Finally, as we have just seen, tariffs may form an integral component of an import substitution policy of industrialization.

Whatever the means used to restrict imports, such restriction always protects domestic firms from competition with producers from other countries. To measure the degree of protection we need to ask by how much do these restrictions cause the domestic prices of imports to exceed what their prices would be if there were no protection. There are two basic measures of protection:
1. the 'nominal' rate of protection;
2. the 'effective' rate of protection.
The *nominal* rate of protection shows the extent, in percentages, to which the domestic price of imported goods exceeds what their price would be in the absence of protection. Thus the nominal (*ad valorem*) tariff rate refers to the final prices of commodities and can be defined simply as:

$$t = \left| \frac{p' - p}{p} \right| \tag{1}$$

where, p' and p are the unit prices of industry's output with and without tariffs respectively.

For example, if the domestic price (p') of an imported automobile is say $5000 whereas the c.i.f. (cost plus insurance and freight) price (p) when it arrives at the importing nation's port of entry is say $4000, then the nominal rate of tariff protection (t) would be 25 per cent.

On the other hand, the *effective* rate of protection shows the percentage by which the *value added* at a particular stage of processing in a domestic industry can exceed what it would be without protection: in other words, it shows by what percentage the sum of wages, interest, profits and depreciation allowances payable by local firms can, as a result of protection, exceed what this sum would be if these same firms had to face unrestricted competition (i.e. no tariff protection) from foreign producers[9]. The effective rate (g) can therefore be defined as:

$$g = \frac{v' - v}{v} \tag{2}$$

where, v' and v are *value added* per unit of output with and without protection, respectively. A more precise formula is

$$g_j = \frac{(t_j - \sum_i a_{i,j} t_i)}{(1 - \sum_i a_{i,j})} \tag{2a}$$

where t_j is the nominal tariff on the final product of industry, j, t_i is the rate of tariff on the intermediate input i and a_{ij} is the free trade value of intermediate input i per unit value of final product of industry j.)

The important difference between nominal and effective rates of protection can be illustrated with an example[10]. Consider a nation without tariffs in which automobiles are produced and sold at the international or world price of $10,000. The value added by labor in the final assembly process is assumed to be $2,000 while the total value of the remaining inputs is $8,000. Assume for simplicity that the prices of these non-labor inputs are equal to their world prices. Suppose that a nominal tariff of 10 per cent is now imposed on imported automobiles, which raises the domestic price of motor cars to $11,000, but leaves the prices of all the other importable, intermediate inputs unchanged. The domestic process of automobile production can now spend $3,000 per unit of output on labor inputs as contrasted with $2,000 per unit before the tariff. The theory of effective protection, therefore, implies that under these conditions the nominal tariff of 10 per cent on the final product automobiles has resulted in an 'effective' rate of protection of 50 per cent for the local assembly process in terms of its value added per unit of output. (It follows, therefore, that for any given nominal tariff rate, the effective rate is greater the smaller the value added of the process; i.e. $g = t\,1 - a$ where t is the nominal rate on final product and a is the proportionate value of the importable inputs in a free market where these inputs are assumed to enter the country duty free).

Most economists argue that the effective rate is the more useful concept (although the nominal or *ad valorem* rate is simpler to measure) for ascertaining the degree of protection and encouragement afforded by a given country's tariff structure to its local manufacturers. This is because effective rates of protection show the *net* effect on a firm or industry of restrictions on the imports of *both* its outputs and inputs. For most countries, both developing and developed, the effective rate normally exceeds the nominal rate, sometimes by as much as 200 per cent. For example, Little, Scitovsky and Scott found that average levels of effective protection exceeded 200 per cent for India and Pakistan during the early 1960s, 100 per cent for Argentina and

Brazil, 50 per cent for the Philippines, 33 per cent for Taiwan and 25 per cent for Mexico[11].

Among the many implications of analyzing effective as opposed to nominal tariff structures with regard to developing countries, two stand out as particularly noteworthy:

1. Most developing countries, as we have seen, have pursued import-substituting programs of industrialization with emphasis on the local production of final consumer goods for which a ready market was presumed to exist already. Moreover, final good production is generally less technically sophisticated than intermediate, capital good production. The expectation was that in time rising demand and economies of scale in finished good production would create strong 'backward linkages' leading to the creation of intermediate goods industries. The record of performance, as we have seen, has been disappointing for most developing countries. Part of the reason for this failure has been that developing country tariff structures have afforded exceedingly high rates of effective protection to final goods industries while intermediate and capital goods have received considerably less effective protection. The net result is an attraction of scarce resources away from intermediate goods production and towards the often inefficient production of highly protected final consumer goods. Backward linkages do not develop, intermediate good import costs rise and, perhaps most important from a long run view, the development of an indigenous capital goods industry focusing on efficient, low-cost, labor-intensive techniques is severly impeded.

2. Even though nominal rates of protection in developed countries on imports from the developing countries may appear relatively low, rates of effective protection can be quite substantial. Raw materials are usually imported duty free while processed products such as roasted and powdered coffee, copra oil and cocoa butter appear to have low nominal tariffs. The theory of effective protection suggests that in combination with zero tariffs on imported raw materials, low nominal tariffs on processed products can represent substantially higher rates of effective protection. For example, if a tariff of 10 per cent is levied on say processed copra oil whereas copra itself can be imported duty free, then if the value added in making oil from copra is 5 per cent of the total value of copra oil, the *process* is actually being protected at 200 per cent! This greatly inhibits the development of food and other raw material processing industries in developing nations and ultimately cuts back on their potential earnings of foreign exchange.

Effective rates of protection against potentially high foreign exchange-earning exportable goods from the Third World can be considerably higher than nominal rates in the developed countries. For example, the effective rate on thread and yarn, textile fabrics, clothing, wood products, leather and rubber goods averaged more than twice the nominal rate on these same items in the US, UK, and the EEC countries during the 1960s[12]. Effective rates on coconut oil were over ten times the nominal rate (150 per cent compared with 15 per cent in the EEC) while those on processed soybean were sixteen times the nominal rate (160 as opposed to 10 per cent) in the European Community.

To sum up, the standard argument for tariff protection in developing countries has four major components:

1. Duties on trade are the major source of government revenue in most LDCs, since they are a relatively easy form of taxation to impose and even easier to collect.
2. Import restrictions represent an obvious response to chronic balance of payments problems.
3. Protection against imports is one of the most appropriate means for fostering industrial self-reliance and overcoming the pervasive state of economic dependence in which most Third World countries find themselves;
4. Finally, by pursuing policies of import restriction, developing countries can gain greater control over their economic destinies while still encouraging foreign businessmen to invest in local import-substituting industries, generating high profits and thus the potential for greater savings and future growth. They can also obtain imported equipment at relatively favorable prices and reserve an already established domestic market for local or locally-controlled producers.

Although the above arguments can be very convincing and some have proven highly beneficial to the developing world, as we discovered in the previous section, many have failed to bring about their desired results. Protection *does* have an important role to play in the development of the Third World – for both economic and non-economic reasons – but it is a tool of economic policy that needs to be employed selectively and wisely, not a panacea to be applied indiscriminately and without reference to both short and long-term ramifications.

3. Foreign exchange rates, exchange controls and the devaluation decision   In section 2.A on import substitution, we briefly discussed the question of foreign currency exchange rates. Remember that a country's 'official' exchange rate is the rate at which its Central Bank is prepared to transact exchanges of its local currency for other currencies in approved foreign exchange markets. Official exchange rates are usually quoted in terms of US dollars – i.e. so many pesos, cruzieros, pounds, shillings, rupees, Bhat, etc., per dollar, For example, the official exchange rate of Kenya shillings for US dollars in 1974 was approximately Shs. 7 per dollar while the Indian rupee was officially valued at approximately 7·6 rupees per dollar. If a Kenyan manufacturer wished to import fabrics from an Indian textile exporter at say a cost of 7,600 rupees, he would need Shs. 7,000 to make the purchase. However, since almost all foreign exchange transactions are conducted in US dollars, the Kenyan importer would need to purchase $1,000 worth of foreign exchange from the Central Bank of Kenya for his 7,000 shillings and then transmit these dollars through official channels to the Indian exporter.

Official foreign exchange rates are not necessarily set at or near the economic 'equilibrium' price for foreign exchange – i.e. the rate at which the domestic demand for a foreign currency such as dollars would just equal its supply in the absence of governmental regulation or intervention. In fact, as we saw in Table 13.2 the currencies of most Third World countries are usually 'overvalued' by the exchange rate. Whenever the official price of foreign exchange is established at a level which, in the absence of any governmental restrictions or controls, would result in an excess of local demand over the available supply of foreign exchange, the domestic currency in question is said to be 'overvalued'.

The economic results of pursuing an intentional policy of currency overvaluation have been succinctly summarized in the following extract from the 1968 *Economic Survey of Asia and the Far East*[13]:

All exporters (who predominantly sold agricultural goods) were required to surrender foreign exchange earnings at the official rate of exchange. This clearly constituted a tax on the agricultural sector of the economy. At the official rate of exchange there existed a large unsatisfied demand for imports. Thus a strict rationing of the entitlement to import through licensing had to be made. The overvalued rate of exchange and the consequent unsatisfied demand for imports naturally meant domestic prices for imports substantially above international prices. This price differential was not absorbed by the government through license fees or import surcharges, but was allowed to be converted into monopoly profit for the license holder, and served as a major source of investible funds in the private sector. The excess demand generated by the strict quantitative control of imports further opened up high profit opportunities for investors in import substituting industries.

In such situations of excess demand, LDC Central Banks have three basic policy options designed to maintain the official rate of exchange. First, they can attempt to accommodate this excess demand by running down their reserves of foreign exchange and/or by borrowing additional foreign exchange abroad and thereby incurring further debts. Second, they can attempt to curtail the excess demand for foreign exchange by pursuing commercial policies and tax measures designed to lessen the demand for imports – e.g. tariffs, physical quotas, licensing, etc. Third, and finally, they can regulate and intervene in the foreign exchange market by 'rationing' the limited supply of available foreign exchange to 'preferred' customers. Such a rationing device is more commonly known as 'exchange control'. It is a policy in wide use throughout the Third World and is probably the major financial mechanism for preserving the level of foreign exchange reserves at the prevailing official exchange rate.

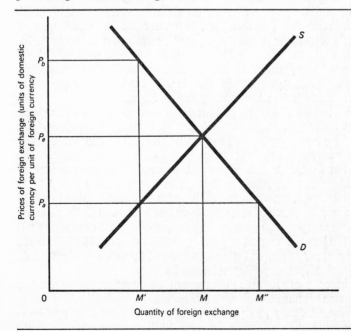

Fig 13.1
The free market and controlled rate of foreign exchange

The mechanism and operation of exchange control can be illustrated diagrammatically with the aid of Fig. 13.1. Under free market conditions the equilibrium price of foreign exchange would be P_e with a total of $0M$ units of foreign exchange demanded and supplied. If, however, the government maintains an artificially low price of foreign exchange (i.e. an overvaluation of its domestic currency) at P_a, then supply of foreign exchange will amount to only $0M'$ units since exports are 'overpriced'. But at price P_a, the demand for foreign exchange will be $0M''$ units with the result that there is an 'excess demand' equal to $M'M''$ units. Some mechanism, therefore, will have to be divised to ration the available supply of $0M'$. If the government were to auction this supply, importers would be willing to pay a price of P_b for the foreign exchange. In such a case the government would make a profit of $P_a P_b$ per unit. Typically, however, such open auctions are not carried out and limited supplies of foreign exchange are allocated through some administrative quota or licensing device. Opportunities for corruption, evasion and the emergence of 'black markets' are thus made possible since importers are willing to pay as much as P_b per unit of foreign exchange.

Why have most Third World governments opted for an overvalued official exchange rate? Basically, as we have seen, they have done so as part of widespread programs of rapid industrialization and import substitution. Overvalued exchange rates reduce the domestic currency price of imports below that which would exist in a free market for foreign exchange, i.e. by the forces of supply and demand. Cheaper imports, especially capital and intermediate producer goods, are needed to fuel the industrialization process. But overvalued exchange rates also lower the domestic currency price of imported consumer goods, especially expensive luxury products. Third World nations wishing to limit such unnecessary and costly imports often need, therefore, to establish import controls (mostly physical quotas) or to set up a 'dual' exchange rate system – one rate, usually highly overvalued to be applied to capital and intermediate good imports and the other, much lower, for luxury consumption good imports. Such dual exchange rate systems, therefore, make the domestic price of imported luxury goods very high while maintaining the artificially low and thus subsidized price of producer good imports. Needless to say, dual exchange rate systems like exchange controls and import licences present serious problems of administration, corruption and evasion.

On the other hand, overvalued currencies reduce the returns to local exporters and to those import-competing industries which are not protected by heavy tariffs or physical quotas. Exporters receive less domestic currency for their products than would be forthcoming if the free market exchange rate prevailed. Moreover, in the absence of export subsidies to reduce the foreign currency price of an LDC's exports, exporters, mostly farmers, become less competitive in world markets since the price of their produce has been artificially elevated by the overvalued exchange rate. In the case of import-competing but unprotected local industries, the overvalued rate artificially lowers the domestic currency price of foreign imports of the same product – e.g., radios, tyres, bicycles, household utensils, etc.

In the absence of effective government intervention and regulation of the foreign exchange dealings of its nationals, overvalued exchange rates have a tendency to exacerbate balance of payments problems simply because they cheapen imports while making exports more costly. As we mentioned in our discussion of the balance of payments, chronic payments deficits resulting primarily from current account transactions (i.e. exports and imports) can possibly be ameliorated by a currency 'devaluation'. Simply defined, a country's currency is 'devalued' or, more strictly, 'depreciated' when the official rate at which its Central Bank is prepared to exchange the local currency for dollars is increased. For example, a devaluation of the Kenya shilling or Indian rupee would occur if their present (1975) official exchange rates of approximately 7 shillings and 7·6 rupees to the dollar were changed to say 10 shillings and/or rupees per dollar. In both instances, US importers of Kenyan and Indian goods would have to pay fewer dollars to obtain the same products as they had to prior to the devaluation. On the other hand, US exports to Kenya and India would become more expensive (i.e. require more shillings and/or rupees to purchase) than before. In short, by lowering the *foreign* currency price of its exports (and thereby hopefully generating more foreign demand) while raising the *domestic* currency price of its imports (and, thereby, lowering domestic demand) Third World nations which devalue their currency hope to improve their trade balance vis-à-vis the rest of the world.

An alternative to a currency devaluation would be to allow foreign exchange rates to fluctuate freely in accordance with changing conditions of international demand and supply. Freely fluctuating or flexible exchange rates are not thought to be desirable, especially in Third World nations heavily dependent on exports and imports, because they are so unpredictable, subject to wide and uncontrollable fluctuations and susceptible to foreign and domestic currency speculation. Such unpredictable fluctuations can wreak havoc with both short- and long-range development plans. We see once again, therefore, that bowing to the 'free market' forces of supply and demand (this time for local and foreign currencies) could subject a wide range of Third World nations to even greater instability and increased vulnerability than market intervention.

The present international system of 'floating' exchange rates, formally legalized at the 1976 Jamaica IMF meeting, represents a compromise between a fixed (artificially 'pegged') and a fully flexible exchange rate system. Under this 'managed' floating system major international currencies are permitted to fluctuate freely but erratic swings are limited through Central Bank intervention. Most developing countries, however, have decided to continue to peg their currencies to those of developed countries. Some like Kenya have gone further and decided to tie their currencies to the movements of a weighted index of the world's major currencies rather than to tie them to a particular currency like the US dollar or the British pound sterling.

One final point about Third World currency devaluations, particularly in the light of previous chapter discussions, is their probable effect on domestic prices. Devaluation has the immediate effect of raising prices of imported goods in terms of the local currency. Shirts, shoes, radios, records, foodstuffs, bicycles, etc., which formerly cost x pesos, now may cost $x + y$ pesos depending on the magnitude of the devaluation. If as a result of these higher prices, domestic workers seek to preserve the 'real' value of their purchasing power, they are likely to initiate increased wage and salary demands. Such increases, if granted, will raise production costs and tend to push local prices up even higher. A wage–price spiral of domestic inflation is thereby set in motion. In fact, a vicious circle of devaluation–domestic wage and price increases–higher export prices–worsened balance of trade–devaluation could result. In effect, the devaluation decision could simply exacerbate the external balance of payments problem while generating galloping inflation domestically. The experience of many Latin American nations with such uncontrollable inflation during the 1950s and 1960s has made them very reluctant users of the tool of currency devaluation.

As for the distributional effects of a devaluation, it is clear that by altering the domestic price and returns of 'tradeable' goods (exports and imports) and creating incentives for the production of exports as opposed to domestic goods, devaluation will benefit certain groups at the expense of others. In general, urban wage earners, those with fixed incomes, the unemployed and those small farmers and rural and urban small-scale producers and suppliers of services who do not participate in the export sector stand to be financially hurt by the domestic inflation that typically follows a devaluation. On the other hand, large exporters (usually large landowners and foreign-owned corporations) as well as the more medium-sized local businesses engaged in foreign trade stand to benefit the most. While we cannot categorically assert that devaluation tends to worsen income distribution without reference to specific countries and situations, we may conclude that the more concentrated is the ownership and control over the export sector in private as opposed to public hands, the greater will be the likelihood of an adverse effect on income distribution. For this reason, among others, international commercial and financial problems (e.g. chronic balance of payments deficits) cannot be divorced from domestic problems (e.g. poverty and inequality) in Third World nations. Policy responses to alleviate one problem can either improve or worsen others. This interaction between problems and policies will be discussed at length in Chapter 16.

4. Conclusions: trade policies and development
In the final analysis, it is not a less developed country's inward or outward looking stance vis-à-vis the rest of the world that will determine whether or not it 'develops' along the lines described in Chapter 3 and in many other parts of this book. Inward-looking, protectionist policies that include tariffs, quotas and exchange rate adjustments do not necessarily guarantee more jobs, higher incomes more equitably distributed, adequate nutrition and health, clean water, and relevant education any more than do outward-looking, non-interventionist policies. In fact, as Professor Streeten[14] so skilfully pointed out when summarizing a Cambridge University conference on trade and development:

A curious paradox came out of the discussion (of the effects of trade on LDC inequalities). It seemed that both inward-looking, import-substituting, protectionist, interventionist policies and outward-looking, market-orientated, non-interventionist policies tend to increase market imperfections and monopolies and reduce the demand for labour-intensive processes, the latter because the market rewards most those factors that are relatively scarce (capital, management, professional skills) and penalizes those in abundant supply and because the market strengthens the ability to accumulate of those who have against those who have not. But though it is paradoxical that both a protectionist 'distorted' system of prices, interest rates, wages and exchange rates and a market-determined one should increase inequalities, there is no contradiction. It is plausible that within a certain social and political framework, both export-orientated market policies and import-substitution-orientated, interventionist, 'distorting' policies should aggravate inequalities, though one set may do this somewhat more than the other. Perhaps economists have been barking up the wrong tree when disputing which set of price policies contributes more to equality. In an inegalitarian power structure, both make for inequality; in an egalitarian power structure, both may make for equality.

The reader will do well to reflect on these observations before reaching any final judgement about trade policies for development, especially within the context of the poverty and inequality issue.

13.4 Economic integration: the potential benefits of looking both outward and inward

One significant variant of the free trade doctrine which can have relevance for many developing countries concerns the question of economic integration. Economic integration arises whenever a group of nations in the same region, preferably of relatively equal size and at equal stages of development, join together to form an economic union by raising a common tariff wall against the products of non-member countries while freeing internal trade among members. In the terminology of integration literature, nations which levy common external tariffs while freeing internal trade are said to have formed a *customs union*. If external tariffs against outside countries differ among member nations while internal trade is free, the nations are said to have formed a *free trade area*. Finally, a *common market* possesses all the attributes of a customs union (i.e. common external tariffs and free internal trade) plus the free movement of labor and capital among the partner states.

1. Some basic concepts

The theory of customs unions and economic integration has a rather treasured place in the modern literature on international trade. It is associated primarily with the work of Professor Jacob Viner of Princeton University in the 1940s. The traditional core of this theory, which focuses on the static resource and production reallocation effects within highly integrated and flexible industrialized nations, is of limited value, however, to contemporary developing nations intent on building up their industrial base. Yet many concepts of the theory of integration do provide valid criteria on which to evaluate the probable short-run success or failure of economic cooperation among Third World countries.

The basic economic rationale for the gradual integration of less developed economies is a long-term dynamic one. It is that integration provides the opportunity for industries which *have not yet been established* as well as for those that have to take advantage of the *economies of large-scale production* that are made possible by expanded markets. Integration, therefore, needs to be viewed as a mechanism to encourage a rational division of labor among a group of countries, each of which is too small to benefit from such a division of labor. In the absence of integration, each separate country may not provide a sufficiently large domestic market to enable local industries to lower their production costs through economies of scale. In such cases, import-substituting industrialization will typically result, as we have seen, in the establishment of high-cost, inefficient local industries.

Moreover, the same industry (e.g. textiles or shoes) may be set up in two or more adjoining small nations. Each will be operating at less than optimal capacity but will be protected against the imports of the other by high tariff or quota barriers. Not only does such duplication result in wasted scarce resources, it also means that consumers are forced to pay a higher price for the product than if the market were large enough for high-volume, low-cost production to take place at a single location.

This leads to a second dynamic rationale for LDC economic integration. By removing barriers to trade among member states, the possibility of *coordinated industrial planning* is created, especially in those industries where economies of scale are likely to exist, such as fertilizer and petrochemical plants, heavy industry like iron and steel, capital goods and machine tool industries, small farm mechanical equipment, etc. But the coordinated planning of industrial expansion which enables all member states to accelerate their rates of industrial growth by assigning given industries to different members takes the partners that much closer to full economic and, eventually, political union. Problems of sovereignty and national self-interest impinge at this stage. To date they have overwhelmed the economic logic of a close and coordinated union. However, as Third World nations, especially small ones, continue to experience the futility of either development in isolation (i.e. autarchy) or full participation in the highly unequal world economy, it is likely that interest will increase in the coming decades in the long-run benefits of some form of economic (and perhaps political) cooperation.

In addition to these two long-term dynamic arguments for integration, there also exist the standard textbook *static* evaluative criteria known as 'trade creation' and 'trade diversion'. Trade creation is said to occur when common external barriers and internal free trade lead to a shift in production from high- to low-cost member states. For example, before integration both country A and country B may produce textiles for their respective local markets. Country A may be a lower cost producer but its exports to country B are blocked by the latter's high tariffs. If A and B form a customs union by eliminating all barriers to internal trade, country A's more efficient low-cost textile industry will cater for both markets. Trade will have been created in the sense that the removal of barriers has led to a shift in country B's consumption from its own relatively high-cost textiles to the lower-cost textiles of country A.

Similarly, trade diversion is said to occur when the erection of external tariff barriers causes production and consumption of one or more member states to shift from lower-cost non-member sources of supply (e.g. a developed country) to higher-cost member producers. Trade diversion is normally considered undesirable since both the world and member states are perceived to be worse off as a result of the diversion of production from more efficient foreign suppliers to the less efficient domestic industries of member states. But this static argument against economic integration ignores two basic facts. First, because of potential economies of scale, the creation of local jobs and the circular flow of income within the integrated region, static trade diversion may turn out to be dynamic trade creation. This is simply a variant of the standard 'infant industry' argument for protection but with the more likely possibility that the infant will grow up as a result of the larger market in which it now operates. Second, if in the absence of integration, each member state were to protect its local import-substituting industry against all lower-cost foreign suppliers, the common external tariff of member states would cause no more trade diversion than would have happened anyway. But, as we just saw, if there are scale economies, the possibility of dynamic trade creation can emerge. Thus, static but useful concepts like trade creation and trade diversion must be analyzed in the dynamic context of growth and development based on the realities of current commercial policies of developing nations, rather than in the theoretical vacuum of traditional free trade models.

Having outlined some basic concepts of economic integration, we can now formulate a set of specific issues against which one can evaluate the successes or failures of various recent integration schemes in the Third World. The questions are the following:

2. Third World regional integration in practice: some case studies[15]

1. Has integration stimulated a more rapid growth rate of internal trade among member states than in its absence?
2. Has the growth of internal trade had the character of 'trade creation' or 'trade diversion' bearing in mind some of the previously discussed limitations of these concepts?
3. How has integration affected the trade of individual member countries?
4. What effect has integration had on the aggregate economic growth rates of member countries?
5. What have been the main obstacles hindering integration?

We can usefully draw on Dr Pazos' recent study to provide preliminary answers to these questions on the basis of contemporary integration experiences of developing countries in Latin America, the Caribbean and Africa. Seven regional groups of varying size, economic structure and levels of development have entered into arrangements to integrate their economies – some more closely than others – since 1960. They are:

1. the *Latin American Free Trade Association* (LAFTA) formed in 1960 and consisting of eleven Latin American countries (see Table 20.2);
2. the *Central American Common Market* (CACM), also formed in 1960 and comprising five Central American nations;
3. the *Andean Group* formed in 1969 and consisting of Bolivia, Chile, Ecuador, Colombia and Peru;
4. the *Caribbean Free Trade Area* (CARIFTA) formed in 1968 and consisting of twelve Caribbean nations; (In July 1973 the Caribbean Free Trade Area was converted into a fully-fledged Caribbean Community.)
5. the *Central African Customs and Economic Union* (CACEU) formed in 1964 and comprising Cameroon, Central African Republic, Congo and Gabon;
6. the *East African Community* (EAC), which has been in existence since colonial times and which consists of Kenya, Uganda and Tanzania;
7. the newly formed (1975) *Economic Community of West African States* (ECOWAS) consisting of fifteen countries – nine French- five English- and one Portuguese-speaking – with a total population of 124 million and an area of 6·5 million square km. ECOWAS will be the largest economic union in Africa.

Table 13.3 summarizes the expansion of trade among member states of the six integration groups between 1960 and 1970. It can be seen

Integration group	Value of exports to area ($ million)				Share of exports to the area in total exports (%)				Annual growth rate of exports to the area (%)		
	1960	1968	1969	1970	1960	1968	1969	1970	1960-8	1969	1970
Latin America											
LAFTA*	564	999	1,206	1,254	8·5	10·7	11·7	10·6	7·4	20·7	3·9
Andean Group†	(40)	(60)	(84)	(109)	(2·5)	(2·2)	(2·9)	(3·3)	(5·2)	(40·0)	(29·8)
CACM‡	33	247	250	286	7·5	26·0	25·7	26·1	28·8	1·2	14·4
Caribbean											
CARIFTA§	27	52	66	—	5·0	5·9	7·2	—	8·6	26·9	—
Africa											
CACEU‖	3	16	21	—	1·7	4·0	4·6	—	23·2	31·2	—
EAC¶	63	116	122	142	14·6	17·1	16·8	17·3	7·9	5·2	16·4

Table 13.3
Intra-trade of integration groups, 1960–70

Source: Pazos, 'Regional integration of trade among less developed countries', *World Development*, 7 (1973), 2, Table 1.

* Latin American Free Trade Association: Argentina, Bolivia, Brazil, Chile, Colombia, Ecuador, Mexico, Paraguay, Peru, Uruguay, Venezeula.

† Andean Group: Bolivia, Chile, Colombia, Ecuador, Peru.

‡ Central American Common Market: Costa Rica, El Salvador, Guatemala, Honduras, Nicaragua.

§ Caribbean Free Trade Area: Barbados, Guyana, Jamaica, Trinidad and Tobago, Antigua, British Honduras, Dominica, Grenada, Montserrat, St Kitts-Nevis-Anguilla, St Lucia, St Vincent.

‖ Central African Customs and Economic Union: Cameroon, Central African Republic, Congo, Gabon.

¶ East African Community: Kenya, Uganda, United Republic of Tanzania.

that in two of the four 'older groups', the CACM and the CACEU, internal trade grew at a phenomenal annual rate of 28·8 and 23·2 per cent respectively during the 1960s. The other two 'older' groups (LAFTA and EAC) showed only moderate rates of growth of between 7 and 8 per cent annually. But it is important to note that in both cases this internal growth rate was significantly higher than the growth rate of total trade for each. This can be seen by the rise in internal trade as a percentage of total trade between 1960 and 1970 for both groups, from 8·5 to 10·6 per cent for LAFTA and from 14·6 to 17·3 per cent for EAC. The relatively slow growth of intra-trade within LAFTA and EAC can be attributed largely to the emergence of new forms of protective restriction in the 1960s designed to permit the weaker partners to catch up slowly with the stronger ones.

Both the Andean Group and the LAFTA, formed in the late 1960s, showed big jumps in their internal trade in 1969. But we must await further data to evaluate the trade expansionary effects of each group. However, the rapid pace at which trade started to expand in CARIFTA and the Andean group testify to the potential capacity of Third World nations to conduct mutually beneficial exchange with each other. Finally, since the bulk of the increase in intra-trade among the various integration groups was concentrated in the manufacturing sector (e.g. in CACM, 74 per cent of all intra-trade is in manufacturing categories), the scope for industrial growth can be greatly strengthened by economic cooperation among various LDCs. Instead of trying to compete with one another for access to heavily-protected manufactured good markets of developed countries, Third World nations may stand a better long-run chance to diversify their economies successfully by trading with one another behind the protective barrier of a common tariff.

With regard to the complex and in some cases irrelevant question of trade creation and trade diversion, Dr Pazos' analysis reveals evidence of the existence of both. But, on the whole, he concludes with respect to CACM (the most carefully analyzed group) that 'integration has created competition among the producers of the five countries and has probably promoted industrial specialization by types of products, thus permitting larger production scales and lower costs'[16]. Thus trade creation does seem to have pervaded the CACM.

Regarding the benefits of integration in terms of growth rates of member-country exports, their GNPs and their intra-country trade balances which often are not uniformly distributed, especially when there is a dominant country in the group (as in the case of Kenya in EAC), all participants of CACM appear to have benefited from an expansion of exports and have also received considerable net benefits in terms of national output and employment rates of growth[17].

Dr Pazos concludes his analysis of the economic effects of integration with regard to the CACM with the observation[18]:

The experience of Central America shows that, under appropriate circumstances, the elimination of restrictions on the mutual trade of a group of developing countries brings about considerable expansion in their commercial interchange, fuller use of industrial capacity, specialization of production, economies of scale, increased industrialization and faster economic growth, without any rise in the number of industrial failures or in the amount of unemployment.

In spite of the impressive record of the Central American Common Market and the early favorable results of the Andean and CACEU experiences, there still remain major stumbling blocks, some real, others psychological and political, in the path of a more widespread Third World movement towards economic integration. The major problems relate to differences in levels of development among prospective members and the consequent expectation among smaller members that a uniform trade liberalization policy will disproportionately benefit the more developed members at their expense. In order for an integration scheme to be successful, it must not penalize any members while assuring that the distribution of the benefits of cooperation are reasonably equitable. If there are severe imbalances among member countries at the outset (as in the case of Kenya vis-à-vis its two East African neighbors) the tendency for unequal gains from trade to emerge and for the widening of the income gap between rich and poor members as a result of free trade will be reinforced. Such unequal benefit distribution is entirely analagous to that between rich and poor nations described in our critique of traditional free trade theory.

However, in the case of regional integration, it is at least possible to redistribute the gains from trade or plan for the more rapid industrial development of weaker members to enable them to 'catch up' through coordinated policy planning. This redistribution or coordination is not possible at the international level. It has been attempted in the EAC (e.g. Kenya provided direct financial transfers to the other two members in the early 1960s) with mixed success. This was due largely to the fact that EAC member states are still able to pursue their own separate and often conflicting industrial development strategies. Moreover, there is no really effective supranational agency to enforce compliance with the provisions of the integration scheme.

3. Conclusions

We may conclude, therefore, that Third World countries at a relatively equal stage of industrial development, with similar market sizes, and with a strong interest in coordinating and rationalizing their joint industrial growth patterns stand to benefit most from the combined inward–outward looking trade policies represented by economic integration. In particular, regional groupings of small nations like those of Central America and Central and West Africa can create the economic conditions (mainly in the form of larger internal markets) on which to accelerate their joint development efforts. In the absence of such cooperation and integration, the prospects for sustained economic progress would be bleak. Moreover by blocking certain forms of trade with the more powerful developed nations and perhaps also restricting or prohibiting the deep penetration of multinational corporations (see below) into their industrial sectors, these nations can provide a better base for their long-run development efforts.

But, while such an integration strategy may seem logical and persuasive on paper (in fact, it may be the only long-run solution to the economic problems of small nations), in practice it requires a degree of statesmanship and a regional rather than nationalistic orientation that is often lacking in many countries. Nevertheless, as time goes on and developing nations begin to see their individual destinies more closely tied to those of their neighbors, and as the pursuit of greater collective self-reliance and self-sufficiency gathers momentum in the late 1970s and 1980s, one might speculate that the pressures for some form of economic integration will gradually overcome the forces of separation. Surely, the collective experience of the six regional groupings briefly reviewed in this section as well as the new West African Community will be closely watched by other Third World regions and may constitute a decisive factor in the latter's decisions whether or not to move towards economic integration.

13.5 Trade policies of developed countries: the need for reform

We have seen that a major obstacle to LDC export expansion, whether in the area of primary products or manufactures, has been the various kinds of trade barriers erected by developed nations against the principal commodity exports of developing countries. In the absence of economic integration or even in support of that effort, the prospects for future LDC trade and foreign exchange expansion depends largely on the international economic policies of developed nations. While internal structural and economic reform may be essential to economic and social progress, an improvement in the competitive position of those industries where LDCs do have a dynamic comparative advantage will be of little benefit either to them or the world as a whole so long as their access to major world markets is restricted by rich country commercial policies.

Four major areas where a developed country's economic and commercial policies stand out as the most important from the perspective of future Third World foreign exchange earnings are:
1. tariff and non-tariff barriers to LDC exports;
2. developed country export incentives;
3. the issue of *adjustment assistance* for displaced workers in industries hurt by freer access of labor-intensive, low-cost LDC exports; and
4. the general impact of rich-country domestic economic policies on developing economies.

1. Rich-nation tariff and The present tariff and non-tariff barriers (e.g. excise taxes, quotas,
non-tariff trade barriers sanitary regulations, etc.) imposed by rich nations on the commodity

exports of poor ones represent the most significant obstacle to the expansion of the latter's export-earning capacities. Moreover, as we have seen, many of these tariffs increase with the degree of product processing, i.e. they are higher for processed foodstuffs compared with basic foodstuffs (e.g. groundnut oil compared with groundnuts) or for shirts as opposed to raw cotton. These high effective tariffs inhibit LDCs from diversifying their own secondary export industries and thus act to restrain their industrial expansion and diversification.

The overall effect of developed country tariffs, quotas and non-tariff barriers (e.g. sanitary laws for meat imports more stringent than domestic regulations) is to lower the effective price received by LDCs for their exports (i.e. worsen their terms of trade), reduce the quantity exported and diminish foreign exchange earnings. Although the burdens which developed-country tariffs impose upon LDC primary and secondary product exports vary from commodity to commodity, the net impact of trade barriers on all products is to reduce Third World foreign exchange earnings by many billions of dollars. In the absence of widespread reductions in these trade barriers and the establishment of special preferences for LDC primary product exports, there can be little optimism about the possibility of accelerating Third World export earnings through trade with the developed nations.

2. Export incentives of developed countries

In addition to restricting the imports of products from the Third World, many developed countries provide generous financial incentives in the form of public subsidies and tax rebates for their own export industries. The Japanese government has made the greatest use of this policy by working closely in support of its private export industries. Although LDC governments also provide export incentives, their limited fiscal capacity prevents them from effectively counteracting the impact of export subsidies in rich countries. The overall effect of this public support of private industries is to make rich country industries more 'competitive' in world markets and to delay the time when Third World industries are able to compete effectively. It is simply another instance of the disproportionate ability of the wealthy to stay on top.

3. The problem of adjustment assistance

One of the major obstacles to the lowering of tariff barriers of rich countries against the manufactured exports of poorer nations is the political pressure exerted by those traditional light manufacturing industries which find their products underpriced by low-cost, labor-intensive foreign goods. Not only can this cause economic disruption for these higher cost domestic industries; it can also lead to a loss of employment for their workers. In classical trade theory the answer to this dilemma would be simple: merely shift these workers from rich countries with their complementary resources to those more capital-intensive industries where a comparative advantage still exists. Everybody will be better off as a result.

Unfortunately, even in the most industrialized and economically integrated societies of the world, the process of adjustment is not so simple. More important, the political power of many of these older industries is such that whenever they feel threatened by low-cost foreign imports, they are able to muster enough support effectively to block competition from the LDCs. Such activities make a mockery of pious statements about the benefits of free trade.

Unless some scheme of 'adjustment assistance' is established by which the governments of developed nations financially assist industries and their workers in the transition to alternative and more profitable activities, trade barriers against competitive Third World exports will continue to be raised. Many such schemes have been proposed. To date, however, none has been really effective in persuading threatened industries and industrial workers to forgo their private interests in the interest of maximum world welfare. This is not surprising. In fact, the typical response of developed country governments has been to subsidize new investment in threatened industries to keep them afloat. Nevertheless, continuous efforts must be made to search for an acceptable program of adjustment assistance which will not unduly penalize displaced workers who often come from the lower income brackets. Without the introduction of such programs in developed nations, the world market for Third World manufactured exports will always remain highly restricted both for new entrants and for the growth of existing suppliers.

4. Domestic economic policies

While it is beyond the scope of this chapter to examine the myriad ways in which the economic welfare of many export-oriented poor nations is tied to the domestic fiscal and monetary policies of rich nations, the importance of this linkage must not be overlooked. The major factor determining the level and growth of Third World export earnings (and this was clearly confirmed by their relatively good performance in the 1960s) has been the ability of rich nations to sustain high rates of economic growth without inflation. Even a low income elasticity of demand for LDC exports can be compensated for by a high rate of income growth in a developed country. It follows that under present international economic relationships, Third World export performance is directly related to the growth and price stability of developed country economies.

But just as the poor are often said to be 'the last to be hired and the first to be fired', so too when international economic disruptions occur, the world's poor nations feel the effects much sooner and more substantially than do the rich nations. The worldwide inflationary spiral of the early and mid-1970s caused by a combination of Keynesian-type excess aggregate 'demand pull' and natural resource, especially petroleum, 'cost-push' factors provides a classic example of this phenomenon. Faced with rampant inflation at home, developed countries were able to call upon traditional macro-economic policies designed to restrict aggregate demand (e.g. lower government expenditure, higher taxes, higher interest rates, a slower growing money supply, etc.) while attempting to control wage and price rises. When rapid inflation is accompanied by growing balance-of-payments deficits and rising domestic unemployment as in the mid-1970s, these 'deflationary' general domestic fiscal and monetary policies tend to be reinforced by specific government actions to curtail imports and control the outflow of foreign exchange. Those hit the hardest by these 'belt tightening' measures are usually the weakest, most vulnerable and most dependent nations of the world – the forty or so 'least developed' countries. While they are not the intended victims of such domestic economic policies, the fact remains that they are the main victims.

Clearly, one cannot blame the developed nations for first looking after their own domestic economic interests. Nevertheless, it would not appear too unreasonable to ask them to try to ease the burden of their spending cutbacks on the poorest nations by giving the exports of these nations some form of preferential treatment. But the lesson is clear. As long as developing nations, either individually or as a group, whether willingly or unwillingly, permit their economies to be linked too closely to the economic policies of rich nations, they will remain its chief, though innocent, victims in times of stress while in times of prosperity their rewards will be minimal. Even more disturbing is the loss of their capacity to control their own economic and social destinies.

The lessons of the 1970s thus revealed to Third World nations, as no economic model could have, their need to make every effort to reduce their individual and joint economic vulnerabilities. One method of achieving this goal is to pursue policies of greater 'collective' self-reliance within the context of mutual economic cooperation and a more cautious attitude towards the further penetration of their economies by products, technologies and corporations from rich countries. While not denying their interdependence with developed nations, many developing countries now realize that in the absence of major reforms of the international economic order, a concentrated effort at reducing their current international economic dependence and vulnerability may be one of the essential ingredients in any successful long-run development strategy.

Notes

1. An important step in this direction, however, was taken at a meeting of the International Monetary Fund held in Jamaica in January 1976. At that meeting the IMF agreed to increase SDR quotas for non-oil exporting LDCs by 50 per cent, thus adding about $1 billion to their reserves. It also agreed to set up a special fund based on the sale of gold to help the developing world balance its deficit payments. In addition, the meeting legalized the IMF's present system of floating exchange rates.
2. For an excellent discussion of these issues see P. P. Streeten, 'Trade strategies for development: some themes for the seventies', *World Development,* 1, no. 6 (1973), 1–10.
3. Ibid., p. 2.
4. See A. Maizels, *Exports and Economic Growth of Developing Countries,* Cambridge U.P. (1968).
5. See Maizels, op. cit., for a lengthy and detailed analysis of this issue.
6. G. K. Helleiner, *International Trade and Economic Development,* Penguin Books, London (1972), 69–70.
7. For the most comprehensive analysis and critique of import substitution policies in developing countries, see I. Little, T. Scitovsky and M. Scott, *Industry and Trade in Some Developing Countries,* London, Oxford U.P. (1970).
8. Helleiner, op. cit., p. 105.
9. Little, Scitovsky and Scott, *Industry and Trade in Some Developing Countries; A Comparative Study,* OECD, Oxford U.P. (1970), 39.
10. Herbert G. Grubel, 'Effective tariff protection: a non-specialist introduction to the theory, policy implications and controversies', in H. Grubel and H. Johnson (eds), *Effective Tariff Protection,* GATT, Geneva (1971), 2.
11. Little, Scitovsky and Scott, op. cit., p. 4.
12. Bela Balassa, 'Tariff protection in industrial countries: an evaluation', *Journal of Political Economy,* October 1965, 580 and 588.
13. UNECAFE, *Economy Survey of Asia and the Far East 1968,* Bangkok (1969), 67.
14. Streeten, op. cit., *World Development,* 1, no. 6 (1973), pp. 3–4.
15. For a useful summary of Third World regional integration experiences, see Felipe Pazos, 'Regional integration of trade among less developed countries', *World Development,* 1, no. 7 (1973), 1–12.
16. Ibid., p. 4.
17. Ibid., pp. 6–9.
18. Ibid., p. 9.

Concepts for review

balance of payments	free trade area
current account	common market
trade surplus versus trade	trade creation
deficit	trade diversion
capital account	export promotion
cash account	import substitution
commercial policies	tariffs
'learning by doing'	quotas
autarchy	non-tariff trade barriers
adjustment assistance	infant industry
export incentives	export duty or subsidy
'outward'- versus 'inward'-looking	official exchange rate
development policies	'overvalued' exchange rate
economic integration	forward and backward
customs union	industrial linkages

Questions for discussion

1. Draw up a Balance of Payments table similar in format to that of Table 13.1 but using the most recent available data from a Third World country. Explain the significance or non-significance of the various entries in the current and capital accounts. What happened to the level of this country's foreign reserves during the year in question?
2. Explain the distinction between primary and secondary 'inward'- and 'outward'-looking development policies.
3. Briefly summarize the range of 'commercial policies' available to Third World countries and why some of these policies might be adopted.
4. What are the possibilities, advantages and disadvantages of 'export promotion' in Third World nations with reference to specific types of commodities (e.g. primary food products, raw materials, fuels, minerals, manufactured goods, etc.).
5. Most less developed countries in Latin America, Africa and Asia have pursued policies of 'import substitution' as major components of their development strategies. Explain the theoretical and practical arguments in support of import substitution policies. What have been some of the weaknesses of these policies in practice and why have the results often not lived up to expectations? Explain.
6. Explain some of the arguments in support of the use of tariffs, quotas and other trade barriers in developing countries.
7. What are the basic static and dynamic arguments for economic integration in less developed countries? Briefly describe the various forms which economic integration can take (e.g. customs union, free trade areas, etc.). What are the major obstacles to effective economic integration in Third World regions?
8. How do the trade policies of developed countries affect the ability of less developed countries to benefit from greater participation in the world economy? How do 'non-trade' domestic economic policies of rich nations affect the export earnings of Third World countries? What is meant by 'adjustment assistance' and why is it so important to the future of Third World manufactured export prospects? Explain.

Further readings Two of the best general sources of information on trade policies and strategies for development are: G. K. Helleiner, *International Trade and Economic Development*, Penguin Books, Middlesex, England (1972) and Paul Streeten, 'Trade strategies for development: some themes for the seventies', *World Development*, **1**, no. 6 (1973).

The following are more specialized readings on the topics covered in this chapter: (*a*) R. L. Allen, 'Integration in less developed areas', *Kyklos*, **14**, fasc. 3 (1961), 315–36; (*b*) B. Balassa, 'The impact of industrial countries' tariff structure on their imports of manufactures from less developed areas', *Economica*, **34**, no. 136 (1967), 372–83; (*c*) B. Balassa, 'Trade policies in developing countries" *American Economic Review*, **61**, no. 2 (1971), 178–87; (*d*) H. Bruton, 'The import-substitution strategy of economic development: a survey', *Pakistan Development Review*, **10**, no. 2 (1970), 123–46; (*e*) C. Cooper and B. Massell, 'Toward a general theory of customs unions for developing countries', *Journal of Political Economy*, **73**, no. 5 (1965), 461–74; (*f*) I. Little, T. Scitovsky and M. Scott, *Industry and Trade in Some Developing Countries: A Comparative Study*, Development Centre, OECD, Oxford U.P. (1970); (*g*) D. Morawatz, *The Andean Group: A Case Study in Economic Integration Among Developing Countries*, MIT Press, Cambridge, Mass. and London (1974); (*h*) A. S. Rojko and A. B. Mackie, 'World demand prospects for agricultural exports of less-developed countries in 1980', *Foreign Agricultural Economic Report*, no. 60, US Department of Agriculture, Economic Research Service, 1970.

Foreign investment and
aid: Old controversies
and new opportunities

What the Third World must ask of the international order is . . . a genuine transfer
of real resources, not the present 'aid' charade.
  Santiago Resolution, April 1973

Two decades of experience with international economic cooperation have convinced many leaders in the developing countries that basic changes in their
economies and social systems are more important than quantitative increases in
external resource transfers.
  Communiqué of Third World social scientists, March 1974[1]

Introduction: the international flow of financial resources

We discovered at the beginning of Chapter 13 that a country's international financial situation as reflected in its balance of payments and its
level of monetary reserves depends not only on its current account
balance (its commodity trade) but also on its balance on capital
account (its net inflow or outflow of private and public financial
resources). Since most Third World countries except the OPEC oil
nations typically incur deficits on their current account balance, a
continuous net inflow of foreign financial resources represents an
important ingredient in their long-run development strategies.

The international flow of financial resources takes two main forms:
private foreign investment, mostly by large multinational corporations
with headquarters in the developed nations, and *public development
assistance* (foreign aid), both from individual national governments
and multinational donor agencies. In this chapter we examine the
nature, significance and controversy over private foreign investment
and foreign aid in the context of the changing world economy.
Although our principal emphasis is on the traditional 'north–south'
flow of development finance (i.e. from developed to less developed
nations), the recent emergence of wealthy Arab oil nations with their
vast surplus of 'petrodollars' does open up exciting new possibilities for
'intra'-Third World development assistance. We explore the significance of this new phenomenon briefly at the end of the chapter.

14.1 Private foreign investment and the multinational corporation

Few developments have played as critical a role in the extraordinary growth of international trade and capital flows during the past two decades as the rise of the multinational corporation (MNC). These huge business firms with their far-flung networks of subsidiaries all marching to the drum of centralized global profit-maximizing decisions of parent companies located in North America, Europe and Japan present a unique opportunity and a host of critical problems for the many developing countries in which they conduct their business.

The growth of private foreign investment in the Third World has been extremely rapid. It has risen from an annual rate of $2·4 billion in 1962 to almost $9 billion by the mid-1970s. But, as we have seen, direct foreign investment involves much more than the simple transfer of capital or the establishment of a local factory in a developing nation. MNCs carry with them technologies of production, tastes and styles of living, managerial services and diverse business practices including cooperative arrangements, marketing restrictions, advertising and the phenomenon of 'transfer pricing', to be discussed shortly. Unlike certain types of foreign aid, the purpose of MNC activities is far from charitable. In many instances, these activities have little to do with the development aspirations of the countries in which they operate. But before analyzing some of the arguments for and against private foreign investment in general and multinational corporations in particular, we outline the character of these enterprises.

1. Multinational corporations: size, patterns and trends Two central characteristics of multinational corporations are their large size and the fact that their world-wide operations and activities tend to be centrally controlled by parent companies. Many MNCs have annual sales volumes in excess of the entire GNPs of the developing nations in which they operate (see Table 14.1). Typically, annual sales run into hundreds of millions of dollars. The five largest MNCs now have annual sales volumes of $10 billion or more, while more than 200 others have annual sales in excess of $1 billion.

Such enormous size confers great economic (and sometimes political) power on MNCs vis-à-vis the countries in which they operate. This power is greatly strengthened by their predominantly 'oligopolistic' market positions, that is, they tend to operate in product markets dominated by a *few* sellers and buyers. They thus have the ability to manipulate prices and profits, to collude with other firms in determining areas of control, and in general to restrict the entry of potential competition through their dominating influences over new technologies, special skills and consumer tastes through product differentiation and advertising.

The largest MNCs have many foreign branches and overseas affiliates. Nearly 200 have subsidiaries in twenty or more countries. Eight of the ten largest are based in the United States, while US firms exercise control over about 30 per cent of all foreign affiliates. Britain, Germany and France together with the United States control over 75 per cent of all MNC affiliates. Latest (1976) estimates put the book value of their total foreign investment in excess of $175 billion with over 80 per cent of that total owned by MNCs in these four countries. Of this total, approximately one-third is located in developing countries. But, given their small size, the LDCs feel the presence of multinational corporations more acutely than do the developed countries.

Rank	Economic Entity	Pro- duct[1] ($b.)	Rank	Economic Entity	Pro- duct[1] ($b.)
1	United States	1068·1	46	Pakistan	8·2
2	USSR	343·1	47	*Chrysler*	8·0
3	Japan	223·0	48	Nigeria	7·9
4	West Germany	196·8	49	Thailand	7·8
5	France	172·0	50	Chile	7·6
6	United Kingdom	135·8	51	*Texaco*	7·5
7	China	128·1	52	U.A.R.	7·5
8	Italy	100·6	53	*Unilever*[2,3]	7·5
9	Canada	89·4	54	*ITT*	7·4
10	India	60·6	55	Portugal	7·1
11	Poland	44·1	56	Bulgaria	7·0
12	Brazil	43·9	57	New Zealand	6·9
13	Spain	37·4	58	Peru	6·7
14	Mexico	36·7	59	Israel	6·6
15	Australia	36·4	60	Taiwan	6·4
16	Netherlands	34·6	61	*Western Electric*	6·1
17	East Germany	34·5	62	*Gulf Oil*	5·9
18	Sweden	34·3	63	Algeria	5·2
19	Czechoslovakia	30·7	64	*British Petroleum*[2]	5·2
20	Argentina	29·0	65	*Philips Gloeilampen*[3]	5·2
21	Belgium	28·7	66	*Standard Oil (Cal.)*	5·1
22	*General Motors*	28·3	67	Puerto Rico	5·1
23	Switzerland	22·9	68	*Volkswagen*[4]	5·0
24	*Standard Oil (NJ)*	18·7	69	*US Steel*	4·9
25	South Africa	18·4	70	Bangladesh	4·7
26	Denmark	17·2	71	*Westinghouse*	4·6
27	Austria	16·5	72	Malaysia	4·5
28	*Ford Motor*	16·4	73	Ireland	4·5
29	Rumania	15·2	74	North Korea	4·4
30	Yugoslavia	15·1	75	Cuba	4·4
31	Iran	13·4	76	South Vietnam	4·3
32	*Royal Dutch/Shell*[2,3]	12·7	77	*Nippon Steel*[5]	4·1
33	Hungary	12·4	78	*Standard Oil (Ind.)*	4·1
34	Turkey	12·3	79	Morocco	4·0
35	Norway	12·2	80	*Shell Oil*	3·9
36	Finland	12·0	81	*du Pont*	3·9
37	Greece	11·3	82	*Siemens*[4]	3·8
38	Venezuela	11·2	83	Saudi Arabia	3·8
39	Indonesia	9·5	84	*Imperial Chem. Ind.*[2]	3·7
40	*General Electric*	9·4	85	*RCA*	3·7
41	Philippines	9·1	86	*Hitachi*[5]	3·6
42	South Korea	8·3	87	*Goodyear*	3·6
43	*IBM*	8·3	88	Hong Kong	3·6
44	Colombia	8·3	89	Iraq	3·6
45	*Mobil Oil*	8·2	90	*Nestle*[6]	3·6

Table 14.1
Ranking of countries and multinational corporations according to size of annual product: 1968

(1): Gross national product for countries and gross sales for corporations.
(2-6) Corporations based outside of the United States, in: (2) the United Kingdom; (3) the Netherlands; (4) West Germany; (5) Japan; or (6) Switzerland.

Sources: Gross national product figures from the *World Bank Atlas* (Washington: World Bank, 1973).
Corporate sales figures from United Nations, Department of Economic and Social Affairs, *Multinational Corporations in World Development* (New York: United Nations, 1973), Table 3.
This table was prepared by Thomas E. Weisskopf for chapter 13 of Richard C. Edwards, Michael Reich & Thomas E. Weisskopf, *The Capitalist System*, revised edition (Prentice-Hall, 1977).

Historically, multinational corporations, especially those operating in developing nations, focused on extractive industries, mainly mineral and raw material production. A few 'agribusiness' MNCs became involved in export-oriented plantation agriculture and local food processing. Recently, however, manufacturing interests have occupied a greater share of their activities. At present, manufacturing accounts for almost 28 per cent of the estimated stock of foreign direct investment in LDCs while petroleum and mining represent 40 per cent and 9 per cent respectively. But the overall importance of MNCs in the economies of Third World nations, especially in the manufacturing and service sectors, is rapidly growing. In the 1960s, MNC private direct investments represented about one-fifth of the total flow of resources to LDCs. Moreover, this flow increased at an annual average rate of 9 per cent. Thus, the stock of foreign private investment increased faster than the GNPs of most poor countries during the past decade.

Given the above brief sketch of the size and importance of multinational corporations, we can now discuss some of the arguments for and against their activities in the context of the development aspirations of Third World nations.

2. Private foreign investment: some 'pros' and 'cons' for development Few areas in the economics of development arouse so much controversy and are subject to such varying degrees of interpretation as the question of the benefits and costs of private foreign investment. If however, we look closely at the essence of this controversy, we will find not so much a disagreement about the influence of MNCs on traditional economic aggregates such as GNP, investment, savings and manufacturing growth rates (though these disagreements do indeed exist) as about the fundamental economic and social 'meaning' of development as it relates to the diverse activities of MNCs. In other words, the controversy over the role and impact of foreign private investment in Third World economies often has as its underlying, though usually unstated, basis a fundamental disagreement about the nature, style and character of a desirable development process. The basic arguments for and against the developmental impact of private foreign investment in the context of the type of development it tends to foster can be summarized as follows:

A. Traditional economic arguments in support of private investment: filling 'gaps' The pro-foreign investment arguments grow largely out of the traditional neo-classical analysis of the determinants of economic growth. Foreign private investment (as well as foreign aid) is typically seen as a way of filling in 'gaps' between the domestically available supplies of savings, foreign exchange, government revenue and skills and the planned level of these resources necessary to achieve development targets. To give a simple example of the 'savings-investment gap' analysis, recall that the basic Harrod–Domar growth model postulates a direct relationship between a country's rate of savings, s, and its rate of output growth, g, via the equation $g = s/k$ where k is the national capital/output ratio. If the planned rate of national output growth, g, is targeted at say 7 per cent annually and the capital/output rate is 3, then the needed rate of annual saving is 21 per cent (since $s = g \times k$). If the saving that can be domestically mobilized amounts to only, say, 16 per cent of GNP, then a 'savings gap' equal to 5 per cent can be said to exist. If the nation can fill this gap with foreign financial resources (either private or public) it will better be able to achieve its target rate of growth.

Therefore, the first and most often cited contribution of private foreign investment to national development (i.e. when this development is defined in terms of GNP growth rates – an important implicit conceptual assumption) is its role in filling the resource 'gap' between targeted or desired investment and locally mobilized savings.

A second contribution, analogous to the first, is its contribution to filling the gap between targeted foreign exchange requirements and those derived from net export earnings plus net public foreign aid. This is the so-called foreign exchange or trade 'gap'. ('Two-gap' models are discussed more fully in the context of foreign aid later in the chapter).

An inflow of private foreign capital can not only alleviate part or all of the deficit on the balance-of-payments 'current account' but it can also function to remove that deficit over time *if* the foreign-owned enterprise can generate a net positive flow of export earnings. Unfortunately, as we discovered in the case of import substitution, the overall effect of permitting MNCs to establish subsidiaries behind protective tariff and quota walls is often a net *worsening* of both the current and capital account balance. Such deficits usually result both from the importation of capital equipment and intermediate products (normally from an overseas affiliate and often at inflated prices) and the outflow of foreign exchange in the form of repatriated profits, management fees, royalty payments and interest on private loans.

The third gap said to be filled by foreign investment is the gap between targeted governmental tax revenues and locally raised taxes. By taxing MNC profits and participating financially in their local operations, LDC governments are thought to be better able to mobilize public financial resources for development projects.

Fourth and finally there is the gap in management, entrepreneurship, technology and skill which is presumed to be partially or wholly filled by the local operations of private foreign firms. MNCs not only provide financial resources and new factories to poor countries: they also are believed to supply a 'package' of needed resources including management experience, entrepreneurial abilities and technological skills which can then be transferred to their local counterparts by means of training programs and the process of 'learning-by-doing'. Moreover, according to this argument, MNCs can educate local managers about how to establish contacts with overseas banks, locate alternative sources of supply, diversify market outlets and, in general, become better acquainted with international marketing practices. Finally, MNCs bring with them the most sophisticated technological knowledge about production processes while transferring modern machinery and equipment to capital-poor Third World countries. Such transfers of knowledge, skills and technology are assumed to be both desirable and productive to the recipient nations.

There are two basic arguments against private foreign investment in general and the activities of MNCs in particular – the strictly economic and the more philosophical or ideological.

B. Arguments against private foreign investment: widening gaps

On the economic side, the four 'gap filling' pro-private foreign investment positions outlined above are countered by the following arguments.

1. Although MNCs provide capital they may *lower domestic savings and investment* rates by stifling competition, failing to reinvest much of their profits, generating domestic incomes for those groups with lower savings propensities, inhibiting the expansion of indigenous firms who might otherwise supply them with intermediate products by their practice of importing these goods from overseas affiliates and imposing high interest costs on capital borrowed by host governments.

2. Although the initial impact of MNC investment is to improve the *foreign exchange* position of the recipient nation, its long-run impact may be to reduce foreign exchange earnings on both current and capital accounts. The current account may deteriorate as a result of substantial importation of intermediate products and capital goods while the capital account may worsen because of the overseas repatriation of profits, interest, royalties, management fees, etc.

3. While MNCs do contribute to *public revenue* in the form of corporate taxes, they can also diminish that revenue as a result of liberal tax concessions, excessive investment allowances, disguised public subsidies and tariff protection provided by the host government.

4. The management, entrepreneurial skills, technology and overseas contacts provided by MNCs may have little impact on developing local sources of these scarce skills and resources and may in fact *inhibit their development* by stifling the growth of indigenous entrepreneurship as a result of the MNCs' dominance of local markets.

But the really significant criticism of MNCs is usually conducted on more fundamental levels than those briefly outlined above. In particular, Third World countries have commonly raised the following objections[2].

1. Their impact on development is very uneven and in many situations MNC activities reinforce dualistic economic structures and exacerbate income inequalities. They tend to promote the interests of the small number of well-paid modern sector workers against the interests of the rest by widening wage differentials. They divert resources away from needed food production to the manufacture of sophisticated products catering primarily for the demands of local elites. And they tend to worsen the imbalance between rural and urban economic opportunities by locating primarily in urban areas and contributing to the accelerated flow of rural–urban migration.

2. MNCs typically produce *inappropriate products* (those demanded by a small rich minority of the local population), stimulate *inappropriate consumption patterns* through advertising and their monopolistic market power, and do this all with *inappropriate* (capital-intensive) *technologies of production*. This is perhaps the major area of criticism of MNCs.

3. As a result of 1 and 2, local resources tend to be allocated towards socially undesirable projects. This in turn tends to aggravate the already sizable inequality between rich and poor and the serious imbalance between urban and rural economic opportunities.

4. MNCs use their economic power to influence government policies in directions unfavourable to development. They are able to extract sizable economic and political concessions from competing LDC governments in the form of excessive protection, tax rebates, investment allowances and the cheap provision of factory sites and essential social services. As a result, the private profits of MNCs may exceed social benefits. In some cases, these social returns to host countries may even be negative! Alternatively, a MNC can avoid much local taxation by artificially inflating the price which it pays for intermediate products purchased from overseas affiliates so as to lower its stated local profits. This phenomenon, known as 'transfer pricing', is a major practice of MNCs and one over which host governments can exert little control so long as corporate tax rates differ from one country to the next.

5. MNCs may damage host economies by suppressing domestic entrepreneurship and using their superior knowledge, worldwide contacts, advertising skills and range of essential support services to drive out local competitors and inhibit the emergence of smaller scale local enterprises.
6. Finally, at the political level, the fear is often expressed that powerful multinational corporations have the ability to gain control over local assets and jobs. They can then exert considerable influence on political decisions at all levels. In extreme cases, they may even, either directly by payoffs to corrupt public officials at the highest levels or indirectly by contributions to 'friendly' political parties, subvert the very political process of host nations (e.g. the ITT experience in Chile).

While the above lists provide a range of conflicting arguments, the real debate ultimately centres on different ideological and value judgements about the nature and meaning of economic development and the principal sources from which it springs. The advocates of private foreign investment tend to be 'free-market, private enterprise, *laissez faire*' proponents who firmly believe in the efficacy and beneficence of the 'free market' mechanism, where this is usually defined as a 'hands-off' policy by host governments. As we have seen, however, the actual operations of MNCs tend to be monopolistic and oligopolistic in practice. Price setting is achieved more as a result of international bargaining and collusion than as a natural outgrowth of free market supply and demand.

C. Reconciling the pros and cons

Those who argue against the activities of MNCs are often motivated more by a sense of the importance of national control over domestic economic activities and the minimization of dominance/dependence relationships between powerful MNCs and Third World governments. They see these giant corporations not as needed agents of economic change but more as vehicles of 'anti-development'. MNCs, they argue, reinforce dualistic economic structures and exacerbate domestic inequalities with their wrong products and inappropriate technologies. Some opponents, therefore, call for the outright confiscation (without compensation) or the nationalization (with some compensation) of foreign-owned enterprises[3]. Others advocate a more stringent regulation of foreign investments, a tougher bargaining stance on the part of host governments, a willingness on the part of LDCs to 'shop around' for better deals and finally, a greater coordination of LDC strategies with respect to terms and conditions of foreign investment. One example of such coordinated strategies was the 1971 decision by the Andean Group in Latin America to require foreign investors to reduce their ownership in local enterprises to minority shares over a 15-year period. Tanzania adopted a similar policy of securing a controlling share of foreign enterprises in line with its 'Arusha Declaration' of 1967 on socialism and self-reliance. As might be expected, however, the annual flow of private foreign investment declined as a result of these more stringent conditions.

In view of the strong anti-MNC sentiment being aired in the capitals of many Third World nations (as indeed in the developed countries as well) and the 'demonstration effect' of the power of OPEC nations to gain increasing control over foreign oil companies, it appears that the phenomenal growth of MNC influence in less developed countries in the 1950s and 1960s will not be matched in the 1970s and 1980s. The arguments both for and against private foreign investment have a certain empirical validity while reflecting important differences in value judgements. Perhaps the only really valid conclusion is that private foreign investment can be an important stimulus to economic and social development so long as the interests of *both* MNC and host country governments coincide (assuming, of course, that they don't coincide along the lines of dualistic development and widening inequalities). As long as MNCs see their role in terms of global output or profit maximization with little interest in the long-run domestic impact of their activities, the accusations of the anti-private investment school of thought will gain increasing Third World acceptance. Perhaps there can be no real congruence of interest between the objectives of MNCs and the priorities of LDC governments. On the other hand, a strengthening of the relative bargaining powers of host-country governments through their coordinated activities, while probably reducing the overall magnitude and growth of private foreign investment, may make that investment better fit the real long-run development needs and priorities of poor nations. The net social benefit of this trade-off between quantity and relevance is likely to have a positive impact on national development. Whatever the outcome, however, it certainly will be interesting and instructive to see what happens to the magnitude, direction and nature of private foreign investment and the role of MNCs over the next decade.

14.2 Foreign aid: the development assistance debate

1. Conceptual and measurement problems In addition to export earnings and private foreign investment, the final major source of Third World foreign exchange is public bilateral and multilateral development assistance, known also as foreign aid.

In principle, all real resource transfers from one country to another (mostly from developed to less developed nations but increasingly from OPEC to other Third World countries) should be included in the definition of foreign aid. Even this simple definition, however, raises a number of problems[4]:

1. Many resource transfers can take disguised forms such as the granting of preferential tariffs by developed countries to Third World exports of manufactured goods. This permits LDCs to sell their industrial products in developed-country markets at higher prices than without such tariff reductions. There is consequently a net gain for LDCs and a net loss for developed countries which amounts to a real resource transfer to the LDCs. Such implicit capital transfers or 'disguised flows' should be counted in quantifying foreign aid flows. Normally, however, they are not.

2. On the other hand, we should not include *all* transfers of capital to LDCs, particularly the capital flows of private foreign investors. For a number of years aid was calculated as the sum of official and private capital flows, although now these two items are listed separately (see Table 14.2). Private flows represent normal commercial transactions, are prompted by commercial considerations of profits and rates of return and, therefore, should not be viewed as aid any more than LDC exports to developed countries should be viewed as aid to the LDCs. Commercial flows of private capital are *not* a form of foreign assistance, even though they may benefit the developing country in which they take place.

Economists have defined foreign aid, therefore, as any flow of capital to LDCs which meets two criteria: (1) its objective should be non-commercial from the point of view of the donor; and (2) it should be characterized by 'concessional' terms, i.e. the interest rate and repayment period for borrowed capital should be 'softer' (less stringent) than commercial terms[5]. Even this definition can sometimes be inappropriate since it could include military aid which is both non-commercial and concessional. Normally, however, military aid is excluded from international measurements of foreign aid flows. The concept of foreign aid, therefore, which is now widely used and accepted is one which encompasses *all official grants and concessional loans, in currency or in kind, which are broadly aimed at transferring resources from developed to less developed nations (and, more recently, from OPEC to other Third World countries) on developmental and/or income distributional grounds.* Unfortunately, there often is a thin line separating purely 'developmental' grants and loans from those ultimately motivated by security and/or commercial interests.

The volume of 'official development assistance' which includes bilateral grants, loans and technical assistance as well as multilateral flows has grown from about an annual rate of $6 billion in 1962 to approximately $10·5 billion in the mid-1970s. However, in terms of the percentage of developed country GNPs allocated to official development assistance, there has been a steady decline from 0·52 per cent in the early 1960s to slightly less than 0·30 per cent in the

	1965*	1970*	1971*	1972	1973
Official	6,198·7	7,983·8	9,030·4	10,253·1	11,995·0
Official Development Assistance (ODA)	5,894·8	6,831·6	7,759·3	8,671·5	9,408·0
Bilateral	5,546·7	5,707·4	6,420·9	6,766·5	7,155·1
Grants and grant-like contributions†	3,713·7	3,323·1	3,634·2	4,369·7	4,481·3
Development lending and capital‡	1,833·0	2,384·3	2,786·4	2,396·7	2,674·0
Contributions to multilateral institutions	348·1	1,124·2	1,338·6	1,905·0	2,252·7
Grants	180·7	553·3	707·4	991·9	1,045·3
Capital subscription payments	167·4	540·6	600·4	862·2	1,120·9
Concessional lending	—	31·5	30·6	50·8	86·4
Other official flows	303·9	1,152·3	1,271·1	1,581·5	2,587·0
Private, at market terms	4,121·3	6,870·6	8,068·2	8,618·8	11,071·6
Private investment and lending‖	3,370·1	4,728·9	5,237·0	7,189·6	9,873·0
Private export credits	751·2	2,141·7	2,831·3	1,429·2	1,198·6
Grants by voluntary agencies	n.a.	858·3	912·8	1,035·9	1,362·2
Total	10,319·7	15,713·1	18,011·3	19,907·8	24,429·0

* Data for New Zealand, which joined DAC in 1973, are unavailable for years prior to 1972.

† Technical assistance, food aid, and other grants.

‡ New development lending, food aid loans, debt reorganization, and equities and other bilateral assets.

§ Official export credits, debt relief, equities and other bilateral assets, and contributions to multilateral institutions.

‖ Direct investment, bilateral portfolio investment, and multilateral portfolio investment.

¶ Voluntary grants were not recorded by DAC before 1970.

Note: Official flows decreased from 60·1 per cent of the total in 1965 to 49·1 per cent of the total in 1973; total ODA fell from 57·1 per cent to 38·5 per cent; and bilateral ODA dropped from 53·8 per cent to 29·3 per cent. ODA contributions to multilateral institutions rose from 3·4 per cent to 9·2 per cent; other official flows increased from 2·9 per cent to 10·6 per cent; and private flows at market terms went from 39·9 per cent to 45·3 per cent.

Source: Report by the Chairman of the Development Assistance Committee, *Development Co-operation, 1974 Review*, OECD, Paris, (1974), 233.

Table 14.2
Net flow of resources from DAC countries to developing countries and multilateral institutions, 1965 and 1970–3

mid-1970s[6]. The United States is still the major supplier of public aid to Third World nations, but its proportion of total development assistance has declined from 59 per cent in 1960 to approximately 35 per cent in the mid-1970s. Tables 14.2 and 14.3 provide recent data on the flow of public and private funds from the developed market economies to the developing world, while Table 14.4 provides information on official assistance from the USSR, Eastern Europe and China from 1969 to 1973. Finally, Table 14.5 shows the flow of development assistance from international donor organizations to developing countries over a similar period.

	1960	1965	1970	1971	1972	1973	1974	1975
Australia	0·38	0·53	0·59	0·53	0·59	0·44	0·53	0·54
Austria	n.a.	0·11	0·07	0·07	0·08	0·13	0·13	0·13
Belgium	0·88	0·60	0·46	0·50	0·55	0·51	0·56	0·62
Canada	0·19	0·19	0·42	0·42	0·47	0·43	0·51	0·51
Denmark	0·09	0·13	0·38	0·43	0·45	0·47	0·49	0·50
France	1·38	0·76	0·66	0·66	0·67	0·58	0·55	0·51
Germany	0·31	0·40	0·32	0·34	0·31	0·32	0·30	0·28
Italy	0·22	0·10	0·16	0·18	0·09	0·14	0·10	0·08
Japan	0·24	0·27	0·23	0·23	0·21	0·25	0·24	0·24
Netherlands	0·31	0·36	0·61	0·58	0·67	0·54	0·61	0·65
New Zealand	n.a.*	n.a.*	n.a.*	n.a.*	0·23	0·27	0·36	0·47
Norway	0·11	0·16	0·32	0·33	0·41	0·45	0·63	0·65
Portugal	1·45	0·59	0·67	1·42	1·79	0·71	0·47	0·42
Sweden	0·05	0·19	0·38	0·44	0·48	0·56	0·69	0·70
Switzerland	0·04	0·09	0·15	0·11	0·21	0·15	0·15	0·15
United Kingdom	0·56	0·47	0·37	0·41	0·39	0·35	0·34	0·32
United States†	0·53	0·49	0·31	0·32	0·29	0·23	0·21	0·20

DAC Total

ODA ($ millions)	1960	1965	1970	1971	1972	1973	1974	1975
current prices	4,665	5,895	6,832	7,762	8,671	9,415	10,706	11,948
1973 prices	7,660	9,069	9,346	9,976	10,059	9,415	9,391	9,452
GNP ($ billions)								
current prices	898	1,340	2,010	2,218	2,550	3,100	3,530	4,100
ODA as % GNP	0·52	0·44	0·34	0·35	0·34	0·30	0·30	0·29
ODA Deflator	60·9	65·0	73·1	77·8	86·2	100·0	114·0	126·4

Table 14.3
Net flow of official development assistance from DAC countries as a percentage of gross national product 1960, 1965, 1970–75

*New Zealand became a member of DAC in 1973. ODA figures for New Zealand are not available for 1960–71.

†In 1949, at the beginning of the Marshall Plan, US Official Development Assistance amounted to 2·79 per cent of GNP.

Note: Countries included are members of OECD Development Assistance Committee, accounting for more than 95 per cent of total Official Development Assistance. Figures for 1973 and earlier years are actual data. The projections for 1974 and 1975 are based on World Bank estimates of growth of GNP, on information on budget appropriations for aid, and on aid policy statements made by governments. Because of the relatively long period of time required to translate legislative authorizations first into commitments and later into disbursements, it is possible to project today, with reasonable accuracy, ODA flows (which by definition represent disbursements) through 1975.

Source: Robert S. McNamara, *Address to the Board of Governors of the World Bank Group,* Washington, DC, 30 September 1974 (Washington, DC: World Bank, 1974).

But just as there are conceptual problems associated with the definition of foreign aid, so too there are measurement and conceptual problems in the calculation of actual development assistance flows. In particular, three major problems arise in measuring aid:

First, one cannot simply add together the dollar values of grants and loans since each has a different significance to both aid-giving and

	1969	1970	1971	1972	1973
Donors					
USSR	474	194	865	581	622
Eastern Europe*	430	188	468	655	486
People's Republic of China	—	709	473	499	378
Total	904	1,091	1,806	1,735	1,486
Recipients					
Africa (excluding South Africa)	146	589	586	419	443†
East Asia (excluding Japan)	12	—	57	—	1
Europe (Malta, Spain, Portugal)	—	—	—	45‡	—
Latin America (excluding Cuba)	31	107	259	331	5
Near East and South Asia	715	395	904	940	1,037§
Total	904	1,091	1,806	1,735	1,486

Table 14.4
Economic aid from USSR, Eastern Europe and China to developing countries, gross commitments, 1969–73

*Bulgaria, Czechoslovakia, German Democratic Republic, Hungary, Poland, and Romania.

†Of this, China committed $335 million, most of it for Zaire, Cameroon, Chad, Upper Volta, and Senegal. Note that China's total commitments to developing countries that year reached $378 million.

‡All from China to Malta.

§India accounted for $455 million, Iran $291 million, Egypt $128 million, and Pakistan $71 million. The USSR and Eastern Europe were the principal donors to this region. Over 85 per cent of USSR commitments went to India, which received $350 million (in the form of grain), and Iran, which received $188 million.

Note: Short-term commitments are excluded. Grants have, since 1954, made up only 5 per cent of the total. Aid has concentrated on the public sector and is tied to the purchases of donor country goods. China probably accounted for most of the 1973 net transfers, i.e., gross disbursements less payments of principal and interest on earlier loans; this is in clear contrast with its position with respect to gross commitments. For 1973, the USSRs net transfer has been estimated at $50 million (its gross flow at $325 million) and Eastern Europe's as negative. Chinese credits are usually the softest: interest-free 10- to 30-year loans with a 10-year grace period. Eastern Europe's are generally 8- to 10-year loans at 3 to 3·5 per cent interest; the USSRs are normally 12-year loans at 2·5 to 3 per cent interest, with grace periods lasting until 1 year after the completion of the project or delivery of the goods.

Source: US Department of State, Bureau of Intelligence and Research, 'Communist states and developing countries: aid and trade in 1973', Research Study INR RS-20, 10 October 1974.

aid-receiving countries. Loans must be repaid and, therefore, 'cost' the donor and 'benefit' the recipient less than the 'nominal' value of the loan itself. Conceptually, therefore, one should deflate or discount the dollar value of interest-bearing loans before adding them to the value of outright grants.

Second, aid can be 'tied' either by *source* (i.e., loans and/or grants have to be spent on the purchase of donor country goods or services) or by *project* (funds cannot be spent on raw materials and intermediate products). In either case, the 'real value' of the aid is reduced because the specified 'source' is likely to be an expensive supplier, otherwise there would be no need to 'tie' the aid (additionally, aid may be tied to the importation of capital-intensive equipment which may impose an additional real resource cost – in the form of higher unemployment – on the recipient nation) or the 'project' itself may require purchase of new machinery and equipment from monopolistic suppliers while existing productive equipment in the same industry is being operated at very low levels of capacity.

Finally, we always need to distinguish between the 'nominal' and 'real' value of foreign assistance, especially during periods of rapid

	1963	1967	1968	1969	1970	1971	1972	1973	1946-73*
International Bank for Reconstruction and Development	394·8	564·7	810·3	1,298·7	1,564·7	1,812·5	1,847·8	1,775·0	16,082·8
International Finance Corportation	20·9	45·6	45·3	83·5	100·4	100·8	106·2	155·1	787·6
International Development Association	256·4	348·8	105·4	369·3	569·4	559·0	671·0	1,706·5	5,595·5
Inter-American Development Bank	183·1	437·6	385·4	489·2	688·1	614·5	536·3	864·7	5,090·9
Asian Development Bank	—	—	5·0	65·6	91·5	223·2	265·9	360·6	1,001·7
African Development Bank	—	—	5·3	0·1	14·6	18·9	22·1	27·8	88·7
UN Development Programme	116·7	178·1	184·5	198·3	178·0	250·0	199·9	182·1	2,407·4
UN Children's Fund and UN regular program of technical assistance and specialized agencies	67·0	42·6	56·5	51·5	53·0	84·4	62·9	76·5	854·2
European Community	123·0	182·3	189·9	141·1	98·5	173·3	188·9	251·9	2,203·8
Total	1,161·9	1,799·7	1,787·6	2,697·3	3,338·2	3,836·6	3,901·0	5,390·2	34,112·6

Table 14.5
Assistance from international organizations to developing countries, gross commitments, FYs 1963 and 1967–73

* Net commitments.
Note: Data for UN programs are calendar-year figures, shown in the fiscal year in which the calendar year ends. All other data are for US fiscal years.
Source: US Agency for International Development, Office of Financial Management, Statistics and Reports Division, *US Overseas Loans and Grants and Assistance from International Organizations: Obligations and Loan Authorizations, 1 July 1945–30 June 1973,* p. 178.

inflation. Aid flows are usually calculated at nominal levels and tend to show a steady rise over time. However, when deflated for rising prices, the actual real volume of aid from most donor countries (notably the United States) has declined substantially during the last decade.

Quoting statistics on the volume, direction and trends in development assistance, however, is of little relevance without an understanding of the ultimate objectives of foreign aid and its role and/or limitations in promoting economic and social development. But this presents difficulties. For the actual definition of aid and the meaning and motives attached to it may vary from donor country to donor country and from one multilateral development assistance agency to another. More important, there are likely to be fundamental differences in attitudes and motivations between donor and recipient countries. Aid is thus a complex and confusing term especially when it is used to cover a variety of resource transfers from one country to another. Many of these, as we have seen, may be military and/or political in nature and have nothing to do with assisting economic development.

Because foreign aid is seen differently by donor and recipient countries, we must first analyze the giving and receiving process from these two often contradictory viewpoints. One of the major criticisms of the literature on foreign aid is that it has concentrated almost exclusively on the motives and objectives of donor countries while devoting little attention to why LDCs accept aid and what they perceive it will accomplish. We therefore examine the aid question first from these differing perspectives. We then summarize the conflicting views of the effects of traditional aid relationships over the past two decades, look at the emerging new aid role of OPEC oil nations and conclude with an analysis of how development assistance can be made more effective.

Donor countries give aid primarily because it is in their political, strategic and/or economic self-interest to do so. While some development assistance may be motivated by moral and humanitarian reasons to assist the less fortunate (e.g. emergency relief programs), there is no historical evidence to suggest that over longer periods of time donor nations assist others without expecting some corresponding benefits (political, economic, military, etc.) in return. We can, therefore, characterize the foreign aid motivations of donor nations into two broad, but often interrelated, categories: political and economic.

2. Why donors give aid

This has been by far the primary motivation of aid-granting nations, especially the major donor country the United States. Foreign aid has been viewed from its very beginnings in the late 1940s under the Marshall Plan, when the United States set out to reconstruct the war-torn economies of Western Europe, as a means of containing the international spread of Communism. When the balance of 'cold war' interests shifted from Europe to the Third World in the mid-1950s, the policy of containment embodied in the US aid program dictated a shift in emphasis toward political, economic and military support for 'friendly' less developed nations, especially those considered geographically strategic. Most aid programs to developing countries were, therefore, oriented more towards purchasing their security and propping up their sometimes shaky regimes than promoting long-term social and economic development. The successive shifts in emphasis from South Asia, to Southeast Asia, to Latin Americas, the Middle East and back to Southeast Asia during the 1950s and 1960s reflects the changes in US strategic and political interests more than changing evaluations of economic need. The relative neglect of Africa throughout the period supports the validity of this proposition.

A. Political motivations

Even the Alliance for Progress, inaugurated in the early 1960s with such fanfare and noble rhetoric about promoting Latin American economic development, was in reality formulated primarily as a direct response to the rise of Fidel Castro in Cuba and the perceived threat of communist takeovers in other Latin American countries. As soon as the security issue lost its urgency, however, and other more pressing problems came to the fore – the war in Vietnam, the growing dollar crisis, the rise in US domestic violence, etc. – the Alliance for Progress stagnated and began to fizzle out. Our point is simply that where aid is seen primarily as furthering donor-country interests, the flow of funds tends to vary in accordance with the *donor's* political assessment of changing international situations and *not* the relative need of different potential recipients.

The experience of other major donor countries like Great Britain and France has been similar to that of the United States. Although obvious exceptions can be cited (e.g. Sweden, Norway, perhaps Canada), it remains widely agreed that donor countries have utilized foreign aid largely as a political lever to prop-up or underpin 'friendly' political regimes in Third World countries; regimes whose continued existence was perceived to be in the 'national security' interests of Western nations. Most 'socialist aid', especially that of the Soviet Union, grew out of essentially the same political and strategic motivations, although the form and content of that 'aid' may have been different.

Within the broad context of political and strategic priorities, foreign aid programs of the developed nations have had a strong economic

B. Economic motivations: 'two-gap' models and other criteria

rationale. In fact, while the political motivation may have been of paramount importance, the economic rationale was at least given greater lip-service as the overriding motivation for assistance.

The principal economic arguments which have been advanced in support of foreign aid are as follows:

1. Foreign exchange   External finance (both loans and grants) can play a critical role in
constraints   supplementing domestic resources in order to relieve savings or more important foreign exchange bottlenecks. This is the familiar 'two-gap' analysis of foreign assistance mentioned briefly in the previous section on private investment[7].

The basic argument of the two-gap model is that most developing countries are faced either with a shortage of domestic savings to match investment opportunities or a shortage of foreign exchange to finance needed imports of capital and intermediate goods. Most two-gap models assume that the savings (domestic real resources) and foreign exchange gaps are unequal in magnitude and that they are mutually independent; that is, there is no substitutability between savings and foreign exchange. (This assumption is obviously unreal but it greatly facilitates the mathematical analysis.)

These assumptions imply that one of the two gaps will be 'binding' or 'dominant' for any LDC at a given point in time. For example, if the savings gap is dominant this would imply that the country is operating at full employment and is not using all of its foreign exchange earnings. It may have enough foreign exchange to purchase additional capital goods from abroad but there is not enough excess domestic labor or other productive resources to carry out additional investment projects. The importation of such capital goods would only direct domestic resources from other activities and probably lead to inflation. As a result, 'excess' foreign exchange, including foreign aid, might be spent on the importation of luxury consumption goods. Such a country is said to have a shortage of 'productive resources' which, from a different viewpoint, can be regarded as a shortage in saving. An outstanding example of 'savings gap' nations would be the Arab oil states (note, however that the savings gap analysis overlooks the possibility that excess foreign exchange *can* be used to purchase productive resources – for example, Saudi Arabia and Iran use their surplus petrodollars to pay for hired labor from other non-oil-exporting countries in the region and overseas). Savings gap countries therefore do not need foreign aid.

Most developing countries, however, are assumed to fall into the second category where the foreign exchange gap is binding. These countries have excess productive resources (mostly labor) and all available foreign exchange is being used for imports. The existence of complementary domestic resources would permit them to undertake new investment projects if they had the external finance to import new capital goods and associated technical assistance. Foreign aid, therefore, can play a critical role in overcoming the foreign exchange constraint and raising the real rate of economic growth.

Algebraically, the simple two-gap model can be formulated as follows:

(*a*) *The 'savings' constraint or gap* – Starting with the identity that capital inflows (i.e. the difference between imports and exports) add to investible resources (i.e. domestic saving), the savings-investment restriction can be written as:

$$I \leqslant F + sY \tag{1}$$

where F is the amount of capital inflows. If F plus sY exceeds I and the economy is at full capacity, a savings gap is said to exist.

(b) *The 'foreign exchange' constraint or gap* – If LDC investment has a marginal import share m_1 (typically ranging from 30 to 60 per cent in most LDCs) and the marginal propensity to import out of a unit of GNP (usually around 10 to 15 per cent) is given by the parameter m_2, then the foreign exchange constraint or gap can be written as:

$$m_1 I + m_2 Y - E \leqslant F \tag{2}$$

where E is the exogenous level of exports.

The term F enters both of the above inequality constraints and, therefore, becomes the critical factor in the analysis. If F, E and Y are initially assigned an exogenous current value, only one of the above two inequalities will prove binding; that is, investment (and therefore the output growth rate) will be constrained to a lower level by one of the inequalities. Countries can therefore be classified according to whether the savings or foreign exchange constraint is binding. More important from the viewpoint of foreign aid analysis is the observation that the impact of increased capital inflows will be greater where the foreign exchange gap (eqn. 2) rather than the savings gap (eqn. 1) is binding. Thus, two-gap models provide a crude methodology for determining the relative need and ability of different LDCs to use foreign aid effectively.

The problem is that such gap forecasts are very mechanistic and are themselves constrained by the necessity of 'fixing' import parameters and assigning exogenous values to exports and net capital inflows. In the case of exports, this is particularly constricting since a liberalization of trade relations between the developed and the developing world would contribute more towards relieving foreign exchange gaps than foreign aid. Although E and F are substitutable in equation (2), they can have quite different indirect effects, especially in the case where F represents interest-bearing loans that need to be repaid. Thus, the alteration of import and export parameters through both LDC and developed country government policy can in reality determine whether the savings or foreign exchange constraint is restricting the further growth of national output (or, in fact, whether neither is binding).

2. Growth and savings

External assistance also is assumed to facilitate and accelerate the process of development by generating *additional* domestic savings as a result of the higher growth rates which it is presumed to induce. Eventually it is hoped that the need for concessional aid will disappear as local resources become sufficient to give the development process a self-sustaining character.

3. Technical assistance

Financial assistance needs to be supplemented by 'technical assistance' in the form of high level manpower transfers to assure that aid funds are most efficiently utilized to generate economic growth. The 'manpower' gap filling is thus analogous to the financial gap filling process mentioned earlier.

4. Absorptive capacity

Finally the amount of aid should be determined by the recipient country's 'absorptive capacity', a euphemism for its ability to use aid funds wisely and productively (often, the way donors want them to be used). Typically, it is the donor countries which decide which LDCs are to receive aid, how much, in what form (i.e. loans or grants, financial and/or technical assistance), for what purposes and under what conditions on the basis of their (i.e. the developed countries') assessment of LDC absorptive capacities. But the total amount of aid rarely has anything to do with Third World absorptive capacities; typically it is a residual and low priority element in donor country expenditure. In most instances, the recipient countries often have had little say in the matter.

C. Economic motivations and self-interest   The above arguments on behalf of foreign aid as a crucial ingredient for LDC development should not mask the fact that even at the strictly economic level, definite benefits accrue to donor countries as a result of their aid programs. The increasing tendency towards providing loans instead of outright grants (interest-bearing loans now constitute about 70 per cent of all aid as compared to less than 40 per cent in earlier periods) and towards 'tying' aid to the exports of donor countries has saddled many LDCs with substantial debt repayment burdens. It has also increased their import costs often by as much as 20 to 40 per cent. These extra import costs arise because aid which is 'tied' to donor country exports limits the receiving nation's freedom to 'shop around' for low cost and suitable capital and intermediate goods. Tied aid in this sense is a 'second best' option to untied aid (and perhaps also freer trade through a reduction of developed country import barriers). It thus may still be desirable from a LDC's economic point of view. As one former US aid official candidly put it[8]:

The biggest single misconception about the foreign aid program is that we send money abroad. We don't. Foreign aid consists of American equipment, raw materials, expert services, and food – all provided for specific development projects which we ourselves review and approve . . . Ninety-three percent of AID funds are spent directly in the United States to pay for these things. Just last year some 4,000 American firms in 50 states received $1·3 billion in AID funds for products supplied as part of the foreign aid program.

Similarly, a former British Minister of Overseas Development once noted that 'About two-thirds of our aid is spent on goods and services from Britain . . . trade follows aid. We equip a factory overseas and later on we get orders for spare parts and replacements . . . [aid] is in our long-term interest'[9].

3. Why LDC recipients accept aid   The reasons why Third World nations, at least until recently, have been very eager to accept aid even in its most stringent and restrictive forms have been given much less attention than why donors provide aid. This is especially puzzling in view of the many instances where both parties may have conflicting rather than congruent motives and interests. Basically, however, one can identify three reasons – one major and two minor – why LDCs have sought foreign aid.

The major reason is clearly economic in concept and practice. Third World countries have often tended to accept uncritically the proposition, typically advanced by developed-country economists, taught in all university 'development' courses, and supported by reference to 'success' cases like Taiwan, Israel and South Korea to the exclusion of many more 'failures', that aid is a crucial and essential ingredient in the development process. It supplements scarce domestic resources; it helps to transform the economy structurally; and it contributes to the achievement of LDC 'take-offs' into self-sustaining economic growth. Thus, the economic rationale for aid in LDCs is based largely on their acceptance of the donor's perceptions of what they, the poor countries, require to promote their economic development.

The basic area of conflict arises, therefore, not out of any disagreement about the role of aid but about its amount and conditions. LDCs, naturally, would like to have more aid in the form of outright grants or longer term low cost loans with a minimum of strings attached. This means the abolition of tying aid to donor exports and the granting of greater latitude to recipient countries to decide for themselves what is in their best long-run development interests.

The two minor though still important motivations for LDCs to seek aid are political and moral. In some countries aid is seen by both donor and recipient as providing greater political leverage to the existing leadership to suppress opposition and maintain itself in power. In such instances 'assistance' takes the form not only of financial resource transfers but military and internal security reinforcement as well. While South Vietnam represents the most dramatic illustration of this 'aid' phenomenom in the 1960s, a number of other Third World nations have this political motivation. The problem is that once aid is accepted, the ability of recipient governments to extricate themselves from implied political and/or economic obligations to donors and to prevent donor governments from interfering in their internal affairs can be greatly diminished.

Finally, we come to the moral motivation. Whether on grounds of basic humanitarian responsibilities of the rich towards the welfare of the poor or because of a belief that the rich nations owe the poor 'conscience money' for past exploitation, many proponents of foreign aid in both developed and developing countries believe that rich nations have an obligation to support the economic and social development of the Third World. They then go on to link this moral obligation with the need for greater LDC autonomy with respect to the allocation and use of aid funds.

4. The effects of aid

The controversy over the economic effects of aid like that related to private foreign investment is fraught with disagreements. On one side are the 'economic traditionalists' who argue that aid has indeed helped to promote growth and structural transformation in many LDCs[10]. There are others who have argued that aid does not promote faster growth but may in fact retard it by substituting for, rather than, supplementing domestic savings and investment and by exacerbating LDC balance of payments deficits as a result of rising debt repayment obligations[11], and tying aid to donor-country exports.

Aid is further criticized for focusing on and stimulating the growth of the modern sector thereby increasing the 'gap' in living standards between the rich and the poor in Third World countries. Some would even assert that foreign aid has been a positive force for 'anti-development' in the sense that it both retards growth through reduced saving and worsens income inequalities[12]. Rather than relieving economic 'bottlenecks' and filling 'gaps', aid (and for that matter, private foreign assistance) not only widens existing savings and foreign exchange resource gaps but may even create new ones, e.g. urban–rural or modern sector–traditional sector gaps.

On the donor side, there has been growing disenchantment in recent years with foreign aid as domestic issues like inflation, unemployment and balance-of-payments problems gain increasing priority over international cold war politics. One often hears the expression 'aid weariness' used to describe the attitudes of developed countries towards foreign assistance. Taxpayers have become more concerned with domestic economic problems especially as they realize increasingly that their tax moneys allocated to foreign aid may be benefiting primarily the small elites of LDCs who may in fact be richer than themselves.

14.3 OPEC and development assistance

1. Surplus 'petrodollars' Instead of looking only at the traditional aid relationships between the developed 'North' and the underdeveloped 'South', we should also take into account the vast new potential for intra-Third World development assistance growing out of the enormous surplus oil revenues currently being generated by the thirteen members of the Organization of Petroleum Exporting Nations (OPEC). In 1974 alone, a total of $54 billion of *surplus* oil revenues was available for 'recycling' to the non-oil-exporting nations. Some estimates are that these surplus revenues may total as much as $300 billion by 1980. While by far the greatest proportion of the 1974 surplus 'petrodollars' were recycled back to the developed industrial nations, a total of $9·5 billion was earmarked for loans and investments in Third World nations with almost $7·2 billion going into direct bilateral assistance (see Table 14.6). It is to be hoped that an even greater proportion of future surplus oil revenues will actually find its way back to the non-oil-exporting developing nations whose economies were hit the hardest by the dramatic increase in international oil prices (an estimated additional import cost of $13 billion in 1974 and 1975).

There are a number of possible ways in which the major oil exporters can play a significant new role in assisting less fortunate Third World countries. To a large degree they are already initiating such a role. For example, the principal Arab members of OPEC (notably Saudi Arabia and Iran) have been extending sizable grants and credits to neighbouring Arab states like Egypt and Syria. Although much of this assistance is in the form of military and political support, a good deal of it is for genuine economic development. Additionally, Arab oil producers have created an Arab Fund for Economic and Social Development with an initial capital endowment of $300 million as well as a Fund for African Development with an initial outlay of $250 million. A few of the Persian Gulf oil states which have close religious and technical ties with Pakistan are stepping up their development assistance to that country. Outside the Middle East, Venezuela has embarked on an ambitious aid programme to assist needy Latin American nations, while Nigeria has recently initiated an $80 million Special African Aid Fund to be administered by the African Development Bank and to provide long-term, low interest loans to the neediest of African nations. Table 14.6 provides a detailed breakdown of bilateral and multilateral OPEC aid commitments and disbursements in 1974 while Table 14.7 shows the major recipients of OPEC bilateral aid during the same year. Note in particular that four countries, Egypt, Syria, Pakistan and India, received almost 84 per cent of all OPEC commitments. Finally, Fig. 14.1 shows how much more active OPEC nations have already become in the aid field in comparison with the developed countries, at least in terms of the percentage of their GNPs being devoted to development assistance.

	Commitments					Disbursements*				
	Bilateral	Multi-lateral	Total	Oil Revenues*	GNP*	Bilateral	Multi-lateral	Total	As Percentage of: Oil Revenues	GNP
	($ millions)			(as percentage of)		($ millions)			(as percentage of)	
Algeria	31	108	139	3·8	1·7	15	45	60	1·1	0·7
Iran	2,802	173	2,975	17·1	10·1	600	2	602	3·4	2·0
Iraq	222	58	280	4·1	2·9	80	35	115	1·7	1·2
Kuwait	957	384	1,341	19·1	15·8	460	70	530	7·6	6·2
Libya	178	241	419	5·5	3·4	45	60	105	1·4	0·9
Nigeria	1	16	17	0·2	0·2	1	15	16	0·2	0·1
Quatar	97	60	157	9·8	7·4	40	20	60	3·7	2·8
Saudi Arabia	2,568	453	3,021	15·1	13·4	650	115	765	3·8	3·4
United Arab Emirates	296	182	478	11·6	10·0	120	45	165	4·0	3·5
Venezuela	20	726	746	7·0	3·6	20	165	185	1·7	0·0
Total	7,172	2,401	9,573	12·1	8·2	2,031	572	2,603	3·3	2·2

* Estimate.

Note: Figures are subject to revision. Some of the disbursement estimates are highly tentative, as are all the comparisons of commitments and disbursements with oil revenue and GNP.

Source: Organization for Economic Co-operation and Development, Development Assistance Directorate, 'Flow of Resources from OPEC Members to Developing Countries', Document No. DD–403, 6 December 1974, Table 2, p. 8.

Table 14.6 OPEC aid commitments and disbursements, 1974

2. Two new initiatives

Of much greater potential significance, however, were two major OPEC initiatives to assist other developing countries to increase their agricultural potential and to overcome short-run balance of payments difficulties. First, OPEC, led by Saudi Arabia, initiated and contributed $600 million towards the establishment in 1976 of a new $1·2 billion International Fund for Agricultural Development. The other $600 million was contributed by the developed nations. The fund doubled the external resources being given or loaned at low interest for long-term agricultural development in Asia, Africa and Latin America and will thus help to alleviate the problem of chronic world hunger. Its financial resources are to be replenished each year with Saudi Arabia being the largest single contributor. The voting power within the new fund is divided one-third for OPEC countries, one-third for the developing nations and one-third for the developed world. Thus, for the first time in history there now exists a major international financial institution which is *controlled* by the Third World. This, indeed, is a remarkable breakthrough in a global economic system which has in the past been totally dominated by the rich nations. It is hoped that it will provide a precedent for future aid relationships in which economically more fortunate developing nations begin to assume increased responsibility for the welfare of their less fortunae colleagues.

The second major OPEC initiative, sponsored jointly by Iran and Venezuela, was the decision taken in January 1976 .o set aside an annual fund of $800 million to assist those Third World countries whose economies were hurt most severely by the fiverold increases in oil prices. This new fund, which represents an equivalent price

	Commitments		Disbursements*	
	($ millions)	(as percentage of total)	(millions)	(as percentage of total)
Arab Countries				
Egypt	3,121*	43·5*	765	37·7
Syria	1,003*	14·0*	325	16·0
Jordan	185*	2·6*	140	6·9
Mauritania	153*	2·1*	25	1·2
Sudan	107	1·5	70	3·4
Somalia	82	1·1	25	1·2
Morocco	80	1·1	25	1·2
Tunisia	54	0·8	15	0·7
Bahrain	21	0·3	10	0·5
Yemen, Arab Rep.	19	0·3	15	0·7
Yemen, People's Dem. Rep.	12	0·2	10	0·5
Other	8	0·1	8	0·4
Africa				
Malagasy Republic	114*	1·6*	—	—
Guinea	16	0·2	5	0·2
Uganda	12	0·2	2	0·1
Senegal	11	0·1	5	0·2
Other	79	1·1	46	2·3
Asia				
Pakistan	957*	13·3*	355	17·5
India	945	13·2	75	3·7
Sri Lanka	86	1·2	35	1·7
Bangladesh	82	1·1	50	2·5
Latin America				
Guyana	15	0·2	15	0·7
Honduras	5	0·1	5	0·2
Europe				
Malta	5	0·1	5	0·2
Total	7,172*	100·0	2,031	100·0

Table 14.7
Recipients of bilateral aid from OPEC
countries 1974

*Estimate.

Note: Figures are subject to revision. Breakdown between Egypt, Syria and Jordan is tentative. Commitment figures for Pakistan include $200 million by Saudi Arabia and Kuwait which were not made public but are believed to have been made.

Source: Organization for Economic Co-operation and Development, Development Assistance Directorate, 'Flow of Resources from OPEC Members to Developing Countries,' Document No. DD-403, 6 December 1974, Table 4, p. 10.

reduction of approximately 8 cents per barrel of oil (at 1975 prices), provides long-term, interest-free loans to aid other developing nations to meet short-term balance of payments deficits and to finance needed development projects and programs. Although initially financed for one year only, the fund if proven successful, will continue to operate until such time as this form of development assistance is no longer necessary.

3. Other possibilities Among the other possible aid strategies which the now wealthy oil exporting nations might pursue are the following:

A. Bilateral Aid Expanded bilateral assistance programs ranging from outright grants to low-interest, long-term concessional loans would obviously be one of the most important mechanisms for recycling surplus petrodollars to needy developing nations. Moreover, direct private or public investment projects in fertilizer and energy production in the poorest countries would assist these nations to meet their current and future food requirements.

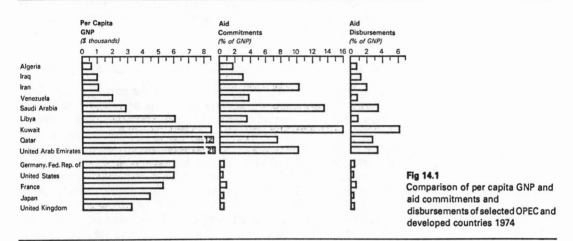

Fig 14.1
Comparison of per capita GNP and aid commitments and disbursements of selected OPEC and developed countries 1974

Sources: The Economist, 15 February 1975, 72, and Report by the Chairman of the Development Assistance Committee, *Development Cooperation, 1974 Review,* OECD Paris, (1974) 44.

B. Expanded financial support for international assistance agencies

An alternative to direct intra-Third World bilateral assistance would be the channelling of more surplus oil revenues into the major international and regional financial institutions such as the World Bank, the International Monetary Fund, and the Asian, African, and Inter-American Development Banks. Such indirect assistance would have the advantage of all multilateral over bilateral assistance: the minimization of political and/or ideological 'strings'.

C. Concessional oil sales

A third possibility would be for OPEC to establish a 'two-tier' or dual price system for their oil sales – a much higher 'market' price for rich industrial nations and a considerably lower 'subsidized' price for Third World oil importers. The problem here as with all dual price systems, is the likelihood of 'black market' operations. In the case of oil, this would probably take the form of the diversion (i.e. re-export) of cheap oil from some Third World nations to the developed nations. An easier and much more feasible possibility, therefore, would be for OPEC nations to sell their oil at a common world price but allow poor Third World Nations to purchase this oil at concessional terms – e.g. payment over a 40- to 50-year period at say 3 per cent interest. In effect, at currently high international interest rates, the 'grant' component of such long-term credits would be in excess of 50 per cent (i.e. the 'real' cost to Third World importers would be less than half of the actual market price had they been required to borrow funds to purchase the oil at higher world market interest rates and with considerably shorter repayment periods of 10 to 20 years).

D. Looking to the future

Despite the economic hardships which the quadrupling of international oil prices has had on most less developed nations (see Ch. 17), the oil-exporting countries are nevertheless riding a crest of popularity among their Third World colleagues. They are experiencing this strong sense of identification largely because they have shown that it is possible for small countries, acting together, to bring the big industrial giants to their economic knees. But such 'good will' and peer group identification will quickly vanish if wealthy OPEC nations do not rapidly seize the opportunity to step into the foreign aid vacuum and assume their important new role of economic leadership within the Third World.[13].

14.4 Conclusions: towards a new view of foreign aid

The combination of 'aid disillusionment' on the part of many Third World recipients and 'aid weariness' among some traditional developed country donors does not augur well for the continuation of past relationships. But we would argue that this is desirable rather than disheartening. Dissatisfaction on both sides creates the possibility for new arrangements and new relationships of greater congruence of interest and motivation on the part of both donor and recipient. The OPEC-sponsored International Fund for Agricultural Development and the $1 billion fund for balance of payments adjustments are two outstanding examples of such new aid relationships. A lower total volume of aid from the developed nations but one which is geared more to the real development needs of recipients and which permits them a greater degree of flexibility and autonomy in meeting their own development priorities would on balance represent a positive step. The rising proportion of development assistance funds now being channelled through multilateral assistance agencies whose political motives are presumably less narrowly defined compared with those of individual donor countries, is also a welcome development. It tends to minimize one of the major criticisms of past foreign aid practices, that is, the linking of economic aid to political conditions.

More aid is better than less aid for some of the reasons outlined earlier. But from the viewpoint of LDC recipients whatever the source and volume of aid the more it takes the form of outright grants and concessional loans, the less it is tied to donor exports, the more local autonomy is permitted in its allocation and the more it is supplemented by the reduction of donor-country tariff and non-tariff trade barriers against Third World exports, the greater will be the development impact of this foreign assistance. (In fact, many argue that better opportunities for profitable trade with the industrial nations are much more vital to Third World economic growth than quantitative increases in development assistance.) Although it may seem wishful thinking to imagine that rich Western countries (both capitalist and socialist) will move in the direction of such real development-oriented trade and aid policies that at first glance appear to be against their economic self-interests, on closer examination this viewpoint may not be so far-fetched after all.

As the realities of global interdependence slowly penetrate the political perceptions of developed nation governments, and perhaps eventually their populace as well, it may begin to dawn on them that their real long-run economic and political interests do in fact lie with the achievement of broad-based development in Third World nations. Eliminating poverty, minimizing inequality and in general raising levels of living for the masses of LDC peoples may just turn out to be in the most fundamental 'self-interest' of developed nations, not because of any humanitarian ideals (though one would hope that these are present) but simply because in the long-run there can be no two futures for mankind, one for the very rich, the other for the very poor, without the proliferation of global conflict.

Enlightened self-interest, therefore, may be the only peg on which to build the hope for a 'new international economic order', one in which both foreign assistance and private foreign investment can begin to make a real and lasting contribution to Third World development.

Notes

1. From 'Self reliance and international reform', *World Development*, 2, no. 6 (1974).
2. P. P. Streeten, 'The multinational enterprise and the theory of development policy', *World Development*, 1, no. 10 (1973).
3. The question of whether or not 'nationalized' foreign enterprises or confiscated domestic private property (e.g. large but unproductive land holdings) should be compensated and, if so, at what amount is typically a political issue. In general, however, such compensation should depend on (*a*) the manner in which the enterprise or property was acquired; (*b*) the historical and replacement costs of the assets confiscated; (*c*) the nature and record of the enterprise's relations with the government and people of the confiscating country prior to confiscation; and (*d*) the financial benefits and economic returns which have already been reaped prior to confiscation. Compensation should be based on a careful evaluation of the above four factors with (*a*) and (*c*) providing the political criteria and (*b*) and (*d*) the economic rationale for the overall decision. For an early economic defence of policies of confiscation and nationalization of foreign owned property in Third World countries, see Martin Bronfenbrenner, 'The appeal of confiscation in economic development', *Economic Development and Cultural Change*, April 1955, 201–8.
4. Jagdish N. Bhagwati, 'Amount and sharing of aid', in *Assisting Developing Countries: Problems of Debt, Burden-Sharing, Jobs and Trade*, Praeger, New York (1972), 72–3.
5. Ibid., p. 73.
6. Even these figures can be very misleading and exaggerate the actual 'aid' (i.e. concessional) component of development assistance. For a devastating critique of how 'official development assistance' statistics can be very misleading or downright false, see G. Myrdal, *The Challenge of World Poverty*, Pantheon, New York (1970), 10.
7. See H. B. Chenery and A. M. Strout, 'Foreign assistance and economic development', *American Economic Review*, September 1966, 680–733.
8. William S. Gaud, 'Foreign aid: what it is; how it works; why we provide it', *Department of State Bulletin*, LIX, no. 1537 (1968).
9. Statement by Mr Earl Grinstead, reported in *Overseas Development*, November 1968, p. 9. In a similar vein one of the staunchest defenders of the role of foreign aid in the development process, economist Hollis Chenery, admitted that 'In the most general sense, the main objective of foreign assistance, as of many other tools of foreign policy, is to produce the kind of political and economic environment in the world in which the United States can best pursue its own social goals'. H. Chenery, 'Objectives and criteria of foreign assistance', in *The U.S. and the Development Economies*, G. Ranis (ed.), Norton, New York (1964), 88.
10. See, for example, H. B. Chenery and N. G. Carter, 'Foreign assistance and development performance', *American Economic Review*, LXIII, no. 2 (1973), 459–68.
11. For example, by the end of 1975, the Third World was in debt to the tune of over $90 billion, compared with $61 billion at the end of 1973. Amortization and interest payments were more than 9 per cent of gross foreign exchange earnings compared to 7 per cent in 1974. These debt claims will continue to rise rapidly for the remainder of the 1970s.
12. See, for example, Keith Griffen and J. L. Enos, 'Foreign assistance: objectives and consequences', *Economic Development and Cultural Change*, April 1970, 313–27.
13. By early 1976 as a result of diminishing oil revenues and rapidly expanding domestic development programs there were signs of a partial retrenchment among OPEC countries in their aid-giving activities to other Third World nations. The net negative balance on current and capital accounts between other Third World countries and OPEC once again began to widen while OPEC's 'good will' showed signs of evaporating under the pressure of chronic payments deficits, especially in the 'least developed' countries.

Concepts for review

private foreign investment
foreign aid
grants versus loans
foreign monetary reserves
multinational donor agencies
bilateral donor agencies
debt burden
two-gap models
'soft' loans
private transfer payments

'strong' currencies
savings-investment 'gap'
foreign exchange 'gap'
'tied' aid
absorptive capacity
multinational corporations
transfer pricing
'inappropriate' products
technical assistance
aid weariness

Questions for discussion

1. The emergence of giant multinational corporations over the past two decades are said to have altered the very nature of international economic activity. In what ways do these MNCs affect the structure and pattern of trading relationships between the developed and underdeveloped world?
2. Summarize the arguments 'for' and 'against' the role and impact of private foreign investment in less developed countries. What strategies might LDCs adopt to make private foreign investment fit their development aspirations better without destroying all incentives for foreign investors?
3. How important is 'foreign aid' for the economies of the Third World in relation to their other sources of foreign exchange receipts? Explain the various forms which development assistance can take and distinguish between bilateral and multilateral assistance. Which do you think is more desirable and why?
4. What is meant by 'tied aid'? Both capitalist and socialist nations have increasingly shifted from grants to loans and from untied to tied loans and grants during the past decade. What are the major disadvantages of tied aid especially when this aid comes in the form of interest bearing loans?
5. Under what conditions and terms do you think LDCs should seek and accept foreign aid in the future? If aid cannot be obtained on such terms do you think LDCs should accept whatever they can get? Explain your answer.

Further readings

For an economic analysis of private foreign investment and the role and influences of multinational corporations, see: (a) Sanjaya Lall, 'Less developed countries and private foreign direct investment: a review article', *World Development,* **2**, nos. 4 and 5 (1974); (b) Gustav Ranis, 'The multinational corporation as an instrument of development', *Discussion Paper no. 123,* Yale Economic Growth Center, September, 1974; (c) Paul Streeten, 'The multinational enterprise and the theory of development policy', *World Development,* **1**, no. 10 (1973).

For an account of the power and inside workings of multinationals whose decisions shape the lives of all peoples and often transcend national and international laws, see: R. J. Barnet and R. E. Müller, *Global Reach: The Power of Multinational Corporations,* Simon and Schuster, New York (1975).

On the question of the 'benefits' and 'costs' of foreign aid see: (a) Lester B. Pearson (chairman), *Partners in Development: Report of the Commission on International Development,* Praeger, New York (1969), Chs. 1, 6, 7, 8, 9 and 11; (b) Gunnar Myrdal, *The Challenge of World Poverty,* Pantheon, New York (1970), Chs. 10 and 11; (c) J. N. Bhagwati and R. S. Eckaus (eds), *Foreign Aid,* Penguin Modern Economic Readings, Harmondsworth (1970); (d) Charles R. Frank Jr., 'Debt and terms of aid' in *Assisting Developing Countries,* ODC Studies – I, Praeger, New York (1972), 3–66; (e) Jagdish N. Bhagwati, 'Amount and Sharing of Aid' in *Assisting Developing Countries,* ODC Studies – I, New York, (1972) 69–128; (f) George C. Abbot, 'Two concepts of foreign aid', *World Development,* **1**, no. 9 (1973).

Finally, a good review and analysis of OPEC aid programs to developing countries can be found in: Maurice J. Williams, 'The aid programs of the OPEC countries', *Foreign Affairs,* 54, no. 2 (1976), 308–24.

Possibilities and prospects | Part IV

| Chapter 15 | **Development planning: Theory and practice** |

Planning is the exercise of intelligence to deal with facts and situations as they are and find a way to solve problems.
  Jawaharlal Nehru

If we could first know *where* we are, and *whither* we are tending, we could better judge *what* to do, and how to do it.
  Abraham Lincoln

Introduction: the planning mystique

In the three decades since the Second World War, the pursuit of economic development has been crystallized by the almost universal acceptance of development planning as the surest and most direct route to economic progress. Until recently, few in the Third World would have questioned the advisability or desirability of formulating and implementing a national development plan. Planning has become a way of life in government ministries and every five years or so the latest development plan is paraded out with the greatest fanfare.

But why, until recently, has there been such an aura and mystique about development planning and such universal faith in its obvious utility? Basically, because centralized national planning was widely believed to offer the essential and perhaps the only institutional and organizational mechanism for overcoming the major obstacles to development and for ensuring a sustained high rate of economic growth. In some cases central economic planning even became regarded as a kind of 'open sesame' which would allow Third World nations to pass rapidly through the barrier dividing their pitiably low standard of living from the prosperity of their former rulers. But in order to catch up, poor nations were persuaded and became convinced that they required a comprehensive national plan. The planning record, unfortunately, has not lived up to its advance billing and there now exists a growing scepticism about the planning mystique.

In this chapter we examine the role and limitations of development planning as practised in Third World nations both in its own right and within the broader framework of national economic policy formulation. We start with a brief review of the nature of development planning and a summary of general planning issues. After examining the main arguments for and against the role of planning in underdeveloped societies and reviewing different models of economy-wide planning and project appraisal, we conclude with an analysis of the recent history of LDC planning in practice. In Chapter 16 we take up the broader questions of the role and limitations of economic policy for development and examine some of the positive and negative factors (both economic and non-economic) of substantial state intervention in economic activities.

15.1 The nature of development planning[1]

Economic planning may be described as a deliberate governmental **1. Basic concepts**
attempt to coordinate economic decision making over the long run and
to influence, direct and in some cases even control the level and growth
of a nation's principal economic variables (income, consumption, employment, investment, saving, exports, imports, etc.) in order to achieve
a predetermined set of development objectives. An *economic plan* is
simply a specific set of quantitative economic targets to be reached in a
given period of time. Economic plans may be either comprehensive or
partial. A *comprehensive plan* sets its targets to cover all major aspects
of the national economy. A *partial plan* covers only a part of the
national economy – industry, agriculture, the public sector, the foreign
sector and so forth. Finally, the *planning process* itself can be described
as an exercise in which a government first chooses social objectives,
then sets various targets and finally organizes a framework for implementing, coordinating and monitoring a development plan.

In one of its first publications dealing with developing countries in 1951, the United Nations Department of Economic Affairs distinguished *four types of planning,* each of which has been used in one form or another by most LDCs[2]:

First, . . . it [planning] *refers only to the making of a program of public
expenditure, extending over from one to say ten years. Second, it refers
sometimes to the setting of production targets, whether for private or for
public enterprises, in terms of the input of manpower, of capital, or of
other scarce resources, or use in terms of output. Thirdly, the word may
be used to describe a statement which sets targets for the economy as a
whole, purporting to allocate all scarce resources among the various
branches of the economy. And fourthly, the word is sometimes used to
describe the means which the government uses to try to enforce upon
private enterprise the targets which have been previously determined.*

Proponents of economic planning for developing countries argue that the uncontrolled market economy can, and often does, subject these nations to economic stagnation, fluctuating prices, and low levels of employment. In particular, they claim that the market economy is not geared to the principal operational task of poor countries: how to mobilize limited resources in a way that will bring about the structural change necessary to stimulate a sustained and balanced growth of the entire economy. Planning has come to be accepted, therefore, as an essential and pivotal means of guiding and accelerating economic growth in almost all Third World countries.

2. Planning in 'mixed' Most development plans are formulated and carried out within the
developing economies framework of the 'mixed' economies of the Third World. These
economies are characterized by the existence of an institutional setting
in which part of the productive resources are privately owned and
operated while the other part is controlled by the public sector. The
actual proportionate division of public and private ownership varies
from country to country and neither the private nor the public sector
can really be considered in isolation from the other. However, unlike
market economies where there usually exists only a small degree of
public ownership, LDC mixed economies are distinguished by a substantial amount of government ownership and control. The private
sector typically consists of four distinct forms of individual ownership:
1. the traditional subsistence sector consisting of small-scale private
    farms and handicraft shops selling a part of their produce to local
    markets;
2. small-scale individual or family-owned commercial business and
    service activities;
3. medium-sized commercial enterprises in agriculture, industry,
    trade, and transport owned and operated by local entrepreneurs;
4. large jointly owned or completely foreign-owned manufacturing
    enterprises, mining companies and plantations primarily catering
    to foreign markets but sometimes with substantial local sales. The
    capital for such enterprises usually comes from abroad while, as we
    saw in the previous chapter, a good proportion of the profits tends
    to be transferred overseas.

In the context of such an institutional setting, we can identify two
principal components of development planning in 'mixed' economies:
1. The government's deliberate utilization of domestic saving and
    foreign finance to carry out public investment projects and to
    mobilize and channel scarce resources into areas that can be
    expected to make the greatest contribution towards the realization
    of long-term economic objectives (e.g. the construction of railways,
    schools, hydroelectric projects and other components of 'economic
    infrastructure', as well as the creation of import-substituting indus-
    tries).
2. Governmental economic policy (e.g. taxation, industrial licensing,
    the setting of tariffs and the manipulation of quotas, wages, interest
    rates and prices, etc.) to stimulate, direct and in some cases even
    control private economic activity in order to ensure a harmonious
    relationship between the desires of private businessmen and the
    social objectives of the central government.

The compromise nature of this situation between the extremes of
market inducement and collectivist control is readily evident from the
above simplified characterization of planning in mixed-market
economies. Since most developing countries fall into this category, let
us look now at some of the economic and institutional conditions that
have led many to conclude that planning is necessary if Third World
countries are to accelerate their pace of economic development.

15.2 The rationale for planning in developing economies

The widespread acceptance of planning as a development tool rests on
a number of fundamental economic and institutional arguments of
which the following four are most often put forward:

Markets in LDCs are permeated by imperfections both of structure *1. The market failure*
and operation. Commodity and factor markets are often badly *argument*
organized and the existence of 'distorted prices' often means that
producers and consumers are responding to economic signals and
incentives that are a poor reflection of the 'real' cost to society of these
goods, services and resources. It is therefore argued that governments
have an important role to play in integrating markets and modifying
prices. Moreover, the 'failure' of the market to price factors of production correctly is further assumed to lead to gross disparities between
social and private valuations of alternative investment projects (see
below). In the absence of governmental interference, therefore, the
market is said to lead to a misallocation of present and future resources
or, at least, to one which may not be in the best long-run social
interests. This 'market failure' argument is perhaps the most often
quoted reason for the expanded role of government in underdeveloped countries.

A clear statement of this viewpoint was presented in a 1965 report of
a United Nations Conference on Planning which asserted that[3]:

*It is an integral task of planning to achieve the best possible use of scarce
resources for economic development ... The need for using appropriate criteria for selecting projects arose because of the failure of the
market mechanism to provide a proper guideline. In less-developed
economies, market prices of such factors of production as labour,
capital and foreign exchange deviated substantially from their social
opportunity costs and were not, therefore, a correct measure of the
relative scarcity or abundance of the factor in question.*

A more recent publication of the United States Industrial Development Organization (UNIDO) provides the following explicit 'market
failure' rationale for planning in LDCs[4]:

*Governments can not, and should not, take a merely passive role in the
process of industrial expansion. Planning has become an essential and
integral part of industrial development programmes, for market forces,
by themselves, cannot overcome the deepseated structural rigidities in
the economies of developing countries ... Today the need for some
degree of economic planning is universally recognised. It is, of course,
an integral part of the economy of the Soviet Union and the other
centrally planned countries ... In developing countries, planning is
more feasible and more desirable than in developed market economies.
The greater feasibility is a result of the smaller number of variables that
must be taken into consideration, and the greater desirability stems from
the fact that the automatic mechanisms for co-ordination of individual
actions function less satisfactorily in developing than in developed
economies. Planning in developing countries is made necessary by, inter
alia, the inadequacies of the market as a mechanism to ensure that
individual decisions will optimize economic performance in terms of
society's preferences and economic goals ... The inadequacy of the
market mechanism as a means of allocating resources for industrial
development sometimes results from government policy itself or because
the theoretical assumptions (particularly with respect to the mobility of
the factors of production) do not apply to the actual economic situation.
Even more importantly, the market mechanism cannot properly allow
for the external effects of investment.*

2. The resource Third World economies cannot afford to waste their limited financial
mobilization and allocation and skilled manpower resources on unproductive ventures. Invest-
argument ment projects must be chosen not solely on the basis of a partial
productivity analysis dictated by individual industrial capital/output
ratios but also in the context of an overall development program
which takes account of external economies, indirect repercussions and
long-term objectives. Skilled manpower must be utilized where its
contribution will be most widely felt. Economic planning is assumed to
help modify the restraining influence of limited resources by recognizing the existence of particular constraints and by choosing and coordinating investment projects so as to channel these scarce factors
into their most productive outlets. On the other hand, it is argued that
competitive markets will tend to generate less investment, to direct
that investment into socially low-priority areas (e.g. consumption
goods for the rich) and to disregard the extra benefits to be derived
from a planned and coordinated long-term investment program.

3. The attitudinal or It is often assumed that a detailed statement of national economic and
psychological argument social objectives in the form of a specific development plan can have an
important attitudinal or psychological impact on a diverse and often
fragmented population. It may succeed in rallying the people behind
the government in a national campaign to eliminate poverty, ignorance
and disease. By mobilizing popular support and cutting across class,
caste, racial, religious or tribal factions with the plea to all citizens to
'work together' towards building the nation, an enlightened central
government, through its economic plan, is thought to be best equipped
to provide the needed incentives to overcome the inhibiting and often
divisive forces of sectionalism and traditionalism in a common quest
for widespread material and social progress.

4. The foreign aid argument The formulation of detailed development plans with specific sectoral
output targets and carefully designed investment projects has often
been a necessary condition for the receipt of bilateral and multilateral
foreign aid. In fact, some cynics would argue that the real reason why
LDCs construct development plans is to secure more foreign aid. With
a 'shopping list' of projects, Third World governments are better
equipped to solicit foreign assistance and persuade donors that their
money will be applied as an essential ingredient in a well-conceived
and internally consistent plan of action. To a certain extent this is a
charade, but one whose origin lies partially with developed country
desires for sophisticated and detailed project descriptions within the
framework of a comprehensive development plan.

15.3 The planning process: some basic models

1. Characteristics of the While there exist a great diversity of development plans and planning
planning process techniques, there are some basic characteristics of 'comprehensive'
planning that are common to most developing countries. Killick[5] has
listed the following *six characteristics* as representative:
1. Starting from the political views and goals of the government,
   planning attempts to *define policy objectives,* especially as they
   relate to the future development of the economy;
2. A development plan sets out a *strategy* by means of which it is
   intended to achieve these objectives, which are normally translated
   into specific targets;

3. The plan attempts to present a *centrally coordinated, internally consistent set of principles and policies,* chosen as the optimal means of implementing the strategy and achieving the targets, and intended to be used as a framework to guide subsequent day-to-day decisions;
4. It *comprehends the whole economy* (hence it is 'comprehensive' as against 'colonial' or 'public sector' planning);
5. In order to secure optimality and consistency, the comprehensive plan employs a more-or-less *formalized macro-economic model* (which, however, will often remain unpublished), and this is employed to project the intended future performance of the economy;
6. A development plan typically covers a period of, say, 5 years and finds physical expression as a *medium-term plan document,* which may, however, incorporate a longer-term perspective plan and be supplemented by annual plans.

Although the formulation of a comprehensive plan is the goal of most poor countries, it is sometimes necessary to base such plans on a more partial sectoral analysis. In very poor countries with limited data and minimal industrial diversification, partial plans may be the most that can be accomplished. In general, however, the ideal planning process can be broadly conceived as consisting of three basic stages, each of which is associated with a particular type of planning model.

2. Planning in stages: three basic models

Most development plans are based initially on some more-or-less formalized macro-economic model. Such economy-wide planning models can conveniently be divided into two basic catagories: (*a*) *aggregate growth models* involving macro-economic estimates of planned or required changes in principal economic variables; and (*b*) *multi-sector 'input–output' models* which ascertain (among other things) the production, resource, employment and foreign exchange implications of a given set of final demand targets within an internally consistent framework of inter-industry product flows. Finally, the third and probably most important component of plan formulation is the detailed selection of specific investment projects within each sector through the technique of *project appraisal and social cost–benefit analysis.* These three 'stages' of planning – aggregate, sectoral and project – provide the main intellectual tools of the planning authority.

A. Aggregate growth models: projecting macro-variables

The first and most elementary type of planning model used in almost every developing country is the aggregate growth model. It deals with the entire economy in terms of a limited set of those macro-economic variables deemed most critical to the determination of levels and growth rates of national output: savings, investment, capital stocks, exports, imports, foreign assistance, etc. Aggregate growth models provide a convenient method for forecasting output (and perhaps also employment) growth over a 3- to 5-year period. Almost all such models represent some variant of the basic Harrod–Domar model described in Chapter 3.

Recall that the Harrod–Domar model views limited savings as the major constraint on aggregate economic growth. Given targeted GNP growth rates and a national capital/output ratio, the Harrod–Domar model can be used to specify the amount of domestic saving necessary to generate such growth. In most cases, this necessary amount of domestic saving is not likely to be realized on the basis of existing savings functions, and so the basic policy problem of how to generate additional domestic savings and/or foreign assistance is begun. For planning purposes, the Harrod–Domar model is usually formulated as follows[6].

We start with the assumption that the ratio of total output to reproducible capital is constant so that:

$$K(t) = kY(t) \tag{1}$$

where $K(t)$ is capital stock at time t, $Y(t)$ is total output (GNP) at time t and k is the average (equal to the marginal) capital–output ratio. We assume next that a constant share (s) of output (Y) is always saved (S), so that:

$$I(t) = K(t + 1) - K(t) + \delta K(t) = sY = S(t) \tag{2}$$

where $I(t)$ is gross investment at time t and δ is the fraction of the capital stock depreciated in each period. Now if g is the targeted rate of growth of output such that:

$$g = [Y(t + 1) - Y(t)]/Y(t) = \Delta Y(t)/Y(t) \tag{3}$$

then capital must be growing at the same rate since from equation (1) we know that:

$$\Delta K/K = k \, \Delta Y/K = \frac{k \, \Delta Y/Y}{K/Y} = \Delta Y/Y$$

Using equation (2), we therefore arrive once again at the basic Harrod–Domar growth equation (although this time with a capital depreciation parameter):

$$g = \frac{sY - \delta K}{K} = \frac{s}{k} - \delta \tag{3}$$

Finally, since output growth can also be expressed as the sum of labor force growth (n) and the rate of growth of labor productivity (p), equation (3) can be rewritten for planning purposes as:

$$n + p = \frac{s}{k} - \delta \tag{4}$$

Given an expected rate of labor force and productivity growth (labor force growth can be calculated from readily available demographic information while productivity growth estimates are usually based either on extrapolations of past trends or on assumed constant rate of increase), equation (4) can then be used to estimate whether or not domestic savings will be sufficient to provide an adequate number of new employment opportunities to a growing labor force. One way of doing this is to disaggregate the overall savings function $(S = sY)$ into at least two component sources of saving: normally the propensity to save out of wage income, W, and profit income, π.

Thus, we define

$$W + \pi = Y$$

and

$$s_\pi \Pi + s_w W = I \tag{5}$$

where s_π and s_w are the savings propensities from Π and W respectively. By manipulating equation (3) and substituting (5) into it, we arrive at a modified Harrod–Domar growth equation:

$$k(g + \delta) = (s_\pi - s_w)(\pi/Y) + s_w \tag{6}$$

which can then serve as a formula for ascertaining the adequacy of current saving out of profit and wage income. For example, if a 4 per cent growth rate is desired and if $\delta = 0 \cdot 03$, $K = 3 \cdot 0$ and $(\pi/Y) = 0 \cdot 5$, then equation (6) reduces to $0 \cdot 42 = s_\pi + s_w$ [7]. If savings out of capital income amounts to 25 per cent, then wage earners must save at a 17 per cent rate to achieve the targeted rate of growth. In the absence of such a savings rate out of labor income, the government could pursue a variety of policies to raise domestic saving and/or seek foreign assistance.

In countries where inadequate foreign exchange reserves are believed to be the principal constraint on economic growth, the aggregate growth model typically employed is some variant of the 'two-gap' model described in Chapter 14. (Two-gap models are simply Harrod–Domar models generalized to take foreign trade problems into account.) In either case, however, aggregate growth models can provide only a rough first approximation of the general directions which an economy might take. As such, they rarely constitute the operational development plan.[Perhaps, more important, the simplicity and relatively low cost (in terms of data collection) of using aggregate growth models can often blind one to their very real limitations, especially when application is carried out in a much too mechanical fashion. Average capital–output ratios are notoriously difficult to estimate and may bear little relation to marginal capital–output ratios, while savings rates can be highly unstable.] This requires a more disaggregated multi-sector model of economic activity like the well-known input–output approach.

B. Input–output models and sectoral projections

The basic idea

A much more sophisticated approach to development planning is to utilize some variant of the *inter-industry* or *input–output model* in which the activities of the major industrial sectors of the economy are interrelated with one another by means of a set of simultaneous algebraic equations expressing the specific production processes or technologies of each industry. All industries are viewed both as producers of *outputs* and users of *inputs* from other industries. For example, the agricultural sector is both a producer of output (e.g. wheat) and user of inputs from, say, the manufacturing sector (e.g. machinery, fertilizer, etc.). Thus, direct and indirect repercussions of planned changes in the demand for the products of any one industry on output, employment and imports of all other industries can be traced throughout the entire economy in an intricate web of economic interdependence. Given the planned output targets for each sector of the economy, the inter-industry model can be used to determine intermediate material, import, labor and capital requirements with the result that a comprehensive economic plan with mutually consistent production levels and resource requirements can, in theory, be constructed.

Inter-industry models range from simple input–output models, usually consisting of from 10 to 30 sectors in the developing economies and from 30 to 400 sectors in advanced economies, to the more complicated 'linear-programming' or 'activity-analysis' models where checks of feasibility (i.e. what is possible given certain resource constraints) and optimality (what is best among different alternatives) are also built into the model. But the distinguishing characteristic of the inter-industry or input–output approach is the attempt to formulate an internally consistent, comprehensive development plan for the entire economy.

Table 15.1
Hypothetical input–output table

Producing Sector (Outputs)	Agriculture	Extractive industry	Manufacturing	Power	Transportation	Total intermediate demand	Household consumption	Investment	Non-investment expenditure	Exports	Total final demand	Total output
	\[Intermediate Use\]						\[Final Use (Demand)\] — Government					
Agriculture	15(x_{11})	0(x_{12})	20(x_{13})	0(x_{14})	10(x_{15})	45 $\sum_{j=1}^{5} x_{1j}$	35	10	5	30	80(Y_1)	125(X_1)
Extractive industry	0(x_{21})	0(x_{22})	0(x_{23})	0(x_{24})	0(x_{25})	0 $\sum_{j=1}^{5} x_{2j}$	0	10	0	30	40(Y_2)	40(X_2)
Manufacturing	10(x_{31})	0(x_{32})	25(x_{33})	15(x_{34})	5(x_{35})	55 $\sum_{j=1}^{5} x_{3j}$	15	20	5	5	45(Y_3)	100(X_3)
Power	5(x_{41})	15(x_{42})	15(x_{43})	0(x_{44})	15(x_{45})	50 $\sum_{j=1}^{5} x_{4j}$	5	10	10	0	25(Y_4)	75(X_4)
Transportation	5(x_{51})	10(x_{52})	15(x_{53})	0(x_{54})	5(x_{55})	35 $\sum_{j=1}^{5} x_{5j}$	5	8	2	0	15(Y_5)	50(X_5)
Total purchases	35	25	75	15	35	185	60	52	22	65	205	
Imports	15(m_1)	0(m_2)	10(m_3)	30(m_4)	5(m_5)	60(M_T)	5	5	0	0	(10)	60(70)
Government (taxes)	20	5	3	7	2	37	(35)	(0)	(0)	(20)	(55)	37(92)
Households (labour)	40(L_1)	5(L_2)	6(L_3)	5(L_4)	2(L_5)	58(L_T)	1	0	12	0	13	71
Capital (C)	5(C_1)	3(C_2)	5(C_3)	12(C_4)	4(C_5)	29(C_T)	0	0	0	0	0	29
Natural resources (N)	10(N_1)	2(N_2)	1(N_3)	6(N_4)	2(N_5)	21(N_T)	0	0	0	0	0	21
Value added	75	15	15	30	10	145	1	0	12	0	13	158
Total inputs	125	40	100	75	50	390	66	63	34	65	218	608

*Source: M. P. Todaro, *Development Planning: Models and Methods*, Oxford U.P., Nairobi (1971).

Table 15.1 provides a numerical example of a hypothetical input-
output system. For simplicity, we assume the existence of only five
sectors: agriculture (sector 1); extractive industry (sector 2); manufacturing (sector 3); power (sector 4); and transportation (sector 5).
Actual tables can range in size from 20 to 400 sectors with most
developing countries at the lower end of the spectrum.

Note that each sector appears twice; as a producer of outputs (rows 1
to 5) and as a user of inputs (columns 1 to 5). Each row shows how each
industry disposed of its output. For example, the agricultural sector
produced a total output of 125 units (for the present disregard all
algebraic symbols in the parenthesis) (the first entry in the last column)
of which 15 were used by itself as inputs (e.g. seeds), 20 by manufacturing (e.g. coffee or tea for processing) and 10 by transportation (e.g. as
food served on passenger railways). The total intermediate use of
agricultural products, i.e. use for further production, is 45 units. To this
figure must be added the quantity of agricultural goods demanded by
final users. In Table 15.1 this consists of the consumption of 35 units by
households, total government expenditure of 15 units and exports to
foreign countries of 30 units. The sum of total intermediate and total
final demand yields a gross output for agricultural production of 125
units. Similarly, we see that the extractive sector produces a total
output of 40 units of which none is sold on an inter-industry basis to
other sectors while the government purchases 10 units, and 30 units
are exported. The disposition of the total outputs of the other three
sectors can be read from the table in the same manner.

The role of the agricultural sector as a purchaser of *inputs* is shown
by column one. Reading down this column we see that in order to
produce its total output of 125 units, agriculture had to use 15 units of
its own output (e.g. using a portion of maize or bean output for
replanting), 10 units of manufacturing output (e.g. fertilizers, insecticides, etc.), 5 units of power (e.g. to operate rotating water sprays and
other electrical equipment), and 5 units of transportation's product
(e.g. for transporting perishable goods to local markets or to the coast
for export). Thus, the total domestic inter-industry purchases of
intermediate material goods and services by agriculture were 35 units.
The remaining 90 units of total inputs purchased consisted of the
importation of 15 units of foreign goods and the creation of 75 units of
value added in the form of payments of 20 units to the government as
taxes, 40 units to households as wages, 5 units for the use of capital,
and 10 units for the use of land. Thus the value of the total output of
agriculture is equal to the total value of all inputs purchased, i.e. 125
units. This same procedure can be followed in analyzing the
input–output structure of each and every sector of the economy.

The crucial assumption of input–output analysis, that is, the one that
makes the system operationally effective, is the assumption that a
single process production function exists in every industry. Actually,
this assumption has two closely related but distinct constituent parts.
The first is the assumption of *constant returns to scale*. The second, and
by far the more controversial, is the corresponding assumption that *no
substitution among inputs* is possible in the production of any good or
service. An alternative way of stating this is that since there is only one
process or method of production in each industry, the level of output
uniquely determines the level of each input required. Technically we
may say that the production process is characterized by *constant* 'technical coefficients of production', that is, each *additional* unit of new

output is produced by an unchanging proportional combination of material inputs from the other sectors. For example, in Table 15.1 we see that in order to produce its 100 units of output, the manufacturing sector had to purchase 20 units of agricultural output for its intermediate input needs. Dividing 20 by 100 we find that our proportionality assumption indicates that for every unit of manufacturing output, $0 \cdot 20$ units of agricultural products will *always* be required as inputs so long as the production process of the manufacturing sector remains unchanged by the prevailing technology. Similarly, for every unit of its output produced, the manufacturing sector requires $0 \cdot 25$ units of its own goods ($25/100 = 0 \cdot 25$), $0 \cdot 15$ units of power ($15/100 = 0 \cdot 15$ units of transportation ($15/100 = 0 \cdot 15$) as material inputs. These technical coefficients of production for manufacturing were obtained by dividing each element in column 3 of the inter-industry transactions matrix by the total output of the manufacturing sector, 100.

By letting a_{ij} represent the number of units of the ith product (say, manufacturing, where $i = 1, 2, \ldots, n$ and designates the *row* in which the industry is located), necessary to produce *one unit* of output of the jth sector (say transportation, where j also equals any number from 1 to n and designates the *column* location of that particular industry within the transactions matrix), we can derive a 5×5 matrix of 'technical coefficients of production'. For example, a_{13} would designate the coefficient located in the 1st row and 3rd column of the derived technical matrix. It would represent the number of units of the 1st industry (agriculture) required by the 3rd sector (manufacturing) in order to produce a unit of its own (i.e. manufacturing) output. As was noted above, a_{13} in our example would be equal to 20/100 or $0 \cdot 20$.

The calculation of all a_{ij}'s is a relatively straightforward task. Simply divide the number located in the ith row and jth column of the original inter-industry transactions matrix by the total output of industry j. Each column of the new matrix comprises the input coefficients of one particular sector, j. It represents the single-process *production function* of that industry. Thus, the entire 'A' matrix, as the matrix of technical coefficients is often designated (see Table 15.2) summarizes the production processes of the entire economy in the form of goods that flow into and out of each industry. Algebraically,

$$a_{ij} = \frac{x_{ij}}{X_j} \quad \begin{array}{l} i = 1,2,\ldots,n \\ j = 1,2,\ldots,n \end{array} \tag{7}$$

where, x_{ij} represents the number of units of good i used by industry j – that is, the figure in the ith row and jth column of the transactions matrix; and X_j equals the *total output* of industry j shown by the last figure in the jth row of the input–output table.

The matrix of technical coefficients of production for any input–output table with n sectors would consist of $n \times n$ elements. For a table with only 5 sectors, as in our example, the 25 technical coefficients of the matrix would be arranged symbolically as follows:

		Sector 1	Sector 2	Sector 3	Sector 4	Sector 5
	Sector 1	a_{11}	a_{12}	a_{13}	a_{14}	a_{15}
	Sector 2	a_{21}	a_{22}	a_{23}	a_{24}	a_{25}
Table 15.2	Sector 3	a_{31}	a_{32}	a_{33}	a_{34}	a_{35}
A 5 ×5 matrix of technical	Sector 4	a_{41}	a_{42}	a_{43}	a_{44}	a_{45}
coefficients	Sector 5	a_{51}	a_{52}	a_{53}	a_{54}	a_{55}

Using equation (7) to calculate the a_{ij}'s for our hypothetical 5-sector input–output table, we arrive at the 'A' matrix shown in Table 15.3.

	Agri-culture	Extractive industry	Manu-facturing	Power	Trans-portation
Agriculture	15/125 = 0·12	0/40 = 0	20/100 = 0·20	0/75 = 0	10/50 = 0·20
Extractive Industry	0/125 = 0	0/40 = 0	0/100 = 0	0/75 = 0	0/50 = 0
Manufacturing	10/125 = 0·08	0/40 = 0	25/100 = 0·25	15/75 = 0·20	5/50 = 0·10
Power	5/125 = 0·04	15/40 = 0·375	15/100 = 0·15	0/75 = 0	15/50 = 0·30
Transportation	5/125 = 0·04	10/40 = 0·25	15/100 = 0·15	0/75 = 0	5/50 = 0·10

Table **15.3**
The 'A' matrix of technical coefficients for our hypothetical 5 sector economy

Thus, for example, we see that the amount of manufactured goods required to produce a unit of agricultural output, a_{31}, is $0·08$; the amount of power necessary to produce a unit of output of the extractive industry, a_{42}, is $0·375$; the amount of transportation needed to produce a unit of power output, a_{54}, is 0; and the necessary agricultural *input* required to produce a unit of agricultural *output, a_{11},* is $0·12$. Since these coefficients are assumed to be *constant* over time, the input–output table can be utilized to measure the *direct* and the *indirect* effects on the entire economy of any sectoral change in total output or final demand. This can be demonstrated most easily by expressing the input–output system as a set of simultaneous algebraic equations.

The mathematics of input–output analysis consists of two basic sets of equations. First, there is a set of accounting equations, one for each producing sector of the economy. The first of these equations states that the total output of sector 1 is equal to the sum of the separate amounts sold by sector 1 to the other industries plus the amount produced to satisfy final demands. The second equation says the same thing for sector 2, and so on for all n industries. In terms of the input–output table, these equations state that for any sector total output is equal to the sum of all the entries in that sector's row in the table. Thus, an implicit assumption of input–output analysis, common to all general equilibrium models, is that in all sectors the entire product produced is consumed either by other industries as inter-mediate inputs or by final demanders. In short, supply always equals demand. Symbolically, this first set of equations can be expressed as follows:[To facilitate a comprehension of the relationships involved in the mathematical input–output model, the student should refer back to the symbols contained in the parentheses in Table 15.1]
Let

The mathematical input–output model

X_i measure the annual rate of total output (in constant value units) of industry i;

x_{ij} represent the amount of the product of industry i absorbed annually as an intermediate input by industry j; and

Y_i equal the amount of the same product i produced to satisfy 'final demand'.

The overall input–output accounting balance for the entire economy comprising n separate industries or sectors can be described in terms of n linear equations:

$$\sum_{j=1}^{n} x_{ij} + Y_i = X_i \qquad (8)$$

where $i = 1, 2, \ldots, n$.

Each equation states that in all sectors the entire product produced (X_i) is consumed either by the other industries $(\sum_{j=1}^{n} x_{ij})$ or by final demanders (Y_i). For example, in Table 15.1 we have five accounting equations. The one for industry 3, manufacturing, would read as follows:

$$x_{31} + x_{32} + x_{33} + x_{34} + x_{35} + Y_3 = X_3$$

or, substituting the appropriate numerical figures,

$$10 + 0 + 25 + 15 + 5 + 45 = 100.$$

The second and more important set of equations central to input–output analysis is another set of n equations, one for each industry, describing the input–output structure of each industry in terms of a derived set of a_{ij} technical coefficients of production. Thus, the commodity flows, x_{ij}, included in the first balance equations are subject to the following set of structural relationships:

$$x_{ij} = a_{ij}X_j \qquad \begin{matrix} i = 1,2,\ldots,n. \\ j = 1,2,\ldots,n. \end{matrix} \qquad (9)$$

(†Since a_{ij} has already been defined as being equal to x_{ij}/X_i, system (9) is merely another way of expressing this definition of proportionality, that is

$$a_{ij} = \frac{x_{ij}}{X_j} \Rightarrow x_{ij} = a_{ij}X_j.]$$

Substituting for x_{ij} from equation (9) into equation (8) and transposing terms, we obtain the basic input–output system of equations:

$$X_i - \sum_{j=1}^{n} a_{ij}X_j = Y_i \qquad (10)$$

In terms of our hypothetical economy, system (10) would consist of five linear equations that could be written symbolically and numerically as follows:

Symbolic representation
$$X_1 - a_{11}X_1 - a_{12}X_2 - a_{13}X_3 - a_{14}X_4 - a_{15}X_5 = Y_1$$
$$X_2 - a_{21}X_1 - a_{22}X_2 - a_{23}X_3 - a_{24}X_4 - a_{25}X_5 = Y_2$$
$$X_3 - a_{31}X_1 - a_{32}X_2 - a_{33}X_3 - a_{34}X_4 - a_{35}X_5 = Y_3$$
$$X_4 - a_{41}X_1 - a_{42}X_2 - a_{43}X_3 - a_{44}X_4 - a_{45}X_5 = Y_4$$
$$X_5 - a_{51}X_1 - a_{52}X_2 - a_{53}X_3 - a_{54}X_4 - a_{55}X_5 = Y_5$$

Numerical representation
125 – 0·12 (125) – 0·00 (40) – 0·20 (100) – 0·00 (75) – 0·20 (50) = 80
 40 – 0·00 (125) – 0·00 (40) – 0·00 (100) – 0·00 (75) – 0·00 (50) = 40
100 – 0·08 (125) – 0·00 (40) – 0·25 (100) – 0·20 (75) – 0·10 (50) = 45
 75 – 0·04 (125) – 0·375 (40) – 0·15 (100) – 0·00 (75) – 0·30 (50) = 25
 50 – 0·04 (125) – 0·25 (40) – 0·15 (100) – 0·00 (75) – 0·10 (50) = 15

For convenience we can rewrite system (10) in terms of matrix and vector notations as follows. [Students who are unfamiliar with elementary matrix algebra may wish to consult any of a number of introductory texts on mathematics for economists. However, the following presentation should be self explanatory.]

$$\bar{X} - [A] \cdot \bar{X} = \bar{Y} \qquad (11)$$

where: $\bar{X}$ represents a *column vector* of total outputs consisting of n elements (in our example $n = 5$) each of which numerically represents the total output of one of the n industries; [A] is an $n \times n$ square matrix of technical coefficients (Table 15.2) and Y is a column vector of total final demands.

Thus, if the economy were divided into 30 sectors ($n = 30$), system (11) would be a convenient way of avoiding the tedious task of writing out a set of 30 simultaneous linear equations.

We can now pre-multiply both sides of equation (11) by the 'identity' or 'unit' matrix, denoted [I], to obtain the following expression:

$$[I] . \bar{X} - [A] . \bar{X} = \bar{Y} \tag{12}$$

[Note that the 'identity' matrix is merely a square matrix in which all the diagonal elements reading from left to right have a value of 1 while all other elements are equal to 0. Thus, a 3×3 identity matrix would be:

$$[I] = \begin{matrix} 1 & 0 & 0 \\ 0 & 1 & 0 \\ 0 & 0 & 1 \end{matrix}$$

The operation of the identity matrix in matrix algebra has the same effect as the operation of the number 1 in simple algebraic equations, i.e. multiplication leaves the value of all elements in the system unchanged.

Thus, if a column vector (e.g. $\bar{X}$) is pre-multiplied by an identity matrix [I], we obtain the same column vector with unchanged values. For example:

$$\begin{vmatrix} 1 & 0 & 0 \\ 0 & 1 & 0 \\ 0 & 0 & 1 \end{vmatrix} \times \begin{vmatrix} 2 \\ 1 \\ 4 \end{vmatrix} = \begin{vmatrix} (1\cdot2)+(0\cdot1)+(0\cdot4) \\ (0\cdot2)+(1\cdot1)+(0\cdot4) \\ (0\cdot2)+(0\cdot1)+(1\cdot4) \end{vmatrix} = \begin{vmatrix} 2 \\ 1 \\ 4 \end{vmatrix}$$

or,
symbolically $[I] . \bar{X}$

Factoring out the $\bar{X}$ column vectors on the left side of equation (12), we derive a very familiar expression of input–output mathematics, namely:

$$(I\text{-}A) . \bar{X} = \bar{Y} \tag{13}$$

The $(I\text{-}A)$ matrix, often called the 'Leontief matrix' in honor of the 'father' of input–output analysis, is obtained mathematically by subtracting each element of the A matrix from its counterpart in the I matrix.

We come now to the crucial mathematical manipulation of the input–output model, the one that gives the system its predictive and planning potentialities. Given a matrix of a_{ij} technical coefficients of production (assumed to be constant and independent of the volume of output) and a column vector of final demands. $(Y_1, Y_2, \ldots, Y_n)$, system (13) can be solved for all values of total output $(X_1, X_2, \ldots, X_n)$ simply by dividing both sides of (13) by the Leontief matrix, $(I\text{-}A)$, to obtain the following expression:

$$\bar{X} = \frac{Y}{(I-A)}$$

or,

$$\bar{X} = (I - A)^{-1}\bar{Y} \tag{14}$$

[This operation with matrices is quite analogous to the technique of division in elementary algebra. For example, in elementary algebra if we had the equation $(1-a)x = y$ and we wished to solve for x in terms of a and y, we would divide through by $(1-a)$ which is equivalent to multiplying y by the reciprocal of $(1-a)$, i.e.

$$x = \frac{y}{(1-a)} = (1-a)^{-1}y.]$$

The expression $(1-A)^{-1}$ is called the 'inverted' Leontief matrix and is commonly designated by the block letter 'R', i.e. system (14) may be written as:

$$\bar{X} = [R] . \bar{Y} \tag{14a}$$

By inserting any given, predicted, or planned final demand, $Y_{j_{j=1,\ldots,n}}$ into the right-hand side of each equation of system (14a), we can determine the corresponding level of output, $X_{i_{i=1,2,\ldots,n}}$, of commodity i that will be produced as a result of this level of demand. Similarly, and more important, system (14a) can be used to measure the probable effects of any *change* in final demands on the total output of all sectors of the economy. To measure the effects of these changes we merely rewrite (14a) as:

$$\Delta X_i = \sum_{j=1}^{n} r_{ij} \Delta Y_{j_{j=1,2,\ldots,n}} \tag{14b}$$

where the symbol Δ stands for 'the change in' final demand, ΔY, *or 'the change in' total output*, ΔX. (Note that each of the constants, r_{ij} , is a function of *all* the a_{ij} 's and if the production process of any one sector is altered due to technological advancement, better management, etc., more than one r_{ij} (in all probability quite a few of r_{ij} 's) will be affected. Consequently the assumption that the technical coefficients are constant in the short run is vital to the applicability of the input–output model.) For example, if the final demands for the products of the manufacturing industry, sector 3 in Table 15.1, were *expected* to increase or were *planned* to increase by, say 10 units, we could determine how much additional total output would have to be produced *in all 5 sectors* by using the equations in system (14b). Thus, if we are given $\Delta Y_3 = +10$ and we wish to determine ΔX_1, ΔX_2, ΔX_3, ΔX_4 and ΔX_5, the procedure would be as follows[9]:

$$\Delta X_1 = 1\cdot19(\Delta Y_1)+0\cdot11(\Delta Y_2)+0\cdot40(\Delta Y_3)+0\cdot08(\Delta Y_4)+0\cdot34(\Delta Y_5)$$
$$\Delta X_2 = 0\cdot00(\Delta Y_1)+1\cdot00(\Delta Y_2)+0\cdot00(\Delta Y_3)+0\cdot00(\Delta Y_4)+0\cdot00(\Delta Y_5)$$
$$\Delta X_3 = 0\cdot16(\Delta Y_1)+0\cdot19(\Delta Y_2)+1\cdot55(\Delta Y_3)+0\cdot30(\Delta Y_4)+0\cdot30(\Delta Y_5)$$
$$\Delta X_4 = 0\cdot10(\Delta Y_1)+0\cdot50(\Delta Y_2)+0\cdot32(\Delta Y_3)+1\cdot06(\Delta Y_4)+0\cdot41(\Delta Y_5)$$
$$\Delta X_5 = 0\cdot08(\Delta Y_1)+0\cdot31(\Delta Y_2)+0\cdot27(\Delta Y_3)+0\cdot05(\Delta Y_4)+1\cdot18(\Delta Y_5)$$

Since $\Delta Y_1 = \Delta Y_2 = \Delta Y_4 = \Delta Y_5 = 0$ in our simple example, we can eliminate the 1st, 2nd, 4th and 5th terms on the right-hand side of the above five equations and arrive at our answer more directly. Thus,

$$\Delta X_1 = 0\cdot40 \,\Delta Y_3 = 0\cdot40(10) = 4\cdot0$$
$$\Delta X_2 = 0\cdot00 \,\Delta Y_3 = 0\cdot00(10) = 0\cdot0$$
$$\Delta X_3 = 1\cdot5 \ \ \Delta Y_3 = 1\cdot5 \ (10) = 15\cdot0$$

$$\Delta X_4 = 0.32 \, \Delta Y_3 = 0.32(10) = 3.2$$
$$\Delta X_5 = 0.27 \, \Delta Y_3 = 0.27(10) = 2.7$$

As a result of an increase in total *final demand* for manufactured products of 10 units, total *output* of agriculture (X_1) will rise by $4 \cdot 0$ units, output of the extractive industry (X_2) will remain unchanged, and the total outputs of the manufactured (X_3), power (X_4), and transportation (X_5) sectors will rise by $15 \cdot 0$, $3 \cdot 2$ and $2 \cdot 7$ units respectively. Since each sector must purchase inputs from other sectors in order to produce more units of its own outputs, we see that the total *direct* and *indirect* effects of an initial increase in final demand will reverberate throughout the entire economy in a vast maze of economic interdependences until the combined increase in total output of all sectors of the economy is many times the magnitude of the initial stimulus. In short, if we are given, anticipate or plan any change in final demands for any good or combination of goods, the input–output equations of system (14b) would portray the full direct and indirect impact of this change or these changes on all sectors of the economy[10].

a. Determination of employment levels
Before concluding this discussion of the mathematics of the basic input–output model, mention should be made of a few of the other important areas of economic analysis where the model can be of value to planners. For example, we can utilize techniques quite similar to those described above to estimate the impact of any change in final demand or total output on the level of total industrial employment in the economy.

Employment can be thought of as being distributed in certain proportions throughout all industries. In the household row of primary inputs in Table 15.1 is a set of five figures representing the value of the labour input used by each of the five sectors. If these values are all written in terms of some average wage rate in the economy, then the relative magnitude of the various figures would correspond to the relative numbers of workers employed in that sector. For example, if the average annual wage rate in our hypothetical economy was equal to $0 \cdot 001$ units of value and if the household figures in Table 15.1 represented the total value of man-years employed by each sector, then agriculture is employing 40,000 man-years of labor (i.e. $40(1/0 \cdot 001) = 40,000$), extractive industry 5,000 man-years and manufacturing, power and transportation 6,000, 5,000 and 2,000 man-years respectively. Total employment in the five industrial sectors is therefore 58,000 man-years. Since the input–output table is based normally on an accounting period of one year, this implies a total employment of 58,000 workers.

In a manner analogous to the derivation of our technical coefficients of production, we can now derive a row vector of n *labor coefficients,* $l_{i_{i=1,2,\ldots,n}}$, each element of which depicts the number of workers (or man-years of employment) required to produce a *unit* of industry i's output. The labor coefficient is, therefore, calculated as follows for each industry:

$$l_i = \frac{L_i}{X_{i_{i=1,2,\ldots,n}}}$$

where, L_i is the level of employment in industry i, and
X_i is the total output of industry i.

Some extensions of the basic input–output model

For example, the labor coefficients for our five-sector economy would be:

$$l_1 = \frac{40}{125} = 0.32; \quad l_2 = \frac{5}{40} = 0.125; \quad l_3 = \frac{6}{100} = 0.06;$$

$$l_4 = \frac{5}{75} = 0.006; \quad l_5 = \frac{2}{50} = 0.04.$$

The level of employment in each industry is uniquely related to the amount of total output produced by that industry. Thus, to find the amount of labor employed in industry i, we multiply the corresponding labor coefficient l by the total output X of that sector. By summing the products of labor coefficients and total outputs of all industries throughout the economy, the following expression for *total* industrial employment can be derived:

$$L_T = \sum_{i=1}^{n} l_i X_i \tag{15}$$

where L_T represents total industrial employment in the economy. Similarly, a *change* in employment as a result of a *change* in total output can be expressed as:

$$\Delta L_T = \sum_{i=1}^{n} l_i \Delta X_i. \tag{15a}$$

Finally, since we know that $\Delta X_i = \sum_{j=1}^{n} r_{ij} \Delta Y_j$ from equation (14b), the change in employment as a consequence of any given, anticipated or planned change in *final demand* can be calculated by substituting into (15a) so that:

$$\Delta L_T = \sum_{i=1}^{n} l_i \left(\sum_{j=1}^{n} r_{ij} \Delta Y_j \right)$$

or

$$\Delta L_T = \sum_{i=1}^{n} \sum_{j=1}^{n} l_i r_{ij} \Delta Y_j$$

For example, the change in total employment that would result directly and indirectly from our hypothetical increase in the final demand for the products of the manufacturing sector (i.e. $Y_3 = +10$) would be:

$$
\begin{aligned}
L_T &= l_1 r_{13} \Delta Y_3 + l_2 r_{23} \Delta Y_3 + l_3 r_{33} \Delta Y_3 + l_4 r_{43} \Delta Y_3 + l_5 r_{53} \Delta Y_3 \\
&= 0.32(0.40 \times 10) + 0.125(0 \times 10) + 0.06(1.5 \times 10) \\
&\quad + 0.062(0.32 \times 10) + 0.04(0.27 \times 10) \\
&= 1.28 + 0 + 0.90 + 0.211 + 0.108 \\
&= 2.499.
\end{aligned}
$$

Thus, there will be increased employment opportunities for 2,499 workers as a result of a 10 unit or 22 per cent $(10/45) = 0.22)$ rise in final demand for manufactured products. It is interesting to note that the greatest *individual* sector impact on employment is *not* in the manufacturing sector (900 workers) as we might expect, but in the agricultural sector where 1,280 new jobs will be created. It is in unexpected circumstances like these that the potential value of input–output analysis to development planners becomes most evident. (If 'labor' is disaggregated further into skill categories (e.g. skilled, semi-skilled and unskilled) with coefficients for each, the model takes on a 'manpower planning' flavour; that is, once skill requirements have been ascertained and compared with available supplies of that skill, any deficiency can be made up by educating and/or training the appropriate number of workers.)

b. Balance of payments analysis.

The input–output model can be used also in the area of foreign trade to examine the approximate impact of any predicted or planned change in final demand on the balance of payments (current account) position of a given economy. Since foreign trade is an integral aspect of the structure of most developing economies, any comprehensive development plan must include some estimate of future balance of payments situations.

We can use our row vector of intermediate imports in Table 15.1 and our column vector of total outputs to derive a row vector of *import* coefficients, $m_{i_{i=1,2,\ldots,n}}$, one for each sector of the economy. Again, the procedure is exactly analogous to our derivation of labor coefficients, namely:

$$m_i = \frac{M_i}{X_{i_{i=1,2,\ldots,n}}}$$

where *M; is equal to the value of intermediate imports of sectors i*. Thus, the intermediate import coefficients for our five-sector economy would be:

$$m_1 = \frac{15}{125} = 0{\cdot}12; \qquad m_2 = \frac{0}{40} = 0; \qquad m_3 = \frac{10}{100} = 0{\cdot}10;$$

$$m_4 = \frac{30}{75} = 0{\cdot}40; \qquad m_5 = \frac{5}{50} = 0{\cdot}10.$$

Any change in total output or final demand will therefore lead to an induced change in intermediate imports in accordance with the following two expressions:

$$\Delta M_T = \sum_{i=1}^{n} m_i \, \Delta X_i \tag{16}$$

and

$$\Delta M_T = \sum_{i=1}^{n} \sum_{j=1}^{n} m_i r_{ij} \, \Delta Y_j \tag{16a}$$

where ΔM_T represents the change in the total value of intermediate imports. For example, as a result of our 10-unit increase in final demand for manufactured goods, induced intermediate imports will rise by:

$$\Delta M_T = 0{\cdot}12(4) + 0(0) + 0{\cdot}10(15) + 0{\cdot}40(3{\cdot}2) + 0{\cdot}10(2{\cdot}7)$$
$$= 0{\cdot}48 + 0 + 1{\cdot}5 + 1{\cdot}28 + 0{\cdot}27$$
$$= 3{\cdot}53 \text{ units of value}$$

Unless exports are expanded, the increase in final demand could lead to balance of payments difficulties.

c. Non-Human Primary Inputs.

Finally, row vectors of capital and natural resource coefficients (denoted c_i and n_i) representing the amounts of these factors used up per unit of total output can also be derived. Thus,

$$c_i = \frac{C_i}{X_i}_{i=1,2,\ldots,n}$$

and

$$n_i = \frac{N_i}{X_i}_{i=1,2,\ldots,n}$$

would be the formulas for computing capital and natural resource coefficients.
Similarly,

$$\Delta C_T = \sum_{j=1}^{n} c_i \, \Delta X_i \tag{17}$$

or

$$\Delta C_T = \sum_{i=1}^{n} \sum_{j=1}^{n} c_i r_{ij} \, \Delta Y_j \tag{17a}$$

and

$$\Delta N_T = \sum_{i=1}^{n} n_i \, \Delta X_i \tag{18}$$

or

$$\Delta N_T = \sum_{i=1}^{n} \sum_{j=1}^{n} n_i r_{ij} \, \Delta Y_j \tag{18a}$$

would be the corresponding equations relating changes in the utilization of capital (ΔC_T) and natural resources (ΔN_T) required to achieve the increased outputs or final demands. The important question is whether or not the economy has the necessary labor, capital and natural resources to achieve the increased output targets. If sufficient productive factors are unavailable, then the Ministry of Planning will have either to adjust its plan downward in accordance with these factor and material constraints, or solicit foreign technical and/or financial assistance.

Criticisms and conclusions The usefulness of the input–output model as a tool of development planning ultimately depends on the reliability of the 'A' matrix of technical coefficients. For most applications of the model, these coefficients are assumed to be constant, thus implying no technical change in sectoral production processes. Moreover, the coefficients are usually derived from actual inter-industry transactions at least 3 to 5 years *prior* to their use in the planning exercise. One of the major objectives of planning is to transform a developing economy's industrial structure and to improve the production process in a number of industries. The use of unadjusted pre-plan technical coefficients would thus be inappropriate. (Similarly, where import substitution is a major objective of development policy, the use of pre-plan import coefficients for projecting balance of payments situations would clearly be incorrect.) Some account, therefore, must be taken of planned or projected changes in these input coefficients through periodic revisions of the technical coefficients matrix.

The assumption of a single production process in each sector as well as the aggregation of different-size firms into a single industry further limits the practical application of input–output planning techniques.

This is particularly true with regard to employment projections, where choice of technique and size of firm can be critical in determining whether a given increase in output will have a major or a minor effect on job creation. The problem of choice of techniques and alternative labor coefficients can be handled theoretically by using linear and non-linear programming or 'activity analysis' models, but in actual practice such models require a degree of information well beyond that which is available in most LDCs. [11].

Finally, input–output projection models are clearly of greater use to countries with a sizeable industrial base, a relatively large flow of inter-industry transactions and a reliable system of data collection. While this limits the immediate application of the model to only a few of the more industrially advanced Third World countries, those others in the early stages of industrial growth and structural transformation may wish to construct simple input–output tables of, say, only 10 to 20 sectors, if for no other reason than to initiate a system of data collection and sectoral accounts that may yield high planning payoffs in the future.

C. Project appraisal and social cost–benefit analysis

Although most planning agencies in developing countries employ a variant of the basic Harrod–Domar growth model, and some work with simplified input–output sectoral models, the vast majority of day-to-day operational decisions with regard to the allocation of limited public investment funds are based on a 'micro-economic' technique of analysis known as 'project appraisal'. The intellectual as well as the operational linkage among these three major planning techniques, however, should not be overlooked. Macro growth models set the broad strategy, input–output analysis assures an internally consistent set of sectoral targets, while project appraisal is designed to assure the efficient planning of individual projects within each sector. The degree to which these three 'stages' of planning interact will determine to a large extent how successful is the planning exercise.

Social cost–benefit analysis: basic concepts and methodology[12]

The methodology of project appraisal rests on the theory and practice of 'social' cost–benefit analysis. The basic idea of cost–benefit analysis is simple: in order to decide on the worth of project involving public expenditure (or, indeed, in which public policy can play a crucial role), it is necessary to weigh up the advantages (benefits) and the disadvantages (costs) to *society as a whole*. The need for 'social' cost–benefit arises because the normal yardstick of 'commercial profitability' which guides the investment decisions of private investors may not be an appropriate guide for public investment decisions. Private investors are interested in maximizing private profits and, therefore, normally take into account only those variables which affect net profit: receipts and expenditures. Both receipts and expenditures are valued at prevailing market prices for inputs and outputs.

The point of departure for social cost–benefit analysis is that it does not accept that *actual* receipts are a true measure of social benefits and actual expenditures social costs. In other words, where social costs and benefits diverge from private costs and benefits, investment decisions based entirely on the criterion of commercial profitability may lead to a set of 'wrong' decisions from the point of view of 'social welfare', which should be the government's major concern. Although social valuations may differ significantly from private valuations, the practice of cost–benefit analysis is based on the assumption that these divergences can be adjusted for by public policy so that the difference between social benefit and cost will properly reflect 'social profitability' just as the difference between actual receipts and expenditures measures the private profitability of an investment.

Thus, we can define social profit in any period as the difference between social benefits and social costs where these are measured both directly (the 'real' costs of inputs and the real value of outputs) and indirectly (e.g. employment effects, distributional effects, etc.). The calculation of the social profitability of an investment then involves a three-step process[13]:

1. We must first specify the 'objective function' to be maximized – normally 'net' social benefit – with some measure of how different benefits (e.g. per capita consumption, income distribution, etc.) are to be measured and what the 'trade-off' between them might be.
2. In order to arrive at calculations of net social benefit, we need some social measures of the unit values of all project inputs and outputs. Such social measures are often called 'accounting' or 'shadow' prices of inputs and outputs to distinguish them from actual market prices (see below)[14]. In general, the greater the divergence between shadow and market prices, the greater the need for social cost–benefit analysis in arriving at public investment decision rules.
3. Finally, we need some decision criterion to reduce the stream of projected social benefit and cost flows to an index, the value of which can then be used to select or reject a project or to rank it relative to alternative projects.

We briefly examine each of these steps of project appraisal.

1. Setting objectives The 'social worth' of a project must be evaluated in light of national economic and social objectives. As we have seen, the setting of such objectives is the first and most important stage in the formulation of a development plan. Although all plans are designed to maximize 'social welfare' in one form or another, it is essential that the main measures of social welfare be specified and quantified as carefully as possible. Given the difficulty of attaching numerical values to such objectives as national cohesion, self-reliance, political stability, modernization and more generally, 'quality of life', economic planners typically measure the social worth of a project in terms of the degree to which it contributes to the net flow of future goods and services in the economy, that is, by its impact on future levels of consumption.

Recently, a second major criterion, the project's impact on income distribution, has also received increased attention. Rather than focusing on the simple quantitative increase in consumption generated by a particular investment, planners are now also asking how the particular project will benefit different income groups, particularly the low income classes. If preference is to be given to raising the consumption standards of low-income groups, then the 'social worth' of a project needs to be calculated as a 'weighted sum' of the distribution of its benefits, where additional consumption by low-income groups may receive a disproportionately high weight in the social welfare objective function. (The attentive reader will note that this procedure is analagous to that of constructing a 'poverty weighted' index of economic growth, discussed in Ch. 5.)

2. Computing 'shadow' prices and social discount rates The core of social cost–benefit analysis is the calculation and/or estimation of the prices to be used in determining the true value of benefits and the real magnitude of costs. There are many reasons for believing that in developing countries market prices of outputs and inputs do not give a true reflection of social benefits and costs. Among others, the following five are most often cited:

(i) Inflation and currency 'overvaluation'
Many developing countries are beset by rampant inflation with the resultant proliferation of price controls. Such prices do not typically reflect the real 'opportunity' cost to society of producing these goods and services. Moreover, in almost all countries, the government manages the price of foreign exchange. With inflation and unaltered foreign exchange rates, the domestic currency becomes 'overvalued' (see Ch. 13) so that (a) import prices underestimate the real cost to the country of purchasing foreign products and (b) export prices (again in local currency terms) understate the real benefit accruing to the country from a given volume of exports. In short, the 'official' price of foreign exchange in most LDCs does not provide a true reflection of the 'social' costs and benefits of importing and exporting. As a result, public investment decisions based on this price will tend to be biased against export industries and in favour of import substitution.

(ii) Wage rates, capital costs and unemployment
The prevalence in almost all developing countries of 'factor-price' distortions resulting in wage rates exceeding the social opportunity cost (or shadow price) of labor and interest rates understating the social opportunity cost of capital results, as we discovered in Chapter 7, in the widespread phenomenon of unemployment and under-employment and the excessive capital-intensity of industrial production technologies. If governments were to use unadjusted market prices for labor and capital in calculating the costs of alternative public investment projects, they would grossly underestimate the real costs of capital-intensive projects and tend to promote these at the expense of the socially less costly labor-intensive projects. Moreover, if the social welfare objective function places a premium on improved income distribution, the choice of capital-intensive projects would not only underestimate costs, it would also contribute marginally less to improved social welfare than the alternative labor-intensive project.

(iii) Tariffs, quotas and import substitution
As we saw in Chapter 13, the existence of high levels of nominal and effective tariff protection in combination with import quotas and over-valued exchange rates discriminates against the agricultural sector and in favour of the import-substituting manufacturing sector. In addition to reflecting incorrectly the real terms of trade between agriculture and industry , such 'distorted' domestic product prices tend once again to favour upper-income groups (urban manufacturers and modern-sector workers) disproportionately in relation to society's lower income groups (rural farmers as well as the urban and rural self-employed).

(iv) Savings deficiency
Given the substantial pressures for providing higher immediate consumption levels to the masses of undernourished and poorly clothed people, the level and rate of domestic savings in most developing countries is often thought to be sub-optimal. Although the public

understandably places a high premium on present as compared with future consumption and thus does little saving, it is up to the government to adopt a longer term perspective and consider the value of higher levels of present saving on accelerating future income and consumption. According to this argument, governments should use a discount rate that is *lower* than the market rate of interest in order to promote projects that have a longer pay-off period and generate a higher stream of investable surpluses in the future. In short, governments should place a premium on projects which generate savings (i.e. by placing a higher shadow price on saving) as opposed to those which merely generate consumption[15] in order to maximize consumption at some future, unspecified period[16].

(v) The social rate of discount

In our discussion of the shadow price of savings, we mentioned the need for governments to choose appropriate discount rates in calculating the worth of project benefits and costs that occur over time. The 'social rate of discount' (also sometimes referred to as 'social time preference') is essentially a 'price' of time – that is, it is the rate which planners use to calculate the net present value of a time stream of project benefits and costs, where the net present value (NPV) is calculated as

$$NPV = \frac{\sum_t B_t - C_t}{(1 + r)^t} \qquad\qquad 16$$

where B_t is the expected benefit of the project at time t, C_t is the expected cost (both evaluated using shadow prices) and r is the government's social rate of discount. Social discount rates may differ from market rates of interest (normally used by private investors to calculate the profitability of investments) depending on the subjective evaluation that planners place on future net benefits: the higher that future benefits and costs are valued in the government's planning scheme, the lower will be the social rate of discount.

In view of the above five forces leading to considerable product, factor and money price distortions, as well as considerations of external economies and diseconomies of production and consumption (by definition, factors *not* taken into account in private investment decisions), it has been widely argued and generally agreed that a strong case can be made for concluding that a project's *actual* anticipated receipts and expenditures do *not* provide an accurate measure of its social worth in developing countries. It is for this reason primarily that the tools of social cost–benefit analysis for project appraisal are now considered essential to an efficient process of project selection.

3. Choosing projects: some decision criteria Having computed relevant shadow prices (either from an economy-wide programming model or, more likely, by intelligent adjustments of individual market prices), projected a time stream of expected benefits and costs (including indirect or external effects) and selected an appropriate social discount rate, planners are now in a position to choose from among a set of alternative investment projects those thought to be most desirable. They, therefore, need to adopt a decision criterion to be followed. Normally, economists advocate using the Net Present Value (NPV) rule in choosing investment projects; that is, projects should be accepted or rejected according to whether their net present values are positive or negative. (Note the similarity between this project appraisal decision rule and our theory of rural–urban migration of Ch. 9.) As we have seen, however, net present value calculations are very sensitive to the choice of a social discount rate. An alternative approach is to calculate the discount rate which gives the project an NPV of zero, compare this 'internal rate of return' with either a predetermined social discount rate or the market rate of interest and choose those projects where internal rates exceed the predetermined or market rate. This approach is widely used in evaluating educational investments.

Since most developing countries face substantial capital constraints, the choice of investment projects will normally also involve a *ranking* of all those projects that satisfy the NPV rule. Projects are ranked in descending order of their net present values (more precisely, by their benefit/cost ratios which are arrived at by dividing NPV by the constraint on total capital cost, K, that is, an NPV/K ratio is calculated for each project). The project or set of projects (some investments should be considered as a 'package' of projects) with the highest NPV/K ratio is chosen first, then the next highest and so on down the line until all available capital investment funds have been exhausted.

D. Conclusions: planning models and plan consistency

The process of formulating a comprehensive, detailed development plan is obviously a more complicated process than that described by our three-stage approach. It involves a constant dialogue and feedback mechanism between national leaders who set priorities, planners, statisticians, research workers and departmental or ministry officials. Internal rivalries and conflicting objectives (not to mention political pressures from powerful vested-interest groups) are always to be reckoned with. Nevertheless, we hope that the preceding presentation has at least provided students with a 'feel' for the mechanics of planning and demonstrated the ways in which aggregate, input–output and project planning models can be interrelated and used to formulate an internally consistent and comprehensive development plan.

15.4 Important considerations in choosing particular planning models

There are a number of different types of economic models and planning approaches from which a developing nation can choose. The preceding section reviewed three of the most well-known and widely used models. A country about to draw up a development plan will have to decide which method, or combination of methods, is most suitable to its own special circumstances, needs and objectives. The ultimate choice, however, is not simply a matter of drawing any plan out of a hat or hastily taking that approach which seems to have been most successful in some other country. Rather, an intelligent and informed choice will depend on the answers to a number of important questions which must be specifically analyzed before reaching a final decision. Some of the more relevant considerations which have been suggested are the following:

1. Stage of development

The choice of a particular plan or strategy obviously depends on the existing level of a country's economic development. If the economy is still permeated by small-scale subsistence agriculture, a limited monetary sector, and little or no inter-industry relations, then detailed quantitative economy-wide planning can have only limited applicability.

It would probably be more appropriate to concentrate on individual 'social overhead' public investment projects aimed at creating the necessary conditions to initiate economic transformation. Some general idea of possible overall rates of growth of GDP and its major components as well as considerations of population growth, and in the case of most small economies, possibilities of import-substitution and export expansion loom more important at this early stage. Two- or three-gap models to identify constraints and bottlenecks in combination with public project appraisal in a few major sectors would probably be most appropriate at this stage. In the later stages, the likely path of development is often more clearly discernible, and greater detail in planning methods may become more feasible.

2. Institutional structure Another important consideration concerns the institutional structure of the economy and the relative roles envisaged for the public and private sectors in the development process. Where the private sector is not very influential and is expected to play a relatively passive role, the public sector will ordinarily be expected to take up the slack and provide the initial stimulus and continued overall direction. Accordingly, more attention will be devoted to public investment projects and sources of government finance. However, if the private sector is considerably more active, the plan is more likely to concentrate on the creation of favorable conditions in which private economic activity is free to flourish in a manner that contributes to the social good. A corollary of this public-versus-private consideration concerns the general attitude and willingness of the private sector to cooperate with the central government in a joint effort to promote national development. Where there exist conflict between public and private interests, the former will normally have to take precedence over the latter.

3. Availability and quality of statistical information The availability of reliable statistical information represents a third important influence on the choice of particular planning approaches. Where existing data are poor and unreliable, the possibility of employing sophisticated mathematical programming models will be greatly diminished. However, while the complete absence of certain statistical information may preclude the use of particular models, economic planners are sometimes advised to resort to 'educated guesses' or to the adaptation of empirical information from economies in similar circumstances rather than to forgo completely a particularly useful approach merely for lack of full statistical data.

4. Resource constraints The character of the development plan is often greatly influenced by the particular resource constraints or 'bottlenecks' impinging on the economy. The nature and character of resource constraints are often related to the stage of a country's economic development. However, in general, domestic savings and foreign exchange scarcity usually have been regarded as the principal bottlenecks limiting rapid economic progress. If capital constitutes the crucial constraint, every care must be taken to ensure its most effective and productive utilization (e.g. through the intelligent application of social cost–benefit analysis). When depleted foreign exchange reserves emerge as the operative constraint, export promotion and/or some form of import control in conjunction perhaps with increased inflows of foreign aid will assume increased importance in the plan. Other possible economic bottlenecks that might appear during the course of the development process include limited supplies of high-level manpower, inadequate transport facilities and limited government finance.

Finally, the specific long-run social and economic goals and objectives which the less developed nation deems most important must provide the conceptual basis for the entire plan. Those economic goals most commonly mentioned include the following: *5. Priorities and objectives*
(a) a rapid increase in per capita income,
(b) a high level of employment,
(c) a relatively stable price level,
(d) a reduction of poverty and income inequalities,
(e) a favorable balance-of-payments situation, and
(f) a diversified and self-reliant economy.
While each of the above objectives may be desirable in itself, serious conflicts may easily arise if all are pursued with equal intensity. There-fore, it often becomes necessary to determine, in the light of existing social, economic and institutional conditions and constraints, the specific objective, or combination of objectives, which should receive special priority in the development plan. The remaining targets might then constitute some form of associated 'side conditions' or secondary priorities to be realized as far as possible in the course of seeking fulfilment of the priority objectives.

This completes our review of the nature of development planning and the role of planning models. We consider some of the limitations and shortcomings of planning in practice.

15.5 The crisis in planning: problems of implementation and plan failures

After more than two decades of experience with development plan-ning in Third World countries, the results have been generally disap-pointing. In the most comprehensive and exhaustive study of the development planning experience in some fifty-five countries, Albert Waterston concluded that[17]:

an examination of postwar planning history reveals that there have been many more failures than successes in the implementation of develop-ment plans. By far the great majority of countries have failed to realize even modest income and output targets in their plans except for short periods. What is even more disturbing, the situation seems to be worsen-ing instead of improving as countries continue to plan.
In a similar vein, Derek Healey in a review article[8] on development policy over the past twenty years concluded that the results of planned development have been 'sadly disillusioning for those who believed that planning was the only way'.

What went wrong? Why has the early euphoria about planning gradually been transformed into disillusionment and dejection? We can identify two interrelated sets of answers – one dealing with the 'gap' between the theoretical economic benefits and the practical results of development planning and the other associated with more fundamental defects in the planning process, especially as it relates to administrative capacities, political will and plan implementation.

The principal economic arguments for planning briefly outlined in **1. Theory versus planning** section 15.2 – i.e. market failure, divergences between private and **practice** social valuations, resource mobilization, investment coordination, etc. – have often turned out to be weakly supported by the actual planning experience. Commenting on this planning failure, Killick[19] has noted that:

> ... *it is doubtful whether plans have generated more useful signals for the future than would otherwise have been forthcoming; governments have rarely, in practice, reconciled private and social valuations except in a piecemeal manner; because they have seldom become operational documents, plans have probably had only limited impact in mobilizing resources and in coordinating economic policies.*

To take the specific case of the 'market failure' argument and the presumed role of governments in reconciling the divergence between private and social valuations of benefits and costs, the experience of government policy in many LDCs has been one of often *exacerbating* rather than reconciling these divergences. We have touched upon these issues in several of the preceding problem-focused chapters, but to illustrate the point, we recapitulate here four crucial problem areas where private and social valuations tend to diverge and where the impact of government policy has often tended to *increase* rather than reduce these divergences.

A. Factor-prices, choice of technique and employment creation

A presumed conflict between two major planning objectives – i.e. rapid industrial growth and expanded employment opportunities – has typically resulted in the neglect of employment creation in the interest of industrial growth. As we saw in Chapter 8, there need be no such conflict if government policies were more geared to adjusting factor-price signals to the real resource scarcities of developing societies. But, in fact, these private price signals have increasingly diverged from their implicit social valuations partially as a result of public policies which have raised the level of wages above labor's shadow price or scarcity value by various devices such as minimum wage legislation, tying wages to educational attainment, and structuring rates of remuneration at higher levels on the basis of comparable 'international' salary scales. Similarly, we saw how investment depreciation and tax allowances, overvalued exchange rates, low effective rates of protection, quotes and credit rationing at low interest rates served to lower the private cost of capital far below its scarcity or social cost.

The net effect of these factor-price 'distortions' has been the tendency to encourage private and public enterprises to adopt more capital-intensive production methods than would exist if public money attempted to 'get the prices right'. In short, private valuations of benefits and costs often dictate more capital-intensive methods of production while true social valuations would point to more labor-intensive technologies. This divergence between private and social valuations is, as we have seen, one of the major reasons for the slow growth of employment opportunities. Within the mystique of development planning, the more powerful mystique of forced industrialization has remained a high priority for many years. Contrary to the expectations of its most vocal advocates, however, planning has had a far from salutary effect on efficient resource allocation in most developing countries[20]. Planning advocates would probably claim that their arguments still hold. The problem has been 'bad' planning and not the mere fact of planning.

A second major area of divergence between private and social valuations where, until recently, LDC economic policy appears to have been counterproductive to social concerns relates to the widespread phenomena of rural–urban migration. As we discovered in Chapter 9, government policies which are strongly biased in favour of urban development as revealed by the existence of sizeable urban–rural income differentials and disparities in locational economic opportunities have stimulated an excessive outflow of rural migrants in search of limited but highly-paid urban jobs. With growing urban unemployment and stagnating agriculture, the continued heavy influx of rural migrants represents a 'net' social loss to society in the context both of lost agricultural output and higher social costs of their urban accommodation. However, from the private viewpoint of the typical migrant, the existence of urban unemployment and thus a less than unitary probability of finding an urban job is more than compensated for by high urban–rural wage differentials. The 'expected' urban wage still exceeds rural incomes. It is therefore, 'privately' rational in terms of discounted expected benefits and costs for rural dwellers to continue to migrate to the cities in spite of high and rising levels of urban unemployment. However, a social benefit–cost analysis would probably indicate that such continued migration is undesirable.

Again, the heavy urban industrialization bias of most LDC development plans in the 1950s and 1960s combined with relative rural and agricultural neglect, created the conditions and distorted the price signals and economic incentives which have contributed to the urban employment crisis. Rather than narrowing the gap between private and social valuations, the planning experience seems to have widened them. It may thus have exacerbated the misallocation of human resources in many Third World countries.

In Chapter 11, we discovered how economic signals and incentives in many LDCs have served to exaggerate the private valuations of the returns to education to a point where the private demand for ever more years of schooling is greatly in excess of the social payoff. The tendency to ration scarce high-paying employment opportunities by level of completed education in combination with the policy of most LDC governments to subsidize the private costs of education, especially at the higher levels, has led to a situation in which the social returns to investment in further quantitative educational expansion seem hardly justified in comparison with alternative investment opportunities (e.g. the creation of productive employment projects). But, so long as private benefit/cost valuations show high returns and in the absence of effective policies like those suggested in Chapter 11 to alter these signals in accord with social valuations, LDC governments will continue to face extraordinary public pressure to expand school places at all levels.

As a result of these socially incorrect pricing policies, even greater proportions of future government recurrent expenditures will have to be earmarked for educational expansion. Such outlays often amount to more than an investment in idle human resources. The government's financial ability to undertake other public projects will be reduced correspondingly. Educational planning appears, therefore, to have contributed little to reconciling divergences between social and private valuations of investment in schooling.

B. Rural–urban imbalances and migration

C. The demand for education and the employment problem

D. The structure of the economy As a final example of the way in which planning and development policy have often contributed to the maintenance or exaggeration of socially 'incorrect' signals and incentives, consider the emphasis of the 1950s and 1960s on rapid industrialization through import-substitution. We saw in Chapter 13 how a wide range of external and internal pricing policies including special tax concessions to foreign investors, overvalued foreign exchange and how effective tariff rates designed to lower the cost of capital and intermediate good imports, quotas, subsidized interest rates and credit rationing to new industries plus a whole array of bureaucratic industrial licensing procedures have all served to provide an artificial stimulus to import-substituting industrial expansion. But we also learned that for the most part the experience of import substitution, especially in Latin America, has failed to meet planned expectations in terms of the eventual realization of low-cost efficient production by local industries. Moreover, the heavy emphasis on urban industrial growth and the concomitant creation through an economic policy of distorted signals and incentives rewarding private industrial activity has greatly contributed to the stagnation of the agricultural sector.

To take a single case, overvalued exchange rates designed to lower import prices of intermediate goods also raise export prices in terms of foreign currencies. If the nation and the vast majority of its rural people must rely on primary product export earnings, such exchange rate policies designed to stimulate industrialization can make agricultural exports less competitive and be a drain on agricultural expansion. Similarly, most other policies designed to stimulate industrial growth tend to work against the interests of the rural sector. The net result of this relative rural neglect in most development plans, especially during the first two decades of planning, has been the phenomenon of agricultural stagnation and rural poverty described in Chapter 10. But, as we also saw, the lessons of such rural neglect have not been lost on LDC governments and planning for agricultural growth is now gaining the priority attention that it long deserved.

2. Reasons for plan failures In view of the preceding examples, we may conclude that the gap between the theoretical economic benefits of planning and its practical results in most Third World countries has been quite large. The gap between public rhetoric and economic reality has been even greater. While professing to be concerned with eliminating poverty, lowering inequality and creating employment, many LDC planning policies have in fact unknowingly contributed to their perpetuation. Some of the major explanations for this have to do with the failures of the planning process itself. These failures include[21]:

A. Deficiencies in plans and their implementation Plans are often over-ambitious. They try to accomplish too many objectives at once without consideration of conflicting and competing objectives. They are often grandiose in design but vague on specific policies needed to achieve stated objectives and, finally, the gap between plan formulation and its implementation is often enormous, i.e., many plans, for reasons to be discussed below, are never implemented.

B Insufficient and unreliable data The economic wisdom of a development plan depends to a great extent on the quality and reliability of the statistical data on which it is based. When these data are weak, unreliable or simply non-existent as in many poor countries, the accuracy and internal consistency of economy-wide quantitative plans are greatly diminished. Moreover, where these unreliable data are compounded by an inadequate supply of qualified economists, statisticians and other planning personnel (as is also the situation in most poor nations) the attempt to formulate and carry out a comprehensive and detailed development plan is likely to be frustrated at all levels. In such situations, it can be both foolish and a waste of scarce high-level human resources to engage in an extensive planning exercise.

Since most LDCs are 'open economies' with a considerable dependence on the inevitable vicissitudes of international trade, aid and private foreign investment, it becomes exceedingly difficult for them to engage in even short-term forecasting, let alone long-range planning, in the face of such manifest uncertainty. The oil price increases of 1974 obviously caused havoc in most LDC development plans. But the energy crisis was only an extreme case of a general tendency for economic factors over which most LDC governments have little control to determine the success or failure of their development policies. Given such vulnerability to external factors, LDC governments need to retain a maximum flexibility in their economic plans and be ready to make needed adjustments as the occasion arises. In the long run, however, a policy of greater self-reliance and less external dependence provides an obvious but often difficult answer to this dilemma. As was pointed out in Chapter 13, economic integration offers an attractive alternative to both strictly 'outward'- and 'inward'-looking development policies.

C. Unanticipated economic disturbances, both external and internal

Much has been written about the institutional weaknesses of the planning processes of most developing countries. These include, among others, the separation of the planning agency from the day-to-day decision-making machinery of government; the failure of planners, administrators and political leaders to engage in a continuous dialogue and internal communication about goals and strategies; and the international transfer of institutional planning practices and organizational arrangements which may be inappropriate to local conditions.

D. The structure of the economy

In addition, there has been much concern about incompetent and unqualified civil servants; cumbersome bureaucratic procedures; excessive caution and resistance to innovation and change; interministerial personal and departmental rivalries (e.g. finance ministries and planning agencies are often conflicting rather than cooperative forces in LDC governments); lack of commitment to 'national' goals as opposed to regional, departmental, or simply private objectives on the part of political leaders and government bureaucrats, and, finally, in accordance with this lack of national as opposed to personal interest, the widespread phenomenon of political and bureaucratic corruption that is a pervasive problem of many Third World governments.

While it is beyond the scope of this chapter to deal further with these substantial institutional weaknesses, one should not minimize their importance in holding back the necessary structural and institutional reforms to accelerate economic and social development. They are critical factors, in addition to the three previously mentioned, in explaining the widespread failures of contemporary development planning.

E. Lack of 'political will' The ultimate cause of LDC planning failures is not simply lack of economic potential nor even inadequate administrative capacity. Rather, poor plan performance and the growing gap between plan formulation and its implementation is widely attributed to a lack of commitment and 'political will' on the part of many Third World leaders and high level decision makers. Waterson[22] summarizes his analysis of the development planning experience thus:

> *The available evidence makes it clear that in countries with development plans, lack of adequate government support for the plans is the prime reason why most are never carried out. Conversely, the cardinal lesson that emerges from the planning experience of developing countries is that the sustained commitment of a politically stable government is the* sine qua non *for development. Where a country's political leadership makes development a central concern, the people can also be interested through a judicious use of economic incentives. And, although it is never easy to reform administrative and institutional inefficiency, commitment by political leaders is a necessary condition for reform; without it, reform is impossible.*

One might add, parenthetically, that such a political 'will to develop' on the part of national leaders (assuming that by 'development' we mean eliminating poverty, inequality and unemployment as well as promoting aggregate per capita GNP growth) will require an unusual ability to take a long-term view and to elevate national social interests above factional class, caste or tribal interests. It will also necessitate the cooperation of the economic elites who may correctly see their privileged positions challenged by such a 'development' posture.

Thus, a political 'will to develop' entails much more than high-minded purposes and noble rhetoric. It requires an unusual ability and a great deal of political courage to challenge powerful elites and vested interest groups and to persuade them that such development is in the long-run interests of *all* citizens. In the absence of their support, whether freely offered or coerced, a will to develop on the part of politicians is likely to meet with continuous frustration and growing internal conflict.

Notes

1. For a more detailed discussion of planning and planning models see M. P. Todaro, *Development Planning: Models and Methods*, Oxford U.P., Nairobi (1971).
2. United Nations Department of Economic Affairs. *Measures for the Economic Development of Underdeveloped Countries*, New York (1951), 63.
3. United Nations, *Planning the External Sector: Techniques, Problems and Policies*, September 1965, 12.
4. R. Helfgoth and S. Schiavo-Campo, 'An introduction to development planning', *UNIDO Industrialization & Productivity Bulletin*, no. 16, (1970), 11.
5. T. Killick, 'The possibilities of development planning', *Oxford Economic Papers*, July 1976.
6. Lance Taylor, 'Theoretical foundations and technical implications' in Charles R. Blitzer *et al.* (eds), *Economy-Wide Models and Development Planning*, Oxford U.P., London (1975), 37–42.
7. Ibid., p. 39.
8. The following illustration as well as other material in section B is based on Todaro, op. cit., Ch. 2, 17–37.
9. The numerical coefficients $1 \cdot 19, 0 \cdot 11, 0 \cdot 40$, etc., are the actual elements of the 5×5 R matrix using the figures in our hypothetical table. For the derivation of these coefficients see, Todaro, op. cit., pp. 30–1.

10. The precise meaning of 'direct' and 'indirect' impacts can be explained by means of a simple example. Suppose the final demand for automobiles dropped by 10 per cent. The direct impact of this change would naturally be a 10 per cent drop in the production of cars. However, since car manufacturers use steel, rubber, cloth, etc., in producing their cars, they would demand less of these inputs and the *initial* indirect effect of this 10 per cent reduction in car output would be a reduction in the steel, rubber, cloth and other inter-industry outputs that are used as inputs in car production. Finally, with their outputs also curtailed, the steel, rubber, and cloth industries will in turn demand less inputs from other industries. This 'iterative' process of second, third, and fourth round effects of the initial stimulus will continue until practically all sectors of the economy whose output is in any way connected with car production have been affected. Thus, the total effect will be substantially greater than the initial *direct* impact of reduced auto demand.

11. For an introductory discussion of the use of economy-wide programming models, see Todaro, op. cit., Ch. 5.

12. For a good introduction to cost benefit analysis stressing linkages with economic theory see, A. K. Dasgupta and D. W. Pearce, *Cost-Benefit Analysis: Theory and Practice,* Macmillan, London (1972).

13. A. K. Dasgupta, *Economic Theory and the Developing Countries,* Macmillan, London (1974), Ch. 9.

14. For those familiar with the techniques of linear programming, shadow prices are merely the solution values of the 'dual' to a linear programming output or profit maximization problem. See Todaro, op. cit., Ch. 5.

15. Note the implicit change in the objective function from consumption maximization to savings maximization.

16. This approach is advocated by Little and Mirrlees in their book, *Project Appraisal and Planning in Developing Countries,* Basic Books, New York (1974).

17. Albert Waterston, *Development Planning: Lessons of Experience,* Johns Hopkins U.P., Baltimore (1965), 293.

18. Derek T. Healey, 'Development policy: new thinking an interpretation', *Journal of Economic Literature,* X, no. 3, (1973), 761.

19. Killick, op. cit., pp. 3–4.

20. For an extensive analysis of how public policy and the proliferation of controls has tended to exacerbate development problems in seven major developing countries, see Little, Scitovsky and Scott, *Industry and Trade in Some Developing Countries: A Comparative Study,* OECD, Oxford U.P. (1970).

21. Killick, op. cit., p. 4.

22. A. Waterson, *Development Planning: Lessons of Experience,* Johns Hopkins U.P., Baltimore (1965), 367.

Concepts for review

economic planning
economic plan
comprehensive versus partial plans
inducement versus control in planning
centralized versus decentralized planning
development planning
economic infrastructure
market failure
cost–benefit analysis
shadow price
input–output analysis
technical coefficient of production
Leontief Matrix
final demands
policy objectives
plan targets
internal plan consistency
short-, medium- and long-term planning
aggregate, sectoral and inter-industry planning models
project appraisal
'stage of development' in relation to choice of planning technique
social rate of discount
net present value
external economics and diseconomies
internal rate of return
plan implementation
'incorrect' signals and incentives
external economic disturbances
'political will'

Questions for discussion

1. Why do you think so many Third World countries were persuaded of the necessity of development planning? Were the reasons strictly economic? Comment.

2. *Explain* and *comment* on some of the major arguments or rationales, both economic and non-economic, for planning in Third World economies.

3. Planning is said to be more than just the formulation of quantitative economic targets. It is often described as a 'process'. What is meant by the planning process and what are some of its basic characteristics?
4. Compare and contrast three basic types of planning 'models': aggregate growth models, input–output analysis and project appraisal. What do you think are some of the strengths and weaknesses of using 'these' planning models in developing nations?
5. 'A developing country should choose the most sophisticated quantitative planning model when drawing up a comprehensive plan.' Comment on this statement, being sure to include in your answer a discussion of the types of consideration which should be taken into account when choosing a particular kind of planning model.
6. There is much talk today of a so-called 'crisis in Third World planning'. Many have even claimed that development planning has for the most part been a 'failure'. List and explain some of the major reasons for plan failures. Which reasons do you think are the most important? Explain.

Further readings 1. On the nature and role of *development planning* see: (*a*) Jan Tinbergen, *Development Planning*, World University Library, Weidenfeld and Nicolson, London, (1967); (*b*) Michael P. Todaro, *Development Planning: Models and Methods*, Oxford U.P., Nairobi (1971); (*c*) Hollis Chenery (ed.), *Studies in Development Planning*, Harvard U.P., Cambridge, Mass. (1971).
2. For a more advanced treatment of the use of mathematical models in development planning, see: C. R. Blitzer, P. B. Clark and L. Taylor (eds), *Economy-Wide Models and Development Planning*, Oxford U.P., London (1975).
3. An informative and thoughtful study of the methodology and use of cost–benefit analysis for project appraisal in developing countries can be found in I.M.D. Little and J. A. Mirrlees, *Project Appraisal and Planning for Developing Countries*, Basic Books, New York, 1974.
4. Finally, on the planning experience of Third World countries during the last decade as well as a critique of the 'planning mystique' see: (*a*) Albert Waterson, *Development Planning: Lessons of Experience*, Johns Hopkins U.P., Baltimore, Maryland (1965); (*b*) Mike Faber and Dudley Seers (eds), *The Crisis in Planning*, Chatto and Windus, London (1972) (2 vols.), especially the article by Seers on 'The prevalence of pseudo-planning'; (*c*) Tony Killick, 'The possibilities of development planning', *Oxford Economic Papers*, July 1976.

There are extremely powerful structural factors in Latin America which lead to inflation and against which traditional monetary policy is powerless.
Raul Prebish, Director General of the Latin American Institute for Economic and Social Planning, United Nations, Santiago, Chile.

The taxation potential in underdeveloped countries is rarely fully exploited . . . no more than one-fifth or possibly one-tenth of what is due [is collected].
N. Kaldor, Cambridge University

Introduction: An eclectic view of development policy

Although development planning represents the most visible aspect of public economic policy in nations of the Third World, the actual day-to-day policy decisions of LDC governments typically represent unplanned and often *ad hoc* responses to emerging and unforeseen economic crises. Within the broad framework of development objectives, diverse 'macro'-economic policies and public investment projects tend to have less internal consistency and economic rationality than many textbook planning models would lead us to believe. The very real physical, human and administrative resource limitations of most developing countries are sufficient to prevent comprehensive planning from being more than a paper exercise – albeit one which can yield important insights into the functioning of an economy and identify its principal constraints.

In this chapter we provide a broader yet more eclectic view of economic policy in developing countries by taking a critical look at two traditional aspects of government activity in 'mixed' market economies: monetary and fiscal policy. We then examine the interdependence between development problems and policies and conclude by discussing the role and limitations of economic policy in the context of the special circumstances of developing nations.

16.1 Some components of 'macro'-economic policy in developing countries

A fruitful way to examine the economic impact of public policies in developing countries is to pick specific development problems and then analyze how economic policies have affected them in the past and in what ways such policies might be improved in the future. Our discussion throughout Parts II and III of this book has followed this problem-oriented approach. We have seen that major development problems such as poverty, inequality, population growth, unemployment, migration, education, rural development and foreign trade and finance are all affected by and affect government policies. In many cases, policies designed to ameliorate one problem only serve to worsen another. But, by and large, the interdependence between problems and policies is of a complementary rather than a conflicting nature. For example, measures to eliminate poverty and reduce inequality will probably be consistent with stimulating rural development, curtailing rural–urban migration and counteracting the incentives to raise large families. Conversely, measures to promote rural development, to improve educational access, to create urban and rural job opportunities and to expand foreign exchange earnings are likely to contribute towards less poverty and lower inequality.

We return to this theme of the interdependence between problems and policies in a people-oriented development strategy later in the chapter when we attempted to summarize the analysis of preceding chapters. For the present we examine the main components of LDC economic policy by utilizing the traditional textbook division between 'monetary' and 'fiscal' policies [1]. But rather than merely providing a 'shopping list' of different public policies, we concentrate on how LDC monetary and fiscal policy can promote or retard a broad-based strategy of economic and social development.

1. Monetary and financial policies: the limitations of traditional macro-instruments In developed nations, monetary and financial policy plays a major direct and indirect role in governmental efforts designed to expand economic activity in times of unemployment and surplus capacity and to contract that activity in times of excess demand and inflation. Basically, monetary policy works on two principal economic variables – the aggregate supply of money in circulation and the level of interest rates. The supply of money (basically currency plus commercial bank demand deposits) is thought to be directly related to the level of economic activity in the sense that a greater money supply induces expanded economic activity by enabling people to purchase more goods and services with their extra funds. This in essence is the so-called 'monetarist' theory of economic activity. Its advocates argue that by controlling the growth of money supplies, governments of developed countries can regulate their nations' economic activity.

On the other side of the monetary issue are the so-called 'Keynesian' economists who argue that an expanded supply of money in circulation increases the availability of loanable funds. A supply of loanable funds in excess of demand leads to lower interest rates. Since private investment is assumed to be inversely related to prevailing interest rates, businessmen will expand their investments as interest rates fall and credit becomes more available. More investment in turn raises aggregate demand leading to a higher level of economic activity (i.e. more employment and a higher GNP). Similarly in times of excess aggregate demand and inflation, governments pursue 'restrictive' monetary policies designed to curtail the expansion of aggregate demand by reducing the growth of the national money supply, lowering the supply of loanable funds, raising interest rates and thereby inducing a lower level of investment and less inflation.

Although this description of monetary policy in developed countries grossly simplifies a complex process, it does point out two important aspects of monetary policy which developing countries lack. First, the ability of developed country governments to expand and contract their money supplies and to raise and lower the costs of borrowing in the private sector (i.e. through direct and indirect manipulation of interest rates) is made possible by the existence of highly organized, economically independent and efficiently functioning money and credit markets. Financial resources are continuously flowing in and out of savings banks, commercial banks and other nationally controlled public and private 'financial intermediaries' with a minimum of interference. Moreover, interest rates are regulated both by administrative credit controls and market forces of supply and demand so that there tends to be a consistency and relative uniformity of rates in different sectors of the economy and in all regions of the country.

By contrast, many markets and financial institutions in most developing countries are highly *organized,* often externally *dependent,* and spatially *fragmented* [2].

Many commercial banks are merely overseas branches of major private banking institutions in developed countries. Their orientation therefore, like that of multinational corporations, may be more towards external and less towards internal monetary situations. The ability of Third World governments to regulate the national supply of money is further constrained by the 'openness' of their economies and by the fact that the accumulation of foreign currency earnings is a significant but highly variable source of their domestic financial resources. Most important, the commercial banking system of most LDCs restricts its activities almost exclusively to rationing scarce loanable funds to 'credit-worthy' medium- and large-scale enterprises in the modern manufacturing sector. Small farmers and indigenous small-scale entrepreneurs and traders in the manufacturing and service sectors must normally seek finance elsewhere – usually through local moneylenders and 'loansharks' who charge exorbitant rates of interest.

Thus, most developing countries operate under a dual monetary system – a small and largely externally controlled or influenced *organized* money market catering for the financial requirements of a small group of middle and upper class foreign and local businesses in the modern industrial sector, and a large but amorphous *unorganized,* uncontrolled and often usurious money market to which most low-income individuals are obliged to turn in times of financial need. This is just another manifestation of the dual structure of many LDC economies and their tendency, whether intentional or not, to serve the needs of wealthy elites while neglecting the requirements of the relatively poor.

The second major limitation of standard (Western) monetary theory and policy when applied to the structural and institutional realities of most Third World nations is the assumption of a direct linkage between lower interest rates, higher investment and expanded output. (As we shall see below, however, a number of larger and more industrially advanced countries in Latin America (e.g. Brazil and Argentina) have followed a policy of inflationary financed industrial growth in which expansionary monetary policy in conjunction with budgetary deficits resulted in negative 'real' interest rates, high profits, expanded investment and a relatively high rate of industrial output growth.) In reality, as we discovered in Chapter 8 when discussing Keynesian macro-theory, there may be severe structural supply constraints (i.e. low elasticities of supply) inhibiting the expansion of output even when the demand for it increases.

These constraints include poor management, the absence of essential (usually imported) intermediate products, bureaucratic rigidities, licensing restrictions and, in general, an overall lack of interdependence within the industrial sector. Whatever the reasons, structural supply rigidities mean that any increase in the demand for goods and services will not be matched by increases in supply. Instead, the excess demand (in this case for investment goods) will merely bid up prices and lead to or worsen inflation. In some Latin American nations, this 'structural' inflation has been a chronic problem made even worse on the cost side by the upward spiral of wages as workers attempt to protect their 'real' income levels.

2. The emergence of development banking In their attempts to secure systematic finance for sustaining planned industrial expansion, many developing countries have established a new type of financial institution known as 'Development Banks'. These banks are specialized public and private financial institutions which supply medium- and long-term funds for the creation and/or expansion of industrial enterprises. They have arisen in many Third World nations because the existing banks usually focus on either relatively short-term lending for commercial purposes (commercial and savings banks) or, in the case of Central Banks, the control and regulation of the aggregate supply of money. Moreover, existing commercial banks usually set loan conditions which often are inappropriate for establishing new enterprises or for financing large-scale projects. Their funds more often are allocated to 'safe' borrowers – i.e. established industries, many of which are foreign owned or run by well-known local families. True 'venture capital' for new industries rarely finds approval.

In order to facilitate industrial growth in economies characterized by a scarcity of financial capital, development banks have sought to raise capital from two major sources: (1) bilateral and multilateral loans from national aid agencies like the United States Agency for International Development (USAID) and from international donor agencies like the World Bank, and (2) loans from their own governments. However, in addition to raising capital, development banks have had to develop specialized skills in the field of industrial project appraisal. In many cases their activities go far beyond the traditional banker's role of merely lending money to credit-worthy customers. The activities of development banks thus often encompass direct entrepreneurial, managerial and promotional involvement in the enterprises they finance – including government owned and operated industrial corporations. Development banks are thus playing an increasingly important role in the industrialization process of many LDCs.

Although development banks are a relatively new phenomenon in the Third World, their growth and spread has been substantial. In the mid-1940s there were no more than ten to twelve such institutions; by the end of the 1960s, their numbers had increased into hundreds and their financial resources had ballooned into billions of dollars. Moreover, although initial sources of capital came from agencies like the World Bank, as well as bilateral aid agencies and local governments (for example the Industrial Credit and Investment Corporation of India was established in 1954 with a 30-year interest-free advance of 75 million rupees from the Indian government), the growth of Development Bank finance has often been further facilitated by growing participation by private investors, both institutional and individual, foreign and local. For example, almost 20 per cent of the share capital of these banks was foreign owned in 1970 with the remaining 80 per cent derived from local investors.

In spite of their impressive growth and their growing importance for Third World industrial expansion, development banks have come under increasing criticism for their excessive concentration on large-scale loans. Some privately-owned finance companies (also categorized as development banks) refuse to consider loans of less than $20,000 to $50,000. They argue that smaller loans do not justify the time and effort involved in their appraisal. As a result, development finance companies almost totally isolate their activities from the field of aid to small enterprises, even though in most countries such aid is of major importance to the achievement of broadly based economic development. In many regions, it may constitute the bulk of assistance needed in the private sector, both formal and informal. Small-scale entrepreneurs often lacking technical, purchasing, marketing, organizational and accounting skills as well as access to bank credit are thus forced to seek funds in the exploitive unorganized money markets. Unless these small-enterprise financial and technical needs can begin to be served, the long-run impact of development banks, public as well as private, will be confined mainly to assisting a relatively few private corporations and para-statal enterprises to consolidate their combined economic power even further.

We may conclude, therefore, that in spite of the growth of development banks in almost every Third World nation, there still remains a need for the establishment of new types of savings institutions and financial intermediaries. Such institutions should not only mobilize domestic savings from small as well as large savers but, more important, they should begin to channel these financial resources to those small entrepreneurs, both on the farm and in the marginal or 'informal' sector of urban areas, who have until now been almost totally excluded from access to needed credit at reasonable rates of interest [3].

3. Fiscal policy for development
A. Taxation: direct and indirect

In the absence of well-organized and locally-controlled money markets, most developing countries have had to rely primarily on 'fiscal' measures to mobilize domestic resources. The principal 'instruments' of such public resource mobilization have been government tax policies. Typically 'direct' taxes – those levied on private individuals, corporations and property – vary between 20 to 40 per cent of total tax revenue for most LDCs and ranges from between 2 and 5 per cent of their GNPs (see Table 16.1). On the other hand, 'indirect' taxes such as import and export duties as well as 'excise' taxes (i.e. purchase, sales and turnover taxes) comprise the major source of fiscal revenue. Table 16.1 shows the tax structure and revenue sources of twenty-two selected LDCs in the late 1960s.

Country	Direct taxes			Indirect taxes		
	Personal and corporate	Property	Total direct	Foreign import and export duties	Domestic (excise taxes)	Total indirect
Ethiopia	15·6	8·3	23·9	33·3	42·8	76·1
India	19·8	9·3	29·1	17·8	53·1	70·9
Somalia	7·2	1·1	8·3	58·1	33·6	91·7
Indonesia	28·8	2·1	30·9	43·3	25·8	69·1
Congo	14·1	0·1	14·2	62·0	23·8	85·8
Kenya	42·6	0·7	43·3	34·2	22·5	56·7
Pakistan	15·7	5·7	21·4	24·2	54·3	78·5
Korea	33·8	8·3	42·1	16·2	41·0	57·2
Sri Lanka	20·7	2·9	23·6	47·6	28·4	76·0
Thailand	13·6	2·1	15·7	41·5	42·8	84·3
UAR	20·4	8·2	28·6	21·8	31·3	53·1
Philippines	23·9	8·2	32·1	21·4	43·4	64·8
Morocco	29·7	5·5	35·2	19·9	42·4	62·3
Tunisia	29·7	3·8	33·5	13·3	52·0	65·3
Paraguay	11·7	5·8	17·5	50·8	29·0	79·8
Ecuador	11·5	9·9	21·4	56·7	21·6	78·3
Brazil	11·4	1·4	12·8	3·5	70·1	73·6
Honduras	27·2	2·0	29·2	38·4	32·4	70·8
Ghana	23·2	2·7	25·9	49·1	25·0	74·1
Guatemala	12·4	5·6	18·0	32·5	49·4	81·9
Costa Rica	23·1	6·3	29·4	34·2	36·4	70·6
Chile	35·3	6·4	41·7	12·2	45·9	58·1

Table 16.1
The tax structure and revenue sources of selected less developed nations: 1966–8

Source: Montek Ahluwalia, 'The scope for policy intervention', in Chenery, Duloy and Jolly (eds), *Redistribution with Growth: An Approach to Policy*, IBRD, August 1973, Table I.

Traditionally, taxation in developing countries has had two purposes. First, tax concessions and similar fiscal incentives have been thought of as a means of stimulating private enterprise. Such concessions and incentives have typically been offered to foreign private investors to induce them to locate their enterprises in the less developed country. While such tax incentives may indeed increase the inflow of private foreign resources, we discovered in Chapter 14 that the overall benefits of such 'special treatment' of foreign firms is by no means self-evident.

The second purpose of taxation – the mobilization of resources to finance public expenditures – is by far the more important. Whatever the prevailing political or economic ideology of the less developed country, its economic and social progress largely depends on its government's ability to generate sufficient revenues to finance an expanding programme of essential, non-revenue yielding public services such as health, education, transport, communications and other components of the economic and social infrastructure. In addition, most Third World governments are directly involved in the economic activities of their nations through their ownership and control of public corporations and state trading agencies. Direct and indirect tax levies enable the government to finance the capital and recurrent expenditures of these public enterprises, many of which often operate at a loss.

In general, the taxation potential of a country depends on the following five factors:
1. The level of per capita real income;
2. The degree of inequality in the distribution of that income;

3. The industrial structure of the economy and the importance of different types of economic activity (e.g. the importance of foreign trade; the significance of the modern sector; the extent of foreign participation in private enterprises; the degree to which the agricultural sector is commercialized as opposed to subsistence oriented);
4. The social, political and institutional setting and the relative power of different groups (e.g. landlords as opposed to manufacuturers, trade unions, village or district community organizations);
5. The administrative competence, honesty and integrity of the tax-gathering branches of government.

We now examine the principal sources of public tax revenues in the context of this five-fold classification of tax potential. We can then consider how the tax system might be used either to redistribute incomes or simply to expand government economic activity.

As can be seen from Table 16.1, there are basically two categories of taxes – direct and indirect. Direct taxes consist primarily of 'income taxes' on individuals and corporations and 'property taxes'. Indirect taxes largely comprise taxes on foreign trade (import and export duties) and 'excise' taxes on the local consumption of commodities.

1. Personal income and property taxes

The personal income tax yields much less proportionate revenue in the less developed than in the more developed nations. In the latter, the income tax structure is said to be 'progressive', that is, people with higher incomes theoretically pay a larger percentage of that income in taxes. In practice, however, the average level of taxation in countries like the United States does not vary much between middle and upper income groups. This is because of the many tax 'loopholes' of which the wealthy are able to take advantage. In developing countries, a combination of more exemptions, lower rates on smaller incomes, and a general administrative weakness in collecting income taxes means that less than 3 per cent of Third World populations pay income tax. This figure compares with 60 to 80 per cent of the populations of developed nations who pay some form of income tax.

In spite of this limited coverage and the fact that it is administratively too costly and economically regressive to attempt to collect substantial income taxes from the many poor, it is nevertheless true that most LDC governments have not been persistent enough in collecting taxes from the very wealthy. Since it is the highest income groups that offer the greatest potential yield to the tax collector, the large income inequalities prevailing in most Third World countries mean that there is great scope for expanding income tax revenues. Moreover, in those countries where the ownership of property is heavily concentrated and therefore represents the major determinant of unequal incomes (e.g. most of Asia and Latin America), property taxes can be an efficient and administratively simple mechanism both for generating public revenues and for correcting gross inequalities in income distribution. But, as can be seen from Table 16.1, in none of the twenty-two countries listed does the property tax constitute more than 10 per cent of total public revenues. Moreover, in spite of much public rhetoric about reducing income inequalities, the share of property taxes as well as overall direct taxation has remained roughly the same for the majority of Third World countries over the past two decades. Clearly, this phenomenon cannot be attributed to government tax-collecting inefficiencies as much as to the political and economic power and influence of the large landowning classes in many Asian and Latin

American countries. The 'political will' to carry out development plans must therefore include the political will to extract public revenue from the most accessible sources to finance development projects. Where the former is absent, so too will the latter be.

2. Corporate income taxes Taxes on corporate profits, of both domestically- and foreign-owned companies, amount to less than 2 per cent of GDP in most developing countries, compared with more than 6 per cent in most developed nations. The main reason why these taxes generate such limited revenue in Third World countries is that there is relatively less corporate activity in the overall economy, combined with a tendency of LDC governments to offer all sorts of tax incentives and concessions to manufacturing and commercial enterprises. Typically, new enterprises are offered long periods (sometimes up to 15 years) of tax exemption and thereafter take advantage of generous investment depreciation allowances, special tax write-offs and other measures to lessen the incidence of taxation.

In the case of multinational foreign enterprises, the ability of LDC governments to collect substantial taxes is often frustrated. These locally run enterprises are able to 'shift' profits to partner companies in those countries offering the lowest levels of taxation through 'transfer pricing' (discussed in Chapter 14). When local subsidiaries of multinational corporations buy from or sell to partner companies in other countries, the prices in such transactions are merely internal 'accounting' prices of the overall corporation; it makes no difference to the calculation of 'total' corporate profits what price one subsidiary charges another since the cost of one will be offset by the income of the other. For example, in high tax nations, MNC exports to branches in low tax countries can be invoiced at artificially low prices. This practice reduces corporate profits in the high tax country and raises them in the low tax nations. The latter is often referred to as a 'tax haven'. Thus, by means of transfer pricing, multinational corporations are able to shift their profits from one place to another in order to lower their overall tax assessment while leaving their total profits unchanged. So long as such tax havens exist, this profit-shifting practice greatly limits the ability of individual LDCs to increase public revenues by raising taxes on foreign corporations.

3. Indirect taxes on The largest single source of tax revenue in developing countries is the **commodities** taxation of commodities in the form of import, export and excise duties (see Table 16.1). These 'indirect' taxes by which individuals and corporations are taxed indirectly through their purchase of commodities are relatively easy to assess and collect. This is especially true in the case of foreign-traded commodities which must pass through a relatively limited number of frontier ports and are usually handled by a few wholesalers. The ease of collecting such taxes is one reason why countries with extensive foreign trade typically collect a greater proportion of public revenues in the form of import and export duties than do those countries with limited external trade. For example, in open economies with up to 40 per cent of their GNPs derived from foreign trade an average import duty of 25 per cent will yield a tax revenue equivalent of 10 per cent of GNP. By contrast, in countries like India and Brazil with only about 8 per cent of their GNPs derived from exports, the same tariff rate would yield only 2 per cent of GNP in equivalent tax revenues.

Although we discussed import and export duties in the context of LDC trade policies in the last chapter, one further point about these taxes, often overlooked, needs to be mentioned. It is that import and export duties in addition to representing the major sources of public revenue in many LDCs can also be an efficient substitute for corporate income tax. To the extent that importers are unable to pass on to local consumers the full costs of the tax, an import duty can serve as a proxy tax on the profits of the importer (often a foreign company) and only partially a tax on the local consumer. Similarly, an export duty can be an effective way of taxing the profits of producing companies, including those locally based multinational firms which practise 'transfer pricing'. But export duties designed to generate revenue should not be raised to the point of discouraging local producers from expanding their export production.

In selecting commodities to be taxed, whether in the form of duties on imports and exports or excise taxes on local commodities, certain general economic and administrative principles need to be followed to minimize the cost of securing 'maximum' revenue. First, the commodity should be imported or produced by a relatively small number of licensed firms so that evasion can be controlled. Second, the price elasticity of demand for the commodity should be low so that total demand is not choked by the rise in consumer prices that results from the tax. Third, the commodity should have a high income elasticity of demand so that as incomes rise more tax revenue will be collected. Fourth, for equity purposes it is best to tax those commodities like motor cars, refrigerators, imported fancy foods, household appliances, etc., which are consumed largely by the upper-income groups while forgoing taxation on items of mass consumption like basic foods, simple clothing, and household utensils even though these may satisfy the first three criteria set forth above.

In the final analysis, a developing nation's ability to collect taxes needed for public expenditure programmes and to use the tax system as a basis for modifying the distribution of personal incomes will depend not only on the enactment of appropriate tax legislation but more importantly on the efficiency and integrity of the tax authorities who must implement these laws. As Professor Kaldor noted [4] over a decade ago:

4. Problems of tax administration

In many underdeveloped countries the low revenue yield of taxation can only be attributed to the fact that the tax provisions are not properly enforced, either on account of the inability of the administration to cope with them, or on account of straightforward corruption. No system of tax laws, however carefully conceived, is proof against collusion between the tax administrators and the taxpayers; an efficient administration consisting of persons of high integrity is usually the most important requirement for obtaining maximum revenue, and exploiting fully the taxation potential of a country.

Thus, the ability of Third World governments to expand their 'tax nets' to cover the higher income groups and to minimize tax evasion by local and foreign individuals and corporations will largely determine the efficiency of the tax system in achieving its dual function of generating sufficient public revenues to finance expanding development programmes and transferring income from upper to lower income groups in order to reduce poverty and income inequality. Much will depend on the 'political will' to enact and *enforce* such progressive tax programs.

B. Fiscal policy to control The spiralling inflation which spread like wildfire throughout the world
inflation in the 1970s affected every nation in Africa, Asia and Latin America.
In the more developed countries, inflation rates of 12 to 25 per cent per
annum were the highest recorded in many decades. The very economic
and political stability of countries like Great Britain and Italy were
threatened more by this inflation than by any other event since the
Second World War.

Economists have variously attributed the inflation of the 1970s to
two major factors – the upward 'demand-pull' of prices as a result of a
previous decade of 'expansionary' fiscal and monetary policy (and in
the United States, the heavy expenditures on the war in Vietnam), and
the upward 'cost-push' of raw material and commodity prices resulting
from the unprecedented 500 per cent rise in oil prices and the
worldwide failure of agricultural production to keep pace with rising
demand[5]. Given these traditional economic factors of demand-pull
and cost–push inflation, psychological factors also entered the picture
as worker expectations of continuing price rises and a further eroding
of their real incomes caused them to press for ever higher wage
increases. These spiralling wage increases exert further upward pressure on production costs leading to even higher consumer prices. Thus,
inflation has a way of becoming self-generating and extremely difficult
to stop. A number of Latin American nations (e.g. Argentina and
Brazil) were aware of this fact long before the global inflation of the
1970s.

Faced with rising prices and higher levels of unemployment (a
combination of forces unprecedented in modern Western economic
history and which contradicted traditional macro-economic theories
that postulated an inverse relationship between inflation and unemployment), most developed countries, as we have seen, pursued a combination of economic policies. These included: (*a*) slowing monetary
growth and raising interest rates; (*b*) curtailing the growth of government current and capital expenditure; (*c*) raising taxes especially for
middle and upper income groups; (*d*) establishing wage and price
'guidelines' through legislative controls in an effort to curtail the
upward movement of costs and prices; and (*e*) manipulating foreign
exchange rates in general and attempting to cut back specifically on oil
imports in an effort to reduce payments deficits and prevent the further
erosion of their foreign exchange positions. While such restrictive
monetary, fiscal and commercial policies may have imposed severe
economic hardships on their poorest families, developed country governments at least processed the economic tools to cope with the unique
inflationary forces of the 1970s.

But what about the less developed countries? Can their domestic
monetary and fiscal policies also act as an effective brake on the
inflation which they too experienced with even more severe economic
dislocations and hardships than the developed countries? Or must they
resign themselves to minor efforts to modify their domestic rates of
inflation while remaining 'non-players' standing on the sidelines while
the developed countries participate in the fight against inflation? This
second rhetorical question better described the position of most contemporary developing nations in the 1970s.

Unlike the inflationary experience of a number of Latin American
countries in the 1960s – an experience which largely grew out of deficit
– financed expansionary domestic demand policies (see below) combined with production supply inelasticities – the inflation of the 1970s

was for most LDCs largely *external in origin.* Being much more dependent than developed countries on the importation of capital goods,
certain raw materials, intermediate products and consumer goods over
whose prices they have virtually no control, the non-oil-exporting
Third World nations found themselves with equally high or higher
rates of inflation but without many of the economic policy tools with
which to combat this price spiral. Most LDCs had therefore to content
themselves with policies to control the importation of certain non-
necessity goods, to stimulate and promote greater exports to pay for
increased imports, to seek special international foreign exchange credits, to ration limited credit from both domestic and foreign sources to
essential industrial uses, to hold the line on wage increases while
attempting to expand the tax net, and to seek ways to control the rising
prices of essential foodstuffs and basic subsistence commodities consumed by the urban and rural poor, often by means of costly government food subsidy programmes.

While the above components of anti-inflationary LDC economic
policy can help to modify the impact of rising prices, especially for
those income groups who can least afford it, they are nevertheless
insufficient to control domestic inflation. Third World dependence on
the world economy in general and on developed country domestic and
international economic policies in particular (not to mention the
policies of their oil-producing OPEC neighbours) was never more
dramatically illustrated than by the inflation and resource-squeeze
crisis of the 1970s. The most lasting impact of this experience was
probably the realization by many LDCs of the real need for increased
cooperation among themselves in the pursuit of a greater degree of
national or regional self-reliance. In the final analysis, therefore, the
achievement of some form of individual or collective economic independence provides one of the only real vehicles for LDCs to control
inflation by purely domestic measures.

Even before the worldwide inflationary spiral of the 1970s, many
developing nations had come to accept rapid price increases as an
inevitable and sometimes even necessary way of life. Because of the
inadequacy of savings and the difficulty of directing them into productive investments, a number of developing-country governments, most
notably Brazil and Argentina, have intentionally sought to raise the
level of investment and to create modern industries by running chronic
budgetary deficits financed by expanded bank credit. This discriminatory, inflationary financing of chosen sectors of the economy is based on
the rationale that deficit-financed inflation itself can lead to increased
investment for three reasons. First, rising relative prices in certain
sectors of the economy mean greater profits and a higher return on
private investments thereby inducing firms to expand their capacity.
Second, the rapid expansion of bank credit in combination with a
ceiling on nominal interest rates and rising output prices mean that
favored investors can often borrow funds at negative 'real' rates of
interest. If their industries are also highly protected against foreign
competition, a rapid (but socially costly) rate of industrial expansion
can be achieved. Finally, inflation was thought to provide an indirect
mechanism of transferring real income from 'non-savers' (i.e., low-
income workers and small rural and urban enterprises) to a 'saving
group' (wealthy local and foreign industrialists) who are assumed to
reinvest their excess profits and incomes in productive industrial pro-

**C. Inflationary-financed
industrial growth: scope and
limitations**

jects and thus maintain a higher level of investment and growth. On this final point, Little, Scitovsky and Scott concluded in their study of seven developing nations (including Brazil and Argentina) that 'There is no evidence anywhere of inflation having increased the flow of saving'[6].

In his study of the Brazilian experience, Huddle has shown that the policy of providing credit for certain industries through the use of inflationary finance during the past two decades has involved some substantial social costs[7]. First, the gains of such growth are very unevenly distributed. Very large firms having privileged access to subsidized finance become dominant in production even though they may be less efficient than their small- or medium-sized competitors. Second, capital-intensive industries and firms expand at the expense of labour-intensive ones, thus exacerbating the problems of unemployment and surplus labour. Third, deficit-financed inflation can lead to an undesirable pattern of demand which reinforces this tendency towards large scale, capital-intensive enterprises by channelling finance and, as a result, factor incomes to those groups in society whose consumption patterns are oriented towards domestic capital-intensive and/or import-intensive 'luxury' products. Such policies can, therefore, reinforce the dualistic nature of developing economies. Fourth, inflation tends to reduce the level of voluntary savings as individuals attempt to protect their real incomes by further bidding up prices of consumer durables, while the pattern of investment can be distorted as funds are used to produce luxury housing, purchase real estate and build up inventories as a hedge against further inflation. Capacity to resist depreciation becomes the overriding criterion for investment instead of social productivity. Finally, inflation ultimately has a tendency to feed upon itself and become self-reinforcing as budget deficits, wage pressures and occasional devaluations all contribute to a chronic upward spiral of domestic prices. This has been the experience of a number of Latin American countries. Although higher aggregate growth rates may continue to be achieved, rising unemployment and a worsening distribution of income make such growth inimical to 'development'.

We conclude, therefore, that although inflationary financing may, under certain conditions, succeed in generating high rates of industrial expansion, it often does this only at the expense of reinforcing dualistic tendencies within developing countries, increasing levels of unemployment and worsening the distribution of personal incomes. Today, few economists would argue seriously that chronic budgetary deficits financed by expanding bank credit and rising prices can be a significant factor in promoting Third World development.

16.2 The interrelationship between problems and policies

It has been convenient for instruction purposes throughout Parts II and III to isolate major development problems and then to identify an appropriate range of corresponding fiscal, monetary and other public-policy alternatives. In reality, however, all these problems and many of the policy responses are highly interrelated. Problems of Third World poverty and inequality cannot be separated from problems of rapid population growth, rising urban unemployment, stagnating agriculture and unequal and inappropriate educational systems.

Similarly, problems of excessive rural–urban migration and rising urban unemploment cannot be analyzed in isolation from problems of mass rural poverty, highly unequal land tenure arrangements, rapid population growth and the elitist, urban-oriented structure of most formal systems of education. One could go on indefinitely demonstrating the many ways in which development problems and policies are linked in an intricate web of cause and effect.

For illustrative purposes, however, and by way of summarizing much of what has been said in Parts II and III, we look again at five critical development problems analyzed separately in earlier chapters along with some of their major policy implications. Table 16.2 provides a brief summary of the major domestic policy options suggested for coping with the problems of poverty and inequality, population growth, urban unemployment, rural underdevelopment and inappropriate educational structures.

Problem	Policy instruments and/or objectives
1. Poverty and inequality	Asset redistribution (mainly from growth). Land reform. Provision of rural social services. Poverty-focused investments (target groups). Tax and subsidy policies (including direct 'transfer payments'). Job creation – urban and rural. Improved educational access.
2. Excessive population growth	Eradicate poverty (see 1 above). Provide family planning services. Monetary incentives and disincentives. Education and job opportunities for women. Improved maternal and child nutrition and health.
3. Urban unemployment	Reducing migration by eliminating artificial urban–rural incentive and economic opportunity imbalances. 'Getting factor prices right'. Choosing and/or developing appropriate labor-intensive technologies. Poverty-focused rural investments. Modifying urban incentive effects of inappropriate education systems. Slowing population growth (see 2 above).
4. Agricultural stagnation and rural underdevelopment	Rural institutional reforms (land tenure, small-farmer access to credit, information, biological and chemical farm inputs, crop insurance, new seeds). Improved rural education, health delivery, sanitation, water supplies and other social services. Specialized rural training programmes. Rural public works. Export promotion.
5. Inappropriate and unequal education	Modifying educational demands by re-orientation of economic signals and incentives towards rural sector. Improved access through system of loans, subsidies and tuition according to ability to pay. Minimizing excessive credentialization. Promoting non-formal, out-of-school life-time education. Reorienting curricula along functional lines.

Table 16.2
The interrelationship between problems and policies: an illustration

It may be seen that for the most part policies designed to deal with one problem often contribute to the solution of one or more of the others. Thus, for example, policies designed to eliminate poverty such as land reform, asset redistribution, taxes and subsidies, the provision of rural social services and the creation of widespread job opportunities are also policies which should help to curtail rapid population growth, reduce rural–urban migration and promote agricultural progress and rural development. Similarly policies designed to promote rural development such as institutional reforms to aid the small farmer, rural public works programs, the provision of rural social services and economic infrastructure and the restructuring of rural educational systems and training programs also contribute to the alleviation of urban unemployment (e.g. through lowering the incentives to migrate), the reduction of rural fertility levels and the amelioration of living conditions where 80 per cent of Third World poverty is located. Finally, policies designed to make education more relevant for development (e.g. by giving it a more functional and rural-oriented structure or by improving access for lower income groups) can be a major force in promoting rural development, reducing urban unemployment, lowering population growth rates (especially as more women are educated) and providing realistic income earning opportunities for children of low income families.

Note that in Table 16.2 we have left out the whole range of international issues and policies dealing with problems of trade, aid and foreign investment. This was done for convenience of exposition. Clearly, policies designed to minimize the harmful effects of trade, aid and foreign investment while maximizing their beneficial potentialities will have a direct and indirect impact on the five major problem areas depicted in the table.

16.3 Development policy and the role and limitations of the state: concluding observations

We conclude this chapter with some generalizations on the actual formulation of economic policy in the Third World and speculate about the future role and limitations of the state in the 'mixed-market' economies characteristic of most countries of Asia, Africa and Latin America [8].

In view of the somewhat disappointing record of the past two decades, most development economists would now probably agree that their early and almost mystical belief in the efficacy and benefits of central planning in comparison to market forces has not been validated by Third World experience [9]. Moreover, economic policies have more often than not tended to be *ad hoc* responses to recurring and often unexpected crises rather than the playing out of a grand economic design for development. We should never forget that political leaders and decision makers are human beings like the rest of us with all the human idiosyncrasies, foibles and weaknesses. Except in very unusual cases, they will tend to take a parochial (class, caste, tribal, religious, ethnic, regional, etc.) rather than a national point of view. In democracies, politicians will respond first to their political constituencies and the vested interest groups within their home areas. In more autocratic forms of government, whether military dictatorship or strict one-party rule, political leaders will still have a natural tendency to respond to those groups to whom they owe their power or upon whom their continued power depends. We must always bear in mind that economic policies are ultimately made, not by economists or planners, but by politicians. They are thus likely to be more interested in 'muddling through' each emerging crisis and staying in power than necessarily in instituting major social and economic reforms. But if, as many now believe, the coming development crisis is one whose solution will necessitate widespread economic and social reform, we should not dismiss the possibility that the present situation can and will be overcome.

We therefore need to be pragmatic about the role and limitations of economic policies in developing nations. On the one hand, we should avoid the tendency to assume that political leaders and decision makers place the 'national interest' above their own private interests, or base their policies on some notion of 'social welfare' as opposed to the 'private welfare' of those groups to whom they are primarily indebted. On the other hand, we should equally avoid the cynical view that the 'social' interest, and especially the interest of the poor, the weak and the inarticulate, will never be considered short of revolution. Social and political revolutions are notorious vehicles by which one elite replaces another while the welfare of the poor remains largely unaffected (China and more recently Cuba being probably the most notable exceptions). It appears more reasonable, therefore, to base our discussion of the role and limitations of the state on the proposition that most Third World governments are beset by conflicting forces, some elitist, others egalitarian, and that their economic policies will be largely a reflection of the relative power of these competing interests. Although narrow elitist interests have tended to prevail in the past, the groundswell for a more egalitarian development process has now reached the point where politicians and planners can no longer ignore it or camouflage it behind noble but empty rhetoric.

Whatever one's ideological preconceptions about the proper role of government, there can be no denying that over the past two decades governments in developing countries have increasingly claimed responsibility for the management and direction of their economies. It has been said that in many countries, especially in Africa, if the government does not induce development, then it probably will not happen at all. If nothing else, governments in these countries are the most important users of trained manpower. How they deploy these limited human resources thus becomes a crucial issue for the success or failure of the development effort. Moreover, how governments are structured and how they manage development have been vitally important and will continue to be even more so in the future.

In classical economics the role of government was conceived simply in terms of maintaining law and order, collecting taxes and generally providing a minimum of social services. With the Keynesian revolution, the economic role of government was greatly expanded. Governments were assigned prime responsibility within a market economy for stabilizing overall economic activity by means of counter-cyclical monetary and fiscal policies with the objective of maintaining full employment without inflation. At the same time that the Keynesian revolution in Western economic thought was occurring, the Soviet Union was demonstrating to the world the power of central planning to mobilize resources and accelerate industrial growth.

As indigenous leadership replaced colonial leadership in Third World nations, these two 'models' of the role of the state were presented. Impressed by the Soviet planning performance yet still imbued with a history of private enterprise from colonial days, most LDCs adopted the system of 'mixed' market combined with planning, with, as we have seen, a relatively heavy emphasis on central coordination and public participation in all aspects of economic activity. Given the increasing concern with questions of poverty and inequality, however, the role of the state today has increased to an even greater extent in spite of the consensus that planning has not worked the magic that some believed it would and that many public corporations are notoriously inefficient users of valuable financial and human resources.

Thus there seems to be a general agreement today among economists and others that LDC governments should *not* do *less,* but that they should do *more* and do it *better* than in the past. Most would agree that the machinery of many Third World governments has become too cumbersome. There are too many ministries often with competing interests, too many public corporations and too many boards of one kind or another. Governments are criticized for being too centralized and too urban-oriented in both staff and outlook. Civil servants and other trained personnel are often poorly utilized, badly motivated and in most respects less productive than they should be. There is too much corruption and too little inventiveness and innovation. Bureaucratic red tape and ossified procedures and processes sap originality and flexibility. In short, contemporary LDC governments are criticized for being not too different from almost any other government around the world!

But, whether one likes it or not, Third World governments must inevitably bear a greater responsibility for the future well-being of their countries than do those in the more developed nations. As their primary tasks of nation-building (in the newly independent countries) and generating rapid economic growth (in all LDCs) are gradually supplemented by preoccupations with problems of poverty, unemployment and inequality, Third World governments are forging a new role, one that will require innovation and change on a scale that has rarely occurred in the past. Central to this new role will be institutional and structural reform in the fields of land tenure, taxation, asset ownership and distribution, educational and health delivery systems, credit rationing, labor market relations, pricing policies, the organization and orientation of technological research and experimentation, the organization of state trading corporations and public sector enterprises, and the very machinery of government and planning itself.

Whether or not such a transition from a purely growth-oriented development strategy to one also emphasizing the elimination of poverty and the reduction of inequality will require major political transformations as some have suggested[10], or whether the existing leadership can respond to the new environment of development by initiating and carrying out major institutional reforms is a moot point. But whatever the nature of the response, one can certainly predict that the public sector, whether centralized or decentralized, whether jointly with private enterprise or on its own, will in the coming decades continue to claim increasing responsibility for the 'commanding heights' of most Third World economies. It is hoped, therefore, that LDC governments have learned much from their experiences of the past two decades and that future successes will more than compensate for any past inadequacies.

Notes

1. In reality, LDC governments have at least *four* major 'policy instruments' at their disposal, namely: (1) fiscal policy; (2) monetary and financial policy; (3) legislative controls (e.g. on foreign exchange, prices, wages, industrial licensing, immigration, etc.); (4) miscellaneous policy interventions including creation of 'para-statal' organizations (e.g. marketing boards, public utilities, research institutions), nationalization, exhortation for voluntary action, requests for foreign aid, anti-monopoly laws, land reform, etc. In this chapter we focus only on (1) and (2). Instruments (3) and (4) have been dealt with elsewhere.

2. One of the earliest and best descriptions of unorganized and fragmented nature of money markets in developing countries can be found in U Tun Wai, 'Interest rates outside the organized money markets', *IMF Staff Papers*, November 1957.

3. For one suggested approach to this problem, see C. Loganathan, 'A new deal in development banking' *Development Digest*, October 1972, 25–36.

4. N. Kaldor, 'Taxation for economic development', *Journal of Modern African Studies*, **1,** no. 1 (1963).

5. For a provocative analysis from a Marxist perspective of US macro policy during the 1960s and how it contributed to the inflation and international instability of the 1970s, see J. R. Crotty and L. A. Rapping, 'The 1975 Report of the President's Council of Economic Advisors: a radical critique', *American Economic Review,* December 1975.

6. Little, Scitovsky and Scott, *Industry and Trade in Some Developing Countries: A Comparative Study,* OECD, Oxford U.P. (1970), 77.

7. Donald L. Huddle, 'Inflationary financing, industrial expansion and the gains from development in Brazil', *Program of Development Studies,* Rice University, Paper no. 60, Winter 1975.

8. Although, based on the Chinese experience and the growing pressures for egalitarian reforms, some Third World countries are likely to turn to even greater public ownership and control over domestic resources in the coming decades, it is fair to assume that the vast majority will remain 'mixed' in overall economic structure with a probably increasing direct and indirect role being played by the state.

9. See, for example, Little, Scitovsky and Scott, op. cit., Ch. 9, and Derek Healey, 'Development policy: new thinking about an interpretation', pp. 792–4.

10. See, for example, A. Shourie, 'Growth poverty and inequalities', *Foreign Affairs,* **51,** no. 2 (1973).

Concepts for review

monetary and fiscal policies
inflation: cost-push, demand-pull and structural
restrictive versus expansionary monetary policy
financial intermediary
'organized' money markets
deficit financed inflationary growth
'unorganized' money markets
development banks
direct versus indirect taxes
progressive versus regressive taxation
tax 'loopholes'
expansionary fiscal policies
contractionary fiscal policies
recession

Questions for discussion

1. The current debate on the role and limitations of development planning in 'mixed' Third World economies turns on the age-old economic question of how much economic activity should be guided by 'market' forces and how much state intervention there should be. Where do you come out in this debate in relation to planning v. the market? Explain the reasoning behind your answer.

2. 'Keynesian' type macro *monetary* and *fiscal* policies have proved to be effective instruments of government economic policy in developed nations but their relevance and effectiveness in most Third World economies is greatly limited. Comment on this statement, being sure to include in your discussion a description of various types of monetary and fiscal policies.

3. What is meant by the terms 'inflation' and 'recession'. Is it possible for an economy to experience an inflation and a recession simultaneously? If so, can you give some recent examples of this phemomenon explaining how such 'reflation' could come about? If not, explain why not.

4. Distinguish between 'demand-pull', 'cost-push', and 'structural' inflation. Is it possible to have them all occurring simultaneously? Explain.

5. What policy alternatives (both fiscal and monetary) do Third World governments possess in coping with the type of worldwide inflation which occurred during the first half of the 1970s? Is it possible for most LDCs to control this type of inflation

completely or must they attempt to contain its excesses while relying ultimately on the effectiveness of developed nation anti-inflationary policies? Explain your answer.

Further readings On fiscal and monetary policy for Third World nations, see: (*a*) W. Arthur Lewis, *Development Planning: The Essentials of Economic Policy,* Harper and Row, New York (1966);   (*b*) Derek T. Healey, 'Development policy: new thinking about an interpretation', *Journal of Economic Literature,* X, no. 3 (1972);   (*c*) R. I. McKinnon, *Money and Capital in Economic Development,* The Brookings Institution, Washington DC 1973;   (*d*) E. S. Nassef, *Monetary Policy in Developing Countries,* The Netherlands Rotterdam U.P. (1972);   (*e*) Loganathan, *Development Savings Banks and the Third World,* Praeger, New York (1973);   (*f*) J. H. Adler, 'Fiscal policy in a developing country', in K. Berrill (ed.), *Economic Development with Special Reference to East Asia,* St Martins Press (1965);   (*g*) R. J. Chelliah, 'Trends in taxation in developing countries', *IMF Staff Papers,* July 1971;   (*h*) Richard M. Bird and Oliver Oldman (eds), *Readings on Taxation in Developing Countries,* revised edition, Johns Hopkins U.P. (1970).

I believe that with all the dislocations that we are now experiencing there also
exists an extraordinary opportunity to form for the first time in history a truly
global society, carried by the principle of interdependence.
 Henry Kissinger, former US Secretary of State

More than ever before it is necessary for the world community to take a *global*
approach to the world's resources and to the structure and operation of international economic relationships.
 Statement by Third World social scientists[1]

Introduction: the new interdependence

We live today in an increasingly 'interdependent' world and, perhaps
some day, a 'world without borders' to borrow the title of a provocative
book by Lester R. Brown. For Third World countries, this dependence
on rich nations is and has always been a stark fact of their economic
lives. It is the principal reason for their heightened interest in promoting greater individual and collective self-reliance. At the same time,
the developed countries of the world who once prided themselves on
their apparent self-sufficiency are rapidly discovering that in an age of
increasingly scarce natural and mineral resources they too are growing
economically more dependent on the policies of certain groups of
developing countries. All indications point to the fact that by the
beginning of the twenty-first century no nation or region will be able to
survive economically in complete isolation from others. Let us therefore conclude this book with a brief survey of this new global economic
interdependence and then close with some comments on the growing
Third World demand for a 'new international economic order'.

17.1 Manifestations of emerging global economic interdependence: energy, food and natural resources

If the 1950s and 1960s could be described as the era of nationalism and
cold war politics, the 1970s and 1980s will probably come to be known
as the decades of global interdependence. The world-wide inflation

which began in the early 1970s pushed the world economy to the brink of chaos. Global food scarcities caused by a combination of rising wealth in the developed countries and increasing populations in the poor countries, along with severe drought conditions in parts of Africa and Asia, alerted the world to the fact that massive starvation was not a remote possibility. Grain and soybean prices doubled and tripled largely to the detriment of the very poor in Asia, Africa and Latin America and to the benefit primarily of the United States which currently accounts for almost three-fourths of the world's net grain exports. On top of these food price rises, the countries of the Persian Gulf and their colleagues in OPEC dramatically increased international oil prices by 400 per cent, thus threatening the viability of the world economy as no other event had since the Great Depression. Rising oil prices in turn caused the prices of fertilizer (for which petroleum is a significant input) to increase sharply. This exacerbated an already dangerous world food situation. While this inflation in the prices of basic goods affected rich and poor nations alike, it fell most heavily on the poorest of the Third World nations, thereby further increasing the real gap between them and the rest of the world.

But even though world price inflation demonstrated once again the enormous vulnerability of the poorest of Third World nations to international economic setbacks, the vulnerability of rich-country economies to rapidly rising natural resource prices dramatically illustrated that, at least in the case of minerals and basic raw materials, their dependence on access to Third World resources is far greater than anyone had thought. In all probability, it will be even greater in the future. Let us, therefore, examine the growing global interdependence with reference to three critical commodities: energy, food and natural resources.

1. Energy and the world economy If anyone ever doubted that energy and energy supplies (e.g. oil, coal, natural gas and hydroelectric power) are the foundations of modern industrial economies, the 'energy shock' of the mid-1970s dramatically proved the point. In 1970, the developed nations comprising one-third of the world's population were consuming annually almost 85 per cent of world energy production. But the non-oil-producing Third World countries also rely heavily on oil to fuel their growing industrial and agricultural economies. The massive and unprecedented 400 per cent increase announced by members of the Organization of Petroleum Exporting Countries in 1974 resulted in enormous additions to their total export revenues, rising from some $14·5 billion in 1972 to over $110 billion in 1974. Admittedly, a vast proportion of these revenues is derived from the principal oil-importing developed nations like Great Britain, France, Italy, Japan and the United States. But the oil import bill of the non-OPEC developing countries – numbering about ninety – rose from $4 billion in 1973 to over $15 billion in 1974, an increase of more than $10 billion or 250 per cent. *That increase in the cost of imports alone amounted to more than the total value of all official foreign aid provided to these countries by the developed world.*

The oil price explosion, irrespective of its eventual outcome, clearly demonstrated the following points about the world economy of the mid-1970s:

1. Almost all of the *developed countries* are net importers of oil. Their ultimate dependence upon the pricing policies of an organized

group of Third World nations was thus vividly revealed. Japan, for example, depends on imports for 99 per cent of its petroleum needs while Western Europe imports 96 per cent of its requirement. Their economies were shaken in a manner attributable to no other single event in the previous 30 years. For the foreseeable future, therefore, the oil-exporting countries are in positions of immense power. The six Middle-East nations, for example, account for little more than 1 per cent of world's population but control over half of the world's known reserves of petroleum and a far greater share of total exportable reserves. The nature of their newly discovered economic power is not being lost sight of by other Third World nations. Many LDCs are now attempting to form OPEC-like cartels for other minerals, raw materials and primary products over which they exert some substantial control.

2. The non-oil-exporting, *less developed countries,* especially those with large modern sectors and limited export markets also are vulnerable to rapid increases in the price of fuels. For illustrative purposes, however, we can distinguish between four groups of Third World countries according to their vulnerability to rapid energy cost increases. The first group consists of countries like Colombia, Mexico, Bolivia and Peru which are largely self-sufficient in oil and are, therefore, not directly affected. Others like Malaysia, Morocco and Brazil are also less seriously affected because the prices of their own scarce exportable raw materials have also been rising gradually. A third category consists of nations like South Korea, Hong Kong, Taiwan and Singapore. These countries are all closely integrated into the world economy primarily through their import of raw and intermediate materials for processing into manufactured goods. The energy component of their imports is, therefore, large but they are able to pass on most of their extra energy and raw material costs in the form of higher prices to buyers of their manufactured export products. Moreover, the dynamism of their economies is such that they have relatively good access to export credits and foreign financial support.

The fourth and last category of nations consist of those forty or so Third World countries which are extremely vulnerable to rapid world price increases for petroleum and other products (see the category of 'least developed countries' in Appendix 2.1). Included among these countries are most of those in sub-Saharan Africa, South Asia (India, Pakistan and Bangladesh), Central America and a few separate countries like Uruguay, Chile and possibly the Philippines. Together they constitute almost 50 per cent of the population of Third World countries (excluding China). For them, the economic consequences of rising resource and commodity prices are overwhelmingly adverse. They are the poorest of countries, with the lowest anticipated economic growth rates and the most limited margin for economic manoeuvring. Having large accumulated debt burdens and limited foreign exchange earning capacities, they are unlikely to have any access to short-term credit. This is the most dependent and vulnerable group of all.

3. The *direct* dependence of *both* developed and less developed nations on energy imports is compounded in the case of the less developed countries by the indirect effects of their economic dependence and vulnerability to the economic policies of rich nations. This indirect dependence is manifested in the latter coun-

tries' ability to adjust their economies to the altered international circumstances. For example, in their efforts to combat the negative effects of higher import prices for energy and raw materials and the more general inflationary trend, wealthy countries are likely to cut back on foreign travel and foreign assistance. These and related policies can exacerbate an already difficult foreign exchange position for the least developed nations.

4. Finally, as was discussed in Chapter 14, much will depend on how the newly discovered 'petro-dollar' wealth of OPEC nations is 'recycled' in world financial markets (i.e. how they invest their enormous surplus oil revenues). If it almost all goes back to the developed countries, as most of it has and probably will, then the overall result may be a transfer of scarce financial resources from poor to rich nations through the intermediary of the oil-producing states. For example, if 90 per cent of Arab oil revenues come from developed countries and 10 per cent from the LDCs and if, after domestic use, 95 per cent of the excess revenue is reinvested in rich-country economies, then in effect the non-oil producing LDCs are financing Arab investments in rich countries. On the other hand, if the thirteen OPEC countries reaffirm their historic ties with other Third World nations and use their surplus funds to invest in the economies of poor nations, then their extraordinary wealth could greatly help to stimulate economic and social improvements in less fortunate nations.

2. Raw materials and mineral resources

No nation or continent is endowed with *all* the raw materials essential for the functioning of a modern industrial economy. As these materials become increasingly scarce, their very uneven distribution throughout the world could thrust previously weak nations into positions of considerable economic power in much the same manner as that experienced by the oil-producing states. World mineral interdependence and, especially, the growing raw material dependence of rich nations on poor ones, is a new and vital component of the growing economic interdependence of all nations. Raw material interdependence in particular has two main aspects.

First, the consumption of nearly all essential minerals, both metallic and non-metallic, is rapidly rising. Those countries of North America and especially Western Europe which industrialized earliest have almost depleted many of their indigenous supplies of basic raw materials. According to Lester Brown [2],

the rich countries, particularly the United States, Japan and those of Western Europe, with their steadily rising consumption of minerals required to support their affluence, are becoming increasingly dependent on the poor countries with their largely unexploited mineral reserves. In western Europe, consumption of eleven basic industrial raw materials – bauxite, copper, lead, phosphate, zinc, chrome ore, manganese ore, magnesium, nickel, tungsten and tin – exceeds production. In the case of copper, phosphates, tin, nickel, manganese ore and chrome ore, nearly all needs must now be met from imports.

Table 17.1 shows that the United States' dependence on raw material imports in 1970 included the need to import more than half its supplies of aluminium, manganese, nickel, tin, zinc and chromium. By 1985 iron, lead and tungsten will probably be added to the list bringing it to a total of nine of the basic thirteen industrial raw materials. By the year 2000 the United States will more than likely be dependent primarily on foreign sources for all its basic industrial raw materials with the probable exception of phosphate. Its total imports of energy fuels and minerals which cost $8 billion in 1970 is projected to increase to almost $64 billion by the turn of the century. As competition for dwindling reserves of high grade minerals sharply increases over the coming decades, the United States as well as the other industrialized countries will become increasingly vulnerable to external forces beyond their control. These forces will originate from supplier nations, mostly in the Third World, whose international bargaining power will be on the rise, especially if organizations similar to OPEC are formed for other scarce minerals.

Raw material	Per cent imported			
	1950	1970	1985	2000
Aluminium	64	85	96	98
Chromium	n.a.	100	100	100
Copper	31	0	34	56
Iron	8	30	55	67
Lead	39	31	62	67
Manganese	88	95	100	100
Nickel	94	90	88	89
Phosphorus	8	0	0	2
Potassium	14	42	47	61
Sulphur	2	0	28	52
Tin	77	n.a.	100	100
Tungsten	n.a.	50	87	97
Zinc	38	59	72	84

Table 17.1 US dependence on imports of principal industrial raw materials with projections to year 2000

Source: Lester R. Brown, *World Without Borders*, Random House, N.Y. (1972), 194.

The second aspect of raw material interdependence, therefore, is the fact that known reserves of a number of minerals are highly concentrated in few, mostly Third World, locations around the globe. For example, four less developed countries (Chile, Peru, Zambia and

Mineral	Major LDC suppliers with per cent supplied by each		Total per cent supplied by LDCs
Aluminium Bauxite	Jamaica	53·5	88·2
	Surinam	27·4	
	Guyana	7·3	
Cobalt	Zaire	34·5	43
	Zambia	8·5	
Copper	Peru	23·2	37·9
	Chile	14·7	
Iron ore	Venezuela	30·6	30·6
Lead	Peru	22·0	31·7
	Mexico	9·7	
Manganese	Gabon	26·3	55·5
	Brazil	18·8	
	Zaire	10·4	
Tin	Malaysia	64·3	96·5
	Thailand	23·3	
	Bolivia	8·9	
Tungsten	Bolivia	18·0	39·0
	Peru	12·0	
	Thailand	9·0	

Table 17.2 US imports of selected minerals from principal LDC suppliers

Source: Overseas Development Council, *Agenda for Action: 1974,* Washington, Table C-10.

Zaire) supply almost all of the world's exports of copper. Three others (Bolivia, Malaysia and Thailand) supply over 70 per cent of all tin traded in international markets. Mexico, Peru and Australia account for almost 60 per cent of the world's traded supply of lead. With regard to phosphate and potash, two of the three principal nutrients in the chemical fertilizer so important to international agricultural production, we find that Canada supplies most of the world's potash while Morocco, Tunisia, Senegal, Joga and the United States control most of the phosphates. The range and concentration of important LDC suppliers of these and other essential minerals to the United States (and, even more so, to other developed countries) is indicated by Table 17.2.

The above discussion reveals that the prospect of economic *collective bargaining* by major Third World suppliers of scarce raw materials emphasizes the very real nature of the growing dependence of rich countries on the poor ones.

Growing resource scarcities promise to modify current international economic and political relationships among nations with the likely elevation of the relative influence and power of certain Third World countries in the international hierarchy. Whatever the probable outcome, however, it can no longer be said that international dependence runs only from poor countries to rich countries.

3. World food shortages The 1970s also witnessed the transition from a previous era of commercial food surpluses to one of global shortages, rising prices and growing national concern primarily among the least developed countries. While droughts in parts of Africa and Asia exacerbated the short-term seriousness of the world food problem, its long-term trend has been in the direction of a narrowing gap between total world production and world consumption. Food prices are likely to remain much higher than they were during the previous decade and, one continent, North America, is emerging as the only major source of exportable world food supplies. Almost half of the world's population will continue to be overwhelmingly dependent on North American food surpluses. For example, despite improved harvests in 1975–6, the world's developing countries still had to import 46 million metric tons of cereal, most of which come from North America. Estimates by the International Food Policy Research Institute in Washington DC show that LDCs as a group will probably have food deficits averaging anywhere from 95 to 100 million metric tons by the year 1985. But rising prices of petroleum and fertilizer, major imports of most poor countries, greatly deplete those foreign exchange funds that would ordinarily be used to buy food from these large grain suppliers.

Although high food prices and periodic grain shortages represent at most an inconvenience to the affluent in both rich and poor nations, to the very poor they may mean the difference between life and death. For the approximately 700 million people in thirty-two Third World countries who already survive on the margin of nutritional subsistence or who spend 80 per cent of their incomes on food, there are no second chances when prices double, or a crop fails, or the rains don't come. Moreover, when global food reserve stocks are low (they had fallen from 26 per cent of annual world grain consumption in 1961 to less than 7 per cent by 1974), the capacity of developed nations to respond collectively with food aid to emergency areas of drought, floods or crop failures is severely diminished. This was dramatically illustrated by the general failure of the World Food Conference held in Rome in 1974 to come up with more than token transfers of food grains to starving nations. Table 17.3 shows how rapidly world grain reserves have fallen since 1970 while Table 17.4 shows the degree to which developing countries have become large net importers of grain during the first half of the 1970s.

	Reserve stocks of grain (millions metric tons)	Grain equivalent of idled US cropland	Total reserves	Reserves as days of annual grain consumption	
1961	154	68	222	95	
1962	131	81	212	88	
1963	125	70	195	77	
1964	128	70	198	77	
1965	113	71	184	69	
1966	99	79	178	66	
1967	100	51	151	55	
1968	116	61	177	62	
1969	136	73	209	69	
1970	146	71	217	69	
1971	120	41	161	51	
1972	131	78	209	66	**Table 17.3**
1973	106	24	130	40	Indicators of world food security,
1974*	90	—	90	26	1961–74

*Preliminary.
Source: Lester R. Brown with Erik P. Eckholm, *By Bread Alone,* Praeger, New York (1974), 60.

	FY 1970– FY 1972 Average	FY 1972	FY 1973	FY 1974	
Developed market economies	31·9	41·9	62·4	58·4	
United States	39·8	42·8	73·1	72·5	
Canada	14·8	18·3	18·8	13·1	
Australia and New Zealand	10·6	10·8	5·8	9·9	
South Africa	2·5	3·7	0·4	4·0	
European Community (nine members)	−16·6	−14·0	−13·4	−13·0	
Other Western Europe	−4·8	−4·5	−5·3	−8·9	
Japan	−14·4	−15·0	−17·0	−19·2	
Centrally planned economies	−6·8	−13·0	−32·2	−15·9	
Eastern Europe	−7·6	−9·2	−8·0	−4·8	
USSR	3·9	−4·3	−19·6	−4·4	
China	−3·1	−15·4	−4·6	−6·7	
Developing countries	−19·1	−26·9	−23·2	−30·3	
North Africa and Middle East	−9·2	−11·9	−8·1	−14·9	
South Asia	−5·7	−5·4	−4·5	7·0	
Southeast Asia	3·2	3·3	1·2	2·5	
East Asia	−8·4	−9·2	−10·4	−10·2	
Latin America	3·2	−2·0	–	0·7	
Central Africa	−1·9	−2·0	−2·0	−2·1	
East Africa	−0·3	0·3	0·6	0·7	
Other	−0·2	−0·2	−0·3	−0·3	**Table 17.4**
Total world exports	107·6	111·2	141·8	151·0	World net grain trade, FYs 1970–74

Note: Negative figures indicate net imports.
Source: US Department of Agriculture, Economic Research Service, *The World Food Situation and Prospects to 1985,* Foreign Agricultural Economic Report No. 98, December 1974, p. 4.

What are the principal factors behind the dramatic alteration of the world food situation? We can identify four. On the demand side, we have:

1. The combined effects of rising population and affluence. On the supply side, there are the four critical resource constraints of land, water, energy and fertilizer as manifested in
2. the limited scope for expanding areas of cultivation,
3. the growing shortage of water for agricultural production, and
4. rising energy costs slowing down the growth of high energy and fertilizer-intensive agriculture.

Together, rapidly rising demand and slowly growing supply are pushing up the international prices of vital foods. We now turn to discuss specifically the international determinants of world food demand and supply[3].

A. Determinants of food demand: population and affluence

In the 1960s the world food problem was perceived primarily as a race against time between rising numbers of people in Third World countries and total food supplies. The race always seemed to remain fairly close but there was a general optimism that new break-throughs in the technology of food production – the so-called 'green revolution' – would ultimately declare food the winner. In the long run population growth would have to be reduced. But for the immediate future it appeared that famine and starvation were an unlikely occurrence.

What these watchers of the race between food and population failed to realize and what the 1970s vividly revealed was the fact that, in addition to Third World population growth, rising affluence in the developed nations was becoming a major factor in the annual increases in food demands. While population growth still remains the dominant source of expanding food demand (e.g. with world population growing at approximately 2 per cent per year, maintaining current levels of world per capita consumption will require a doubling of food production every 30 or so years), rising income levels account for an ever increasing proportion of this demand. For example, in terms of the demand for basic food grains (wheat, corn and rice) which dominate world consumption patterns, people in the less developed nations consume approximately 181 kg per person per year. Nearly all of this is consumed *directly* as bread, maizemeal and rice to meet minimum energy requirements. On the other hand, the average North American consumes over 450 kg per year. But out of this total, only 65 kg is consumed directly in the form of bread, pastry and breakfast cereals. The remaining 345 kg per capita is consumed *indirectly* in the form of meat, milk and eggs, that is, 385 kg of cereal grains per capita are used to feed livestock and poultry, the products of which are then consumed by the North American public.

The agricultural resources (mainly land, water, energy and fertilizer) required to produce this output for an average North American are often five to seven times that of his Asian or African counterpart. Moreover, as per capita incomes rise, a significant share of this additional income is spent on high-quality beef and poultry which in turn means greater indirect consumption of feed grains and soybeans, much of which will have to be imported. This only exacerbates an already tight world food market and can mean less direct consumption for the poorest in Third World nations.

B. Constraints on supply: land, water, energy and fertilizers

Basically, there are four critical factors of modern agricultural production which are serious resource constraints on its expansion: land, water, energy and fertilizer. The principal mechanisms for expanding world food supplies fall into two basic categories:

1. Increasing the total amount of land under cultivation, or
2. Raising yields on existing arable land through the more intensive use of water, energy and fertilizer.

Both cases represent increases in agricultural *inputs* which should lead to higher *outputs* in accordance with the basic economic theory of production. But, in the contemporary world, the possibilities of increasing these production inputs are restricted by the following factors:

Historically, enlarging the area of cultivation has been the traditional *Land expansion* approach to expanding agricultural production. But the potential for further expansion of farm acreage is limited today by the growing competition for land use by industrial development, urbanization, new town development and transportation.

Water was once thought to be a 'free' good, that is, it was thought to be *Fresh water expansion* present in such plentiful supplies that one person's use of it would not impair its availability to another. But it is far from 'free' for modern agriculture. In fact, it is a scarce and critical input. There are many regions of the world, particularly in Africa, where the availability of sufficient water could turn unproductive land into a productive resource. The principal way of achieving this is through irrigation projects made possible by the damming up of natural waterways. But most of the world's rivers that are suitable for damming and irrigation have already been developed. Any future efforts to expand fresh water supplies for agriculture will require alternative techniques such as river diversion (but this creates serious problems when a river flows between more than one country), desalting ocean water or cloud-seeding to create and manipulate rainfall in dry agricultural areas. Unfortunately, the outlook for these efforts is, at present, not very promising.

An alternative source of intensifying agricultural production on exist- *Energy expansion* ing land is through the application of greater energy inputs through the use of mechanized farm equipment such as tractors, seeders, reapers, and combines. However, as we have already seen, the sharp international price increases in energy supplies make such efforts extremely costly. In fact, high energy prices are more than likely to hold down total food production, especially in energy-intensive areas like North America and the Soviet Union, unless food prices rise equally fast.

In addition to land, fresh water and energy, supplies of fertilizer are *Fertilizer expansion* becoming increasingly more costly as a result of substantially higher prices for phosphate and potash and alternative uses for the petroleum inputs into fertilizer production. The process of manufacturing chemical fertilizers requires large amounts of costly energy inputs. In the face of these rising costs and the enormous expansion of world demand for fertilizer, it is clear that future prices will continue to rise. In 1974, for example, fertilizer prices almost quadrupled. Third World countries had to pay many hundreds of millions of dollars more for their fertilizer imports than in previous years. Worse still, many nations could not even obtain adequate supplies at any price. Included among these nations were the very populous and food-scarce countries of South and

Southeast Asia (e.g. India, Pakistan, Bangladesh and the Philippines). A continuation of high prices and limited supplies of chemical fertilizer means lower per capita outputs and increased food import needs for these nations over the coming years. Unfortunately, this increase in basic food needs usually occurs at times when world food prices are also high and global grain reserves are at dangerously low levels.

It should be evident from the preceding description of the prospects for world food demand and supply that many of the 'least developed' Third World countries are likely to become even more dependent on future food imports from the developed regions, mainly the United States but also Canada and the Soviet Union. With world demand outpacing supply, rising prices will mean greater burdens on the very poor. Worse still, shortages of vital agricultural resource inputs such as energy and fertilizer will probably lead to some form of world food 'rationing'. With the United States controlling almost three-quarters of exportable world grain supplies, the use of food as a new and deadly weapon of 'political blackmail' against hungry Third World nations becomes a distinct and frightening possibility[4].

It becomes all the more urgent, therefore, for such populous, food-short nations as Bangladesh, India, Indonesia and much of sub-saharan Africa as well as parts of Latin America to itensify their efforts to expand food production through the promotion of labor-intensive and energy-saving small- and medium-scale commercial farm development. This is where the greatest and least-costly output potential lies. We discussed and reviewed the possible nature of such labor-intensive agricultural and rural development strategies in Chapter 10.

17.2 Some concluding observations: global interdependence and the 'new international economic order'

Our discussion in this final chapter has touched upon many of the economic and non-economic manifestations of the growing interdependence of nations. We have seen that whereas a decade or so ago this interdependence was perceived primarily in terms of the dependence of poor nations on the rich ones, today developed countries are rapidly discovering that in a world of growing mineral and raw material scarcities, their future economic well-being will depend increasingly on the international economic policies of many Third World countries. Let there be no misunderstanding, however. The poor nations are and will continue to remain considerably more vulnerable to the economic events and policies of rich nations than the other way around. But their international bargaining power is undoubtedly on the rise.

The events of the 1970s have underlined the fact that the world is in the midst of a fundamental and profound economic transformation. For decades, the developed nations experienced continuous economic progress based on ever expanding industrial production and rising exports to each other and to the less developed countries. Raw material inputs were cheap and in plentiful supply. It was a 'buyers' market – i.e. sellers (mostly LDCs) had to compete vigorously with each other to find markets for their abundant raw materials. More simply, supply increases continuously exceeded demand expansion.

But today, for the first time since the Great Depression of the 1930s, there is a worldwide 'sellers' market for many goods – i.e. more buyers (demands) must compete with one another to obtain limited supplies.

The growing list of scarce items goes beyond oil, food and fertilizer. It includes timber, minerals, cotton and man-made textiles among others. What will happen to countries, both rich and poor, in such a situation of scarcity?

One thing is clear. The new era of scarcity is bound to alter international economic relations. It may even lead to a major revision of the international economic system as demanded by Third World nations and as adopted by the Special Session of the UN General Assembly in April 1974 in the form of the controversial Declaration and Action Programme on the Establishment of the New International Economic Order[5]. Those countries rich in minerals and basic raw materials, both rich and poor, will discover either a greater or, at least, a new economic power. Those without such natural resource supplies, especially those in Third World countries, will find their already economically vulnerable position even weaker. As scarcities become more pronounced, there will be the ever present threat of 'economic warfare' among nations – i.e. individual resource-rich countries may use their resources as a weapon to extract exorbitant demands out of economically desperate resource-poor nations.

Our point here is that the question of how limited supplies of scarce resources, such as energy and certain raw materials, and commodities such as food grains are 'rationed' and who gets 'access' to these supplies will assume increasing economic and political importance in future years. The outcome will probably be determined by *both* economic and non-economic considerations. Over the last decade, the world has witnessed a rapid international shift, especially for the developed countries, from the basic question of how to get *access* to foreign markets (both developed and Third World) where finished products could be *sold,* to the very different present question of how to get *access* to markets (both less developed and developed) where raw materials can be *purchased.*

With this shifting world economic situation, the names and numbers of 'players' as well as the 'rules' of the international power game have changed rapidly. No longer is it simply a competitive or cooperative game among a select group of rich countries vying for poor country markets to sell their expensive manufactures in return for cheap primary products and natural resources. Resource-rich Third World nations will undoubtedly have a much greater impact on the future functioning and status of the world economy. Whether or not they act as spokesmen for the larger issues of Third World development on behalf of their less fortunate compatriots remains to be seen.

The crucial question is whether or not this emerging new economic interdependence among all nations, both developed and underdeveloped, will lead to greater cooperation or greater conflict. The newly discovered resource and raw material bargaining potential of Third World nations may turn out to be the lever that has long been needed to make the more developed countries realize that the economic futures of *both* groups of nations are intimately linked. No longer can rich nations totally dominate the established international economic order without inviting harmful retaliation. Cooperation becomes essential[6]. On the other hand, the potential for economic conflict will probably become even more pronounced if resource-rich Third World countries attempt to 'over-exploit' their real new strengths. Such a strategy may merely invite heavy retaliation from the still more powerful rich nations who, as we have seen, may begin to use food as a counter-weapon against the Third World's raw materials. The only feasible outcome of this emerging new international interdependence is one in which *everyone* either wins or loses. In the interdependent world of the last quarter of the twentieth century, there cannot in an 'ultimate' sense be simultaneous winners and losers.

With each passing year, rich and poor nations alike share an increasingly common destiny. The world community must begin to realize that a 'new international economic order' is not only *possible,* it is *essential.* Such a new international economic order should be based on the principle that *each* nation and *each* individual's development is intimately bound to the development of *every* nation and *every* individual. The future of *all* mankind is linked more closely today than ever before. All indications are that it will become even more interdependent in the coming decades. Let us hope, therefore, that reason and good sense will prevail so that the 'First', 'Second' and 'Third' Worlds can truly become part of 'One World' – forged together by a common economic destiny and guided by the humane principles of peace, brotherhood and mutual respect.

Notes

1. *World Development,* 2, no. 6 (1947), 54.
2. Lester Brown, *World Without Borders,* Random House, New York (1972), 193.
3. For a more comprehensive discussion of these detriments, see Lester Brown and Erik P. Eckholm, 'Food: growing global insecurity', in *Agenda for Action 1974,* Praeger, New York (1974), Ch. 4.
4. In fact, a 1974 report of the US Central Intelligence Agency (CIA) entitled *Potential Implications of Trends in World Population, Food Production and Climate* specifically addresses itself to the possibility of using food as a political lever to influence the policies of needy nations.
5. For an example of the kinds of demands now being put forward by the developing countries, see *The Communique of the Third World Forum Conference* in Karachi, Pakistan, January 1975, which is reproduced as Appendix 17.2.
6. A promising first step towards such co-operation was taken at the 27-member International Energy and Raw Materials Conference held in Paris in December 1975. It was agreed there that four specialist commissions (on energy, raw materials, development problems and international finance) would be set up to tackle the world's major economic problems and to search for equitable global solutions.

Questions for discussion
1. The 1970s ushered in an era in which, for the first time, developed nations began to recognize their growing dependence on and vulnerability to the policies of certain Third World groups of nations. Briefly describe this new source of developed country dependence. Can you think of areas other than oil where such dependence might emerge in the future?
2. The actions of OPEC in 1973–4 dramatically demonstrated that coordinated action by Third World nations in the area of physical resource control could substantially benefit a diverse group of LDCs. Do you think the future will bring greater cooperation among Third World nations in the area of international 'collective bargaining'? What are some of the major obstacles?
3. 1974 was also a year in which the first World Food Conference was held in Rome bringing all nations together to discuss the 'world food crisis'. Do you believe that there is such a global food crisis and, if so, what are its origins?
4. How are the world food and energy crisis interrelated? What is meant by global 'food reserves'? Who controls these reserves and what position might Third World nations adopt with regard to assuring access to these reserves? Explain your answer.

5. In an era of growing mineral and raw material resource scarcities, problems of **Questions for discussion**
   non-price *rationing* and *access* assume increasing importance while traditional alloca-
   tions by the international pricing mechanism become relatively less important.
   Explain the meaning and comment upon this statement.
6. Can the growing objective of greater 'self-reliance' in Third World nations be
   reconciled with the tendency towards greater global economic and non-economic
   'interdependence'? Explain your answer.

In addition to current newspaper and magazine articles which almost every day have **Further readings**
some piece on energy, food, and/or inflation, a good, non-technical discussion of global
interdependence can be found in: Lester R. Brown, *World Without Borders,* Random
House, New York (1972).

For an anlaysis of the world food and energy crisis as these affect Third World nations
see: (*a*) James P. Grant, 'Engergy shock and the development prospect' in *Agenda for
Action: 1974,* ODC, Praeger, New York (1974);   (*b*) Lester R. Brown and Erik P.
Eckhelm, 'Food: growing global insecurity' in the same volume.

Finally, for statements by Third World social scientists on many of these issues, see:
'Self-reliance and international reform', *World Development,* 2, no. 6, (1974), 52–5, as
well as the Santiago Declaration of April 1973 and the Communique of the Third World
Forum of January 1975. These latter two documents, reflecting the collective views of
some fifty leading Third World economists, are reproduced for the reader's information
as Appendices 17.1 and 17.2 of this chapter.

Appendix 17.1

1. A group of social scientists from the Third World met in Santiago from 23 to 25 **Santiago declaration of Third World**
   April 1973 and reviewed some of the external and internal elements of the crisis **social scientists, April 1973**
   confronting the Third World today, since the voice of the majority of mankind is
   seldom heard, and certainly is never decisive, in international forums.
2. The Third World, with 70 per cent of the world population, subsists on only 20 per
   cent of the world income – and even this meagre income is so maldistributed
   internally as to leave the bulk of its population in abject poverty. Collectively, the
   Third World faces a situation where its per capita income is one-fourteenth of that in
   the developed world; it produces many of the mineral and agricultural resources of
   the world but barely gets enough to eat; its participation in world trade decreases
   steadily; it suffers the worst forms of economic deprivation; 800 million of its total
   population of 2,600 million are illiterates, almost 1,000 million suffer from malnutrition or hunger, 900 million have a per capita income of less than 30 cents a day.
3. In the field of ideas, the Third World has frequently lived with concepts of development, with performance criteria and with economic strategies which were often
   externally conceived and largely inappropriate.
4. It is time that the intellectuals of the Third World re-examine the established
   development strategies and seek alternative strategies more relevant to their own
   needs:
   ● which extend beyond material progress to integrate the cultural and social values
     of their societies;
   ● which benefit the bulk of the population, and not only a privileged minority – and
     this through appropriate social, economic and structural changes; and
   ● which reflect a creative interaction between indigenous thinking and external
     experience and which are based on appropriate technology and financed largely
     by indigenous resources.
5. This search for more relevant development strategies would require an effort of
   unprecedented proportions to which we must commit ourselves, and which must be
   carried out in close contact with the broad mass of our people.
6. Similar effort is also necessary to re-examine the international order in which the
   Third World finds itself today.
7. One of the dominant features of the present-day world order is the unequal
   relationship between the developed and the developing countries. The developing
   countries are poor and weak and, in any international bargaining, they are conveniently ignored or easily squeezed.
8. What the Third World must ask of the international order is protection of its
   legitimate interests in the trade field, not trade concessions; a genuine transfer of
   real resources, not the present 'aid' charade; a powerful voice in the shaping of a
   new monetary system, not formal representation in the Group of Twenty.

9. But such demands must be based on constructive thought, not negative agitation. They must be supported by a relevant research effort in the Third World and mobilization of its best brainpower to devise appropriate strategies, negotiating positions and policy options.

10. What is required is nothing short of an intellectual revolution. This intellectual revolution must be carried to every university, every institute of learning and every thinking forum in the Third World.

11. We have decided, therefore, to organize an intellectual Forum of the Third World.

12. This Forum will be open to all the social scientists from the Third World with a predominant interest in the development of their societies.

13. The Forum will organize its activities in such a way as to:
    - express views on international issues affecting the Third World and its relations with the developed world;
    - provide an intellectual platform for an exchange of views on alternative development strategies and their policy implications;
    - provide intellectual support to developing countries in devising their policy options and negotiating alternatives on all relevant issues;
    - stimulate and organize relevant socio-economic research through regional and national research institutes in Africa, Asia and Latin America.

14. We hope that this Forum will receive widespread support in the Third World so that it becomes truly representative. We are also confident of the wide support of the intellectuals of the whole world.

15. For we come together in a spirit of intellectual enquiry to find real answers to our genuine problems and to give positive ideas on the great issues of our time.

Appendix 17.2

Communique of Third World Forum conference in Karachi, 1975

1. An inaugural meeting of the Third World Forum was held in Karachi from 5 to 10 January 1975 to discuss critical elements in the national and international economic order as well as to discuss means of action to meet the continuing crisis in the relationship between the industrialized and the developing countries.

2. The participants to the Forum supported the objectives stated in the Santiago Declaration [see Appendix 17.1] and agreed on the need for a continued intellectual revolution to overcome the dependence of the Third World and for profound changes in the internal and external order that the developing countries face today. They felt that they could best make a contribution to the promotion of these aims by organizing a Third World Forum on a permanent basis. The delegates accordingly considered and adopted a constitution to found such a Forum.

Functions and organization of the forum

3. It was agreed that, in line with the Santiago Declaration, the principal functions of the Forum would be to:
    (a) provide an intellectual platform for an exchange of views on alternative development strategies and their policy implications;
    (b) provide intellectual support to the Third World countries in devising their policy options and negotiating alternatives on all relevant development issues;
    (c) stimulate and organize relevant socio-economic research, particularly through the regional and national research institutes, in the Third World;
    (d) foster the interchange of relevant ideas and research, identify the areas of Third World interdependence and, to this end, seek to influence appropriate international, regional and national decision-making bodies to recognize and protect the legitimate rights and interests of the people of the Third World;
    (e) provide support to programmes of action on all types of co-operation among developing countries by;
        (i) suggesting areas, methods, and types of action that would be most effective for mutual co-operation;
        (ii) defining areas in which the Third World countries could offer assistance or could benefit from assistance provided by other Third World countries;
        (iii) examining and analyzing mutual co-operation in all fields, including science and technology, with the purpose of facilitating the exchange of ideas, information and an efficient transfer of these between Third World countries;

(*f*) express views on international issues affecting the Third World and its relations with the developed world.

4. It was agreed that the membership to the Forum will be open to leading social scientists, eminent experts and other intellectuals, both men and women from the Third World acting in their personal capacities.

5. The following were elected to form the first Executive Committee of the Forum for a period of two years. It was decided to enlarge the membership of the Executive Committee to sixteen at a later stage as the total membership of the Forum expands.
   1. Enrique V. Iglesias
   2. Enrique Oteiza
   3. Oscar Pino-Santos
   4. Samir Amin
   5. Justinian Rweyemamu
   6. Ikenna Nzimiro
   7. Mohamed Said al Attar
   8. Mahbub ul Haq
   9. Gamani Corea

6. The Executive Committee was authorized to prepare concrete plans for the permanent location of the secretariat of the Forum in a Third World country and for the financing of its activities.

National development strategies

7. The participants considered the need for the new development strategies, more responsive to the aspirations of their masses. They agreed that, while there could be many separate roads to development, the new strategies must be based on at least the following principles:
   - the real focus should be on the satisfaction of basic human needs and on a meaningful participation of the masses in the shaping of economic and social change;
   - the policies of self-reliance should be encouraged, with emphasis on a self-confident and creative use of local resources, manpower, technology and knowledge, and with growing stress on collective self-reliance between the societies of the Third World;
   - the concepts of development should embrace the political needs and cultural patterns of their societies, so that life styles in the Third World do not become a pale imitation of somebody else's experience but a proud extension of their own value systems.

8. The participants also reviewed the national development strategies of a few selected countries which had adopted a distinctive style of their own. They agreed that there should be a greater exchange of experience in economic development between the developing countries themselves, with more organized publications and visits to one another than the traditional visits to the centres of the developed countries.

9. In order to promote these concerns, the Forum agreed to:
   (*a*) sponsor specific studies on national development strategies,
   (*b*) discuss and disseminate the results of such studies, and
   (*c*) organize seminars and visits for a more orderly exchange of development experience. The participants authorized the Executive Committee to develop a concrete programme of action to implement these concerns.

New international economic order

10. The participants reviewed the nature of the current inequitable world order and discussed specific proposals for the establishment of a more just international economic order.

11. The participants agreed that the present crisis in the world system was neither a 'normal' economic recession nor the result of the oil problem. It, in fact, marked the gradual crumbling of an old order in which a group of rich nations constituting the developed centre continuously expanded by the use of energy and raw materials provided by the poor nations at the periphery at cheap prices. The increase in the price of oil by the OPEC could, therefore, be seen as a part of the struggle of the Third World to obtain a better deal from the world order. But this struggle would

neither be complete nor meaningful until other poor nations at the periphery also obtained a fairer deal and unless the present polarization between the countries at the centre and those at the periphery was changed by different patterns of collective self-reliance among the Third World countries.

12. The participants discussed a number of specific proposals to improve the prospects of the Third World in the present world order. These proposals included:
    - the establishment of a Commodity Bank to strengthen commodities in a weak bargaining position;
    - the promotion of producers' associations for suitable commodities for ensuring better supply management and for creating countervailing power against the existing concentration of control at the buying end;
    - more control over the creation and distribution of international credit by the Third World;
    - bold policy and institutional measures to promote trade among the countries of the Third World including the establishment of payment unions within the Third World;
    - a new alliance of interdependence including the flow of investments towards agriculture production to various Third World countries;
    - a conference of principal creditors and debtors to reach an agreement on the basic principles of a long term settlement of the past debt that the developing countries have accumulated;
    - the termination of all unfavourable contracts, leases and concessions given to the multinational corporations by the developing countries for the exploitation of their natural resources and their renegotiation;
    - establishment of a Third World Development Bank financed by OPEC and other Third World countries;
    - a new and more automatic basis for international transfer of resources to the poor nations from traditional sources which could be financed from a development process on non-renewable resources exported from the Third World to the industrialized countries, royalties from ocean bed mining and link between SDRs and aid;
    - democratization of control over international financial institutions by obtaining at least 50 per cent of the voting power for the Third World;
    - setting up of institutions of intellectual self-reliance within the Third World financed by a trust fund of the order of $1 billion.

13. In connection with these initiatives the participants considered that close cooperation between OPEC and other parts of the Third World was vital in the next stage of this continuing struggle if the Third World was to succeed in its efforts to obtain more justice from the world order and if oil-exporting countries were to expect to consolidate and maintain their gains.

14. It was agreed that, in order to prepare a concrete programme of action (*a*) various proposals should be placed in a clear time perspective, (*b*) they should be backed up by concrete studies so as to carry both conviction and weight, and (*c*) there should be an identification of the specific fora and implementation machinery through which they ought to be pursued. Besides the need for concrete elaboration of the above proposals the following studies were identified to examine the legitimacy of existing international economic relations.
    - the present margins between producers return and consumers price for important commodity exports of the Third World;
    - the waste and inefficiencies in the consumption as well as the production patterns;
    - the magnitude of the existing debt as compared with the surpluses which were extracted from the developing world during the colonial era and the surpluses now being extracted through unjust trade and investment patterns;
    - the systematic intellectual biases which have been diffused in much of the literature produced in the developed world on such questions as economic development, international trade, welfare economics and project-criteria;
    - the means by which the media in the developing world could develop its own network aimed at informing the peoples of the Third World of each other's needs, aspirations and achievements.

15. The participants authorized the Executive Committee to prepare a concrete plan of studies, including the identification of individuals and institutions for preparing these studies within specified time periods and the selection of fora and instruments through which implementation of concrete proposals should be pressed.

Appeal to other intellectuals

16. The Forum appealed to all intellectuals of the Third World to get organized behind these concerns of vital importance to their societies and to initiate action at all levels to create a climate for more equitable national and international orders.

The Forum concluded by extending its warm thanks to the Government of Pakistan for its generous invitation to hold the plenary session in Karachi and to the National Bank of Pakistan for the excellent arrangements for the conduct of the conference, to the news media of Pakistan for their extensive coverage and support for the activities of the Forum and to the people of Pakistan who are an essential part of the struggle which the entire Third World is waging and for which the Third World Forum was established on a permanent basis during its historic meeting in Karachi. The Forum expressed its deep appreciation to the Governments of Sweden and Canada for providing funds for the meeting.

Glossary

The following glossary of terms is designed to cover most of the major concepts and organizations, both regional and international, discussed in the text. Note that the *italicized* words which appear in any definition are themselves defined elsewhere in the glossary.

absolute (cost) advantage: if country A can produce more of a commodity with the same amount of real *resources* than country B (i.e. at a lower absolute *unit cost*), country A is said to have absolute cost advantage over country B. See also *comparative advantage*.

absolute poverty: a situation where a population or section of a population is able to meet only its bare *subsistence* essentials of food, clothing and shelter in order to maintain minimum *levels of living*. See also *international poverty line* and *subsistence economy*.

absorptive capacity: the ability of a country to effectively 'absorb' foreign private or public financial assistance, i.e. to use the funds in a productive manner.

adjustment assistance: the process of providing public financial assistance to workers and industries hurt by the importation of lower-cost competitive foreign goods. Such assistance allows them to 'adjust' to a new occupation during a transitional period.

'advanced' capitalism: *economic system* characterized by private ownership but with a major role played by the *public sector*. Most developed *market economies* like those in North America, Western Europe, Japan and Australia are examples of advanced capitalism.

AID: see *USAID*.

age structure (of population): the age composition of a given population. For example, in LDCs, the age structure of the population is typified by a large portion of population under 15 years old, a slightly smaller proportion aged between 15 and 45 years and a very small proportion above 45 years old.

aggregate consumer demand: that part of the total demand (*aggregate demand*) for goods and services in the economy attributed to the demands of households for consumer goods and services within a specific period, usually one year. See also *consumption*.

aggregate demand: a measure of the real purchasing power of the community. Commonly referred to as the total effective demand or total expenditure, it normally comprises private *consumption* (C) private and public *investment* (I) government expenditure (G) plus net exports (X–M).

agrarian system: the pattern of land distribution, ownership and management; also the social and *institutional* structure of the agrarian economy. Many Latin American and Asian *agrarian systems* are characterized by concentrations of large tracts of land in the ownership of a few powerful *landlords*. *Rural development* in many LDCs may require extensive reforms of the existing *agrarian system*.

agricultural extension services: services offered to farmers usually by the government in the form of transmitting information, new ideas, methods and advice about, for instance, the use of fertilizers, control of pests and weeds, appropriate machinery, soil conservation methods, simple accounting, etc., in a bid to stimulate high *farm yields*.

agricultural labor productivity: the level of agricultural output per unit of labor input, usually measured as output per man-hour or man-year. It is very low in LDCs compared to developed countries. See also *labor productivity* and *farm yields*.

agricultural mechanization: the extensive use of machinery in farm production activities thereby reducing the amount of labor input necessary to produce a given level of output. See also *labor-saving technological progress*.

'appropriate' technology: the 'right type' of *production technique,* i.e. one that employs *factors of production* in their 'least cost' or 'correct' proportions. For example, a technology that employs a higher proportion of labor relative to other factors in a labor abundant economy is in general more appropriate than one which uses smaller labor proportions relative to other factors. See also *factor price distortion, principle of economy* and *neo-classical price incentive model.*

ADB: Asian Development Bank: a regional development bank located in Bangkok whose major objective is to assist the development of Asian nations through the provision of *loans* and *technical assistance.*

asset ownership: the ownership of land, *physical capital* (factories, buildings, machinery, etc.), *human capital* and financial resources which are employed to generate income for their owners. The distribution of asset ownership is a major determinant of the distribution of personal income in any non-socialist society. See also *income distribution.*

autarchy: a *closed economy* that attempts to be completely *self-reliant.*

average cost: the total cost of production of a commodity incurred by a producer during a period divided by the number of units of output produced in that period. See also *unit cost.*

average propensity to consume (APC): the proportion of total income expended on *consumption*; derived by dividing total consumption expenditure, C, by total income, Y, – i.e. $APC = C/Y$. See also *marginal propensity to consume.*

average propensity to save (APS): the proportion of total income, Y, that is set aside as *savings, S* – i.e., $APS = S/Y$. See also *marginal propensity to save* and *savings ratio.*

balance of payments (table): a summary statement of a nation's financial transactions with the outside world. See also *current account, capital account* and *cash account.*

balanced trade: a situation where the value of a country's exports and the value of its imports of visible items are equal.

barter transactions: the trading of goods directly for other goods in economies not fully monetized.

basic science and **technological innovation** (relationship between): basic science refers to a systematic, scientific and objective investigation aimed at bringing into existence 'new' knowledge or tools; while technological innovation has to do with the application of *inventions* of basic science (such as the new tools or knowledge) to perform tasks in a more efficient way.

'big push theory' of development: theory stating that all LDCs require to 'take off' into a period of self-sustaining *economic growth* is a massive investment program designed to promote rapid *industrialization* and the building up of *economic infrastructure.*

bilateral assistance (aid): see *foreign aid.*

birth rate, crude: number of children born alive each year, per thousand population, e.g. a crude birth rate of 20 per 1,000 is the same as a 2 per cent increase. See also *general fertility rate* and *death rate.*

black market: a situation in which there is illegal selling of goods at prices above a legal maximum set by the government. It occurs due to relative *scarcity* of the goods concerned and the existence of an excess demand for them at the established price. See also *rationing* and *exchange control.*

brain drain: the emigration of highly educated and skilled professional and technical manpower from the developing to the developed countries.

CACM: Central American Common Market: an economic union formed in 1960 and consisting of five central American nations: Costa Rica, El Salvador, Guatemala, Honduras and Nicaragua.

capital: see *physical capital* and *human capital.*

capital account: that portion of a country's *balance of payments table* which shows the volume of *private foreign investment* and public *grants* and *loans* that flow into and out of a country over a given period, usually one year. See also *current account* and *cash account.*

capital accumulation: increasing a country's stock of real *capital,* i.e. net investment in fixed assets. To increase the production of capital goods necessitates a reduction in the production of consumers' goods. 'Economic' development largely depends on the rate of *capital accumulation.*

capital-intensive technique: more capital-using process of production; i.e., that which uses a higher proportion of capital relative to other *factors of production* such as labor or land per unit output.

capital–output ratio: a ratio which shows the units of *capital* that are required to produce a unit of output over a given period of time. See *Harrod–Domar equation.*

capital-saving technological progress: arises as a result of some *invention* or *innovation* which facilitates achievement of higher output levels using the same quantity of capital inputs.

capital stock: total amount of physical goods existing at a particular time period which have been produced for use in the production of other goods (including services).

capitalism: see *pure market capitalism* and *advanced capitalism.*

cash account: the 'balancing' portion of a country's *balance of payments* table showing how cash balances (*foreign reserves*) and short-term financial claims have changed in response to *current* and *capital account* transactions.

cash crops: crops produced entirely for the market, e.g. coffee, tea, cocoa, cotton, rubber, pyrethrum, jute, wheat, etc.

centralized planning: the determination by the state of what shall be produced and how *factors of production* shall be allocated among different uses. In a free enterprise economy consumers decide what shall be produced through their demands. While maximum amount of central planning is found in Soviet type economies, LDCs and developed countries do show increasing state planning in an attempt to maintain *full employment.* Central planning is done at the 'center' and then dictated to various sections in the economy.

ceterus paribus: a Latin expression widely used in economics meaning 'all else being equal' – i.e. all other variables are held constant.

'character' of economic growth: the distributive implications of the process of *economic growth*; for example, participation in the growth process, asset ownership, etc. In other words, how that *economic growth* is achieved and who benefits.

Chinese People's commune: a multi-purpose political, administrative and organizational unit covering the full range of economic, social and administrative activities necessary and feasible in a rural community. The people's agricultural communes is the basis of *rural development* in China. Communal ownership includes all the rural land, all means of agricultural production and commune-owned industries.

closed economy: an economy in which there are no foreign trade transactions or any other form of economic contacts with the rest of the world. See also *autarchy* and *'inward-looking' development policies.*

cognitive skills: the ability to perceive and understand abstract concepts and think logically; to have knowledge and/or be aware of a range of relevant information.

collusion: an agreement among sellers of a commodity (or commodities) to set a common price and/or share their commodity market.

'command' socialism: a type of *economic system* where all *resources* are state owned and their allocation and degree of utilization are determined by the centralized decisions of planning authorities rather than by a *price system.* The USSR is the most outstanding example of a command socialist economy.

commercial policy: policy encompassing instruments of 'trade protection' employed by countries to foster industrial promotion, export diversification, employment creation and other desired development oriented strategies. They include *tariffs, physical quotas* and *subsidies.*

common market: a form of *economic integration* in which there is free internal trade, a common external tariff, plus the free movement of labor and capital among partner states. The *European Economic Community* (EEC) provides an example. See also *customs union* and *free trade area.*

comparative advantage: a country has a comparative advantage over another if in producing a commodity it can do so at a relatively lower *opportunity cost* in terms of the foregone alternative commodities that could be produced. Taking two countries, A and B, each producing two commodities, X and Y, country A is also said to have comparative advantage in the production of X if its *absolute advantage* margin is greater or its absolute disadvantage is less in X than in Y.

complementary resources: factors of production that are necessarily used along with others to produce a given output or to accomplish a specific task, e.g. manhours of farm labor are complementary to a hectare of land in the production of maize; machinery and equipment are complementary to labor in the construction of a road, etc.

comprehensive plans: those *economic plans* that set their targets to cover all the major sectors of the national economy.

constraints – see *economic constraint.*

consumer sovereignty: the notion central to '*Western*' *economic theory* that consumers determine what and how much shall be produced in an economy. The free play of the *price system* and *market mechanism* is then assumed to equilibrate consumer demand with producer supply of that commodity.

consumption: that part of total *national income* devoted to expenditure on *final goods* and services by individual consumers during a given period of time, typically one year. Total private consumption is assumed to be directly related to the level of aggregate personal income.

consumption diseconomies: problems (costs) that occur to individuals or society as a whole as a result of the unpopular consumption habits of another individual. Examples include alcoholism, poor individual hygiene, drug addiction, etc.

consumption economies: advantages (benefits) that accrue to individuals or society as a whole as a result of increases in the consumption of certain types of goods or services by other individuals – e.g., education, health care, etc.

consumption possibility line: in international *free trade* theory a locus of points showing the highest possible consumption combinations that can be attained as a result of trade. Graphically, the *consumption possibility line* is represented by the international price line at its tangency to the domestic *production possibility curve* of a country.

cost/benefit analysis: a basic tool of economic analysis in which the actual and potential *costs* (both *private* and *social*) of various economic decisions are weighed against actual and potential *private* and *social benefits*. Those decisions or projects yielding the highest benefit/cost ratio are usually thought to be most desirable. See also *project appraisal*.

cost–push inflation: *inflation* that results primarily from the upward pressure of production costs, usually because of rising raw material prices (e.g. oil) or excessive wage increases resulting from trade union pressures. See also *demand-pull* and *structural inflation*.

current account: that portion of a *balance of payments table* which portrays the market value of a country's 'visible' (e.g. commodity trade) and 'invisible' (e.g. shipping services) exports and imports with the rest of the world. See also *capital account* and *cash account*.

curative medicine: medical care which focuses on curing rather than preventing disease. Requires extensive availability of hospitals and clinics. See also *preventive medicine*.

customs union: a form of *economic integration* in which two or more nations agree to free all internal trade while levying a common external *tariff* on all non-member countries. See also *common market* and *free trade area*.

death rates, crude: yearly number of deaths per thousand population – e.g. an annual crude death rate of 15 per thousand or 1·5 per cent of the population. See also *birth rate* and *infant mortality*.

decentralized planning: regionalized or sectoral planning as opposed to planning at the center. See *centralized planning*.

decile: a 10 per cent proportion of any numerical quantity, e.g. a population divided into deciles would be one which was divided into ten equal numerical groups. See also *quintile*.

decreasing costs: if *increasing returns* exist then a given proportionate change in output will require a smaller proportionate change in quantities of factor inputs thus implying a fall in cost per unit of output because input costs will be expected to rise less than proportionately with output. In short, a fall in *average costs* of production as output expands.

deficit expenditure: amount by which planned government expenditure exceeds realized tax revenues. *Deficit expenditure* is normally financed by borrowed funds and its major object is to stimulate economic activity by increasing the purchasing power within an economy (i.e its *aggregate demand*).

demand curve: graphical representation of the quantities of a commodity or resource that would be bought over a range of prices at a particular time, when all other prices and incomes are held constant. When demand curves of all consumers in the market are aggregated a 'market demand' curve is derived showing the total amount of the good which consumers are willing to purchase at each price.

demand-pull inflation: *inflation* that arises because of the existence of excess Keynesian *aggregate demand,* i.e., when total effective demand exceeds the productive capacity (aggregate supply) of the economy.

demographic transition: the phasing out process of *population growth rates* from a virtually stagnant growth stage characterized by high *birth* and *death rates,* through a rapid growth stage with high birth rates and low death rates, to a stable, low growth stage in which both birth and death rates are low.

demonstration effects: the effects of transfers of alien ways of life upon nationals of a country. Such effects are mainly cultural and attitudinal in nature, e.g. *consumption* habits, modes of dressing, patterns of education, leisure and recreation, etc.

dependence: a corollary of *dominance*; a situation where the LDCs have to rely on developed country domestic and international *economic policy* to stimulate their own *economic growth*. *Dependence* can also mean that the LDCs adopt DC education systems, their technology, economic and political systems, attitudes, *consumption* patterns, dress, etc.

dependency burden: that proportion of the total population of a country falling in the ages of 0–15 and 64+ which is economically unproductive and therefore not counted in the labour force. In many LDCs the population under the age of 15 accounts for almost as much as half of the total population thus posing a burden to the generally small productive labour force and to the government which has to allocate *resources* on such things as education, public health, housing, etc. for the *consumption* of people who don't contribute to production.

devaluation: a lowering of the 'official' *exchange rate* between one country's currency and those of the rest of the world – e.g. a 10 per cent devaluation of the Kenya shilling would entail a change from its present (1976) rate of approximately Shs. 8·0 per dollar to Shs. 8·80 per dollar.

development (meaning of): the process of improving the quality of all human lives. Three equally important aspects of development are: (1) raising people's living levels, i.e. their incomes and *consumption* levels of food, medical services, education etc., through 'relevant' *economic growth processes*; (2) creating conditions conducive to the growth of people's *self-esteem* through the establishment of social, political and *economic systems* and *institutions* which promote human dignity and respect; and (3) increasing people's *freedom to choose* by enlarging the range of their choice variables, e.g. increasing varieties of consumer goods and services.

development banks: specialized public and private *financial intermediaries* providing medium- and long-term credit for the creation or expansion of industrial enterprises in developing countries.

development plan: the documentation by a government planning agency of the current national economic conditions, proposed public expenditures, likely developments in the *private sector*, a macro-economic projection of the economy, and a review of government policies. Many LDCs publish 5-year *development plans* to announce their economic objectives to their citizens and others.

diminishing returns: the principle that if one *factor of production* is fixed and constant additions of other factors are combined with it, the *marginal productivity* of *variable factors* will eventually decline. The major assumptions of this principle are that at least one factor is fixed, units of the variable factor are identical, and there exists no *technical progress*. For example, if a fixed land area is combined with constant additions of labour using simple tools to produce coffee, output will initially increase but as more and more labour units are added, average output per man-hour/year declines as also do marginal additions to total product. See also *'surplus' labor*.

disguised underemployment (unemployment): a situation in which available work tasks are split among *resources* (typically labour) such that they all seem fully employed, but in reality much of their time is spent in unproductive activities.

disposable income: the income that is available to households for spending and saving after personal income taxes have been deducted.

division of labor: allocation of tasks among the workers such that each one engages in tasks that he performs most efficiently. *Division of labor* promotes worker specialization and thereby raises overall *labor productivity*. It has its historical origins in Adam Smith's *Wealth of Nations*.

dominance: in international affairs, a situation in which the developed countries have much greater power than the less developed countries (LDCs) in decisions affecting important international economic issues; e.g. the prices of agricultural commodities and raw materials in world markets. See also *vulnerability* and *dependence*.

doubling time (of population): period that a given population size takes to increase itself by its present size. *Doubling time* is approximated by dividing any numerical growth rate into 72 – e.g. a population growing at 2 per cent per year will double in size approximately every 36 years.

dualism: the coexistence in one place of two situations or phenomena (one desirable and the other one not) which are mutually exclusive to different groups of a society; e.g., extreme poverty and affluence, modern and traditional economic sectors, growth and stagnation, university education among a few and mass illiteracy, etc.

dual price system: government-operated pricing mechanism whereby producers of, say, a staple crop are paid a different price from the one consumers (mostly urban consumers) are charged. In short, any two-price system, one for sellers and the other for buyers.

EAC: East African Community: an integrated economic grouping of the three East African countries – Kenya, Uganda and Tanzania – established by the Treaty of East African Cooperation of 1967 following the Philip Commission Report of 1966. Cooperation takes the form of running jointly a number of common public services by the three governments (railways, airways, ocean and lake transport, research) and a *customs union* in which there is internal *free trade* and a common external *tariff* on imports. Cooperation in East Africa dates back to colonial times.

ECA: Economic Commission for Africa: a regional branch of the *UnitedNations* system located in Addis Ababa, Ethiopia and devoted to the analysis of economic developments and trends in African nations. Statistical bulletins and technical analyses of economic trends in individual countries and groups of countries in various regions of Africa are regularly published. See also *ECLA* and *ECAFE*.

ECAFE: Economic Commission for Asia and the Far East: a regional branch of the *United Nations* system located in Bangkok, Thailand and devoted to the technical and statistical analysis of economic developments and trends in the diverse countries of Asia and the Far East. See also *ECA* and *ECLA*.

ECLA: Economic Commission for Latin America: A regional branch of the *United Nations* system located in Santiago, Chile and devoted to the regular publication of technical and statistical analyses of economic trends in Latin America as a whole and in individual Latin American nations. See also *ECA* and *ECAFE*.

ECOWAS: Economic Community of West African States: A recently formed (1975) economic community of 15 West African Countries – 9 French, 5 English and 1 Portuguese – with a total population of over 125 million and a land area of 6·5 million square miles. It is the largest example of *economic integration* in Africa and includes such countries as Nigeria, Ghana, Upper Volta, Senegal, Niger and Chad.

economic 'constraint': a barrier to the attainment of a set target (e.g. *economic growth*) in a particular period of time. For example, physical *capital* has long been thought of as the major 'constraint' on *economic growth* in LDCs.

economic disincentives (for fertility reduction): economic disadvantages (costs) and risks of having small families, e.g. parents' insecurity during their old age (no children or too few children to care for them), shortages of parents' farm labor supply, etc.

economic efficiency (in production): in traditional *Western economic theory*, a situation in which all *resources* are fully employed and no *resource* can be reallocated to another use without some loss of output. This condition is satisfied when the *marginal products* of all real *resources* in use are equal. See also *optimization* and *economy, principle of*.

economic good: any commodity or service which yields 'utility' to an individual or community and which must be paid for in money terms in a monetary economy, or 'in kind' in a non-monetary economy.

economic growth: the steady process by which the productive capacity of the economy is increased over time to bring about rising levels of *national income*. Rapid *economic growth* has been a major preoccupation of economists, planners and politicians in LDCs in the last two or three decades because it has been thought to be 'a major precondition determining *levels of living*. Emphasis is now shifting to problems of *income inequality, poverty* and *unemployment*.

economic incentives (for fertility reduction): economic motivations aimed at encouraging parents to limit their families to a specified size. Such economic incentives include: free or subsidized education for children of families within the specified family size, free or subsidized medical treatment for small families, high wages for mothers with few children, etc.

economic infrastructure: the underlying amount of *capital accumulation* embodied in roads, railways, waterways, airways and other forms of transportation and communications plus water supplies, financial institutions, electricity and public services such as health, education, etc. The level of infrastructural development in a country is a crucial factor determining the pace and diversity of economic development.

economic integration: the merging to various degrees of the economies and economic policies of two or more countries in a given region. See also *common market, customs union, free trade area, trade creation* and *trade diversion*.

economic plan: a written document containing government policy decisions on how *resources* shall be allocated among different uses in order to attain a targeted rate of *economic growth* over a certain period of time. See *economic planning, centralized planning, planning model* and *plan implementation*.

economic planning: a deliberate and conscious attempt by the State to formulate decisions on how the *factors of production* shall be allocated among different uses or industries, thereby determining how much of total *goods* and services shall be produced in the ensuing period(s). See also *economic plan* and *centralized planning*.

economic policy: statement of objectives and the methods of achieving these objectives (*policy instruments*) by government, political party, business concern, etc. Some examples of government economic objectives are maintaining *full employment*, achieving a high rate of *economic growth*, reducing *income* and regional development *inequalities*, maintaining prices stability, etc. *Policy instruments* include fiscal policy, monetary and financial policy and legislative controls (e.g. price and wage control, rent control, etc.).

economic principles: basic concepts of economic theory which provide the tools of economic analysis. Examples of economic principles are the principle of substitution, the *principle of economy*, the *principle of diminishing returns*, the concept of *scarcity*, etc.

economizing spirit: the act of minimizing the real *resource* costs of producing any level of output. In general, allocating scarce *resources* with great care. See also the *optimization principle*.

economic system: the organizational and institutional structure of an economy including the nature of *resource* ownership and control (i.e. private versus public ownership and control). Major economic systems included *subsistence economy, pure market capitalism, advanced capitalism, market socialism, command socialism* and *'mixed' systems* that characterize most LDCs.

economic 'variable': a measure of economic activity such as income, consumption and price that can take on different quantitative values. Variables are classified either as 'dependent' or 'independent' in accordance with the economic model being used.

economies of scale: these are economies of growth resulting from expansion of the scale of productive capacity of a firm or industry leading to increases in its output and decreases in its cost of production per unit of output.

economy, principle of: see *principle of economy*.

educational certification: the phenomenon by which particular jobs require specified levels of education. Applicants must produce 'certificates' of such completed schooling in the *formal educational system*.

EEC: European Economic Community: a European economic federation (*common market*) established under the Treaty of Rome in 1957 with a view of abolishing inter-state *tariffs* within the federation in order to increase trade volume (and hence GDP) of member states. The current membership of EEC includes: West Germany, Luxembourg, Great Britain, Italy, Denmark, Austria, Switzerland, France and the Netherlands.

elasticity of demand: see *price elasticity of demand* and *income elasticity of demand*.

elasticity of factor substitution: a measure of the degree of 'substitutability' between *factors of production* in any given *production process* when relative factor prices change.

employment 'gap': (1) *deflationary:* amount by which employment at equilibrium national output falls short of employment that would obtain at capacity output. (2) *inflationary:* amount by which prices at equilibrium national output exceeds that which would obtain at capacity or *potential output* level. The employment gap is a major Keynesian concept but one that has limited relevance for many LDCs.

enclave economies: those economies found among LDCs in which there exist small pockets of economically developed regions (often due to the presence of colonial or foreign firms engaged in plantation and mining activities) with the rest of the larger outlying areas experiencing very little progress. See also *dualism*.

equilibrium price: the price at which the quantity demanded of a good is exactly equal to the quantity supplied. It is often referred to as the price at which the market clears itself. See also *price system*.

equilibrium wage rate: the wage rate that equates the demand for and supply of labor – i.e. the wage at which all the people who want to work at that wage are able to find jobs and also at which the employers are able to find all the workers they desire to employ. In other words, it is the wage rate that clears the labour market.

exchange control: a governmental policy designed to restrict the outflow of domestic currency and prevent a worsened *balance of payments* position by controlling the amount of *foreign exchange* which can be obtained or held by domestic citizens. Often results from *overvalued exchange rates*.

exchange rate: the rate at which central banks will exchange one country's currency for another (i.e. the 'official' rate). Rates are normally expressed in terms of dollars, e.g. X pesos per dollar. See also *overvalued exchange rate* and *devaluation*.

export dependence: a situation where a country relies heavily on exports as the major source of finance needed for carrying out development activities. This is the situation of many LDCs who must export *primary products* to earn valuable *foreign exchange*.

export incentives: public *subsidies*, tax rebates and other kinds of financial and non-financial measures designed to promote a greater level of economic activity in export industries.

export promotion: purposeful governmental efforts to expand the volume of a country's exports through *export incentives* and other means in order to generate more *foreign exchange* and improve the *current account* of its *balance of payments*.

external diseconomies of production: these are the increased costs that a single firm or a group of firms faces in increasing its output beyond a certain level, because of problems for which the firm or the group of firms concerned is not responsible. Such diseconomies include: increases in clearing costs due to pollution of other firms, transport delays due to too many vehicles on the road, etc.

external economies of production: increases in output (or decreases in costs) of an individual firm over a certain range of production and plant scale due to production advantages it derives from the expansion activities of other firms – e.g. its use of new equipment that has been invented by an outside group of growing firms. See also *internal economies of production.*

factors of production: *resources* or *inputs* required to produce a *good* or service. Basic categories of *factors of production* are: land, labor and *capital.*

factor endowment trade theory: the neo-classical model of *free trade* which postulates that countries will tend to specialize in the production of those commodities which make use of their abundant *factors of production* (land, labor, *capital,* etc.). They can then export the surplus in return for imports of the products produced by factors with which they are not sufficiently endowed. The basis for trade arises because of differences in relative factor prices and thus domestic price ratios as a result of differences in factor supplies. See also *comparative advantage.*

factor mobility: the unrestricted transference or free voluntary movement of factors of production between different uses and geographic locations.

factor-price distortions: situations in which *factors of production* are paid prices which do not reflect their true *scarcity* values (i.e. their competitive market prices) because of institutional arrangements which tamper with the free working of market forces of supply and demand. In many LDCs the prices paid for *capital* and *intermediate producer goods* are artificially low because of special capital depreciation allowance, tax rebates, investment subsidies, etc. while labor is paid a wage above its competitive market value partly because of trade union and political pressures. *Factor-price distortions* can lead to the use of 'inappropriate' techniques of production. See also *neo-classical price incentive model* and *appropriate technology.*

factor-price equalization: in *factor endowment theory of free trade* the proposition that because countries trade at a common international price ratio, factor prices among trading partners will tend to be equalized given the assumption of identical technological possibilities for all commodities across countries. The prices of the more abundantly utilized *resources* will tend to rise while those of the relatively scarce factors fall. Over time, international factor payments will tend towards equality, e.g. real wage rates for labour will be the same in Britain or Botswana.

'false paradigm' model of underdevelopment: the proposition that *Third World* countries have failed to develop because their development strategies (usually given to them by Western economists) have been based on an 'incorrect' model of development; one that overstressed *capital accumulation* without giving due consideration to needed social and *institutional* change.

family planning programs: public programs designed to help parents to plan and regulate their family size in accordance with their ability to support such a family. The program usually includes supply of contraceptives to adult population, education on the use of birth control devices, mass media propaganda of benefits derived from smaller families, etc.

FAO: Food and Agricultural Organization: a department of *United Nations* based in Rome, Italy, whose major concern is to expand world food production in order to meet food intake requirements of the growing world population. FAO researches into modern methods of increasing *farm yields* and educates farmers on their use. It also works in collaboration with such bodies as the World Food Council, Overseas Food Organization, etc.

farm yields: a quantitative measure of the productivity of a given unit of farm land in producing a particular commodity – usually measured in terms of output per hectare (e.g. so many kilos of rice per hectare).

farmer cooperatives: associations of farmers mainly engaged in cash crop production to enable them to reap the benefits of *economies of scale.* Large tracts of farm land are jointly owned and operated by the cooperative with profits being shared in accordance with a prearranged pattern of distribution (not necessarily equal for all farm families).

fertility rate, general: yearly number of children born alive per thousand women within the child bearing age bracket (normally between the ages of 15 and 49 years). See also *crude birth rate.*

final goods: commodities that are *consumed* to satisfy wants rather than passed on to further stages of production. Whenever a *final good* is not *consumed* but is used as an *input* instead, it becomes an *intermediate good.*

financial intermediary: any financial institution, public or private, which serves to channel loanable funds from savers to borrowers. Examples include commercial banks, savings banks, *development banks,* finance companies, etc.

First World: the new economically advanced *capitalist* countries of Western Europe,

North America, Australia, New Zealand and Japan. These were the first countries to experience sustained and long-term *economic growth*.

fixed inputs: *Inputs* which do not vary as output varies. A hectare of land for example is a *fixed input* on a small family farm because it can be used to produce different quantities of, say, maize output without its size changing. See also *variable inputs*.

fixed input coefficients: a phenomenon in the economics of production in which any level of output requires a fixed ratio of *factor* inputs – e.g. 3 units of labor are always required to produce 10 units of output so that in order to produce 50 units of output, 15 units of labor will be required. The labor (input) coefficient (L/Q) in the case would be $0 \cdot 3$ ($= \frac{3}{10}$).

flexible institutions: *institutions* that are self-responsive or can be made to respond to changing *development* requirements. For example, a system of land tenure that can adjust itself or be adjusted to allow for a more equitable redistribution of land would represent such a flexible institution. See also *rigid institutions*.

flexible wages: wages that adjust upwards or downwards depending on the directions of forces of demand for and supply of labor, e.g. if the demand for labor increases (decreases) or its supply decreases (increases), 'cereris paribus', wages will increase (decrease).

foreign aid: the international transfer of public funds in the form of *loans* or *grants* either directly from one government to another (*bilateral assistance*) or indirectly through the vehicle of a *multilateral assistance* agency like the *IBRD* (*World Bank*). See also *tied aid* and *private foreign investment*.

foreign exchange: claims on a country by another held in the form of currency of that country. Foreign exchange system enables one currency to be exchanged (or be converted into) for another, thus facilitating trade between countries. See also *exchange rate* and *foreign reserves*.

foreign reserves: the total value (usually expressed in dollars) of all gold, dollars and *Special Drawing Rights* (*SDRs*) held by a country as both a reserve and a fund from which international payments can be made.

'formal' educational system: the organized and 'accredited' school system with licensed teachers, standard curricula, regular academic years and recognized certification. Encompasses primary, secondary and tertiary educational institutions. See also *non-formal educational system*.

free market: see *pure market capitalism,* and *price system* and *market mechanism*.

free trade: trade in which goods can be imported and exported without any barriers in the form of *tariffs, physical quotas* or any other kind of restriction.

free trade area: a form of *economic integration* in which there exist free internal trade among member countries but each member is free to levy different external tariffs against non-member nations. See also *customs union, common market* and *LAFTA*.

freedom to choose (of a society): a situation in which a society has at its disposal a variety of alternatives from which to satisfy its wants. See also *development* (meaning of).

full employment: (1) a situation where everyone who wants to work at the prevailing wage rate is able to get a job, or alternatively (2) a situation whereby some job seekers cannot get employment at the going wage rate but *open unemployment* has been reduced to a desired level, e.g. 2 per cent.

functional distribution of income: the distribution of income to *factors of production* without regard to the ownership of the factors. See *factor shares* and *marginal productivity*.

gains from trade: the increase in output and consumption resulting from specialization in production and *free trade* with other economic units including persons, regions, or countries.

GATT: General Agreement on Tariffs and Trade: an international body set up in 1947 to probe into the ways and means of reducing tariffs on internationally traded goods and services. Between 1947 and 1962 GATT held about seven conferences but met only with moderate success. Its major success was achieved in 1967 during the 'Kennedy Round' of talks when tariffs on primary commodities were drastically slashed.

gini coefficients: an aggregate numerical measure of *income inequality* ranging from zero (perfect equality) to one (perfect inequality). It is graphically measured by dividing the area between the perfect equality line and the *Lorenz curve* by the total area lying to the right of the equality line in a Lorenz diagram. The higher the value of the coefficient the higher the *inequality of income distribution* and the lower it is the more equitable the *distribution of income*. See also *Lorenz curve* and *'skewed' distribution of income*.

good: see *economic goods*; also *final goods*.

grants: an outright *transfer payment* usually from one government to another (*foreign* *aid*), i.e. a gift of money or *technical assistance* which does not have to be repaid. See also *loans* and *tied aid*.

Green Revolution: the revolution in grain production associated with the scientific discovery of new hybrid seed varieties of wheat, rice and corn which have resulted in high *farm yields* in many LDCs.

gross domestic product (GDP): the total monetary value calculated at market prices of all final *goods* and *services* produced in an economy over a given period of time, typically one year. See also *Gross National Product, National Income* and *National Expenditure*).

gross national product (GNP): the sum total of all incomes that accrue to the *factors of production* in a particular geographical region over a given time period – i.e., *GDP* 'plus' all incomes that accrue to residents of that region from their investments in foreign countries 'less' incomes that accrue to foreigners as a result of their investments in that region.

growth: see *economic growth*.

'growth poles': more economically and socially advanced regions than others around them – e.g. urban centres vis-à-vis rural areas in LDCs. Large-scale economic activity tends to cluster around such 'growth poles' due to economies of agglomeration – i.e. lower costs of locating an industry in an area where much *economic infrastructure* has been built up.

'hard' loan: see *loans*.

Harrod–Domar equation: this is a functional economic relationship in which the *growth rate of Gross Domestic Product* (g) depends directly on the *national savings rate* (s) and inversely on the national *capital/output ratio* (k) so that it is written as $g = s/k$. The equation takes its name from a synthesis of analyses of growth process by two economists (Sir Roy Harrod of Britain and E. V. Domar of the USA).

hidden momentum (of population growth): a dynamic latent process of population increase that continues even after a fall in *birth rates* because of a large youthful population that widens the population's parent base. Fewer children per couple in the succeeding few generations will not mean a smaller or stable population size because at the same time there will be a much larger number of child bearing couples. Thus a given population will not stabilize until after two or so generations.

hidden unemployment (of labor): a situation in which labor is fully employed but is unproductive either because the workers are incapacitated, sick, uneducated, hungry, unmotivated or are using unsuitable tools in their tasks. See also *underemployment* and *disguised unemployment*.

hybrid seeds: seeds produced by cross-breeding plants or crops of different species through scientific research. See also *Green Revolution*.

human capital: productive *investments* embodied in human persons. These include skills, abilities, ideals, health, etc., that result from expenditures on education, on-the-job training programs and medical care. See also *physical capital*.

IBRD: International Bank for Reconstruction and Development (World Bank): an international financial institution forming part of the *United Nations* system and based in Washington DC (United States). One of its main objectives is to provide 'development funds' to needy *Third World* nations (especially the poorest countries) in the form of *interest*-bearing *loans* and *technical assistance*. The *World Bank* operates with funds borrowed primarily from rich nations but increasingly from *OPEC* countries as well. See also *IDA*.

IDA: International Development Association: an international body set up in 1960 to assist the *World Bank (IBRD)* in its efforts to promote economic development of the underdeveloped countries by providing additional *capital* on a low *interest* basis (i.e. through *'soft' loans*) especially to the poorest of the poor developing countries.

IFC: International Finance Corporation: an international financial institution that was set up in 1956 to supplement the efforts of *World Bank* in providing development *capital* to private enterprises (mainly industrial) of the under-developed countries.

ILO: International Labour Organization: one of the *United Nations* functional organizations based in Geneva whose central task is to look into problems of world manpower supply, its training, utilization, domestic and international distribution, etc. Its aim in this endeavour is to increase 'world output' through maximum utilization of available human *resources* and thus improve *levels of living* for people.

IMF: International Monetary Fund: an autonomous international financial institution that originated from the Bretton Woods Conference of 1944. Its main purpose is to regulate the international Monetary Exchange System that also evolved at the same conference but has since been modified. In particular, one of the central tasks of *IMF* is to control fluctuations in *exchange rates* of world currencies in a bid to alleviate severe *balance of payments* problems.

imperfect competition: a market situation or structure in which there are relatively few buyers and sellers of similar but differentiated products. Examples include *monopoly* and *oligopoly*. See also *perfect competition*.

imperfect market: a market where the theoretical assumptions of *perfect competition* are violated by the existence of, for example, a small number of buyers and sellers, barriers to entry, non-homogeneity of products and imperfect information. The three imperfect markets commonly analyzed in economic theory are *monopoly, oligopoly* and monopolistic competition.

import substitution: a deliberate effort to promote the emergence and expansion of domestic industries by replacing major imports such as textiles, shoes, household appliances, etc., with locally produced substitutes. Requires the imposition of protective *tariffs* and physical *quotas* to get the new industry started. See also *infant industry*.

income distribution: see *functional distribution of income* and *size distribution of income*.

income effect: the implicit change in *real income* resulting from the effects of a change in a commodity's price on the quantity demanded.

income elasticity of demand: the responsiveness of the quantity demanded of a commodity to changes in the consumer's income, measured by the proportionate change in quantity divided by the proportionate change in income.

income 'gap': the gap between the incomes accruing to the bottom poor and the top rich sectors of a population. The wider the gap the higher the inequality in the *income distribution*. Also used to refer to the gap between *income per capita* levels in rich and poor nations.

income in 'kind': a household's or firm's income in the form of goods or services instead of in the form of money. Payments in a *barter* and *subsistence economy* are mainly made in 'kind'.

income inequality: the existence of disproportionate distribution of total *national income* among households whereby the share going to rich persons in a country is far greater than that going to the poorer persons (a situation common to most LDCs). This is largely due to differences in the amount of income derived from ownership of property and to a lesser extent the result of differences in earned income. Inequality of personal incomes can be reduced by steeply *progressive income* and *wealth taxes*. See also *Gini coefficient* and *Lorenz Curve*.

income per capita: total *GNP* of a country divided by the total population. Per capita income is often used as an economic indicator of the *levels of living* and *development*. It, however, can be a 'biased' index because it takes no account of *income distribution* and the ownership of the *assets* which are employed to generate part of that income.

increasing returns: a disproportionate increase in output which results from a change in the scale of production. In traditional economic theory, increasing returns (and thus decreasing costs) will occur until a certain output level has been reached and thereafter *diminishing returns* (increasing costs) are assumed to set in. Some industries (e.g. utilities, transportation) are characterized by increasing returns over a wide range of output. This leads to *monopoly* situations. See also *economies of scale*.

increasing opportunity cost: in a state of *full employment* the shifting away of increasing amounts of productive *resources* from the production of one commodity, say automobiles, to another, say food, involves an *opportunity cost*. The *opportunity cost* of producing a given increase in automobiles is the amount of food production forgone. As more and more cars are produced at the expense of food there will be increasing opportunity costs of additional auto production. This gives rise to the phenomenon of the ('concave') *production–possibility curve* in economic theory.

indirect taxes: taxes levied on goods purchased by the consumer (and exported by the producer) for which the taxpayer's liability varies in proportion to the quantity of particular goods purchased or sold. Examples of indirect taxes are customs duties (*tariffs*), excise duties, sales taxes and export duties. The indirectness of such taxes arises because the consumer or producer can avoid paying them by not consuming or producing the taxed goods. They are a major source of tax revenue for most LDCs as they are easier to administer and collect than *direct taxes* (e.g. income and property taxes).

industrialization: the process of building up a country's capacity to 'process' raw materials and to manufacture goods for consumption or further production – e.g. setting up firms and acquiring plant and equipment (including *human capital*) to process agricultural products and extracted raw materials or to make manufactures such as radios, cars, tinned foods, ploughs, clothes, etc.

infant industry: a term given to a newly established industry usually set up behind the protection of a *tariff* barrier as part of a policy of *import substitution*. Once the industry is no longer an 'infant', the protective tariffs are supposed to disappear but they often do not.

infant mortality: the deaths among children between birth and 1 year of age. *Infant mortality rate* measures the number of these deaths per 1,000 live births.

inferior good: a good whose demand falls as consumer incomes rise. The *income elasticity of demand* of an inferior good is thus negative.

inflation: a period of above normal general price increases as reflected, for example, in the consumer and wholesale price indices. More generally, the phenomenon of rising prices. See also *cost-push, demand-pull* and *structural inflation*.

informal sector: that part of the urban economy of LDCs characterized by small competitive individual or family firms, petty retail trade and services, *labor-intensive* methods of doing things, low *levels of living*, poor working conditions, high *birth rates*, low levels of health and education, etc. But it is often thought of as providing a major source of urban employment and economic activity.

infrastructure: see *economic infrastructure*.

innovation: the application of *inventions* of new production processes and methods into production activities as well as the introduction of new products. Innovations may also include the introduction of new social and institutional methods of organization and management commensurate with modern ways of conducting economic activities. See *inventions* and *modernization ideals*.

inputs: goods and services – e.g. raw materials, man-hours of labor, etc. – used in the process of production. See also *factors of production* and *resources*.

institutions: norms, rules of conduct and generally accepted ways of doing things. *Social institutions* refer to well-defined and formal organizations of society that govern the way that society operates – e.g., class system, private versus communal ownership, educational system etc. – while *economic institutions* include the banking systems, the mechanism of resource allocation, the *economic system* and general role of public versus private activity. Finally, *political institutions* refer to the systems that govern the operations of the government of a particular society – e.g. formal power structures, political parties (e.g. *Socialist* and Democratic parties), mechanism of getting into power, etc.

integrated rural development: the broad spectrum of rural development activities encompassing the simultaneous fostering of small-farmer agricultural progress; improvement of *levels of living* (incomes, employment, education, health and nutrition, housing and other social services) for the rural people; reducing inequality in the distribution of rural incomes and urban–rural imbalances in incomes and economic opportunities; and the capacity of the rural sector to sustain and accelerate the pace of these improvements over time.

integration: see *economic integration*.

interdependence: interrelationship between *economic* and *non-economic variables*. Also in international affairs, the situation in which one nation's welfare depends to varying degrees on the decisions and policies of another nation, and vice-versa. See also *dependence, dominance* and *vulnerability*.

interest: the payment (or price) for the use of borrowed funds. See also *interest rate, social discount rate, time preference*, etc.

interest rate: the amount that a borrower must pay a lender over and above the total amount borrowed expressed as a percentage of the total amount of funds borrowed – e.g. if a man borrowed 100 rupees for 1 year at the end of which he had to repay 110 rupees, the *interest rate* would be 10 per cent per annum.

intermediate producer goods: goods that are used as *inputs* into further levels of production, for example, leather in shoe manufacture, iron ore into steel production, etc. See also *final goods*.

internal economies (diseconomies) of production: these are the advantages (lower costs) in the case of economies or the *constraints* (additional costs) in the case of diseconomies to a single firm as its scale of production expands. They include: decreasing or increasing administrative costs, improved or worsened coordination problems, shortages of appropriate manpower skills, etc. See also *external economies* and *diseconomies of production*.

international poverty line: an arbitrary international *real income* measure, usually expressed in constant dollars (e.g. $50), used as a basis for estimating the proportion of the world's population that exist at bare levels of *subsistence* – i.e. those whose incomes fall below this poverty line.

investment: that part of *national income* or *expenditure* devoted to the production of *capital goods* over a given period of time. 'Gross' investment refers to total expenditure on new *capital goods*, while 'net' investment refers to the additional *capital goods* produced in excess of those that wear out and need to be replaced.

invention: the discovery of something new, for example, a new product (e.g. *hybrid corn*) or a new production process (e.g. a cheaper and more efficient way of producing synthetic rubber). See also *innovation*.

'investment' in children (process of): the process by which parents raise the 'quality' and hence the 'earning capacity' of children by providing them with an education in expectation of future returns. In this sense, children in poor societies are viewed as *capital goods* and a source of old age security. See also *human resources*.

invisible hand: this term has its origin in Adam Smith's famous book *Wealth of Nations* written in 1776. It argues that the unbridled pursuit of individual self interest automatically contributes to the maximization of the social interest. See also *laissez faire, perfect competition* and *pure market capitalism*.

'inward' looking development policies: policies that stress economic *self-reliance* on the part of LDCs, including the development of indigenous *'appropriate'* technology, the imposition of substantial protective *tariffs* and *non-tariff trade barriers* in order to promote *import substitution* and the general discouragement of private *foreign investment*. See also *autarchy* and *outward-looking development policies*.

Keynesian economics: that branch of *Western macro-economic theory* focusing on the determination of aggregate income and employment in an *advanced capitalist, market economy*. Named after its originator, Lord John Maynard Keynes, the famous British economist of the 1930s.

Keynesian model: model developed by Lord John Maynard Keynes in the early 1930s to explain the cause of economic depression and hence the unemployment of that period. The model states that unemployment is caused by insufficient *aggregate demand* (AD) and it can be eliminated by, say, government expenditure that would raise AD and activate idle and/or underutilized resources and thus create jobs.

labor or capital-augmenting technological progress: the *technological progress* that adds to the effectiveness (productivity) of the existing quantity of labor (or capital), e.g. labor by general education, on-the-job training programs etc.; and capital by *innovation* and new *inventions*. See also *labor-saving technological progress*.

labor-intensive technique: More labor-using method of production, i.e. that which uses proportionately more labor relative to other *factors of production*. See also *capital-intensive technique*.

labor productivity: the level of output per unit of labor input, usually measured as output per man-hour or man-year.

labor-'saving' technological progress: associated with the achievement of higher output using unchanged labor inputs as a result of some *invention* (e.g. the computer) or *innovation* (such as assembly line production).

labor theory of value: in classical international trade theory, the proposition that relative commodity prices depend on relative amounts of labor used to produce those commodities. Much of Marxist economics is based on the labor theory of value.

LAFTA: Latin American Free Trade Association: an economic federation of eleven Latin American states formed in 1960 and within which all commodities are traded free of tariff. Each member state however may charge tariffs and legislate other trade restrictions on goods entering it from countries that are not members of the federation. The primary purpose of LAFTA is to encourage trade creation in the economically integrated area; its current membership includes: Brazil, Argentina, Chile, Venezuela, etc.

laissez faire: an expression often used to represent the notion of free enterprise, market capitalism. See also *perfect competition* and *pure market capitalism*.

landlord: a proprietor of a freehold interest in land with rights to lease out to tenants in return for some form of payment for the use of the land.

land reform: deliberate attempt to reorganize and transform existing *agrarian systems* with the intention of improving the distribution of agricultural incomes and thus fostering *rural development*. Among its many forms, *land reform* may entail provision of secured tenure rights to the individual farmer; transfer of land ownership away from small classes of powerful land owners to tenants who actually till the land; appropriation of land estates for establishing small new settlement farms; instituting land improvements and irrigation schemes, etc.

latifundios: very large landholdings in Latin American *agrarian system*, capable of providing employment for over twelve people each, owned by a small number of *landlords* and comprising a large proportion of total agricultural land. Holders of *minifundios* are often required to offer unpaid seasonal labor to latifundios.

'laws' versus *tendencies*: a law is a universal truth – i.e. it holds in all situations and its validity is independent of the social and/or political context in which it is observed – e.g. in the physical sciences, the law of gravity holds whether an experiment is conducted in North America, the USSR, China, Botswana or Brazil. On the other hand, *tendencies* (as in the case of economics) are only inclinations of behaviour or phenomena that may occur under similar conditions but are not always true in different social contexts.

levels of living: the extent to which a person, a family or group of people can satisfy their material and spiritual wants. If they are able to afford only a minimum quantity of food, shelter and clothing their *levels of living* are said to be very low. On the other hand if they do enjoy a greater variety of food, shelter, clothing and other things such as good health, education, leisure, etc., then clearly they are enjoying relatively high *levels of living.* See *development* (meaning of).

life expectancy (at birth): time period, normally in years, that a baby is expected to live after it has been born alive. In LDCs, this time period is roughly 48 years for male children and 52 years for female children. In developed countries, it is approximately 70 years for male children and 72 years for female children. See also *birth rate.*

life sustenance: those basic goods and services like food, clothing and shelter that are necessary to sustain an average human being at the bare minimal *level of living.*

literacy: the ability to read and write. Literacy rates are often used as one of the many social and economic indicators of the state of 'development' within a country.

loans: the transfer of funds from one economic entity to another (e.g. government to government, individual to individual, bank to individual, etc.) which must be repaid with *interest* over a prescribed period of time 'Hard' loans refer to those given at 'market' rates of interest whereas 'soft' loans are given at 'concessionary' or low rates of interest. See also *grants.*

Lorenz curve: a graph depicting the variance of the *size distribution of income* from perfect equality. See also *Gini coefficient.*

luxury goods: goods whose demand is generated in large part by the higher income groups within a country. Luxuries are regarded as suitable objects of taxation from the social point of view (in order to 'improve' income distribution) as they are not considered 'necessary' for 'life maintenance'. Examples of luxuries in a less developed economy are very expensive motor cars, imported expensive clothing, cosmetics, jewellery, television sets, etc.

macro-economics: that branch of economics which considers the relationships between broad economic aggregates such as *national income,* total volumes of *saving, investment, consumption* expenditure, employment, *money supply,* etc. It is also concerned with determinants of the magnitudes of these aggregates and their rates of change through time. See also *Keynesian economics.*

'macro' population–development relationship: a general cause-and-effect relationship between development process and population growth. Development causes population growth rates to slow down and stabilize by providing *economic incentives* that motivate people to have smaller families. Population growth (in the absence of a population problem) in turn, affects development in many ways, e.g. it increases *aggregate demand* that stimulates increases in national output, provides more people for national defence, etc.

malnutrition: a state of ill-health resulting from an inadequate or improper diet – usually measured in terms of average daily protein consumption.

Malthusian population 'trap': an inevitable population level envisaged by the Reverend Thomas Malthus (1766–1834) at which population increase was bound to stop because after that level the life-sustaining resources that increase at an arithmetic rate would be insufficient to support human population which increases at a geometric rate. Consequently, people would die of starvation, diseases, wars, etc. The Malthusian population 'trap' therefore represents that population size that can just be supported by the available resources.

manpower planning: the long-range planning of skilled and semi-skilled manpower requirements and the attempt to gear educational priorities and investments in accordance with these future *human resource* needs.

marginal cost: the addition to total cost incurred by the producer as a result of varying output by one more unit.

marginal product: the increase in total output resulting from the use of one additional unit of a variable *factor of production.*

marginal propensity to consume (MPC): the change in consumption, C, divided by the change in income, Y, that brought it about, i.e., $MPC = \Delta C/\Delta Y$.

marginal propensity to save (MPS): the change of saving, S, that results from a given change in income, Y, that is, the ratio of change in saving to the change in income so that $MPS = \Delta S/\Delta Y$ or dS/dY in calculus. By definition $MPC + MPS = 1$. See *marginal propensity to consume (MPC).*

marginal utility: the satisfaction derived by consuming one additional or one less unit of a good. A consumer's marginal utility is said to be maximized if his marginal utility per last unit of expenditure on that good, is equal to marginal utilities of all other goods available to him, divided by their respective prices.

market economy: a free private enterprise governed by a *price system* and *market mechanism*. See also *perfect competition* and *pure market capitalism*.

market failure: a phenomenon which results from the existence of market imperfections (e.g. monopoly power, factor immobility, lack of knowledge, etc.) which weaken the functioning of a free market economy – i.e. it 'fails' to realize its theoretical beneficial results. Market failure often provides the justification for government interference with the working of the free market.

market mechanism: the system whereby *prices* of commodities or services freely rise or fall when the buyer's demand for them rises or falls or the seller's supply of them decreases or increases. See *price system*.

market socialism: economic system in which all resources are owned by the State but their allocation in the economy is done primarily by a *market price system*. See also *'Command' Socialism*.

mass production: large scale production of goods or services achieved primarily through automation, specialization and the *division of labor*.

micro-economics: that branch of economics which is concerned with individual decision units – firms and households – and the way in which their decisions interact to determine relative prices of goods and factors of production and how much of these will be bought and sold. The 'market' is the central concept in micro-economics. See also *price system* and *traditional economics*.

micro-economic theory of fertility: an extension of the theory of economic behavior of individual firms and households to the family formation decisions of individual couples. The central proposition of this theory is that family formation has costs and benefits and thus the sizes of families formed will depend on these costs and benefits. If the costs of family formation are high (low) relative to its benefits, the rates at which couples will decide to bring forth children will decline (increase). See also *'opportunity cost' of a woman's time, (general) fertility rate, (crude) birth rate, economic incentives* and *disincentives of fertility reduction,* etc.

microfundios: very small landholdings in Latin American *agrarian system* which are further divisions of *minifundios* as a result of growing populations on crowded areas of poor land, e.g. in Guatemala *microfundios* yield an average income that is less than one-third of that provided by the minifundios.

minifundios: landholdings in the Latin American *agrarian system* which are considered too small to provide adequate employment for a single family. They are too small to provide the workers with a *level of living* much above the bare survival minimum. Holders of *minifundios* are often required to provide unpaid seasonal labor to *latifundios* and to seek outside low-paid employment to supplement their meager incomes. See also *latifundios* and *microfundios*.

mixed commercial farming: the first step in the transition from *subsistence* to *specialized farming*. This evolutionary stage is characterized by the production of both staple crops and cash crops and, in addition, simple animal husbandry.

'mixed systems': *economic systems* that are a mixture of both *capitalist* and *socialist* economies. 'Mixed' economic systems characterize most developing countries. Their essential feature is the coexistence of substantial *private* and *public* activity within a single economy. See also *market socialism* and *advanced capitalism*.

model: an analytical framework used to portray functional relationships among economic-*models*.

modernization ideals: ideals regarded by some as necessary for sustained economic growth. They include *rationality, economic planning,* social and economic equalization, and improved *institutions* and attitudes.

money income: the income accruing to a household or firm expressed in terms of some monetary unit, e.g. 1,000 rupees or pesos per year.

money supply: sum total of currency in circulation plus commercial bank demand deposits (M_1) plus sometimes savings bank time deposits (M_2).

moneylender: in Asia, a person who lends money at higher than market rates of *interest* to peasant farmers to meet their needs for seeds, fertilizer and other inputs. Activities of moneylenders are often unscrupulous and can help to accentuate landlessness among the rural poor.

monopoly: a market situation in which a product which does not have close substitutes is being produced and sold by a single seller. See also *perfect competition* and *oligopoly*.

monopolistic market control: a situation in which the output of an industry is controlled by a single producer (or seller), or a joint group of producers governed by joint decisions.

multilateral assistance agency: see *foreign aid*.

multinational corporation (MNC): an international or transnational corporation with headquarters in one country but branch offices in a wide range of both developed and developing countries. Examples include General Motors, Coca Cola, Firestone, Philips, Renault, British Petroleum, Exxon, ITT, etc.

national expenditure: total expenditure on *final goods* and services in an economy over a given time period. National expenditure (E) includes: consumption expenditure (C), investment expenditure (I) government expenditure (G) and expenditure on exports by foreigners (X) less expenditure on imports by domestic residents (M). Thus $E = C + I + G + X - M$.

national income: total monetary value of all *final goods* and services produced in an economy over some period of time, usually a year. See also *gross national product (GNP)* and *national expenditure*.

necessary condition: a condition that must be present although need not be enough for an event to occur, e.g. *capital* formation is a necessary condition for sustained *economic growth* (i.e. before increases (growth) in output can occur, there must be tools to produce it). But for this growth to be continued, social, *institutional* and attitudinal changes must also occur.

necessity goods: life sustaining items, e.g. food, shelter, protection, medical care, etc. These are items that are essential for a good life. See also *luxury goods*.

'neo-classical' price incentive model: model whose main proposition is that if market prices are to influence economic activities in the right direction, they must be adjusted to remove *factor price distortions* by means of subsidies, taxes, etc. so that factor prices may reflect the true *opportunity cost* of resources being used. See also *'appropriate' technology*.

neo-classical economics: see *traditional (Western) economics*.

neo-colonial model of underdevelopment: model whose main proposition is that under-development exists in *Third World* countries because of exploitive economic, political and cultural policies of developed nations towards less developed countries, e.g. inappropriate transfers of technology, unequal trading relationships, misdirected assistance programmes, etc.

non-economic variables: elements of interest to economists in their work, but which are not given a monetary value or expressed in numerals because of their intangible nature. Examples of these include: beliefs, values, attitudes, norms and power structure. Sometimes *non-economic variables* are more important than the quantifiable economic variables in promoting development.

'non-formal' education: basically, any 'out of school' program that provides basic skills and training to individuals. Examples include adult education, on-the-job training programmes, agricultural and other extension services, etc. See also *'formal' educational system*.

non-renewable resources: natural resources whose quantity is fixed in supply and cannot be replaced. Examples include petroleum, iron ore, coal and other minerals. See also *renewable resources*.

'non-tariff' trade barrier: barriers to *free trade* that take forms other than *tariffs* such as *quotas*, sanitary requirements for imported meats and dairy products, etc.

normal and superior goods: goods whose purchased quantities increase as the incomes of consumers increase. Such goods have a positive *income elasticity of demand*. See also *inferior goods*.

normative economics: the notion that economics must concern itself with what 'ought to be'. Thus, it is argued that economics and economic analysis always involve *value judgements*, whether explicit or implicit, on the part of the analyist or observer. See *positive economics*.

OECD: Organization for Economic Cooperation and Development: an organization of twenty countries from the Western World including all of those in Europe and North America. Its major objective is to assist the economic growth of its member nations by promoting cooperation and technical analysis of national and international economic trends.

oligopoly: a market situation whereby there are a few sellers and many buyers of similar but differentiated products. *OPEC* provides a good example of international oligopoly. See also *imperfect competition*.

oligopolistic market control: exists when a market structure has a small number of rival but not necessarily competing firms dominating the industry. Thus, all recognize the fact that they are interdependent and can maximize their individual advantages through explicit (cartel) or implicit (collusion) joint actions.

OPEC: Organization of Petroleum Exporting Countries: an organization consisting of the thirteen major oil-exporting countries of the Third World who act as a 'cartel' or *oligopoly* to promote their joint national interests. Members include Saudi Arabia, Nigeria, Algeria, Venezuela, Libya, Kuwait, United Arab Emirates, Iran, Iraq, Ecuador, Qatar, Gabon and Indonesia.

open economy: an economy that engages in foreign trade and has financial and non-financial contacts with the rest of the world, e.g. in areas such as education, culture, technology, etc. See also *closed economy* and *outward-looking development policies*.

open unemployment: includes both *voluntary* and involuntary *unemployment*. Voluntarily unemployed persons are those unwilling to accept jobs for which they could qualify probably because they have means of support other than employment. Involuntary unemployment is a situation in which job-seekers are willing to work but there are no jobs available for them. *Open unemployment* is most conspicuous in the cities of less developed countries. See also *underemployment, surplus labor,* and *disguised unemployment*.

opportunity cost: in production, the real value of resources used in the most desirable alternative – e.g. the 'opportunity cost' of producing an extra unit of manufactured good is the output of, say, food that must be forgone as a result of transferring resources from agricultural to manufacturing activities; in consumption, the amount of one commodity that must be forgone in order to consume more of another. See also *increasing opportunity cost*.

'opportunity cost' of a woman's time: real or monetary wage or *profits* that a woman sacrifices by deciding to stay home and bring forth children instead of working for a wage or engaging in profit making self-employment activities. The higher the opportunity cost of a woman's time involved in bearing children, the more unwilling she will be to bring forth more children – at least in terms of the *micro-economic theory of fertility*.

optimization, principle of: a principle which states that in order to minimize costs in production or maximize 'satisfaction' in *consumption,* scarce *resources* should be used in the economically most 'efficient' manner while *goods* and *services* should be consumed so that the last unit of expenditure yields the same marginal utility for all individuals. See also the *principle of economy, appropriate technology, economic efficiency,* etc.

'organized' money market: the formal banking system in which loanable funds are channelled through recognized and licensed *financial intermediaries*. See also *'unorganized' money market*.

output-employment lag: a phenomenon in which employment growth 'lags' substantially behind output growth – normally, when output grows at a rate of three to four times that of employment as it has in most modern sectors of 'developing nations'.

outward-looking development policies: policies that encourage *free trade,* the free movement of capital, workers, enterprises and students, a welcome to *multinational corporations* and an open system of communications. See also *open economy*.

'overvalued' exchange rate: an *exchange rate* that is 'officially' set at a level higher than its real or 'shadow' value – i.e. 7 Kenya shillings per dollar instead of say, 10 shillings per dollar. Overvalued rates cheapen the real cost of imports while raising the real cost of exports. They often lead to a need for *exchange control*.

'package' of policies: a set of multidimensional economic and social policies aimed for example at removing inequalities and improving living standards for the masses. In short, a set of different but mutually reinforcing policies designed to achieve a single or multiple objective.

partial plans: those that cover only a part of the national economy, e.g. agriculture, industry, tourism, etc.

per capita food production: total food production divided by the total population.

per capita income: see *income per capita*.

perfect competition: a market situation characterized by the existence of (1) very many buyers and sellers of (2) homogeneous goods or services with (3) perfect knowledge and (4) free entry so that no single buyer or seller can influence the price of the good or service. See also *price system, laizze faire, Western economics* and *pure market capitalism*.

personal income: the amount of *money income* received by households over a given period of time. Note that some incomes are earned (as a result of rendering productive services) but not currently received (e.g. undistributed profits and contributions for social insurance), while some incomes received by the household sector are not earned through current productive activity, e.g. *transfer payments*. Personal income is derived by adding to *national income* the various incomes received by the households but not earned, and subtracting those that are earned but not received.

physical capital: tangible investment goods, e.g. plant and equipment, machinery, building, etc. See also *human capital*.

plan: see *economic plan* and *development plan*.

plan implementation: the practical carrying out of the objectives set forth in the *development plan*. Some of the difficulties encountered in attempting to attain plan targets result from insufficient availability of economic resources (physical and financial capital, skilled manpower, etc.), insufficient foreign aid, the effects of inflation, and, most importantly, lack of *political will*.

planning model: a mathematical model (e.g. an input–output or 'macro' planning model) designed to simulate quantitatively the major features of the economic structure of a particular country. Planning models provide the analytical and quantitative basis for most national and regional *development plans*. See also *economic plan* and *plan implementation*.

policy instruments: see *economic policy*.

political economy: the attempt to merge economic analysis with practical politics – i.e. to view economic activity in its political context. Much of 'classical' economics was *political economy* and today 'political economy' is increasingly being recognized as necessary for any realistic examination of development problems.

policy: see *economic policy*.

political will: a determined, deliberate, purposeful, independent decision, conclusion or choice upon a course of action by persons in political authority such as elimination of inequality, poverty and unemployment through various reforms of social, economic and institutional structures. Lack of 'political will' is often said to be one of the main obstacles to development and the main reason for the failure of many *development plans*. See *plan implementation*.

population density: the number of inhabitants per unit area of land, e.g. per square mile.

population increase (rate of): rate at which a given population size grows over a period of time, say, one year. Part of this rate, that which results entirely from increases in the number of births is called the *rate of natural increase of population,* to distinguish it from the rate resulting from, say, immigration.

'positive' economics: The notion that economics should be concerned with 'what is', was, or will be. It addresses itself to questions such as, what government policies will generate faster GNP growth; what government policies will reduce unemployment, inflation, inequality, etc. Answers to these questions are supposedly based on facts or empirical observation. See also *'normative' economics*.

potential output: the aggregate capacity output of a nation – i.e. maximum quantity of goods and services that can be produced with available resources and a given state of technology.

poverty: see *absolute poverty*.

poverty line: see *international poverty line*.

preventive medicine: medical care that focuses on the prevention of sickness and disease through immunology and health education. See also *curative medicine*.

present consumption: expenditure on goods and services that satisfy short-term wants – e.g. expenditures on food, cinema, entertainment, etc. *Future consumption* refers to expenditures on consumer items that yield want-satisfying benefits over a long time period, normally beyond one year, such as expenditure on cars, residential houses, furniture, etc. See also *consumption*.

price: monetary or real value of a resource, commodity or service. The role of prices in a *market economy* is to *ration* or allocate resources in accordance with supply and demand; additionally, relative prices should reflect the relative scarcity values of different resources, goods or services. See *price system*.

price elasticity of demand: the responsiveness of the quantity of a good demanded to change in its price, expressed as the percentage change in quantity demanded divided by the percentage change in price.

price elasticity of supply: the responsiveness of the quantity of a commodity supplied to change in its price, expressed as the proportionate change in quantity supplied divided by the proportionate change in price.

price system: the mechanism by which scarce resources, goods and services are allocated by the free upward or downward movements of prices in accordance with the dictates of supply and demand in a *market economy*. See also *perfect competition* and *pure market capitalism*.

primary industrial sector: part of the economy that specializes in the production of agricultural products and the extraction of raw materials. Major industries in this sector include: mining, agriculture, forestry and fishing.

primary products: products derived from all extractive occupations – farming, lumbering, fishing, mining and quarrying – viz. foodstuffs and raw materials.

principles – see *economic principles*.

principle of economy: the proposition in *perfect competition* that for a given level of *resources* (inputs), producers will tend to minimize costs for a given level of output or maximize output for a given cost. The need to 'economize' arises because resources are 'scarce' and are therefore not free.

private benefits: gains that accrue to a single individual — e.g. profits received by an individual firm. See also *social benefits*.

private-cost: the direct monetary outlays or costs of an individual economic unit, e.g. the private costs of a firm are the direct outlays on *fixed* and *variable inputs* of production.

private foreign investment: the investment of private foreign funds in the economy of a developing nation, usually in the form of *import substituting* industries by *multinational corporations (MNCs)*. See also *foreign aid.*

private sector: that part of an economy whose activities are under the control and direction of non-governmental economic units such as the households or firms. Each economic unit owns its own *resources* and uses them mainly to maximize its own well-being.

production function: a technological or engineering relationship between the quantity of a good produced and the quantity of *inputs* required to produce it.

productivity gap: the difference between per capita product, say, the agricultural population, i.e. *agricultural labour productivity,* in LDCs and that in developed countries. It has tended to be wide because of differences in the application of technological and biological improvements.

production process: see *production technique.*

production–possibility curve: a curve on a graph indicating alternative combinations of two commodities or categories of commodities (e.g. agricultural and manufactured goods) that can be produced when all the available *factors of production* are efficiently employed. Given available resources and technology, the *P–P* curve sets the boundary between which combination is attainable and which it is unobtainable. See also *opportunity cost* and *production function.*

production technique: method of combining *inputs* to produce required output. A production technique is said to be *appropriate* ('best') if it produces a given output with the least cost (thus being *economically efficient*) or with the least possible quantity of real resources (*technically efficient*). A technique may be *labor-intensive* or *capital-intensive.*

profit: the difference between the market value of output and the market value of *inputs* that were employed to produce that output. Alternatively, a firm's or farm's profits can be defined as the difference between total revenue and total cost.

profit maximization: making as large as possible the profits of a firm or farm. Producers often desire to find the level of output which results in maximum profits, at least according to a fundamental assumption of *Western economic theory.*

progressive income tax: a tax whose rate increases with increasing personal incomes – i.e., where the proportion of personal income paid by a rich person in taxes is higher than that paid by a poorer person. A progressive tax structure therefore tends to improve *income distribution.* See also *regressive tax.*

project appraisal: the quantitative analysis of the relative desirability (profitability) of investing a given sum of public and/or private funds in alternative projects – e.g. building a steel mill or textile factory. *Cost/benefit* analysis provides the major analytical tool of *project appraisal.*

public sector: that portion of an economy whose activities (economic and non-economic) are under the control and direction of the state. The state owns all resources in this sector and uses them to achieve whatever goals it may have – e.g. to promote the economic welfare of the ruling elite or to maximize the well-being of society as a whole. See also *private sector.*

pure market capitalism: *economic system* in which all resources are privately owned and their allocation is done exclusively by a *price system.* See also *perfect competition, market economy, invisible hand* and *laissez faire,*

quintile: a 20 per cent proportion of any numerical quantity, e.g. a population divided into quintiles would be one which was divided into five equal numerical groups. See also *decile.*

quota: a physical limitation on the quantity of any item that can be imported into a country, e.g. so many automobiles per year.

rate of natural increase (of population): see *population increase, rate of.*

rationality: one of the foundations (with regard to people's behavior) upon which traditional or *Western economic theory* is built. An economically 'rational' person is one who will always attempt to maximize satisfaction or profits, or minimize costs. The notion of rationality as one of the modernization ideals means the replacement of age-old traditional practices by modern methods of 'objective' thinking and logical reasoning in production, distribution and consumption. See also *rational choice, principles of economy* and *optimization and profit maximization.*

rationing: a system of distribution employed to restrict the quantities of goods and services that consumers or producers can purchase or be allocated freely. It arises because of excess demand and inflexible prices. *Rationing* can be by coupons, points or simply administrative decisions with regard to commodities, by academic credentialization with regard to job allocation, by industrial licences with regard to capital good imports, etc. See also *black market.*

'rational' choice: a choice commensurate with logical reasoning. In economic theory it is often assumed that everyone behaves rationally in his economic activities. See, for example, the *principle of economy, profit maximization, principle of optimization* and *rationality*.

real income: the income that a household or firm receives in terms of the real goods and services it can purchase. Alternatively, it is simply *money income* adjusted by some price index.

recession: a period of slack general economic activity as reflected in rising unemployment and excess productive capacity in a broad spectrum of industries.

redistribution policies: policies geared to reducing inequality of incomes and economic opportunities in order to promote *'development'*. Examples include *progressive tax* policies, provision of services financed out of such taxation to benefit persons in the lower income groups, rural development policies giving emphasis to raising *levels of living* for the rural poor through *land reform* and other forms of *asset* and wealth redistribution, etc.

regressive tax: if the ratio of taxes to income as income increases tends to decrease, the tax is called 'regressive', i.e. relatively poor people pay a larger proportion of their income in taxes than do relatively rich people. A regressive tax therefore tends to worsen *income distribution*. See also *progressive tax*.

renewable resources: natural resources which can be replaced so that the total supply is not fixed for all time as in the case of *non-renewable resources*. Examples include timber and other forest products.

rent: in the context of macro-economics it refers to the share of *national income* going to the owners of the productive resource, land (i.e., landlords). In everyday usage, the price paid for rental property, e.g. buildings and housing. In the theory of micro-economics it is a short form for 'economic rent' – i.e. the payment to a *factor* over and above its highest *opportunity cost*.

replacement fertility: level of *fertility* at which child-bearing women have just enough daughters to 'replace' themselves in the population. This keeps the existing population size constant through an infinite number of succeeding generations. See also general *fertility rate*, and *birth rate*.

research and development (R and D): a scientific investigation with a view towards improving the existing quality of human life, products, profits, *factors of production* or just plain knowledge. There are two categories of R and D. (1) 'basic' R and D, i.e. one without a specific commercial objective and (2) 'applied' R and D, i.e. one with a commercial pursuit.

resources, physical and human: *factors of production* used to produce goods and services to satisfy wants. Land and capital are frequently referred to as *physical resources* and labour as the *human resource*. See also *fixed* and *variable inputs*.

resource endowment: a nation's supply of *factors of production*. Normally such endowments are supplied by nature, e.g. mineral deposits, raw materials, timber forests, labor, etc. See also *factor endowment theory of trade*.

rigid institutions: *institutions* that are designed in such a way that they cannot be adjusted or adjust of themselves to accommodate *development* requirements, e.g. a social system – typically a clan unit – that has conservative values which render it resistant to *modernizing ideals* is often referred to as a 'rigid institution'.

risk: a situation in which the probability of obtaining some outcome of an event is not precisely known, that is, known probabilities cannot be precisely assigned to these outcomes but their general level can be inferred. In everyday usage a risky situation is one in which one of the outcomes involves some loss to the decision maker, for example, changes of demand, weather and tastes. See also *uncertainty*.

rural development: see *integrated rural development*.

rural support systems: systems which need to be created to stimulate the productivity of both small- and large-scale agricultural farms. These include making more effective and efficient the rural *institutions* directly connected with production, e.g. banks, *moneylenders,* public credit agencies, seed and fertilizer distributors; and provision of services such as technical and educational *extension services,* storage and marketing facilities, rural transport and feeder roads, water, etc.

savings: that portion of *disposable income* not spent on *consumption* by households plus profits retained by firms. Savings are normally assumed to be positively related to the level of income (personal or national).

savings ratio: savings expressed as a proportion of *disposable income* over some period of time. It shows the fraction of *National Income* that is saved over any period. The savings ratio is sometimes used synonymously with the *average propensity to save*. See also *Harrod–Domar Equation*.

'scale neutral' technological progress: *technological progress* which can lead to the achievement of higher output levels irrespective of the size (scale) of the firm or farm – i.e. it is equally applicable to small as well as to large-scale production processes. An often cited example is the hybrid seeds of the *Green Revolution* which theoretically can increase yields on both small and large farms (if *complementary resources* such as fertilizer, irrigation, pesticides, etc. are available).

scarcity: in economics, the term referring to a situation which arises when there is less of something (e.g. an *economic good, service* or *resource*) than people would like to have if it were free. The quantity of goods and services are scarce relative to people's desire for them because the economy's resources used in their production are themselves scarce. Scarcity therefore gives rise to the need for efficient allocation of resources among alternative competing uses through, for example, the free *market mechanism* in *capitalist* economies or through a centralized *command system* in planned economies.

scatter diagram: a two-dimensional graph on which numerical values of statistically observed variables are plotted in pairs, one measured on the horizontal axis and the other on the vertical axis.

Second World: the now economically advanced *socialist* countries. Major *Second World* countries include: the Soviet Union and other Soviet-type economies of eastern Europe such as Poland, Czechoslovakia, Yugoslavia, etc. See also *First World* and *Third World*.

secondary industrial sector: the 'manufacturing' portion of the economy that uses raw materials and *intermediate products* to produce *final goods* or other intermediate products. Industries such as motor assembly, textile and building and construction are part of this sector.

self-esteem (of a society): feeling of 'human worthiness' that a society enjoys when its *social, political* and *economic systems* and *institutions* promote human respect, dignity, integrity, self-determination, etc. See *development* (meaning of).

self-reliance: reliance on one's own capabilities, judgement, resources, skills in a bid to enhance political, economic, social, cultural, attitudinal and moral independence. Countries may also desire to be self-reliant in particular aspects such as food production, manpower and skills, etc. Increasingly, the term 'collective' *self-reliance* is being used in *Third World* forums.

shadow price: price that reflects the true *opportunity-cost* of a resource.

sharecropper: in the *agrarian systems* of LDCs the tenant peasant farmer whose crop produce has to be shared with the *landlord*. The *landlord* usually appropriates a large share of the tenant's total crop production.

shifting cultivation: peasant agricultural practice in Africa in which land is tilled by a family or community for cropping until such time that it has been exhausted of fertility. Thereafter the family or community moves to a new area of land which is prepared for cropping as the previous one while leaving the former to regain fertility until eventually it can be cultivated once again.

size distribution of income: the distribution of income according to size class of persons, e.g. the share of total income accruing to say the poorest 40 per cent of a population or the richest 10 per cent, without regard to the sources of that income (e.g. if it comes from wages, interest, rent or profits). See also *functional distribution of income, Lorenz curve* and *Gini coefficient.*

'skewed' distribution of income: skewness is a lack of symmetry in a 'frequency distribution'. If income is perfectly distributed such a distribution is said to be symmetrical. A skewed distribution of income is one diverging from perfect equality. Highly 'skewed' distribution of income occurs in situations where the rich persons, say the top 20 per cent of the total population, receive more than half of the total *national income*. See also *Lorenz curve* and *Gini coefficient.*

small farmer: farmer owning a small family-based plot of land on which he grows subsistence crops and perhaps one or two cash crops, relying almost exclusively on family labour.

small-scale industry: industry whose firms or farms operate with small-sized plants, low employment and hence have small output capacity. *Economies of scale* do not normally exist for such firms or farms but they often tend to utilize their limited *physical, human* and financial *resources* more efficiently than many large-sized firms or farms.

social benefits: gains or benefits that accrue or are available to the society as a whole rather than solely to a private individual – e.g., the protection and security provided by the police or the Armed Forces; the *external economies* afforded by an effective health delivery system; and the widespread benefits of a literate population. See *private benefits.*

social cost: the cost to society as a whole of an economic decision, whether private or public. Where there exist *external diseconomies* of production (e.g. pollution) or consumption (alcoholism), *social costs* will normally exceed *private costs* and decisions based solely on private calculations will lead to a misallocation of resources.

'social' discount rate: the rate at which the society 'discounts' potential future *social benefits* to find out whether such benefits are worth their present *social cost. The rate used in this discounting procedure is usually the social opportunity cost* of the funds committed.

social science: that branch of study that concerns itself with human society, its behaviour, activities and growth, e.g., sociology, history, philosophy, political science, economics, etc.

social system: term used to refer to the *organizational* and *institutional* structure of the society including its *value premises,* attitudes, power structures and traditions. Major social systems include: political set-ups, religions, clans, etc.

socialism: see *command socialism* and *market socialism.*

'soft' loan: see *loans.*

special drawing rights (SDRs): a new form of international financial asset – often referred to as 'paper gold' – created by the *International Monetary Fund (IMF)* in 1970 and designed to supplement gold and dollars in settling international *balance of payments* accounts. At present 75 per cent of the total SDR issue is distributed to twenty-five industrial nations while only 25 per cent is distributed among the more than one hundred developing countries that participate in the international monetary system.

specialization: a situation in which *resources* are concentrated in the production of a relatively few commodities rather than a wider range of commodities. See also *comparative advantage* and *division of labor.*

specialized farming: the final and most advanced stage of the evolution of agricultural production in which farm output is produced wholly for the market. It is most prevalent in advanced industrial countries. High farm yields are ensured by a high degree of *capital formation, technological progress,* and scientific *research and development.* See also *subsistence farming* and *commercial farming.*

spread effects: impacts that are felt beyond the initial place of action. Sometimes referred to as 'echo' effects. The spread effects for example of increasing medical services are: a reduction in death rates, a rise in *life expectancy* at birth, healthy and productive labour force, etc.

'stages of growth' theory of development: this theory of development is associated with the American economic historian W. W. Rostow. According to Rostow, before a country can achieve development, it must inevitably pass through the following stages: (*a*) traditional and stagnant low per capita stage; (*b*) transitional stage (in which the 'pre-conditions for growth' are laid down); (*c*) the 'take-off' stage (beginning of *economic growth* process); (*d*) industrialized, mass production and consumption stage (*development* stage).

staple food: a leading or main food consumed by a large section of a country's population, e.g. maize meal in Kenya, Zambia and Tanzania, rice in Southeast Asian countries, yams in West Africa, mandioca in Brazil, etc.

structural inflation: *inflation* that arises as a result of supply inelasticities and structural rigidities (e.g. inefficient marketing and distribution systems) in the industrial sectors of the economy. A form of *demand-pull inflation* but can exist with considerable excess capacity and unemployment.

structural theory of underdevelopment: hypothesis that underdevelopment in *Third World* countries is due to underutilization of *resources* arising from structural and/or *institutional* factors that have their origins in both domestic and international *dualistic* situations. 'Development', therefore, requires more than just accelerated *capital* formation as espoused in the *Stages of growth* and *'false paradigm'* models of development.

structural transformation: the process of transforming the basic industrial structure of an economy so that the contribution to *national income* by the manufacturing sector increasingly becomes higher than that by the agricultural sector. More generally, an alteration in the industrial composition of any economy. See *primary, secondary* and *tertiary industrial sectors.*

subsidy: a payment by the government to producers or distributors in an industry to prevent the decline of that industry (e.g. as a result of continuous unprofitable operations), an increase in the prices of its products, or simply to encourage it to hire more labour (as in the case of a wage subsidy). Examples of subsidies are export subsidies to encourage their sale abroad, subsidies on some foodstuffs to keep down the cost of living especially in urban areas, farm subsidy to encourage expansion of farm production to achieve *self-sufficiency* in food production, etc.

subsistence economy: an economy in which production is mainly for own consumption and the standard of living yields no more than the basic necessities of life – food, shelter and clothing. See also *subsistence farming.*

subsistence farming: farming in which crop production, stock rearing, etc., is mainly for 'own-consumption' and is characterized by low productivity, *risk* and *uncertainty*. See also *subsistence economy*.

sufficient condition: a condition which when present causes an event to occur, e.g. being a university student is a sufficient condition to get a loan under university education loan schemes. See also *necessary condition*.

supply curve: a positively sloped curve relating the quantity of a commodity supplied to its price.

'surplus' labor: the excess supply of labor over and above the quantity demanded at the going 'free' market wage rate. In Arthur Lewis' two-sector model of economic development, surplus labor refers to that portion of the rural labor force whose *marginal productivity* is zero or negative. See also *underemployment*.

synthetic commodity substitutes: commodities that are artificially produced but of like nature with and substitutes for the natural commodities, e.g. those involving rubber, cotton, wool, camphor, pyrethrum, etc. Producers of raw materials, mainly LDCs, are becoming more and more vulnerable to competition from synthetics from industrialized countries as a result of the latter's more advanced state of scientific and technical progress.

tariff (ad valorem): a fixed percentage tax (e.g. 30 per cent) on the value of an imported commodity levied at the point of entry into the importing country.

technical assistance: *foreign aid* (either *bilateral* or *multilateral*) which takes the form of the transfer of expert personnel, technicians, scientists, educators, economic advisers, consultants, etc., rather than a simple transfer of funds.

technological progress: increased application of new scientific knowledge in form of *inventions* and *innovations* with regard to *capital*, both *physical* and *human*. Has been a major factor in stimulating the long-term *economic growth* of contemporary developed countries. See also *labor augmenting, labor-saving capital-augmenting* and *scale neutral technological progress*.

tenant farmer: one who farms on land held by a *landlord* and therefore lacks secure ownership rights and has to pay for the use of that land, e.g. by surrendering part of his output to the owner of the land. Examples are found in the Latin American and Asian *agrarian systems*. See also *sharecropper*.

terms of trade (commodity): the ratio of a country's average export price to its average import price. A country's *terms of trade* are said to 'improve' when this ratio increases and to 'worsen' when it decreases, i.e. when import prices rise at a relatively faster rate than export prices (the experience of most LDCs over the past two decades).

tertiary sector: the 'services' and commerce portion of an economy. Examples of services include: repair and maintenance of *capital goods*, haircuts, public administration, medical care, transport and communications, teaching, etc. See also *primary* and *secondary sectors*.

Third World: the present 118 or so developing countries of Asia, Africa, the Middle East and Latin America. These countries are mainly characterized by *low levels of living*, high rates of *population growth*, low levels of *per capita income* and general economic and technological *dependence* on *First* and *Second World* economies.

Third World or 'development' economics: the economics of the less developed nations of Africa, Asia and Latin America which addresses itself mainly to problems of *economic growth*, poverty, unemployment and inequality.

tied aid: *foreign aid* in the form of *bilateral loans* or *grants* which require the recipient country to use the funds to purchase goods and/or services from the donor country – thus the aid is said to be 'tied' to purchases from the assisting country.

'total' factor productivity: total monetary value of all units of output per unit of each and every *factor of production* in an economy. It is a measure of the average productivity of all factors employed in an economy.

trade (as an engine of growth): *free trade* has often been described as an 'engine of growth' because it encourages countries to *specialize* in activities in which they have *comparative advantages* thereby increasing their respective production efficiencies and hence their total outputs of goods and *services*.

trade creation: a situation in the theory of *customs unions* that occurs when, following the formation of the union, there is a shift in the geographic location of production from higher-cost to lower-cost member states. See also *trade diversion*.

trade diversion: occurs when the formation of a *customs union* causes the locus of production of formerly imported goods to shift from a lower cost non-member state to a higher cost member nation. See also *trade creation*.

trade-off: the necessity of sacrificing ('trading off') something in order to get more of something else – e.g. sacrificing *consumption* now for *consumption* later by devoting some present *resources* to *investment*. See also *opportunity cost*.

traditional (Western) economics: the economics of *capitalist market economies* characterized by *consumer sovereignty, profit maximization, private enterprise* and *perfect competition*. The major focus is on the efficient allocation of scarce resources (see *economic efficiency*) through the *price system* and the forces of supply and demand. See also *micro-economics, macro-economics, Keynesian economics, laissez faire, invisible hand, market economy* and *'Western' economic theory*.

transfer payment: any payment from one economic entity to another that takes the form of a 'gift' – i.e. it is not for a service rendered and it need not be repaid. Examples include unemployment insurance, food stamps, welfare payments, *subsidies*, bilateral *grants,* etc.

transfer pricing: an accounting procedure usually designed to lower total taxes paid by *multinational corporations (MNCs)* in which intracorporate sales and purchases of goods and services are artificially invoiced so that profits accrue to those branch offices located in low tax countries ('tax havens') while offices in high tax countries show little or no taxable profits.

'trickle down' theory of development: the prevalent view of the 1950s and 1960s in which *development* was seen as purely an 'economic' phenomenon in which rapid gains from the overall growth of *GNP* and *per capita income* would automatically bring benefits (i.e. 'trickle down') to the masses in the form of jobs and other economic opportunities. The main preoccupation was therefore to get the growth job done while problems of *poverty, unemployment* and *income distribution* were of secondary importance.

UN: United Nations: a global organization set up at the end of the Second World War with the basic aim of cultivating international cooperation among countries and hence ensuring that any conflicts or misunderstanding between or among countries would be resolved by peaceful means. At present the UN has a membership of 141 countries drawn from both the developed and less developed nations. The *United Nations* has its headquarters in New York, but many of its organs have headquarters elsewhere.

uncertainty: a situation in which the probability of obtaining the outcome(s) of an event is not known. There is thus a plurality of possible outcomes to which no objective probability can be attached. See also *risk*.

UNCTAD: United Nations Conference on Trade and Development: a body of *United Nations* whose primary objective is to promote *international trade* and commerce with a principal focus on trade and *balance of payments* problems of developing nations. Its first Secretary General was Raul Prebisch of Latin America.

underdevelopment: economic situation in which there are persistent *low levels of living* with the following characteristics: absolute poverty, low *per capita incomes,* low rates of *economic growth,* low *consumption* levels, poor health services, high *death rates,* high *birth rates, vulnerability* to and *dependence* on foreign economies, and *limited freedom to choose* between variables that satisfy human wants. See also *development*.

underemployment: a situation in which persons are working less, either daily, weekly, monthly, or seasonally, than they would like to work. See also *open unemployment* and *surplus labor*.

underutilization of labor: operation of labor force at levels below their capacity or potential output. See also *open unemployment, underemployment, disguised underemployment, voluntary unemployment,* etc.

UNESCO: United Nations Educational, Scientific and Cultural Organization: a major organ of the *United Nations* system located in Paris and charged with the responsibility of promoting 'international understanding' by: (*a*) spreading ideas or knowledge through the educational process; (*b*) encouraging multi-racial coexistence through reconciliation of cultural values of different societies; and (*c*) sponsoring educational, cultural and scientific exchange programs that make it possible for educators, artists, writers and scientists from a wide variety of countries and cultures to meet and exchange ideas and knowledge.

UNDP: United Nations Development Program: a member of the *United Nations* family system of world bodies whose major function is to promote *development* in *Third World* countries. Major development oriented projects financed and carried out by UNDP include: initiation of nutrition, health and education programs, building up agricultural, industrial and transport infrastructure, etc.

unit cost: the average total cost per unit of output of any *economic good* or service.

'unorganized' money market: the informal and often usurous credit system that exists in most developing countries (especially in rural areas) where low income farms and firms with little collateral are forced to borrow from moneylenders and 'loansharks' at exorbitant rates of interest. See also *'organized' money market*.

urbanization: economic and demographic growth process of urban centres.

USAID: United States Agency for International Development: a *bilateral assistance agency* of the United States government whose primary objective is to assist *Third World* countries in their *development* efforts as part of United States foreign policy. The 'economic' assistance given by USAID normally takes the form of educational *grants,* special interest *loans* and *technical assistance.* However, much of AIDs activity also consists of 'non-economic' (mostly military) assistance to 'friendly' LDC governments.

variable: see *economic variables.*

variable inputs: *inputs* or *resources* whose required use in a *production function* will vary with changes in the level of output. For example, in the production of shoes, labor is usually a variable *input* because as more shoes are produced, more labor must be used. See also *fixed inputs.*

values and value premises: principles, standards, or qualities considered worthwhile or desirable. A value judgement is one based on or reflecting one's personal or class beliefs. See also *normative economics.*

'vent for surplus' theory of trade: states that the opening up of world markets to developing countries through international trade provides them with the opportunity to take advantage of formerly underutilized land and labor resources to produce larger *primary product* outputs, the surplus of which can be exported to foreign markets. Such economies will usually be operating at a point somewhere inside their *production possibility frontiers* so that trade permits an outward shift of such a production point.

vested interest (groups): group of persons that have acquired rights or powers in any sphere of activities within a nation or in international affairs which they often struggle to guard and maintain. Examples of powerful *vested interest* groups in developing countries include *landlords,* political *elites,* and wealthy private local and foreign investors.

vicious circle: a self-reinforcing situation in which there are factors which tend to perpetuate a certain undesirable phenomenon – e.g., low incomes in poor countries lead to low consumption which then leads to poor health and low labor productivity and eventually to the persistence of poverty.

Index